THE PLACE OF LAW

THE PLACE OF LAW

The Role and Limits of Law in Society

LARRY D. BARNETT

Routledge
Taylor & Francis Group
LONDON AND NEW YORK

First published 2011 by Transaction Publishers

2 Park Square, Milton Park, Abingdon, Oxfordshire OX14 4RN
711 Third Avenue, New York, NY 10017

Routledge is an imprint of the Taylor & Francis Group, an informa business

First issued in paperback 2017

Library of Congress Catalog Number: 2011008126

Library of Congress Cataloging-in-Publication Data

Barnett, Larry D.
The place of law : the role and limits of law in society / Larry D. Barnett.
p. cm.
Includes index.
ISBN 978-1-4128-4258-7
1. Law—Social aspects—United States. 2. Law and the social sciences. 3. Sociological jurisprudence. I. Title.
KF380.B364 2011
340'.115—dc22

2011008126

ISBN 13: 978-1-4128-4258-7 (hbk)
ISBN 13: 978-1-138-51662-5 (pbk)

Contents

Preface

Being at the start of a book, a preface is perhaps an oddity inasmuch as it was written after the book manuscript was finished. Whether or not its placement in a book is curious, however, a preface serves an important function. Through a preface, the author can convey to readers some of personal history of, and insights derived from, a scholarly project that has consumed much time and energy. The preface, accordingly, furnishes readers with perspective on the materials that follow. In one sense, then, a preface is like a rear-view mirror on a motor vehicle—it supplies a picture of what lies behind what lies ahead.

Law is a multifaceted phenomenon that presents innumerable topics for research, but *The Place of Law* deals with just a small slice of law. In brief, *The Place of Law* is concerned with the societal causes and consequences of the concepts and doctrines of law on socially significant patterns of human activity. The scope of *The Place of Law* is further cabined because its thesis is confined to sovereign, technologically advanced, structurally complex, democratic nations. *The Place of Law* thus neither encompasses all facets of the institution of law in all types of societies nor, within a society, covers all types of activities that are targeted by law or all types of actors participating in the institution of law. The book, rather, tackles a single aspect of law in a single type of society and thus does not develop, and does not purport to develop, a theory, i.e., a set of propositions that posit relationships between variables applicable to the entirety of law. For the topic and societal context with which it deals, the book merely suggests a few—but hopefully useful—propositions about a certain aspect of the institution of law.

The propositions of *The Place of Law*, readers will note, emphasize the social side of law, and in doing so, the propositions rest on the assumption that a society contains a domain that is social and a domain that is economic. That assumption is probably not controversial despite the conceded difficulty of pinpointing the boundary between the two domains, but the assumption needs to be explicitly acknowledged because it underlies the book. *The Place of Law* makes the distinction between these domains when, inter alia, it directs attention to the social antecedents and effects of law that is intended to regulate economic matters. In particular, the social aspects of law that on the surface seems to deal solely with the economic domain are illustrated in the book by two statutes in the United States—the federal Investment Company Act and Investment Advisers Act. These are not commonly studied statutes, even in the field of securities law, and statutes on other topics that implicate economics (e.g., taxation of personal income) would undoubtedly have been equally suitable as examples. However, the Investment Company Act and Investment Advisers Act are of major economic significance in the United States, and because they have a distinctly social character, I use them to underscore the inescapable relevance of the social domain to law that appears to be only within the domain of economics.

The chapters of *The Place of Law* result from my training both as a lawyer and as a sociologist. Of course, training in two disciplines may not make an author an expert in either one, but in writing this book, the fact that I had a foot in each world hopefully proved valuable. Disciplines differ substantively—e.g., in their concepts, analytical approaches, and research techniques—and the differences permit each discipline to make a distinct contribution to studies of a phenomenon. Familiarity with two disciplines, therefore, offers a potentially major advantage over familiarity with just one.

What can law and sociology each contribute to the development of knowledge about the institution of law? In this endeavor, a scholar who has been trained in law benefits from the ability to uncover and delve into the flexibility of the concepts and doctrines of law. In the United States, that flexibility is remarkable, but flexibility presumably exists in the law of all nations of the type encompassed by *The Place of Law*. Indeed, flexibility in the content of law is probably inherent in modern societies given the relatively rapid pace at which these societies evolve. However, a lawyer who has not had graduate-level training in empirical sociology is at a material disadvantage in ascertaining the reasons for changes in law, because a lawyer whose schooling has been solely in law is unlikely to be familiar with the concepts, data, and quantitative methods of sociology—resources that can help explain why law undergoes alteration. The marriage of sociology and law, therefore, brings together disciplines that possess a natural compatibility. Indeed, the marriage of sociology and law makes partners of disciplines that are at least as compatible as the marriage of economics and law, and it is regrettable that the union of economics and law has been embraced by U.S. law schools while the union of sociology and law has not.

The combination of two disciplines is especially advantageous to the advance of human understanding when the knowledge-building resources of one or both disciplines are improving. For sociology, those resources have grown dramatically over the last several decades. *The Place of Law*, I hope, has taken advantage of the progress that has been made in the data sets, statistical methods, and research literature of sociology and cognate social sciences. Although the advances happened gradually, even imperceptibly, they are impressive when considered in the aggregate, and if the pace of progress continues, the stock of knowledge about law can grow rapidly in the future through research using the tools of sociology.

In light of the potential contribution of sociology to knowledge about the nature of law, a comment is in order regarding the general neglect of sociological concepts and research in scholarship originating in law schools in the United States. To the extent that scholars in U.S. law schools today have an interest in the social/behavioral sciences, their interest is confined to economics and, to a lesser degree, psychology. The neglect of sociology is probably attributable to many factors, but I believe that two are primary. One is the emphasis in American culture on individualism, an emphasis that blocks recognition of and creates resistance to group-level explanations of the components of social life, including law. Notably, the faculty members of U.S. law schools manifest this emphasis not only in their scholarship but also in their teaching. If a macrosociological approach to law was adopted, U.S. law schools would be broadly changed, and the change would include significant modifications in pedagogy, especially in courses on subjects that raise broad societal issues (e.g., courses dealing with constitutional law). Sadly, law school students in the United States are unlikely to benefit in the near future from sociological insights, partly because teachers and scholars in law, like humans in general, typically do not rush to embrace fundamental intellectual shifts.

The neglect of sociology in U.S. law schools, however, is not entirely due to the belief that the individual is paramount. That neglect seems also to stem from the reputation that sociology as a discipline has developed. While it is understandably an uncomfortable problem for sociologists to confront, the reputation of their discipline in the United States is poor, having evidently declined precipitously during the second half of the twentieth century.[1] I can only hope that Ph.D. programs in sociology have been graduating, and will in the future graduate, skilled empiricists whose research will be rigorous in quality, substantial in quantity, and not biased by political ideology or personal agenda. Without such research, a material rise in the prestige of sociology is not possible. Unfortunately, however, even if sociologists produce a large volume of well-designed empirical research, the reputation of their discipline cannot be expected to improve quickly, because social phenomena generally are slow to change. As a result, an appreciable upgrading of the reputation of sociology will almost certainly require decades, and scholarship and teaching in U.S. law schools will probably continue to ignore sociology for a long time.

By the time a book is finished, its author is cognizant that, in completing the project, significant assistance was received from numerous individuals. However, an author can easily overlook some persons who helped; contributions are not necessarily peripheral even though at the time they seemed unimportant. Consequently, while the preparation of *The Place of Law* benefited from the assistance of many people, I am all too aware that the individuals I name below may not comprise a complete list of those who provided important help.

Let me begin with the person without whom this book would not have been undertaken. He is Irving Louis Horowitz, the editorial director of Transaction Publishers. Professor Horowitz, after reading one of my law review articles, encouraged me to write a book on the sociology of law, and later—after seeing another of my law review articles—suggested that the book be built on these articles. Seven of the nine chapters in *The Place of Law* accordingly come from articles I originally published in law reviews, although three of the seven chapters are extensively modified versions of the articles on which they are based. The two chapters that are not from my law review articles were written in order to introduce the macrosociological thesis of the book (Chapter 1) and to discuss matters pertinent to quantitative research on the societal conditions that shape the content of law (Chapter 9).

I would be remiss if I did not also acknowledge the staff members of the Widener University law school library who often provide me with assistance and who have done so for many years. They are Enza Klotzbucher, Mary Jane Mallonee, and Kelly Pierce. The library is excellent for a number of reasons, among which is the presence on the staff of Enza, Mary Jane, and Kelly. I have relied on their help for such a long time that I fear I may at times take them for granted.

Last, but certainly not least, I must mention the contribution of Linda Rae Barnett, my wife of almost half a century. Linda Rae disproves a remark about marriage—a remark attributed to the playwright Oscar Wilde—that "Bigamy is having one wife too many. Monogamy is the same." She has generously accepted the heavy demands that scholarship places on the time of a spouse, and the book is a testament to her understanding.

Wilmington, Delaware
February 2011

Note

1. *Compare* "Jobs and Occupations: A Popular Evaluation," *Opinion News*, September 1, 1947, 3, 4–5 (finding that, in a national sample survey of U.S. adults conducted in 1947, sociologists ranked twenty-seventh among ninety occupations that were rated on their "general standing") *with* Dennis J. Downey et al., "The Status of Sociology within the Academy: Where We Are, Why We're There, and How to Change It," *American Sociologist* 39 (2008): 193, 199 (finding that, in a sample survey conducted during academic year 2006–2007, deans in U.S. colleges of arts and sciences chose sociology from a list of twenty-five disciplines as one of the two disciplines that were lowest in prestige).

1

Introduction

The important thing in science is not so much to obtain new facts as to discover new ways of thinking about them.

William Henry Bragg[1]

I. The Study of Law

Humans cannot know with certainty what is real and what is not. They can only aspire to do so, in part because their perceptions are molded not only by the stimuli they can see and hear but also by the assumptions they bring to the stimuli. Since assumptions commonly exist and affect perceptions,[2] humans frequently take for granted that certain things are real and are inclined to perceive accordingly.[3] When this happens, incorrect assumptions are retained. Only when perceptions serve to test the accuracy of relevant assumptions are improvements possible in human understanding of reality.

Scholars, of course, are not immune from the effects of assumptions on perceptions. The rigor of scholarly work reduces error, but it does not eliminate error. In the short run, therefore, scholars may not advance knowledge even though in the long run they are engaged in a self-correcting enterprise. When scholars rely on unsuitable intellectual frameworks, they will include in their studies the wrong explanatory (independent) and/or output (dependent) variables, and they may also employ unsuitable research methods.[4] Colloquially put, scholars at any particular point in time may get it wrong.

A central thesis of the instant book is that a fundamental defect exists in some widespread assumptions regarding, and hence perceptions of, the institution of law. If scholarship on law is being led astray by currently accepted beliefs about law, as I contend in this book, progress in understanding law as a societal institution will be impeded until another view of law is accepted.

In advancing the above argument, however, I need to point out that the instant book is not concerned with all aspects of law. Rather, the book deals with just two questions—though these questions are at the heart of the institution of law. First, why is law an evidently universal, enduring institution in societies that are characterized by a relatively high level of economic development and a relatively high degree of social complexity? Second, why do the concepts and doctrines of the institution of law differ between jurisdictions (e.g., states or nations) at one point in time and vary within a particular jurisdiction over time? The two questions should be prominent in the study of law, but usually they remain in the background and are not considered. As a consequence, answers to the questions are not sought with the evidence that is available, or can be developed, from well-designed quantitative social science research.

By relying on existing quantitative research and providing some of its own, the instant book suggests answers to the two questions posed in the preceding paragraph and offers a framework for the study of law.[5] The answers and framework are necessarily tentative, but they merit consideration even though they conflict with prevailing assumptions. Advances in knowledge involve the interplay of ideas and empirical research, and the advances often require the former for the latter.[6] Thus, where the proposed framework is ahead of existing knowledge, the framework can serve a useful function by guiding future research to test it.

In addition to the preceding caveat, let me point out that this book does not provide an all-encompassing, i.e., "grand," framework for law. It does not do so for at least three reasons:

1. The framework for law that I propose is concerned with, and only with, law on activities that are fundamental aspects of social organization, i.e., activities that are deeply embedded in social life. The framework is not intended to apply to law dealing with mechanical aspects of a society, e.g., law designating the date by which income tax returns must be filed with government each year and law specifying the length of time a government-issued license is valid for a pet or for the operation of an automobile.
2. The framework for law that I propose is intended to apply only to law in sovereign nations that are economically advanced and socially complex. The framework may not be appropriate for developing nations or for societies with small populations and relatively simple social structures.
3. The framework for law that I propose has been derived from a relatively brief period in history and is evaluated with evidence from that period. However, the character and functions of the institution

of law may change from one historical era to another in a society. My framework, therefore, may be useful only in a particular setting at a single point in history.

The second and third reservations above are especially important in evaluating scholarship on law, and they extend beyond the instant book. Assessments of the utility of a framework for or a theory of law must recognize the possibility that the nature and societal role of law are not the same across all societies at a single point in time and are not the same within a single society at all points in time.

A. Scope of Law

An additional matter that must be addressed is the referent of the word "law." A study of law presupposes a definition of "law." Of course, every definition is to some extent arbitrary, and a single definition of a word will not encompass everything that everyone would include as a referent of the word. Nonetheless, a useful definition of law can be formulated for this book. Specifically, I define "law" as *the formally expressed rules that a government, following accepted procedures, adopts and interprets for the purpose of regulating behavior and organization.*[7] Law, that is, attempts to steer its target. As such, law is a means to ends—a tool that is employed by a society to attain certain goals.

Law as so defined has three key elements. First, a rule for behavior or organization is deemed to be law only if the governing body of a jurisdiction has adopted the rule.[8] A rule is thus not regarded as law unless it emanates from a government source, viz., a legislative or judicial body or an executive-branch administrative agency. Second, to regulate, a rule must involve (a) expectations for conduct or arrangements in the jurisdiction and (b) sanctions aimed at encouraging conformity to the expectations. While the sanctions can be (and probably most often are) penalties, they may also be rewards. Third, to be "formally expressed," a rule must be in written form, and government must be responsible for the writing.

While the exact boundary between rules that are law and rules that are not will undoubtedly be uncertain in particular situations, rules that are not law must be taken into account in order to understand the nature of law. Unfortunately, rules that are not law have traditionally been within the province of sociology and anthropology, but their relevance to law should not be ignored simply because of disciplinary lines. The scope of an area of study is fixed only by convention, and at least three reasons argue against continuing to stress just law in scholarship on law.

The first reason, which is important for the political process, is that law evidently does not have the type and magnitude of impact on a society that it is generally thought to have. Instead, rules outside law are likely to be primarily, if not almost entirely, responsible for sustaining social life. Until the limited role of law in the social order is appreciated, law will continue to be viewed as a relatively easy cure for societal ills, and the political process will be driven to satisfy the anxieties of constituents by adding or amending statutes. Emphasis on the political process, however, fails to take into account the appreciable body of social science research indicating that law does not substantially and permanently alter the incidence of behavior patterns in a society.[9] Because the institution of law is unable to provide effective, enduring solutions to social problems, a society must find these solutions elsewhere (if solutions can be found at all) and must come to appreciate the senselessness of social disorder stemming from politics.

Scholarship on law should consider rules that are not law for a second reason as well. Specifically, the concepts and doctrines of law in a society are shaped by the non-law concepts and doctrines of the society. What exists inside the institution of law depends on what exists outside, and the study of law cannot yield a full understanding of law if non-law rules are disregarded. If the framework I propose is useful, the institution of law operates within a societal context and is inextricably tied to that context. When the societal context of law is neglected, the current and evolving content of law cannot be explained, and the future content of law cannot be predicted.[10]

A third reason for including rules beyond the borders of law in studies of law is that rules outside law, and hence rules inside law, are responses to societal conditions. An awareness of rules outside of law thus provides an impetus to research on the societal circumstances that shape the rules of government for behavior and organization in a society. In particular, studies of the impact on law of societal characteristics—i.e., of the relationship to law of jurisdiction-level attributes—are necessary to dispel the belief that important, lasting concepts and doctrines of law arise randomly or are due to individual personalities.

B. Change in Societal Perceptions

Perceptions of "reality" are neither universal across space nor constant over time. Societies that have dissimilar central postulates—i.e., that have dissimilar cultures[11]—will differ in their perceptions of reality, and a society whose culture changes will alter its perceptions.[12] Indeed, a major change in culture creates epochs,[13] i.e., periods that are differentiated by what the society believes to be reality. Assumptions regarding and perceptions of gender and sex roles are illustrative. The evolution of these assumptions and perceptions in the United States can be traced through opinions written by the highest court of the nation, i.e., the U.S. Supreme Court.[14] An opinion of the Court is a useful indicator of the understanding that American society had of the role that was appropriate for each sex at the time the opinion was written. Once this understanding is known, the social pressures to sustain then-current sex role ideals can be inferred.

Two opinions of the U.S. Supreme Court, written approximately nine decades apart, illustrate the marked shift that has taken place in assumptions and perceptions regarding gender. At the start of the twentieth century, a woman was generally thought in the United States to be inescapably subservient to a man and to be unable to provide for herself. The following passage is in an opinion of the Court written in 1908:

> Even though all restrictions on political, personal and contractual rights were taken away, and she [i.e., a woman] stood, so far as statutes are concerned, upon an absolutely equal plane with him [i.e., a man], it would still be true that she is so constituted that she will rest upon and look to him for protection; that her physical structure and a proper discharge of her maternal functions—having in view not merely her own health, but the well-being of the race—justify legislation to protect her from the greed as well as the passion of man.[15]

By the end of the twentieth century, however, societal assumptions and perceptions relevant to gender were much different. Stereotypes of women and of men had become unacceptable,[16] and classifications grounded on the sex attribute could be employed only to compensate for disadvantages previously imposed on members of one sex.[17] Thus, in 1996, the U.S. Supreme Court wrote:

> "[G]eneralizations about 'the way women are,' estimates of what is appropriate for *most women*, no longer justify denying opportunity

> to women whose talent and capacity place them outside the average description."[18]

When the twentieth century ended, in short, American social values were more concerned with individuals than gender, and required that responses to an individual be based on the abilities and skills of the individual. A sex-based policy or practice was unacceptable unless the distinction between women and men was proven to stem from an inherent, relevant biological difference between the sexes.[19]

The experience of the United States during the twentieth century demonstrates that the gender-relevant assumptions and perceptions of a society, and the law stemming from them, are not fixed by the biological attribute of sex. They exist, instead, in a societal setting that varies across time and space. Indeed, while the United States rejects sex-role traditionalism in its law, Europe accepts sex-role traditionalism in furnishing women with support through law.[20]

C. Change in Individual Perceptions

Changes in the key assumptions and perceptions of a society over the course of time, however, occur in spite of a generally strong resistance to such change among humans at any particular time. For individuals, the assumptions that shape perceptions of the "real" character of social and physical environments have a strong tendency to persist, and these assumptions do not seem to be replaced easily or often by assumptions that break with the past.[21] Although the reasons for resistance to such change cannot be listed with certainty, they may include, inter alia, the physical structure of the human brain, psychological discomfort in the human individual that is caused by change, and/or convention-reinforcing feedback loops that are embedded in human groups. In the instant chapter, however, the reasons are not of concern. The point to be emphasized is that inertia is an integral part of the human condition and, therefore, exists in all scholarly endeavors, including science.[22]

The aversion of individuals to perceptual change would be an unimportant topic suitable merely for idle conversation except that this aversion can have serious practical consequences. For example, the aversion causes continued reliance on past solutions to problematic situations when the situations have altered and the responses of the past can no longer correct the problems efficiently, or at all.[23] In the case of situations that have remained the same but that are poorly comprehended, the aversion is an impediment to the discovery of approaches that deal with the situations effectively. In a scholarly discipline, the aversion to perceptual change thus prevents the abandonment of a theory or framework for a phenomenon in spite of evidence that the theory or framework fails to account adequately for the phenomenon. The aversion thus retards the acceptance of new understandings of a phenomenon that are more complete, or at least more promising, and hinders the accumulation of knowledge.

II. Societal Beliefs about the Nature of Law

The study of the institution of law illustrates the preceding point. Scholarship on all topics is affected by assumptions and perceptions, and scholarship on law is no exception. In this part of Chapter 1, I consider three of the assumptions that support the perception of law that seems to prevail in the United States today. The three assumptions are:

1. A jurisdiction undergoes a change in its law (a) *because* its constitution is construed by the judiciary or (b) *because* a statute is adopted by the legislature or is interpreted by a judicial body or an administrative agency. Under assumption #1, then, the concepts and doctrines of law are believed to be the work of government.
2. The government actions that are responsible for the content of law are determined through and by politics, e.g., through and by elections, lobbying, and appointments and nominations of government officers. Under assumption #2, the political process is thought to drive government action and, hence, to explain the concepts and doctrines of law.
3. Regulation by law is essential for assuring that the behavior expected of others will occur; by supporting expectations for behavior, law makes possible interpersonal and intergroup relationships, i.e., social life.[24] Given its indispensable role in sustaining society, law-based regulation for an activity is adopted when the activity offends strongly held societal values. When law already exists to regulate such an activity, the government expands enforcement of the law and/or increases the penalties for violating it. Under assumption #3, law is considered to be fundamental to the stability of society.

The preceding assumptions appear to be widely accepted, but are they correct? Given the definition of law that has been adopted in this book,[25] assumption #1 is accurate, though just superficially. Assumption #1 is wanting because it leads to analyses that explore no more than the surface of law. Notably, the assumption is prevalent in U.S. law schools and is thus routinely imparted in the education of lawyers.

While assumption #1 has some justification, albeit shallow, assumptions #2 and #3 are indefensible and need to be thoroughly reassessed. I discuss next the reasons I am dubious about these two assumptions, and in subsequent chapters, I identify difficulties in some other popular beliefs about the institution of law.

A. The Political Process

Let me begin by pointing out that, as a set, the three assumptions involve a common matter—viz., whether, how, and why law differs between jurisdictions and evolves over time within jurisdictions. Perhaps surprisingly, the causes of differences and changes in law are not well understood. In discussions of the processes and sources of change, however, emphasis often seems to be placed on politics. I turn, therefore, to the phenomenon of politics, the subject of assumption #2.

Admittedly, politics is involved in the adoption, revision, and repeal of law, but a particular political figure or event—even one receiving considerable attention—is not necessarily the cause of a specific concept or doctrine of law. Regrettably, the belief that the political process is a vital influence on the content of law is taken for granted, and the supposed influence of politics in formulating law typically goes unquestioned. The possibility is ignored that politics is determined by factors embedded in society and that in the long run politics contributes little or nothing of its own to law because it is the product of macro-level forces.

To understand a phenomenon, all of the links in the chain that lead to the phenomenon must be identified and the exact role of each link must be ascertained. In the framework for law that I advocate, politics and its personalities and events are believed to have no major, enduring impact on the content of law[26] even though they occupy a temporal position between societal characteristics and law.[27] Any material impact of politics is expected to be brief, and any long-term impact of politics is expected to be no more than minor. Instead, my framework—whose objective is to explain differences between jurisdictions and change within jurisdictions in the concepts and doctrines of law—posits that the causes of law are society-level factors, that these factors drive politics, and that the significant attention that politicians and political events receive (especially in the mass media) is accordingly unwarranted. In other words, although the political process is a salient mechanism for transmitting societal pressure to alter existing law on an activity, politics is not, in my framework, the *source* of the pressure. Instead, the conditions of social life generate the pressure, and the pressure is transmitted through politics and through other means, e.g., private conversations between legislators and individuals with whom they have a close, personal relationship.[28]

Is there a cogent empirical reason for doubting that elected and appointed individuals have a unique, significant influence on the formulation of law? I believe that there is.[29] A notable aspect of change in law is that nations often concurrently yet independently adopt the same or similar law. Let me give one example.[30] From the 1960s to the 1980s, most of the countries in Western Europe altered their law on divorce and expanded the grounds for dissolving a marriage.[31] During the same historical period, almost every state in the United States enacted legislation that accepted divorce without evidence of fault.[32] Each nation and U.S. state that acted, however, had its own political figures. The preceding point is critical—while political processes and political figures were involved in the liberalization of divorce law, the individuals who were the political figures, though advancing the same idea, differed from one jurisdiction to another. Political processes and figures are unable to explain a particular shift in law when the shift involves like content but different individuals.[33]

What, then, accounts for the common outcome (i.e., liberalized divorce law) in these jurisdictions? If developments in law have causes, chance cannot explain the joint occurrence of an identical (or similar) change in the law of different jurisdictions during the same period of history. Instead, the most likely explanation for the common outcome is that the political domain was being propelled by one or more macro-level forces and that all of the jurisdictions were simultaneously subject to the same force(s). The easing of law-created restrictions on divorce involved politics, of course, but the easing was not produced by politics. The foregoing proposition is plausible (even though it has not been directly tested) because research has unearthed definite ties between societal attributes and law on topics other than divorce.[34]

B. Regulatory Law and Societal Stability

Let me turn now to the assumption that law is indispensable for minimizing disruptions in social life and that enforcement of the doctrines of law is essential to maintaining societal equilibrium. This is assumption #3, and like assumption #2, I believe it is erroneous. A recent study of homicide illustrates the questionable accuracy of assumption #3. No interpersonal act is more violent and destructive than homicide, and if the institution of law does not respond to homicide in ways that have the potential to reduce the occurrence of homicide in the future, the institution will probably not be a useful safeguard against other types of socially disruptive acts. The study is thus notable in finding that higher rates of homicide in U.S. counties *reduced* the probability of conviction for defendants who were charged with homicide and *shortened* the length of the prison terms imposed on defendants who were convicted of homicide.[35] The findings are the opposite of what popular beliefs about law would anticipate, and while assumption #3 cannot be dismissed on the basis of a single study, confidence in the accuracy of the assumption is obviously undermined by the study.

In my framework, regulatory law is adopted, revised, or reinterpreted for an activity that is within the core of social life—but *after*, not before, the activity becomes more frequent and/or more salient. This point is illustrated by the above study: As the homicide rate increased, prosecutors and judges evidently altered the construction of law on homicide through, for example, plea bargaining and trial rulings. The point is also illustrated by two other significant aspects of social life—divorce and abortion—and I discuss each below. As I hope to make clear, divorce and abortion provide reason to doubt the accuracy of assumption #3. Because of the availability of data, my discussion is confined to divorce and abortion in the United States.

1. Divorce

If the framework I am proposing is correct, divorce without fault was authorized by law due to mounting societal pressure for such law. To assess the foregoing proposition, I begin with a measure of the incidence of divorce. The measure that seems to be used most often in social science research is the number of divorces per one thousand population. However, this measure can yield a misleading picture of change over time in the likelihood of divorce, because its denominator includes individuals who are not married (e.g., minors who, because of their age, are ineligible to marry). The latter individuals may not comprise the same share of the denominator in every time period, and when they do not, the divorce rate as gauged by the number of divorces per one thousand population will be affected. To illustrate, an increase in the number of births, by expanding the denominator, will reduce the number of divorces per one thousand population even when the risk of divorce remains constant.

To ascertain whether the likelihood of divorce changed over time, I will focus on differences between marriage cohorts in the incidence of divorce by specific durations of marriage. Such a focus avoids the potential errors contained in other measures.[36] A marriage cohort is composed of all marriages that take place during a particular year or range of years, and an examination of numerous marriage cohorts at a given length of marriage can reveal whether the risk of divorce increased in the period prior to the arrival of no-fault divorce. Length of marriage must be taken into account because as time passes, an increasing percentage of the marriages within a cohort will end in divorce; the failure to control length of marriage can thus produce mistaken conclusions regarding trends in the likelihood of divorce. If the likelihood of divorce for a given marital duration rose from early to recent marriage cohorts, marriage was progressively weakening, and if marriage was becoming less attractive before the advent of no-fault divorce, the onset of law authorizing no-fault divorce can plausibly be attributed to societal pressure for it.

Fortunately, estimates exist on the incidence of divorce by marital duration in marriage cohorts prior to, as well as during the initial part of, the period (1970–1989) when no-fault divorce became available by statute in the United States.[37] The estimates cover calendar years through 1975 and were published by the National Center for Health Statistics, an agency of the U.S. government.[38] Data extending beyond 1975, though including a longer marital history for each cohort, are unnecessary for my analysis, because by 1975 most states had provided some no-fault statutory ground for divorce[39] and because my primary objective is to ascertain whether the likelihood of divorce was changing *before* no-fault divorce became available by state statute.

The data are graphed in Figure 1.1.[40] The horizontal axis of the figure gives the calendar year (1948 through 1971) in which the marriages of a cohort occurred, and the vertical axis specifies the cumulative (i.e., total) percentage of marriages that had been dissolved by divorce up to a particular marriage anniversary. The trend lines in the figure show the percentages of dissolved marriages over time at different marital durations (marriage anniversaries). The shortest marital duration in the figure is the fourth anniversary, and the longest is the fifteenth anniversary; in addition, the cumulative incidence of divorce is provided

Figure 1.1 Cumulative Percentage of Marriages Ended by Divorce
By year and length of marriage

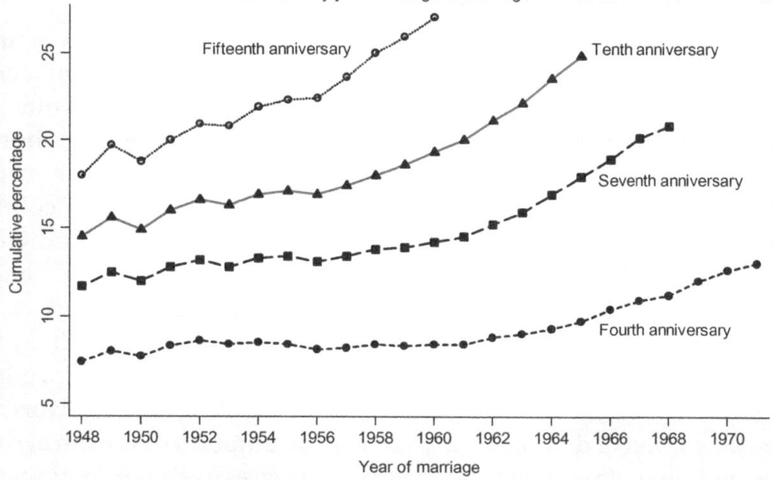

for the seventh anniversary and for the tenth anniversary. Because 1975 is the final calendar year covered by the data, the last marriage cohort included in Figure 1.1 differs between marriage anniversaries. To illustrate, the data in the figure for the fourth anniversary end with the marriage cohort of 1971 since the fourth anniversary for the 1971 cohort occurred in 1975.

Marriage anniversary	**Marriage cohorts covered in Figure 1.1**
Fourth	1948 through 1971
Seventh	1948 through 1968
Tenth	1948 through 1965
Fifteenth	1948 through 1960

Figure 1.1 shows that, beginning with the marriage cohort of 1950, a substantial secular rise took place in the likelihood of divorce by the seventh marriage anniversary, by the tenth marriage anniversary, and by the fifteenth marriage anniversary. The incidence of divorce up to the seventh anniversary, for example, was 12.0 percent in the cohort of 1950 (whose seventh anniversary was in calendar year 1957) and was

15.2 percent in the cohort of 1962 (whose seventh anniversary was in calendar year 1969). Even for the fourth anniversary, the incidence of divorce increased, although the increase did not commence until the 1962 cohort (whose fourth anniversary was in 1966). Once started, the increases were appreciable for all lengths of marriage and caused recent marriage cohorts to attain given levels of divorce earlier than temporally distant cohorts.[41]

The magnitude of the increases in divorce likelihood prior to the arrival of no-fault divorce are given numerically in Table 1.1, which presents for each marriage anniversary (a) the percentage of marriages in the 1950 marriage cohort that had been terminated by divorce as of the first calendar year each anniversary was reached by the 1950 cohort (see column 2); (b) the percentage of marriages that had been terminated by divorce as of 1969 in the last marriage cohort that arrived at each anniversary in 1969 (see columns 3 and 4); and (c) the change from (a) to (b) measured in percentages (see column 5). The amounts in column 5 were computed for each anniversary by subtracting (a) from (b), dividing by (a), and multiplying by 100. The amounts in column 5 are thus percentages, not percentage points, and are the changes in divorce risk by marriage anniversary from the calendar years in column 2 to 1969.

Column 5 of Table 1.1 reveals that, before the period when divorce without fault became available in states—i.e., before 1970–1989—the likelihood of divorce rose fully one-fourth at marriage anniversaries

Table 1.1 Cumulative Divorce Rate for 1950 Marriage Cohort, and Increase in Cumulative Divorce Rate to 1969, by Marriage Anniversary

Marriage anniversary (column 1)	Cumulative divorce rate: 1950 marriage cohort in specified calendar year (column 2)	Cumulative divorce rate in 1969 for marriage cohort in column 4 (column 3)	Marriage cohort (column 4)	Percentage increase in cumulative divorce rate: columns 2–3 (column 5)
Fourth	7.7% in 1954	9.7%	1965	26.0
Seventh	12.0% in 1957	15.2%	1962	26.7
Tenth	14.9% in 1960	18.6%	1959	24.8
Fifteenth	18.8% in 1965	21.9%	1954	16.5

of ten years or less. At the fifteenth anniversary, the increase was smaller, with the risk of divorce growing by one-sixth. However, all of the percentages in column 5 do not involve the same length of time. For instance, the percentage in column 5 for the fourth anniversary represents change in the divorce rate over a fifteen-year period, but the percentage in column 5 for the fifteenth anniversary represents change in the divorce rate over just a four-year period. In order to compare marital durations, accordingly, percentages *per year* are required. When the percentages in column 5 are recalculated to take into consideration the number of years over which the divorce rate changed, the pace of the increase in the divorce rate is found to vary directly with marital duration. To be exact, the percentages per year for the fourth, seventh, tenth, and fifteenth anniversaries are 1.7, 2.2, 2.8, and 4.1, respectively. Clearly, the risk of divorce in the decade-and-a-half following marriage grew at a not-inconsequential clip prior to the availability of no-fault divorce.

Figure 1.1 and Table 1.1, in short, furnish evidence that, in the last half of the 1950s and in the 1960s, pressure to ease the requirements of law for dissolving a marriage was intensifying in the United States.[42] However, the increases in the incidence of divorce at this time were almost certainly not the sole factor creating the pressure for legislation to allow divorce without fault. A secular rise in the divorce rate had been occurring in the United States since at least the last third of the nineteenth century,[43] but no-fault divorce was not approved by legislatures until the last third of the twentieth century. An explanation of the legislative action on no-fault divorce, consequently, must include one or more other societal factors that emerged after World War II and that added to the impact of the growing divorce rate.

One such factor is suggested by Table 1.2. The percentages in the table include persons in the specified ages who had ever married, whether or not they were currently married.[44] As the table reveals, there were increases between 1950 and 1960 in the percentages of men and of women, at both age 20–24 and at age 25–29, who were or had been married.[45] Two points are noteworthy. First, the 1950–1960 change was larger in absolute amount for men who were 20–24 years old than for women in that age range, and the change for men occurred against an appreciably smaller base. During the 1950s, therefore, a materially larger proportional increase took place among men than among women in the percentage ever married at age 20–24. Because the change among men 20–24 years old was also considerably larger

Table 1.2 Percentage of Persons in the United States Who Had Ever Married, by Year, Age, and Sex

Year	Persons 20–24 years old		Persons 25–29 years old	
	Males (%)	Females (%)	Males (%)	Females (%)
1950	40.9	67.7	76.2	86.7
1960	46.9	71.5	79.2	89.5
1970	44.5	63.7	80.4	87.8
1980	31.8	48.8	67.9	78.4

than the change among men 25–29 years old, marriage became more acceptable in this decade to the members of the sex-age group that had been relatively unwilling to enter it. Second, the percentages ever-married were noticeably smaller in 1980 than in 1960 in every age-sex group, but the 1960-to-1980 declines were bigger at age 20–24 than at age 25–29. Of greater importance, the 1960-to-1980 decline in the percentages at age 20–24 was much larger among women than men, and as a result, the sex gap in the percentage ever-married at age 20–24 was appreciably smaller in 1980 than in 1950 or in 1960. Together, the preceding indicate that marriage and its incidents were especially prominent concerns in U.S. society during the 1950s and became less so by the end of the two decades that followed.[46] The 1950s, in short, differed from later decades in a way that was sociologically significant.

If scholarship on law is to understand the adoption of law, including law permitting divorce without fault, it must at least consider society-wide developments because these developments may not be coincidence. Figure 1.1, Tables 1.1 and 1.2 when juxtaposed suggest a plausible explanation for the appearance of no-fault divorce in state statutes beginning in 1969. In this regard, the reader should keep in mind that the societal pressure leading to the adoption of legislation authorizing no-fault divorce would have required time to have its effect and that only one state out of fifty did not adopt such legislation over the two decades that followed 1969.

My hypothesis is that, during the 1950s, the expanded prevalence of marriage raised the salience of the marital relationship, while increases in the incidence of divorce, especially in the late 1950s and the 1960s, made more salient the grounds allowed by law for dissolving the marital relationship. Acting in concert, the foregoing changes initiated pressure on the institution of law to remove conspicuous law-based impediments to exiting marriage.[47] From a sociological perspective, fault as a ground for divorce is incompatible with the character of a society that, like the United States, is rapidly changing and structurally complex. In such a setting, many marriages unavoidably are or become unworkable. Moreover, the growth in the prevalence of marriage during the 1950s may have combined synergistically rather than additively with the increasing likelihood of marital failure during the late 1950s and the 1960s. If so, the two changes would have been especially likely to create pressure on legislatures to provide for divorce without fault. Finally, the pressure may have been intensified by the subsequent growth of a reluctance to marry. The declines in entry into marriage that occurred between 1960 and 1970, although not large, signaled an erosion of the societal importance of marriage, and the declines between 1970 and 1980 indicated that the pace of this erosion accelerated.

2. Abortion

The advent of law authorizing no-fault divorce in the United States should be considered only an instance of the general proposition that law on an activity embedded in the fabric of a society changes after, not before, the activity has become more common or significant in the society. Indeed, by the time a doctrine of law on a socially important activity is adopted, most of the change in the activity may have already taken place. Law thus recognized that marriage—an arrangement at the core of social life—could be ended without evidence of spousal fault after more young people had entered marriage and then exited it through divorce under existing law.

Is the proposition applicable to numerous societal phenomena? An affirmative answer to the question garners indirect support from an impressive body of social science research. As I will point out in later chapters, well-designed studies find that law has just a small and/or brief impact on the frequency and prevalence of a variety of socially salient activities. These findings can be explained by the proposition that developments in society precede and are responsible for developments in law.

Here, however, I want to support the proposition with another concrete illustration. I do so with the emotionally charged and politically contentious subject of abortion. Politicians may claim, and many people (including some scholars) may believe, that the incidence of mortality among women from unlawfully induced abortions is high and that many women in the United States will die if government adopts law designed to restrict access to abortion.[48] The claim, however, is inconsistent with the incidence of mortality among women from illegal (i.e., unlawfully induced) abortions in the years before law on abortion was liberalized in the United States.[49] Although perhaps surprising, that incidence was evidently quite low.[50] Indeed, prior to the period when law in the United States was rewritten to relax the prerequisites for legally terminating a pregnancy—a period that started in the last half of the 1960s[51]—the general safety of unlawfully induced abortions was known and had been acknowledged. In 1960, the medical director of the Planned Parenthood Federation of America—an organization that has favored the elimination of law-based restrictions for terminating pregnancies—stated that "abortion, whether therapeutic or illegal, is in the main no longer dangerous."[52]

What is an appropriate time span in the United States for assessing the incidence of mortality among women from unlawfully induced abortions? I will rely on the years around 1960 for two reasons. First, law-based restrictions on abortion were removed shortly thereafter. Prior to the ruling in 1973 of the U.S. Supreme Court in Roe v. Wade,[53] sixteen states modified their law to ease restrictions on inducing abortions, and these states began to do so in 1967.[54] Second, while the number of women dying from abortion had markedly declined from 1940 to 1950[55]—a decline that seems to be attributable to the discovery and use of antibiotics[56] and perhaps to an increase in abortions done by skilled physicians[57]—the number that died was relatively stable from 1950 to 1965.[58]

How many women died annually from aborting pregnancies in the period before law on abortion was changed? Although the precise number is unknown, data from the National Center for Health Statistics indicate that a mean of 292 women died per year from abortion during 1958–1962.[59] However, this number is not restricted to deaths from illegal abortions; it also includes deaths due to lawfully induced abortions, spontaneous abortions (miscarriages), and "undetermined causes." Unfortunately, deaths from spontaneous abortions and undetermined causes are combined into a single category for 1958–1962, but assuming that deaths from undetermined causes in 1958–1962 are the same proportion of all deaths in these two categories in 1968 and 1969 (when frequencies are first reported separately for each category), deaths from undetermined causes were roughly three-fourths of the deaths in the two categories in 1958–1962.[60] If deaths from undetermined causes[61] are then assigned to unlawfully induced abortions and to lawfully induced abortions in proportion to the incidence of deaths reported for each of the foregoing categories (unlawfully induced abortions and lawfully induced abortions) in 1958–1962,[62] the mean number of women who died in this period from an illegal abortion was 237 per year.[63]

Although a pregnant woman was more likely to die from an unlawfully induced abortion than from a lawfully induced abortion during the period before law on abortion was liberalized,[64] the risk of death posed by illegal abortion was relatively small.[65] The magnitude of this risk can be understood by reference to the annual number of abortions in the United States during the pre-reform period. The total number of abortions is thought to have been in the vicinity of one million each year,[66] all but eight thousand of which were illegal.[67] Because the number of lawfully induced abortions was negligible, I will initially assume that 1 million illegal abortions were performed annually in the United States.

With these assumptions, less than three-hundredths of 1 percent of women who had an illegal abortion died as a result.[68] However, let us suppose that the number of women who died yearly from illegal abortions was five times larger than the estimate above (i.e., 237); in other words, let us assume that 80 percent of all abortion-related deaths among women from unlawfully induced abortions were not counted and that the annual number of these deaths was thus approximately 1,200. The latter estimate (1,200) is likely to be far higher than the actual number, because mortality from illegal abortion was probably no more than two times larger than the estimate of 237.[69] The calculations below can accordingly be expected to provide a substantial overstatement of the mortality rate. The calculations, nonetheless, are useful for illustrating the point that the abortion-related death rate among women who had an illegal abortion was very low during the period that preceded the liberalization of law on abortion.

If 1,200 women died annually from unlawfully performed abortions, the mortality rate due to abortion among women who had illegal abortions is higher than the initial calculation, but it is still only about one-tenth of 1 percent.[70] The low mortality rate is further illustrated by retaining the assumption that 1,200 women died each year from an illegal abortion and making the assumption that the annual number of illegal abortions was 500,000 rather than 1,000,000. Let us suppose, in short, that 80 percent of abortion-caused deaths among women having illegal abortions were excluded from my count and that the yearly number of illegal abortions was just half the number I used in the prior calculations. With these assumptions, only one-quarter of 1 percent of all women who had an unlawfully induced termination of a pregnancy before the liberalization of law on abortion died as a consequence of their abortion.[71]

III. Lineage and Organization of the Book

If the thesis I am advancing is correct, the institution of law in a democratic nation is a reactive mechanism, following rather than leading the social system of the nation. To be exact, changes in doctrines of law that address activities at the core of social life are made necessary by changes in these activities, because doctrines of law must acknowledge existing societal needs and endorse prevailing social values. Whether law accepts or attempts to suppress a particular activity[72] will be determined by whether, and the degree to which, the activity fits or conflicts with social values.[73]

Although the thesis of the present book is inconsistent with popular assumptions about law,[74] the essence of the thesis is far from novel. The book is part of a long-standing intellectual tradition—namely, the theory of structuralism and functionalism in the sociology of law.[75] The book belongs to this tradition[76] because of its twin premises that law is molded by macro-level attributes of society[77] and serves to preserve (and, when necessary, strengthen) the stability of society.[78] The book thus incorporates central assumptions of structuralism and functionalism. However, the book departs from the traditional version of structuralism and functionalism in at least two significant respects, which I consider next.

First, the book contends that the societal contributions of law differ from the contributions that have been posited by theories in structuralism and functionalism. The book is particularly out of the mainstream of such theories in rejecting the notion that law provides a major benefit to society by effectively regulating behavior and that law, being an effective regulator, is a useful tool for (re)shaping society.[79] Although this notion seems to have been, and seems to remain, popular in the United States, empirical studies cast doubt on its accuracy with regard to social issues.[80]

A second aspect of the book distinguishes it from theoretical works on the sociology of law that are in the tradition of structuralism and functionalism. During the past quarter of a century, the social sciences have made major strides in the quality (as well as in the quantity) of their research. The improvements in quality have probably been due to several factors. Obvious factors include advances in statistical techniques; acquisition of longitudinal data, especially time-series data; and growth in the power, and reductions in the price, of computer technology. All of these developments are recent, and the quantitative social science research they have made possible form a cornerstone of the instant book.

Of course, the social science research completed during the last quarter-century was unavailable to writers who made earlier attempts to build theory in the sociology of law. Each of these writers (including the two discussed in Part III-A infra) was accordingly handicapped. However, quantitative research can no longer be neglected when building theory. The macrosociological framework for law proposed in the present book is thus based on, or at least suggested by, quantitative research conducted in the last few decades. The framework, I hope, will assist in understanding law, but the reader should appreciate that the framework is suggestive, not definitive. In spite of the appreciable body of well-designed quantitative research that has accumulated, there are still large gaps in knowledge, not-inconsiderable limitations in measurement methods, and possible defects in hypothesis-testing procedures (especially with regard to the use of tests of statistical significance). Consequently, much more research is needed along with improvements in research methodology, and the framework I propose for law as a societal institution is unavoidably tentative.

A further comment may be helpful regarding quantitative research. While I believe that quantitative research is essential to answering a range of important questions regarding law, the reader should keep in mind that no single quantitative study is conclusive and that every quantitative study will contain at least one limitation (perhaps in the population it examined) and flaw (perhaps in the measurement of variables). However, compared to personal experience, which has evidently been the principal basis to date for theory in the sociology of law, quantitative research has at least two major advantages—(a) it allows, if it does not demand, a higher degree of precision and (b) it facilitates verification of findings through follow-up studies by other investigators. These advantages give quantitative research a substantial edge over personal experience in adding to the store of knowledge—which, of course, is the goal of scholarship. During the nineteenth century, empiricism (including quantitative research) displaced personal observation as the accepted source of knowledge,[81] and the success of empiricism presumably occurred because of its superiority in building knowledge.

A. Lineage of the Book

I turn now to a synopsis of the writings of two sociologists whose analyses of law make them notable intellectual forerunners of the framework that is posited in the present book. While their conclusions regarding law are not identical to mine, their analyses share some important similarities with the analysis of law in this book. The two sociologists are Émile Durkheim and Donald Black.

Durkheim, whose writings have had a profound impact on the sociological theory of structuralism and functionalism, thought that the content of law in a society embodies the social character of the society.[82] According to Durkheim, whose chief works were published during the last decade of the nineteenth century and the first decade of the twentieth century,[83] two polarities of interpersonal ties (i.e., of social cohesion) exist for societies, and the polarities arise from differences in the degree to which roles in the economy, as well as roles in social life, are specialized. Durkheim, who labeled the polarities "mechanical solidarity" and "organic solidarity," contended that the differences in social structure associated with the polarities are manifested in and measured by differences in law.[84] His thesis thus considered society-level factors to be present in the institution of law and to be determinants of the content and societal function of the institution.

Of notable relevance to the present book, Durkheim explicitly identified or implicitly suggested two factors that he believed generate change in the structure of a society and hence in its law. These factors are fundamental to my line of reasoning, because I too believe they have acted (and will continue to act) as important macro-level influences on law. The factors are (a) the size and density of population[85] and (b) the utility and availability of knowledge and technology.[86] Each factor affects every individual in a society but is beyond the control of any particular individual, and each factor is the result of macro-level forces, e.g., migration patterns in the case of change in population density and social values in the case of change in knowledge/technology. Both factors are thus central to a sociological study of law.

In addition to the scholarship of Émile Durkheim, a book by Donald Black is within the lineage of my work.[87] In his book, which was published in 1976, Black was concerned with differences in law between societies at one point in time and with change in law in a society over time. Such differences and change were explained by reference to factors that are part of the sociological theory of structuralism and functionalism. The propositions that Black formulates to explain this variation are supported mainly with case studies drawn from anthropology and history.

Let me illustrate the sociological variables that Black employs to account for spatial and temporal variation in law. One proposition proposed by Black is that the amount of law in a society is proportional to, and the result of, the degree to which the society is stratified.[88] Law thus becomes larger in quantity as stratification increases. However, the manner in which Black measures the amount of law places the proposition outside my framework. In particular, Black counts every law-related occurrence in the institution of law. Such occurrences include, for example, each filing of a complaint or application, each arrest and conviction, and each award of damages. They also include every instance when law is promulgated, e.g., each statute, court decision, and administrative-agency rule and interpretation.[89] The proposition proffered by Black thus deals with numerical tallies of events that take place within the institution of law. My focus, on the other hand, is not with the volume of law but, rather, with the referents of the concepts of law and with the substance of the doctrines of law, i.e., with the foci and stated rules of law.

The quantity of law is not the sole focus of the propositions proffered by Black. The way in which law is applied is a variable inherent in some of his propositions. For instance, Black suggests that the institution of law deals not just more frequently but also more severely with parties that occupy low positions in the stratification hierarchy of a society than with parties that occupy high positions.[90] When the institution of law handles cases in which the parties are not at the same stratification level, Black contends, the institution is harsher towards the injuring party to the degree that the injuring party is lower in rank than the injured party, i.e., to the degree that the former party is below the latter party in the stratification hierarchy.[91] Similarly, the institution of law is expected by Black to be more likely to treat an injuring party unsympathetically when the social marginality of the injuring party increases and is greater than that of the injured party.[92]

As the previous paragraph implies, Black assumed in his book that the control of social life is the chief, and perhaps sole, function of law,[93] and his propositions are constructed largely on this assumption. Indeed, Black posits that the quantity of law in a society rises when there are declines in such control by other societal institutions.[94] However, while the attempt by Black to explain law with structural sociological variables moves the study of law in a needed direction, the relationships posited by his propositions may not exist if law does not serve the function on which his propositions are grounded.

Black, however, was not alone in assuming that law controls behavior. Durkheim, too, regarded law as a key source of social control, but Durkheim treated law in a more nuanced fashion. Specifically, Durkheim believed that law is an effective mechanism for regulation not only because it compels particular behaviors but also because it inspires commitment to society.[95] In the latter respect, my book can be traced to Durkheim.

B. Organization of the Book

The remainder of the instant book has been divided into two parts—one concerned with concepts and the other with explanations. Chapters 2 through 5 focus on concepts that place law in a societal setting and highlight its social character. One concept, which is the subject of Chapters 2 and 3, is social productivity, which directs attention to aspects of law that are neglected by its alternatives, i.e., economic productivity and social capital. Another concept, which is the subject of Chapters 4 and 5, is social values. Chapter 4 contends that long-term and widespread change in social values created the foundation for the recent upheaval in finance in the United States. Chapter 5 considers the concept of social values in conjunction with the concept of morality. This chapter suggests that the concepts together furnish a basis for explaining, at least partially, a change that occurred over the course of four decades in a particular doctrine of law in the United States. By doing so, Chapter 5 serves as a transition to the three chapters that follow.

Chapters 6–8 deal largely with quantitative studies that investigate whether sociological, demographic, and economic conditions of jurisdictions are temporal antecedents, and hence possible causes, of specific doctrines of law in these jurisdictions. Because such studies promise to alter current assumptions about law, their importance cannot be understated. To the degree that sociological, demographic, and/or economic characteristics of jurisdictions are related to the concepts and doctrines of law in the jurisdictions, each society furnishes the setting in which its institution of law operates and imposes the context that shapes the content of its law. Because the line of research found in Chapters 6–8 is essential to developing a useful macrosociological theory of law, key aspects of this research are discussed in Chapter 9.

Notes

1. The Quotations Page, http://www.quotationspage.com/quotes/Sir_William_Bragg (accessed April 7, 2011).
2. Alice H. Eagly and Shelly Chaiken, "Attitude Structure and Function," in *The Handbook of Social Psychology*, ed. Daniel T. Gilbert et al. (Boston, MA: McGraw-Hill, 1998), vol. 1, 4th ed., 269, 293–94; Susan T. Fiske and Shelley E. Taylor, *Social Cognition* (New York: McGraw-Hill, 1991), 2nd ed., 99, 121–22, 150.
3. Mark E. Koltko-Rivera, "The Psychology of Worldviews," *Review of General Psychology* 8 (2004): 3, 22–27.
4. Thomas S. Kuhn, *The Structure of Scientific Revolutions* (Chicago, IL: University of Chicago Press, 1996), 3rd ed., 10–18.
5. The thesis of this book and the propositions it advances are not a theory if theory is "[a] scheme or system of ideas or statements held as an explanation or account of a group of facts or phenomena; ...a statement of what are held to be the general laws, principles, or causes of something known or observed." *Oxford English Dictionary* 17 (1989), 2nd ed., 902. The instant book does not claim to offer a comprehensive set of propositions on the institution of law as a whole, and it does not articulate the relationships of subsets of the propositions to one another. Rather, the propositions in the book cover only certain aspects of the institution of law and, as to these aspects, are not systematized. Accordingly, the ideas proposed in the chapters of the book are more appropriately labeled a framework, i.e., they furnish an elementary structure for studying some of the phenomena within the institution of law.
6. Mansoor Niaz, "The Quantitative Imperative vs the Imperative of Presuppositions," *Theory & Psychology* 15 (2005): 247.
7. The participants in a society may receive benefits in the form of services and monetary payments through law-established programs. Such programs in the United States include, inter alia, Medicaid and Social Security. Regulation is involved in these programs, but is ancillary to them. Larry D. Barnett, *Legal Construct, Social Concept* (1993), 165.
8. The population covered by the law of a jurisdiction can be numerically small or large, and can be confined to a single locality or spread over a substantial geographic area. For the framework proposed in the instant book, however, the population must be in a nation that is sovereign, economically advanced, and socially complex.
9. Supporting quantitative social science research is cited infra in Parts III-E and V-B of Chapter 3 (notes 160–63, 165, and 209) and in Part II of Chapter 8 (notes 66 and 67).

10. The possibility and benefit of predicting law are discussed infra in Part V of Chapter 5.
11. Edgar H. Schein, "Culture: The Missing Concept in Organization Studies," *Administrative Science Quarterly* 41 (1996): 229, 236 (defining the word "culture" as "the set of shared, taken-for-granted implicit assumptions that a group holds and that determines how it perceives, thinks about, and reacts to its various environments").
12. Karen Miller-Loessi and John N. Parker, "Cross-Cultural Social Psychology," in *Handbook of Social Psychology*, ed. John Delamater (New York: Kluwer Academic/Plenum Publishers, 2003), 529, 533–35 (summarizing research that finds cross-cultural differences in the perception of phenomena). See Alan Page Fiske et al., "The Cultural Matrix of Social Psychology," in *Handbook of Social Psychology*, ed. Daniel T. Gilbert et al. (Boston, MA: McGraw-Hill, 1998), vol. 2, 4th ed., 915 (finding that psychological processes can differ between cultures). Cf. Perry den Brok et al., "Cultural Influences on Students' Perceptions of Videotaped Lessons," *International Journal of Intercultural Relations* 27 (2003): 355 (finding that the cultural background of students affected students' perceptions of teachers).
13. *Webster's Third New International Dictionary* (unabr. ed. 1993), 766 (defining the word "epoch" to include "a period of time during which a particular type of culture is dominant in an area").
14. Barnett, supra note 7, at 47–55.
15. Muller v. Oregon, *United States Reports* 208 (1908), 412, 422. The passage from *Muller* that is reproduced in the text was used again by the U.S. Supreme Court in 1915. Miller v. Wilson, *United States Reports* 236 (1915), 373, 380–81. The passage is evidently an accurate measure of the views regarding sex roles that were generally accepted by Americans at the start of the twentieth century. Jay Kleinberg, *Women in American Society 1820-1920* (British Association for American Studies, 1990), BASS Pamphlet No. 20, http://www.baas.ac.uk/index.php?option=com_content&view=article&id=227:jay-kleinberg-women-in-american-society-1820-1920&catid=18&Itemid=11 (accessed April 7, 2011). During the first half of the twentieth century, the preference for traditional sex roles evidently varied, declining in the 1920s and subsequently returning to its prior level. Barnett, supra note 7, at 47–51. In the 1930s, despite the instability and uncertainties caused by the economic depression, Americans wanted traditional sex roles. In 1938, for example, a survey of a national sample of adults found that 78 percent of all adults, including 75 percent of all women, disapproved "of a married woman earning money in business or industry if she has a husband capable of supporting her." George H. Gallup, *The Gallup Poll: Public Opinion 1935-1971* (1972), vol. 1, 131. The movement in the United States toward current sex-role ideals evidently started at some point during the second half of the twentieth century. See Part IV in Chapter 5 infra.
16. J. E. B. v. Alabama ex rel. T.B., *United States Reports* 511 (1994), 127, 135; Larry D. Barnett, "The Roots of Law," *American University Journal of Gender, Social Policy & the Law* 15 (2007): 613, 632–34 [hereinafter *The Roots of Law*]. Pages 632–34 in *The Roots of Law* are reproduced in Part II of Chapter 6 infra.

17. United States v. Virginia, *United States Reports* 518 (1996), 515, 533–34.
18. Ibid., 550. The quoted passage embodies prevailing social values at the end of the twentieth century in the United States. In 1997 and 1999, for example, at least seven out of ten adults in the United States disagreed "completely" or "mostly" with the statement that "women should return to their traditional roles in society." The Pew Research Center for the People & the Press Poll Database (Q.21J), http://people-press.org/questions/?qid=334750&pid=51&ccid=51#top and http://people-press.org/questions/?qid=407834&pid=51&ccid=51#top. See also Richard J. Harris and Juanita M. Firestone, "Changes in Predictors of Gender Role Ideologies among Women: A Multivariate Analysis," *Sex Roles* 38 (1998): 239, 245, 249 (finding substantial movement toward sex-role equality in the social values of adult United States women between 1974 and 1994).
19. United States v. Virginia, *United States Reports* 518 (1996), 515, 532–33; Nevada Dep't of Human Res. v. Hibbs, *United States Reports* 538 (2003), 721, 728–29.
20. Julie C. Suk, "Are Gender Stereotypes Bad for Women? Rethinking Antidiscrimination Law and Work-Family Conflict," *Columbia Law* Review 110 (2010): 1, 60 (noting that law in Europe does not place as much emphasis on countering sex role stereotypes as United States law and that anti-discrimination law in Europe is built on the expectation that women more often than men have family-care responsibilities).
21. Donald C. Langevoort, "Where Were the Lawyers? A Behavioral Inquiry Into Lawyers' Responsibility for Clients' Fraud?" *Vanderbilt Law Review* 46 (1993): 75, 100–1.
22. Juan Miguel Campanario, "The Parallelism between Scientists' and Students' Resistance to New Scientific Ideas," *International Journal of Science Education* 24 (2002): 1095.
23. José J. Cañas et al., "Cognitive Flexibility and Adaptability to Environmental Changes in Dynamic Complex Problem-Solving Tasks," *Ergonomics* 46 (2003): 482, 496–98.
24. See Heyer v. Flaig, 449 P.2d 161, 164 (Cal. 1969).
25. See the text accompanying note 7 supra.
26. Through the political process, however, certain political figures and events may be given credit for specific legislation. Catherine L. Carpenter, "Legislative Epidemics: A Cautionary Tale of Criminal Laws that Have Swept the Country," *Buffalo Law Review* 58 (2010): 1.
27. The political process is nonetheless critical in determining government action that directly affects behaviors and arrangements that are outside the core of social life. Illustrations of the importance of politics include the military involvement undertaken in Vietnam by the United States government during the third quarter of the twentieth century and the military incursion into Iraq launched by the United States government during the first decade of the twenty-first century. Both military actions are largely attributable to the particular individuals who had been elected to the office of President, and neither of the individuals was removed from office by impeachment. The election and impeachment of Presidents are inherently political. Indeed, elections and impeachments are considered in United States jurisprudence to be political matters. Patrick M. Garry,

"A Different Model for the Right to Privacy: The Political Question doctrine as a Substitute for Substantive Due Process," *University of Miami Law Review* 61, no. 8 (2006): 169, 171. See generally Rachel E. Barkow, "More Supreme than Court? The Fall of the Political Question Doctrine and the Rise of Judicial Supremacy," *Columbia Law Review* 102 (2002): 237 (reviewing the history of the political question doctrine).

28. The pressure may not be consciously exerted on legislators, judges, and administrative-agency rulemaking personnel. The pressure may occur in informal discussions of the activity that is the subject of the law.
29. Former U.S. President Ronald Reagan remarked that "[p]olitics is supposed to be the second oldest profession. I have come to realize that it bears a very close resemblance to the first." The Quotations Page, http://www.quotationspage.com/quotes/Ronald_Reagan. The point of the remark is that, on issues that are important to a society, the occupants of elected offices accede to the wishes of their constituencies, and the occupants of appointed offices do so as well (though perhaps not consciously). My contention in this book is that the constituents are responding to the properties of society.
30. For other examples, see the following: Julia L. Ernst et al., "The Global Pattern of U.S. Initiatives Curtailing Women's Reproductive Rights: A Perspective on the Increasingly Anti-Choice Mosaic," *University of Pennsylvania Journal of Constitutional Law* 6 (2004): 752, 759 (law on abortion); Aaron Xavier Fellmeth, "State Regulation of Sexuality in International Human Rights Law and Theory," *William and Mary Law Review* 50 (2008): 797, 817–18 (law on homosexuality). In addition, *compare* Jean R. Sternlight, "In Search of the Best Procedure for Enforcing Employment Discrimination Laws: A Comparative Analysis," *Tulane Law Review* 78 (2004): 1401, 1430–31, 1451 *with The Roots of Law*, supra note 16, at 632–35 (law on discrimination). Pages 632–35 of *The Roots of Law* are reproduced infra in Part II of Chapter 6.
31. Antony W. Dnes and Robert Rowthorn, *The Law and Economics of Marriage and Divorce* (New York: Cambridge University Press, 2002), 218–20; Shaakirrah R. Sanders, "The Cyclical Nature of Divorce in the Western Legal Tradition," *Loyola Law Review* 50 (2004): 407, 430–31.
32. The first state to provide a no-fault ground for divorce did so in 1969, and by the end of the 1980s, forty-nine of the fifty U.S. states had adopted a version of no-fault divorce. Lynn D. Wardle, "No-Fault Divorce and the Divorce Conundrum," *BYU Law Review* 79 (1991): 83, 87–90, 138. Because the legislation of the first state to act (California) was not in force until the following year, no-fault divorce did not become available in that state until 1970. Ibid., 83.
33. Politics, of course, is a potential explanation of substantial *differences* in law between jurisdictions at a single time point and between distant time points in a single jurisdiction. However, such differences may also be explained—and my framework contends that they are indeed explained—by societal properties.
34. Larry D. Barnett, *Mutual Funds, Hedge Funds, and the Public-Private Dichotomy in a Macrosociological Framework for Law* (Interuniversity Center for Research on the Sociology of Law, Information and Legal

Institutions, Working Paper No. 34, 2008), 11–13, http://www.cirsdig.it/Pubblicazioni/barnett.pdf (accessed April 7, 2011).

35. Mark Cooney and Callie Harbin Burt, "Less Crime, More Punishment," *American Journal of Sociology* 114 (2008): 491.
36. Differences between birth cohorts in the percentage ever divorced by a given age are less accurate as a gauge of long-term change in the likelihood of divorce than differences between marriage cohorts in the percentage of marriages that end in divorce by a specific duration of marriage. The percentage of each birth cohort that marries affects the percentage of each birth cohort that divorces, and the former percentage can vary appreciably over time. U.S. Census Bureau, *Detailed Tables — Number, Timing and Duration of Marriages and Divorces: 2004 Table 1* (2007), http://www.census.gov/hhes/socdemo/marriage/data/sipp/2004/tables.html (accessed April 7, 2011).
37. Wardle, supra note 32, at 83, 87–90, 137–38. In reporting the number of states by year that had a no-fault ground for divorce, Wardle presumably gives the year in which states approved legislation authorizing a no-fault ground. For example, Wardle reports that in 1969 eight states had a no-fault ground for divorce. Ibid., 138. However, the year of approval of legislation is not necessarily the year of its implementation. Supra note 32. I have added one year to each of the years given by Wardle on the assumption that (a) the legislation for a state was not in force until the year following its approval or (b) the legislation was not in force until late during the year in which it was approved, resulting in relatively few divorces on a no-fault ground that year.
38. Alexander A. Plateris, "Divorces by Marriage Cohort," in *Vital and Health Statistics*, Series 21, no. 34 (National Center for Health Statistics, DHEW Publication No. (PHS) 79-1912) (1979), http://www.cdc.gov/nchs/data/series/sr_21/sr21_034.pdf (accessed April 7, 2011). Estimates for years after 1975 are available in, e.g., U.S. Census Bureau, "Number, Timing, and Duration of Marriages and Divorces: 2001," *Current Population Reports*, Series P70-97 (2005): 6, table 2. However, duration-specific estimates of marriage termination by marriage cohort after 1975 are not as detailed as those for the period to 1975 and do not cover all of the marriage cohorts that are of interest here.
39. Wardle, supra note 32, at 137–38.
40. All of the data in Figure 1.1 are from Plateris, supra note 38, table 4.
41. Plateris, supra note 38, at 2. Some portion of the rise in divorce rates that followed the implementation of no-fault divorce law in states may have been due to the introduction of no-fault divorce. Divorce rates can be affected temporarily (even though they are not affected permanently) by a change in divorce law. Frans van Poppel and Joop de Beer, "Measuring the Effect of Changing Legislation on the Frequency of Divorce: The Netherlands, 1830–1990," *Demography* 30 (1993): 425; Thorsten Kneip and Gerrit Bauer, "Did Unilateral Divorce Laws Raise Divorce Rates in Western Europe?" *Journal of Marriage and Family* 71 (2009): 592, 602, 604.
42. The primary determinant of divorce rates for marriages is the period in which the divorces happen, not the year in which the marriages occur. Anne Babette Wils, "Period and Cohort Effects on Divorce Rates," *Popnet*

18 (1990): 11, 16. Because divorce rates are affected mainly by divorce period, the enactment of legislation authorizing divorce without proof of fault is evidently explained by the society-level factors that were then operating to raise divorce rates.

43. Samuel H. Preston and John McDonald, "The Incidence of Divorce Within Cohorts of American Marriages Contracted Since the Civil War," *Demography* 16 (1979): 1, 3–6.
44. States generally allow marriage at age sixteen with parental consent and at age eighteen without parental consent. Homer H. Clark, Jr., *The Law of Domestic Relations in the United States* (St. Paul, MN: West Publishing, 1988), 2nd student ed., 91.
45. The percentage in each cell of Table 1.2 was derived by subtracting from 100 the percentage of never-married persons in the age-sex category for that cell. The percentages of never-married persons were obtained or calculated from the following sources:

    1950: U.S. Census Bureau, *Census of Population: 1950*, Vol. II, Part I: United States Summary. Section 4: Detailed Characteristics: United States Summary Table 102 (1953), http://www2.census.gov/prod2/decennial/documents/21983999v2p1_TOC.pdf (accessed April 7, 2011).

    1960: U.S. Bureau of the Census, *United States Census of Population: 1960*, Vol. II: Subject Reports. Marital Status Table 1 (PC(2)-4E) (1966), http://www2.census.gov/prod2/decennial/documents/41927943v2p4a-4e_TOC.pdf (accessed April 7, 2011).

    1970: U.S. Census Bureau, *1970 Census of Population and Housing*, Vol. II: Subject Reports. Marital Status Table 1 (PC(2)-4C) (no date), http://www2.census.gov/prod2/decennial/documents/42045395v2p4a4c_TOC.pdf (accessed April 7, 2011).

    1980: U.S. Bureau of the Census, *1980 Census of Population*, Vol. 2: Subject Reports. Marital Characteristics Table 1 (PC80-2-4C) (1985), http://www.census.gov/prod/www/abs/decennial/1980cenpopv2.html (accessed April 7, 2011).
46. American social values during the 1950s have been characterized as traditional. E.g., Dan T. Carter, "The Rise of Conservatism since World War II," *Magazine of History* (January 2003): 11, 13; Anne McLeer, "Practical Perfection? The Nanny Negotiates Gender, Class, and Family Contradictions in 1960s Popular Culture," *NWSA Journal* (Summer 2002): 80, 82–83. However, the accuracy of the characterization can be tested to only a limited degree with quantitative measures and systematically gathered data. National sample surveys furnish some support in finding that, prior to the 1960s, slightly more than half of all adults in the United States thought that it was "not all right" for "either or both parties to a marriage to have had previous sexual experience"; only about three out of ten thought it was "all right" or "all right for men only." Tom W. Smith, "The Sexual Revolution?" *Public Opinion Quarterly* 54 (1990): 415, 421. Approval of sexual intercourse prior to marriage was evidently constant until the 1960s and began to rise only at some point during the 1960s. Ibid., 416.
47. The importance that social values attach to marriage in the United States was presumably the reason for law-based actions during the 1990s to promote and preserve marriage. These actions, however, had no more than

a trivial effect. Amy M. Donley and James D. Wright, "For Richer or For Poorer: The Impact of State-Level Legislation on Marriage, Divorce, and Other Outcomes," *Sociological Spectrum* 28 (2008): 133, 145, 153.

48. E.g., Jennifer L. Ernst and Matthew Barge, *Abortion Distortions* (August 22, 2005), http://www.factcheck.org/society/abortion_distortions.html (accessed April 7, 2011) (critiquing claim by a U.S. senator that five thousand women will die annually if the U.S. Supreme Court overrules its 1973 decision invalidating statutes that barred or severely limited access to abortion prior to fetus viability); Cass Sunstein, "Neutrality in Constitutional Law (with Special Reference to Pornography, Abortion, and Surrogacy," *Columbia Law Review* 92 (1992): 1, 37 (quoting estimate that "before Roe, 5,000 to 10,000 women died per year as a result of incompetently performed abortions").
49. In the event a reader suspects that my position is politically motivated, I want to make explicit that no conscious political ideology lies behind the analyses in the instant book. The political ideology of an author should not be present in scholarship, and I have attempted to exclude mine in writing this book.
50. For evidence that unlawfully induced abortions were generally safe in Britain before that country liberalized its law on abortion, see Colin Francome, "Estimating the Number of Illegal Abortions," *Journal of Biosocial Science* 9 (1977): 467, 477 table 5, 478.
51. See the text accompanying note 54 infra.
52. Mary Steichen Calderone, "Illegal Abortion as a Public Health Problem," *American Journal of Public Health* 50 (1960): 948, 949.
53. *United States Reports* 410 (1973), 113.
54. See Part II-A in Chapter 6 infra.
55. Willard Cates, Jr. et al., "Trends in National Abortion Mortality, United States, 1940–1974: Implications for Prevention of Future Abortion Deaths," *Advances in Planned Parenthood* 11 (1976): 106, 108.
56. Ibid., 111.
57. Christopher Tietze, "The Effect of Legalization of Abortion on Population Growth and Public Health," *Family Planning Perspectives* 7 (1975): 123, 127. Licensed physicians may have performed abortions more often by expansively interpreting the statutory grounds for abortion. Kristin Luker, *Abortion and the Politics of Motherhood* (Berkeley: University of California Press, 1984), 72, 80–82.
58. Cates et al., supra note 55, at 108.
59. Tietze, supra note 57, at 125, 126 & figure 1, 127 & table 4. The procedure for assigning cause of death can affect the count of deaths from a particular cause such as abortion. Ibid., 126.
60. In 1968 and 1969, deaths from undetermined causes among women who had an abortion were $(54 + 56)/(22 + 16 + 54 + 56) = 100/148 = 0.74 \times 100 = 74\%$ of all deaths from both spontaneous abortions and undetermined causes. Calculated from Ibid., 127, table 4.
61. According to the National Center for Health Statistics, 175 women died annually during 1958–1962 as the result of either a spontaneous abortion or, after having an abortion, an undetermined cause. Tietze, supra note 57, at 127, table 4. In 1958–1962, therefore, the number of women who

died yearly from an undetermined cause after an abortion was 0.74 x 175 = 130. The proportion 0.74 is derived from note 60 supra.

62. In 1958–1962, yearly deaths among women due to illegal abortion as a proportion of all deaths due to both illegal abortions and lawfully induced abortions was 112/117 = 0.96. Calculated from Tietze, supra note 57, at 127, table 4.
63. Of the 130 women who were estimated in note 61 supra to have died each year from an undetermined cause following an abortion, the proportion that was computed supra in note 62 indicates that 125 died from an illegal abortion (0.96 × 130 = 125). These 125 deaths do not include the deaths from illegal abortions that were recorded by the National Center for Health Statistics (NCHS). According to the NCHS, 112 women died annually from illegal abortion during 1958–1962. Tietze, supra note 57, at 127, table 4. Consequently, the total number of women who died each year during 1958–1962 from an illegal abortion would be 125 + 112 = 237.
64. Ibid., 127 table 4.
65. In judging the mortality risk to women from an unlawfully induced abortion, a focus on rates and percentages is preferable to a focus on absolute numbers. Absolute numbers can inject political ideology into discussions of abortion. Such ideology is inappropriate in social science scholarship.
66. Christopher Tietze, "Abortion on Request: Its Consequences for Population Trends and Public Health," *Seminars in Psychiatry* 2 (1970): 375.
67. Council on Scientific Affairs, American Medical Association, "Induced Termination of Pregnancy Before and After Roe v Wade," *JAMA* 268 (1992): 3231, 3234.
68. The percentage was computed as follows: 237/1,000,000 = 0.000237 × 100 = 0.0237%.
69. Tietze, supra note 66, at 375.
70. The percentage was computed as follows: 1,200/1,000,000 = 0.0012 × 100 = 0.12%.
71. The percentage was computed as follows: 1,200/500,000 = 0.0024 × 100 = 0.24%. A lower estimate of the annual number of illegal abortions at this time is 200,000. Brian W. Clowes, "The Role of Maternal Deaths in the Abortion Debate," *Saint Louis University Public Law Review* 13 (1993): 327, 332. An estimate of 200,000 cannot be summarily dismissed inasmuch as it is within the range of credible estimates, though at the low end of the range. Christopher Tietze et al., "Report of the Statistics Committee (May 29, 1957)," in *Abortion in the United States: A Conference Sponsored by the Planned Parenthood Federation of America and The New York Academy of Medicine*, ed. Mary Steichen Calderone (New York: Hoeber-Harper, 1958), 178, 180. However, even if illegal abortions numbered only 200,000 a year, just six-tenths of 1 percent of all women who had such abortions died from terminating their pregnancies (1,200/200,000 = 0.006 × 100 = 0.60%). The latter calculation is based on the assumption that 80 percent of all women who died from abortion were missed in my count, but as indicated in the text accompanying note 69 supra, the actual percentage is probably much lower than 80 percent. If so, use of the assumption materially inflates the death rate among women from unlawfully induced abortions.

72. One activity that law in the United States can be expected to accept widely in the future is physician assistance to terminally ill, mentally competent individuals who request assistance in ending their lives. See Part V in Chapter 8 infra.
73. When multiple social values bear on an activity, whether law accepts or seeks to eliminate an activity may depend on, inter alia, the rank of the most relevant value in the hierarchy of values and the degree to which that value is reinforced by other values.
74. See Part I-A in Chapter 5 infra. The thesis is especially at variance with the widespread belief in the ability of law to solve social problems. An illustration of the popularity of this belief is provided by a national sample survey of adults in the United States that was conducted in 1993. The survey found that 63 percent of respondents thought the frequency of violent crime would be curbed "a lot" if there were "longer jail terms for those convicted of violent crimes." Times Mirror Center for The People & The Press, *Public Backs Clinton on Gun Control* (1993), 9, http://people-press.org/http://people-press.org/files/legacy-pdf/19931210.pdf (accessed April 7, 2011) . Of course, the likelihood and length of imprisonment are affected by, inter alia, provisions of law, and they may change with the adoption of new provisions. The 1993 survey also found that 41 percent of all respondents expected the frequency of violent crime to be curbed "a lot" if there were "stricter gun control laws." (Ibid.) According to surveys conducted in 1989 and 1993, approximately two out of three adults in the United States supported "stricter gun control laws." John T. Young et al., "Guns," *Public Opinion Quarterly* 60 (1996): 634, 641.
75. A. Javier Treviño, *The Sociology of Law: Classical and Contemporary Perspectives* (New Brunswick, NJ: Transaction Publishers, 2008), 311–33.
76. See Part IV in Chapter 6 infra.
77. See Part III-A infra in Chapter 1.
78. Treviño, supra note 75, at 332.
79. See Ibid., 319, 328, 332.
80. Supporting studies are cited in (a) Part III-E and Part V-B in Chapter 3 infra and (b) Part II in Chapter 8 infra. However, regulation may be effective for some types of economic problems. Barnett, supra note 7, at 162–63.
81. W. T. Murphy, *The Oldest Social Science? Configurations of Law and Modernity* (Oxford: Clarendon Press; New York: Oxford University Press, 1997), 120–22.
82. Treviño, supra note 75, at 239–41; John R. Sutton, *Law/Society: Origins, Interactions, and Change* (Thousand Oaks, CA: Pine Forge Press, 2001), 35–41.
83. Treviño, supra note 75, at 234, 241–42.
84. Ibid., 234–39; Sutton, supra note 82, at 35–40.
85. Roger Cotterrell, *Émile Durkheim: Law in a Moral Domain* (Stanford, CA: Stanford University Press, 1999), 83; Leo F. Schnore, "Social Morphology and Human Ecology," *American Journal of Sociology* 63 (1958): 620, 622–23.
86. Durkheim contended that improvements in the technologies for communication and transportation were the source of change in law. Schnore, supra note 85, at 622–23. Improvements in the effectiveness and efficiency of

technology result generally from advances in knowledge, which advances may be facilitated by technologies that have previously been developed.
87. Donald Black, *The Behavior of Law* (New York: Academic Press, 1976).
88. Ibid., 13.
89. Ibid., 21.
90. Ibid.
91. Ibid., 24–25.
92. Ibid., 49–51.
93. Ibid., 2.
94. Ibid., 107.
95. Cotterrell, supra note 85, at 20–21.

Sociological Concepts and Law

2

Social Productivity*

Chapter 2 proposes a concept—social productivity—to complement the widely used concepts of social capital and economic productivity. All three concepts are concerned with structured groups, which include organizations, institutions, and societies, but each concept focuses on a different aspect of such groups. Social productivity deals with the *social outputs* of groups; social capital emphasizes the *social resources* of groups; and economic productivity deals with the economically relevant goods and services of groups. Three social outputs of organized groups are identified: (1) reputation, (2) symbols, and (3) trust and perceptions of fairness. These social outputs are critical to a group not only because they affect the degree of commitment to the group by its participants but also because they affect the responses to the group by nonmembers. From the perspective of social productivity, government adopts law in order to preserve the reputation of important groups, provide symbols, and promote trust. The chapter illustrates the concept of social productivity by examining federal law on investment companies and investment advisers.

I. Introduction

In the economic sector, productivity is—and is widely acknowledged to be—a critical variable determining the pecuniary success or failure of profit-seeking entities that supply goods and services. Economic productivity, however, affects not just the profitability of particular business enterprises, but the material wealth of society as a whole. All else being equal, the material prosperity of a society is a function of: (1) the ability of the goods that are manufactured and the services that are furnished in an economy to satisfy what consumers perceive to be their needs; and (2) the influence that the prices of those goods and services exert on the purchasing power of the basic consuming units in a society (individuals, households, and families) and, in turn, on their standard of living. Productivity, by affecting the monetary cost of goods and services, is a key variable in the economy.[1]

While an economic concept of productivity is undeniably important in explaining the material wealth of groups, personal observation suggests that a full understanding of organized groups—including business firms—requires a *sociological* concept of productivity. The need for such a concept is illustrated by a number of significant instances during the last several decades in which Americans in decision-making positions failed to appreciate and concern themselves with the critical, albeit often subtle, social consequences of policies and actions. According to available evidence, these consequences weakened the social system by creating, inter alia, alienation from and mistrust of the system.[2] The instances were harmful to the fabric of society not because the activities involved were found to be unlawful but because they eroded implicit expectations that decision-makers would act in a fair manner and in the group's long-term interests. In these (and undoubtedly other) instances, fundamental principles of group dynamics were ignored.

The instances that injured the social system, in short, breached unwritten rules that defined social equity for Americans. Through civil actions and/or criminal prosecutions in courts, violations of rules of law may be rectified and confidence in society restored, but government does not supply justice for violations of rules that are implicit in social life. Since the cohesion of society is reduced when justice is not obtainable for breaches of implicit rules that are basic to interpersonal relationships, government converts some of these rules into law through legislative, administrative agency, or judicial action. Thus, when relationships between individuals became difficult or impossible because of uncertainty whether a particular form of conduct (e.g., fraud or violence) would occur, common law developed to penalize such conduct and allow each participant in a relationship to expect that all participants will act in a manner consistent with the requirements of the relationship:

> [T]he early common law posited "rights and duties upon the relationship of parties within the socio-economic system rather than upon factors, such as consensual agreement, dependent on the will of individual litigants" and such relationship concepts served as the major framework of the legal structure.[3]

Because the protection and promotion of interpersonal relationships were important goals of law in its initial stage, they are presumably part of the foundation of law. As such, they help to explain both the emergence and the continued existence of law in society. It follows, then, that law must support social life and that when existing law fails to do so, the rules (and occasionally the concepts) of law change in order to furnish this support. Changes in law, although not immediate, occur because the evolution of law cannot be divorced from, but must reflect, the evolution of society.

With the preceding points in mind, let me review notable instances in which concern was lacking for the social consequences of group policies and actions. For each instance, I present data from responses to questions included in national sample surveys of the adult population in the United States. The responses are measures of the reactions of the public to the instances and are indicators of changes in commitment to the social order.

One of the instances, and chronologically the earliest, was the United States' military engagement in Vietnam during the 1960s and early 1970s.[4] The engagement came to be widely questioned, but the executive branch of the federal government continued the engagement and even sought (unsuccessfully) to prevent newspapers from publishing a document that it expected would further public doubts regarding its Vietnam policy.[5] Moreover, as the historical record now reveals, the President of the United States obtained congressional authorization for large-scale military involvement in Vietnam by falsifying evidence, and contrary to his public statements, he recognized that military intervention by the United States would not succeed.[6] Among the negative social consequences of the use of American military force in Vietnam is that, in sample surveys of the adult population conducted during the 1979–1980 period, three out of five respondents expressed the belief that the United States' Vietnam policy made "suckers" of Americans who served in the military to implement the policy.[7] Moreover, for the last quarter of a century, no fewer than three out of five survey respondents thought that the United States military involvement in Vietnam "was more than a mistake, it was fundamentally wrong and immoral."[8] Such reactions undoubtedly increased mistrust of government and thereby eroded the attachment of Americans to their society. Indicative of the magnitude of the error of the Vietnam policy is that Congress in 1973 enacted legislation to limit the ability of the President to commit United States military forces.[9]

A second instance of group policies and actions harmful to the fabric of the societal system in the United States involves financial practices at salient charities. These financial practices do not entail illegal activity; indeed, the requirements of law appear to have been fully satisfied.[10] Under applicable law, some charities—i.e., organizations that have charitable goals and come within section 501(c)(3) of the federal Internal Revenue Code[11]—pay their key personnel substantial compensation even though a provision of the Code is designed to prevent unreasonable compensation.[12] Table 2.1 lists selected national charities that seem especially generous in compensating their top managers. The columns in the table, respectively, provide the name of the charity (in alphabetical order); the city in which the headquarters of the charity is located (since cities vary in their cost of living); the highest and lowest compensation of (the range of compensation paid to) the three officers or employees who received the largest compensation amounts[13]; and the last month of the fiscal year in which the compensation was paid. (The fiscal year used in the table is the last for which information is available.) Among the three best-compensated officers or employees of the American Cancer Society, for example, the highest compensation was $1,212,293 and the lowest compensation was $667,909 during the fiscal year ending in August 2008.

In determining the compensation amounts to be reported in the third column of Table 2.1, I included salaries as well as contributions to deferred-compensation and employee-benefit plans. However, I omitted sums received from expense accounts, other allowances, and bonuses. (The footnotes in the first column report some of the significant bonus and incentive payments to officers/employees.) The third column thus reports total compensation whose components seem likely to continue, but the reader should keep in mind that the amounts in the third column may not be fully comparable across organizations because of differences in the manner in which compensation was recorded in the source of the information.[14]

The organizations in the table are well-established and relatively well-known. Given the publicity that has appeared over the past quarter of a century regarding financially self-serving conduct of officers of charities, it is not surprising that, in a survey conducted in 1996 of adults in the United States, approximately one-half of the respondents believed their personal view was characterized "very well" by the statement "[y]ou have to be careful about charity groups these

Table 2.1 Highest and Lowest Compensation Amounts of the Three Persons Paid the Largest Compensation by Selected National Charities

Charity	Headquarters location	Compensation range	Fiscal year ending
American Cancer Society	Atlanta, Georgia	$1,212,293 $667,909	8/2008
American Heart Association[15]	Dallas, Texas	$1,142,569 $552,958	6/2009
American Lung Association	New York, New York	$450,999 $303,014	6/2009
American National Red Cross[16]	Washington, D.C.	$600,886 $444,023	6/2009
Boy Scouts of America	Irving, Texas	$1,163,472 $580,478	12/2008
CARE USA (Cooperative for Assistance and Relief Everywhere)[17]	Atlanta, Georgia	$405,754 $257,293	6/2009
Cystic Fibrosis Foundation[18]	Bethesda, Maryland	$624,639 $443,736	12/2008
Easter Seals[19]	Chicago, Illinois	$638,200 $324,000	8/2009
Girl Scouts of the United States	New York, New York	$554,239 $313,274	9/2008
March of Dimes Foundation	White Plains, New York	$627,104 $323,231	12/2008
National Kidney Foundation[20]	New York, New York	$574,299 $287,086	6/2009
Save the Children Federation	Westport, Connecticut	$420,886 $275,143	9/2008
United Negro College Fund[21]	Fairfax, Virginia	$522,018 $311,981	3/2009
World Wildlife Fund[22]	Washington, D.C.	$449,699 $261,156	6/2009

days, because some of them are dishonest or waste money."[23] Moreover, three out of ten adults in surveys conducted during the last half of the 1990s rejected the view that "[m]ost charitable organizations are honest and ethical..." when using the money donated to them.[24] Charities have thus generated widespread misgivings and suspicion.

The negative view of charities undoubtedly was accompanied by increased alienation from society[25] and contributed to the impetus for government action designed to penalize the individuals at tax-exempt organizations who authorize or receive excessive compensation.[26]

A final illustration of group policies and actions that have inflicted a social toll comes from the compensation of top-tier officers of business enterprises in the United States. Such compensation has increased dramatically in recent decades. One measure of the change is the ratio of the average compensation of chief executive officers to the average compensation of production workers: In 1980, the ratio was approximately 40 to 1; in 1990, the ratio was approximately 85 to 1; and in the early 2000s, the ratio was estimated to be roughly 400 to 1.[27] In less than a quarter of a century, the compensation gap between the top and the bottom of the organizational chart in the business sector grew tenfold.

How does the public perceive the financial compensation received by executives of business firms and the compensation disparity in the organizational pyramid? In samples of the adult population as a whole since 1987, at least three out of five respondents have thought that business executives are "paid too much."[28] Of greater importance is that surveys conducted since the late 1990s indicate that approximately seven out of ten adults have relatively little trust in employers to "treat their employees fairly."[29] Business leaders are evidently viewed by the public as putting their own interests first,[30] a situation to which the growing compensation disparity between highly paid executives and most employees almost certainly contributed. In 2003, the federal government began combating excessive compensation of business leaders with existing provisions of the Internal Revenue Code,[31] an undertaking that undoubtedly stemmed in part from the widespread belief in the unfairness of the compensation of business leaders.

Given the instances described above, this chapter develops the concept of *social productivity*. The concept, I believe, can make a contribution to research on the way organized groups function, thereby advancing our ability to explain the character of such groups. The uniqueness of the concept lies in its focus on the *social consequences* for groups of policies that are implemented and actions that are taken by the groups. These policies and actions include (but are not confined to) the content and application of law by government.

The groups to which the concept is relevant may be of any size and may have a primarily economic purpose (as in the case of business enterprises), a primarily social or psychological purpose (as in the case of religious entities), or a combination of economic and social purposes (as in the case of families). The social consequences of their policies and actions need to be emphasized, because these consequences are a central aspect of social life, but they have not been systematically identified and extensively examined in empirical social science research.[32] The concept of social productivity directs attention to such consequences; in doing so, it can promote research that advances knowledge about the conditions under which the social effects of group policies and actions on the groups are positive and the conditions under which the social effects of group policies and actions on the groups are negative. For example, a society's values are a factor shaping the ideal characteristics of leaders in business firms[33] and probably in other groups as well. Whether a group is benefited or damaged by its leaders may depend in large part on the degree to which the policies and actions of the leaders generate results that are consistent with the value-based ideals that society has for the leaders.

In sum, the policies and actions of groups have social consequences that can mold, in favorable and unfavorable ways, the character and performance of the groups[34]—even their ability to survive.[35] However, the social consequences of group policies and actions will not receive the attention they deserve until researchers and group leaders are sensitive to them. This sensitivity will be more frequent if there is a concept that focuses attention on such consequences. Economic productivity has justifiably become a key concept in economics and business, but it cannot fully explain the variation found in economic efficiency and effectiveness and, hence, in wealth. Indeed, economic productivity apparently results in large part from the social character of groups. For example, personal efficacy, planning, task completion, and trust in others—which appear to be manifestations of a single underlying value or attitude—differ between groups and affect earnings from employment to roughly the same degree as human capital.[36] Accordingly, this chapter suggests a concept—social productivity—that is parallel to economic productivity. The concept of social productivity, however, is sociological rather than economic in nature, and therefore draws upon a very different intellectual background.

II. Definitions and Context

Every organized group possesses patterned arrangements for conducting activities that it regards as essential, and through these arrangements—which constitute the social structure of the group—the participants in the group carry on their lives. In a group that is deemed a society, the arrangements are denoted by the term "institutions" because they are fundamental, salient, and defining subsystems of the society.[37] Consequences that are social in nature and that can promote or impair the operation of society emanate from every institution, even the economy.[38]

Although the importance of the economy as an institution cannot be understated, this chapter will focus just indirectly on the economy. Another institution that is critical to the functioning of society—government and law—will be used to discuss the concept of social productivity and suggest its utility.[39] The concept of social productivity is probably applicable to most subjects within law, and for each suitable subject, it can undoubtedly be applied to all sources of law, viz., statutes, agency rules, constitutions, and government-authorized (e.g., court) interpretations of the foregoing. I will emphasize statutory law governing securities—in particular, statutes pertinent to investment companies and investment advisers. My discussion, accordingly, will implicate securities markets and indirectly involve the economy.

In this regard, two related points that are important to the discussion should be made explicit: Social science research on securities and securities markets is conducted almost entirely within the fields of economics and finance rather than sociology[40]; at the same time, while economists have systematically conceptualized economic productivity and its elements,[41] sociologists have not done so for social productivity.[42] This chapter will therefore apply an unused sociological concept to a topic that has been explored infrequently from a sociological perspective.

Why has the concept of productivity matured in economics but not been recognized in sociology? The answer in part may be that, as a discipline, economics has a longer history than sociology, but whatever the reason(s), the need to understand law requires the use of every science that adds to knowledge about law. Benefits are derived from a science to the extent the science applies useful concepts, develops accurate hypotheses, and formulates coherent theories. The discipline of economics has gained from the concept of economic productivity, and even though social productivity may not prove to be as central to sociology as economic productivity has become to the study of economic phenomena, our understanding of law is likely to benefit from the concept of social productivity.

I should add that some of the findings of research on economic productivity are likely to have counterparts in social productivity.

For example, the relationship between economic productivity and the economic wealth of a population is apparently nonlinear, i.e., all else being equal, the amount by which income responds to a unit of change in economic productivity varies with the level of economic productivity at which the unit of change occurs.[43] Similarly, the social consequences of a policy or action probably vary in magnitude with the degree of cohesiveness of the group that is involved and with the strength of the forces (e.g., the growth of knowledge) that are affecting the group. Because of thresholds, small differences in the macro-level attributes of groups, and small differences in the magnitude of macro-level forces affecting groups, are likely to be associated with wide variations in the social effects of policies and actions.

Social productivity and its context will now be described in greater detail. Social productivity occurs when an organized group of individuals[44] creates social things that become attributes of the group and affect its functioning. These social things—the outputs of social productivity—necessarily entail and result from interactions between the participants in the group. In turn, the interaction patterns, which manifest perceived group needs and dominant group values, lead to the policies, actions, reactions to—and even the viability of—the group. For example, a law school whose faculty has been dominated by cronyism and mediocrity is likely to possess a substantially poorer reputation than a law school at which significant faculty contributions to understanding law-related phenomena have consistently been encouraged and obtained through publications.[45] The reputations of the two schools differ because a major force that has molded (and that can be expected to continue molding) the social structure of the United States is the growth of knowledge,[46] which American cultural values prize.[47] Therefore, it is not surprising that, at a university, the reputation of other programs and disciplines, too, is a function of the contributions that their faculty members make to knowledge.[48]

The concept of social productivity should logically have been identified and formalized long ago by sociologists, but it was not. In one respect, social productivity is comparable to social capital,[49] a sociological concept that is becoming popular in the social sciences. The two concepts are alike insofar as both highlight significant, and to some extent previously studied, phenomena.[50] However, social capital and social productivity differ in at least two key respects. First, social capital emphasizes the social *resources* of a group; thus, it is not mainly concerned with the social *consequences* for groups of group functioning. These consequences, however, are the exclusive focus of social productivity. Second, to the extent the concept of social capital has led to the study of the consequences for groups of group activity, positive consequences have been emphasized.[51] The concept of social productivity, however, is as much concerned with negative consequences as with positive consequences. Social productivity, therefore, encourages research on the conditions under which (a) a group experiences numerically more negative effects than positive effects from the way(s) in which it operates and (b) the magnitude and duration of the negative effects exceed those of any positive effects. Researchers need to identify these conditions, and group leaders need to avoid them.

Event sequences, then, are the focus of social productivity—the functioning of groups leads to certain outcomes, and the outcomes have consequences. Thus, social movements in a society can be a forerunner of changes in law and policy. However, little is known regarding how, and by how much, social movements shape law and policy. This situation is unfortunate because "the effects of social movements are often indirect, unintended, and sometimes even in contradiction to their goals."[52] Law, too, has effects that are unnoticed, unanticipated, and/or counterintuitive.[53] Such effects, moreover, are probably not uncommon because a society, being a system, is characterized by interacting components that appear to influence one another synergistically. Thus, while not taught in law schools, the most significant consequences of the institution of law in the United States are unlikely to be ascertainable from the wording of statutes, agency regulations, and court rulings.

To summarize, social productivity, by focusing on the *social results* of group functioning, considers the outputs of groups and suggests the importance of understanding the effects of the outputs. Law, as an institution of a society, is involved in the interrelationships that characterize the societal system, and the surface of law must be penetrated to determine the manner in which legal doctrine works in the societal system. What a doctrine of law was intended or expected to achieve, and what it actually achieves, may often differ. Hence, rigorous research on the impacts of law, although just in its infancy, offers potential benefits that cannot be underestimated.

III. Social Productivity and Societal Institutions

All concepts are abstractions, but the concept of social productivity has practical importance because it bears on the functioning of organized groups, including society and its subsystems (institutions). The matters addressed by the concept are significant because they involve the consequences for an organized group of its policies and actions—not just consequences that dissipate quickly and leave no mark but, more importantly, consequences that endure and generate effects of their own. For the societal institution of government and law, the concept focuses on the social outcomes of, inter alia, the content and application of statutes enacted by legislatures, rules adopted by administrative agencies, and doctrines formulated by courts. Moreover, the concept concentrates not only on the long-term social benefits, but also on the long-term social losses, that stem from the policies and actions of a group. For example, negative outcomes—outcomes that reduce the effectiveness and efficiency of a group—can be expected if self-seeking conduct dominates leaders of the group and/or if the social or economic resources of the group are squandered. If even a few salient members act to obtain immediate personal benefits for themselves without regard to the costs to the group,[54] the outputs of social productivity can lead to a cycle whose long-term effects are destructive to the group. Such outcomes, which seem likely to have serious ramifications for society when the group involved is a societal subsystem (i.e., an institution), may be the sociological equivalents of the damage to the physical and biological environment that results from what biologist Garrett Hardin labeled the "tragedy of the commons."[55] Just as unfettered "[f]reedom in a commons brings ruin to all" in terms of natural resources and ecosystems,[56] the exploitation for personal gain of the assets of a group, though benefiting the gainers, can substantially erode the operation of the group.

When the social outputs of an important type of organized group injure society, new law will emerge to prevent such outputs in the future, or existing law will be used to punish transgressors responsible for the outputs. To the extent that law is successful, the social system will be more cohesive and more stable. For example, to avert long-term harm to social life from self-serving conduct and personal aggrandizement, the legal concept of fiduciary duty requires the person subject to the duty to protect the welfare of the party to whom the duty is owed. Thus, a fiduciary duty in client relationships is imposed on both investment advisers[57] and lawyers in order to safeguard the societal subsystems of finance and law, respectively. For lawyers, the model ethics rules of the American Bar Association (ABA) obligate a lawyer to advance the interests of each client, and to some extent this obligation continues after the lawyer has ceased to represent the client.[58] In certain circumstances the obligation of a lawyer may extend to a person who is not formally a client of the lawyer.[59]

A point meriting emphasis is that the outputs of groups are not always easy to identify and simple to measure. Indeed, the failure of sociologists to develop the concept of social productivity may be attributable, in part, to problems of operationalizing (i.e., specifying the means of observing and measuring) the concept. Social productivity was intentionally defined as the generation of social *things*[60]—a word encompassing that which is hard to designate with specificity or describe with precision[61]—because it necessarily extends to outcomes that are not readily delineated (as well as to outcomes that are easily operationalized). Nonetheless, the concept of social productivity, by increasing sensitivity to the positive and negative consequences of group actions and policies, can encourage empirical research designed to assess the extent of these consequences, and ascertain the conditions under which they occur.[62] As a corollary, lawyers and sociologists will less often assume that statutes, court decisions, and administrative agency rules achieve their intended objectives and cause no unintended effects. Probably because members of the legal profession are trained as advocates and not in social science research methods, they have generally been insensitive to the need to assess (and unaware of how to assess) whether espoused legal doctrines promote the desired social goals. Unfortunately, sociologists seem to share this insensitivity—possibly because sociologists have lacked a concept that promotes attention to the social consequences of group policies and actions.

To recapitulate, an organized group produces social things, and these things and their consequences determine how, and how well, the group performs. Since the outputs and their consequences seem to be often neglected by group decision-makers and by researchers, a concept is apparently required that, in addressing the results of group functioning, increases sensitivity to what happens socially when a group operates. The concept seems particularly appropriate to a group that is a society, which contains identifiable subsystems (i.e., institutions) that must act to preserve the larger system (society). Among the institutions of society are government and law, and even when law is crafted with care, its consequences may not be anticipated or recognized.

IV. Standards for Behavior and Societal Institutions

Standards for behavior are an inherent feature of an organized group,[63] and at the level of a society, the most conspicuous institution that establishes such standards is government. The standards created by government constitute law, but as the discussion below will make clear, standards for behavior are not confined to government and law.

Standards for behavior have two components: (1) expectations for behavior and (2) sanctions to promote conformity to the expectations. Each of the preceding can be informal or formal: Expectations are informal when they are unwritten, and they are formal when they are written and systematically collected (i.e., codified). Sanctions are informal when they are applied by group members through interpersonal pressure, and they are formal when they are applied by an entity. Informal standards (i.e., expectations and sanctions) for behavior are undoubtedly utilized by all organized groups, and in some groups, formal standards are also employed. I will focus exclusively on the latter, i.e., on formal standards.

Formal expectations and sanctions, it should be noted, are found in at least three institutions: (1) the economy—whose entities (e.g., business corporations) develop and enforce standards for their personnel, procedures, products, and services; (2) religion—whose faiths generate standards for their members and operations; and (3) government—whose legislatures, courts, and executive-branch agencies promulgate and implement standards for behavior. The word "law" in this chapter will denote exclusively the standards adopted by government for its own behavior, for the behavior of other groups, and for the behavior of individuals. The most salient law applicable to government is found in constitutions; the main body of law applicable to other groups and to individuals is found in statutes and agency rules.

In general terms, law results inter alia from socially recognized needs,[64] and the concepts and principles that dominate law at a given point in time reflect the needs that society has identified.[65] Conversely, law is unaffected by needs that are not recognized by society, and often a need remains unidentified by society until it creates a crisis. Thus, needs recognized by society do not determine the content of law instantaneously; rather, they do so with a time lag—which varies with the nature and intensity of the need. To use an example from securities law, the problems in the mutual fund industry that became publicly known starting in September 2003[66] began to generate changes in law before the end of 2003.[67] The quick response occurred because mutual funds are, and are acknowledged as being, an important vehicle in the United States for finance and personal economic security. However, mutual funds will be unable to serve effectively the interests of society if their managers are widely thought to prefer interests other than those of their shareholders. Society cannot allow finance as a societal sub-institution, and a significant component of the economy as an institution, to suffer permanent damage from its social outputs—in particular, damage to the reputation and level of public trust in mutual funds. Therefore, the institution of government and law responded promptly.

At this point, it may be helpful to state the key propositions that underlie the present chapter. The propositions are key components, although not the sole components, of a framework for understanding law as an institution. The framework, I believe, is indispensable to the study of law as a societal institution. Without the framework, for example, the content of law at any one point in time, and the evolution of law over time, cannot be explained.

> Proposition I: Law, as an institution (i.e., subsystem) of society, acts to increase the cohesiveness, and hence the stability, of society.

Proposition I suggests that law is a servant rather than a master of the social system. In its doctrines and concepts (i.e., content) and in its application (i.e., enforcement), law strengthens social life, or changes so that it does so, thereby countering forces that reduce societal cohesiveness.

> Proposition II: Legal doctrines and their applications change when existing law does not or cannot add to the cohesiveness of society.

Under Propositions I and II, then, a large portion of law is explainable by what law *contributes socially* to the society of which it is part. The degree to which law is valuable to society is determined by the socially beneficial things that law directly and indirectly generates, and law will change in order to provide these benefits. Consequently, the evolution of law, although often popularly attributed to particular personalities, is a response to shifts in the needs and values of society. However, while law that is unacceptable to the social system will ultimately be replaced, such law may not be—and probably is not typically—changed immediately. Depending on the extent of its incompatibility with societal conditions, law that is not in harmony with the needs and values of society may be widely ignored until it changes (as happened during the Prohibition era in the United States[68]).

> Proposition III: The content and application of law are determined by and directed at, inter alia, the social outputs of organized groups.

An important implication of Proposition III should be noted. Proposition III suggests that much of the content and application of law is a response to the social productivity of organized groups in a society—i.e., to the social outputs of group operation and to the consequences of these outputs. Among these groups are the institutions of society. Thus, the institution of government and law has social outputs that can reshape the content of law.

V. The Outputs of Social Productivity

What types of social things does an organized group produce?[69] There are, I believe, three main social outputs. The outputs are reviewed below, but the reader should keep in mind that they are organized alphabetically rather than ranked in terms of their significance to a society. Indeed, all three social outputs matter to a group. Moreover, social outputs can overlap substantively and may exhibit modest correlations with one another when, and if, measured quantitatively. Finally, additions to the list of important social outputs may be appropriate or necessary. The present list of three may not be exhaustive.

The social outputs of organized groups that will be discussed below are (1) reputation, (2) symbols, and (3) trust and perceptions of fairness.[70] Two significant group outputs that will *not* be discussed are the demographic variables that alter the nature and size of a population—viz., fertility, mortality, and migration—and knowledge and technology. Both of these outputs are partially social in character and can be of inestimable importance in molding society. By way of example, each of the demographic variables, acting alone or in conjunction with the others, helps to shape the age structure of the population, and in the United States, the combined action of the demographic variables has affected, inter alia, legal doctrine on the age of majority.[71] The demographic variables have also raised population numbers and density, thereby leading the judiciary to constrict the right of privacy.[72] Turning to knowledge and technology, advances in the technology for broadcasting have influenced social patterns,[73] and therefore broadcasting has become the subject of federal regulatory law.[74] Nonetheless, I do not treat either the three demographic phenomena or knowledge-technology as social outputs because they are insufficiently social in nature.[75] The products of group operation that I have identified are entirely or almost entirely social, and the demographic phenomena as well as knowledge-technology possess major non-social aspects.

Let me illustrate. The demographic phenomena, in determining the population size of geographic areas, can be driven by climate and weather-related events[76]; the fertility of a population is influenced by the extent to which childbearing is rendered difficult or impossible by medical conditions[77]; and rates of mortality, at any one time as well as over time, are affected by the physical health of the population[78]—a variable that manifests inter alia genetic factors[79] and the presence or absence of environmental contaminants.[80] The acquisition of sophisticated knowledge and technology on a broad range of matters requires appreciable financial support for scientific research,[81] which is not possible in a society that lacks sufficient wealth[82] to supply funds for such research.[83] Moreover, technology is, to a large extent, comprised of equipment devoted to economic activity. The three outputs of social productivity considered in this chapter, on the other hand, are phenomena having purely (or almost purely) *social* qualities.

A. Reputation

Every group, like every individual, develops a reputation: A group is judged by outsiders in terms of its attributes and compared with other groups. Research by social psychologists has found, not surprisingly, that a group's reputation shapes the way the group is treated by both members and nonmembers.[84] Notably, a relatively low-status group is less likely than a relatively high-status group to attract members and to generate identification with the group by its members, particularly when membership in the former group is not ascribed and can be altered.[85] Accordingly, reputation, by its very nature, helps to determine a group's position in society. Moreover, the impact on a group of its reputation may be substantially greater than the impact of the current attributes of the group: research suggests that the price of a particular type of consumer product is raised far more by a belief in the excellence of the product than by the present quality of the product.[86] Thus, reputation evidently exerts a very appreciable influence on the degree to which a group is sought after.

The preceding discussion is pertinent to business firms and to the professions that are central to this chapter—sociology and law. Unfortunately, sociologists and legal scholars have neglected the importance of reputation. I will discuss at length the reputation of sociologists and lawyers, as well as factors that have apparently interacted with their reputations to affect members of each profession. The discussion, I hope, will underscore the significance of reputation to a group and the damage that can be inflicted by a poor reputation.

The reputation of particular occupations has been the subject of some research conducted by sociologists, but the topic ought to have attracted substantially more of their attention. As indicated earlier with regard to law schools, substantial variation exists between universities in the status of a specific academic unit, i.e., a particular department or school. Furthermore, within each university, substantial variation in reputation exists between academic disciplines, a phenomenon in which sociologists have a personal stake. As a discipline, sociology seems generally not to be held in high regard even though the sophistication of sociological research has improved dramatically over the past quarter of a century. To some extent, the status accorded to sociology is wanting because many sociologists failed to recognize the importance of rigorous standards and anticipate the negative impact this failure would have on the image of their field. Indeed, a past president of the American Sociological Association complained in 1989 that, despite advances in its research, "[s]ociology is not a high-quality discipline" in terms of the students it attracts and the courses it offers, a situation accompanied by (and perhaps attributable in part to) a repudiation of exacting standards by numerous leaders of the Association; during the 1970s, the former president observed, "...'quality' was a dirty word..." in the American Sociological Association.[87] The improvements in sociological research that have occurred since the 1980s stem from markedly better data sets and statistical methods, indicating that sociologists as a whole will continue to produce high-quality research. Unfortunately, however, the contributions of sociology almost certainly have been (and are likely to continue to be) impeded by the reputation of the discipline. That reputation, by increasing skepticism about sociology and resistance to accepting a sociological perspective, has impeded progress in understanding law as an institution.

The profession of sociology thus illustrates the concept of social productivity. The decline in reputation apparently suffered by sociologists in North America and Europe over the last several decades[88] seems not to have been experienced by other social science disciplines. The decline may have taken place because sociology did not fulfill the expectations of the public that as a science it would furnish significant practical benefits and/or because sociologists came to be widely viewed as polemicists advancing political agendas rather than as scientists.[89] Whatever the reason, the tarnished reputation of sociology has undoubtedly had serious consequences for the discipline.

Let us consider one such consequence. Specifically, the reputation of sociology was undoubtedly an important (though certainly not the sole) factor contributing to the precipitous decline in the number of college students completing undergraduate degrees in sociology during the 1970s and the first half of the 1980s. The number of bachelor's degrees in sociology that were awarded in the United States fell from a high of 35,491 in the 1973–1974 academic year to 11,968 in the 1984–1985 academic year—a decline of two-thirds (66.3 percent) in little more than a decade. The decrease in sociology undergraduate degrees occurred even though, during the same period in the United States, the total number of bachelor's degrees conferred in all disciplines rose by 3.6 percent.[90]

The change in the number of bachelor's degrees in sociology, however, should not be considered in isolation. Rather, it can be compared to the changes that occurred in the number of bachelor's degrees in economics and in political science/government. Political science/government may furnish an especially apt yardstick for sociology, because in their central topics, the two disciplines seem to be more similar to each other than economics is to sociology. Figure 2.1 presents the number of bachelor's degrees awarded in each of the three disciplines from the 1949–1950 academic year through the 2006–2007 academic year.[91] The horizontal axis in the figure shows the year that ended the academic year; e.g., 1950 on the horizontal axis is academic year 1949–1950.

Figure 2.1 makes clear that the reduction in bachelor's degrees in sociology from 1973–1974 to 1984–1985 was unmatched in magnitude by either of the other two social science disciplines. In political science/government, the number of bachelor's degrees fell during the same period, but the drop was just 16 percent (from 30,744 in 1973–1974 to 25,834 in 1984–1985). The percentage reduction in political science/government, accordingly, was just one-fourth of the percentage reduction in sociology. In economics, the number of

Figure 2.1 Number of Bachelor's Degrees in Selected Social Sciences
United States by Academic Year

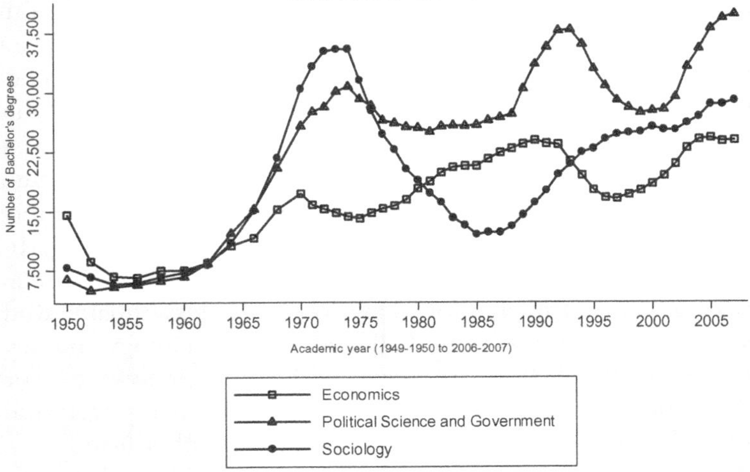

bachelor's degrees rose 45.0 percent (from 14,285 in 1973–1974 to 20,711 in 1984–1985).

A related measure of the change in the reputation of sociology and its attractiveness for undergraduate students may be the percentage of all bachelor's degrees that were conferred each year in sociology. At its peak in 1973–1974, the number of bachelor's degrees in sociology (35,491) comprised 3.8 percent of the total number of bachelor's degrees. Since then, a third of a century has elapsed, but the percentage has not returned to its level in 1973–1974. Indeed, the percentage of all bachelor's degrees that were conferred in sociology in 2006–2007—the latest year for which data are available—is only half of the percentage in 1973–1974. In 2006–2007, to be exact, the number of bachelor's degrees in sociology (28,960) was just 1.9 percent of all bachelor's degrees even though the number of bachelor's degrees in sociology in 2006–2007 was larger than in any year since bottoming in 1984–1985. The fact that sociology has been unable to reach the level of acceptance it had among undergraduates thirty-three years earlier is an indicator of obstacles that the discipline is encountering. One likely obstacle is reputation.[92]

The reader should recognize, furthermore, that the above data for sociology are *net* changes and that the sharp decrease in the number of undergraduates majoring in sociology from 1973–1974 to 1984–1985 probably stemmed from sizeable increases in two categories of students—(a) students who never entertained sociology as a major and (b) students who initially elected (or at least considered) sociology as a major but, after enrolling in one or more sociology courses, decided to pursue a bachelor's degree in another discipline. The increases in both categories are likely to have been attributable in part to the reputation of sociology. However, while the impact of reputation on category (a) would have been direct, the impact of reputation on category (b) would have been indirect. In the case of category (b), the reputation of sociology would have reduced the average academic ability of students enrolled in sociology courses; as less-capable students became a larger proportion of all students in sociology courses, the intellectual level of these courses would have been lowered; and the reduced quality of sociology courses would have encouraged students (especially more-capable students) to major in other fields.

Happenings, of course, have consequences. Thus, the increased rejection of sociology by undergraduates is likely to have magnified another problem that is evidently attributable in large part to the reputation of sociology—namely, the problem of graduate-student quality. Even before the decline in undergraduate enrollments that started in 1973–1974, graduate-degree programs in sociology had been attracting substantially fewer talented students than most other disciplines, including political science and economics,[93] and the numerical loss of undergraduate students that sociology experienced in the 1970s and early 1980s is likely to have exacerbated the problem. If the decline in undergraduate enrollments over time reduced the quality of graduate students, the reputation of sociology would have been harmed, but even without an impact on graduate-student quality, the decline in undergraduates would at least have reinforced the reputation of the discipline.

In spite of the increase in bachelor's degrees in sociology since the mid-1980s, other evidence indicates that the reputation of the discipline has not appreciably improved. Surveys by the American Sociological Association of sociology departments having undergraduate degree programs in 1991–1992 and 2001–2002 found that the number of full-time faculty was rising at the time of the first survey but falling at the time of the second survey.[94] Since the declining numbers of full-time faculty in undergraduate sociology departments cannot be attributed to enrollments, they probably stem in large part from the reputation of sociology, which causes universities to be reluctant to support the discipline. If so, the reputation of sociology has created a self-reinforcing, destructive cycle that fosters a disregard of the current quality of sociological research and hampers the development of sociology as a science. The practical result has been to limit our insights into the nature and workings of law as an institution.

Because the present chapter involves not only the discipline of sociology but also the discipline of law, it is appropriate to consider the reputation of lawyers. Furthermore, inasmuch as the juxtaposition of sociology with other fields (viz., political science/government and economics) furnished perspective on the state of sociology, the discussion below compares lawyers with physicians in order to understand the condition of the profession of law.

Simply stated, the reputation of lawyers is far worse than the reputation of physicians. Although the reputation of physicians is not as good today as a quarter of a century ago, it has declined less than the reputation of lawyers. Table 2.2 presents data for 1977, 1992, and 2009 from national sample surveys of adults in the United States. Interviewees in each survey were asked whether they regarded the occupation of "lawyer" and the occupation of "doctor" as having "very great prestige," "considerable prestige," "some prestige," or "hardly any prestige at all." On logical grounds, the prestige of an occupation is a correlate or component of the reputation of the occupation. Between 1977 and 2009, the reputation of the profession of law deteriorated dramatically—the percentage responding that lawyers have "very great prestige" fell by more than one-fourth while the percentage responding that lawyers have "hardly any prestige at all" almost quadrupled. Another way of viewing the change is that, in 1977, the percentage of respondents who described lawyers as having "very great prestige" was 7.2 times larger than the percentage of respondents who described lawyers as having "hardly any prestige at all." In 2009, however, the two percentages were appreciably closer, with the former just 1.4 times larger than the latter. While the reputation of doctors also eroded from 1977 to 2009, the reputation of lawyers suffered much more. During this period, to be exact, the decrease in "very great prestige" was twice as large for lawyers (ten percentage points) than for physicians (five percentage points),[95] and the growth in "hardly any prestige at all" was seven times larger for lawyers (fourteen percentage points) than for physicians (two percentage points).

Table 2.2 Reputation of Lawyers and Doctors[96]

Occupation/response (%)	Year		
	1977	1992	2009
Lawyers			
"Very great prestige"	36	25	26
"Considerable prestige"	37	29	22
"Some prestige"	20	28	33
"Hardly any prestige at all"	5	16	19
Don't know; refused	2	1	0
Total (%)	100	99	100
Doctors			
"Very great prestige"	61	50	56
"Considerable prestige"	29	33	28
"Some prestige"	7	13	13
"Hardly any prestige at all"	1	4	3
Don't know; refused	2	1	0
Total (%)	100	101	100

Reputation, of course, is not the sole factor bearing on the attractiveness of a group. The economic utility of the group—in this case, the economic contribution of lawyers to society—also affects the degree to which nonmembers (e.g., students) are drawn to the group. The economic value of expertise in law appears to considerably surpass the economic value of expertise in sociology.[97] As a result, the number of students pursuing a law degree in the United States has not experienced a protracted, severe decline during the last several decades. This situation is quite unlike the experience of sociology. Indeed, the number of first-professional degrees (i.e., Juris Doctor or Bachelor of Laws) awarded by ABA-approved law schools has generally grown over time: 27,756 such degrees were conferred in the 1973–1974 academic year and 36,687 in the 1984–1985 academic year, a 32 percent increase in the period during which bachelor's degrees in sociology decreased precipitously. In the 2009–2010 academic year, 44,004 first-professional degrees were conferred by ABA-approved law schools.[98]

However, while law schools in the United States are attracting appreciable numbers of students—due partly to the economic value of training in law—lawyering as an occupation is characterized by a set of serious, and seemingly interrelated, problems that have been described as a crisis in professionalism. In addition to a sharp decline in reputation, a substantial number of practicing attorneys evidently are dissatisfied with lawyering as an occupation and are engaging in offensive conduct.[99] At the same time, the number of attorneys who leave law for another occupation may be rising.[100] The situation may be partially attributable to the personality characteristics of practicing attorneys,[101] which may (1) generate behavior that is incompatible with good interpersonal relationships, (2) reduce the collective reputation of lawyers, and (3) increase the personal dissatisfaction of lawyers with their occupation. The preceding three effects, however, may not be concurrent but rather sequential. Specifically, the behavior of lawyers may be eroding their reputation with the public, and the impaired reputation may, in turn, be raising the level of occupational dissatisfaction within the legal profession. Research in social psychology indicates that the reputation of a group is a factor in the satisfaction and commitment of its members: a group with an unfavorable reputation, compared to a group with a favorable one, will have more members who do not identify with the group and who are not satisfied with it, especially when these members may be able to join a group with a better reputation.[102] Furthermore, members who do not identify with their group are more likely than members who do identify to divorce themselves from the problems of the group and to desire membership in another group.[103] A self-reinforcing cycle may thus exist: personality attributes may be responsible for lawyer behavior that is damaging the reputation of law as an occupation, which in turn may encourage lawyers to leave the profession. The remaining lawyers will then be the ones who are most likely to exhibit the behavior that injures the reputation of the profession.

B. Symbols

Symbols[104] are used by an organized group—especially a group that is large in size[105]—to strengthen the tie that its participants have to the group.[106] However, in some circumstances, a symbol can cause participants to distance themselves from their group. Unfortunately, the role of symbols in group cohesion, and the conditions under which symbols generate commitment to or alienation from a group, appear to be barely understood, because only a few rigorous, quantitative social science studies have been conducted on the social role of symbols. Indeed, of the three social outputs of groups that I have identified, symbols seem to have received the least attention in research on group functioning. The situation should not be surprising, however, because symbols assume a variety of forms and some may not be easily recognized as symbols.[107] In the United States, school mascots are illustrative of symbols[108] and pertinent to government action and law. One such mascot[109] is the Indian figure symbolizing the University of Illinois. In the 1990s, that mascot became the subject of action by the state legislature and governor[110] as well as a ruling by the United States Department of Education.[111] Another symbol, and one that is especially salient, is the United States flag. The social significance of the flag has generated federal statutes that specify the circumstances and manner in which the flag is to be displayed[112] and that mark the anniversary of the official adoption of the flag's current design.[113] Moreover, a federal statute designates May 1 of every year as Loyalty Day, states that it is "a special day for the reaffirmation of loyalty to the United States," and asks the President to have the flag displayed on all federal buildings on that day.[114] Statutes such as these exist because, in the words of the United States Supreme Court, "[t]he very purpose of a national flag is to serve as a symbol of our country...."[115] The flag's role as a symbol was indicated by its public display[116] and increased sales after the attacks on the country on September 11, 2001. From September 11, 2001 to May 2002, Wal-Mart alone sold 4.9 million American flags, more than four times the number it sold during the corresponding interval one year earlier.[117] For a while, moreover, manufacturers and retailers could not immediately fill the demand for flags.[118]

However, the symbols that society employs are not necessarily obvious and tangible, as is the case with flags. Law itself performs a symbolic function and possesses considerable "symbolic power."[119] Therefore, law can act sociologically as cement for the social order. At the same time, however, law may furnish symbols that are incompatible, and the symbol that prevails is an indicator of the relative importance of the societal values involved. To society, the importance of law is found not in what law *says* but in what law *does*: law is driven not by the wording of statutes, agency rules, constitutions, and court decisions, but by underlying sociological factors. For example, the United States Supreme Court has repeatedly held that the First

Amendment guarantee of free expression does not allow government to penalize individuals who intentionally destroy, damage, or deface the American flag for the purpose of communicating a message of political dissent.[120] The Constitution expresses societal ideals,[121] and the Court's decisions gave priority to the Constitution as a symbol of the ideal of freedom of political expression over the flag in its physical form and as a symbol of the United States.[122] Although there is irony in the use of one symbol (the Constitution) to permit damage to another symbol (the country's flag), the First Amendment embodies values concerned with forms of personal liberty that are a defining feature of American culture.[123] That those values appear in the *First* Amendment to the Constitution is no coincidence.

Law acts as a symbol of important social values not only through new legal doctrines that emerge from constitutional (and statutory) interpretation but also through existing law—especially criminal law—that is applied to "high profile" personalities. For example, the prosecution, guilty pleas, and punishment of Andrew and Lea Fastow stemming from financial misdeeds at the Enron Corporation[124] endorse a principle of group dynamics that every organized group must follow if it is to retain the commitment of its members. The principle is that all members of the group, regardless of their position and prominence, must abide by generally applicable and accepted standards of behavior. Because the principle is fundamental to group cohesion, it is a value that permeates law.[125] The punishment of the Fastows for violating behavioral standards established by law is unlikely to deter similar conduct by others,[126] but the case is nonetheless important sociologically. By symbolizing the principle that government will hold every person to the same rules of behavior, the successful prosecution of the Fastows helped to bond Americans to their society and thereby strengthened the social order.[127]

C. Trust and Perceptions of Fairness

In the context of social productivity, trust is the supposition by an individual or a group that the conduct of another (individual or group) will be satisfactory to the party making the supposition.[128] Fairness is difficult to define, however, because it evidently is multifaceted. Indeed, fairness may be defined by as many as four different (albeit related) phenomena.[129] One of the four, procedural fairness, is concerned with whether the parties affected by a decision-making procedure believe that the procedure conforms to accepted standards for behavior. Both trust and procedural fairness are critical elements of law. In the words of the Supreme Court of California: "Our system [of law] relies for its validity on the confidence of society; without a belief by the people that the system is just and impartial, the concept of the rule of law cannot survive."[130]

In this chapter, trust and perceptions of fairness are considered together, because empirical evidence indicates that the degree to which the members of a group trust their group and its leaders is not clearly distinguishable from the degree to which the members believe their group and its leaders act equitably.[131] Future empirical research may yield results that dispute this conclusion, but even if trust and perceptions of fairness are found to be distinct factors that operate independently to a considerable extent, their referents appear to be sufficiently related to warrant linking them. I therefore treat trust and perceived fairness as a single construct, which I label simply "trust/fairness."

In social science, a concern with trust/fairness did not become prevalent until the 1990s,[132] perhaps because the elevated level of anti-statist individualism in American social ideology during the several preceding decades[133] inhibited a focus on group attributes. As a result, social science studies of trust/fairness are limited in number. Fortunately, however, social scientists are beginning to conduct empirical research on the manner in which and the degree to which variations in the level of trust/fairness influence groups. Although the research that has been completed permits only tentative conclusions, it (as well as theory) indicates that trust/fairness is a critical aspect of groups and must not be ignored in drafting and implementing law.

If theoretical work on trust/fairness is correct, (1) a high level of trust/fairness is necessary for the development of structural complexity in a society,[134] and (2) law is not an effective substitute for trust/fairness in maintaining a structurally complex society when levels of trust/fairness are low and challenges to key social values are widespread.[135] Assuming that these propositions are proven empirically, the social order in a structurally differentiated country like the United States requires considerable trust/fairness, but the ability of law to affect the level of trust/fairness varies with societal conditions. Therefore, from a sociological perspective, the wording of the prescriptions and proscriptions found in law is not important. Rather, law is important to the extent it is able to preserve and increase societal stability by, inter alia, generating trust/fairness.

What conclusions can be drawn from presently available empirical studies of trust/fairness? Research on employees has found that a higher level of trust/fairness promotes greater employee commitment to and involvement in the employing organization, as well as greater employee acceptance of decisions made by persons in authority.[136] Research comparing different nations suggests that a higher level of interpersonal trust is associated with stability of democratic forms of government,[137] with government efficiency and adequacy of educational systems and physical infrastructure (e.g., roads and telecommunications),[138] and—of particular relevance to Part VI infra in this chapter—with a larger and more-active financial sector.[139] However, these are not the sole benefits that are evidently derived from increased trust; empirical research has found that the social fabric is advantaged in other ways, too, as the level of trust rises.[140]

Finally, it should be kept in mind that even groups focusing mainly on economic profit have noneconomic products, and one of these products is trust/fairness. However, variations in trust/fairness evidently cannot be fully explained with traditional economic principles, which have been confined to estimations of personal benefit and advantage.[141] An understanding of trust/fairness, rather, requires the insights of sociology and social psychology.

VI. Investment Companies, Investment Advisers, and the Regulation of Conflicts of Interest

As an illustration of the conceptual scheme that has been developed, I consider the regulation of conflicts of interest[142] under the Investment Company Act[143] and the Investment Advisers Act,[144] both of which were enacted by Congress in 1940 (and are therefore commonly denominated the "1940 Acts").[145] The former statute is concerned with certain types of collective vehicles for owning securities[146]; the latter statute deals with the entities and individuals responsible for managing securities portfolios for others, including the collective vehicles regulated under the Investment Company Act. One indicator of the importance of investment companies and investment advisers in the United States is that, in every year from 2000 through 2010, more than four out of five households in the country-owned shares of at least one mutual fund.[147] Anything that endangers collective vehicles for securities investments thus threatens the public welfare.

Conflicts of interest are of concern to the law when they affect conduct, or are viewed as able to affect conduct, in ways that implicate principles fundamental to social life. Conflicts of interest, of course, can accompany or involve investments in securities.[148] In terms of investment companies and investment advisers, conflicts of interest can reduce trust in, and injure the reputation of, the companies and advisers. In order to symbolize principles that are essential to group life and that can strengthen the social order, law prohibits conflicts of interest and penalizes them with civil and/or criminal sanctions that group participants deem just. To this end, standards directed at conflicts of interests have been imposed and enforced by law for behavior in and by organizations that invest in securities on behalf of others or that are responsible for decisions on these investments.[149]

Because securities are the centerpiece of the activities upon which the Investment Company Act and Investment Advisers Act focus, I begin with a discussion of the concept of a security.

A. Securities

Neither of the 1940 Acts define—i.e., identify the essential features of—a security. Instead, the Acts merely enumerate types of securities.[150] However, application of the concept of social productivity to investment companies and investment advisers can be fully appreciated only with an understanding of the elements of a security. What makes a security a security? The question probably cannot be answered definitively since the attributes of a security may change with the passage of time as society and its economy evolve and new types of securities emerge. Moreover, Congress intended the concept to have a broad scope and an expansive application.[151] Thus, while most of the items listed as securities in the two statutes are precise and relatively unambiguous (e.g., "treasury stock," "put," and "straddle"), one notable item is not. Specifically, a security includes "in general, any interest or instrument commonly known as a 'security'...."[152] Under the statutes, then, the word "security" has no border and its referents are unclear.

However, the indefiniteness of the statutory lists has been reduced to some degree by the United States Supreme Court.[153] In *Reves v. Ernst & Young*,[154] a case involving the Securities Exchange Act, the Court concluded that a security necessarily involves an investment.[155] The concept of "investment" was left undefined, but under the Securities Act, the Court has observed that Congress wanted the word security to be "capable of adaptation to meet the countless and variable schemes devised by those who seek the use of the money of others on the promise of profits."[156] The latter statement is consistent with the generally accepted definition of the word "investment" in an economic context,[157] and when juxtaposed with the Court's conclusion in *Reves*, the statement suggests that a security involves, inter alia, the commitment of financial resources to an endeavor from which the party making the commitment seeks pecuniary gain.[158]

However, an investment is just one element of a security; other elements must also be present for a security to exist. Real estate and paintings can be investments, but direct ownership of real estate and paintings does not entail ownership of securities. In addition to an investment, what must be present? At a minimum, a security requires "a financial instrument eligible to participate in a public market,"[159] and the instrument must be capable of being reasonably regarded as a security by the participants in a social system who acquired the instrument.[160] Unless investors can have a rational belief that the instruments they hold are securities, they are not protected by federal securities statutes.[161] Moreover, instruments may be deemed securities as a matter of law if investors reasonably believe that the instruments are securities "even where an economic analysis of the circumstances of the particular transaction might suggest that the instruments are not 'securities' as used in that transaction."[162] Thus, the categorization of an instrument—as a security or as not a security—appears to be influenced by social factors and will vary over time. Whether an investor is reasonable in considering an instrument to be a security is likely to depend on the cultural subgroup of the investor,[163] and even if a single reasonable belief could be identified for society as a whole, that belief can be expected to evolve as social–economic conditions change. An instrument that is not deemed a security in one subgroup of society or in one historical period may be deemed a security in another subgroup or at another time.[164]

In short, a security is a social phenomenon as much as it is an economic phenomenon. While little, if anything, seems to be known about the social dimensions of securities—a situation that will continue until these dimensions become the subject of well-designed research—their centrality to the business of investment companies and investment advisers makes the concept of social productivity germane to that business and to its regulation. For example, a basic standard for behavior imposed by federal securities law requires securities issuers and investment companies to reveal and communicate information to investors in an adequate manner, because disclosure is necessary to maintain trust in, and a belief in the fairness of,[165] securities markets.[166] Trust and perceived fairness are social products of group functioning, and if they are absent from securities markets, securities will not be a viable means of promoting economic activity.[167]

B. Directors of Investment Companies

As a matter of law, the directors of an investment company—a subject considered both here and infra in Chapter 3—are guardians of the interests of both the company and its shareholders.[168] Sociologically, they are symbols of this fiduciary duty. As symbols of a fiduciary obligation, the directors affect the reputation of the company and the degree to which the company is trusted and perceived to be fair by its shareholders.[169] Conflicts of interest, however, can reduce or appear to reduce the ability of directors to fulfill their fiduciary duty, and therefore are of concern to the law. Unfortunately, conflicts of interest can easily arise in an investment company because of the relationship that normally exists between the company and its investment adviser. An investment company, which is usually created by its investment adviser, generates income for the adviser through the fees it pays the adviser, but all else being equal, these fees reduce the profits earned by the company and hence by the company's shareholders. Shareholders, of course, seek to maximize their profits, a goal that requires investment companies to minimize costs. Accordingly, the fees paid by an investment company to its investment adviser promote a divergence between, on the one hand, the goals of the company and its investors and, on the other hand, the goals of the adviser.[170] Because most advisers control the investment companies they advise,[171] directors of an investment company can be aligned with the adviser and are subject to a palpable conflict of interest. The Investment Company Act addresses this situation as well as others that involve conflicts of interest.[172]

An investment vehicle that qualifies as an investment company under the Investment Company Act must be registered with the Securities and Exchange Commission[173] and is accordingly subject to section 10(a) of the Act.[174] Section 10(a) allows 60 percent of the directors of a registered company to have certain types of ties to the company and/or to an investment adviser or principal underwriter for the company.[175] Therefore, by statute, a majority of an investment company's directors can be "interested" in the company, and only a minority of the directors must be "disinterested," i.e., free of such ties.[176] In addition, the statute normally permits the current interested directors to control nominations of the individuals who will serve as disinterested (i.e., independent) directors,[177] and this control may limit the degree to which nominally independent directors will act adversely to the interests of the investment adviser. However, the independent directors, as the "watchdogs" for the shareholders, were expected by Congress to bear the main responsibility for protecting the shareholders.[178] For example, a registered investment company that has a board of directors must obtain the approval of a majority of its independent directors before it can contract with an investment adviser,[179] and the independent directors are obligated to secure a contract that maximizes the interests of the company and its investors.[180] Given the importance of independent directors to preserving the trust of investors, since 2002 the Commission, through its authority to promulgate rules, has required an investment company that uses any of ten Commission rules for an exemption from a provision of the Investment Company Act to have a board that is comprised of a majority of independent directors. Furthermore, the independent directors on a board of such an investment company must nominate the independent directors.[181]

Under what conditions is a director classified as "independent"? The Investment Company Act answers this question by specifying attributes that create "interest" in the investment company. An individual with any of the listed attributes is interested in the investment company and is disqualified from serving as an independent director of the company.[182] Disqualifying attributes are of two general types and may stem either from the investment company or from an investment adviser or principal underwriter for the investment company.[183] First, an individual, and a member of the immediate family of an individual,[184] cannot be an independent director of an investment company if the individual possesses, at the time he or she is classified as independent or interested, certain kinds of connections either to the company or to an investment adviser or a principal underwriter for the company. An individual with any of the designated connections is an "affiliate" of the company, adviser, or underwriter[185] and will be an interested director of the company.[186] Connections that prevent an individual from serving as an independent director of an investment company include, inter alia, ownership of 5 percent or more of the outstanding voting securities of (1) the investment company or of (2) an investment adviser or principal underwriter for the company. Other types of disqualifying connections include control by the individual of, or control over the individual by, (1) or (2)[187]; current employment of the individual by, or current service by the individual as, an officer of (1) or (2); and current membership on the board of directors of (2). As already noted, the connections designated by the Act that disqualify the individual from being an independent director also disqualify every member of the immediate family of the individual.[188]

A prohibited affiliation, however, is not the only attribute that bars service as an independent director of an investment company. In addition, a prohibited relationship must not exist with the company, with an investment adviser or a principal underwriter for the company, or with certain of their affiliates. The kinds of relationships that are prohibited by the Act are economic in nature and significant in magnitude. Two examples may be helpful. First, an individual is disqualified from being an independent director of an investment company if, at any time since the start of the company's last two completed fiscal years, the individual or a partner of the individual has been a lawyer for the company, for an investment adviser to the company, or for a principal underwriter of the company.[189] Second, an individual cannot serve as an independent director of an investment company if the Commission has found that, within the period since the start of the last two completed fiscal years of the company, the individual had "a material business relationship" with the company, with an investment adviser or a principal underwriter for the company, or with certain of their affiliates.[190] Such relationships, which can arise from positions held by the individual or from transactions in which the individual participated, evidently are not uncommon and are not easily recognized.[191] Indeed, some of these relationships may exist in situations that on the surface seem unobjectionable.[192]

C. Fiduciary Duty of Investment Advisers

The Investment Advisers Act defines an investment adviser as:

> any person who, for compensation, engages in the business of advising others, either directly or through publications or writings, as to the value of securities or as to the advisability of investing in, purchasing, or selling securities, or who, for compensation and as part of a regular business, issues or promulgates analyses or reports concerning securities.[193]

Under the definition, the clients of investment advisers can include not only investment companies[194] but also other types of entities that individuals use to invest collectively in securities.[195] Individuals and entities investing directly in securities can also be clients of investment advisers. Thus, the clientele of investment advisers is heterogeneous and supplies advisers with sizeable assets to invest in securities. Indeed, investment advisers managed an estimated $19 trillion in assets in 2002, between one-third and two-fifths of which were assets of investment companies.[196]

Given the amount of wealth they control, investment advisers are an important component of the financial institution in the United States and its securities markets. As a result, the institution is unavoidably affected by the reputation of investment advisers and by the degree to which the public believes that advisers are trustworthy and treat investors fairly. If investment advisers are poorly regarded and/or are thought to be untrustworthy and unfair, the effectiveness of the financial institution will be hampered.[197] In short, the basis for government regulation of investment advisers is intrinsically sociological.

The Investment Advisers Act, by symbolizing the principle that advisers treat all of their clients equally, promotes the reputation of advisers and confidence in them. Section 206 of the Act prohibits fraud by investment advisers[198] and even extends to advisers not required to register with the Securities and Exchange Commission.[199] Notably, an adviser can violate section 206 with conduct that does not financially injure a client[200]: a misrepresentation or omission of a material fact suffices to breach the section. Moreover, the misrepresentation or omission need not involve existing clients but can involve advertising that is directed toward potential clients.[201] Under the Act, in short, advisers have a broad fiduciary duty.

The intolerance of the Investment Advisers Act for breaches of trust is illustrated by a case in which a corporate adviser and its officers were penalized for conduct whose motivation seems to have been entirely benevolent. The case involved an investment adviser that divided sixty-five client accounts into two categories.[202] One category contained forty-five of the accounts, and those accounts paid an annual management fee to the adviser that ranged from 1.0 percent to 1.5 percent of their market value, which averaged slightly more than $2 million. The other category contained the remaining twenty accounts, most of which were opened by personal friends of the two officers of the corporate adviser; these accounts were not charged advisory fees, and their average market value was approximately $70,000.[203] Section 206 was breached when "hot IPOs" were purchased and sold quickly for short-term profits. The adviser often acquired such securities as long-term investments for the accounts of clients, and in such instances, the securities were allocated using objective, fully disclosed criteria. However, the securities that were the subject of short-term trades were disproportionately assigned to the accounts in the second category—the accounts of the less-wealthy clients—based on the belief of the officers of the adviser as to which of these clients were currently in need of money. Because fidelity is owed to every client, the Commission ruled that the latter allocation practice needed to be revealed to all clients and that, by failing to make the disclosure, the advisor violated section 206. For the violation, the corporate adviser was fined $100,000 and its officers were censured.[204]

An investment adviser is thus not permitted to act as a present-day Robin Hood. Because the profit available from securities investments is limited, investment advisers, absent the consent of their clients, cannot favor one set of clients and disadvantage another set. If investment advisers are to make a positive contribution to the functioning of society, they must be regarded by securities investors as trustworthy and fair. Thus, advisers must possess a reputation not only for being competent but also for treating all of their clients equally. The Investment Advisers Act advances these social goals by symbolizing important principles of group dynamics through its written provisions and through actions (administrative proceedings) enforcing them.

D. Compensation of Investment Advisers

Section 17(e)(1) of the Investment Company Act is perhaps the most prominent provision of the 1940 Acts directed at the compensation of investment advisers.[205] The section states:

> It shall be unlawful for any affiliated person of a registered investment company, or any affiliated person of such person—(1) acting as agent, to accept from any source any compensation (other than a regular salary or wages from such registered company) for the purchase or sale of any property to or for such registered company or any controlled company thereof, except in the course of such person's business as an underwriter or broker.[206]

By its terms, the section covers both a party (entity or individual) affiliated with a registered investment company and a party affiliated with an affiliated party. The former party is commonly denominated a "first-tier affiliate" of the company, while the latter party is a "second-tier affiliate" of the company. Section 17(e)(1) encompasses investment advisers—as well as their directors, officers, and employees—because of the definition of affiliation in section 2(a)(3) of the Act.[207] An investment adviser to an investment company is a first-tier affiliate of the company under subsection (E) of section 2(a)(3), while the officers, employees, and directors of the investment adviser, as first-tier affiliates of the adviser under subsection (D), are second-tier affiliates of the investment company.[208]

The financial fortunes of investment companies depend, of course, on whether the investment merit of securities is accurately assessed. Section 17(e)(1) seeks to facilitate these assessments by removing an extraneous factor: the section bars compensation that can tempt first-tier and second-tier affiliates to act for their own benefit in choosing securities for the portfolio of their investment company. "The objective of section 17(e)(1) is to prevent affiliated persons from having their judgment and fidelity impaired by conflicts of interest."[209] However, to breach section 17(e)(1), the compensation need not alter any decision of an affiliate regarding portfolio securities or cause economic injury to the investment company.[210] Compensation violates the section if it merely creates for an affiliate a conflict of interest that exposes the investment company to possible injury. The compensation, moreover, is evidently not required to have economic value or even a physical form. Compensation exists under section 17(e)(1) when an affiliate subjectively views as a benefit that which has been accepted.[211] Consequently, a tangible item such as a family heirloom that has emotional meaning to the affiliate, but no determinable monetary worth, can apparently be compensation. An intangible item, such as a title, probably can be compensation, too. In short, anything can constitute unlawful compensation if it entices an affiliate and poses a risk that the affiliate will be unable to assess objectively the likelihood that a security will generate a profit for the investment company.

A civil action by the Securities and Exchange Commission against a corporate investment adviser and its president illustrates the scope of section 17(e)(1).[212] The historical context of the case is noteworthy. During the 1970s, computers were very expensive and not widely used, but the president of the adviser recognized that computers, with their ability to process large amounts of quantitative data, could supply information that would be useful in judging whether particular securities held promise as investments. Because neither the investment adviser nor the registered investment company it advised could afford a computer, the president obtained the money for a computer from a broker. However, the benefits and the burdens of the arrangement were split. The investment adviser received the payments from the broker, and in exchange for the payments to the adviser, the investment company directed virtually all of its securities trading, and hence brokerage expenditures, to the broker. The arrangement created a conflict of interest for the adviser (a first-tier affiliate of a registered investment company) and the president (a second-tier affiliate of a registered investment company),[213] because acceptance of the payments (compensation) was an inducement for them to use the brokerage business and expenditures of the investment company to offset the cost to the broker of the payments.

In short, conflicts of interest for the investment adviser and its president produced benefits for the adviser at the expense of the investment company it managed, and the arrangement violated section 17(e)(1). The Commission, therefore, censured the investment adviser and its president. The section was *not* breached by the effort of the adviser and its president to maximize the effectiveness of the adviser through access to a computer. Rather, the adviser and its president breached the section because they had a duty of loyalty to the investment company. This duty obligated them to use the broker(s) offering the best service to the investment company, but their ability to fulfill the duty was compromised by the money that the broker supplied. Notably, the president was held to have breached the section even though there appears to have been no evidence that he personally profited from the arrangement.[214]

Investment advisers have utilized the brokerage businesses of their investment companies in another way to generate income for themselves. Advisers select the brokers that handle the securities transactions of their investment companies, and these brokers benefit from the brokerage expenditures of the companies. However, brokers have been chosen as a reward for recruiting investors for the investment companies. An open-end fund is especially susceptible to this practice because it continuously sells its shares and, in principle, is not limited in the number of shares it can sell. Since an investment adviser to an investment company is paid fees for managing the money that the company obtains from investors, the adviser can earn additional compensation by steering the brokerage business and expenditures of the investment company to brokers that sell or have sold shares of the company. The compensation to the adviser, however, may tempt the adviser to choose brokers for the investment company that produce the compensation, not brokers that offer the best service. As of December 2004, a Commission rule prohibited registered open-end management investment companies from considering the marketing or sale of their shares when choosing brokers.[215] The Commission expressly predicated the rule on the inescapable conflict of interest for an investment company and its investment adviser from employing a broker for portfolio transactions of the investment company in order to compensate the broker for promoting the company.[216] This practice can damage investors' trust in the mutual fund industry as well as the industry's reputation. In addition, the practice creates an incentive for brokers to recommend to their clients the funds that provide the largest brokerage commissions rather than the funds that are best suited to the needs of the clients.[217]

VII. Conclusion

In this chapter, I have proposed a concept that focuses on the social consequences of group policies and actions. The concept deals with an inherent aspect of every organized group. A group necessarily responds to problems it perceives, and the responses—which may include the enforcement of existing law and/or the development of new law—have social consequences for the group inasmuch as symbols are created, reputations are shaped, and trust in others is affected. The perceived problems are important in their own right, of course, and because they are salient, legal scholars and researchers in the social sciences are attracted to them. Thus, this chapter has examined the manner in which conflicts of interest are handled by the Investment Company Act and Investment Advisers Act. However, the chapter has used conflicts of interest and their treatment by the 1940 Acts merely to illustrate[218] a more fundamental matter, namely, the social outcomes of group policies and actions that address problematic situations. Unfortunately, these outcomes and their ramifications are usually not considered by the leaders and members of the groups, or by social scientists in their research. However, because it is often the case that "discovery consists in seeing what everyone else has seen and thinking what no one else has thought,"[219] the acquisition of insight can be aided by a new concept.

Although the social effects of group activity may not be anticipated by the leaders and members of a group, the effects need to be considered because they may not be beneficial for the group. Indeed, the effects may be harmful to the group, and the harm may be serious and long-lasting. For some types of groups and/or group policies and actions, furthermore, social effects that are unanticipated and detrimental may be as common as those that are anticipated and beneficial. Because an organized group is a set of interrelated components (i.e., a system), a group characterized by even a modest degree of complexity will contain communication networks and self-reinforcing loops that operate in ways difficult to discern in advance. Accordingly, the social outcomes of group policies and actions, and the ramifications of such outcomes for the effectiveness and efficiency of groups, must be appreciated. That appreciation is more likely if there is an established concept that promotes sensitivity to the social consequences of group life.

When considering government and law, questions that are political in nature attract widespread interest. Should candidate M or candidate N be elected? Should individual X or individual Y be appointed? Should person A be nominated for a judicial position by the Governor of the State or President of the United States? However, "politics is the art of the possible,"[220] and the political process is merely a means to an end, not an end in itself. Moreover, political issues can shift rapidly; as a successful politician once noted, "A week is a long time in politics."[221] Accordingly, politics should not distract researchers and group decision-makers from matters that are more fundamental and less ephemeral. The content of law on all topics and from all sources should be formulated with recognition of the enduring aspects of groups. In particular, whether group policies and actions will be socially beneficial rather than injurious must be a central consideration in deciding on courses of action. In terms of law, the social impacts of proscriptions and prescriptions require thorough investigation when—and ideally before—they are incorporated into statutes, agency rules, constitutional provisions, and court decisions.

Social science evidence indicates that in recent decades the United States has experienced a variety of related changes in social patterns that are indicative of a decline in the cohesiveness of social life,[222] i.e., of a decline in community.[223] These changes are probably attributable in part to forces such as globalization and technological advances that have generated important economic shifts, e.g., in the level and distribution of wealth.[224] Because of the separation of intellectual disciplines, there is insufficient recognition that economic transformations can have serious social consequences. In particular, "[e]conomic distress appears to depress social networks, trust, and tolerance, while elevating anomia and crime."[225] In future years, the restructuring of the American economy can be expected to continue, and the pace of change may even intensify.[226] To the extent that economic stress reduces community—i.e., harms social cohesiveness—society can be expected to respond, and the response is likely to include changes in law. The resulting law, however, will not necessarily be beneficial. Law will probably not aid society if it attempts directly to suppress the social problems that define an erosion of community[227]; government is more likely to advance the public interest—i.e., to have positive social outputs—if it addresses the policies and actions of entities that contribute to these problems.[228]

Unfortunately, current research furnishes relatively little guidance on the conditions under which positive social impacts are obtained from government and law, and until much more empirical research is conducted, new forms of government regulation will be shaped by guesswork. The regulation of securities is one avenue by which law in the United States can further the operation of American society, and the concept of social productivity, by fostering sensitivity to inadequately studied topics, may stimulate research that will advance our understanding of how to maximize the effectiveness of statutes such as the Investment Company Act and the Investment Advisers Act.

Notes

*Chapter 2 is a substantial revision of Larry D. Barnett, "Social Productivity, Law, and the Regulation of Conflicts of Interest in the Investment Industry," *Cardozo Public Law, Policy, & Ethics Journal* 3 (2006): 793.

1. Paul A. Samuelson and William D. Nordhaus, *Economics*, 13th ed. (New York: McGraw-Hill, 1989). Economic productivity is defined as "the ratio of total output to a weighted average of inputs," where "inputs" are the physical implements such as the equipment, tools, labor, land, and raw materials that are employed in producing goods and services. Ibid., 505, 972.
2. See infra notes 7–8, 23–24, 28–29, and accompanying text.
3. Heyer v. Flaig, 449 P.2d 161, 164 (Cal. 1969) (quoting Matthew O. Tobriner and Joseph R. Grodin, "The Individual and the Public Service Enterprise in the New Industrial State," *California Law Review* 55 (1967): 1247, 1249).
4. The agreement that ended hostilities involving United States military forces in Vietnam was signed and became effective in January 1973. "Bygone Days," *Commercial Appeal* (January 24, 1998): C5.
5. New York Times v. United States, *United States Reports* 403 (1971), 713.

6. Eric Alterman, "Listening to Lyndon," *American Prospect* (January 28, 2002): 34.
7. Louis Harris & Associates (November 17–December 19, 1979, November 1979–March 1980), Roper Center for Public Opinion Research. Respondents in these surveys expressed their agreement or disagreement with the following statement: "Veterans of the Vietnam War were made suckers, having to risk their lives in the wrong war in the wrong place at the wrong time."
8. Gallup Organization (November 17–26, 1978; October 29–November 6, 1982; October 15–November 10, 1998), Roper Center for Public Opinion Research.
9. War Powers Resolution, Pub. L. No. 93-148, 87 Stat. 555 (1973) (codified as amended at 50 U.S.C. §§ 1541–1548 (2006)).
10. For a study of civil and criminal breaches of fiduciary duties imposed by law on tax-exempt organizations, see Marion R. Fremont-Smith and Andras Kosaras, "Wrongdoing by Officers and Directors of Charities: A Survey of Press Reports 1995–2002," Harvard Center for Nonprofit Organizations Working Paper No. 20 (September 2003).
11. 26 U.S.C. §§ 170(a), 501(c)(3) (2006). An organization qualifying under section 501(c)(3) is exempt from the federal income tax on corporations, and donors to the organization can deduct the amount of their donations in calculating their federal income tax.
12. 26 U.S.C. § 4958 (2006 & Supp. I 2009). The statute was adopted in 1996. Pub. L. No. 104-168, 110 Stat. 1475 (1996). For a summary and discussion of the statute and the implementing regulations adopted by the Internal Revenue Service, see James J. Fishman, "Improving Charitable Accountability," *Maryland Law Review* 62 (2003): 218, 253.
13. By generously compensating *three* officers or employees, the charities in Table 2.1 have demonstrated a pattern of such compensation.
14. The information in Table 2.1 was derived from Form 990 (Return of Organization Exempt from Income Tax), which a charity is required to file annually with the Internal Revenue Service. 26 U.S.C. § 6033(b) (2006). The latest Form 990 for each organization in Table 2.1 was obtained from the National Center for Charitable Statistics of the Urban Institute at http://nccs.urban.org (follow the link "Find an Organization") (accessed June 10, 2010).
15. An officer/employee whose compensation was $720,661 received an additional $94,041 in "bonus and incentive compensation."
16. The officer/employee whose compensation was $600,886 was paid an additional $41,400 in "bonus and incentive compensation." An officer/employee whose compensation was $440,189 received an additional $110,000 in "bonus and incentive compensation." Several other officers/employees were paid substantial "bonus and incentive compensation." For example, an officer/employee whose compensation was $411,793 received an additional $134,089 in "bonus and incentive compensation"; an officer/employee whose compensation was $390,690 received an additional $65,000 in "bonus and incentive compensation"; and an officer/employee whose compensation was $430,167 received an additional $41,250 in "bonus and incentive compensation."

17. An officer/employee whose compensation was $186,278 received an additional $22,005 in "bonus and incentive compensation."
18. The compensation shown is the total amount received from the Cystic Fibrosis Foundation and related organizations. The officer/employee whose compensation was $624,639 received an additional $115,418 in "bonus and incentive compensation" from the Cystic Fibrosis Foundation and related organizations. The officer/employee whose compensation was $443,736 received an additional $68,615 in "bonus and incentive compensation" from the Cystic Fibrosis Foundation and related organizations. An officer/employee whose compensation was $468,938 received an additional $72,754 in "bonus and incentive compensation" from the Cystic Fibrosis Foundation.
19. The officer/employee whose compensation was $638,200 was paid an additional $142,800 in "bonus and incentive compensation." An officer/employee whose compensation was $599,000 received an additional $30,800 in "bonus and incentive compensation."
20. The officer/employee whose compensation was $574,299 was paid an additional $94,050 in "bonus and incentive compensation"; the officer/employee whose compensation was $287,086 was paid an additional $44,072 in "bonus and incentive compensation." An officer/employee whose compensation was $320,812 was paid an additional $58,229 in "bonus and incentive compensation."
21. The officer/employee whose compensation was $522,018 received an additional $188,301 in "bonus and incentive compensation"; the officer/employee whose compensation was $311,981 received an additional $72,724 in "bonus and incentive compensation." An officer/employee whose compensation was $357,217 received an additional $68,310 in "bonus and incentive compensation." Other officers/employees were paid "bonus and incentive compensation" in amounts up to $44,500.
22. The officer/employee whose compensation was $449,699 received an additional $60,000 in "bonus and incentive compensation." The officer/employee whose compensation was $261,156, and an officer/employee whose compensation was $280,417, each received an additional $35,000 in "bonus and incentive compensation."
23. Public Agenda Foundation (December 3–18, 1996), Roper Center for Public Opinion Research.
24. Gallup Organization (May 4–June 16, 1996) and Roper Center Institute for Social Inquiry (March 14–31, 1997), Roper Center for Public Opinion Research.
25. See Toshio Yamagishi et al., "Uncertainty, Trust, and Commitment Formation in the United States and Japan," *American Journal of Sociology* 104 (1998): 165.
26. U.S. Dep't of Treasury, Excise Taxes on Excess Benefits Transactions, 67 Fed. Reg. 3076 (January 23, 2002); Mark Taylor, "Tax Exemptions: Sanctions with Bite Could Affect Hospitals," *Modern Healthcare* (January 28, 2002): 12; Jessi Hempel and Amy Borrus, "Now the Nonprofits Need Cleaning Up," *Business Week*, June 21, 2004, 107.
27. "Where's the Stick?" *Economist*, October 11, 2003, 13.

28. *NBC News & Wall Street Journal* (September 21–22, 1987), I.C.R. Survey Research Group (May 1–5, 1992), and Harris Interactive (July 10–11, 2002), Roper Center for Public Opinion Research.
29. Peter D. Hart Research Associates (January 31–February 4, 1997, August 10–13, 2002), Roper Center for Public Opinion Research. In each survey, the question was: "Generally speaking, how much would you say that you trust employers to treat their employees fairly—do you trust them a great deal, quite a bit, just some, or not much at all?" The alternatives "just some" or "not much at all" were selected by 74 percent of all respondents in 1997 and by 66 percent in 2002. Ibid.
30. One highly regarded management expert has observed that the level of compensation of chief executive officers at businesses has alienated the managers below them and eroded teamwork within these businesses. Peter Drucker and Brent Schlender, "Peter Drucker Sets Us Straight," *Fortune*, January 12, 2004, 114.
31. Derrick P. Neuhauser, "Executive Compensation Compliance Initiative," *Tax Adviser* 35 (2004): 265; Louis Lavelle, "Everybody Should be a Little Nervous," *Business Week*, December 22, 2003, 42.
32. A distinction is often made between social science and behavioral science. Under that classification, social psychology should be designated a social science, not a behavioral science.
33. Felix C. Brodbeck et al., "Cultural Variation of Leadership Prototypes Across 22 European Countries," *Journal of Occupational & Organizational Psychology* 73 (2000): 1.
34. David F. Caldwell and Charles A. O'Reilly, III, "The Determinants of Team-Based Innovations in Organizations: The Role of Social Influence," *Small Group Research* 34 (2003): 497; Andrea L. Sinclair, "The Effects of Justice and Cooperation on Team Effectiveness," *Small Group Research* 34 (2003): 74.
35. See Joel A. C. Baum and Christine Oliver, "Institutional Linkages and Organizational Mortality," *Administrative Science Quarterly* 36 (1991): 187. The accounting firm of Arthur Andersen illustrates the demise of a business organization (group) attributable to the social consequences of policies and actions of the organization. The social conditions responsible for the extinction of Arthur Andersen involved shifts in the values of the firm that were accompanied by decreases in social cohesiveness. Notably, many of the changes in the firm were small in magnitude and barely perceptible at the time they occurred. Susan E. Squires et al., *Inside Arthur Andersen: Shifting Values, Unexpected Consequences* (Upper Saddle River, NJ: FT Prentice Hall, 2003), 172.
36. Maria Szekelyi and Robert Tardos, *Attitudes that Make a Difference: Expectancies and Economic Progress* (Institute for Research on Poverty, Univ. Of Wisconsin–Madison, Discussion Paper No. 1003-93, 1993), 21, 24, 53–54. For the relative impact on earnings of the underlying value/attitude compared to human capital (as measured by educational attainment), see the zero-order correlation coefficients in Tables 4.B and 5.
37. Sociologically, an institution is a set of statuses and roles (a) that a society defines and endorses and (b) that involve interpersonal relationships through which a socially approved type of activity takes place in the society.

Howard B. Kaplan, "The Concept of Institution: A Review, Evaluation, and Suggested Research Procedure," *Social Forces* 39 (1960): 176, 179.

38. E.g., Caroline Hodges Persell, "The Interdependence of Social Justice and Civil Society," *Sociological Forum* 12 (1997): 149.

39. While an argument can be made that government and law are distinct institutions, they are closely intertwined and difficult to separate. Accordingly, government and law will be considered to be a single institution. I will often refer to the institution as "law" because of my knowledge of and familiarity with this aspect of the institution.

40. See Lisa A. Keister, "Financial Markets, Money, and Banking," *Annual Review of Sociology* 28 (2002): 39, 53.

41. Paul Schreyer and Dirk Pilat, "Measuring Productivity," *OECD Economic Studies*, no. 33 (2001): 127.

42. The term "social productivity" seems to be essentially absent from the literature in sociology. One recently published article that reports the findings of a sociological study employs the phrase "socially productive organization," but the article uses the phrase just once and only with reference to membership in community groups. Kim Perren et al., "Men's Organizational Affiliations in Later Life: The Influence of Social Class and Marital Status on Informal Group Membership," *Aging & Society* 23 (2003): 69, 70. The literature in economics occasionally uses the term "social productivity." E.g., Uma Lele, "Women and Structural Transformation," *Economic Development & Cultural Change* 34 (1986): 195, 215; Ganti Subrahmanyam, "Real Money Balances as a Factor of Production: Some New Evidence," *Review of Economics & Statistics* 62 (1980): 280. When the term has been used in economics, however, either no effort has been made to develop and specify its aspects or the focus of the term has been an economic phenomenon. The situation in law is identical to the situation in economics, perhaps because law draws upon economics more often than it draws upon any other social science discipline.

    Two notable law review articles applied the sociological concept of social capital: Jason Mazzone, "Towards a Social Capital Theory of Law: Lessons from Collaborative Reproduction," *Santa Clara Law Review* 39 (1998): 1; Jason Mazzone, "When Courts Speak: Social Capital and Law's Expressive Function," *Syracuse Law Review* 49 (1999): 1039. However, social capital and social productivity, while related, have different referents: The former deals with the social *resources* of groups while the latter deals with the social *consequences* of group functioning. Further differences between the two concepts are discussed later in Part II of this chapter.

43. See Carl D. Lantz and Pierre-Daniel G. Sarte, "Consumption, Savings, and the Meaning of the Wealth Effect in General Equilibrium," *Economic Quarterly* 87 (2001): 53.

44. As defined in this chapter, a group is "organized" when (1) it persists over a minimum period of time, (2) its members have some minimum level of interpersonal ties, and (3) it has developed a structure, including identifiable (even if shifting) leaders and standards for the behavior of group members. (Standards for behavior are discussed in Part IV infra.) A group that lasts just a short time is "organized" if it terminates on a date set in advance as long as the group, while in existence, is characterized by interpersonal

bonds between its members and a structure. Conversely, a group is not "organized" when its members lack durable ties to one another and when it has failed to develop a structure.

45. See Brian Leiter, "Measuring the Academic Distinction of Law Faculties," *Journal of Legal Studies* 29 (2000): 451. In the Leiter study, a numerical score was computed for the scholarly output and impact of faculty members at sixty-six law schools in the United States; the law schools were selected because they were expected to place among the schools highest on this variable. Ibid., 460. The score for and the names of each of the forty schools that had the highest scores are reported by Professor Leiter, who also presents the score from *U.S. News & World Report* for the subjective reputation of each of these schools. Ibid., 492–94, tables A10–11. Professor Leiter did not calculate the correlation coefficient between the two sets of scores, but using Stata (version 8.2), I found the zero-order product-moment coefficient to be .71. Thus, in the absence of controls for other factors that might be affecting the relationship between the two scores, fully half ($r^2 = (.71)^2 = .504$) of the variation in reputation at the forty schools can be explained by variation in the scholarly output and impact of their faculties.
46. Larry D. Barnett, *Legal Construct, Social Concept* (New York: Aldine De Gruyter, 1993), 21–23.
47. See Princeton Survey Research Associates, November 1–2, 2001, Roper Center for Public Opinion Research.
48. Warren O. Hagstrom, "Inputs, Outputs, and the Prestige of University Science Departments," *Sociology of Education* 44 (1971): 375, 382–83, table 4 (biology, chemistry, mathematics, and physics); Kenneth A. Borokhovich et al., "Finance Research Productivity and Influence," *Journal of Finance* 50 (1995): 1691, 1705–6 (business).
49. The term "social capital" was first proposed by James S. Coleman. James S. Coleman, "Social Capital in the Creation of Human Capital," *American Journal of Sociology* 94 (1988): S95.
50. As to social capital, see Alejandro Portes, "Social Capital: Its Origins and Applications in Modern Sociology," *Annual Review of Sociology* 24 (1998): 1, 21.
51. Ibid., 15.
52. Marco G. Guigni, "Was It Worth the Effort? The Outcomes and Consequences of Social Movements," *Annual Review of Sociology* 24 (1998): 371, 386.
53. E.g., Jennifer K. Robbennolt, "Determining Punitive Damages: Empirical Insights and Implications for Reform," *Buffalo Law Review* 50 (2002): 103; Charles Lave and Patrick Elias, "Did the 65 MPH Speed Limit Save Lives?" *Accident Analysis & Prevention* 26 (1994): 49.
54. Benefits are not necessarily tangible. They may also be intangible, e.g., ranks and tributes.
55. Garrett Hardin, "The Tragedy of the Commons," *Science* 162 (1968): 1243.
56. Ibid., 1244.
57. See discussion infra Part VI.
58. *Model Rules of Prof'l Conduct R. 1.3 cmt.*, 1.7, 1.9 (2003). This obligation was initially recognized by the American Bar Association in 1908 when

the Association adopted the Canons of Professional Ethics. However, the scope of the obligation at that time was narrower than it is today. James M. Altman, "Considering the A.B.A.'s 1908 Canons of Ethics," *Fordham Law Review* 71 (2003): 2395, 2468–70.

59. Fickett v. Superior Court, 558 P.2d 988 (Ariz. Ct. App. 1976); *Model Rules of Prof'l Conduct R. 1.18* (2003).
60. See supra Part II.
61. *Random House Dictionary of the English Language 1971*, 2nd ed. (New York: Random House, 1987).
62. Some of the methodological problems confronting such research are discussed in Chester L. Britt et al., "A Reassessment of the D.C. Gun Law: Some Cautionary Notes on the Use of Interrupted Time Series Designs for Policy Impact Assessment," *Law & Society Review* 30 (1996): 361.
63. Supra note 44.
64. Recognized needs, however, do not act by themselves in molding the content of law. Dominant social values also shape legal doctrine. See Thomas R. Marshall, *Public Opinion and the Supreme Court* (Boston, MA: Unwin Hyman, 1989), 78–80. Moreover, the nature and importance of the social values involved may determine whether new legal doctrine originates through legislation, through action by the executive branch of government (e.g., agency rulemaking), or through interpretation or amendment of the constitution of the jurisdiction.
65. See Drazen v. New Haven Taxicab Co., 111 A. 861, 863 (Conn. 1920) ("[s]ociety progresses, and law develops to meet its needs"). The concept of societal need is discussed infra in Part IV of Chapter 7.
66. Lauren Young and Mike McNamee, "Mutual Funds: In the Scandals' Wake, A Raft of New Rules," *Business Week*, January 12, 2004, 126.
67. Compliance Programs of Investment Companies and Investment Advisers, Investment Advisers Act Release No. IA-2204 and Investment Company Act Release No. IC-26299, 68 Fed. Reg. 74,714 (December 24, 2003) (codified at 17 C.F.R. pts. 270, 275, 279).
68. James M. Sgueo, "The Role of Control States in Today's Society," *StateWays*, September 1, 2003, 11.
69. My discussion focuses on organized groups regardless of scale, whether large (i.e., a society and its institutions) or small. Such groups below the scale of a societal institution include (a) private-sector social service organizations that are or purport to be eleemosynary and (b) business organizations that seek financial profit from the activities in which they engage. Organizations that blend the preceding are also included. (The latter are discussed in Laura D'Andrea Tyson, "Good Works—With a Business Plan," *Business Week*, May 3, 2004, 32.) However, the discussion extends beyond organizations that have a legal status (e.g., corporations and partnerships) and encompasses organized groups that are not recognized by law as entities distinct from their members, e.g., unincorporated groups having a civic or recreational purpose.
70. The three social phenomena I have identified—reputation, symbols, and trust and perceptions of fairness—may be regarded as *resources* of groups, or they may be regarded as *outcomes* of group functioning. In either case, each of the three phenomena can vary between groups. However, if the three phe-

nomena are deemed to be group resources, they are components of social capital; if they are deemed to be outcomes of group life, they are aspects of social productivity. If (as I believe) the consequences of law must be understood, social productivity is more useful than social capital in the study of law, and the three phenomena, therefore, are more fruitfully viewed as outcomes, i.e., approached from the perspective of social productivity.

71. Larry D. Barnett, "The Roots of Law," *American University Journal of Gender, Social Policy & Law* 15 (2007): 613, 620–26. Pages 620–26 in this article are reproduced infra in Part I-C of Chapter 6.
72. Larry D. Barnett, "Population Growth, Population Organization Participants, and the Right of Privacy," *Family Law Quarterly* 12 (1978): 37.
73. Meyer F. Nimkoff, "Obstacles to Innovation," in *Technology and Social Change*, ed. Francis R. Allen et al. (New York: Appleton-Century-Crofts, 1957), 56.
74. Delbert C. Miller, "Radio and Television," in *Technology and Social Change*, supra note 73, 157; Communications Act of 1934, 47 U.S.C. § 151 (2006).
75. As to demographic phenomena, *compare* Halliman H. Winsborough, "Demography," in *Encyclopedia of Sociology*, vol. 1, ed. Edgar F. Borgatta and Marie L. Borgatta (New York: Macmillan, 1992), 451 *with* Douglas S. Massey, "What I Don't Know About My Field but Wish I Did," *Annual Review of Sociology* 26 (2000): 699. As to the social character of the development of knowledge and technology, see Hornell Hart, "Acceleration in Social Change," in *Technology and Social Change*, supra note 73, at 27, 54–55; Robert K. Merton, "Puritanism, Pietism, and Science," in *The Sociology of Science*, ed. Bernard Barber and Walter Hirsch (New York: Free Press of Glencoe, 1962), 33; Bernard Barber, *Social Studies of Science* (New Brunswick, NJ: Transaction Publishers, 1990), 97–113.
76. Reid A. Bryson and Thomas J. Murray, *Climates of Hunger* (Madison: University Of Wisconsin Press, 1977); Glenn Deane and Myron P. Gutmann, "Blowin' Down the Road: Investigating Bilateral Causality between Dust Storms and Population in the Great Plains," *Population Research & Policy Review* 22 (2003): 297.
77. Anjani Chandra and Elizabeth Hervey Stephen, "Impaired Fecundity in the United States: 1982-1995," *Family Planning Perspectives* 30 (January–February, 1998): 34.
78. Richard G. Rogers et al., *Living and Dying in the USA: Behavioral, Health, and Social Differentials of Adult Mortality* (Basingstoke, Hampshire: Stockton, 2000), 195, 309.
79. Anne Maria Herskind et al., "The Heritability of Human Longevity: A Population-based Study of 2872 Danish Twin Pairs Born 1870–1900,' *Human Genetics* 97 (1996): 319; Ivan A. Iachine et al., 'How Heritable is Individual Susceptibility to Death? The Results of an Analysis of Survival Data on Danish, Swedish and Finnish Twins," *Twin Res*earch 1 (1998): 196; Anatoli I. Yashin et al., "Half of the Variation in Susceptibility to Mortality Is Genetic: Findings from Swedish Twin Survival Data, *Behavioral Genetics* 29 (1999): 11. *Contra* Birgit Ljungquist et al., "The Effect of Genetic Factors for Longevity: A Comparison of Identical and Fraternal Twins in

the Swedish Twin Registry," *Journal of Gerontology: Medical Science* 53A (1998): M441.

80. Douglas Dockery and Arden Pope, "Epidemiology of Acute Health Effects: Summary of Time-Series Studies," in *Particles in Our Air: Concentrations and Health Effects*, ed. Richard Wilson and John D. Spengler (Cambridge, MA: Harvard School Of Public Health, 1996), 123, 146.
81. Stephan Fuchs, *The Professional Quest for Truth* (Albany: State University of New York Press, 1992), 89–90, 180; *House Science Comm.*, 105th Cong., 2nd Sess., *Unlocking Our Future: Toward a New National Science Policy* (Comm. Print 1998).
82. To be affluent, a society must have access to mineral resources. See *Comm. on Resources and Man, Nat'l Academy of Sciences–Nat'l Research Council, Resources and Man* (1969). Advanced science, consequently, presupposes the availability to society of plentiful minerals.
83. See Sayre P. Schatz, "The Role of Capital Accumulation in Economic Development," *Journal of Development Studies* 5 (1968): 39.
84. Nyla R. Branscombe et al., "The Context and Content of Social Identity Threat," in *Social Identity: Context, Commitment, Content*, ed. Naomi Ellemers et al. (Malden, MA: Blackwell Publishers, 1999), 35, 43–46.
85. Naomi Ellemers, "The Influence of Socio-structural Variables on Identity Management Strategies," *European Review of Social Psychology* 4 (1993): 27.
86. Stuart Landon and C. E. Smith, "The Use of Quality and Reputation Indicators by Consumers: The Case of Bordeaux Wine," *Journal of Consumer Policy* 20 (1997): 20; Stuart Landon and Constance E. Smith, "Quality Expectations, Reputation, and Price," *Southern Economic Journal* 64 (1998): 628.
87. Hubert M. Blalock, Jr., "The Real and Unrealized Contributions of Quantitative Sociology," *American Sociological Review* 54 (1989): 447, 457, 458. Professor Blalock was president of the American Sociological Association in 1979. American Sociological Association, ASA Presidents by Date of Service, http://www.asanet.org/about/past_presidents.cfm (accessed December 4, 2009).
88. Regrettably, there are no time-series data that directly measure the reputation of sociology in the population generally or among college and university students during the last half-century. Nonetheless, some evidence exists that, within colleges and universities, sociology at the present time has a reputation that is poor relative to other disciplines. See Dennis J. Downey et al., "The Status of Sociology within the Academy: Where We Are, Why We're There, and How to Change It," *American Sociologist* 39 (2008): 193.
89. Randall Collins, "Sociology: Proscience or Antiscience?" *American Sociological Review* (1989): 124, 124 ("[i]n recent years there have been a variety of assaults on the conception of sociology as a science"); Alan Wolfe, "Social Skills," *New Republic*, April 23, 2007, 56 (estimating that half of all sociologists now devote themselves to political, not scientific, pursuits).
90. The number of bachelor's degrees conferred each year in sociology, and the number of bachelor's degrees conferred each year in all disciplines, were obtained from *Nat'l Ctr. for Educ. Statistics, Digest of Education Statistics*

2008, tables 268, 317, http://nces.ed.gov/programs/digest/2008menu_tables.asp (accessed April 7, 2011).

91. The data in Figure 2.1 are from *Nat'l Ctr. for Educ. Statistics, Digest of Education Statistics 2008*, Table 317, http://nces.ed.gov/programs/digest/2008menu_tables.asp (accessed April 7, 2011). This source does not furnish, and hence the figure does not include, data for 1950–1951 or for each second academic year thereafter through 1968–1969. From 1969–1970 onward, data on every academic year are supplied and included in the figure.
92. From the 1993–1994 academic year through the 2006–2007 academic year, as Figure 2.1 shows, the number of bachelor's degrees in sociology exceeded the number of bachelor's degrees in economics. Ibid. Reputation is not the sole determinant of decisions made by undergraduates regarding their major, of course, and the larger number of students completing bachelor's degrees in sociology than in economics beginning in 1993–1994 indicates that the impact of the reputation of sociology was being partially offset by other factors. Nonetheless, the substantially lower percentage of all bachelor's degrees awarded in sociology during 2006–2007 (viz., 1.9 percent) than during 1973–1974 (3.8 percent) is evidence that the reputation of sociology (a) is worse today than during the period that ended in 1973–1974 and (b) is hurting the discipline. As to (b), see Downey et al., supra note 88, at 194–95.
93. James A. Davis, *Great Aspirations* (Chicago, IL: Aldine Publishing, 1964), 144–47.
94. Roberta Spalter-Roth, "Has Sociology Suffered the Declines Predicted Ten Years Ago?" *Footnotes* 31 (2003): 1, 11, http://www.asanet.org/footnotes/feb03/indextwo.html (accessed December 4, 2009).
95. However, the percentage of United States adults who believe that lawyers have "very great prestige" has risen since bottoming in 2002 at 15 percent. Harris Interactive, *Firefighters, Scientists and Doctors Seen as Most Prestigious Occupations*, August 4, 2009, http://www.harrisinteractive.com/vault/Harris-Interactive-Poll-Research-Pres-Occupations-2009-08.pdf (accessed April 7, 2011).
96. Louis Harris & Associates (October 8–16, 1977 and April 22–27, 1992), Roper Center for Public Opinion Research; Harris Interactive, supra note 95, at 3.
97. For 2007, 2008, and 2009, the National Compensation Survey provided data on the mean hourly earnings both for "law teachers, postsecondary" and for "sociology teachers, postsecondary." U.S. Dep't of Labor, Bureau of Labor Statistics Data: National Compensation Survey, http://data.bls.gov/cgi-bin/dsrv?nw. The average compensation of law teachers at the postsecondary level was between 1.7 and 1.8 times larger than the average compensation of sociology teachers at the postsecondary level. The disparity in reported earnings, however, did not take into account differences that may exist between the two occupations in the average number of years of occupational experience.
98. American Bar Association, Enrollment and Degrees Awarded, http://www.americanbar.org/groups/legal_education/resources/statistics.html (accessed April 7, 2011).

99. Susan Daicoff, "Lawyer, Know Thyself: A Review of Empirical Research on Attorney Attributes Bearing on Professionalism," *American University Law Review* 46 (1997): 1337, 1344–47.
100. Maura Dolan, "Miserable with the Legal Life: More and More Lawyers Hate Their Jobs, Surveys Find," *Los Angeles Times*, June 27, 1995, A1. Accurate data do not exist on the number of attorneys who reject law as an occupation and move into a different occupation, but the number of California attorneys on inactive status with the state Bar increased from one in ten in 1980 to one in four (in, presumably, 1995). Ibid. See Hindi Greenberg, "Lawyers in Transition," *San Francisco Attorney*, June–July 1999, http://www.sfbar.org/about/sfam/junejuly99/transition.html (accessed April 12, 2005); Karen Uhlenhuth, "More Lawyers Taking the Out-Law Trail," *Omaha World-Herald*, February 18, 1996, 1G.
101. Daicoff, supra note 99, at 1420–25. See Lawrence R. Richard, "Psychological Type and Job Satisfaction Among Practicing Lawyers in the United States," *Capital University Law Review* 29 (2002): 979.
102. Ellemers, supra note 85.
103. Heather J. Smith et al., "Social Identity and the Context of Relative Deprivation," in *Social Identity: Context, Commitment, Content*, ed. Naomi Ellemers et al. (Malden, MA: Blackwell Publishers, 1999), 205, 223–24.
104. The word "symbol" refers here to "[s]omething that stands for, represents, or denotes something else (not by exact resemblance, but by vague suggestion, or by some accidental or conventional relation); esp. a material object representing or taken to represent something immaterial or abstract, as a being, idea, quality, or condition." *Oxford English Dictionary*, vol. 17, 2nd ed. (1989), 451.
105. Groups with a small number of members may require fewer symbols to maintain internal cohesion and thus not generate as many symbols as groups with a large number of members. A small group may have less of a need for symbols in part because, compared to a large group, the members of a small group experience face-to-face interaction more often and with a higher proportion of other members of their group. Face-to-face interaction is likely to bolster social cohesiveness in most situations.
106. In addition to improving group cohesion, symbols can promote the demand for the products and services of entities engaged in commerce. For a business, a trademark is a symbol of the goodwill that the trademark owner possesses with the public, and a firm may devote substantial resources to increasing its goodwill and, hence, the value of its trademark. See Jerome Gilson et al., *Trademark Protection and Practice*, vol. 1, (Newark, NJ: Matthew Bender, 2001), §§ 1.03[6], 1.03[7].
107. The racing horse Seabiscuit was (and, given the popularity of the recent movie about him, is) an example of a symbol that reflected the values of Americans. See Robert Denerstein, "Racing Away from Cynicism: 'Seabiscuit' Betting on Romantic Appeal," *Rocky Mountain News*, July 26, 2003, 14D (claiming "Seabiscuit came to symbolize hope and second chances"); Rupert Cornwell, "Four-Legged All-American Hero Diverts Nation," *The Independent (London)*, August 4, 2003, 9 (stating Seabiscuit "is the equine embodiment of how Americans love to imagine themselves: scrappy underdogs who manage to beat the odds").

108. Dave Walters, "The Nickname Game," *Tampa Tribune*, December 11, 1998, 9 (observing that a school is symbolized by its mascot, which "defines its identity and is a rallying point for communities across the nation").
109. Another school mascot was the focus of Crosby v. Holsinger, 852 F.2d 801 (4th Cir. 1988) (holding that a Virginia public high school did not violate the First Amendment when it banned the school's "Johnny Reb" mascot because, as a symbol of the Confederacy, it alienated black students from the school).
110. See Timothy S. Rooney, "House Supports Chief Illiniwek as Symbol," *Chicago Sun-Times*, April 23, 1995, 7; Michael Gillis, "Chief Illiniwek's Fate Left Up to University," *Chicago Sun-Times*, October 21, 1995, 6; Editorial, "Tradition, Sensibilities and Chief Illiniwek," *St. Louis Post-Dispatch*, November 8, 1995, 6B.
111. "Mascot Ruling Upsets Indians at the University of Illinois, *New York. Times*, December 3, 1995, § 1, at 44.
112. 4 U.S.C.A. §§ 6, 7 (West 2005 & Supp. 2009).
113. 36 U.S.C. § 110 (2006).
114. 36 U.S.C. § 115 (2006). The statute is in addition to 4 U.S.C. § 6(e) (2006), which mandates the daily display of the flag "on or near the main administration building of every public institution."
115. Texas v. Johnson, *United States Reports* 491 (1989), 397, 405.
116. Rick Bragg, "After the Attacks: The Flag," *New York. Times*, September 17, 2001, A1.
117. "Patriotism Fuels Flag Purchases," *USA Today*, September 10, 2002, 1D. See also *Briefly*, *St. Petersburg Times*, September 14, 2001, 13A.
118. Hilary E. MacGregor, "The Peace (Flag) Makers," *Los Angeles Times*, December 2, 2001, § 5, at 1; Leslie Walker, "Merchants Make Their War Plans," *Washington Post*, October 11, 2001, E01.
119. New Jersey v. T.L.O., *United States Reports* 469 (1985), 325, 373 (Stevens, Marshall, and Brennan, JJ., dissenting).
120. Spence v. Washington, *United States Reports* 418 (1974), 405; Texas v. Johnson, *United States Reports* 491 (1989), 397, 405; United States v. Eichman, *United States Reports* 496 (1990), 310. The United States. Supreme Court is unclear whether the First Amendment protects only individuals who own, or reasonably believe they own, the flag that is the subject of their action. In *Johnson*, for example, the Court ruled that, under the First Amendment, a statute that criminalized physical abuse of the United States flag could not be violated by a person who burned the flag as part of a political protest. The flag had been removed from a building by another demonstrator. *United States Reports* 491, at 399. However, the majority opinion in *Johnson* makes no reference to whether the defendant realized that he lacked the permission of the owner to burn the flag.
121. United States v. Robel, *United States Reports* 389 (1967), 258, 264.
122. Texas v. Johnson, *United States Reports* 491, at 419 ("[o]ur decision is a reaffirmation of the principles of freedom and inclusiveness that the flag best reflects...").
123. Nat'l Labor Relations Bd. v. Catholic Bishop of Chi., *United States Reports* 440 (1979), 490, 501 ("[t]he values enshrined in the First Amendment plainly rank high 'in the scale of our national values[]'").

124. Mary Flood and Clifford Pugh, "Lea Fastow Expresses 'regret' at Sentencing; Wife of ex-Enron CFO Faces Year in Prison," *Houston Chronicle*, May 7, 2004, A19; Carrie Johnson, "Lea Fastow Sentenced to 1-Year Term," *Washington Post*, May 7, 2004, E1.
125. The United States Supreme Court has expressed the principle as follows:

> Our whole system of law is predicated on the general fundamental principle of equality of application of the law. 'All men are equal before the law,' 'This is a government of laws and not of men,' 'No man is above the law,' are all maxims showing the spirit in which Legislatures, executives and courts are expected to make, execute and apply laws.

Truax v. Corrigan, *United States Reports* 257 (1921), 312, 332.
126. David Weisburd et al., "Specific Deterrence in a Sample of Offenders Convicted of White-Collar Crimes," *Criminology* 33 (1995): 587; cf. Lisa Stolzenberg and Stewart J. D'Alessio, "'Three Strikes and You're Out': The Impact of California's New Mandatory Sentencing Law on Serious Crime Rates," *Crime & Delinquency* (1997): 457 (state statute requiring a mandatory prison sentence upon conviction of a felony for persons with prior felony convictions did not generally reduce, in metropolitan areas of the state, the rate of a composite index of six reported crimes, viz., willful homicide, forcible rape, robbery, aggravated assault, burglary, and motor vehicle theft); Tamasak Witayapanyanon, Criminal Justice Policy in the United States: A Pooled Time-Series Analysis of Sentencing Reform Impacts (1989) (unpublished PhD dissertation, Northern Illinois University) (changes in state laws governing prison sentencing did not halt rises in state rates of murder, rape, robbery, and aggravated assault).
127. Some symbols generated by government and law may reduce societal cohesion. Affirmative action is a government policy and a doctrine of law that may operate in part as a symbol of social values in the United States. With regard to values, affirmative action can symbolize support for equality of opportunity, or it can be a symbol that the selection of individuals is not based on merit and skill. In the latter event, affirmative action is seen by Americans as inconsistent with an ideal they hold and is rejected as reverse discrimination. See Leatta M. Hough and Frederick L. Oswald, "Personnel Selection: Looking toward the Future–Remembering the Past," *Annual Review of Psychology* 51 (2000): 631, 651. In *Regents of the Univ. of Cal. v. Bakke, United States Reports* 438 (1978), 265, 295, Justice Powell observed:

> *All* state-imposed classifications that rearrange burdens and benefits on the basis of race are likely to be viewed with deep resentment by the individuals burdened. The denial to innocent persons of equal rights and opportunities may outrage those so deprived and therefore may be perceived as invidious.... One should not lightly dismiss the inherent unfairness of, and the perception of mistreatment that accompanies, a system of allocating benefits and privileges on the basis of skin color and ethnic origin.

An analysis of attitudinal data from the 1990 General Social Survey found that affirmative-action programs targeting race rather than income substantially decreased the support of Whites not only for social policies promoting equal outcomes (e.g., quotas) but also for social policies promoting equal opportunities. Lawrence Bobo and James R. Kluegel, "Opposition to Race-Targeting: Self-Interest, Stratification Ideology, or Racial Attitudes?" *American Sociological Review* 58 (1993): 443. However, no studies to date have employed quantitative data either to (1) identify the manner in which affirmative action as a symbol directly and indirectly alters the level of cohesion in society, or to (2) estimate whether the net impact of affirmative action as a symbol has been to increase or decrease the cohesion of American society. The second question should be answered with time-series data rather than with cross-sectional data (such as that used by Bobo and Kluegel, supra), and time-series data may be necessary to answer the first question, too.

128. Sim B. Sitkin and Nancy L. Roth, "Explaining the Limited Effectiveness of Legalistic "Remedies" for Trust/Distrust," *Organization Science* 4 (1993): 367, 368.
129. Jason A. Colquitt, "On the Dimensionality of Organizational Justice: A Construct Validation of a Measure," *Journal of Applied Psychology* 86 (2001): 386.
130. Clancy v. Superior Court, 705 P.2d 347, 351 (Cal. 1985). See also Wheat v. United States, *United States Reports* 486 (1988), 153, 160 ("[f]ederal courts have an independent interest in ensuring that... legal proceedings appear fair to all who observe them").
131. Daniel J. Koys and Thomas A. DeCotiis, "Inductive Measures of Psychological Climate," *Human Relations* 44 (1991): 265.
132. In the practice of law, however, fairness and perceptions of fairness have long been of concern. Leslie W. Abramson, "Appearance of Impropriety: Deciding When a Judge's Impartiality 'Might Reasonably Be Questioned,'" *Georgetown Journal of Legal Ethics* 14 (2000): 55, 66–67; Roberta K. Flowers, "What You See Is What You Get: Applying the Appearance of Impropriety Standard to Prosecutors," *Missouri Law Review* 63 (1998): 699.
133. Francis Fukuyama, *Trust* (New York: Free Press, 1995), 278–79, 313. See Barry R. Schaller, "A Legal Prescription for Bioethical Ills," *Quinnipiac Law Review* 21 (2002): 183, 403 (referring to "the unbalanced individualistic philosophy that has dominated during the latter half of the past century").
134. Niklas Luhmann, *Trust and Power* (Chichester: Wiley, 1979), 8, 25–26.
135. Sitkin and Roth, supra note 128, at 369–71.
136. J. Barton Cunningham and James MacGregor, "Trust and the Design of Work: Complementary Constructs in Satisfaction and Performance," *Human Relations* 53 (2000): 1575; Ian R. Gellatly, "Individual and Group Determinants of Employee Absenteeism: Test of a Causal Model," *Journal of Organizational Behavior* 16 (1995): 469, 481; Sandra L. Robinson, "Trust and Breach of the Psychological Contract," *Administrative Science Quarterly* 41 (1996): 574; Stephen P. Schappe and Annette C. Doran, "How Does Fair Treatment Affect Employee Commitment to an Organization? A Field Study of Financial Holding Company Employees," *Mid-Atlantic Journal of Business* 33 (1997): 191; Tom R. Tyler and Peter Degoey, "Trust in Organizational Authorities: The Influence of Motive Attributions on Willingness to Accept Decisions," in *Trust in Organizations*, ed. Roderick

M. Kramer and Tom R. Tyler (Thousand Oaks, CA: Sage Publications, 1996), 331.

137. Ronald Inglehart, *Modernization and Postmodernization* (Princeton, NJ: Princeton University Press, 1997), 180–97.
138. Rafael La Porta et al., "Trust in Large Organizations," *American Economic Review* 87 (May 1997): 333, 336.
139. César Calderón et al., "Development and Efficiency of the Financial Sector and Links with Trust: Cross-Country Evidence," *Economic Development & Cultural Change* 51 (2002): 189.
140. See note 110 in Chapter 3.
141. Tyler and Degoey, supra note 136, at 344. In the words of H. L. Mencken, "it is mutual trust, even more than mutual interest[,] that holds human associations together." The Quotations Page, http://www.quotationspage.com/quotes/H._L._Mencken/ (accessed December 5, 2009).
142. As used in this chapter, a conflict of interest arises from two or more goals each of which is attractive but only one of which can be achieved. A person subject to a conflict of interest must choose one of the goals and sacrifice the goal(s) not chosen. See *In re* BH&P, Inc., 103 B.R. 556, 563 (Bankr. D. N.J. 1989).
143. 15 U.S.C. §§ 80a-1 to -64 (2006).
144. 15 U.S.C. §§ 80b-1 to -21 (2006).
145. Investment Company Act, ch. 686, title I, 54 Stat. 789 (1940); Investment Advisers Act, ch. 686, title II, 54 Stat. 847 (1940).
146. The assets of an investment company are composed of a portfolio of securities that are acquired with the assets obtained from the purchasers of the securities issued by the investment company. 15 U.S.C. § 80a-3 (2006). The staff of the Securities and Exchange Commission has taken the position that the defining attributes of the securities in the portfolio of the investment company differ from the defining attributes of the securities issued by the investment company. Merrill Lynch, Pierce, Fenner, & Smith, Inc., SEC No-Action Letter, [1982–1983 Transfer Binder] Fed. Sec. L. Rep. (CCH) ¶ 77,310, at 78,145 (October 28, 1982), available at 1982 SEC No-Act. LEXIS 3036. The position of the Commission staff is disputed by C. Steven Bradford, "Expanding the Investment Company Act: The SEC's Manipulation of the Definition of Security," *Ohio State Law Journal* 60 (1999): 995.
147. Michael Bogdan et al., "Ownership of Mutual Funds, Shareholder Sentiment, and Use of the Internet, 2010," *Investment Company Institute Research Fundamentals* 19 (2010): 19 (Figure A1), http://www.ici.org/pdf/fm-v19n6.pdf. (accessed April 7, 2011).
148. Royce de R. Barondes, "Professionalism Consequences of Law Firm Investments in Clients: An Empirical Assessment," *American Business Law Journal* 39 (2002): 379; Mathew L. A. Hayward and Warren Boeker, "Power and Conflicts of Interest in Professional Firms: Evidence from Investment Banking," *Administrative Science Quarterly* 43 (1998): 1.
149. See discussion infra in Parts VI-B, VI-C, and VI-D of Chapter 2 and in Parts I and II of Chapter 3.
150. The same types of securities are covered by the two 1940 Acts. The securities covered are listed in section 2(a)(36) of the Investment Company

Act and in section 2(a)(18) of the Investment Advisers Act. 15 U.S.C. §§ 80a-2(a)(36), 80b-2(a)(18) (2006).

151. Tcherepnin v. Knight, *United States Reports* 389 (1967), 332, 338 (finding "Congress did not intend to adopt a narrow or restrictive concept of security" and sought "a flexible rather than a static" interpretation of the concept) (internal quotation marks omitted).
152. 15 U.S.C. §§ 80a-2(a)(36), 80b-2(a)(18) (2006).
153. The cases discussed in this paragraph involved the Securities Act and the Securities Exchange Act. The types of securities covered by these Acts are almost identical to the types of securities covered by the 1940 Acts. For the list of securities in the Securities Act, see 15 U.S.C. § 77b(a)(1) (2006). For the list of securities in the Securities Exchange Act, see 15 U.S.C. § 78c(a)(10) (2006).
154. Reves v. Ernst & Young, *United States Reports* 494 (1990), 56.
155. Ibid., 61.
156. Sec. & Exch. Comm'n v. W. J. Howey Co., *United States Reports* 328 (1946), 293, 299.
157. "Investment" in its economic sense is "the investing of money or capital," and invest(ing) is "to employ (money) in the purchase of anything from which interest or profit is expected." *Oxford English Dictionary*, vol. 8, 2nd ed. (1989), 46, 48.
158. Minn. Educ. Ass'n, SEC No-Action Letter (November 4, 1982), [1982–1983 Transfer Binder] Fed. Sec. L. Rep. (CCH) ¶ 77,316, at 78,177, 78,179, available at 1982 SEC No-Act. LEXIS 3033, at *1 (staff reply).
159. Scott FitzGibbon, "What Is a Security? – A Redefinition Based on Eligibility to Participate in the Financial Markets," *Minnesota Law Review* 64 (1980): 893, 919.
160. Sec. & Exch. Comm'n v. Int'l Scanning Devices, Inc., No. Civ-74-351, [1977–1978 Transfer Binder] Fed. Sec. L. Rep. (CCH) ¶ 96,147, at 92,164, 92,175, available at 1977 U.S. Dist. LEXIS 16501, at *39 (April 6, 1977) (stating instruments were securities because they "were reasonably believed to be investment securities by the purchasers, and... reasonable people with the information that these investors had would consider them to be securities"). *Accord, In re* Nat'l Mort. Equity Corp. Mort. Pool Certificates Sec. Litig., 723 F. Supp. 497, 503 (C.D. Cal. 1989).
161. United Housing Found., Inc. v. Forman, *United States Reports* 421 (1975), 837, 850 (asserting that an instrument must "lead a purchaser justifiably to assume that the federal securities laws apply"). *Accord,* Landreth Timber Co. v. Landreth, *United States Reports* 471 (1985), 681, 687.
162. Reves v. Ernst & Young, *United States Reports* 494, at 66.
163. *See* Verónica Benet-Martínez and Zahide Karakitapoğlu-Aygün, "The Interplay of Cultural Syndromes and Personality in Predicting Life Satisfaction: Comparing Asian Americans and European Americans," *Journal of Cross-Cultural Psychology* 34 (2003): 38, 55–56; Michael Harris Bond and Peter B. Smith, "Cross-Cultural Social and Organizational Psychology," *Annual Review of Psychology* 47 (1996): 205.
164. See Joel Seligman, "The Obsolescence of Wall Street: A Contextual Approach to the Evolving Structure of Federal Securities Regulation," *Michigan Law Review* 93 (1995): 649, 651, 672.

165. See Colquitt, supra note 129.
166. Notice of Adoption of Rule 144, Exchange Act Release No. 5223 (January 11, 1972), [1971–1972 Transfer Binder] Fed. Sec. L. Rep. (CCH) ¶ 78,487, at 81,049, 81,051, available at 1972 SEC LEXIS 49.
167. Sec. & Exch. Comm'n v. Capital Gains Research Bureau, *United States Reports* 375 (1963), 180, 201 (a "climate of fair dealing... is... essential to maintain public confidence in the securities industry and to preserve the economic health of the country").
168. E.g., Smith v. Van Gorkom, 488 A.2d 858, 872 (Del. 1985). Cf. Lynn A. Stout, "On the Proper Motives of Corporate Directors (Or Why You Don't Want to Invite Homo Economicus to Join Your Board)," *Delaware Journal of Corporate Law* 28 (2003): 1 (considering whether and why corporate directors are motivated to advance the interests of their companies).
169. See Enderle v. Trautman, Civil No. A3-01-22, 2001 U.S. Dist. LEXIS 20181, at *21 (N.D. December 3, 2001) ("trust.... is essential to establishing a fiduciary relationship").
170. Interpretive Matters Concerning Independent Directors of Investment Companies, Investment Company Act Release No. IC-24083, 64 Fed. Reg. 59877 (November 3, 1999) [hereinafter Release No. IC-24083].
171. Role of Independent Directors of Investment Companies, Investment Company Act Release No. IC-24082, 64 Fed. Reg. 59826, 59827 (November 3, 1999).
172. Another type of conflict of interest is dealt with by § 17(a) of the Act. The section bars, inter alia, an affiliated person of a registered investment company, and a person affiliated with an affiliated person, from engaging in specified transactions with the investment company. 15 U.S.C. § 80a-17(a) (2006).
173. 15 U.S.C. § 80a-7 (2006).
174. 15 U.S.C. § 80a-10(a) (2006).
175. 15 U.S.C. § 80a-10(a) (2006).
176. In certain circumstances, the Investment Company Act mandates that disinterested directors constitute a majority of the board of a registered investment company. 15 U.S.C. § 80a-15(f)(1)(A) (2006).
177. An exception provided by the Investment Company Act is that individuals who fill vacancies for independent directors on the board of a registered investment company must be nominated by the independent directors of the company when the vacancies have occurred because the investment adviser (or a person affiliated with the investment adviser) to the company has received a benefit from the sale of any interest in the adviser. 15 U.S.C §§ 80a-16(b), 80a-15(f)(1)(A) (2006).
178. Burks v. Lasker, *United States Reports* 441 (1979), 471, 484–85. In addition, see Part II in Chapter 3 infra.
179. 15 U.S.C. § 80a-15(c) (2006).
180. The Act, in requiring the independent directors to approve a contract with an investment adviser, "imposes upon the directors the fiduciary duty to use these powers intelligently, diligently and solely for the interests of the company and its stockholders." Brown v. Bullock, 194 F. Supp. 207, 235 (S.D.N.Y. 1961), *aff'd*, 294 F.2d 415 (2d Cir. 1961).

181. Role of Independent Directors of Investment Companies, Investment Company Act Release No. IC-24816, 66 Fed. Reg. 3734, 3736–37 (January 16, 2001).
182. 15 U.S.C. §§ 80a-2(a)(3), 80a-2(a)(19) (2006).
183. Attributes that arise through the investment adviser or principal underwriter are disqualifying because of 15 U.S.C. §§ 80a-2(a)(19)(A)(iii), 80a-2(a)(19)(B) (2006).
184. A member of the immediate family is "any parent, spouse of a parent, child, spouse of a child, spouse, brother, or sister, and includes step and adoptive relationships." 15 U.S.C. § 80a-2(a)(19) (2006).
185. 15 U.S.C. § 80a-2(a)(3) (2006).
186. The distinction between affiliation and interest is underscored by Twentieth Century Investors, Inc., SEC No-Action Letter (February 19, 1972), [1971–1972 Transfer Binder] Fed. Sec. L. Rep. (CCH) ¶ 78,628, at 81,334, available at 1972 SEC No-Act. LEXIS 805.
187. 15 U.S.C. § 80a-2(a)(9) (2006) (definition of "control").
188. 15 U.S.C. §§ 80a-2(a)(3), 80a-2(a)(19)(A)(i)-(A)(ii), 80a-2(a)(19)(B)(i)-(B)(ii) (2006).
189. 15 U.S.C. §§ 80a-2(a)(19)(A)(iii), 80a-2(a)(19)(A)(iv), 80a-2(a)(19)(B)(iv) (2006).
190. 15 U.S.C. §§ 80a-2(a)(19)(A)(iii), 80a-2(a)(19)(A)(vii), 80a-2(a)(19)(B)(vii) (2006). Subsections (A)(vii) and (B)(vii) of section 2(a)(19) cover both a material business relationship and a material professional relationship, and either one will prevent an individual from being an independent director. 15 U.S.C. § 80a-2(a)(19) (2006). To date, however, neither the commissioners nor the staff of the Commission have clearly distinguished a "professional" relationship from a "business" relationship, let alone identified the elements of each. A professional relationship possesses noneconomic attributes that a business relationship lacks. Larry D. Barnett, "When is a Mutual Fund Director Independent? The Unexplored Role of Professional Relationships under Section 2(a)(19) of the Investment Company Act," *DePaul Business & Commercial Law Journal* 4 (2006): 155, 172, 177–78.
191. See Release No. IC-24083, supra note 170.
192. S & P Counselors Fund, Inc., SEC No-Action Letter (January 2, 1972), [1971–1972 Transfer Binder] Fed. Sec. L. Rep. (CCH) ¶ 78,619, at 81,319, available at 1972 SEC No-Act. LEXIS 153 (staff declined relief to an investment company director for co-authorship of, and shared royalties from, a revised edition of a book to be written with an individual who was a director of the investment adviser and chair of the board of the parent of the adviser, and for use of the library facilities of the parent of the investment adviser and principal underwriter while preparing the revision, which would require a maximum of nine months).
193. 15 U.S.C. § 80b-2(a)(11) (2006).
194. The Investment Company Act defines an "investment adviser" in reference to investment companies. 15 U.S.C. § 80a-2(a)(20) (2006).
195. Certain collective investment vehicles (e.g., pension plans qualifying under the Internal Revenue Code) are deemed by section 3(c) of the Investment Company Act not to be investment companies. See 15 U.S.C. § 80a-3(b),

(c) (2006). These vehicles, however, may be managed by investment advisers.

196. Proxy Voting by Investment Advisers, Investment Advisers Act Release No. IA-2059, 67 Fed. Reg. 60841 (September 26, 2002).

197. As the United States Supreme Court has observed, "'It requires but little appreciation... of what happened in this country during the 1920's and 1930's to realize how essential it is that the highest ethical standards prevail' in every facet of the securities industry." Sec. & Exch. Comm'n v. Capital Gains Research Bureau, Inc. *United States Reports* 375 (1963), 180, 186–87.

198. 15 U.S.C. § 80b-6 (2006). Section 206 provides:

> It shall be unlawful for any investment adviser, by use of the mails or any means or instrumentality of interstate commerce, directly or indirectly— (1) to employ any device, scheme, or artifice to defraud any client or prospective client; (2) to engage in any transaction, practice, or course of business which operates as a fraud or deceit upon any client or prospective client; (3) acting as principal for his own account, knowingly to sell any security to or purchase any security from a client, or acting as broker for a person other than such client, knowingly to effect any sale or purchase of any security for the account of such client, without disclosing to such client in writing before the completion of such transaction the capacity in which he is acting and obtaining the consent of the client to such transaction....; (4) to engage in any act, practice, or course of business which is fraudulent, deceptive, or manipulative....

199. Rules Implementing Amendments to the Investment Advisers Act of 1940, Investment Advisers Act Release No. 1633, 62 Fed. Reg. 28112, 28127 n.172 (May 22, 1997). See *In re* Henry Weingarten, Investment Advisers Act Release No. IA-2019 (March 19, 2002), 77 S.E.C. Docket 477, available at 2002 SEC LEXIS 646, http://www.sec.gov/litigation/admin/ia-2019.htm (accessed April 7, 2011).

200. *In re* Deutsche Asset Mgmt., Inc., Investment Advisers Act Release No. IA-2160 (August 19, 2003), 2003 SEC LEXIS 1977, at *10, http://www.sec.gov/litigation/admin/ia-2160.htm (accessed April 7, 2011).

201. 17 C.F.R. § 275.206(4)-1 (2009).

202. *In re* Account Mgmt. Corp., Investment Advisers Act Release No. IA-1529 (September 29, 1995), 60 S.E.C. Docket 962, available at 1995 SEC LEXIS 2554. Account Management Corporation was found to have violated § 206(2), which is reproduced at supra note 198. Its officers were held to have aided and abetted the violation, thereby making them subject to sanctions under § 203(e) of the Act. 15 U.S.C. § 80b-3 (2006).

203. Average market values were computed from *In re* Account Mgmt. Corp., supra note 202, at Part III-A-2(a).

204. *In re* Account Mgmt. Corp., supra note 202.

205. 15 U.S.C. § 80a-17(e) (2006). Another compensation-relevant provision of the Investment Company Act is section 36(b), which imposes on the investment adviser to a registered investment company a fiduciary duty with regard to compensation that the company pays the adviser or an affiliate of the adviser. 15 U.S.C. § 80a-35(b) (2006). A provision of the Investment Advisers Act that deals with the compensation of advisers is section 205. 15 U.S.C. § 80b-5 (2006).

206. 15 U.S.C. § 80a-17(e) (2006).
207. 15 U.S.C. § 80a-2(a)(3) (2006).
208. Ibid.
209. United States v. Deutsch, 451 F.2d 98, 109 (2d Cir. 1971), *cert. denied, United States Reports* 404 (1972), 1019.
210. Ibid.; *In re* Stein Roe & Farnham, Investment Company Act Release No. 17316 (January 22, 1990), [1989–1990 Transfer Binder] Fed. Sec. L. Rep. (CCH) ¶ 84,512, at 80,575, 80,576, available at 1990 SEC LEXIS 71, at *4.
211. United States v. Ostrander, 999 F.2d 27, 31 (2d Cir. 1993).
212. Investors Research Corp. v. Sec. & Exch. Comm'n, 628 F.2d 168 (D.C. Cir.), *cert. denied, United States Reports* 499 (1980), 919.
213. The president of the investment adviser was also the president of the investment company. Ibid. He was therefore a first-tier affiliate, as well as a second-tier affiliate, of the company. 15 U.S.C. § 80a-2(a)(3)(D) (2006). However, the president is treated in the text as a second-tier affiliate because section 17(e)(1) has wider application under this approach.
214. Indeed, the Commission stated in part:

> This is not a garden variety kickback case in which an investment company's manager and its portfolio broker concoct [s]ome fraudulent scheme for the sole purpose of lining their own pockets at the shareholder's expense.... We do not condone what was done. Bu[t] realism constrains us to recognize that the respondents were confronted by a difficult problem and that their belief that the law permitted them to resolve it as they did may well have been entertained in good faith.

In re Investors Research Corp., Investment Company Act Release No. 10223, 46 S.E.C. 1209, 1216-17, at 1978 SEC LEXIS 1655, at *18.
215. Prohibition on the Use of Brokerage Commissions to Finance Distribution, Investment Company Act Release No. 26591, 69 Fed. Reg. 54728, 54730 (September 9, 2004).
216. Ibid., 54731 ("[t]he practice of directing brokerage for sales involves substantial conflicts of interest that can harm shareholders").
217. Ibid., 54730. In noting this danger, the Commission also stated: "Because of the lack of transparency of brokerage commissions and their value to a broker-dealer, customers are unlikely to appreciate the extent of this conflict." Ibid. However, the conflict of interest is likely to be uncovered at some point, and knowledge of the conflict can be expected to disillusion investors with investment companies (and brokers).
218. Part VI supra of this chapter does not cover all sections of the 1940 Acts that are concerned with conflicts of interest. Among the other provisions of the 1940 Acts that are pertinent to conflicts of interest are sections 17(a) and 17(d) of the Investment Company Act and sections 205(a) and 206 of the Investment Advisers Act. 15 U.S.C. §§ 80a-17(a), 80a-17(d) (2006); 15 U.S.C. §§ 80b-5(a), 80b-6 (2006).
219. The Quotations Page, http://www.quotationspage.com (quoting Albert Szent-Gyorgyi) (accessed December 2, 2009).
220. The Quotations Page, http://www.quotationspage.com (quoting Otto von Bismarck) (accessed December 2, 2009).

221. The observation was made by Harold Wilson, who was Prime Minister of Britain from 1964 to 1970 and from 1974 to 1976. Wikiquote, http://en.wikiquote.org/wiki/Harold_Wilson (accessed December 2, 2009).
222. Robert D. Putnam, "Civic Disengagement in Contemporary America," *Government & Opposition* 36 (2001): 135; Robert D. Putnam, "Tuning In, Tuning Out: The Strange Disappearance of Social Capital in America," *PS: Political Science & Politics* 28 (1995): 664.
223. For a definition of community, see David W. McMillan, "Sense of Community," *Journal of Community Psychology* 24 (1996): 315.
224. Shifts in the level and distribution of wealth in the United States are found in data on the net worth of the American population. In terms of the level of wealth, mean and median net worth (holding constant the purchasing power of the dollar) rose from 1962 to 1989 and fell from 1989 to 1995. In terms of the distribution of wealth, the concentration of net worth increased between 1962 and 1995: The wealthiest one-fifth of the American population held 81.2 percent of all net worth in 1962 and 83.9 percent in 1995; the wealthiest 1 percent of the American population held 33.5 percent of all net worth in 1962 and 38.5 percent in 1995. Most of the increase in the concentration of net worth occurred during the 1980s. Lisa A. Keister and Stephanie Moller, "Wealth Inequality in the United States," *Annual Review of Sociology* 26 (2000): 63, 67–68. The trend toward wealth concentration also appears in the pre-tax income of households: Households with the largest one-fifth of total pre-tax income in the United States received 43.8 percent of such income in 1967, 49.2 percent in 1998, 50.5 percent in 2006, and 50.3 percent in 2009. The entire increase took place after 1980. Arthur F. Jones, Jr. and Daniel H. Weinberg, U.S. Census Bureau, "The Changing Shape of the Nation's Income Distribution 1947-1998," *Current Population Reports*, Series P60, no. 204 (2000): Table 2, http://www.census.gov/prod/2000pubs/p60-204.pdf; U.S. Census Bureau, Table A-2: Selected Measures of Household Income Dispersion, 1967 to 2009 (no date), http://www.census.gov/hhes/www/income/data/historical/inequality/taba2.pdf (accessed April 7, 2011).
225. Persell, supra note 38, at 163. Professor Persell applies the term "civil society" to the set of variables she lists as effects of economic change. I believe the concept of community more aptly describes the factor that underlies these variables and ties them together.
226. Pete Engardio et al., "The New Global Job Shift," *Business Week*, February 3, 2003, 50. See also Aaron Bernstein, "Shaking Up Trade Theory," *Business Week*, December 6, 2004, 116.
227. Social behaviors deemed problematic are generally not reduced appreciably and permanently by direct government regulation. Supra note 126; Barnett, supra note 46, at 17, 24–36, 162–67; Britt et al., supra note 62; Larry D. Barnett, "Law as Symbol: Appearances in the Regulation of Investment Advisers and Attorneys," *Cleveland State Law Review* 15 (2007): 289, 299–301; Larry D. Barnett, "The Regulation of Mutual Fund Boards of Directors: Financial Protection or Social Productivity?" *Journal of Law & Policy* 16 (2008): 489, 528–531. The present book reproduces infra my article *Law as Symbol* and my article *The Regulation of Mutual Fund Boards*

of Directors. The former article is in infra Chapter 8; the latter article is in infra Chapter 3.

228. Attempts to block the forces responsible for economic restructuring will almost certainly be ineffective in the long run and may have consequences that are not only unanticipated but unwanted. Regulation seems most likely to protect society from damaging activities when it is imposed on organizations (e.g., investment companies) rather than on individuals.

3

Social Productivity and the Regulation of Mutual Fund Boards of Directors*

Section 2(a)(19) of the Investment Company Act classifies directors of mutual funds and other types of investment companies as either interested or not interested. Section 10(a) of the Act requires that directors who are deemed not interested by section 2(a)(19) must comprise at least 40 percent of the board of an investment company that needs to register with the Securities and Exchange Commission. Section 10(a) is based on the assumption that only non-interested directors consistently protect the shareholders of investment companies from financial exploitation. The assumption exists even though all directors, regardless of their classification by section 2(a)(19), are subject under state law to the same fiduciary duties and to the same test for determining whether they breached a fiduciary duty. Notably, social science studies on the accuracy of the assumption have reached contradictory conclusions. However, a considerable body of research casts doubt on the effectiveness of law as a mechanism to regulate social behavior in general. Thus, Chapter 3 suggests that law regulating the composition of the boards of directors of investment companies does not markedly reduce the frequency with which investment company shareholders are financially exploited but, instead, benefits society in ways captured by the concept of social productivity. In particular, Chapter 3 hypothesizes that section 2(a)(19) serves as a symbol of a commitment by society to combating shareholder exploitation and thereby aids in bonding individuals to the social system. Section 2(a)(19) can also be expected to preserve public trust in, and protect the reputation of, investment companies.

"The conventional view serves to protect us from the painful job of thinking."

—John Kenneth Galbraith[1]

I. Introduction

During the last quarter of a century, mutual funds in the United States achieved a remarkable degree of public acceptance as a means of investing in securities. The change is manifested in both the number and assets of mutual funds. Between 1980 and 2008, for example, the number of mutual funds grew from fewer than 600 to more than 8,000, and the assets managed by mutual funds expanded from approximately $135 billion to $9.6 trillion.[2] The increased popularity of mutual funds has made the funds an important factor in the financial well-being of Americans—in 2008, mutual fund shares were owned by 45 percent of all U.S. households, and mutual funds held almost one-fifth of the total financial assets of U.S. households.[3] Given the current importance of mutual funds, instances of exploitation of fund shareholders may damage the economic welfare of individuals and reduce investments in securities by the public.

Under its mandate to protect investors in mutual funds, the Securities and Exchange Commission ("Commission") has, since 2001,[4] devoted considerable attention to the boards of directors of the funds.[5] In particular, the Commission has acted to require funds to fill more seats on their boards with "independent" directors and thus to exceed the minimum percentage of independent directors specified by Congress in the Investment Company Act ("Act"), the principal federal statute governing mutual funds.[6] Accordingly, we next explore the basis of the actions that have been taken by Congress and the Commission to regulate the composition of fund boards.

II. The Investment Company Act and Investment Company Directors

The analysis undertaken in the instant chapter involves three basic concepts, viz., "investment company," "mutual fund," and "director." The Act defines an investment company in pertinent part as an entity that (a) issues securities to its investors and that (b) employs, or proposes to employ, the assets received from investors to engage in the business of seeking profit from securities issued by other entities.[7] An investment company, therefore, not only issues securities of its own but holds a portfolio of securities of other issuers, and if securities are absent at either point, an investment company does not exist under the Act.[8]

While the Act specifies the nature of an investment company, it is silent on the nature of a "mutual fund." In the securities industry, however, a mutual fund is generally regarded as an investment company (a) that publicly sells the securities it issues; (b) that, when requested by investors holding its securities, redeems these securities[9]; and (c) that manages the securities in its portfolio.[10] To use the nomenclature of the Act, a mutual fund is an open-end management investment company.[11] Accordingly, mutual funds are one type of investment company, and while the present chapter refers frequently to mutual funds, its discussion of directors is applicable to all types of investment companies that have directors.[12] Indeed, mutual funds and investment companies are, in one sense, almost coextensive because the net assets of mutual funds in 2008 constituted 92.8 percent of the net assets of all investment companies.[13]

The third concept requiring definition is that of "director." The Act considers a director to be

> any director of a corporation or any person performing similar functions with respect to any organization, whether incorporated or unincorporated, including any natural person who is a member of a board of trustees of a management company created as a common-law trust.[14]

Under the Act, therefore, a person may be a director of an entity even though the entity is not a corporation. For example, a person managing a limited partnership that is an investment company will be treated by the Act as a director of the partnership if the responsibilities of the person are comparable to the responsibilities of a director of a corporation.[15]

At the present time, the Act classifies directors as interested or as not interested. Conventional wisdom in the regulation of investment companies is that independent (i.e., not interested) directors are essential to protecting investment company shareholders from financial exploitation. Thus, the staff of the Commission has described independent directors as fulfilling a "critical role" in preventing actions that take advantage of investment company shareholders,[16] and one court has characterized independent directors as performing "a vital function" in safeguarding the shareholders.[17]

The implication of this position is that, even though fairness is at the heart of the fiduciary duties of all directors,[18] the interested directors of an investment company will not consistently be fair to the shareholders of the company. The misgivings about interested directors seem to be a result, or at least a concomitant, of the apparent belief of Congress and the Commission that, because the interested directors are involved in certain types of situations that are personally important to them and/or to other persons having ties to them, the interested directors possess an incentive to sacrifice the goals of the shareholders when dealing with matters which implicate these situations. The prevailing approach to regulating mutual fund boards, in short, reflects a lack of confidence in interested directors.[19]

When is a director designated as independent? The answer requires an understanding of the detailed criteria specified by the Act for determining the status of a director. The criteria that prevent a director from being independent have changed since the Act became law in 1940. As originally enacted, the Act prohibited an entity that was required to register with the Commission as an investment company[20] from filling more than 60 percent of the seats on its board of directors with persons who were an investment adviser to, affiliated with an investment adviser to, or an officer or employee of the investment company.[21] Directors who were not in any of the preceding categories were regarded as independent,[22] and Congress believed that such directors were essential to representing the shareholders of the company.[23] As discussed in Part II-A later, Congress subsequently amended the criteria for determining the status of a director, but the label "independent" continues to be conferred only on directors who are free of all of the ties that troubled Congress.

The reader will note both from the discussion supra and from the discussion in Part II-A infra that the Act makes the concept of affiliation a key factor in the status of a director. The Act considers affiliation to exist between two persons when, inter alia, (a) at least 5 percent of the voting securities[24] of one person[25] directly or indirectly are owned by or can be voted by the other person; (b) one of the persons directly or indirectly controls or is controlled by the other or is, along with the other person, controlled by a third person[26]; or (c) one person is currently an "officer, director, partner, copartner, or employee" of the other person or, if the other person is an investment company, is currently its investment adviser.[27] The Act has included the concept of affiliation since its enactment in 1940, and notably, the definition of the concept has not changed. However, subsequent legislation altered the role of affiliation in determining whether a director is independent. This legislation is discussed next.

A. Section 2(a)(19) of the Investment Company Act

In 1970, Congress reexamined the statutory criteria establishing the status of a director and concluded that the criteria adopted in 1940 were not furnishing sufficient protection to the shareholders of investment companies.[28] Consequently, the framework for defining an independent director was reworked,[29] and with some modifications, the framework devised in 1970 is still in effect. As with the original (1940) legislation, the board of a registered investment company is required by the Act to fill no less than 40 percent of its seats with independent directors, but in 1970 Congress introduced into the Act the concept of an "interested" person[30] and thus distinguished interested directors from independent directors.[31] The concept of the interested person, which is defined by section 2(a)(19) of the Act,[32] is the foundation of the current structure of investment company boards. Under this structure, a maximum of 60 percent of the directors of a registered investment company can be "interested" in the company.[33]

In general terms, a person is not an independent director if she or he is interested in the investment company either directly through ties to the company itself or indirectly through ties to an investment adviser or principal underwriter for the company.[34] Given the congressional goal of preventing harm to the shareholders of investment companies, the ties of a person that are included in section 2(a)(19) are evidently those believed likely to create a significant temptation for the person to disadvantage the investment company and its shareholders in favor of (a) the person and/or (b) an individual or entity having ties to the person. A director will be independent only if the director possesses *none* of the ties listed by the Act; a director having *any* of the ties will not be independent, i.e., will be "interested."[35]

The main concern of the Act, accordingly, is with conflicts of interest[36]—situations in which an individual is pulled toward mutually exclusive alternatives and is prevented, or appears to be prevented, from basing decisions on the relative merits of each alternative for the investment company and its shareholders. If a society is to operate effectively, however, its organizations, including its business organizations, must avoid conflicts of interest because such conflicts, inter alia, generate distrust in and damage the reputation of the organizations as well as make the organizations socially dysfunctional symbols. Trust, reputation, and symbols seem to be fundamental aspects of every organized group, and they either promote or reduce the effectiveness of the group.[37]

Thus, in mandating that some directors of registered investment companies be non-interested persons, Congress was attempting to protect society as a whole. The responsibility of independent directors to deal with conflicts of interest became a central tenet of the Act in an attempt to protect shareholders from the damaging effects of such conflicts.[38] Independent directors, being free from the conflicts of interest that Congress found problematic, were expected to be the shareholders' defense against financial abuse.[39] In the words of the U.S. Supreme Court, Congress intended the independent directors to perform "the role of 'independent watchdogs,' who would 'furnish an independent check upon the management' of investment companies."[40]

If a person can be an independent director of an investment company only if she or he is not "interested" in the investment company, in an investment adviser to the company, or in a principal underwriter for the company, when is a person interested? The statutory determinants of interest are listed in the two subsections—(A) and (B)—of section 2(a)(19) of the Act and have undergone some refinement since 1970. The review below deals with the two subsections as they are currently written.[41]

The statutory determinants of whether a person is an interested director of an investment company are more easily explained by starting with subsection (B) and subsequently considering subsection (A). Subsection (B) specifies the types of situations that make a person interested in an investment adviser or principal underwriter for the investment company. Subsection (A), on the other hand, specifies the types of situations that make a person interested in the investment company itself, and under subsection (A)(iii), any person interested in an investment adviser or principal underwriter for an investment company pursuant to subsection (B) is interested in the investment company.[42]

In what circumstances does subsection (B) cause a person to be interested in an investment adviser or principal underwriter for an investment company? Such interest exists when, inter alia, the person is affiliated with the investment adviser or principal underwriter,[43] has certain types of kinship ties to someone who is so affiliated,[44] or is aware of having a direct or indirect beneficial interest in a security that has been issued by the investment adviser, by the principal underwriter, or by a party controlling either of them.[45]

A person is also interested in an investment adviser or principal underwriter when that person is, or is a partner or employee of, another person and the latter (i.e., other person) has served as legal counsel for the investment adviser or principal underwriter at any time since the beginning of the last two completed fiscal years of the investment company.[46] Further, a person is interested in an investment adviser or principal underwriter when that person is, or is affiliated with, a person that during the previous six months has executed securities transactions or distributed securities for, had principal transactions with, or extended a loan to, inter alia, an investment company served by the investment adviser or principal underwriter.[47]

Finally, an individual is interested in an investment adviser or principal underwriter when the Commission has issued an order designating the individual as interested because, at any time since the start of the last two completed fiscal years of the investment company, the individual has had "a material business or professional relationship" with the investment adviser or principal underwriter or with the principal executive officer of, or a person in control of, either the adviser or underwriter.[48]

While subsection (B) specifies the determinants of interest in an investment adviser or principal underwriter for an investment company, subsection (A) specifies the circumstances in which interest exists in the investment company per se.[49] The clauses of subsection (A), in focusing on the investment company, parallel the clauses of subsection (B) with one exception. The exception is that, under subsection (A), interest in an investment company cannot arise from a beneficial interest in a security issued by the company unless at least 5 percent of the voting securities of the company are owned or controlled, or can be voted, by the person whose status is in question.[50] As indicated above, however, a person knowingly holding a beneficial interest in a security that has been issued by the investment adviser or principal underwriter for an investment company, or by a person controlling the investment adviser or principal underwriter, is interested in the investment company, and any quantity of such a security suffices to make the holder interested in the company.[51]

To recapitulate, the Act requires an investment company that must be registered with the Securities and Exchange Commission to fill at least 40 percent of the seats on its board with directors who do not possess any of the interest-generating ties listed in the Act and who, accordingly, are deemed to be independent. Because of the importance attached to independent directors, the requirement that 40 percent of the directors be independent is merely a statutory minimum. As discussed in Part II-B infra, the Commission, under its congressionally delegated authority to promulgate rules,[52] has raised the required percentage for almost all registered investment companies.

B. Securities and Exchange Commission Rules

Since July 2002, mutual funds using any of ten specified rules promulgated by the Securities and Exchange Commission to gain an exemption from a mandate of the Act have been required by the Commission to fill a majority of the seats on their boards with independent directors and to assign the responsibility for selecting and nominating the independent directors solely to the independent directors.[53] Because use of the rules was widespread, nine out of ten funds were estimated to be covered by the requirement.[54] Illustrative of the ten rules[55] was the rule allowing a fund and specified affiliates to engage in securities transactions with one another[56]; a fund that relies on the rule to avoid violating the ban on such transactions imposed by section 17(a) of the Act[57] must have a board that is comprised of a majority of independent directors who are chosen by the independent directors. The ten rules that were designated involve activities that the Commission concluded are characterized by inescapable conflicts of interest between the fund and its management.[58] The Commission believed that with a majority of seats on the board of a fund that relies on any of the rules, the independent directors would be able

> to control the fund's "corporate machinery," i.e., to elect officers of the fund, call meetings, solicit proxies, and take other actions without the consent of the [investment] adviser... [and] have a more meaningful influence on fund management and represent shareholders from a position of strength.[59]

Did fund investors receive appreciable added protection from the requirement that independent directors form a majority of the membership of fund boards? The answer seems to be in the negative because "few funds," according to the Commission, had boards whose membership was altered by the requirement.[60] Nonetheless, independent directors may be helpful in protecting shareholders. Unfortunately, there is a dearth of rigorous social science research on whether, and the extent to which, fund shareholders benefit from independent directors, from any particular number or percentage of independent directors, or from a requirement that independent directors be chosen by independent directors. Indeed, the three studies I now review are apparently the sole pertinent studies thus far completed.

In the first of these studies, tests of statistical significance indicated that the financial performance of domestic-stock mutual funds, while unrelated to the *percentage* of board seats held by independent directors, increased with the *number* of independent directors.[61] However, whether the relationship between the number of independent directors and fund performance was due to the status of directors under section 2(a)(19) has been questioned,[62] and whether there was an effect that was sufficiently large to be of practical consequence is uncertain.[63] In the second of the studies, the financial performance of mutual funds that invested in equity securities was weakly and *inversely* related to the percentage of board seats occupied by independent directors; i.e., fund performance declined to some extent as the fraction of independent directors rose.[64] In the third and most recent of the studies, the proportion of independent directors on the boards of mutual funds whose portfolios tracked an index of U.S. stocks was found not to have a statistically significant relationship to the investment return of the fund.[65]

In light of the inconsistent findings of the three studies, whether mutual fund shareholders financially benefit from independent directors is uncertain. However, even if the three studies furnished evidence of such a benefit, none of the studies was available when the Commission acted. Thus, the Commission adopted the requirements that independent directors constitute a majority of an investment company board and nominate the independent directors because the requirements *seemed* desirable.[66]

The unproven assumption that independent directors are key to protecting mutual fund shareholders was also present in an attempt by the Commission in 2004 to increase further the percentage of seats on investment company boards for such directors. Under a policy approved on a split vote of the commissioners but not yet implemented, a fund that relies on any of the ten rules to avoid breaching the Act would be required to place independent directors in three out of every four seats on its board; if such a fund has a board with just three members, at least two directors would need to be independent.[67] The proposed requirement, therefore, would raise the percentage of independent directors from 50 percent to 75 percent for a covered fund having four or more directors. In addition, the individual chairing the board would need to be an independent director.[68] However, neither requirement can be implemented until the Commission, pursuant to a court decision,[69] receives and assesses additional evidence on the cost of the requirements to investment companies. The Commission has requested comments and evidence pertinent to the proposed requirements[70] but has not acted on submitted materials even though the submission period ended in August 2006.

III. Fiduciary Duties of Investment Company Directors

In believing that it is the independent directors of investment companies who safeguard the shareholders of the companies from company-related financial exploitation,[71] current law assumes that there is an unacceptable probability the interested directors (as defined in section 2(a)(19) of the Act) will financially abuse the fund's investors. The established view suggests that shareholders will be financially injured by interested directors considerably more often than by independent directors because interested directors are subject to inherent conflicts of interest from exposure to situations where their goals and the goals of the shareholders differ.[72] Thus, interested directors are seen as inclined to act in ways that favor them or persons linked to them, and instances of exploitation of shareholders by interested directors are thought to result from selfishness. Financial injuries to shareholders caused by independent directors, on the other hand, are thought to result from errors in assessing the advantages and disadvantages of particular courses of action.

Conflicts of interest admittedly exist for the interested directors of investment companies, but should the assumption be made that these conflicts render interested directors an actual or probable menace to the investors in the companies? State law has a clearly expressed set of fiduciary duties for directors of entities, including investment companies, and the duties are imposed on *all* directors, interested as well as independent.

Before discussing the duties of directors, the reader should note that an investment company can be structured as a corporation, as a business trust, or as a limited partnership.[73] However, as explained in Part II supra, the structure of an investment company is irrelevant to whether a person is a director, because under the definition of "director" in the Act, persons are directors if their functions "with respect to any organization, whether incorporated or unincorporated," are "similar" to those of a director of a corporation.[74] The definition, accordingly, is not confined to a person on the board of a corporation but extends to a general partner of an investment company that is a limited partnership and to a trustee of an investment company that is a business trust.[75]

Because Delaware is the leading U.S. jurisdiction in the field of corporation law,[76] its view of directors is particularly instructive. As the Supreme Court of Delaware makes clear in the passage quoted below, directors are deemed to be fiduciaries. The passage is phrased in terms of corporations, but the position it states is not limited to directors of corporations because fiduciaries of all types and in all settings are subject to similar requirements of law[77]:

> The fiduciary nature of a corporate office is immutable. As this Court stated long ago:
>
> > Corporate officers and directors are not permitted to use their position of trust and confidence to further their private interests. While technically not trustees, they stand in a fiduciary relation to the corporation and its shareholders....
>
> ...
>
> Thus, directors are required to demonstrate both their utmost good faith and the most scrupulous inherent fairness of transactions in which they possess a financial, business or other personal interest which does not devolve upon the corporation or all stockholders generally.[78]

Pursuant to this doctrine, the failure of a director to fulfill a fiduciary duty renders the offending director liable for damages that stem from the failure.[79] However, while the potential for liability is assumed to shape the conduct of directors for the benefit of the public, the fact that the duties apply to interested directors seems to be overlooked.

The duties of interested directors that are expressed in doctrines of law may be simply words, of course, and have no influence on the behavior of directors. After all, the human capacity for selfishness and shortsightedness should never be underestimated, and directors may pursue their own, immediate goals regardless of principles embodied in law. From a macrosociological perspective, however, doctrines of law as widespread and prominent as the fiduciary duties of directors exist because they reflect the character of the society in which the law is embedded and endorse behavioral patterns valued or needed by the system.[80] Consequently, directors' fiduciary duties in state law are important—though they may be important in ways that are not widely understood and acknowledged.

With this background, I review the fiduciary duties of directors, and given the topic of the instant chapter, I do so in the context of investment companies. The review begins with the duty of care and then considers the duty of loyalty, both of which are well-entrenched and widely accepted in state law for a director of a corporation[81] and for a director (general partner) of a limited partnership.[82] Following the discussion of the duty of care and of loyalty, I consider the requirement contained in state law that the directors of an entity act in good faith. Good faith is taken up separately because, as explained in Part III-B infra, uncertainty currently exists as to whether good faith will achieve the status of a fiduciary duty and, if it does, what its content will be.

While corporations and limited partnerships are traditional (or at least popular) arenas for examining director duties, business trusts appear not to be. Thus, business trusts and the duties of their directors (i.e., trustees) merit comment here. For mutual funds, the law on business trusts of three states—Delaware, Maryland, and Massachusetts—is of primary importance because mutual funds that operate as business trusts seem normally to be established under the law of one of these states.[83] In states that have decided the issue, the directors of a business trust are generally deemed to have a fiduciary relationship to the holders of beneficial interests in the trust.[84] The fiduciary relationship includes both a duty of care and a duty of loyalty.[85] The Delaware statute on business trusts, however, allows the document that governs a business trust to alter or remove fiduciary duties of a trustee, although the document cannot "eliminate the implied contractual covenant of good faith and fair dealing."[86] The current wording of the section became effective on August 1, 2006,[87] but even in the absence of the legislative prohibition on removing the obligations of good faith and fair dealing, it was unlikely that Delaware courts would allow a trustee of a business trust to escape these obligations.[88] In Delaware, then, a trustee of a business trust cannot avoid the requirements—good faith and fairness—that are inherent in and central to the role of a director.[89]

By way of summary, the duties of care and of loyalty are applicable both to the directors of an investment company that is structured as a corporation and to the directors of an investment company that is structured as a limited partnership. These duties seem generally applicable as well to the directors of an investment company that is a business trust.[90] When examining each duty, accordingly, the three structures need not be distinguished, and as used in this chapter, the terms "investment company" and "fund" will encompass all of them.

A. Duty of Care and Duty of Loyalty

We begin with the content of the fiduciary duty of care and the fiduciary duty of loyalty. Although the two duties overlap and are thus not fully separable,[91] they can be distinguished as concepts[92] in terms of the type of conduct expected of a fiduciary. Specifically, the duty of care mandates reasonable caution and foresight by a fiduciary in handling the affairs of the entity to which, or the individual to whom, the duty is owed; the duty of loyalty, on the other hand, forbids a purposeful action by a fiduciary in the context of a conflict of interest that advantages the fiduciary and disadvantages the person owed the duty.[93] In the words of one court:

> The duty of loyalty... is rooted in intentional tort law. Thus, this aspect of fiduciary duty is commonly expressed in the form of a prohibitive rule. In short, a fiduciary... must not abuse his position of trust in order to advance his own selfish interests. On the other hand, the duty of due care is rooted in negligence principles, and is commonly expressed affirmatively. The fiduciary, therefore, must exercise at least that degree of care that a reasonably prudent person would devote to his own affairs under like circumstances.[94]

To understand more fully the two duties, it is helpful to identify what the directors of an entity do in their role as directors. At least three functions are expected to be performed by a director of an entity. Specifically, a director is expected to (a) monitor the affairs of the entity, (b) inquire into entity-related matters about which the director receives information that suggests a major problem exists in the entity, and (c) make decisions for the entity.[95] In carrying out each of these functions, directors are subject both to a duty of care and to a duty of loyalty.

For investment company directors, the chief functions appear to be the first and third,[96] and because both functions implicate the business judgment rule, the rule must be satisfied by directors when performing these functions. In terms of the first function, the requirements of the business judgment rule must be met when directors decide whether an activity in their organization will be monitored. If the directors decide to monitor the activity, they must also satisfy the rule in selecting the manner in which the activity will be monitored.[97] In terms of the third function, directors must meet the requirements of the rule with regard to the procedure they follow in reaching decisions for the entity but not necessarily with regard to the substance of the decisions.[98]

The business judgment rule is thus a centerpiece of law relevant to both the duty of care and the duty of loyalty of directors. When directors have satisfied the rule, they have not breached either duty.[99] But what is the rule? One major text on corporation law contends that a single business judgment rule does not exist.[100] The unease that exists with the rule is illustrated by three current or former members of the Delaware judiciary who, in a law review article, wrote:

> [A] standard formulation of the business judgment rule in Delaware is that it creates a presumption that (i) a decision was made by directors who (ii) were disinterested and independent, (iii) acted in subjective good faith, and (iv) employed a reasonable decision making process.[101]

At the same time, however, the authors contend that the rule as formulated is not employed by Delaware courts to evaluate the inherent merits of a board action as the basis for determining whether the action breached the directors' duty of care and/or duty of loyalty. Instead, according to the authors, the rule as stated establishes a presumption that places on plaintiffs the burden to prove such a breach.[102] The determinations of a court that matter with respect to the business judgment rule, the authors argue, concern whether the requirements specified in their description of the rule have been met, and the substance of the board decision is irrelevant to the outcome of the judicial process.[103] In essence, then, the rule identifies the circumstances in which the directors of an entity escape liability for a loss arising from an action they approved, but the merits of the board decision are not involved in the burden-assigning presumption of the rule.

If any element of the business judgment rule is not satisfied when the directors of an entity make a decision—e.g., if the directors participating in the decision were subject to a conflict of interest or were acting in bad faith—the rule will be unavailable to the directors as a defense. In this event, the directors responsible for the decision will be liable for losses sustained by the entity they serve unless they are able to establish that the decision, and the procedure employed to reach it, were fair to the entity.[104] The latter standard, in requiring directors to prove both the substantive fairness and the procedural fairness of the decision to avoid liability, is more demanding than the business judgment rule.[105]

B. Good Faith

In addition to a duty of care and a duty of loyalty, courts may have also started to recognize in the director role a duty to act in good faith.[106] Whether good faith will be accepted in U.S. law as a fiduciary duty is uncertain, and because a common-law fiduciary duty of good faith is only in the process of emerging—if it emerges at all—its content is yet to be determined.[107] However, the meaning of the phrase "good faith" in law applicable to directors will be consistent with the meaning of the phrase to the public generally because the concepts and doctrines of law arise from, and are molded by, the society in which law operates.[108] Notably, the *Oxford English Dictionary* defines "good faith" to include "fidelity... [in] fulfilling one's trust."[109] Thus, an obligation of good faith for directors that is manifested in law can be expected to entail, in large part, conduct that preserves and promotes trust in interpersonal relationships. By doing so, law would express the vital role of trust in promoting the effective operation of a society.[110]

A macrosociological treatment of the institution of law approaches the doctrines (as well as the concepts) of the institution as mechanisms that in the long run facilitate, rather than undermine, the functioning of society. If this perspective correctly describes the institution, the doctrines and concepts of law ultimately embody the requisites for effective group operation. Accordingly, an emphasis on interpersonal trust in the obligation of good faith may be attributable to, and a means of rectifying, the apparent erosion or abandonment during the twentieth century of such an emphasis in the law-defined duty of loyalty,[111] and it may not be coincidence that the Supreme Court of Delaware recently subsumed good faith under the duty of loyalty.[112]

Specifically, the Supreme Court of Delaware has taken the position that bad faith is necessary, though not sufficient, to render directors liable for losses resulting from action or inaction by them as directors and that, because liability for bad faith stems from a breach of the duty of loyalty, good faith is inherent in loyalty.[113] Thus, the court, in endorsing the fiduciary duty of loyalty, reinforced for directors an obligation (albeit not a fiduciary duty) of good faith. Notably, by placing good faith within the duty of loyalty, the court directed attention to the ties that individuals have to one another and, hence, to pertinent groups, and it implicitly acknowledged that the ability of groups to operate successfully depends in part on the degree to which their members have trust in and are committed to the groups. The position adopted by the court, in short, manifested a principle of group dynamics.[114]

If the preservation or augmentation of interpersonal trust is an underlying concern of good faith, what substantive components might good faith contain as a fiduciary duty or as a component of a fiduciary duty? One scholar has suggested that the foundation of good faith as a fiduciary duty in a business setting should be comprised of four elements: (a) the personal integrity needed to sustain social life, (b) adherence to societal norms of decency in business operations, (c) conformity to important standards and mandates that have been established for business entities, and (d) commitment to fulfilling the particular office held in a business entity.[115]

With these elements, good faith prohibits a director of an entity from making decisions for the entity based on a personal *non*-financial motive when the shareholders will be financially injured.[116] Since apart from good faith the duty of loyalty mandates that directors not approve action or inaction by the entity that financially harms its shareholders when the directors have a personal financial reason for approving the action or inaction,[117] an essential aspect of the director role is the protection of shareholders from financial abuse. Notably, the Supreme Court of Delaware, in an en banc opinion, has indicated that a commitment to preventing avoidable economic harm to shareholders, as well as promoting economic gain for shareholders, is encompassed by the obligation of good faith applicable to directors of a corporation.[118] Because the expectations that are embodied in law for directors are essentially the same in every type of investment company having a board,[119] a director of an investment company must have a commitment to the financial concerns of the company's shareholders even if the investment company is a limited partnership or a business trust.

C. Summary

Parts III-A and III-B of this chapter advanced several key points. First, the members of an investment company board are subject to three obligations—care, loyalty, and good faith—and at least the first two of these obligations are fiduciary in nature, i.e., expressions of a societal demand for ethical conduct in business (and other) relationships rather than contractual provisions for specified conduct in relationships.[120] Second, the three obligations, which are embedded in state law and derive from the social setting in which the law of a state exists, cover *all* directors of all investment companies.

The three obligations thus apply to the interested directors of investment companies. The third point, which parallels the second, is that the test determining whether a fiduciary duty has been breached is the same for all directors. State law, that is, offers no safe haven for investment company directors of a particular stripe, and directors who are interested, as well as directors who are not interested, under section 2(a)(19) of the Investment Company Act are treated alike by state law. Under state law, then, interested directors should not differ from independent directors in the degree to which they protect investment company shareholders from financial abuse.

D. In re *Nuveen Fund Litigation*

In a case that illustrates the duties of investment company directors, the directors of two closed-end funds[121] were alleged to have breached their duty of care in approving the issuance and sale of additional shares by each fund after the initial blocks of shares offered by the funds had been purchased by investors.[122] As a presumably conventional closed-end investment company, each fund would have sold its shares to the public but would not have redeemed these shares at the request of their owners.[123] Investors who, after purchasing shares of either fund, wanted to dispose of the shares would have sold them to other persons who desired to acquire the shares as an investment. Following the initial sale of shares by the fund, then, transactions in fund shares would have occurred between investors. However, the market price of the shares in such transactions frequently differs from the net asset value of the shares,[124] although the market price and the net asset value of shares of closed-end funds tend to move in the same direction and movements in the former are on average smaller than movements in the latter.[125]

In the instant litigation, the complaint alleged that, because each fund invested only in bonds and the additional shares of the fund were sold when interest rates were low, the directors breached their duty of care in failing to anticipate that the bonds acquired by the funds with the proceeds from the sale of the additional shares would unavoidably damage the long-term investment performance of each fund.[126] The reason for this damage, the plaintiffs claimed, was that the market price of the newly acquired bonds would decline in the future when interest rates increased and the decline would reduce the net asset value of fund shares.[127] In addition, the complaint alleged that the directors did not fulfill their duty of care because they failed to understand that, in violation of the funds' articles of incorporation, the additional shares were priced to sell at less than the net asset value of shares presently outstanding, which caused investors who owned shares just prior to the sale of the additional shares to suffer a financial loss.[128] Finally, the complaint alleged that at least two of the directors approving the sale of the additional shares were motivated by self-interest stemming from ties they had to the investment adviser and the parent of the adviser.[129] The self-interest existed, according to the complaint, because the proceeds from the sale of the additional shares would increase the assets of the funds and thereby result in the payment by the funds of larger advisory fees to the adviser.[130] In effect, therefore, the plaintiffs contended that the two directors had also breached their duty of loyalty to the funds.[131]

With regard to the fund boards, each fund had seven directors, and the individuals who were the directors of one fund were also the directors of the other fund.[132] All seven directors of each fund were named as defendants, and two of the seven had the status of interested directors under section 2(a)(19) of the Act.[133]

The decision of the federal district court resulted from a motion to dismiss filed by the five directors who were designated by the funds as independent.[134] Employing the business judgment rule,[135] the court focused on whether the independent directors, by relying entirely on materials supplied by the funds' investment adviser and its parent, had utilized a reasonable procedure in evaluating the effect that the additional shares would have on the future investment performance of the funds.[136] In doing so, the court followed the view of the business judgment rule presented in Part III-A supra. However, this view may not have been followed in considering the allegation that the articles of incorporation of the funds were breached by the price that the board set for the additional shares. On this issue, the court's opinion is not altogether clear, and even though the directors claimed they had relied on counsel from an outside law firm, the court may have believed that the merits of the board's decision were pertinent.[137]

Two matters that were not discussed in the opinion of the court are noteworthy. First, all seven directors of the funds had evidently voted to approve the issuance and sale of the additional shares, and the plaintiffs had alleged that two of the directors were interested persons under section 2(a)(19) due to their ties to the investment adviser and its controlling parent.[138] However, the motion to dismiss had been filed by the five directors who were independent under section 2(a)(19), not by the two directors who were interested, and the court opinion thus does not analyze the law applicable to the two interested directors and their votes. Such an analysis would have been instructive.

A second and equally important question omitted by the court was whether any of the fund directors who were denominated as independent had a conflict of interest pertinent to the business judgment rule. Such a conflict of interest would have raised the issue of whether the affected director fulfilled his/her obligations under state law. In particular, one director who was evidently classified by the funds as independent pursuant to section 2(a)(19)[139] could have been incorrectly classified due to subsection (B)(vii).[140] At some point in the past, the fund director in question had been chairman of the parent (and hence the entity in control) of the funds' investment adviser,[141] and if he had held this position at any time since the start of the most recent two completed fiscal years of the funds, he might have been found under subsection (B)(vii) to be currently involved in a "material business or professional relationship" with the parent.[142] Such a relationship would be deemed to exist in the present even though the fund director was no longer chairman of the parent, and it would make the director interested in the investment adviser because subsection (B)(vii) covers a person (e.g., a parent) that controls the adviser. If the director was still interested in the adviser, he would be an interested director of the funds.[143]

When does a position that is no longer held create an ongoing material business or professional relationship? If the position was occupied during the time period covered by subsection (B)(vii), a material business or professional relationship will exist if the position could

> impair a director's independence by providing incentives for the director to place his or her own interests over the interests of fund shareholders. The key factors in evaluating whether a director's position with [an entity specified by the subsection] would tend to impair his or her independence include the level of the director's responsibility in the position and the level of compensation or other benefits that the director receives or received from the position.[144]

Given the above test for whether a relationship is material, in what situations would a director of the funds who was formerly chairperson of the parent of the investment adviser to the funds have a current material business relationship with the parent and, hence, a current conflict of interest? Otherwise expressed, what circumstances would provide the director, as former chairperson of the parent, with a continuing incentive to place the welfare of the parent and adviser ahead of the welfare of the funds? A number of possibilities can be imagined. For example, a current material business relationship would presumably exist if there was more than a negligible possibility that, at the time the board authorized the funds to issue and sell additional shares, the parent would award its former chairperson a lucrative consulting contract or would steer clients to a business managed by its former chairperson.[145] These examples, although hypothetical, are plausible because the parent in the instant case was not a small entity but a "multi-million dollar" firm supplying financial services as an investment banker and investment adviser.[146]

E. Director Status under Section 2(a)(19) and Director Liability for Board Decisions

The test quoted above[147] for whether a business or professional relationship is material was articulated by the staff of the Securities and Exchange Commission for two provisions of section 2(a)(19) of the Act—namely, subsections (A)(vii) and (B)(vii)[148]—but it has an important feature in common with the business judgment rule: Under the subsections and under the rule, evaluations of investment company directors are based on specifics.[149] Generalities such as category labels, accordingly, do not determine the outcome of these evaluations. In terms of the business judgment rule, an investment company director who participated in a particular decision and who had a conflict of interest or was acting in bad faith with regard to the matter that was decided would be liable under state law for a loss resulting from the decision unless the decision was fair.[150] The status of the director under section 2(a)(19)—whether the director is interested or not interested—is not relevant to liability. However, a conflict of interest that was created for the director by the matter decided is relevant, whether or not the conflict had a bearing on the status of the director under the Act.

To illustrate, section 2(a)(19) provides that a director of an investment company is not interested in the company if, inter alia, the director has not served as an attorney for the company or its investment adviser at any time since the start of the previous two completed fiscal years of the company and is not a member of a law firm any of whose partners or employees have done so.[151] Nonetheless, a director who is not interested under this provision would be unable to assess impartially a given matter if the director's spouse would obtain a significant financial benefit from the decision on the matter by the board of the company. Within the scope of state law, then, a fund director would have a conflict of interest regarding a board decision if a current or former position or relationship leads the director to anticipate personal gain from board approval or disapproval of an action by the fund and thus "tend[ed] to impair"[152] the director's judgment on behalf of the fund with respect to the matter. In this situation, the director could not rely on the business judgment rule as a defense because the rule does not shield from liability a director who promotes a board decision with knowledge that he or she will obtain a unique financial benefit from the decision.[153]

For a fund director then, the fiduciary duties found in state law are unaffected by section 2(a)(19) because the Act does not preempt state law on the fiduciary duties of fund directors.[154] Indeed, the Commission has expressly acknowledged that the fiduciary duties of investment company directors embodied in state law are separate from, and in addition to, the mandates of the Act.[155] Within the Act, nonetheless, section 2(a)(19) is important, and its role is significant. In particular, the status of an individual established by the section can affect the eligibility of the individual for a seat on an investment company board,[156] and this status is the basis for assigning certain board tasks to the individuals who are directors.[157]

Because under state law the liability of an investment company director for a decision made as a director is determined by whether the director directly or indirectly could or did benefit personally from the decision in question, the test for interest under state law differs from and is much broader than the activities and relationships listed in section 2(a)(19) of the Act. Specifically, interest is present under state law if *any* factor renders a director of an entity incapable of making for the entity a decision that is grounded solely on the advantages or disadvantages of the decision to the entity.[158] In the words of the Supreme Court of Delaware, interest exists in a particular matter whenever a connection of a director to an individual or an entity

> is so close that the director's independence may *reasonably* be doubted. This doubt might arise either because of financial ties, familial affinity, a particularly close or intimate personal or business affinity or because of evidence that in the past the relationship caused the director to act non-independently vis a vis an interested director.[159]

For investment company directors, the implication of the preceding points is of major practical significance, and it is central to the instant chapter. Two investment company directors who are similarly situated with regard to a given matter will be subject to the same standard of review under state law for ascertaining whether, in their action on the matter, they breached a fiduciary duty even though one director qualifies as interested under section 2(a)(19) of the Act and the other does not. When adjudicating an allegation of a breach of duty by a director, state law focuses on the character of the matter being decided by the board and on whether the director directly or indirectly gained, or was in a position to gain, a unique personal advantage from the decision reached.

If the status of a director under section 2(a)(19) of the Act is irrelevant to the director's risk of liability under state law for decisions as a director, then directors designated as interested by the section may be no more likely than directors designated as independent to use their board seats to benefit themselves at the expense of shareholders. Notably, social science research has often found that regulatory law fails to achieve its goal(s). This research, which I discuss next, buttresses the argument that directors of an investment company make decisions for the company unaffected by their status under section 2(a)(19).

In illustrating social science research on the impact of regulatory law, I begin with studies of government regulation directed at economic activity. As to such activity, state statutes prohibiting employment policies that either mandate union membership or mandate abstention from union membership have been found not to influence appreciably the proportion of nonagricultural workers who are union members.[160] In addition, statutes and executive-branch actions directed at controlling hospital costs have not consistently and substantially done so.[161] As an example of government regulation directed at activity that is largely social in nature, state statutes requiring minors to attend school until they reach a specified age have generally not had a material impact on the school enrollment rates of minors.[162] Moreover, statutes permitting divorce only when fault exists seem to have had little effect on the divorce rate because the adoption of statutes allowing divorce without fault evidently has had no more than a short-term impact on the probability of marriage dissolution[163] (even though critics of no-fault statutes have believed the statutes substantially increase the incidence of divorce[164]).

The preceding studies are not alone. An impressive body of well-designed quantitative research on a variety of social problems has found that law intended to regulate behavior, including law that criminalizes behavior, does not have a large, enduring impact on the frequency of the behavior.[165] The reason for the lack of a substantial, permanent impact probably lies in societal complexity. The studies cited were conducted in relatively complex social systems, i.e., social systems whose populations and institutions are heterogeneous. However, because a complex system is characterized by multiple causal pathways and feedback loops, complexity in a society is likely to hamper regulation and render law incapable of having an appreciable, sustained influence on conditions in the society. Accordingly, if the law that was examined in these studies was making or had made a positive societal contribution, it did so mainly in other ways, e.g., by acting as a symbol that contributed to social cohesion.[166]

It should not be surprising, then, that social science research on operating companies has failed to uncover uniform, material inter-company differences in economic performance attributable to the proportion of board seats held by "outside" directors (i.e., directors who are not employees of the firm on whose board they serve) or independent directors generally.[167] Since law is evidently not often effective as a regulatory tool, the mandates and classifications it develops should not be expected to engineer society to a material degree. Of course, operating companies are not investment companies, but as pointed out supra in Part II-B, social science studies completed to date have not yielded consistent findings as to whether the economic returns of investment companies generally are influenced to a meaningful extent by the composition of their boards under section 2(a)(19).[168] Of course, if board composition is a distinct and major influence on investment performance, existing studies would have uncovered the effect, and their findings would be in agreement and unambiguous. The studies, however, do not demonstrate such an effect. Differences in the long-term investment performance of funds as a whole, therefore, are likely to be due to fund-related factors other than the number and proportion of board seats occupied by independent directors as defined by section 2(a)(19).[169]

The concepts and doctrines of law exist for a reason, however, and as a result, investment performance should not be the sole criterion for judging the composition of mutual fund boards under section 2(a)(19) even though investments are made in mutual funds for the purpose of economic gain.[170] An additional, but equally important, criterion should be whether the number and proportion of interested directors and independent directors influence the functioning of the social system by, for example, affecting the frequency of scandals involving funds. Unlike the criterion of investment performance—which is economic—the second criterion is sociological, and while investment performance is widely accepted as a criterion for evaluating funds, the sociological criterion is largely ignored.

The importance of the sociological criterion, however, cannot be overstated. The social products of an organization such as an investment company include reputation and trust, and although these products have yet to be explored fully by social science, they seem to be critical in the long run to the organization and to society in general.[171] For instance, the negative publicity involved in a scandal damages not just the reputation of and trust in the particular organization(s) in which a socially accepted rule of behavior was violated, but it can also harm the reputation of and trust in the societal segment in which the violation occurred.[172] The damaged segment may be all of the organizations comprising a particular industry in the economy (e.g., all mutual funds), and under some conditions, it may encompass the entire institution or sub-institution in which the industry operates (e.g., the financial sector). Even if the damage is limited to a particular industry, however, the operation of society is impaired to some extent.[173] Consequently, a sociological criterion, and not just an economic criterion, is needed to evaluate investment company boards. Unfortunately, a sociological criterion raises questions that rigorous social science studies have yet to answer.

IV. The Macrosociological Nature of Investment Company Regulation

By way of review, federal law governing mutual funds is grounded on skepticism regarding the willingness or ability of interested directors to safeguard fund investors from financial abuse. This skepticism exists in spite of the explicit recognition that state law contains fiduciary duties for directors and that interested directors are subject to the same duties as independent directors. Under state law, the care and loyalty with which interested directors perform their tasks as directors must match that of independent directors. Given this parity, the skepticism directed at interested directors is illogical.

In addition to involving a logical inconsistency, law on the interested directors of mutual funds is accompanied by the belief that the prevalence of interested directors on fund boards substantially affects the investment returns of the funds. The accuracy of this belief, however, seems dubious in light of existing social science studies.[174] These studies are buttressed by a substantial body of social science research that has found regulation to be relatively ineffective in altering societal patterns.[175] Consequently, it is at least plausible, and may indeed be probable, that the relationship between board composition and fund performance is weak or nonexistent.

If we postulate that the status of directors under section 2(a)(19) does not appreciably influence the financial performance of mutual funds as a whole—i.e., if interested directors do not pose the economic threat to the funds and their shareholders that is commonly assumed—two questions must be answered. First, what advantages accrue to society from the congressionally established maximum percentage of interested directors on fund boards and from the actions of the Securities and Exchange Commission to reduce this percentage? Second, can regulatory approaches that do not impose a maximum on the percentage of board seats held by interested directors benefit society as much as, or more than, regulatory approaches that do? The answer to the first question will inform the answer to the second.

The first question implicates the macrosociological proposition that (a) the concepts and doctrines dominant in the institution of law facilitate the operation of the society in which they exist and (b) when these concepts and doctrines hinder the social system, they are abandoned and replaced by concepts and doctrines that strengthen the social order.[176] This two-part proposition leads to the conclusion that, if interested directors have no appreciable effect on the profitability of investments in fund shares, existing law on the percentage of interested directors on fund boards arose because it benefits the social system in some other way(s). The functioning of a social system is improved by the creation and preservation of trust,[177] and the legislative history of the Act discloses that the Act was adopted to promote trust in entities that are vehicles for collective investments in securities so that the entities would contribute to the growth of the United States economy.[178] Thus, even though a concern with trust is rarely made explicit (let alone stressed) in court opinions and Commission releases, Congress evidently had an underlying sociological purpose in limiting the percentage of investment company board seats held by interested fund directors.

Trust, however, is not the only dimension of society affected by the regulation of investment company boards. Through this regulation, Congress and the Commission have probably also protected the reputation of investment companies and created symbols of governmental concern with the welfare of investors.[179] Symbols are important for maintaining and improving the operation of groups,[180] and in regulating investment company boards of directors, federal legislation seems to be inescapably symbolic. The macrosociological concept of social productivity encompasses these outputs (viz., symbols, trust, and reputation) of societal institutions and other organized groups, including business firms.[181] Because the concept of social productivity deals with an important aspect of the institution of law, it can aid in understanding the emergence and role of the doctrines and concepts of law in a society.[182]

In sum, the success of legislation, agency rules, agency enforcement efforts, and court decisions should be judged at least as much by a sociological yardstick as by one that is economic. This will not happen, however, until the macrosociological character of law is acknowledged, because an important contribution of a macrosociological perspective is recognition that law can benefit society in ways other than by altering the incidence of targeted behavior. The effects of law are broad, as well as subtle and elusive, and there must be an awareness of *all* of these effects in order to understand the role of law in a social system.

V. Penalties for Shareholder Exploitation

I turn now to the second question raised in Part IV supra. If law-regulating investment company boards primarily involves social productivity and is primarily concerned with reinforcing the social system, can law strengthen society without focusing on the number or percentage of board seats held by interested directors? I believe that the question has an affirmative answer, and I suggest below an approach that has not heretofore been applied to investment companies. I emphasize, however, that well-designed social science research does not exist at the present time to evaluate my suggestion. Barring an emergency, novel law and policies should be adopted, and actions to enforce them should be undertaken, only *after* exacting research indicates that their goals will be achieved without major, undesired side effects.

A. A Proposal

The starting point for my proposal is the remarkable growth that has occurred in the number of mutual funds in the United States during the last quarter of a century. This growth is visible in Figure 3.1, which uses data from the Investment Company Institute and covers the period from 1940 through 2008.[183] Mutual funds today operate in a buyer's market and must actively pursue investors,[184] and an important reason for the intense competition is the enlarged number of funds. The numerical growth in funds has also created a greater potential for incidents of shareholder exploitation because, all else being equal, more funds present more opportunities for such exploitation.

Both of the time series in the figure reveal a rapid rise in the number of mutual funds starting in the first half of the 1980s. Given the current number of funds and the level of competition between them, the prospect of adverse publicity is presumably a concern of directors and officers of the funds and their investment advisers. A recent study reveals the damage that funds can suffer from unfavorable publicity. The study estimated the asset outflows from mutual funds following disclosure in the *Wall Street Journal* that the entities managing the funds were being investigated or had been penalized by the Securities and Exchange Commission during the period from

Figure 3.1 Number of Mutual Funds in the United States
1940 to 2008

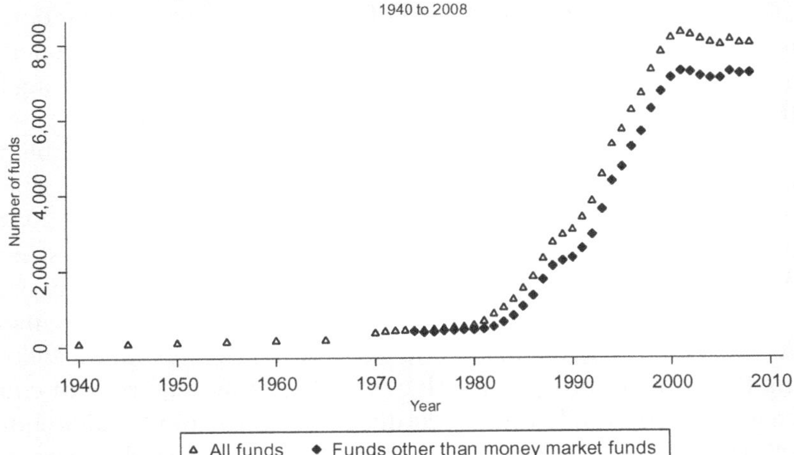

1994 through 2004.[185] For the particular funds that were the focus of the Commission and that were managed by an entity that was penalized, outflows were found to average 22 percent of the assets of the funds in the twelve months after the Commission action was reported in the *Wall Street Journal*.[186] At the same time, average outflows of 7 percent of assets were experienced by funds that were not involved in an investigation or penalty but that belonged to a fund family having a fund that was involved.[187] Because substantial outflows occurred not only from the particular funds that were subjects of Commission attention but also from other funds in the same family, it is clear that shareholders react when they learn that the entity managing their fund may have disregarded, or in fact did disregard, the welfare of fund investors, and the reaction generalizes to other funds in the same family.[188]

Unfortunately, the study could not ascertain whether board composition under section 2(a)(19) of the Act affected the likelihood that a fund would become the focus of a Commission investigation or be involved in a Commission sanction,[189] but the central finding of the study is nonetheless important—shareholders financially punish a fund and its fund family when they learn that the fund manager is even suspected of unlawful conduct. Because the shareholders' reactions remove substantial assets from the funds, they reduce the fees that the funds pay their investment advisers since the fees are calculated as a percentage of fund assets.[190] The possibility of such reactions is presumably an incentive for directors and other affiliates of funds, including the investment advisers of funds, to be wary of any action or inaction that is or might be legally unacceptable and that can generate adverse publicity. The incentive, moreover, is likely to be as strong for the interested directors as for the independent directors.

What means are available to the Commission that will publicize instances in which affiliated persons of funds have exploited shareholders? In a number of cases, the Commission has required investment advisers that breached the antifraud section of the Investment Advisers Act ("Advisers Act")[191] to furnish a copy of the Commission's order identifying the breach and penalty both to current clients by certified or registered mail[192] and also, for the twelve months following the order, to prospective clients.[193] The same requirement could be imposed on funds when their directors have exploited shareholders or have failed to prevent other fund affiliates from doing so. The requirement as to funds is evidently authorized by section 9(f)(1) of the Investment Company Act.[194] By its terms, the section applies when any provision of the Act, or any rule or regulation promulgated by the Commission under the Act, has been breached in the past, is being breached currently, or can be expected to be breached in the future.[195] In such a situation, the Commission can order an end to the violation by both the person(s) committing the violation and "any other person" that was involved in, and that had actual or constructive knowledge of, the violation.[196] Notably, the order may further

> require such person to comply, or to take steps to effect compliance, with such provision, rule, or regulation, upon such terms and conditions and within such time as the Commission may specify in such order.[197]

Because a "person" can be an entity,[198] section 9(f)(1) applies to investment companies of all types.

Instances in which investors in a mutual fund are exploited by an affiliate of the fund threaten a tenet that permeates the entire Act,[199] and such a fund will probably fail to make adequate disclosure of incidents of investor exploitation in the periodic reports it must file with the Commission[200] pursuant to section 30 of the Act,[201] at least until after the Commission has learned of the exploitation. Under section 34(b), disclosure in these reports must be complete, and the content of the reports cannot imply, let alone explicitly assert, that there has been no exploitation of fund shareholders when there has been.[202] However, the likelihood does not seem high that a fund will voluntarily and fully disclose such exploitation until after at least one inaccurate report that could have disclosed the exploitation has been submitted to the Commission. If the exploitation is due to conduct by a director (or other affiliate) of the fund and involves the purchase of property (e.g., securities) from the fund, or the sale of property to the fund, without prior Commission approval, section 17(a) of the Act will have been violated.[203] If the director (or other affiliate) benefited financially from the transaction while acting as an agent of the fund or another person, section 17(e)(1) also may have been violated.[204]

In short, a breach of section 34(b) by a fund, or a breach of section 17[205] by a director of a fund that can be imputed to the fund, is a basis for penalizing the fund. For a breach of either section, the Commission could require that the fund supply to current and prospective investors a salient notice of the manner in which its investors were exploited. The Commission might also prohibit the fund from seeking new investors for a specified period of time.[206]

If the proposal outlined above is implemented, funds would face not only the prospect of adverse publicity in the mass media for an instance of investor exploitation but also the possibility that they would be compelled to call the attention of current and potential investors to the exploitation and the resulting Commission action. Since investment advisers that have run afoul of the antifraud section of the Advisers Act have been required to inform their clients of the violation(s) in this manner,[207] the proposal is not without some precedent. Certified mail is unlikely to be disregarded by a recipient, and the notification to shareholders, by suggesting regulatory vigilance on the part of the Commission, can be expected to symbolize government concern with protecting investors and to assist in restoring trust in mutual funds. The proposal, in short, has the potential to improve the social productivity of investment company regulation.

B. Discussion

The above proposal, if adopted, would join other approaches used by the Securities and Exchange Commission to respond to instances of financial abuse of mutual fund investors. As the mutual fund scandal that emerged in 2003 demonstrates, the Commission already penalizes exploiters. My proposal would not displace such penalties but would add to them. In protecting the integrity of the social system, however, prevention of conduct that has not occurred is likely to be preferable to penalties for conduct that has already occurred, and my proposal employs penalties.

A common assumption in the United States is that penalties reduce the future occurrence of the behavior targeted by the penalties, i.e., that penalties contribute to deterring unwanted conduct,[208] and thus penalties for an activity that has happened are employed with the expectation that the penalties will contribute to preventing future activity of the same type. Unfortunately, this assumption is just that—an assumption. Notably, social science research strongly suggests that penalties, and the possibility of penalties, for criminal conduct have generally no more than a minimal deterrent effect.[209] Because civil sanctions are less severe than criminal sanctions, there is no reason to anticipate that civil penalties in any form—whether the mandatory notifications that are included in my proposal or the disgorgement and fines that the Commission already imposes[210]—will be effective in averting substantial amounts of socially harmful conduct by directors, regardless of their status under section 2(a)(19) of the Act.[211]

Nonetheless, penalties can benefit a society. While penalties qua penalties may not appreciably curb the frequency of an activity, penalties can symbolize a societal commitment to established social values and thereby serve "not so much to guide society, as to comfort it."[212] In doing so, penalties are likely to help in cementing a social system.[213] Moreover, through as well as apart from their symbolism, penalties may reinforce trust in the social system and promote the reputation of the types of entities targeted by the penalties. There is a possibility, of course, that such consequences—i.e., enhanced societal cohesiveness, augmented trust, and improved entity reputation—will reduce the incidence of some types of socially undesirable behavior. However, the deterrence is unlikely to be large in magnitude and, if it occurs, would be indirect—the penalties would strengthen the social system, and the strengthened social system would prevent socially damaging conduct.

While penalties seem to help in maintaining a social system, penalties may contribute less than prevention to reinforcing the fabric of a society.[214] If so, approaches that prevent shareholder exploitation but that do not involve penalties are advisable in efforts to preserve the attractiveness to investors of entities for collective investments in securities. Effective non-penalty approaches will be difficult to identify, but one possibility is suggested by a recent study. The study found that, all things being equal, the investment return of mutual funds whose portfolios were dedicated to equity securities generally increased with the amount of money that the directors of the funds had personally invested in their funds.[215] If the relationship between director investments and fund performance reflected a greater personal concern with the funds by the directors who were investors, a requirement that an individual commit a specified minimum sum to a fund in order to be a director of that fund may prevent shareholder exploitation because directors of a fund who are also investors in the fund are likely to take actions to avert such exploitation. However, while prevention is prudent, none of the current provisions of the Investment Company Act explicitly authorizes the Securities and Exchange Commission to compel investments by directors in their funds, let alone compel specified minimum investments, and Congress would need to amend the Act to provide the Commission with this authority. Whether Congress would adopt such an amendment is an open question.

Finally, regardless of the form it takes and the activity it targets, regulation should be informed by the findings of rigorous social science research. Because well-designed studies conducted to date support the conclusion that deterrence of conduct injurious to mutual funds and their investors is unlikely to be achievable through law, the mailed notification that I proposed would probably not prevent substantial amounts of future misconduct, at least partly because the notification would reach current shareholders only after many if not most of them had learned of the misconduct through other means (e.g., newspaper articles) and had reacted to the disclosure. If the mailed notification would be unlikely to generate appreciable additional redemptions of shares from the fund involved in the scandal and from other funds in the same family, fund directors and officers may be minimally concerned by the notification requirement.

However, every approach to regulating mutual fund boards should be assessed with a sociological criterion, not just an economic criterion, because each approach requires an examination of the influences and reactions of society, elusive and subtle as these influences and reactions may be. Government regulation stems from and affects society in ways that can be understood with the tools of sociology, and studies of the regulation of investment companies can be enriched by, and can enrich, the sociology of law.[216] For example, the statute adopted by Congress establishing the maximum percentage of interested directors on an investment company board, as well as the penalties imposed by the Securities and Exchange Commission for instances of shareholder exploitation, are likely to furnish symbols supporting the social order as well as promote trust in the financial sector. In doing so, these regulatory measures would enhance the credibility of, and hence commitment to, the social system among participants in the system, and the benefit to the social system would occur even if, as seems probable, the measures do not directly or indirectly curb the frequency with which shareholders are financially exploited.[217] By its very nature, a social system requires its participants' commitment, and the extent of this commitment is presumably a determinant of the degree to which the system operates effectively. Thus, in efforts to understand government regulation of investment companies, research employing a macrosociological perspective is essential, and the exclusive use of an economic perspective is a mistake.

Notes

*Chapter 3 is a revised version of Larry D. Barnett, "The Regulation of Mutual Fund Boards of Directors: Financial Protection or Social Productivity?" *Journal of Law and Policy* 16 (2008): 489.

1. The Quotations Page, http://www.quotationspage.com/quotes/John_Kenneth_Galbraith (accessed April 8, 2011).
2. Investment Company Institute, *2009 Investment Company Fact Book*, 49th ed. (2009), 110, http://www.ici.org/about_ici/annuals/fact_books (accessed April 8, 2011). The data in the text on the number and assets of funds include money market funds. The number of funds from 1940 to 2008 is graphically depicted infra in Figure 3.1.
3. Ibid., 10, 72. Money market funds are evidently counted in the percentage of households with an investment in a mutual fund.
4. Role of Independent Directors of Investment Companies, Investment Company Act Release No. IC-24816, 66 Fed. Reg. 3734 (January 16, 2001) [hereinafter Release No. IC-24816].
5. Sec. & Exch. Comm'n, Exemptive Rule Amendments of 2004: The Independent Chair Condition, A Report in Accordance with the Consolidated Appropriations Act (April 2005), available at 2005 SEC LEXIS 1031.
6. Investment Company Act, 15 U.S.C. §§ 80a-1 to -64 (2006). The managers of the securities portfolios of mutual funds and other investment companies are investment advisers under the Investment Advisers Act and subject to that Act. 15 U.S.C. §§ 80b-2(a)(11), -3(a) (2006). In addition, the Securities Act and the Securities Exchange Act apply to mutual funds because the funds issue securities that are offered and sold to investors. 15 U.S.C. § 80a-24 (2006); 15 U.S.C. §§ 77a to 77z-3 (2006); 15 U.S.C. §§ 78a to 78mm (2006).
7. 15 U.S.C. § 80a-3(a) (2006).
8. See generally C. Steven Bradford, "Expanding the Investment Company Act: The SEC's Manipulation of the Definition of Security," *Ohio State Law Journal* 60 (1999): 995 (discussing and rejecting the position of the Securities and Exchange Commission that the criteria determining whether instruments are securities differ between the instruments issued by an investment company to its investors and the instruments in the portfolio of the investment company).
9. The Act defines a "redeemable security" in section 2(a)(32). 15 U.S.C. § 80a-2(a)(32) (2006).
10. Investment Company Institute, supra note 2, at 190; John Downes and Jordan E. Goodman, *Barron's Finance & Investment Handbook*, 4th ed. (Hauppauge, NY: Barron's Educational Series, Inc., 1995), 442. This definition is also used by the Securities and Exchange Commission. See, e.g., Compliance Programs of Investment Companies and Investment Advisers, Investment Company Act Release No. IC-26299, 68 Fed. Reg. 74,714, 74,714 (December 24, 2003).
11. 15 U.S.C. §§ 80a-4(3), -5(a) (2006).
12. Unit investment trusts, which are one of the three types of investment companies enumerated by the Act, do not have boards of directors. 15 U.S.C. § 80a-4 (2006). For an explanation of unit investment trusts, see Thomas S. Harman, "Emerging Alternatives to Mutual Funds: Unit Investment

Trusts and Other Fixed Portfolio Investment Vehicles, *Duke Law Journal* 1987 (1987): 1045.

13. Computed from Investment Company Institute, supra note 2, at 9.
14. 15 U.S.C. § 80a-2(a)(12) (2006).
15. Integrated Resources, Inc., SEC No-Action Letter, 1979 SEC No-Act. LEXIS 2940, at *1–2 (June 1, 1979).
16. Interpretive Matters Concerning Independent Directors of Investment Companies, Investment Company Act Release No. IC-24083, 64 Fed. Reg. 59,877, 59,877 (November 3, 1999) (statement of staff position) [hereinafter Release No. IC-24083].
17. Papilsky v. Berndt, No. 71 Civ. 2534, 1976 U.S. Dist. LEXIS 14442, at *43 (S.D.N.Y. June 24, 1976).
18. J. Robert Brown, Jr., "Disloyalty without Limits: "Independent" Directors and the Elimination of the Duty of Loyalty," *Kentucky Law Journal* 95 (2006): 53, 57.
19. See Burks v. Lasker, 441 U.S. 471, 485 (1979), where the United States Supreme Court writes that the welfare of shareholders was "entrusted" by Congress to the non-interested directors and thus implies that Congress did not trust the interested directors to prevent the exploitation of shareholders. Ibid., at 485, 485 n.15.
20. Investment Company Act of 1940, ch. 686, §§ 3, 6, 7, 54 Stat. 789, 797, 802 (1940) (codified as amended at, respectively, 15 U.S.C. § 80a-3 (2006) and 15 U.S.C. §§ 80a-6, -7 (2006)). Section 3 of the Act designates the features of an investment vehicle that make the vehicle an investment company; section 7 requires an investment company to register with the Commission unless the investment company is exempt from registration under section 6.
21. Investment Company Act of 1940, ch. 686, § 10(a), 54 Stat. 789, 806 (1940). A limited exception to the maximum was provided in section 10(d). If the conditions of section 10(d) were met, all but one of the directors of a registered investment company could be affiliated with the investment adviser to the company or could be officers or employees of the company. Ibid., § 10(d), 54 Stat. at 807. The conditions creating affiliation are discussed in the text infra. Section 10(d) was intended to cover an investment company established by an investment adviser specifically for clients not having substantial assets available for securities investments. Senate Comm. on Banking and Currency, Investment Company Act of 1940 and Investment Advisers Act of 1940, S. Rep. No. 76-1775, at 14 (3rd sess. 1940). Section 10(d) was amended in 1970 and now allows all but one of the directors of a registered investment company that satisfies specified criteria to be "interested" in the investment adviser to the company or to be officers or employees of the company. Investment Company Amendments Act of 1970, Pub. L. 91-547, § 5, 84 Stat. 1413, 1416 (codified at 15 U.S.C. § 80a-10(d) (2006)). The criterion of "interest" is discussed in Part II-A infra of the instant chapter.
22. Senate Comm. on Banking and Currency, Investment Company Act of 1940 and Investment Advisers Act of 1940, S. Rep. No. 76-1775, at 14 (3rd sess. 1940).
23. Tannenbaum v. Zeller, 552 F.2d 402, 406 (2nd Cir.), *cert. denied*, 434 U.S. 934 (1977).

24. The Act currently defines a "voting security" in section 2(a)(42). 15 U.S.C. § 80a-2(a)(42) (2006). The statutory definition of "voting security" has not been revised since the Act was adopted in 1940. See Investment Company Act of 1940, ch. 686, § 2(a)(40), 54 Stat. 789, 796 (1940). For interpretations of section 2(a)(42) by the staff of the Commission, see Real Estate Investment Trusts, SEC No-Action Letter, 1998 SEC No-Act. Lexis 1145, at *4 (November 4, 1998) (staff reply); Wells Fargo Alternative Asset Management, LLC, SEC No-Action Letter, 2005 SEC No-Act. Lexis 116, at *7–8 (January 26, 2005) (staff reply).
25. Under the Act, a "person" is either "a natural person or a company." 15 U.S.C. § 80a-2(a)(28) (2006). The statutory definition of "person" has not changed since the Act was adopted in 1940. See Investment Company Act of 1940, ch. 686, § 2(a)(27), 54 Stat. 789, 794 (1940).
26. The Act defines "control" in section 2(a)(9). 15 U.S.C. § 80a-2(a)(9) (2006). The statutory definition of "control" has not been altered since the Act was adopted in 1940. See Investment Company Act of 1940, ch. 686, § 2(a)(9), 54 Stat. 789, 791–92 (1940).
27. Investment Company Act of 1940, ch. 686, § 2(a)(3), 54 Stat. 789, 791 (1940) (codified at 15 U.S.C. § 80a-2(a)(3) (2006)).
28. S. Comm. On Banking and Currency, Investment Company Amendments Act of 1969, S. Rep. No. 91-184, at 32 (1st Sess. 1969); H. Comm. On Interstate and Foreign Commerce, Investment Company Amendments Act of 1970, H. Rep. No. 91-1382, at 13–14 (2nd Sess. 1970).
29. Investment Company Amendments Act of 1970, Pub. L. No. 91-547, 84 Stat. 1413.
30. Investment Company Amendments Act of 1970, Pub. L. No. 91-547, §§ 2(a), 5, 84 Stat. 1413, 1413, 1416.
31. S. Comm. On Banking and Currency, Investment Company Amendments Act of 1969, S. Rep. No. 91-184, at 33 (1st Sess. 1969); H. Comm. On Interstate and Foreign Commerce, Investment Company Amendments Act of 1970, H. Rep. No. 91-1382, at 14 (2nd Sess. 1970).
32. 15 U.S.C. § 80a-2(a)(19) (2006).
33. 15 U.S.C. § 80a-10(a) (2006). As explained in note 21 supra, section 10(d) of the Act allows more than 60 percent of the directors of a qualifying investment company to be interested.
34. The Act defines "investment adviser" in section 2(a)(20) and "principal underwriter" in section 2(a)(29). 15 U.S.C. §§ 80a-2(a)(20), -2(a)(29) (2006). These statutory definitions have not changed since the adoption of the Act in 1940. Investment Company Act of 1940, ch. 686, §§ 2(a)(19), 2(a)(28), 54 Stat. 789, 793, 794 (1940).
35. It may be helpful to note here that the Commission has taken the position that an individual who serves as a director of a registered investment company can act just for herself or himself, and not as an agent or as a delegate of another individual or an entity, except in certain situations involving a limited partnership. Investment Company Act Release IC-19658, 58 Fed. Reg. 45,834, 45,836 (August 31, 1993); 17 C.F.R. § 270.2a19-2(a) (2009). The position taken by the Commission—viz., that an entity normally cannot be a director of a registered investment company—may not have been intended by Congress. Larry D. Barnett, "When is a Mutual Fund

Director Independent? The Unexplored Role of Professional Relationships under Section 2(a)(19) of the Investment Company Act," *DePaul Business & Commercial Law Journal* 4 (2006): 155, 165 n.54 [hereinafter *When is a Mutual Fund Director Independent?*].

36. See Role of Independent Directors of Investment Companies, Investment Company Act Release No. IC-24082, 64 Fed. Reg. 59,826, 59,827 (November 3, 1999) [hereinafter Release No. IC-24082].
37. See Part V in Chapter 2 supra.
38. Personal Investment Activities of Investment Company Personnel and Codes of Ethics of Investment Companies and Their Investment Advisers and Principal Underwriters, Investment Company Act Release No. IC-21341, 60 Fed. Reg. 47,844, 47,847 (September 14, 1995) ("The role of independent fund directors in policing conflicts of interest is central to the Investment Company Act.").
39. Release No. IC-24082, supra note 36, at 59,827–28.
40. Burks v. Lasker, 441 U.S. 471, 484 (1979) (citation omitted).
41. 15 U.S.C. § 80a-2(a)(19) (2006).
42. 15 U.S.C. § 80a-2(a)(19)(A)(iii) (2006).
43. 15 U.S.C. § 80a-2(a)(19)(B)(i) (2006).
44. 15 U.S.C. § 80a-2(a)(19)(B)(ii) (2006). Section 2(a)(19)(B)(ii) covers individuals who are related as spouses, as parent and child, as siblings, as child and spouse of a parent of the child, or as parent and spouse of a child of the parent. The preceding relationships are included even if they are step or adoptive in nature and apply to both subsection (A) and subsection (B) of section 2(a)(19). 15 U.S.C. § 80a-2(a)(19) (2006).
45. 15 U.S.C. § 80a-2(a)(19)(B)(iii) (2006).
46. 15 U.S.C. § 80a-2(a)(19)(B)(iv) (2006).
47. 15 U.S.C. §§ 80a-2(a)(19)(B)(v), 80a-2(a)(19)(B)(vi) (2006).
48. 15 U.S.C. § 80a-2(a)(19)(B)(vii) (2006).
49. 15 U.S.C. § 80a-2(a)(19) (2006).
50. Such a person would be affiliated with the investment company. 15 U.S.C. § 80a-2(a)(3)(A) (2006). A person affiliated with an investment company through holdings or control of voting securities is interested in the company. 15 U.S.C. § 80a-2(a)(19)(A)(i) (2006).
51. 15 U.S.C. §§ 80a-2(a)(19)(A)(iii), 80a-2(a)(19)(B)(iii) (2006). See SAFECO Asset Management Co., SEC No-Action Letter, [1977–1978 Transfer Binder] Fed. Sec. L. Rep. (CCH) 81,425, at 88,911, 88,912 (December 2, 1977), available at 1977 SEC No-Act. Lexis 2834 (SEC staff concluded that an individual who had an indirect beneficial interest in just 0.63 percent of the common stock of the entity that controlled the investment adviser and principal underwriter for a family of investment companies would be an interested director of the investment companies).
52. 15 U.S.C. § 80a-37(a) (2006).
53. Release No. IC-24816, supra note 4.
54. Ibid., 3747 n.120.
55. Ibid., 3736 n.17 (identifying and summarizing the ten rules).
56. 17 C.F.R. § 270.17a-7 (2009).
57. 15 U.S.C. § 80a-17(a) (2006).
58. Release No. IC-24816, supra note 4, at 3736.

59. Ibid.
60. Release No. IC-24082, supra note 36, at 59,830.
61. Bill Ding and Russ Wermers, *Mutual Fund Performance and Governance Structure: The Role of Portfolio Managers and Boards of Directors* (November 9, 2009), 11–12, 32–35, 57, http://ssrn.com/abstract=683721 (accessed April 8, 2011). Some measures of the financial performance of funds were negatively affected when independent directors comprised more than 75 percent of all directors. Ibid. 57.
62. Alan R. Palmiter, "The Mutual Fund Board: A Failed Experiment in Regulatory Outsourcing," *Brooklyn Journal of Corporate, Finance & Commercial Law* 1 (2006): 165, 200.
63. See Ding and Wermers, supra note 61, at 22 (concluding from Fama–MacBeth regression that "board independence is not an important influence in ongoing fund performance.").
64. Felix Meschke, *An Empirical Examination of Mutual Fund Boards* (Univ. of Minnesota, Twin Cities, Carlson School of Management, Working Paper, March 15, 2007), 17–18, 33–34, 36, http://ssrn.com/abstract=676901 (accessed April 8, 2011) . Based on tests of statistical significance, the percentage of board positions held by independent directors was not clearly related to the performance of funds whose portfolios consisted of debt securities. Ibid., 33, 35, 37.
65. John C. Adams et al., *Internal Governance Mechanisms and Operational Performance: Evidence from Index Mutual Funds* (November 11, 2009), 6, 14, 27, http://ssrn.com/abstract=1356364 (accessed April 8, 2011). The regression coefficient for the *proportion* of seats on a board held by independent directors is reported only for all funds included in the study. Ibid., 27 (panel A of Table 3). A regression coefficient was also estimated for a dummy variable measuring whether boards of stock-index funds were comprised exclusively of independent directors, and the coefficient is reported for the relationship of the variable to the investment return of each of two types of stock-index funds. Fund type was defined by the market capitalization of the issuers in the portfolio of the fund. The regression coefficient for the dummy variable was positive and statistically significant for index funds that tracked large-capitalization companies but was not statistically significant for index funds that tracked small- and mid-capitalization companies. Only among stock-index funds for large-capitalization issuers, accordingly, was investment return affected by whether all of the directors were independent. Ibid., 23, 30. However, even if the regression coefficients for the dummy variable had been positive and statistically significant for stock-index funds that tracked small- and mid-capitalization companies as well as for stock-index funds that tracked large-capitalization companies, the variable does not seem to have contributed much to differences in investment return among U.S. mutual funds as a whole. Few funds that are not index funds are likely to have a board without a single interested director, i.e., a board composed entirely of independent directors. Approximately nine out of ten U.S. mutual funds are not index funds. In 2008, the number of U.S. mutual funds that invested solely in stocks was 4,830, of which just 368 were index funds. Investment Company Institute, supra note 2, at 114, 155.

66. Cf. Palmiter, supra note 62, at 208 ("At worst the fund board creates an illusion of investor protection.").
67. Investment Company Governance, Investment Company Act Release No. IC-26520, 69 Fed. Reg. 46,378, 46,389 (August 2, 2004) [hereinafter Release No. IC-26520].
68. Ibid.
69. Chamber of Commerce v. Sec. & Exch. Comm'n, 443 F.3d 890 (D.C. Cir. 2006).
70. Investment Company Governance, Investment Company Act Release No. IC-27395, 71 Fed. Reg. 35,366 (June 19, 2006).
71. See supra notes 16–19 and accompanying text.
72. Although it has not been articulated with precision, the established view probably does *not* assume that the interested directors of a fund act for their own benefit in all situations where the goals of the interested directors diverge from the goals of the fund's investors. Rather, the established view seems to assume that interested directors act for their own benefit in a significant and unacceptable proportion of situations that involve such divergence. See generally Lynn A. Stout, "On the Proper Motives of Corporate Directors (or, Why You Don't Want to Invite Homo Economicus to Join Your Board)," *Delaware Journal of Corporate Law* 28 (2003): 1 (suggesting from social and behavioral science research that directors frequently, and perhaps typically, act for the benefit of others).
73. Mutual funds are either corporations or business trusts, and both are common among mutual funds. Investment Company Institute, supra note 2, at 174; John H. Langbein, "The Secret Life of the Trust: The Trust as an Instrument of Commerce," *Yale Law Journal* 107 (1997): 165, 171 n.40. Investment companies can also be limited partnerships. Executive Discount Realty Co., SEC No-Action Letter, 1993 SEC No-Act. LEXIS 731, at *4 (April 1, 1993). The Act defines the word "company" to cover, inter alia, corporations, trusts, and partnerships. 15 U.S.C. § 80a-2(a)(8) (2006). Consequently, all three structures come within the definition of an investment company.
74. 15 U.S.C. § 80a-2(a)(12) (2006). See supra text accompanying note 14 for the full definition.
75. Integrated Resources, Inc., SEC No-Action Letter, 1979 WL 14861, at *1 (June 1, 1979); Sheldon A. Jones et al., "The Massachusetts Business Trust and Registered Investment Companies," *Delaware Journal of Corporate Law* 13 (1988): 421, 435 n.91, 451.
76. David L. Cohen, "Theories of the Corporation and the Limited Liability Company: How Should Courts and Legislatures Articulate Rules for Piercing the Veil, Fiduciary Responsibility and Securities Regulation for the Limited Liability Company?" *Oklahoma Law Review* 51 (1998): 427, 472 n.252.
77. Tamar Frankel, "Fiduciary Law," *California Law Review* 71 (1983): 795, 795, 797, 804, 818.
78. Mills Acquisition Co. v. Macmillan, Inc., 559 A.2d 1261, 1280 (Del. 1989) (internal citations omitted).
79. Franklin A. Gevurtz, *Corporation Law* (St. Paul, MN: West Group, 2000), 301.

80. Larry D. Barnett, "The Roots of Law," *American University Journal of Gender, Social Policy & Law* 15 (2007): 613, 615–26 [hereinafter *The Roots of Law*]. Pages 615–26 in *The Roots of Law* are reproduced infra in Part I of Chapter 6.
81. Gevurtz, supra note 79, at 273–86.
82. Unif. P'ship Act § 404, 6 U.L.A. 143 (2001); Rev. Unif. Ltd. P'ship Act § 403(a), 6A U.L.A. 365 (2003). See also Boxer v. Husky Oil Co., 429 A.2d 995, 997 (Del. Ch. 1981) ("When the provisions of the Uniform Partnership Act and the Uniform Limited Partnership Act are read together, it is clear that the general partner in a limited partnership owes a fiduciary duty to the limited partners."); *accord, In re* Fid. Am. Fin. Corp., 43 B.R. 74, 77 n.7 (E.D. Pa. 1984).
83. Larry E. Ribstein and Erin Ann O'Hara, "Corporations and the Market for Law," *University of Illinois Law Review* 2008 (2008): 661, 705.
84. Herbert B. Chermside, Jr., Annotation, *Modern Status of the Massachusetts or Business Trust,* A.L.R. 88 (1978): 3d 704, 753; William K. Sjostrom, Jr., "Tapping the Reservoir: Mutual Fund Litigation Under Section 36(a) of the Investment Company Act of 1940," *University of Kansas Law Review* 54 (2005): 251, 274 ("[S]tate courts have generally analogized the duties of trustees of business trusts to those of directors of corporations."); 13 Am Jur. 2D *Business Trusts* §§ 57–59 (2009).
85. Arthur B. Laby, "Resolving Conflicts of Duty in Fiduciary Relationships," *American University Law Review* 54 (2004): 75, 80; Cede & Co. v. Technicolor, Inc., 634 A.2d 345, 367 (Del. 1993).
86. Del. Code Ann. tit. 12, § 3806(c) (2007).
87. 75 Del. Laws 418 (2006), http://legis.delaware.gov (using Bill Search to locate session law, select GA 143 from Session menu, select HB from Bill Type menu, and enter 445 for No.) (accessed April 8, 2011).
88. Tamar Frankel, "The Delaware Business Trust Act Failure as the New Corporate Law," *Cardozo Law Review* 23 (2001): 325, 332.
89. The Supreme Court of Delaware acknowledges that these requirements are fundamental to the role of a director of a corporation. See text accompanying note 78 supra. See also Brown, supra note 18, at 57 ("The sine qua non of a director's fiduciary duty is fairness.").
90. Section 36(a) of the Act authorizes the Securities and Exchange Commission to ask a federal court to impose injunctive and/or other relief on, inter alia, a director of a registered investment company for violating a "fiduciary duty involving personal misconduct." 15 U.S.C. § 80a-35(a) (2006). Because it does not distinguish investment companies by their structure, the section applies to all investment companies that have a board of directors. However, section 36(a) may cover just the duty of loyalty of investment company directors. See Jacobs v. Bremner, 378 F. Supp. 2d 861, 866 (N.D. Ill. 2005).
91. Fed. Deposit Ins. Corp. v. Gonzalez-Gorrondona, 833 F. Supp. 1545, 1549 (S.D. Fla. 1993); Omnibank of Mantee v. United S. Bank, 607 So.2d 76, 84 (Miss. 1992).
92. Sean J. Griffith, "Good Faith Business Judgment: A Theory of Rhetoric in Corporate Law Jurisprudence," *Duke Law Journal* 55 (2005): 1, 40.
93. Ibid. *In re* Chavez, 140 B.R. 413, 424 (W.D. Tex. 1992).

94. Wright v. Nimmons, 641 F. Supp. 1391, 1402 (S.D. Tex. 1986).
95. Melvin A. Eisenberg, "The Duty of Care of Corporate Directors and Officers," *University of Pittsburgh Law Review* 51 (1990): 945, 951–52, 956, 958–59. The functions of directors of a corporation—the focus of Professor Eisenberg's article—are also the functions of persons qualifying as directors of an investment company that is a business trust or a limited partnership. As explained in note 73 supra, investment companies that are mutual funds are established as business trusts if they are not established as corporations, and investment companies can also take the form of limited partnerships.

    Directors of a non-corporate investment company necessarily carry out the third function listed in the text (i.e., decision-making for the entity) because the function inheres in their role as directors. In addition, the first two functions of directors are embedded in the supervisory responsibilities of the directors of investment companies. As the Securities and Exchange Commission has pointed out, "[d]irectors are generally responsible under state law for the oversight of all of the operations of a mutual fund, and the Investment Company Act assigns many specific responsibilities to fund boards." Release No. IC-26520, supra note 67, at 46,379 n.8. Because mutual funds can be business trusts, the Commission's statement applies to the directors (i.e., trustees) of funds formed as business trusts. The statement also applies to the directors (i.e., general partners) of investment companies that are limited partnerships. See UNIF. P'SHIP ACT § 401(F), 6 U.L.A. 133 (2001); REV. UNIF. LTD. P'SHIP ACT § 403(A), 6A U.L.A. 365 (2003).
96. See Release No. IC-26520, supra note 67, at 46,379 n.8. The second function occurs just sporadically in the typical company. Eisenberg, supra note 95, at 956. Because the second function is presumably infrequent in investment companies as well, it is not discussed further.
97. Eisenberg, supra note 95, at 955–56. If directors do not monitor a particular activity because they have inadvertently overlooked it, their mistake must have been reasonable under the circumstances in which it occurred. Gevurtz, supra note 79, at 274–78. But see *In re* Caremark Int'l, Inc. Derivative Litig., 698 A.2d 959, 970 (Del. Ch. 1996) (requiring directors to act in good faith in selecting a system to detect and disclose problems in the organization).
98. Gevurtz, supra note 79, at 286–88; *In re Caremark Int'l, Inc. Derivative Litig.*, 698 A.2d at 967–68.
99. Stephen Fraidin and Radu Lelutiu, "Strategic Alliances and Corporate Control," *Case Western Reserve Law Review* 53 (2003): 865, 890–91; Cede & Co. v. Technicolor, Inc., 634 A.2d 345, 368 (Del. 1993) (The business judgment rule "is premised on a presumption that the directors have severally met their duties of loyalty... and that the directors have collectively, as a board, met their duty of care."). See also Dennis J. Block et al., "The Duty of Loyalty and the Evolution of the Scope of Judicial Review," *Brooklyn Law Review* 59 (1993): 65, 67 (contending that the duties of care and loyalty create a standard of conduct for directors and describing the business judgment rule as "a specific application of this directorial standard of conduct").
100. Gevurtz, supra note 79, at 279. See also John H. Matheson and Brent A. Olson, "Shareholder Rights and Legislative Wrongs: Toward Balanced

Takeover Legislation," *George Washington Law Review* 59 (1991): 1425, 1488 (describing the business judgment rule as "amorphous" and plagued by "vagueness and various manifestations").

101. William T. Allen et al., "Function over Form: A Reassessment of Standards of Review in Delaware Corporation Law," *Business Law* 56 (2001): 1287, 1298.
102. See generally Basic Inc. v. Levinson, 485 U.S. 224, 245 (1987) (explaining that presumptions can function to impose the burden of proof on one party and stem from "considerations of fairness, public policy, and probability, as well as judicial economy").
103. Allen et al., supra note 101, at 1297; William T. Allen et al., "Realigning the Standard of Review of Director Due Care with Delaware Public Policy: A Critique of Van Gorkom and Its Progeny as a Standard of Review Problem," *Northwestern University Law Review* 96 (2002): 449, 457.
104. Block et al., supra note 99, at 69; Bud Roth, "Entire Fairness Review for a "Pure" Breach of the Duty of Care: Sensible Approach or Technicolor Flop," *Delaware Law Review* 3 (2000): 145, 165–67.
105. Lyman P. Q. Johnson, "The Audit Committee's Ethical and Legal Responsibilities: The State Law Perspective," *South Texas Law Review* 47 (2005): 27, 46.
106. Melvin A. Eisenberg, "The Duty of Good Faith in Corporate Law," *Delaware Journal of Corporate Law* 31 (2006): 1, 4, 74. A portion of a June 2006 opinion of the Supreme Court of Delaware is consistent with the contention of Professor Eisenberg that a duty of good faith is being recognized. *In re* Walt Disney Co. Derivative Litig., 906 A.2d 27 (Del. 2006) (en banc). On the one hand, the court reasoned that "[a] vehicle is needed to address... doctrinally" situations in which the duties of care and loyalty have not been breached by a director, and this "doctrinal vehicle is the duty to act in good faith." Ibid., 66. On the other hand, the court also stated that it was not deciding whether "good faith is a duty that, like the duties of care and loyalty, can serve as an independent basis for imposing liability upon corporate officers and directors." Ibid., 67 n.112. In November 2006, the Supreme Court of Delaware adopted a position that is inconsistent with the contention of Professor Eisenberg. Stone v. Ritter, 911 A.2d 362, 369–70 (Del. 2006), which is discussed infra in the text accompanying notes 112 and 113.
107. *In re Walt Disney Co. Derivative Litig.*, 906 A.2d at 63–64 (en banc) (describing a duty of good faith as "not a well-developed area of our corporate fiduciary law" and "up to this point relatively uncharted").
108. *The Roots of Law*, supra note 80, at 615–26, 677–80. The cited pages in *The Roots of Law* are reproduced, respectively, in Part I and in Part IV-B of Chapter 6 infra.
109. *Oxford English Dictionary*, vol. 5, 2nd ed. (1989), 679 (definitions 10 and 11.a. of "faith"). Accord, *Random House Dictionary of the English Language*, 2nd ed. (New York: Random House, 1987), 822 (definition of "good faith").
110. Stephen Knack, "Social Capital and the Quality of Government: Evidence from the States," *American Journal of Political Science* 46 (2001): 772, 775, 779, 782 (finding that the overall performance of state govern-

ment in the United States rises with the level of trust characterizing the state population); Daniel Lederman et al., "Violent Crime: Does Social Capital Matter?" *Economic Development & Cultural Change* (2002): 509, 526, 529 (finding that, in cross-country data, the degree of social trust is inversely related to the homicide rate); Isabel Neira et al., "An Empirical Analysis of Social Capital and Economic Growth in Europe (1980-2000)," *Social Indicators Research* 92 (2009): 111, 125 (finding in data on European nations that the level of trust is directly related to gross domestic product per person); Richard Rosenfeld et al., "Social Trust, Firearm Prevalence, and Homicide," *Annals of Epidemiology* 17 (2007): 119, 124 (finding in data on counties and sets of counties in the United States that the degree of social trust is inversely related to the homicide rate). Additional supporting empirical studies are summarized and cited in Larry D. Barnett, "Social Productivity, Law, and the Regulation of Conflicts of Interest in the Investment Industry," *Cardozo Public Law, Policy, & Ethics Journal* 3 (2006): 793, 827 [hereinafter *Social Productivity & Law*]. Page 827 in *Social Productivity & Law* is reproduced supra in Part V-C of Chapter 2.

111. Lawrence E. Mitchell, "Fairness and Trust in Corporate Law," *Duke Law Journal* 43 (1993): 425.
112. Stone v. Ritter, 911 A.2d 362, 369–70 (Del. 2006). In so ruling, the court regarded good faith not as a fiduciary duty but, rather, as an *element* of a fiduciary duty, viz., the duty of loyalty.
113. Ibid.
114. See *The Roots of Law*, supra note 80, at 615 and nn.4–5. Notes 4 and 5 in *The Roots of Law* are reproduced in Part I of Chapter 6 infra, where they are notes 4 and 5.
115. Eisenberg, supra note 106, at 5, 22–25.
116. Ibid., 57–58. See *Stone*, 911 A.2d at 370 (Del. 2006); Blake v. Smith, No. 03-0003-B, 2006 Mass. Super. LEXIS 668, at *21 (Mass. Super. Ct. 2006).
117. E.g., Margaret M. Blair & Lynn A. Stout, *A Team Production Theory of Corporate Law*, 85 VA. L. REV. 247, 298–99 (1999).
118. See *In re* Walt Disney Co. Derivative Litig., 906 A.2d 27, 66–67 (Del. 2006) (en banc).
119. See notes 81–85 supra and accompanying text.
120. See Robert W. Hillman, "Closely-Held Firms and the Common Law of Fiduciary Duty: What Explains the Enduring Qualities of a Punctilio?," *Tulsa Law Review* 41 (2006): 441, 442, 448–49.
121. Under the Act, a closed-end fund is a management investment company that issues securities that are not redeemable by the company. 15 U.S.C. §§ 80a-2(a)(32), -5(a)(2) (2006).
122. *In re* Nuveen Fund Litigation, No. 94 C 360, slip op., 1995 U.S. Dist. LEXIS 19482 (N.D. Ill., December 21, 1995) (report of magistrate judge) [hereinafter *Report of Magistrate Judge*]; *In re* Nuveen Fund Litigation, No. 94 C 360, slip op., 1996 U.S. Dist. LEXIS 8077 (N.D. Ill., May 17, 1996) (district court opinion) [hereinafter *District Court Opinion*].
123. See *Report of Magistrate Judge*, supra note 122, at *7; *District Court Opinion*, supra note 122, at *4. Closed-end funds that satisfy specified conditions

can periodically redeem shares they have issued. 17 C.F.R. § 270.23c-3 (2009). See generally Sec. & Exch. Comm'n, Exemptive Rule Amendments of 2004: The Independent Chair Condition, A Report in Accordance with the Consolidated Appropriations Act, 2005, 2005 SEC LEXIS 1031 (April 2005), at *65–67 (discussing Rule 23c-3). I assume that the two funds did not take advantage of Rule 23c-3 and regularly redeem their shares, because neither the *Report of the Magistrate Judge* nor the *District Court Opinion* mentions the Rule.

124. See Downes and Goodman, supra note 10, at 233 (defining "closed-end fund" and "closed-end management company"). The "net asset value" of a share is computed by subtracting the total liabilities of a fund from the total market value of the assets of the fund, including the securities in its portfolio, and dividing the result by the number of outstanding shares of the fund. Ibid., 449–50 (defining "net asset value").
125. Peter Klibanoff et al., "Investor Reaction to Salient News in Closed-End Country Funds," *Journal of Finance* 53 (1998): 673, 678, 681 (finding that, for thirty-nine single-country closed-end funds during the period January 1986 through March 1994, weekly changes in share price were 36 percent less than weekly changes in net asset value).
126. *Report of Magistrate Judge*, supra note 122, at *13–14.
127. Ibid.
128. Ibid., *10–11, *13; *District Court Opinion*, supra note 122, at *6–7.
129. *Report of Magistrate Judge*, supra note 122, at *16.
130. Ibid., *2, *4, *9–10.
131. See Strougo v. Scudder, Stevens & Clark, Inc., 964 F. Supp. 783, 800 (S.D.N.Y. 1997) (concluding on facts similar to those of *Nuveen* that plaintiffs had alleged a violation by fund directors of their duty of loyalty to the fund because plaintiffs claimed the directors had a financial incentive to favor the investment adviser to the fund).
132. *Report of Magistrate Judge*, supra note 122, at *3–4.
133. Ibid., *4. The two directors were interested directors of the funds because they were interested persons of the investment adviser to the funds. 15 U.S.C. § 80a-2(a)(19)(A)(iii) (2006). Two factors made these directors interested persons of the adviser, although either factor by itself would have sufficed. First, each of the two directors was a director of the adviser. *Report of Magistrate Judge*, supra note 122, at *3. As directors of the adviser, they were affiliated with the adviser, and this affiliation caused them to be interested in the adviser. 15 U.S.C. §§ 80a-2(a)(3)(D), -2(a)(19)(B)(i) (2006). Second, both directors owned stock issued by the corporation that was the parent of the adviser and that controlled the adviser. *Report of Magistrate Judge*, supra note 122, at *3–4. An owner of a security issued by an entity in control of an investment adviser is interested in the adviser. 15 U.S.C. § 80a-2(a)(19)(B)(iii) (2006).
134. *District Court Opinion*, supra note 122, at *1.
135. Ibid., *12.
136. Ibid., *13–22.
137. *See* Ibid., *24 (concluding that the plaintiffs adequately alleged that the directors, in relying on counsel, had not fulfilled their duty of care).
138. See supra note 133.

139. The district court described the fund director in question as independent, and the plaintiffs evidently did not contest this designation. *District Court Opinion*, supra note 122, at *1, *8.
The fund director in question had been chairman of the investment adviser to the funds. *Report of Magistrate Judge*, supra note 122, at *4. The position of chairperson is not described. If, as chairman, the fund director was a director and/or officer of the adviser, he would have been affiliated with the adviser, and hence interested in the adviser and the funds, but only while he was a director/officer of the adviser. 15 U.S.C. §§ 80a-2(a)(3)(D), 80a-2(a)(19)(A)(iii), 80a-2(a)(19)(B)(i) (2006).
140. Subsection (B)(vii) provides that interest in the investment adviser or principal underwriter for an investment company exists on the part of "any natural person whom the Commission by order shall have determined to be an interested person by reason of having had at any time since the beginning of the last two completed fiscal years of such investment company a material business or professional relationship with such investment adviser or principal underwriter or with the principal executive officer or any controlling person of such investment adviser or principal underwriter." 15 U.S.C. § 80a-2(a)(19)(B)(vii) (2006). See generally *When is a Mutual Fund Director Independent?*, supra note 35, at 165–78 (distinguishing "professional" relationships from "business" relationships and discussing the former under subsections (A)(vii) and (B)(vii) of section 2(a)(19)). A ruling by the Commission that a director is interested in the investment adviser or principal underwriter for an investment company under subsection (B)(vii), or is interested in the investment company under subsection (A)(vii) (infra note 148), does not operate retroactively; the director is deemed to be interested only after the ruling. S. Comm. On Banking and Currency, Investment Company Amendments Act of 1969, S. Rep. No. 91-184, at 33 (1st Sess. 1969); H. Comm. On Interstate and Foreign Commerce, Investment Company Amendments Act of 1970, H. Rep. No. 91-1382, at 14 (2nd Sess. 1970).
141. *Report of Magistrate Judge*, supra note 122, at *3, *4.
142. A seven-member board can have a maximum of four interested directors under section 10(a) of the Act (7 x 0.60 = 4.2). 15 U.S.C. § 80a-10(a) (2006). Even though two of the seven directors of the Nuveen funds were interested (see supra note 133 and accompanying text), an additional board member of each Nuveen fund could have been an interested director without placing the boards in violation of section 10(a). Compliance with section 10(a), however, has no bearing on whether a director has breached a fiduciary duty under state law.
143. 15 U.S.C. §§ 80a-2(a)(19)(A)(iii), 80a-2(a)(19)(B)(vii) (2006). Subsection (A)(iii) deems a member of the board of directors of an investment company to be interested in the company if the director is "any interested person of any investment adviser of or principal underwriter for such company." 15 U.S.C. § 80a-2(a)(19)(A)(iii) (2006).
144. Release No. IC-24083, supra note 16, at 59,879.
145. Ibid., 59,880–81. If an individual chaired the parent of the investment adviser at the time he or she voted as a fund director to approve an action by the fund, the position as chair of the parent could by itself have produced

a material business relationship with the investment adviser. Ibid., 59,880.

146. *District Court Opinion*, supra note 122, at *3–4.
147. Supra note 144 and its accompanying text.
148. Subsection (A)(vii) provides that interest in an investment company exists on the part of

> any natural person whom the Commission by order shall have determined to be an interested person by reason of having had, at any time since the beginning of the last two completed fiscal years of such company, a material business or professional relationship with such company or with the principal executive officer of such company or with any other investment company having the same investment adviser or principal underwriter or with the principal executive officer of such other investment company.

15 U.S.C. § 80a-2(a)(19)(A)(vii) (2006). Subsection (B)(vii) is reproduced in note 140 supra.

149. Release No. IC-24083, supra note 16, at 59,879 (stating the view of the Commission staff that, under subsections (A)(vii) and (B)(vii), whether the independence of a director might be impaired by a business or professional relationship depends on "the particular facts of each case"); Cede & Co. v. Technicolor, Inc., 634 A.2d 345, 367 (Del. 1993) (asserting that the business judgment rule applies to "the business transaction at hand" and "a particular transaction").
150. See supra notes 104 and 105 and accompanying text.
151. 15 U.S.C. §§ 80a-2(a)(19)(A)(iv), 80a-2(a)(19)(B)(iv) (2006).
152. According to the reports of the Senate and House committees that drafted section 2(a)(19), Congress wanted a director of an investment company to be deemed interested under subsections (A)(vii) and (B)(vii) when the director had a material business or professional relationship with specified parties, i.e., a relationship that "might tend to impair" the director's ability to represent shareholders. S. Comm. On Banking and Currency, Investment Company Amendments Act of 1969, S. Rep. No. 91-184, at 33 (1st Sess. 1969); H. Comm. On Interstate and Foreign Commerce, Investment Company Amendments Act of 1970, H. Rep. No. 91-1382, at 14 (2nd Sess. 1970). The "might tend to impair" standard, however, arguably should not be confined to subsections (A)(vii) and (B)(vii). Rather, *all* of the subsections of section 2(a)(19) may reflect a concern with situations and arrangements that "might tend to impair" the ability of a director to advance the welfare of shareholders. Furthermore, a plausible argument can be made that the phrase "tend to impair" is appreciably broadened by the use of the word "might" and that Congress believed that interest should exist when a situation or arrangement produced even a low probability of swaying a director.
153. Aronson v. Lewis, 473 A.2d 805, 812 (Del. 1984). See Allen et al., supra note 101 and accompanying text.
154. Clarke Randall, "Fiduciary Duties of Investment Company Directors and Management Companies Under the Investment Company Act of 1940," *Oklahoma Law Review* 31 (1978): 635, 644.
155. Release No. IC-26520, supra note 67, at 46,380, 46,392 n.32 (statement of commissioners); Release No. IC-24083, supra note 16, at 59,878 (statement of staff).

156. 15 U.S.C. § 80a-10(a) (2006).
157. These tasks are reviewed in Palmiter, supra note 62, at 171–76.
158. *In re* Oracle Corp. Derivative Litig., 824 A.2d 917, 920 (Del. Ch.), *appeal denied*, 829 A.2d 141 (Del. 2003).
159. Beam v. Stewart, 845 A.2d 1040, 1051 (Del. 2004) (emphasis in original). *Accord*, McCabe v. Foley, 424 F.Supp. 2d 1315, 1324–25 (M.D. Fla. 2006).
160. Keith Lumsden and Craig Petersen, "The Effect of Right-to-Work Laws on Unionization in the United States," *Journal of Political Economy* 83 (1975): 1237.
161. John J. Antel et al., "State Regulation and Hospital Costs," *Review of Economics & Statistics* 77 (1995): 416, 421–22.
162. John K. Folger and Charles B. Nam, *Education of the American Population* (Washington, DC: Bureau of the Census, U.S. Department of Commerce, 1967), 24–27; William M. Landes and Lewis C. Solman, "Compulsory Schooling Legislation: An Economic Analysis of Law and Social Change in the Nineteenth Century," *Journal of Economic History* 32 (1972): 54, 86; Linda Nasif Edwards, "An Empirical Analysis of Compulsory Schooling Legislation, 1940–1960," *Journal of Law & Economics* 21 (1978): 203, 221–22.
163. The most persuasive study supporting this conclusion is by Frans van Poppel and Joop de Beer, "Measuring the Effect of Changing Legislation on the Frequency of Divorce: The Netherlands, 1830-1990," *Demography* 30 (1993): 425. In the van Poppel and de Beer study, which was confined to The Netherlands, the divorce rate was measured by the annual number of divorces per 10,000 married males during a 160-year period (viz., 1830–1990). Ibid., 430. A no-fault divorce statute was adopted in The Netherlands in 1971. Ibid., 430. None of three major changes that occurred in divorce law during the 160 years covered by the study, including the introduction of no-fault divorce in 1971, had a long-term, appreciable effect on the divorce rate. Ibid., 438–39.

    Of the research done to date on the impact of no-fault divorce law on the incidence of divorce, the study by van Poppel and de Beer is the most convincing for several reasons. First, the study covered a long time span during which three important changes in divorce law occurred, and it found that the response of the divorce rate to all three changes was the same. The impact of divorce law, then, was consistent and exhibited a pattern. Second, the changes in law were assessed with a statistical technique whose estimates of relationships between variables are unaffected by serial dependency in data. Ibid., 427. Divorce rates for multiple time points can be expected to exhibit serial dependency because the rate at any one time point is likely to be affected by the rate at the preceding time point. Third, the denominator of the divorce rate used by van Poppel and de Beer was the number of married males, not the total population. Ibid., 430. As a result, their measure of the likelihood of divorce was limited to persons who were exposed to the possibility of divorce.

    The findings of the van Poppel and de Beer study are supported by more recent research examining the impact of divorce law on divorce rates in eighteen countries of Western Europe. Thorsten Kneip and Gerrit Bauer,

"Did Unilateral Divorce Laws Raise Divorce Rates in Western Europe?," *Journal of Marriage and Family* 71 (2009): 592. In addition, the findings of the van Poppel and de Beer study are consistent with recent research on the impact of divorce law in the United States. Justin Wolfers, "Did Unilateral Divorce Laws Raise Divorce Rates? A Reconciliation and New Results," *American Economic Review* 96 (2006): 1802. In particular, the Wolfers study concluded that, although law allowing unilateral no-fault divorce raised divorce rates in the United States, the effect was relatively small and disappeared within ten years. Ibid., 1814–16. Other research on the impact of divorce law in the United States has yielded disputed findings. E.g., *compare* Norval D. Glenn, "Further Discussion of the Effects of No-Fault Divorce on Divorce Rates," *Journal of Marriage & Family* 61 (1999): 800, *with* Joseph Lee Rodgers et al., "The Effect of No-Fault Divorce Legislation on Divorce Rates: A Response to a Reconsideration," *Journal of Marriage & Family* 59 (1997): 1026 *and* Joseph Lee Rodgers et al., "Did No-Fault Divorce Legislation Matter? Definitely Yes and Sometimes No," *Journal of Marriage & Family* 61 (1999): 803. However, when differences and changes in statutes governing divorce are statistically related to the crude divorce rate in the United States, jurisdiction-level differences and changes in demographic, economic, and social attributes of the population appear to have a considerably stronger relationship to the divorce rate. Thomas B. Marvell, "Divorce Rates and the Fault Requirement," *Law & Society Review* 23 (1989): 544, 551, 557.

164. Robert M. Gordon, Note, "The Limits of Limits on Divorce," *Yale Law Journal* 107 (1998): 1435, 1436, 1439–40.

165. E.g., Amy M. Donley and James D. Wright, "For Richer or For Poorer: The Impact of State-Level Legislation on Marriage, Divorce, and Other Outcomes," *Sociological Spectrum* 28 (2008): 133; Ann E. Horvath-Rose et al., "Capping Kids: The Family Cap and Nonmarital Childbearing," *Population Research & Policy Review* 27 (2008): 119, 134; Marc Poitras and Daniel Sutter, "Policy Ineffectiveness or Offsetting Behavior? An Analysis of Vehicle Safety Inspections," *Southern Economic Journal* 68 (2002): 922, 932. Other pertinent research is cited and reviewed by: Anne H. Gauthier, "The Impact of Family Policies on Fertility in Industrialized Countries: A Review of the Literature," *Population Research & Policy Review* 26 (2007): 323, 339, 342; Larry D. Barnett, "Law as Symbol: Appearances in the Regulation of Investment Advisers and Attorneys," *Cleveland State Law Review* 15 (2007): 289, 300–01 nn.65–67 [hereinafter *Law as Symbol*]. Also see infra note 209. *Law as Symbol* is reproduced with revision in Chapter 8 infra; in Chapter 8, see notes 66–67.

Law can also have inconsistent effects on a targeted problem; that is, law may improve one dimension of a problem and have no impact on, or worsen, another dimension of the problem. E.g., David Neumark and Wendy A. Stock, "The Labor Market Effects of Sex and Race Discrimination Laws," *Economic Inquiry* 44 (2006): 385, 411–14 (finding with census data on individuals that state statutes prohibiting sex-based differentials in pay increased the earnings of employed white women and of employed black women but reduced the level of employment among both, and finding that state statutes prohibiting race-based employment discrimination raised the earnings, but did not affect the level of employment, of black men relative to white men).

166. *Law as Symbol*, supra note 165, at 299–301. Pages 299–301 in *Law as Symbol* are reproduced infra in Part II of Chapter 8.

167. Dan R. Dalton et al., "Meta-Analytic Reviews of Board Composition, Leadership Structure, and Financial Performance," *Strategic Management Journal* 19 (1998): 269, 271, 278–80. The same conclusion is reached by Donald C. Clarke, "Three Concepts of the Independent Director," *Delaware Journal of Corporate Law* 32 (2007): 73, 75. Cf. James D. Westphal, "Board Games: How CEOs Adapt to Increases in Structural Board Independence from Management," *Administrative Science Quarterly* 43 (1998): 511, 512, 529 (finding that changes in board composition may not have their anticipated effects because chief executive officers adapt to the changes by personally influencing directors).

168. See text accompanying supra notes 61–65.

169. Cf. Christine Parker and Vibeke Lehmann Nielsen, "Corporate Compliance Systems: Could They Make Any Difference?" *Administration & Society* 41 (2009): 3, 27–8 (finding that implementation by business firms of compliance programs consistent with the requirements of law governing competition and consumer protection was "patchy at best" and that the presence or absence of formal compliance programs increased compliance with the law no more than the values and general competence of the managers of the businesses).

170. Indeed, a profit motive on the part of investors is essential if the instruments issued by mutual funds are to qualify as securities. Fund investors typically seem to hold investment contracts. See generally Sec. & Exch. Comm'n v. Edwards, 540 U.S. 389, 393, 395 (2004) (identifying, from prior cases, the elements of an investment contract). An investment contract is deemed by the Act to be a security. 15 U.S.C § 80a-2(a)(36) (2006). A profit motive is an element of an investment contract. United Housing Found. v. Forman, 421 U.S. 837, 852–53 (1975).

171. *Social Productivity & Law*, supra note 110, at 806–09, 812–27. Pages 806–9 and 812–26 in *Social Productivity & Law* are reproduced in Part III and Part V, respectively, of Chapter 2 supra.

172. Ari Adut, "A Theory of Scandal: Victorians, Homosexuality, and the Fall of Oscar Wilde," *American Journal of Sociology* 111 (2005): 213, 219–21.

173. Public misstatements of material facts, or omissions of material facts from public communications, by officers of mutual funds are also pertinent to the sociological criterion. Such misstatements and omissions can reduce trust in the funds and damage the reputation of the funds. To the extent that misstatements and omissions do so, they hamper the funds in raising capital for economic activity. Congress has recognized that the federal securities statutes, including the Investment Company Act, were adopted to preserve trust in securities markets. *When is a Mutual Fund Director Independent?*, supra note 35, at 158–59. See Dura Pharm., Inc. v. Broudo, 544 U.S. 336, 345 (2005) ("The [federal] securities statutes seek to maintain public confidence in the marketplace.").

174. See Ding and Wermers, supra note 61; Meschke, supra note 64; Adams et al., supra note 65. Also see supra note 63.

175. See sources cited supra notes 160–63, 165.
176. United States v. Trottier, 9 M.J. 337, 344 (C.M.A. 1980) ("The law is not an end in itself; more properly it is a means to accomplish the ends of an ordered society. When change occurs in the conditions of that society upon which the law is based, the law, in turn, must respond thereto.").
177. Supra note 110.
178. *When is a Mutual Fund Director Independent?*, supra note 35, at 159.
179. *Social Productivity & Law*, supra note 110, at 832. Page 832 in *Social Productivity & Law* is reproduced supra in Part VI-B of Chapter 2.
180. Ibid., 821–25; *Law as Symbol*, supra note 165, at 290–91. Pages 821–25 in *Social Productivity & Law* are reproduced supra in Part V-B of Chapter 2. Pages 290–91 in *Law as Symbol* are reproduced infra in Part I of Chapter 8.
181. *Social Productivity & Law*, supra note 110. *Social Productivity & Law* is reproduced supra in Chapter 2. The concept of social productivity is more useful than the concept of social capital when considering law. Social capital is concerned with the resources of a group (including an institution) and the advantages and disadvantages furnished by these resources to the participants in the group. Social productivity, on the other hand, focuses on the social outputs of a group and the effects of these outputs. When the effects of the outputs are harmful to the functioning of the social system, they become a concern to law, which as a societal institution attempts to deal with the (negative) effects. The concept of social productivity, therefore, is relevant to law. Of course, the institution of law itself has consequences, and doctrines of law can be expected to respond to any such consequences that damage the social system.
182. The macrosociological framework for law that I am proposing considers the political process, as the forerunner of legislation and agency rules, to be an indicator of societal conditions. This point is implicit in the remark that "[p]olitics is the art of the possible." Otto von Bismarck, *quoted in* The Quotations Page, Otto von Bismarck Quotes—The Quotations Page, http://www.quotationspage.com/quotes/Otto_von_Bismarck/ (accessed December 10, 2009). In my framework, therefore, criticisms that are directed at the current content of section 2(a)(19) of the Act, and at Commission rules pertinent to the section, should prompt a study of the social system in which the Act exists and the Commission operates.

    The political process is involved in choosing judges, too, and is an indicator of the societal conditions that shape judicial rulings and opinions. See *The Roots of Law*, supra note 80, at 636–37. Pages 636–37 in *The Roots of Law* are reproduced infra in Part III of Chapter 6.
183. Investment Company Institute, supra note 2, at 114.

    For the period from 1940 until 1970, the Investment Company Institute reports the number of funds for each fifth year, but starting in 1970, the number is reported for every year. Through 1973, furthermore, the data of the Institute combine money market funds with other types of mutual funds (viz., funds investing in longer-term debt securities and funds investing in equity securities), and a separate count of money market funds is furnished beginning only with 1974. Based on these numbers, Figure 3.1 contains one time series (denoted by hollow triangles) that represents all mutual funds, including money market funds; the data in this time series are for each fifth year from 1940 to 1970 and then for every year through 2008. The second time series in the figure represents funds that are *not* money market funds, i.e., funds that invest in stocks and/or in debt securities having maturities exceeding those of money market instruments. The second time series (denoted by solid diamonds) includes every year from 1974 through 2008. Ibid.

184. See Prohibition on the Use of Brokerage Commissions to Finance Distribution, Investment Company Act Release No. IC-26356, 69 Fed. Reg. 9726, 9729 (March 1, 2004) (characterizing as "intense" the degree of competition for investors when funds distribute their shares through brokers); Political Contributions by Certain Investment Advisers, Investment Advisers Act Release No. IA-2910 (August 3, 2009), 2009 SEC Lexis 2713, at *114 (describing as "keen" the level of competition between investment advisers to have government-sponsored savings plans choose funds they manage as investment options for plan participants).
185. Stephen Choi and Marcel Kahan, "The Market Penalty for Mutual Fund Scandals," *Boston University Law Review* 87 (2007): 1021, 1026.
186. Ibid., 1029, 1042.
187. Ibid., 1050. Outflows from funds that were not involved in a Commission investigation or penalty, but that were in the same family as a fund that was involved, were larger in total number of dollars than outflows from the fund involved because the former funds collectively had more assets than the latter funds. Ibid., 1051.
188. The negative reaction of investors to funds that were not involved in a Commission investigation or sanction, but that were part of a fund family having a fund that was investigated or sanctioned, is attributable to the psychological process of stimulus generalization. See *Law as Symbol*, supra note 165, at 297–98 (explaining stimulus generalization). Pages 297–98 in *Law as Symbol* are reproduced infra in Part II of Chapter 8.
189. Stephen Choi and Marcel Kahan, *The Market Penalty for Mutual Fund Scandals* (New York Univ. Ctr. for Law & Econ., Working Paper No. 06-07, 2006), 25, 27.
190. 15 U.S.C. § 80b-5 (2006).
191. 15 U.S.C. § 80b-6 (2006).
192. For certified and registered mail, the U.S. Postal Services supplies proof of mailing as well as proof of the date and time of attempted or actual delivery. As a means of confirming delivery, a return receipt can be obtained for a certified letter and a registered letter. Registered mail differs from certified mail in that insurance is available for registered mail to a maximum of $25,000. U.S. Postal Service, A Customer's Guide to Mailing, Adding Extra Services, http://pe.usps.com/text/dmm100/adding.htm (accessed February 3, 2008). For investment companies that send a copy of a Commission order to shareholders, there would seem to be no need for insurance, and certified mail would suffice.
193. E.g., In the Matter of Account Mgmt. Corp., Admin. Proc. File No. 3-8857, Investment Advisors Act Release No. 1529, 1995 SEC LEXIS 2554, at *18, *19 (September 29, 1995); In the Matter of CapitalWorks Inv. Partners, LLC, Admin. Proc. File No. 3-12324, Investment Advisers Act Release No. 2520, 2006 SEC LEXIS 1306, at *9, *10 (June 6, 2006).

194. 15 U.S.C. § 80a-9(f)(1) (2006).
195. Ibid.
196. Ibid.
197. Ibid.
198. 15 U.S.C. § 80a-2(a)(28) (2006).
199. The objectives of the Act include protecting investors from intentional injuries such as those that occur when funds are operated for the benefit of, inter alia, their directors, officers, or investment advisers. 15 U.S.C. § 80a-1(b)(2) (2006).
200. 17 C.F.R. §§ 270.30b1-1, 270.30b1-5 (2009).
201. Section 30 applies to investment companies registered with the Commission. 15 U.S.C. §§ 80a-29(a), 80a-29(b) (2006). Mutual funds, as the term is used in the instant chapter, are by definition registered.
202. Section 34(b) of the Act requires the inclusion in reports of truthful statements and prohibits omissions that cause the included statements to be "materially misleading." 15 U.S.C. § 80a-33(b) (2006). Under federal securities law, a statement that is literally accurate can be materially misleading if, by context or wording, it prevents a reasonable person from comprehending the facts. McMahan & Co. v. Wherehouse Entertainment, Inc., 900 F.2d 576, 579 (2d Cir. 1990), *cert. denied,* 501 U.S. 1249 (1991).
203. 15 U.S.C. §§ 80a-17(a), 80a-17(b) (2006). Section 17(a) covers both first-tier and second-tier affiliated persons of a registered investment company. Ibid. Directors of a fund are first-tier affiliates of the fund under section 2(a)(3)(D). 15 U.S.C. § 80a-2(a)(3)(D) (2006).
204. 15 U.S.C. § 80a-17(e)(1) (2006). Section 17(e)(1) applies to first-tier and second-tier affiliated persons of an investment company that is registered with the Commission. Directors of a fund are first-tier affiliates of their fund through section 2(a)(19)(3)(D) of the Act. 15 U.S.C. § 80a-2(a)(3)(D) (2006). Under section 17(e)(1), the affiliated persons must be serving as an agent of either their fund or another person. Investors Research Corp. v. Sec. & Exch. Comm'n, 628 F.2d 168, 176 (D.C. Cir.), *cert. denied,* 449 U.S. 919 (1980). Section 17(e)(1) prohibits the acceptance of "compensation" by such agents, but compensation does not include either (a) profits earned from transactions in securities in the course of an underwriting or brokerage business or (b) acceptance of "a regular salary or wages from" the investment company. 15 U.S.C. § 80a-17(e)(1) (2006). Outside of these exclusions, the term "compensation" is construed broadly and includes anything that the recipient views as a benefit. United States v. Ostrander, 999 F.2d 27, 31 (2d Cir. 1993). This expansive definition of compensation is not confined to the Act but seems to be found generally in law. E.g., United States v. Rosenthal, 9 F.3d 1016, 1023 (2d Cir. 1993). Section 17(e)(1) is discussed in more detail in *Social Productivity & Law,* supra note 110, at 839–41. Pages 839–41 in *Social Productivity & Law* are reproduced supra in Part VI-D of Chapter 2.
205. A breach of section 17 could also include a violation of section 17(d), which prohibits a first-tier and second-tier affiliated person of a registered investment company from engaging in a joint transaction with the company in which the affiliated person is acting as a principal unless the transaction complies with Rule 17d-1. 15 U.S.C. § 80a-17(d) (2006); 17 C.F.R. § 270.17d-1 (2009).

206. See *In re* Gintel Asset Mgmt., Inc., Admin. Proc. File No. 3-10930, Investment Advisors Act Release No. 2079, 2002 SEC LEXIS 2868, at *33, *41 (November 8, 2002). In *Gintel Asset Management*, an investment adviser that violated the antifraud section of the Investment Advisers Act and the prohibition imposed by the Investment Company Act on trading in securities with an affiliated registered investment company was (a) required to mail a copy of the Commission order to existing clients and (b) barred for one year from "soliciting, marketing, or advertising" to recruit new clients. Ibid.
207. See supra note 193 and its accompanying text.
208. Ctr. for Survey Research, Univ. of Virginia (January 27–April 14, 1996), Roper Center for Public Opinion Research (finding in a survey of United States adults that, to reduce crime, "tougher laws and penalties" were believed by 59 percent of respondents to "help a lot" and by 28 percent to "help somewhat"); Princeton Survey Research Assoc. (August 23–25, 1994), Roper Center for Public Opinion Research (finding in a survey of United States adults that "tougher laws and penalties" were believed by 68 percent of respondents to "help a lot," and by 22 percent of respondents to help "somewhat," as a deterrent to "crime, including white collar crime").
209. Supporting research is found in *Law as Symbol*, supra note 165, at 300 n.65; note 65 in *Law as Symbol* is reproduced infra in Part II of Chapter 8, where it is numbered note 66. In addition, see Chester Britt et al., "A Reassessment of the D.C. Gun Law: Some Cautionary Notes on the Use of Interrupted Time Series Designs for Policy Impact Assessment, *Law & Society Review* 30 (1996): 361 (discussing important features of social science research design for assessing the impact of law, and finding with time-series data and an appropriate control group that the law of a local government regulating the possession of handguns did not affect the homicide rate).

    Contrary to what is popularly assumed, the frequency of crime may determine the probability and severity of punishment for committing crime. Mark Cooney and Callie Harbin Burt, "Less Crime, More Punishment," *American Journal of Sociology* 114 (2008): 491, 493–94. A study of counties in the United States found that higher homicide rates both (a) reduced the likelihood that defendants who had been charged with murder would be convicted and (b) shortened the length of the sentence that was imposed on defendants who had been convicted of murder. Ibid., 511–14.
210. E.g., *In re* Banc of Am. Capital Mgmt, LLC, Investment Company Act Release No. 26756, 2005 SEC LEXIS 291 (February 9, 2005).
211. The fiduciary duties of directors under state law are a form of regulation. Because regulatory law generally seems to have little measurable impact on the occurrence of the conduct with which such law is concerned, the fiduciary duties of directors probably do not often stop either interested directors or non-interested directors from financially exploiting shareholders. Whether directors financially exploit shareholders seems attributable, instead, to factors other than the fiduciary duties of directors and the status of directors under section 2(a)(19).
212. Thurman W. Arnold, *The Symbols of Government* (London: H. Milford, Oxford University Press, 1935), 34.

213. Unfortunately, sociologists have yet to identify with rigorous quantitative research the degree to which, and the paths by which, the symbolism of penalties benefits a society.
214. Cf. Ezzat A. Fattah, "Some Reflections on Crime Prevention Strategies in Large Metropolitan Centres of the 21st Century," *European Journal of Crime, Criminal Law & Criminal Justice* 7 (1999): 130, 131, 135, 141, 146–48 (concluding that the incidence of crime cannot be reduced by law-imposed penalties but may be reduced by certain prevention strategies).
215. Martijn Cremers et al., *Does Skin in the Game Matter? Director Incentives and Governance in the Mutual Fund Industry* (Yale Int'l Ctr. for Fin., Working Paper No. 06-34, 2006), 13–14, 23, http://ssrn.com/abstract=686167 (accessed April 8, 2011) . Another study, which included funds with portfolios consisting of debt securities as well as funds with portfolios consisting of equity securities, found a relationship between the amounts that independent directors personally invested in their funds and the financial performance of the funds. However, the causal direction of the relationship was unclear; i.e., the performance of the funds may have been the antecedent, rather than the effect, of the amount that the directors put into their funds. Meschke, supra note 64, at 17–18.
216. Serious problems of quality in sociology became obvious during the 1980s in the United States. The problems, which were largely caused by sociologists themselves, had developed over the course of the two or three preceding decades. Hubert M. Blalock, Jr., "The Real and Unrealized Contributions of Quantitative Sociology," *American Sociological Review* 54 (1989): 447, 457–58; see Irving Louis Horowitz, *The Decomposition of Sociology* (New York: Oxford University Press, 1993), 12–13, 24. The problems have not been cured; rather, they are continuing and evident today. Alan Wolfe, "Social Skills," *New Republic,* April 23, 2007, 56 (estimating that half of all sociologists are currently advancing a political agenda, not science); Horowitz, supra, at 9, 16–17 (concluding that sociology is in danger of becoming "a pseudoscience" due to the large proportion of sociologists who are political ideologues). For empirical sociologists, however, major improvements in data sets and statistical techniques since the 1980s have dramatically increased the sophistication of their research. Unfortunately, the higher quality of sociological research has evidently failed to enhance the reputation of sociology as a discipline, probably because just a small segment of the professoriate in sociology produces rigorous quantitative research. Dennis J. Downey et al., "The Status of Sociology within the Academy: Where We Are, Why We're There, and How to Change It," *American Sociologist* 39 (2008): 193, 200–1, 203–6 (reporting the results of a survey conducted during the 2006–7 academic year of deans, associate deans, and assistant deans in the College of Arts and Sciences at universities in the United States). Cf. Bruce Keith and Nicholas Babchuk, "The Quest for Institutional Recognition: A Longitudinal Analysis of Scholarly Productivity and Academic Prestige among Sociology Departments," *Social Forces* 76 (1998): 1495 (finding that scholarly articles and books published by faculty members in Ph.D.-granting departments of sociology had just a limited impact on the reputation within sociology of their departments). Nonetheless, the improved data sets and statistical techniques in sociology

permit studies of the sociological aspects of law with a degree of rigor that was not possible a quarter of a century ago. Such studies will be essential to understanding the manner in which law functions in a social system.

217. Palmiter, supra note 62, at 200, 207; Meschke, supra note 64, at 18–19, 38 (finding that the percentage of board seats held by independent directors is not related to the incidence of suits against mutual funds filed by shareholders and the Securities and Exchange Commission).

4

Social Values*

In 2008, the United States experienced a severe contraction in the availability of credit, a marked reduction in the price of common stocks, and an appreciable increase in interest rates on debt instruments issued by business entities and by state and local governments. The premise of Chapter 4 is that this upheaval, although economic in form and sudden in occurrence, stemmed from change that was sociological in character and that started in prior decades. Specifically, the 2008 upheaval in finance is traced to (a) an increased prevalence among Americans of social values stressing hedonism, materialism, and short-term concerns and (b) the suboptimum intellectual skills of the population that this shift in social values is hypothesized to have produced. Quantitative evidence in support of the thesis is presented, and implications of the thesis for provisions of the Investment Company Act are discussed.

I. Introduction

When Americans attempt to account for unwanted large-scale events, they normally focus on the actions of particular individuals. Perhaps because the culture of the United States has traditionally deemphasized the group and favored the individual,[1] conditions and processes in society itself usually escape attention as the source of problems that are broad in scope and intense in magnitude. The inclination of Americans to blame specific people for an adverse societal event, however, ignores an important sociological proposition—that individuals, as members of a society, live in a *social system*, and that a society, being a system, is more than the sum of the individuals in it. Because a society is a system composed of general patterns of social conduct—i.e., because a society is an organized arrangement of recurring interpersonal activities—massive happenings and continuing behaviors that are serious problems for a society are unlikely to be due to action or inaction by identifiable individuals.[2] Rather, a major occurrence in a society, including a major occurrence that is harmful to the society, is related to the character of the society itself.

To use sociological terminology, a society is a set of institutions, i.e., patterns of interpersonal behavior that are central to the continuation of the society.[3] Being components of a system, the institutions of a society are linked. Moreover, the interpersonal activities that are the building blocks for the institutions of a society involve, and are affected by, feedback loops that can create unanticipated difficulties and that can unexpectedly magnify the severity of difficulties, both those foreseen and those unforeseen. Important social problems, in short, manifest conditions and processes embedded in the society in which the problems occur, and when explaining the origin of such problems, Americans need to recognize that "we have met the enemy, and not only may he be ours, he may be us."[4]

Regrettably, the preceding sociological points are typically not considered by law school faculty members, but the points are important because, inter alia, they lead to an awareness that a society can respond to attempted interventions, including interventions by the institution of law, in unwanted ways and with unwanted consequences. Indeed, the systemic character of a society may be responsible for frequent deviations from what was envisioned and desired by the members of the society and its institutions. The instant chapter thus employs a sociological framework, a framework that can aid in understanding the role of law in society.

Given that the systemic nature of social life is customarily overlooked in efforts to identify the causes of problems, an editorial published in September 2008 in a United States newspaper was unusual in explicitly placing responsibility for the upheaval then occurring in U.S. financial markets not on a numerically small group of market professionals but, instead, on Americans generally. "Greed," the editorial explained, "has permeated every level of American society, from the Wall Street bankers and brokers to the middle-class homeowner."[5] Of course, if the upheaval in finance in 2008 had its genesis in the very fabric of the social system rather than in a particular occupation or particular set of individuals, the operation of the finance sector involves matters that are not solely economic. Indeed, this contention is a centerpiece of the instant chapter. Specifically, I will argue that the upheaval stemmed largely from long-term changes in the fabric of the social system in the United States and that, therefore, a key cause of the upheaval was sociological.

Because the concepts and doctrines of the institution of law are products of the society in which they are found,[6] the 2008 disruption of U.S. financial markets can be expected to have ramifications for law. The disruption—which has been described as a "meltdown,"[7] "emergency,"[8] and "crisis"[9] in finance—has had global repercussions,[10] and the finance sector in the United States is likely to be changed by it. Indeed, the finance sector may undergo a restructuring to a degree that is sweeping in scope and historic in significance.[11] If such a restructuring takes place, it will alter U.S. law. Under my premise that sociological conditions were central to creating the 2008 disruption, these conditions must be included when explaining the change in law that results from the disruption.

Before we turn to the key events that marked the 2008 upheaval in financial markets, a point to keep in mind is that, although scholarship by law school faculty members has not come to terms with the sociological nature of the institution of law, that scholarship bears a special responsibility to do so. Scholarship in the discipline of law is employed by courts in writing opinions,[12] and it may also be used in the future by administrative agencies and legislatures. Because publications by scholars in the field of law have practical applications, the publications should contribute to understanding *all* of the causes of a phenomenon that implicates law. The articles and books written by scholars in law on the financial market upheaval of 2008 thus need to examine the contribution of social forces and processes to the upheaval. If these publications do not do so, their utility will be unnecessarily diminished.

II. The Financial Market Upheaval of 2008

The upheaval that occurred in the finance sector in 2008 involved a severe contraction in the availability of credit, a marked reduction in the price of common stocks,[13] and an appreciable increase in interest rates on debt instruments issued by business entities and by state and local governments.[14] The immediate antecedent of the upheaval, according to a number of observers, was a rapid and substantial decline in the market value of owned homes in the United States.[15] The home-price decline produced the upheaval as that decline and a material increase in residential foreclosures reinforced each other.[16] However, the home-price decline was able to trigger the upheaval only because homeownership is widespread in the United States. The popularity of homeownership, in turn, is partially a function of social values,[17] a factor evidencing the systemic character of society.

Although home prices started to fall in 2006, the decline was gradual until the last half of 2007. The S&P/Case-Shiller National Home Price Index,[18] which covers single-family homes in the United States as a whole and is computed for each calendar quarter at the end of the quarter,[19] was 90 percent higher in the second quarter of 2006 than it had been in January 2000, the base period.[20] Between the second quarter of 2006 and the third quarter of 2007, however, the Index fell almost ten percentage points, and during each of the next two quarters, it declined at an even faster quarterly pace—roughly ten percentage points in the fourth quarter of 2007 and about eleven percentage points in the first quarter of 2008. Further (though smaller) quarterly declines were experienced in the second and third quarters of 2008. The result was that the Index was approximately forty percentage points lower in the third quarter of 2008 than at its peak in the second quarter of 2006. At that point (i.e., by the fourth quarter of 2008), the upheaval in finance was unavoidable if it had not already started.[21]

If the decrease in the market price of owned homes in the United States triggered the financial crisis of 2008, an explanation is needed of why it did so. In a system, an immediate antecedent does not activate a major occurrence by itself. Rather, a change in a society brings about a large-scale effect because of certain conditions in the society, and although identifying all of these conditions is not a simple task, they must be uncovered to understand the effect being investigated—here, the upheaval in finance that occurred in 2008.

In order to locate the range of antecedents of the upheaval in finance, we must ascertain the principal factors that formed the economic context of the home-price decline. These factors, while more-distant antecedents of the upheaval, are important because they were links in the chain of causation. When considering the economic factors, however, the social conditions that lay behind them must not be neglected, in part because social conditions have a major bearing on whether and how government regulates finance. Social conditions can lead to (or prevent) a financial problem in a society, because they involve, inter alia, a set of assumptions regarding the prerequisites for a maximally effective economy. The assumptions shape the nature and extent of regulation of the economy,[22] and when a particular set of assumptions is displaced by a different set—which involves change in the social character of a society—one historical era ends and another starts. In the final analysis, then, the structure and regulation of finance result from a set of ideas that has been accepted by society.[23]

Two related economic factors, acting in combination, were apparently central forerunners of the home-price decline that became the immediate antecedent of the 2008 upheaval in finance.[24] As will be evident below, the factors did not materialize suddenly; instead, they developed over an extended time span. The course of each factor over time is visually depicted in a graph below (Figures 4.1 and 4.2). Each graph covers a period that ends in 2008 and uses data on the United States for the fourth quarter of every calendar year included in its time series.

One of the factors responsible for making the home-price decline the immediate antecedent of the 2008 upheaval in finance was the percentage of all housing units in the United States that were occupied by their owners.[25] Yearly data on this percentage are available from 1965 onward[26] and appear in Figure 4.1. An unmistakable, rapid rise in the percentage begins in the mid-1990s. Owner-occupied housing units as a share of all housing units increased from 64.2 percent in 1994 to 69.0 percent in 2005, and then decreased to 67.5 percent in 2008.[27] The 1994–2005 increase has been attributed in large part to the concurrent expansion of lending to "subprime" borrowers,

Figure 4.1
Percentage of Housing Units Occupied by Owner

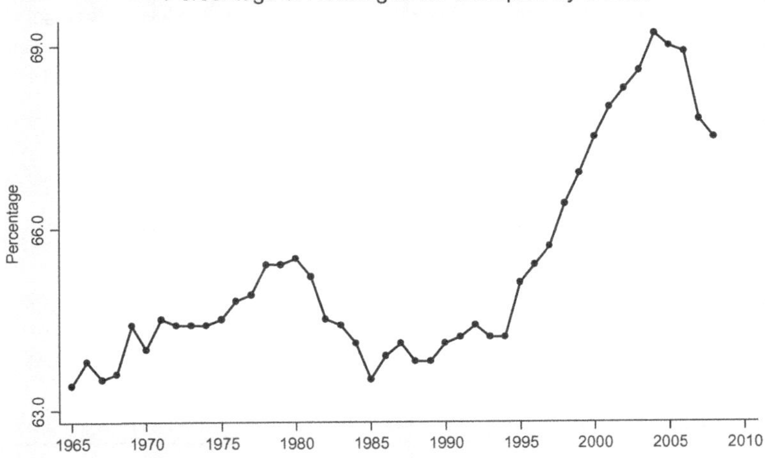

i.e., borrowers who are unable to obtain a loan with a relatively low interest rate because they have been classified as having a high likelihood of defaulting on their financial commitments.[28] In addition, the decline of interest rates during the same period has been viewed as a factor that encouraged the ownership of housing, and the acquisition of more-expensive housing, than would have been acceptable under conventional criteria.[29]

The second factor that made the home-price decline the immediate antecedent of the upheaval in finance was the pressure placed on household income from the financial obligations associated with ownership of a home. Figure 4.2 presents, for the period from 1980 to 2008, the estimated percentage of the total disposable personal income of household members that was devoted each year to payments on mortgages and to payments for mortgage-related expenses, viz., homeowners' insurance and property taxes.[30] A substantial rise in the percentage is evident starting in the last half of the 1990s. To be exact, the portion of household income allocated to mortgages and related expenses went from 8.65 percent in the fourth quarter of 1998 to 11.25 percent in the fourth quarter of 2007.[31]

The decline that began in 2006 in the market price of homes, then, occurred after the segment of the population experiencing financial

Figure 4.2
Percentage of Household Income Devoted to Housing Ownership

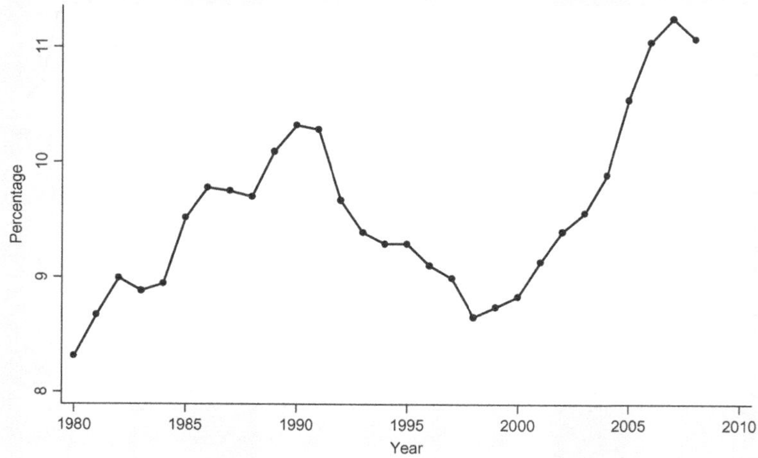

pressure from homeownership had appreciably expanded in size. The increases that had occurred since the mid-1990s in the prevalence of homeownership were accompanied by growth in the share of household income devoted to homeownership expenses. The home-price decline was thus tied to other changes that had taken place in U.S. society, and as residential foreclosures accompanied the decline and became more common, the financial sector was severely disrupted.

III. Sociological Concepts and Financial Market Exigencies

Sociology is a discipline with many specialties and numerous concepts, and it can contribute to understanding exigencies in finance. Two of the concepts traditionally used in sociology[32] seem especially promising as avenues to understanding the upheaval in finance that occurred in 2008. These are the concepts of *social values* and *collective behavior*. Social values are believed to explain, or at least describe, differences between societies at any one point in time[33] and changes within a particular society over time.[34] Collective behavior is considered to be a salient and not-uncommon aspect of social life. The two concepts, accordingly, have become central to the sociological enterprise.

Before the concepts of social values and collective behavior can be discussed, however, each must be defined. In the instant chapter, social values will refer to the ideals that are accepted by the members of a society and that influence the conduct of the members in a variety of situations and over an extended period of time.[35] Values are thus conceptions of the aims of social life that are broad in scope and enduring in duration.

Collective behavior, on the other hand, cannot be readily defined. Sociologists seem not to have agreed on its key elements[36] even though they uniformly accept that certain types of phenomena—e.g., crowds, panics, and riots—involve collective behavior.[37] Declines in securities prices that are large and rapid, including those experienced in 2008, involve collective behavior because panic occurs during the declines and, indeed, is a factor contributing to them.[38] While the central dimensions of collective behavior have yet to be identified by the professionals who study the phenomenon,[39] I will employ the concept of collective behavior to refer to conduct that involves numerous individuals, that has a shared objective or purpose, and that occurs during the same period of time. The conduct of individuals that comprises collective behavior, however, is not merely the sum of the conduct of each individual; the behavior is *collective* because the conduct of each participant affects, and is affected by, the conduct of other participants. The conduct of participants in collective behavior, moreover, exhibits some degree of spontaneity (popularly known as "emotion"); the participants in an instance of collective behavior may not have a single set of leaders; and a large proportion of the participants may not interact face-to-face or intend to exchange communications. Collective behavior can involve individuals who are strangers if the conduct of some of them prompts and/or reinforces the conduct of others.

Unfortunately, the sociological specialty of collective behavior seems not to have developed a cohesive body of knowledge that includes relatively precise estimates of the magnitude of relationships between pertinent variables and that is derived from a substantial number of empirical (let alone quantitative) studies. The situation may be due to the serious impediments confronting research on collective behavior,[40] but whatever the reason(s), the situation is likely to account, at least in part, for the present inability of sociologists to agree on a definition of collective behavior as a phenomenon. Simply put, useful knowledge regarding collective behavior is limited.[41] Accordingly, the instant chapter will not consider collective behavior further, but readers should be aware that sociologists will in time unearth important aspects of collective behavior that will shed light on events such as the 2008 upheaval in finance.[42]

The remainder of the chapter will focus on social values, the change that the United States has experienced in specific social values during the last several decades, and one consequence of the change in values that is especially important for American society. In particular, I concentrate on social values characterizing the population of the United States with regard to hedonism, materialism, and time horizon—three dimensions that can be distinguished as concepts but that are probably correlated empirically.[43] In terms of hedonism, the question is the extent to which personal pleasure is emphasized and pursued in a society. In terms of materialism, the question is the extent to which goods and services classifiable as luxuries are sought in a society instead of intellectual and spiritual development. In terms of time horizon, the question is the extent to which short-term considerations or long-term considerations matter in a society. To illustrate time horizon, short-term considerations are manifested, inter alia, in the desire for rewards quickly (often labeled "immediate gratification") rather than rewards later ("deferred gratification"). Social values that endorse hedonism, materialism, and a short-term orientation are relevant to the instant chapter because they and their impact on the intellectual skills of the U.S. population are likely antecedents of the financial sector upheaval of 2008.[44] As a result of these social values and the suboptimum analytical acumen to which they led, Americans invested and spent in ways and to an extent that were imprudent. A severe disruption in the operation of financial markets, with its large-scale effect on the economy, was the eventual outcome.

IV. Change in Social Values in the United States

I now present quantitative data bearing on the extent of and change in social values that measure hedonism, materialism, and time horizon among Americans. The evidence considered as a whole supports the conclusion that hedonism, materialism, and short-term considerations have been appreciably more widespread among Americans in recent years than in the past, but the reader should be aware that the evidence is neither as complete nor as exact as I would like. In particular, I was able to locate just two studies that have repeatedly drawn samples over time from the U.S. population and asked members of the samples to answer questions revealing the members' social values on hedonism, materialism, and/or time horizon. While neither of the two studies utilized a question that was both facially valid[45] and pertinent,[46] each study asked a question that gauges indirectly at least one of the values. Data from both studies are reported below in Part IV-A. To supplement the two studies, Part IV-A also presents quantitative data that reveal change over time in several manifestations of the values of interest here. In Part IV-B, I review data on the intellectual skills of the U.S. population and contend that these skills have been damaged by the shift that has occurred in social values on hedonism, materialism, and time horizon. Shifts in values are important not only in their own right but also for the societal problems they create.[47]

A. Measures of Social Values

I begin with the two studies that asked respondents to answer a question concerned with the social values on which I am focusing. The first is the Monitoring the Future ("MTF") study, which began in 1975 and is a recurring, annual survey of a nationwide sample of students who are in their last year of high school prior to graduation, i.e., who are enrolled in their senior year of high school.[48] Every year the questionnaire for the MTF study has asked the respondents to "disagree," "mostly disagree," "mostly agree," "agree," or "neither" disagree nor agree with the statement that "To me, work is nothing more than making a living."[49] Responses to the statement are presumed to measure the presence or absence of hedonism.

Figure 4.3 presents the yearly percentages of high school seniors who, in responding to the statement on whether "work is nothing more than making a living," answered either "agree" or "mostly agree" and who, by doing so, portrayed themselves as hedonistic. The percentages are shown for each sex, because the indicators of hedonism—i.e., the responses "agree" and "mostly agree"—are found among females as a group noticeably less often than among males as a group. Figure 4.3 covers the entire period for which MTF data have been published, viz., 1975 through 2008.[50]

Figure 4.3 reveals secular change over time in the prevalence of hedonism among males and among females. Specifically, a steady and substantial rise in hedonism took place from the first half of the 1980s to the last half of the 1990s, at which point the prevalence of hedonism reached a plateau. The increase in hedonism, however, was somewhat larger among males than females, and as a result, the sex gap in this plateau is greater than the sex gap during the early part

Figure 4.3 Hedonism among High School Seniors

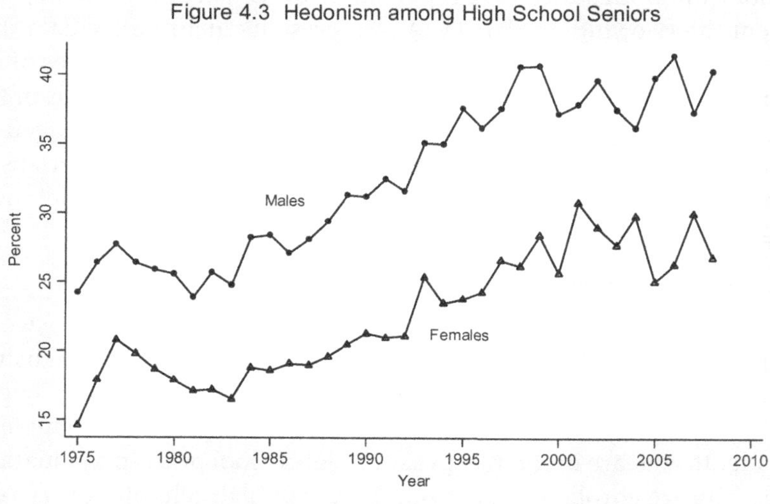

of the period covered by Figure 4.3. To illustrate, the gap in percentage points ranged from 8.5 to 9.6 in 1975–1976 and from 8.0 to 9.8 in 1985–1986. In 1995–1996, however, the gap in percentage points ranged from 11.9 to 13.8, and in 2005–2006, it ranged from 14.7 to 15.1. In the latest year for which data are available (2008), the sex gap was 13.5 percentage points.

The second study that probed pertinent social values through responses to a question asked of cross-sections of the U.S. population is the General Social Survey ("GSS"). The GSS has been conducted annually or biennially since 1972 and obtains data on a variety of characteristics of adults (i.e., persons eighteen years of age and older) who reside in the United States, although interviewees were limited to English-speaking adults until 2006.[51] The GSS is relevant here because it has frequently included a question on the aspects of employment that respondents consider most important. Specifically, interviewees have been shown a card naming five aspects of employment and asked to designate "which one thing on this list you would most prefer in a job." One of the aspects named was "high income."[52] Income level, of course, affects the ability of the income recipients to acquire consumable goods and services. Responses to this question, accordingly, can be expected to reveal, albeit imperfectly, the prevalence of materialism and hedonism.[53] The question was asked in almost every year from 1973 through 1994 that the GSS was conducted, but after 1994, it was not asked again until 2006.[54]

Given the utility of the question and the lengthy time span for which data on it are available, I turn to the percentages of Whites[55] in each year who considered "high income" the most desirable feature of a job.[56] The data are for respondents of both sexes who were 20–29 years old.[57] Two reasons account for the age restriction. First, to the extent that the values of the age group 20–29 diverge from the values of older age groups and are largely unaffected by the aging process, the values of the population as a whole will, ceteris paribus, move gradually toward the values that are held by persons at age 20–29 because, with the passage of time, the members of the older cohorts die and are replaced by the members of the younger cohorts. Second, persons who were 20–29 years old in the 1970s are likely to have still been economically active during the years immediately preceding the financial sector upheaval of 2008. Indeed, during the decade prior to the upheaval, aging and cohort succession had probably placed members of this age group in influential positions in finance, and aging had evidently led a large proportion of them to become securities investors.[58] The social values of persons 20–29 years old thus offer useful evidence of the social values that led to the 2008 upheaval in finance.

What do the data reveal? Among Whites 20–29 years old, high income was ranked as the most important aspect of a job by 12.8 percent in 1973 and by 9.9 percent in 1974. In every subsequent year in which the question was asked, however, the percentages were materially larger, although quite variable. In 1976 and 1977, the percentages were 20.9 and 16.6, respectively, and during the 1980s, the percentages ranged from 16.2 to 35.1. From 1990 to 1994, the percentages were between 20.4 and 25.1, and in 2006, the last year the question was included in the GSS, 18.8 percent regarded high income as the most preferred aspect of a job. Although the post-1975 percentages cover a substantial range, the data for 1973–2006 as a whole suggest that, after the first half of the 1970s, hedonism and materialism became much more common in the United States and their prevalence remained elevated.

I turn now to another type of evidence. While social values are abstractions from human behavior, they are embodied in behavior. Behavioral patterns are observable, of course, and can be (and have been) measured. We can thus take advantage of quantitative data on behavioral patterns manifesting hedonism, materialism, and/or a short-term time horizon. These manifestations include the following:

- Obesity, which evidently becomes more probable with increases in physical inactivity and amount of food (especially fat) consumed,[59] grew steadily more common among adults 20–74 years old in the United States between 1960–1962 and 2003–2006.[60] Adjusting for change over time in the age distribution of persons 20–74 years old, obesity was two-and-a-half times more prevalent in 2003–2006 than it had been in 1960–1962.[61]
- The median number of square feet of floor area in new single-family houses that were sold in the United States fluctuated around 1,600 during the period 1978–1985 but rose to approximately 2,200 during the period 2004–2008.[62] Between the former period and the latter period, consequently, the median amount of living space acquired by U.S. residents buying a new one-family house increased by 37 percent.
- Of all new cars that were sold annually in the United States, the fraction classified as "small" decreased from no less than one out of two during model years 1975 through 1995 to fewer than two out of five in model year 2008.[63]
- The ratio of total household debt—i.e., consumer debt and mortgage debt—to disposable personal income in the United States rose

> appreciably from the first half of the 1950s to the last half of the 1960s, remained at a plateau until the middle of the 1980s, and then increased rapidly.[64] The result was that total household debt was 108 percent of disposable personal income in 2004 and 128 percent in 2008.[65] While an increase in mortgage debt accounted for most of the growth in household debt, consumer debt materially expanded, too.[66] During the two decades that preceded the financial crisis of 2008, Americans thus became steadily more reliant on borrowed money to finance their consumption of goods and services rather than defer consumption until they had accumulated the money for it.[67]

The debt of households, however, is not the sole form of debt that manifests the extent of hedonism, materialism, and short-term thinking in a society. The debt of governments at the state and local level is also a useful indicator. Compared to the federal government, state and local governments are (or at least are widely believed to be) more closely attuned and responsive to the everyday wishes of their respective populations.[68]

Figure 4.4 provides a yardstick for the debt per capita of state and local governments in the United States during the period from 1960 to 2006 (the latest year for which data were available). The yardstick was

Figure 4.4 Inflation-Adjusted Debt Per Capita of State and Local Governments in the United States: 1960 to 2006

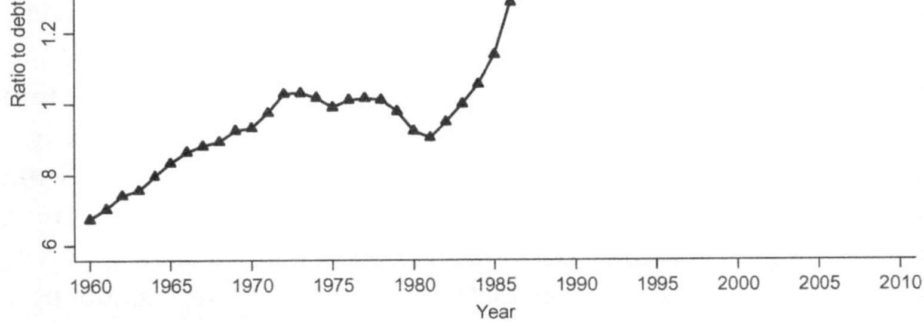

developed with a two-step procedure. In the first step, the number of dollars per capita owed by state and local governments in each year[69] was multiplied by the Consumer Price Index for the same year.[70] In the second step, the amounts obtained in the first step were divided by the amount obtained in the first step for 1983. In Figure 4.4, therefore, 1983 is the base year, i.e., 1983 is set at 1.00, and the per-capita debt of state and local governments in a given year is the ratio of the per-capita debt in that year to the per-capita debt in 1983. The calculation procedure allows Figure 4.4 to show change over time in the debt per capita of state and local governments with the purchasing power of U.S. currency held constant.

Figure 4.4 reveals that an increase in the level of indebtedness of state and local governments occurred after 1960 and continued until the first half of the 1970s. From 1972 to 1978, the indebtedness of state and local governments was essentially unchanged, and it then declined slightly until 1982. After 1982, however, indebtedness began a long-term, substantial rise, and in 2006, indebtedness was 1.87 times (i.e., 87 percent) larger than in 1983. Over the last two decades covered by Figure 4.4, in short, the constituents of state and local governments sought and obtained infrastructure and services by having these governmental entities borrow the necessary money. The result was an appreciable enlargement of state and local government debt per capita. Because change in the purchasing power of the U.S. dollar has been statistically controlled, the increase in debt from the early 1980s onward that is visible in Figure 4.4 cannot be attributed to inflation. Nor can the increase be attributed to simple numerical growth in the population because indebtedness has been measured per person.

B. Social Values and Intellectual Skills

There is reason to believe that, during the last half of the twentieth century, intellectual acumen among younger cohorts, while rising, was not increasing as rapidly as it had among cohorts that were at the same age at prior points in time.[71] Although relatively little is known about this change—for instance, whether it happened gradually over numerous cohorts or abruptly over just a few cohorts—available evidence strongly suggests that the intellectual abilities of the U.S. population have not been maximized. Among U.S. adults 19–64 years old in 2003, for example, fewer than one out of five was deemed to be "proficient" in prose and quantitative literacy; one out of eight or nine (depending on age category) was classified as "below basic" in prose literacy; and approximately one out of five was considered to be "below basic" in quantitative literacy.[72]

Scholars have recognized that the emergence of suboptimum intellectual skills creates serious potential problems for the United States,[73] and I believe that it was a factor in the upheaval that took place in the financial sector during 2008. Specifically, my contention is that the financial-sector upheaval of 2008 was the outcome of a number of antecedents that occurred in sequence. The immediate antecedent of the upheaval was imprudent investing and spending by individuals and entities. The unwise investing and wasteful spending that preceded the upheaval, however, did not occur in a societal vacuum. Instead, they temporally followed and were produced by broad social changes. At least two such social changes can be identified: (a) hedonism, materialism, and a short-term time horizon became more widespread among Americans and (b) the foregoing shift in social values prevented the members (especially the youthful members) of the population from maximizing their intellectual abilities.[74]

In short, my thesis is that social values in the United States were the root of the financial-sector upheaval of 2008. In proposing this thesis, I assume that social values as to hedonism, materialism, and time horizon are intertwined, i.e., are a set of values, and that, if this set is affecting one dimension of a society, it is affecting other dimensions, too. Research has found that, during the 1980s and first half of the 1990s, social values favoring materialism had a negative impact on the level of trust in others.[75] Accordingly, the increased prevalence of social values promoting hedonism, materialism, and time horizon is a plausible factor causing an array of societal problems, including impairment of intellectual skills.

What approach most accurately assesses the intellectual abilities of the population of a country? When countries are competing economically with each other, as they increasingly are, the most appropriate assessment is a comparison of the countries in terms of the performance by their residents on standardized tests. I follow this approach and compare the United States with other countries that are members of the Organization for Economic Cooperation and Development ("OECD"). All comparisons are based on data for fifteen-year-old students in the latest year for which data are available.[76] The comparisons illustrate the disquieting degree to which the intellectual abilities of the U.S. population are wanting. Notably, the general ranking of the United States among OECD countries has been roughly the same for several decades.[77] Accordingly, the intellectual skills of U.S. teenagers in recent years do not merely foreshadow the intellectual skills of the future adult population of the United States; they are also indicative of the intellectual skills of a large share of the current adult population.

- On a measure of mathematics literacy, the average score in the United States was significantly lower than the average score in twenty-three of thirty OECD countries; the average score in the United States was significantly higher than the average score in only four of the thirty countries.[78]
- On three scales measuring science literacy, the average combined score in the United States was significantly lower than the average combined score in sixteen of thirty OECD countries; the average combined score in the United States was significantly higher than the average combined score in just five of the thirty countries.[79]
- On a test of problem-solving ability, the average score in the United States was significantly lower than the average score in twenty-two of twenty-nine OECD countries; the average score in the United States was significantly higher than the average score in just three of the twenty-nine countries.[80]

To conclude Part IV, the evidence presented indicates that broad, fundamental change has occurred in the character of U.S. society since the middle of the twentieth century. The evidence is consistent with my thesis that the upheaval in finance during 2008 stemmed from conditions that emerged over a relatively long time span and that became part of the fabric of U.S. society. The upheaval thus did not result merely from mismanagement in the financial sector and/or from inadequate government regulation.[81] If the thesis is correct, its implications for the regulation of investment companies in the United States should be explored. I turn now to that task.

V. Investment Company Act

In a remarkably short period of time, investment companies have become an important and salient component of the financial resources of Americans. Few developments in the history of finance in the United States are likely to match, in magnitude and speed, the post-1980 embrace of investment companies by Americans and the corresponding growth in the assets of these companies. The significance of U.S. investment companies—particularly mutual funds[82]—may be understood by placing them in a global context: Mutual funds in the

United States are responsible for managing more wealth than mutual funds in any other nation as measured by the market value of assets under management.[83] Indeed, in 2008, the net assets of mutual funds in the United States comprised fully half (50.6 percent) of the net assets of all mutual funds in the world.[84] Given this proportion and the strong links now existing between securities markets in the United States and securities markets in other countries,[85] U.S. law on mutual funds is important to the finance sector globally.

What is an investment company under U.S. law? The answer is found in the Investment Company Act ("Act"),[86] which was adopted by Congress in 1940.[87] In general terms, the Act classifies an entity as an investment company if the entity (a) issues securities to individuals and entities in exchange for financial assets, (b) uses these assets to invest in securities of other issuers, and (c) is unable to qualify for a statutory exclusion from investment company status.[88] An investment company is thus an entity that pools assets from the holders of its securities, i.e., from its investors, in order to acquire securities issued by others and seek a monetary profit for its securities holders. An entity that is deemed by the Act to be an investment company is subject to the requirements of the Act and to regulation by the Securities and Exchange Commission ("Commission") pursuant to the Act.[89]

The Investment Company Act recognizes different types of investment companies,[90] but in terms of wealth under management, open-end management investment companies[91]—i.e., mutual funds[92]—are the main type. An indicator of the importance of mutual funds in the United States to the finance sector of the country is that the investment portfolios of the funds in December 2008 had a market value of approximately $9.6 trillion.[93] The wealth managed by mutual funds has important societal ramifications, because 82 percent of it derives from the 45 percent of U.S. households that are fund investors[94] and because it represents more than one-fifth of the retirement assets of U.S. households.[95] Given that a large fraction of Americans have a monetary stake in mutual funds and have entrusted the funds with a sizeable fraction of their retirement assets, the utility of U.S. law applicable to the funds is of the utmost importance to Americans individually and collectively.[96]

In light of the societal significance of the Investment Company Act, I examine sections of the Act that seem especially pertinent to exigencies in securities markets. In particular, I have chosen sections of the Act for review that may have reduced damage to securities markets from the 2008 upheaval in finance or that, with revision, may minimize such damage from future upheavals.[97] In this regard, the determination of whether these sections were beneficial, or can be altered so that they will be beneficial, should take into consideration the sociological antecedents of the 2008 upheaval. As attributes of U.S. society, the sociological antecedents of the 2008 upheaval can shape the content of U.S. law,[98] and they are accordingly important for assessing statutory provisions on investment companies.

A. Sections 3(c)(1) and 3(c)(7)

Subsections 1 and 7 of section 3(c)[99] of the Act are based on the public—private dichotomy that is widespread in American society and, hence, in its law.[100] The subsections establish conditions under which an entity will not be classified as an investment company even though the entity would be designated an investment company by section 3(a).[101] An entity that meets the requirements of either subsection 1 or subsection 7 is not an investment company under the Act and is not governed by any of the provisions of the Act (with exceptions[102] to be reviewed infra[103]).

Subsection 1, which was included in the Act when it was adopted in 1940,[104] covers an entity when the securities that the entity has issued to investors have a maximum of one hundred beneficial owners and have not been publicly offered for sale.[105] Congress incorporated subsection 1 into the Act because it wanted to prevent the regulation of "private companies in which there is no significant public interest,"[106] but believed that an entity was operating in the private sphere only if both criteria specified in the subsection were satisfied. An entity cannot escape investment company status through subsection 1, accordingly, unless one hundred or fewer persons beneficially own the securities of the entity *and* these securities were sold privately.

Subsection 7, too, is directed at preventing government regulation of private entities,[107] but unlike subsection 1, subsection 7 does not limit the number of investors.[108] Under subsection 7, which was adopted in 1996,[109] an entity is not an investment company if (a) all of its investors (with certain exceptions) are "qualified purchasers" when they acquire the securities issued by the entity and (b) the offer of the securities to investors is conducted by the entity in a manner that is not public. Because "qualified purchasers" are individuals and entities with investments amounting to no less than $5 million,[110] they were presumed by Congress to be experienced, knowledgeable investors.[111]

A vehicle for investing in securities can develop a portfolio that has substantial monetary value, but an entity (e.g., a mutual fund) that is an investment company under section 3 of the Act is subject to section 18 and to the ceiling it imposes on borrowing.[112] A vehicle for investing in securities that satisfies either subsection 1 or subsection 7 of section 3(c), on the other hand, is not classified as an investment company and escapes the limitation on borrowing imposed by the Act. The latter type of vehicle includes hedge funds. Thus, hedge funds, which meet the requirements of one of the subsections, are not circumscribed by section 18 in their ability to borrow.[113] Borrowing, of course, allows a fund to acquire a larger quantity of securities than could be acquired with just the money provided by its investors, and borrowing can thus increase not only profits but losses.[114] Because their investments can be made with an appreciable amount of borrowed money,[115] hedge funds are thought to have played a major role in the marked decline that took place during 2008 in the prices of common stocks and corporate debt securities.[116]

What are the implications for subsections 1 and 7 of the greater prevalence of hedonism, materialism, and short-term time horizon that now characterize the U.S. population? Although the implications are undoubtedly multiple and complex, I discuss just one here. In particular, I believe that one likely result of current social values is that, ceteris paribus, hedge funds are able to attract a substantially larger number of individuals as investors than they would otherwise attract, because Americans are more inclined than in the past to seek immediate monetary rewards and consider such rewards obtainable.[117] At the same time, unfortunately, individuals who are willing to entrust financial resources to a hedge fund are not on average as capable of understanding the risks of hedge-fund investments as they would have been with the intellectual skills they could have acquired.

The preceding conclusion, if correct, suggests that subsections 1 and 7 should be amended in a way that appreciably reduces the proportion of the U.S. population that is eligible to invest in hedge funds. For example, the subsections might be revised to mandate that an individual be an "experienced investor" in order to invest as a principal in a hedge fund. The definition of the concept of "experienced investor" would differ from the definition of the concept of "accredited investor" in the Securities Act and Regulation D under the Securities Act.[118] To be an "experienced investor" under the Investment Company Act, an individual would need to demonstrate a personal history of investing in securities, and perhaps other types of property (e.g., commodities),[119] as a principal and/or as an agent; the personal history would need to have involved the investment of a specified and substantial minimum amount of money; and the investment history would need to have occurred over a designated minimum number of years. Otherwise stated, an entity that, but for subsection 1 or subsection 7, would be an investment company could not accept an individual as an investor under the suggested revision of the subsections unless the individual met standards considerably more restrictive than the current net worth and income standards that an individual is required to meet in order to be an "accredited investor" under Regulation D.[120]

B. Section 7(d)

As a nation becomes enmeshed in a global economy, it can be expected to experience an increase in cross-country financial activities. With globalization, accordingly, a vehicle for investing in securities that was established and is located outside the United States is likely to seek opportunities to recruit investors within the United States. The Investment Company Act, through section 7(d),[121] addresses this situation. The section was designed to prevent a foreign investment company from exposing the U.S. public to risks from activities and arrangements that Congress believed were unacceptable for domestic investment companies.[122]

Section 7(d) applies to an entity the activities of which meet the criteria for an investment company stated in section 3 of the Act but which was formed under the law of a country other than the United States. Unless the entity (i.e., foreign investment company) registers with, and subjects itself to the jurisdiction of, the Securities and Exchange Commission, it and its underwriters are prohibited by section 7(d) from utilizing interstate commerce or mail in the United States (a) to make a public offer to sell the securities it issues or (b) to sell such securities, or deliver such securities after sale, if the sale/delivery is connected to a public offer. Although section 7(d) is inapplicable to nonpublic offers and sales,[123] section 3(c)(1) allows no more than one hundred U.S. residents to invest in a foreign investment company that privately offers and sells its securities using interstate commerce or mail.[124] Section 3(c)(7), on the other hand, permits such a foreign investment company to have an unlimited number of U.S. residents as investors, but only if the investors are qualified purchasers.[125]

While section 7(d) explicitly allows a foreign investment company to engage in a public offering and sale of its securities in the United States by registering with the Commission, registration is possible only if the company meets a series of conditions and secures Commission approval.[126] As a result, section 7(d) is believed to be the reason that just a small number of foreign investment companies have chosen to offer and sell their securities publicly in this country.[127] However, the impact of the section in excluding many foreign investment companies from the United States seems to have had an unintended effect—even public offers and public sales by foreign investment companies that would be advantageous to U.S. investors have been prevented.[128] As a result, the Commission recommended in 1973 and in 1984 that Congress amend section 7(d) to expand the conditions under which a foreign investment company can offer and sell its securities publicly in the United States.[129]

Section 7(d) was not revised in response to the recommendations of the Commission.[130] However, during the quarter of a century since the last recommendation was made, the ties between the U.S. economy and the economies of other nations have expanded. The pressure to modify section 7(d) is likely to have intensified, therefore, and an effort to rewrite the section in the foreseeable future would not be surprising.

Should Congress decide to revise section 7(d), the concerns arising from the shift in social values and its impact on intellectual skills, discussed supra in Part V-A with regard to subsections (c)(1) and (c)(7) of section 3, need to be addressed, both because the concerns have a bearing on foreign investment companies and because the concerns exacerbate a problem that is unique to these companies. This problem—i.e., the problem for section 7(d) and foreign investment companies that is magnified by the change in social values and its effect on intellectual acumen—involves a principle from the field of linguistics. When a foreign investment company makes a public offer of its securities in the United States, differences between the English language and the language of the country that is the home of the foreign investment company pose a potential hurdle to preparing a prospectus that communicates, effectively and thoroughly, concepts that are important to U.S. investors.[131] Concepts are conveyed by, inter alia, words in a language, but a word typically has multiple referents and can carry subtle connotations. Because the meaning of a word depends on the situation and culture[132] in which the word is utilized,[133] the concept represented by a word in one language may not be fully understood, let alone correctly explained, by persons who have been reared in another language.[134] If section 7(d) is to be amended so that a larger number of foreign investment companies are permitted to recruit investors from the U.S. public, Congress as well as the Commission will need to confront the problems of communication posed by differences between English and the language(s) used in the country of a foreign investment company that seeks Commission approval to offer and sell shares of the company publicly in the United States. This problem is made more difficult by the suboptimum intellectual skills of the U.S. population, but it may be mitigated if a rule of the Commission under section 7(d), as revised, mandates that a foreign investment company must have its English-language prospectus and sales materials written by an individual (a) who is fluent both in English and in the language(s) of the home country of the investment company, *and* (b) who has lived for an appreciable period in both the United States and the home country.[135] Residence in the home country allows an individual to learn the subtle meanings of words that are difficult, if not impossible, to acquire through language training in a classroom located elsewhere.

C. Section 12(d)(1)

An investment company that buys or otherwise comes to own more than a small percentage of the shares issued by one or more other investment companies—i.e., a fund of funds—poses a number of risks beyond those that are common to all securities investments. The investors in a fund of funds, of course, are subject to such risks. Moreover, when redeemable shares[136] are issued by a fund of funds to its investors and are acquired by a fund of funds for its portfolio, a number of risks exist for the investment companies that are in the portfolio of the fund of funds, and even for the financial sector as a whole. Two risks of a fund of funds merit attention here. The first is that the investors in a fund of funds may be unaware of all of the types of securities in which they have a financial interest and may not recognize when the fund of funds has a potential for investment losses that is substantially greater than the investors realize.[137] The risk arises because investors in a fund of funds have a financial interest in securities not just directly but indirectly as well—the investors in a fund of funds own shares of the fund of funds, and they also have an interest in the securities that comprise the portfolios of the underlying funds, i.e., the individual funds that are currently held by the fund of funds. Complexity is thus built into a fund of funds, and the complexity is not conducive to a full understanding of the character of a fund of funds by its investors.[138]

The second risk of a fund of funds exists when the fund of funds issues redeemable shares to its investors and owns redeemable shares issued by other investment companies ("underlying funds"). A redeemable share requires its issuer to transfer cash or securities in its portfolio to the redeeming party in an amount equal to the current market value of the share redeemed.[139] In the context of a fund of funds, the risk stemming from redeemable shares can materialize in at least three ways.

First, a fund of funds that issues redeemable securities may experience a substantial redemption from its investors and be forced to redeem shares of some or all underlying funds. Second, even though investors in the fund of funds are not withdrawing, a fund of funds may decide to exercise its right to redeem shares of underlying funds. In either event, a redemption demand made on a single underlying fund that manages sizeable assets, or on numerous underlying funds that in combination manage sizeable assets, can force the underlying fund(s) to sell a large quantity of portfolio securities. The result may be an appreciable decline in the market price of the portfolio securities that are sold by the underlying fund(s), and even in the market price of securities generally.[140]

A third way in which redeemable securities held by a fund of funds can create risk is that the fund of funds may threaten, explicitly or implicitly, to redeem shares of an underlying fund. The potential for a significant redemption by a fund of funds can lead to actions by the underlying fund that would otherwise not occur. For example, concern with a potential redemption can affect decision making by the manager of the underlying fund as to the amount of cash to have on hand and as to particular securities to have in the portfolio of the fund.[141] The Investment Company Act, however, was adopted partly because of the damage to the public welfare inflicted by investment companies that were responsive to the wishes of other investment companies or the persons controlling the latter.[142]

The above risks were among those that subsections (A), (B), and (C) of section 12(d)(1)[143] were designed to reduce or eliminate, especially insofar as the risks emanate from funds of funds located outside the United States.[144] These subsections impose quantitative limits[145] on an investment company in acquiring the shares of another investment company and/or in selling its shares to another investment company,[146] unless each of the investment companies is not (and need not be) registered with the Securities and Exchange Commission. However, as pointed out in Part V-A supra, subsections (A)(i) and (B)(i) of section 12(d)(1) apply to an investment vehicle that, while satisfying section 3(a) of the Act, is not required to register because the vehicle meets the requirements of either section 3(c)(1) or section 3(c)(7).[147] Such a vehicle is subject to subsections (A)(i) and (B)(i) of section 12(d)(1) even though it is otherwise not regarded by the Act as an investment company.

Under subsection (A)(i),[148] an investment company can currently own a maximum of 3 percent of the outstanding voting shares of any other investment company, a limit that is supplemented in subsection (A)(ii)[149] by a requirement that the acquiring investment company commit no more than 5 percent of its assets (measured by market value) to securities issued by the acquired investment company. An additional restraint is contained in subsection (A)(iii),[150] which allows an investment company to invest a maximum of 10 percent of the market value of its assets in securities issued by two or more investment companies.

Under subsection (B)(i),[151] an open-end investment company that is (or that is required to be) registered with the Commission cannot sell its voting shares to another investment company, whether or not registered, if the open-end investment company is aware that the sale will result in ownership of more than 3 percent of its outstanding voting shares by the acquiring investment company. Subsection (B)(ii),[152] furthermore, allows such sales only if a maximum of 10 percent of the outstanding voting shares of the open-end investment company will be owned by two or more investment companies, whether registered or unregistered.

Subsection (C) is the counterpart of subsection (B) for a closed-end investment company, i.e., a fund that issues nonredeemable securities.[153] Under subsection (C),[154] a maximum of 10 percent of the outstanding voting shares of a registered closed-end fund can be acquired by a registered investment company or an unregistered investment company.[155] Because of subsection (C), accordingly, a fund of funds that includes, or wants to include, a registered closed-end fund in its portfolio is subject to the same quantitative limit that subsection (B)(ii) applies to a registered open-end fund.

Congress believed that subsections (A)–(C) were adequate to deal with the risks that it concluded funds of funds posed to the public welfare,[156] but Congress adopted the subsections in 1970.[157] Since then, four decades have elapsed, and the United States has undergone considerable change. Given the shift in social values and its effect on intellectual skills (as described supra in Part IV), has the ability of the subsections to handle the risks posed by funds of funds been undermined?

In answering the question, I begin with the problem that investors in a fund of funds will not thoroughly understand the types of securities that determine the investment performance of the fund of funds. This problem is likely to have been exacerbated by the changes that have occurred in U.S. society over the last four decades. Compared to the decades that preceded the final quarter of the twentieth century, a larger proportion of Americans today, ceteris paribus, probably can be attracted to investment vehicles that may produce substantial profits quickly. However, because of changes in U.S. society, the intellectual skills of Americans are lower than would otherwise be the case. The result is that an unnecessarily large proportion of individuals can be lured by a type of investment vehicle that they do not fully understand because they lack the intellectual acumen to formulate relevant questions and analyze the information that such questions would uncover.

A second problem created by societal change since the middle of the twentieth century involves the potential for conflicts of interest in a fund of funds. In judging whether subsections (A)–(C) adequately safeguard the public welfare at the present time, consideration should be given to a statutory exception to the quantitative limits of the three subsections. The exception is in subsection (G) of section 12(d)(1),[158] which subsection was added in 1996.[159] In pertinent part, subsection (G) authorizes a family of open-end investment companies that are registered with the Commission to establish and offer publicly a registered open-end investment company that confines its portfolio to other open-end funds in the family and certain other types of securities.[160]

Conflicts of interest are a central concern of the Investment Company Act,[161] and such conflicts are more than a remote possibility when a fund invests in funds within the same family. Indeed, conflicts of interest may be unavoidable when a fund of funds belongs to the same set of investment companies as its underlying funds. An investment adviser has a fiduciary duty to each of its clients,[162] but if all of the funds involved in a fund of funds created under subsection (G) are served by the same investment adviser—i.e., if the selection of portfolio securities for the fund of funds and for the underlying funds is the responsibility of a single-investment adviser—the loyalties of the investment adviser are divided. In serving the fund of funds, the adviser has a duty to make the decisions that are best for the fund of funds, but in serving the underlying funds, the adviser is obligated to be loyal to the underlying funds. Because situations can develop that require the fund of funds to act in a manner that is harmful to one or more of the underlying funds, the interests of the fund of funds can diverge from the interests of one or more underlying funds.

To illustrate, assume that a family of funds has established a fund of funds pursuant to subsection (G) and that fund X and fund Y in the family are eligible for the portfolio of the fund of funds. Assume further that the investment objective, strategy, and/or performance of fund X appreciably change and that fund X has become more suitable than fund Y to the fund of funds. Assume finally that the fund of funds currently does not invest in fund X but that (a) it invests in fund Y and (b) its investment in fund Y is a significant percentage of the assets of fund Y. In this situation, the fund of funds should substitute fund X for fund Y, but the substitution will work to the detriment of fund Y because the latter will lose a significant portion of its assets. If the same entity is the investment adviser to the fund of funds, to fund X, and to fund Y, the adviser suffers from an irreconcilable conflict of interest. On behalf of the fund of funds, the adviser should mandate the substitution by ordering that the fund of funds redeem the shares of fund Y it holds and use the proceeds of the redemption to purchase shares of fund X. On behalf of fund X, the adviser should welcome this decision. However, on behalf of fund Y, the adviser should oppose the substitution. The action by the investment adviser that is required for one client in the above situation is incompatible with the action that is required for another client, preventing the investment adviser from fulfilling its fiduciary duty both to the fund of funds and to fund Y.

To summarize, a fund of funds that is operated by a family of open-end funds and that includes in its portfolio other funds in the family—i.e., a fund of funds created under subsection (G) of section 12(d)(1)—probably cannot avoid conflicts of interest when all of the funds are served by the same investment adviser.[163] While economic and business considerations have been used to justify a one-family fund of funds,[164] the rationale for subsection (G) has been undermined by social change. A one-family fund of funds can be problematic for investors because of conflicts of interest, and investors accordingly need to—but may not—appreciate the ramifications of the conflicts. A factor that may prevent investors from understanding the consequences of the conflicts of interest in a one-family fund of funds is the change in social values that occurred in the United States during the last half of the twentieth century. The increased prevalence of hedonism, materialism, and short-term time horizon described in Part IV-A supra can logically be expected to have reduced the inclination of Americans to investigate an unfamiliar, complex vehicle for investing in securities. A compounding factor is the suboptimum intellectual proficiency of the U.S. population that resulted from this shift in social values.[165] The intellectual deficit that has developed suggests that a large segment of the population lacks the analytical skill necessary to comprehend the import of the conflicts of interest that can affect a one-family fund of funds.

VI. Conclusion

Probably all societies are characterized by significant inertia, but an unwillingness of their individual members to change is not the reason, or at least not the chief reason, that a society typically exhibits constancy over time. Individuals reside in a social system, which is composed of interdependent components with self-sustaining features such as enforcement mechanisms and feedback loops. A society, therefore, is structured to behave in the same manner and to move in the same direction as it has in the past, and in the normal course, the properties of a society do not change rapidly.[166] Evolution, not revolution, typifies a social system and the patterns of behavior in it.

Given the inertia that characterizes social life, can a society reorganize quickly in response to an event that poses a serious, recognizable threat to it or to one of its central components? The upheaval in finance that occurred during 2008 is evidently such a threat to the United States, but whether the upheaval will swiftly and substantially alter the direction of the country seems improbable. Even in the unlikely event that the social values of Americans were to be suddenly transformed,[167] the level of intellectual skill created in the population by the set of values that were displaced cannot be materially raised in a brief period. The change in social values that has been the focus of the instant chapter will thus have long-lasting consequences. Two illustrations may help to underscore this point. First, a high level of monetary debt in a country will be reduced only insofar as income can be and is diverted from other uses to debt repayment. However, such a diversion will create difficulties for the uses to which the money was formerly devoted, will encounter resistance from the sectors of the economy that depended on these uses, and will be retarded by the social values that promoted these uses. Second, if the cognitive skills of individuals decline after young adulthood, as research in psychology suggests they do,[168] suboptimum analytical ability will be eliminated or made less common in a population mainly by the passage of decades as mortality removes the now-older individuals, i.e., the individuals with suboptimum ability. In short, neither heavy debt nor deficient intellectual skill in a population can be cured rapidly.

The thesis of the instant chapter, then, is that a social problem not only can generate an economic problem but that, when it does, the social problem will impede a solution to the economic problem. Further, a social problem will be resistant to solution if, as is likely, the social problem is embedded in the fabric of the society in which the problem is found. As a result, while the institutions of a society are connected to one another, the links between institutions do not ensure that change needed in the economy will be supported or facilitated by another institution or by properties of the society as a whole (including social values). On the contrary, change required in the economy of a country may be retarded by social conditions that are widespread in the country.

The thesis of the chapter is pertinent to the institution of law and to its role in U.S. society. Because social problems that have arisen from the fabric of a society are difficult to remedy, law should not be expected to yield instant and visible results when it is directed at these problems. Notably, well-designed quantitative studies of a variety of social patterns have found that the impact of law is not large and lasting.[169] Therefore, while the current upheaval in finance can be expected to produce change in law bearing on finance[170]—with new statutory provisions enacted by Congress and new rules promulgated by executive-branch agencies—the rewritten law should not be expected to reshape, markedly and promptly, the social conditions underlying the crisis in the financial sector. Given the empirical evidence currently available, social engineering, whether attempted through law or through another institution such as religion, seems unable to effect permanent, substantial change in a society, at least if the society is a democracy. Colloquially stated, law is not a magic bullet for social problems.

Nonetheless, law is important sociologically. The importance of law, however, lies in its *social products*—or perhaps I should say *social byproducts*—rather than in its ability to alter the frequency of targeted social activities. Specifically, law benefits a society through the symbols it furnishes, the reputations it helps entities to (re)build, and the trust it promotes in entities and in institutions.[171] Law, in other words, aids a society by increasing social integration, and by doing so, it can help to cure problems that the society faces. The contribution of law to reducing social problems, however, is indirect, which prevents law from having an impact on such problems that is both immediate and large.

In the long run, the upheaval in the finance sector that was experienced during 2008 may help to alter prevailing assumptions about law, and to the extent that these assumptions come to be questioned, the upheaval will have educational value. The role that law evidently plays in the United States differs from the view of law that has been common among Americans for almost half a century—a view that, simply stated, is wrong. Rather than being an effective tool with which to confront social problems, as is popularly believed, the institution of law is a response to and is molded by the society in which it exists.[172] This view, of course, is contrary to the hopes that many advocates and their supporters have for law, but such hopes are based on overly optimistic beliefs about law. Until Americans come to accept that law does not offer speedy, permanent solutions to their social problems—until Americans become realistic as to the role of law in society—there will be unnecessary public frustration with the political process and unnecessary public disillusionment with the institution of law.

Notes

*Chapter 4 is a revised version of Larry D. Barnett, "The Financial Sector Upheaval of 2008: Sociological Antecedents and Their Implications for Investment Company Regulation," *Hastings Business Law Journal*, 5 (2009): 229. Parts II and IV of Chapter 4 have been updated with more recent data.

1. Michael Dominic Meuti, "Legalistic Individualism: An Alternative Analysis of Kagan's Adversarial Legalism," *Hastings International & Comparative Law Review* 27 (2004): 319, 335
2. Larry D. Barnett, "The Roots of Law," *American University Journal of Gender, Social. Policy & the Law* 15 (2007): 613, 615, 673–74 [hereinafter

The Roots of Law]. Page 615 and pages 673–74 in *The Roots of Law* are reproduced in Part I and Part IV-A, respectively, of Chapter 6 infra.

3. Formally defined, an institution is a set of statuses and roles (a) that a society defines and endorses and (b) that involve interpersonal relationships through which a socially approved type of activity takes place in the society. Howard B. Kaplan, "The Concept of Institution: A Review, Evaluation, and Suggested Research Procedure," *Social Forces* 39 (1960): 176, 179.
4. Walt Kelly, *quoted in* The Quotations Page, Rand Lindsly's Quotations, http://www.quotationspage.com/quote/22720.html (accessed December 30, 2009).
5. Editorial, "We All Have a Role in the Financial Failures of U.S.," *Greeley Tribune (Colo.)*, September 28, 2008 [page number unspecified], available at LexisNexis ALLNWS library. See generally Evan Cornog, Commentary, *Newhouse News Service*, May 26, 2006 (noting the prevalence and acceptance of selfishness in the United States), available at LexisNexis ALLNWS library.
6. Quantitative social science studies supporting this proposition are reviewed in Larry D. Barnett, *Mutual Funds, Hedge Funds, and the Public-Private Dichotomy in a Macrosociological Framework for Law* (Univ. of Messina Interuniversity Centre for Research on Sociol. of Law, Info. and Legal Institutions, Working Paper No. 34, 2008), 11–13, available at http://www.cirsdig.it/indexeng.html (accessed April 8, 2011) [hereinafter *The Public-Private Dichotomy*]. The proposition is discussed further in *The Roots of Law*, supra note 2, at 615, 636–37, 672–74. Pages 615, 636–37, and 672–74 in *The Roots of Law* are reproduced in Part I, Part III, and Part IV, respectively, of Chapter 6 infra.

   The proposition that the content of law is determined by societal conditions rather than particular individuals seems not to be widely accepted, and its corollary is apparently unpopular as well. The corollary is that regulatory law (i.e., law that is designed to regulate) does not directly shape patterns of social activity in a society to an appreciable degree and for an appreciable length of time. Social problems, therefore, are largely unresponsive to attempts by the institution of law to eliminate them or reduce their extent. For citations to quantitative social science research that finds law is relatively ineffective in changing social patterns, see Larry D. Barnett, "Law as Symbol: Appearances in the Regulation of Investment Advisers and Attorneys," *Cleveland State Law Review* 55 (2007): 289, 300–1 nn.65 and 67 [hereinafter *Law as Symbol*]; Larry D. Barnett, "The Regulation of Mutual Fund Boards of Directors: Financial Protection or Social Productivity?" *Journal of Law & Policy* 16 (2008): 489, 528–31 nn. 163–66 and 168, 545 n. 217 [hereinafter *Regulation of Mutual Fund Boards*]. Notes 65 and 67 in *Law as Symbol* are reproduced as revised in Part II of Chapter 8 infra, where they are numbered notes 66 and 67. Notes 163–66, 168, and 217 in *Regulation of Mutual Fund Boards* are reproduced as revised in Part III-E and Part V-B of Chapter 3 supra, where they are numbered notes 160–63, 165, and 209, respectively.

   Even though regulatory law does not control social behavior, its societal role is important. By manifesting societal conditions and by evolving in response to change in these conditions, regulatory law contributes to the cohesiveness of the social system even though it does not directly alter targeted social patterns. Specifically, law strengthens societal cohesiveness, and thereby assists in the operation of society, by furnishing symbols, (re)building interpersonal and intergroup trust, and (re)establishing the reputation of important societal segments. *Regulation of Mutual Fund Boards*, supra at 534–37, 545–46; Larry D. Barnett, "Social Productivity, Law, and the Regulation of Conflicts of Interest in the Investment Industry," *Cardozo Public Law, Policy, & Ethics Journal* 3 (2006): 793 [hereinafter *Social Productivity*]. Pages 534–37 and 545–46 in *Regulation of Mutual Fund Boards* are reproduced in Part IV and Part V-B, respectively, of Chapter 3 supra. *Social Productivity* is reproduced supra in Chapter 2.

7. E.g., Byron Acohido, "Tech Firms' Outlook Less Rosy; Near-term Forecasts Could Be Pared Back," *USA Today*, October 10, 2008, 9A.
8. E.g., Sam Zuckerman, "Bailout Plan Back on Track in Congress, Pelosi Says," *San Francisco Chronicle*, September 27, 2008, A1.
9. E.g., Sebastian Mallaby, "Main Street's Rescue," *Washington Post*, October 10, 2008, A19.
10. Steve Maich et al., "Edge of Disaster," *Maclean's*, September 29, 2008, 44.
11. Pete Engardio, "Forget Adam Smith. Whatever Works," *Business Week*, October 27, 2008, 22.
12. Dennis Archer, "The Importance of Law Reviews to the Judiciary and the Bar," *Detroit College of Law Review* 1991 (1991): 229.
13. From January 1, 2008 through December 31, 2008, the total investment return of the S&P 500 stock index was –37.0 percent. Total investment return is computed from both change in the price of a share of stock and payment of cash dividends per share. *Standard & Poor's, S&P 500*, http://www2.standardandpoors.com/portal/site/sp/en/us/page.topic/indices_500/2,3,2,2,11,31,2008,0,0,0,0,0,0,0,0,0.html (accessed January 1, 2009). The calendar-year price decline of the S&P 500 was larger in 2008 than in any calendar year since 1937. Elizabeth Stanton, *U.S. Stocks Post Steepest Yearly Decline Since Great Depression*, http://www.bloomberg.com/apps/news?pid=20601084&sid=a5RkfQG30k1k&refer=stocks (accessed January 1, 2009).
14. Jeremy R. Cook and Michael McDonald, "Muni Sales Dry Up as States Face $42 Billion Deficit (Update 1)," *Bloomberg*, December 31, 2008, http://www.bloomberg.com/apps/news?pid=20601015&sid=aE_Syu_H1HRM&refer=munibonds (accessed April 8, 2011); Gabrielle Coppola and Bryan Keogh, "Company Bond Sales Fall as Recession Drives Rates Up (Update 2)," *Bloomberg*, December 31, 2008, http://www.bloomberg.com/apps/news?pid=20601009&sid=a2Czskdlu1EY&refer=bond (Accessed April 8, 2011).
15. Vikas Bajaj and Louise Story, "Mortgage Crisis Spreads Past Subprime Loans," *New York Times*, February 12, 2008, A1; Engardio, supra note 11, at 23; Russell Grantham, "Financial Shake-Up: Collapses Create Nervous Consumers, Risking a Deep Depression," *Atlanta Journal-Constitution*, September 21, 2008, 1B. The Secretary of the U.S. Department of the Treasury has stated that "[t]he U.S. housing correction was clearly the spark that ignited the financial crisis." Henry M. Paulson, Jr., Remarks at the Ronald Reagan Presidential Library, http://www.treas.gov/press/releases/hp1285.htm (accessed November 20, 2008).

16. "A Helping Hand to Homeowners," *Economist*, October 25, 2008, 92; Maich et al., supra note 10; Steve Maich, "Facts and Fairy Tales of Paulson's Bailout," *Maclean's*, October 20, 2008, 47. The proportion of mortgage loans that were in foreclosure started to rise in 2006, and the rise continued through the third quarter of 2008. "Is Housing Close to a Bottom?" *Business Week*, December 22, 2008, 11. From the second quarter of 2006 to the third quarter of 2008, the proportion increased from less than 2 percent to more than 5 percent. Ibid.
17. Richard Harris and Chris Hamnett, "The Myth of the Promised Land: The Social Diffusion of Home Ownership in Britain and North America," *Annals of the Association of American Geographers* 77 (1987): 173, 174–75.
18. S&P/Case-Shiller Home Price Indices, S&P/Case-Shiller U.S. National Home Price Index (Excel spreadsheet), http://www2.standardandpoors.com/portal/site/sp/en/us/page.topic/indices_csmahp/0,0,0,0,0,0,0,0,0,2,1,0,0,0,0,0.html (accessed November 25, 2008). The Index is widely accepted as a measure of home prices. Kimberly Blanton, "Boston House Prices Show Some Spring," *Boston Globe*, July 30, 2008, C1; David Leonhardt and Vikas Bajaj, "Drop Foreseen in Median Price of Homes in U.S.," *New York Times*, August 26, 2007, A1.
19. *Standard & Poor's, S&P/Case-Shiller Home Price Indices: Index Methodology* 27 (2008), http://www2.standardandpoors.com/spf/pdf/index/SP_CS_Home_Price_Indices_Methodology_Web.pdf (accessed April 9, 2011). The Index uses the selling price of each structurally unchanged single-family home in the United States that is sold in a transaction in which the selling price is determined by bargaining; the Index is constructed from all such transactions. Ibid., 16–18.
20. Ibid., 14, 33. While the Index employs a single month for the base period, it uses three months for measuring change from the base period. Ibid., 6.
21. See Paul Syvret, "U.S. May See a Silver Lining in Bank's Demise," *Courier Mail* (Australia), July 17, 2009, 2 (noting that the collapse of the U.S.-based investment bank Lehman Brothers in September 2008 is generally regarded as the beginning of the crisis in finance).
22. Charles R. Morris, *The Trillion Dollar Meltdown* (New York: Public Affairs, 2008), 27, 34–35, 54. The principle in the text is illustrated by testimony to a committee of the House of Representatives in October 2008 by Alan Greenspan, who answered affirmatively and unequivocally when asked whether the economic philosophy he followed as chair of the Federal Reserve Board of Governors had one or more erroneous assumptions. Edmund Andrews, "Greenspan Concedes Error on Regulation," *New York Times*, October 23, 2008, http://www.nytimes.com/2008/10/24/business/economy/24panel.html?_r=1&hp&oref=slogin (accessed April 8, 2011). Mr. Greenspan chaired the Board of Governors of the U.S. Federal Reserve System from 1987 to 2006. Wikipedia, http://en.wikipedia.org/wiki/Alan_greenspan (accessed December 31, 2009).
23. Cf. Michael J. Sandel, *Democracy's Discontent* (Cambridge, MA: Belknap Press of Harvard University Press, 1996), 224–27 (attributing to social ideology the manner in which government regulates the economy through law and policy).

24. The discussion here is intended to be no more than suggestive. Quantitative research will be necessary to uncover all of the economic factors that were important contributors to the upheaval, to ascertain the sequence in which the factors operated, to determine the direct and indirect effects of each factor, and to identify the nature and magnitude of these effects.
25. The numerator for the proportion is the number of housing units in the United States that were occupied by their owners. Housing units are classified as "owner-occupied" if the owner-occupants regard the units as their usual place of residence whether or not the owner-occupants purchased their units with loans that have yet to be fully repaid; thus, a housing unit is considered to be occupied by its owner even when the owner-occupant is a mortgagor. Homeownership rates are based on the civilian noninstitutionalized population, which includes, inter alia, civilians who are in households, military personnel who are in households that are off a military post, and military personnel who are in households that are on a military post and contain a family member who is a civilian adult. U.S. Census Bureau, Differences between the Homeownership Rate Estimates from the American Community Survey, the Current Population Survey/Housing Vacancy Survey, and the American Housing Survey, http://www.census.gov/hhes/www/housing/homeownershipfactsheet.html (accessed November 30, 2004).
26. The data are from U.S. Census Bureau, Table 14: Homeownership Rates for the U.S. and Regions: 1965 to Present, http://www.census.gov/hhes/www/housing/hvs/historic/index.html (accessed June 5, 2010).
27. Ibid. The total number of housing units in the United States was also growing throughout most of this period. See U.S. Census Bureau, Table 7: Estimates of the Housing Inventory for the United States: 1965 to Present, http://www.census.gov/hhes/www/housing/hvs/historic/index.html (accessed June 5, 2010).
28. A. Brooke Overby, "Mortgage Foreclosure in Post-Katrina New Orleans," *Boston College Law Review* 48 (2007): 851, 898–99; Richard A. Brown and Susan E. Burhouse, "Implications of the Supply-Side Revolution in Consumer Lending," *Saint Louis University Public Law Review* 24 (2005): 363, 369–70.
29. Todd J. Zywicki, "An Economic Analysis of the Consumer Bankruptcy Crisis," *Northwestern University Law Review* (2005): 1463, 1499–1500. The decline in interest rates for housing loans in the United States as a whole is illustrated by the mean interest rate on a thirty-year fixed-rate mortgage loan at the time the lender committed to making the loan. The rate decreased from a yearly average of 8.38 percent in 1994 to 5.87 percent in 2005. Freddie Mac [Fed. Home Loan Mortgage Corp.], Monthly Average Commitment Rate and Points on 30-Year Fixed-Rate Mortgages since 1971, http://www.freddiemac.com/pmms/pmms30.htm (accessed June 5, 2010). The yearly average was 6.41 percent in 2006, 6.34 percent in 2007, and 6.03 percent in 2008. Ibid.
30. Federal Reserve Board, Household Debt Service and Financial Obligations Ratios (September 22, 2008), https://www.federalreserve.gov/releases/housedebt/default.htm (accessed June 5, 2010). The graph uses data for the fourth quarter of each year.

31. Ibid.
32. Steven Hitlin and Jayne Allyn Piliavin, "Values: Reviving a Dormant Concept," *Annual Review of Sociology* 30 (Karen S. Cook and John Hagan eds., 2004): 359; Benigno E. Aguirre and E. L. Quarantelli, "Methodological, Ideological, and Conceptual-Theoretical Criticisms of the Field of Collective Behavior: A Critical Evaluation and Implications for Future Study," *Sociological Focus* 16 (1983): 195.
33. Shalom H. Schwartz, "A Theory of Cultural Values and Some Implications for Work," *Applied Psychology* 48 (1999): 23, 32–40.
34. Ronald Inglehart and Wayne E. Baker, "Modernization, Cultural Change, and the Persistence of Traditional Values," *American Sociological Review* 65 (2000): 19, 49.
35. Hitlin and Piliavin, supra note 32, at 361–62.
36. Clark McPhail, "The Crowd and Collective Behavior: Bringing Symbolic Interaction Back In," *Symbolic Interaction* 29 (2006): 433, 455.
37. Hank Johnston and Shoon Lio, "Collective Behavior and Social Movements in the Postmodern Age: Looking Backward to Look Forward," *Sociological Perspectives* 41 (1998): 453, 454–55.
38. Brenda Spotton Visano, "Financial Manias and Panics," *American Journal of Economics & Sociology* 61 (2002): 801.
39. The lack of agreement among sociologists on a definition of collective behavior may be due to the lack of a clear boundary between collective behavior and occurrences known as social movements. Sociologists have attempted to link research on collective behavior and research on social movements, but they have had limited success in doing so. Johnston and Lio, supra note 37, at 454. The difficulty of tying collective behavior and social movements may stem at least partly from the absence of an unambiguous line between the two phenomena.
40. Stephen Vider, "Rethinking Crowd Violence: Self-Categorization Theory and the Woodstock 1999 Riot," *Journal for the Theory of Social Behaviour* 34 (2004): 141, 141–42, available at EBSCOhost.
41. Indeed, research on collective behavior has yet to answer basic questions about such behavior. David Schweingruber and Clark McPhail, "A Method for Systematically Observing and Recording Collective Action," *Sociological Methods & Research* 27 (1999): 451, 458–61.
42. Research on collective behavior in financial markets may find that the frequency and impact of such collective behavior has changed over the course of history. Such change may have occurred because, inter alia, of the development and adoption of new technologies, e.g., broadcasting, cell telephones, and email. Daniel J. Myers, "Racial Rioting in the 1960s: An Event History Analysis of Local Conditions," *American Sociological Review* 62 (1997): 94, 97.
43. See Keith Hayward, "Situational Crime Prevention and its Discontents: Rational Choice Theory versus the 'Culture of Now,'" *Social Policy & Administration* 41 (2007): 232, 239–41 (describing general theoretical models that link hedonism, materialism, and a short-term time horizon in present-day societies); James E. Burroughs and Aric Rindfleisch, "Materialism and Well-Being: A Conflicting Values Perspective," *Journal of Consumer Research* 29 (2002): 348, 359, 365 (finding in a small sample that a high

level of materialism in individuals tends to be accompanied by a high level of hedonism).

44. E.g., Victor Davis Hanson, "Why the U.S. Economy will Brebound Before Others," *San Jose Mercury News (Cal.)*, October 30, 2008, [page not specified] (contending that the 2008 upheaval in finance occurred because Americans were characterized by "greed [that] drove us to demand even more than we had earned" and because Americans were in "a hypnotic trance of self-indulgence").

45. A facially valid question would attempt to tap these values with an explicit reference to the values. However, data produced by facially valid questions designed to measure social values can produce erroneous data to the extent that current values diverge from traditional values, because in answering questions, survey respondents tend to rely on the values endorsed by their cultural heritage. Matthew J. Streb et al., "Social Desirability Effects and Support for a Female American President," *Public Opinion Quarterly* 72 (2008): 76, 78–80. Traditionally, hedonism and materialism have been disfavored by the religious faiths that dominate the United States. Alexis de Tocqueville, *Democracy in America*, ed. J. P. Mayer and Max Lerner, trans. George Lawrence (New York: Harper & Row , 1966), 514–16 (1840). Not surprisingly, therefore, an inverse relationship has been found among individuals between degree of religious commitment and strength of materialism. Wendy M. Rahn and John E. Transue, "Social Trust and Value Change: The Decline of Social Capital in American Youth, 1976-1995," *Political Psychology* 19 (1998): 545, 560. In light of the teachings of the main religions in the United States, a substantial number of Americans are likely to be unwilling to admit that they approve, or at least do not disapprove, of hedonism and materialism, and can be expected to misstate their personal view when responding to questions explicitly referencing these values. Data from facially valid questions thus probably understate the extent of hedonism and materialism.

46. One of the two studies asked whether respondents believed that "[p]eople are too much concerned with material things these days." Jerald G. Bachman et al., *Monitoring the Future: Questionnaire Responses from the Nation's High School Seniors, 2006* (item number 6000) (2008), 104, http://www.monitoringthefuture.org/pubs.html#refvols (accessed April 8, 2011). The question measures the respondents' evaluation of the degree to which materialism exists among other individuals or among individuals generally. Because the question does not measure the degree to which the respondents personally are materialistic, I concluded that it does not permit an accurate assessment of the extent of materialism in the United States. Accordingly, data from the question are not employed here.

47. Of course, social problems can be avoided by the content of and change in values, but that did not happen in the situation being examined in the instant chapter.

48. Bachman et al., supra note 46, at 2–3, 9–10. The MTF study covers students in public high schools as well as students in private high schools. Ibid., 2, 4.

49. This statement is numbered item 8060 in the MTF study, and given the wording of the statement, agreement with it is evidence of a hedonistic orientation. The questionnaire for the study contained a series of statements

dealing with leisure and work, and item 8060 was the second in the series. (The alternatives available for responding to item 8060 were available for responding to every statement in the series.) Notably, item 8060 was preceded by the statement (item 8050) that "I like the kind of work you can forget about after the work day is over." Ibid., 18, 137, 320–21. Research on responses to questions in sample surveys has found that a prior item can affect responses to the item that follows. Alexander Todorov, "Context Effects in National Health Surveys: Effects of Preceding Questions on Reporting Serious Difficulty Seeing and Legal Blindness," *Public Opinion Quarterly* 64 (2000): 65, 65, 73–74. The wording of item 8050 is likely to have increased the inclination of survey respondents to interpret item 8060 in terms of hedonism.

50. The yearly data in Figure 4.3 are from the individual reference volumes of the MTF study. The volumes are listed at http://www.monitoringthefuture.org/pubs.html#refvols (accessed April 8, 2011)
51. Nat'l Opinion Res. Center, *General Social Surveys, 1972–2010: Cumulative Codebook* (2011), vii, http://www.norc.org/GSS+Website/Documentation (accessed April 8, 2011). Beginning in 2006, adults who spoke only Spanish were interviewed along with adults who spoke English. Ibid.
52. The other four aspects were (1) "No danger of being fired," (2) "Workings [sic] hours are short, lots of free time," (3) "Chances for advancement," and (4) "Work important and gives a feeling of accomplishment." Ibid., 313–14.
53. Income that is not required for minimum necessities may, of course, be spent for other than hedonistic or materialistic purposes. Given the culture of the United States, however, the assumption is likely to be correct that such income will be devoted to activities involving hedonism and materialism.
54. Nat'l Opinion Res. Center, supra note 51, at 2474, 2515.
55. The percentages for Nonwhites are not reported because of the small numbers of Nonwhites in the yearly samples.
56. The mnemonic label of the question was JOBINC. The percentages were obtained from the GSS 1972–2008 Cumulative Datafile, http://sda.berkeley.edu/cgi-bin/hsda?harcsda+gss08. All of the percentages were calculated using the WTSSALL weight. See *Nat'l Opinion Res. Center*, supra note 51, at 2202 (explaining WTSSALL).
57. The percentages are not presented separately for males and for females because doing so would require the use of unacceptably small numbers of respondents.
58. Investment Company Institute, *2009 Investment Company Fact Book*, 49th ed. (2009), 74 [hereinafter *Investment Company Fact Book*], http://www.ici.org/about_ici/annuals/fact_books (accessed April 8, 2011) (reporting that, in 2008, shares of at least one mutual fund were owned by slightly more than half of all U.S. households in which the person who was responsible for making investment and savings decisions was 45–64 years of age).
59. James O. Hill and John C. Peters, "Environmental Contributions to the Obesity Epidemic," *Science* 280 (1998): 1371.
60. Nat'l Center for Health Statistics, U.S. Dep't of Health & Hum. Services, Publ'n No. 2010-1232, *Health, United States, 2009*, (2010), 302 (table 72) http://www.cdc.gov/nchs/data/hus/hus09.pdf (accessed April 8, 2011).

61. Calculated from ibid. for men and women combined. Broken down by sex, the prevalence of obesity increased more among men than among women. Specifically, the ratio of obesity prevalence in 2003–2006 to obesity prevalence in 1960–1962 was 3.1 for men and 2.2 for women. Ibid.

62. Nat'l Ass'n of Home Builders, *Median and Average Square Feet of Floor Area in New One-Family Houses Sold by Location* (2009), http://www.nahb.org/reference_list.aspx?sectionID=819&channelID=311 (MS Excel file) (accessed January 1, 2010).

    The increase in floor space does not seem to have been necessary to accommodate larger numbers of children. Among all families in the United States with their own children who were younger than eighteen years, the mean number of own minor children declined from 1965 until 1984 and then remained essentially constant: In 1965, the mean number was 2.44; from 1984 to 2008, the mean number was in the range of 1.85±0.04. U.S. Census Bureau, Families and Living Arrangements, Historical Time Series: Families, *Table FM-3. Average Number of Own Children Under 18 Per Family, By Type of Family: 1955 to Present* (January 2009), http://www.census.gov/population/www/socdemo/hh-fam.html#ht (Excel spreadsheet) (accessed January 1, 2010). Floor space was thus increasing while the number of own minor children was not.

63. Stacy C. Davis et al., *U.S. Dep't of Energy, Transportation Energy Data Book*, 28th ed. (2009), 4–7, http://kerstech.com/PDFs/Transportation%20Energy%20Data%20Book%202009.pdf (accessed April 9, 2011). Cars are differentiated from and do not include wagons. Ibid. A car (or a wagon) was classified as "small" if it had a maximum of 110 cubic feet of space for passengers and luggage. See ibid. at G-2 (criteria for "minicompact," "subcompact," and "compact" automobiles and wagons).

64. John A. Weinberg, "Borrowing by U.S. Households," *Economic Quarterly* 92 (2006): 177, 179. Unfortunately, an adjustment was not made for changes in the distribution of age in the adult population of the United States during the period covered by the data. Such an adjustment would have produced a more accurate estimate of the ratio of debt to disposable income of households over time, because the ratio varies by age of the household head. Ana M. Aizcorbe et al., "Recent Changes in U.S. Family Finances: Evidence from the 1998 and 2001 Survey of Consumer Finances," *Federal Reserve Bulletin*, January 2003, 1, 22–23.

65. The percentage for 2004 is from Weinberg, supra note 64, at 178. The percentage for 2008 was computed from the following sources: Board of Governors of the Federal Reserve System, Table D.3: Debt Outstanding by Sector, Federal Reserve Statistical Release, Z.1, Flow of Funds Accounts of the United States, (March 12, 2009), 8, http://www.federalreserve.gov/releases/z1/20090312 (accessed April 9, 2011) [hereinafter Board of Governors]; Bureau of Economic Analysis, U.S. Dep't of Commerce, Table 2.1: Personal Income and Its Disposition (December 22, 2009) (annual data), http://www.bea.gov/national/nipaweb/SelectTable.asp?Selected=N (accessed April 9, 2011).

66. Weinberg, supra note 64, at 179; Board of Governors, supra note 65. The ratio of minimum debt payments to income—which ratio takes into account, inter alia, changes in interest rates and maturities on debt—grew

during the mid-1980s, declined until the first half of the 1990s, and then increased. Karen Dynan et al., "Recent Changes to a Measure of U.S. Household Debt Service," *Federal Reserve Bulletin,* October 2003, 417, 420.

67. Personal debt to allow consumption by the individuals incurring the debt or by their children has evidently become more acceptable to Americans. Robert D. Manning, *Living with Debt: A Life Stage Analysis of Changing Attitudes and Behaviors* (no date), 138–40, A.1 (reporting the results of interviews conducted in 2005 with 145 individuals at different stages of the life cycle), http://www.lendingtree.com/livingwithdebt/collateral/full_report.pdf (accessed April 8, 2011).

68. E.g., Richard H. Fallon, Jr., "The "Conservative" Paths of the Rehnquist Court's Federalism Decisions," *University of Chicago Law Review* 69 (2002): 429, 440.

69. These amounts were obtained from various issues of *U.S. Census Bureau, Statistical Abstract of the United States,* an annual print publication whose issues are available at http://www.census.gov/prod/www/abs/statab .html (accessed April 8, 2011); from *Governing Magazine, State and Local Sourcebook,* http://sourcebook.governing.com/index.jsp (follow "U.S." link under "Data by Region," select "Finance," and find "State & Local Debt Per Capita" beneath heading "State & Local Debt") (accessed June 5, 2010); and from *U.S. Census Bureau, State and Local Governments—Indebtedness,* http://www.allcountries.org/uscensus/507_state_and_local_governments_indebtedness.html (accessed June 5, 2010).

70. The base period for the Consumer Price Index was 1982–1984, i.e., the average of prices in 1982–1984 was used to create Consumer Price Index ratios for each year in the time series. *U.S. Census Bureau, Statistical Abstract of the United States: 2009,* 128th ed. (2008), 463 (Table 702), http://www.census.gov/prod/www/abs/statab2006_2009.html (accessed April 8, 2011).

71. Michael J. Handel, "Skills Mismatch in the Labor Market," *Annual Review of Sociology* 29 (2003): 135, 160 (reporting "evidence of decelerating growth of human capital and stability in cognitive test scores"). Cf. Thomas Lord, "Darn it, Professor. Just Tell Us What We Need to Know to Pass Your Course," *Journal of College Science Teaching* 37 (January/February 2008), 71.

72. *Inst. of Educ. Sci., Nat'l Center for Educ. Stat., The Condition of Education 2007: Trends in Adult Literacy* (2007), 155 (Table 18-2), http://nces.ed.gov/programs/coe/2007/pdf/18_2007.pdf (accessed April 9, 2011). Prose literacy was defined as "the knowledge and skills needed to perform prose tasks (i.e., to search, comprehend, and use information from continuous texts, such as paragraphs from stories)." Quantitative literacy was defined as "the knowledge and skills required to perform quantitative tasks (i.e., to identify and perform computations, either alone or sequentially, using numbers embedded in printed materials." Ibid. Performance was divided into four levels: below basic, basic, intermediate, and proficient. Ibid.

The data cited in the sentence in the text are also available at http://nces.ed.gov/programs/coe/2007/section2/table.asp?tableID=693 (accessed April 9, 2011).

73. E.g., Michael Jordan, "Law Teachers and the Educational Continuum," *Southern California Interdisciplinary Law Journal* 5 (1996): 41, 61–64.
74. Grades have markedly increased in colleges and universities in the United States since the 1960s, and the increase in grades has substantially reduced the amount of time that students devote to studying. Philip Babcock, Real Costs of Nominal Grade Inflation? New Evidence from Student Course Evaluations 3–4, 7, 18–20 (2008) (unpublished manuscript, on file with author), http://www.econ.ucsb.edu/~babcock/GradeInflation.pdf. The inflation of grades and the resulting decline in study time are probably manifestations, at least in part, of the expansion of hedonism, and if so, they support the proposition that the growth of hedonism has impaired the intellectual skills of Americans.
75. Rahn and Transue, supra note 45 (reporting an analysis of data from the MTF study and finding that the spread of social values endorsing materialism reduced trust in others).
76. In the comparisons in the text, a difference between the United States and another country was judged to be "significant" if the difference would occur in no more than five out of one hundred samples randomly drawn from the population of fifteen-year-old students in each country. The calculation of significance was made on the assumption (null hypothesis) that fifteen-year-old students in each country have the same average score. The "significance" of a difference between countries, therefore, is a statistical concept.
77. Eric A. Hanushek, "Our School Performance Matters," *Journal of Education* 185 (2006): 1.
78. Stéphane Baldi et al., Nat'l Center for Educ. Stat., Highlights from PISA 2006: Performance of U.S. 15-Year-Old Students in Science and Mathematics Literacy in an International Context, (NCES 2008-016) (2007), at 12 (Table 3), http://nces.ed.gov/pubs2008/2008016.pdf (accessed April 8, 2011). The data in the text are for 2006. The definition of "mathematics literacy" is: "An individual's capacity to identify and understand the role that mathematics plays in the world, to make well-founded judgments and to use and engage with mathematics in ways that meet the needs of that individual's life as a constructive, concerned and reflective citizen." Ibid., 11.
79. Ibid., 6 (Table 2). The data in the text are for 2006. The definition of "science literacy" is: "An individual's scientific knowledge and use of that knowledge to identify questions, to acquire new knowledge, to explain scientific phenomena, and to draw evidence-based conclusions about science-related issues, understanding of the characteristic features of science as a form of human knowledge and enquiry, awareness of how science and technology shape our material, intellectual, and cultural environments, and willingness to engage in science-related issues, and with the ideas of science, as a reflective citizen." Ibid., 5.
80. Mariann Lemke et al., Nat'l Center for Educ. Stat., International Outcomes of Learning in Mathematics Literacy and Problem Solving: PISA 2003 Results from the U.S. Perspective (2004), 29 (Table 3), http://nces.ed.gov/pubs2005/2005003.pdf (accessed April 8, 2011). The data in the text are for 2003. The definition of "problem solving" is: "an individual's capacity

to use cognitive processes to confront and resolve real, cross-disciplinary situations where the solution is not immediately obvious, and where the literacy domains or curricular areas that might be applicable are not within a single domain of mathematics, science, or reading." Ibid., 22.

81. While such mismanagement and regulation undoubtedly occurred in the United States, much of it is likely to be explained by the changes in U.S. society that I describe in the text.
82. At the end of 2008, the assets of U.S. mutual funds represented 92.8 percent of the assets of all investment companies in the United States. Computed from *Investment Company Fact Book*, supra note 58, at 9. 83. Ibid., 167.
83. Ibid., 167.
84. Computed from ibid.
85. David D. Haddock, "Insider Trading: Academic Hostility and SEC Acquiescence: Henry Manne's Insider Trading," *Case Western Reserve Law Review* 50 (1999): 313, 317 (noting that "United States securities markets have become integrated with those of the rest of the world").
86. 15 U.S.C. §§ 80a-1 to -64 (2006).
87. Investment Company Act, ch. 686, tit. I, 54 Stat. 789 (1940).
88. 15 U.S.C. § 80a-3 (2006).
89. 15 U.S.C. § 80a-37, -41 (2006).
90. 15 U.S.C. § 80a-4, -5 (2006).
91. By definition, open-end management investment companies issue redeemable securities. 15 U.S.C. § 80a-5(a)(1) (2006). A redeemable security entitles its owner to receive from the company issuing the security the net asset value of the security at the time of redemption. 15 U.S.C. § 80a-2(a)(32) (2006). Redemption may effected in cash, or it may be effected in kind, i.e., with a security or securities in the portfolio of the company that issued the redeemable security. 17 C.F.R. § 270.18f-1 (2008).
92. *Regulation of Mutual Fund Boards* , supra note 6, at 493–94.
93. *Investment Company Fact Book*, supra note 58, at 110. The market value of fund portfolios, however, had fallen from $12.0 trillion in December 2007. Ibid.
94. Ibid., 72. The percentages in the text are for 2008.
95. Ibid., 100. The proportion in the text is for 2008. The retirement assets of U.S. households comprise approximately one-third of their total financial assets. Investment Company Institute, "The U.S. Retirement Market, 2009," *Research Fundamentals*, May 2010, 39 (Figure A20), http://www.ici.org/pdf/fm-v19n3.pdf. (accessed April 8, 2011).
96. In justifying adoption of the Investment Company Act, Congress explicitly acknowledged the importance of investment companies to "the national public interest and the interest of investors." 15 U.S.C. § 80a-1(b) (2006).
97. Although I argue that law has little direct impact on aspects of and activities in a society that are predominantly *social*, law may be useful for controlling some aspects and activities that are predominantly *economic*. Larry D. Barnett, *Legal Construct, Social Concept* (New York: Aldine de Gruyter 1993), 162–63.
98. *The Roots of Law* , supra note 2; *The Public-Private Dichotomy* , supra note 6, at 39–40.
99. 15 U.S.C. § 80a-3(c) (2006).

100. *The Public-Private Dichotomy* , supra note 6, at 15–18.
101. 15 U.S.C. § 80a-3(a) (2006).
102. 15 U.S.C. § 80a-3(c)(1), -3(c)(7)(D) (2006).
103. The exceptions are sections 12(d)(1)(A)(i) and 12(d)(1)(B)(i). 15 U.S.C. § 80a-12(d)(1) (2006). See infra notes 148, 151, and accompanying text.
104. Investment Company Act, Pub. L. No. 76-768, tit. I, § 3(c)(1), 54 Stat. 789, 798 (1940).
105. 15 U.S.C. § 80a-3(c)(1) (2006).
106. Small Business Investment Incentive Act of 1980, H.R. REP. NO. 96-1341, at 35 (1980), *reprinted in* 1980 U.S.C.C.A.N. 4800, 4817.
107. S. REP. NO. 104-293, at 10 (1996), 1996 WL 367191 (stating that the subsection "expands capital formation opportunities by creating a new exception from registration and regulation under the Investment Company Act for private investment pools").
108. 15 U.S.C. § 80a-3(c)(7) (2006).
109. National Securities Markets Improvement Act of 1996, Pub. L. No. 104-290, § 209, 110 Stat. 3416, 3433–34 (1996).
110. 15 U.S.C. § 80a-2(a)(51)(A) (2006).
111. S. REP. NO. 104-293, at 10 (1996), 1996 WL 367191.
112. 15 U.S.C. § 80a-18 (2006). The ceiling for open-end investment companies differs from the ceiling for closed-end investment companies. Periodic Repurchases by Closed-End Management Investment Companies; Redemptions by Open-End Management Investment Companies, Investment Company Act Release No. IC-18869, 57 Fed. Reg. 34,701, 34,704 (August 6, 1992). Congress explicitly identified borrowing by investment companies as a reason for regulating the companies. 15 U.S.C. § 80a-1(b)(7) (2006).
113. I discuss hedge funds in more depth in *The Public-Private Dichotomy*, supra note 6, at 7–8, 22–23.
114. Securities Trading Practices Of Registered Investment Companies, Investment Company Act Release No. 10666, 44 Fed. Reg. 25,128, 25,129–30 (April 18, 1979).
115. Kevin G. Hall and Robert A. Rankin, "Hedge Funds May Pose a Risk to U.S. Economy," *McClatchy Newspapers*, August 8, 2007 [page number unspecified], http://www.mcclatchydc.com/227/story/18766.html (accessed April 8, 2011) (estimating that hedge funds had assets worth a total of $1.6 trillion in mid-2007 and that some hedge funds used borrowed money to acquire as much as four-fifths of their assets); David Henry and Matthew Goldstein, "Another Blowup for Hedge Funds," *Business Week*, November 24, 2008, 34 (estimating that the amount of money borrowed by hedge funds for investments was six times their capital).
116. Henry and Goldstein, supra note 115; Matthew Goldstein and David Henry, "The Hedge Fund Contagion," *Business Week*, November 3, 2008, 36. Hedge funds did not avoid the losses that occurred in securities markets. An index of hedge funds in North America was estimated to have had an investment return of −10.25 percent from January 1, 2008 through December 31, 2008. Eurekahedge North American Hedge Fund Index, http://www.eurekahedge.com/indices/default.asp (accessed April 1, 2009).
117. See Registration under the Advisers Act of Certain Hedge Fund Advisers, Investment Advisers Act Release No. IA-2333, 69 Fed. Reg. 72,054, 72,057

(December 10, 2004) (noting "the growing exposure of smaller investors, pensioners, and other market participants, directly or indirectly, to hedge funds" and concluding that "[h]edge fund investors are no longer limited to the very wealthy").

118. 15 U.S.C. § 77b(a)(15)(ii) (2006); 17 C.F.R. § 230.501(a) (2008).
119. In recent years, hedge funds have invested in commodities as well as in securities. Goldstein and Henry, supra note 116, at 38.
120. For an individual, the current standards require that, to be an accredited investor, the individual must have (a) a net worth, alone or jointly with her/his spouse, totaling more than $1 million, (b) an annual personal net income of more than $200,000, or (c) an annual joint net income with his/her spouse of more than $300,000. To satisfy (b) and (c), the income amounts specified by Regulation D must have been received during both of the last two years and must be reasonably expected during the present year as well. 17 C.F.R. §§ 230.501(a)(5), 230.501(a)(6) (2008).
121. 15 U.S.C. § 80a-7(d) (2006).
122. See Sec. & Exch. Comm'n, *Protecting Investors: A Half Century of Investment Company Regulation* (1992), 189, http://www.sec.gov/divisions/investment/guidance/icreg50-92.pdf (accessed April 8, 2011).
123. Ibid., 190.
124. Touche, Remnant & Co., SEC No-Action Letter, [1984–1985 Transfer Binder] Fed. Sec. L. Rep. (CCH) ¶ 77,810, at 79,138, 79,141–42 (July 27, 1984).
125. See Goodwin, Procter & Hoar, SEC No-Action Letter (February 28, 1997), 1997 WL 86002. The foreign investment company must choose between section 3(c)(1) and section 3(c)(7); it cannot rely on both sections. Ibid.
126. Applications of Foreign Investment Companies Filed Pursuant to Section 7(d) of the Investment Company Act of 1940, Investment Company Act Release No. IC-13691, 49 Fed. Reg. 55 (January 3, 1984).
127. Sec. & Exch. Comm'n, supra note 122, at 189–90, 192.
128. Ibid., 198.
129. Ibid., 193–94, 198–200. The Division of Investment Management, which is the unit within the Commission that is responsible for interpreting the Investment Company Act, has also suggested changes to section 7(d). Ibid., 205–14. The proposals of the Commission and of the Division were made before section 3(c)(7) and section 2(a)(51) were added to the Act in 1996. Pub. L. No. 104-290, § 209, 110 Stat. 3416, 3433–34.
130. Indeed, section 7(d) has not been amended since the Investment Company Act was adopted in 1940. See Investment Company Act, ch. 686, tit. I, § 7(d), 54 Stat. 789, 803 (1940).
131. See Benjamin Lee Whorf, "Science and Linguistics," in *Language, Thought, and Reality: Selected Writings of Benjamin Lee Whorf*, ed. John B. Carroll (Cambridge: Technology Press of Massachusetts Institute of Technology, 1956), 207. Whorf, a leading linguist, described the function of language as follows: "[T]he world is presented in a kaleidoscopic flux of impressions which has to be organized by our minds—and this means largely by the linguistic systems in our minds. We cut nature up, organize it into concepts, and ascribe significances as we do, largely because we are parties to an agreement to organize it in this way—an agreement that holds

throughout our speech community and is codified in the patterns of our language." Ibid., 213.

132. Benjamin Lee Whorf, "The Relation of Habitual Thought and Behavior to Language, in ibid., 134, 152–59; Naomi Quinn and Dorothy Holland, "Culture and Cognition," in *Cultural Models in Language and Thought*, ed. Dorothy Holland and Naomi Quinn (New York: Cambridge University Press, 1987), 3, 7.
133. Towne v. Eisner, 245 U.S. 418, 425 (1918) (observing that "A word is not a crystal, transparent and unchanged[;] it is the skin of a living thought and may vary greatly in color and content according to the circumstances and the time in which it is used").
134. See Whorf, supra notes 131, 132.
135. The preceding mandate could also require that the persons who prepare the English-language prospectuses and sales materials must be recognized for their language competence. The word "recognized," as it would apply in section 7(d), is admittedly ambiguous, but another section of the Investment Company Act contains a word with a not-dissimilar degree of ambiguity. Specifically, section 17(g) directs a registered management investment company to have a bond that covers losses from larceny and embezzlement of portfolio securities by officers and employees of the company. Section 17(g) and its implementing Commission rule explicitly limit the issuer of the bond to a "reputable" insurance company. 15 U.S.C. § 80a-17(g) (2006); 17 C.F.R. § 270.17g-1(a) (2008). The word "reputable" is not defined in the section or the rule.
136. See supra note 91.
137. H.R. Rep. No. 89-2337, at 322 (1966); Fund of Funds Investments, Investment Company Act Release No. IC-26198, 68 Fed. Reg. 58,226, 58,227 (October 8, 2003) [hereinafter Release No. IC-26198].
138. Release No. IC-26198, supra note 137, at 58,227.
139. An open-end investment company that is registered with the Commission must redeem its securities within seven days unless exceptional circumstances are present or an order has been obtained from the Commission allowing the company additional time. 15 U.S.C. § 80a-22(e) (2006).
140. H.R. Rep. No. 89-2337, at 316–17 (1966).
141. H.R. Rep. No. 89-2337, at 315–17 (1966); Release No. IC-26198, supra note 137, at 58,226–27. See 15 U.S.C. § 80a-1(b)(2) (2006).
142. 15 U.S.C. § 80a-1(b)(2) (2006).
143. 15 U.S.C. § 80a-12(d)(1)(A)-(C) (2006). Subsections (A), (B), and (C) were added in 1970. Investment Company Act Amendments of 1970, Pub. L. No. 91-547, § 7, 84 Stat. 1413, 1417 (1970).
144. Cheapside Dollar Fund Ltd., SEC No-Action Letter, [1971–1972 Transfer Binder] Fed. Sec. L. Rep. (CCH) ¶ 78,389, at 80,872, 80,873 (August 26, 1971), available at 1971 WL 11137.
145. The limitations are subject to exceptions. 15 U.S.C. § 80a-12(d)(1)(D)–(G) (2006).
146. As to the securities specified in subsections (A), (B), and (C) of section 12(d)(1), the calculation of whether an investment company, in acquiring securities issued by another investment company, surpasses each statutory maximum is made by counting not only the securities owned

by the acquiring investment company but also the securities owned by a company controlled by the acquiring investment company. 15 U.S.C. § 80a-12(d)(1)(A)-(C) (2006). To simplify the discussion in the text, however, I will refer just to the acquiring investment company.

147. 15 U.S.C. §§ 80a-3(c)(1), -3(c)(7)(D) (2006). Although a fund that invests in hedge funds must abide by subsections (A)(i) and (B)(i) of section 12(d)(1) in spite of qualifying under section 3(c)(1) or section 3(c)(7), funds of hedge funds may have exacerbated the declines in securities prices that occurred during 2008. Henry and Goldstein, supra note 115.
148. 15 U.S.C. § 80a-12(d)(1)(A)(i) (2006).
149. 15 U.S.C. § 80a-12(d)(1)(A)(ii) (2006).
150. 15 U.S.C. § 80a-12(d)(1)(A)(iii) (2006).
151. 15 U.S.C. § 80a-12(d)(1)(B)(i) (2006).
152. 15 U.S.C. § 80a-12(d)(1)(B)(ii) (2006).
153. 15 U.S.C. § 80a-5(a)(2) (2006).
154. 15 U.S.C. § 80a-12(d)(1)(C) (2006).
155. To ascertain whether the maximum has been exceeded, the shares of the closed-end fund held by the acquiring investment company and by companies under the control of the acquiring investment company are added to the shares of the closed-end fund held by other investment companies that employ the same investment adviser. See supra note 146.
156. S. Rep. No. 91-184, at 30 (1969), *reprinted in* 1970 U.S.C.C.A.N. 4897, 4925, available at 1969 WL 4981; H.R. Rep. No. 91-1382, at 11, 23 (1970).
157. Investment Company Act Amendments of 1970, Pub. L. No. 91-547, § 7, 84 Stat. 1413, 1417 (1970).
158. 15 U.S.C. § 80a-12(d)(1)(G) (2006).
159. National Securities Markets Improvement Act of 1996, Pub. L. No. 104-290, § 202, 110 Stat. 3416, 3426–27 (1996).
160. A fund of funds created under subsection (G) and its underlying funds are subject to some restrictions, including limits on sales loads and distribution-related fees, but the restrictions are not relevant to the discussion here.
161. Provisions of the Act that are concerned with conflicts of interest include sections 1(b)(2), 2(a)(19), 10(a), 10(b), 15(c), and 17(a) through 17(e). 15 U.S.C. §§ 80a-1(b)(2), 2(a)(19), 10(a)–(b), 15(c), 17(a)–(e) (2006).
162. Investors Research Corp. v. Sec. & Exch. Comm'n, 628 F.2d 168, 176 (D.C. Cir.), *cert. denied*, 449 U.S. 919 (1980); Compliance Programs of Investment Companies and Investment Advisers, Investment Company Act Release No. IC-26299, 68 Fed. Reg. 74,714, 74,720 n.68 (December 24, 2003).
163. Even when the fund of funds and the underlying funds have different investment advisers, serious conflicts of interest can occur. If all of the funds have the same directors, the directors are subject to divided loyalties because they have a duty of loyalty to every fund. These divided loyalties can give rise to conflicts of interest and lead to board decisions that injure investors in one or more of the funds. *In re* Vanguard Special Tax-Advantaged Retirement Fund, Inc., Investment Company Act Release No. 14361 (February 7, 1985), 1985 SEC LEXIS 2236, at *12–*14 (Commissioners Treadway and Peters, dissenting).

164. *In re* Vanguard Special Tax-Advantaged Retirement Fund, Inc., Investment Company Act Release No. 14153, 49 Fed. Reg. 36,582. (September 18, 1984).
165. See supra Part IV-B.
166. Societal properties are measured as means, medians, rates, proportions, and percentages. Such measures are inherently resistant to rapid change.
167. Social values on at least some topics are evidently altered by events, i.e., by one or more occurrences that take place during a given period of time and that have a largely uniform impact throughout the population. Karin L. Brewster and Irene Padavic, "Change in Gender-Ideology, 1977-1996," *Journal of Marriage & Family* 62 (2000): 477, 485–86; David J. Harding and Christopher Jencks, "Changing Attitudes toward Premarital Sex: Cohort, Period, and Aging Effects," *Public Opinion Quarterly* 67 (2003): 211, 225. However, the magnitude of period effects, especially relative to the magnitude of the effects of aging and of differences between cohorts, has yet to be established for social values generally. Unfortunately, the effect of any one of the three factors (i.e., age, cohort, and period) cannot be separated statistically from the effects of the other two. Norval D. Glenn, "Cohort Analysis," *Quantitative Applications in the Social Sciences*, Monograph # 5 (1977), Sage Publications, Inc. Series: Quantitative Applications in the Social Sciences.
168. Timothy A. Salthouse, "What and When of Cognitive Aging," *Current Directions in Psychological Science* 13 (2004): 140.
169. See supra note 6.
170. See Press Release, The White House, Declaration of the Summit on Financial Markets and the World Economy ¶ 9 (November 15, 2008), http://georgewbush-whitehouse.archives.gov/news/releases/2008/11/20081115-1.html (accessed April 8, 2011) (statement of leaders of twenty nations calling for increased government regulation of finance).
171. *Regulation of Mutual Fund Boards*, supra note 6, at 546, 548–49. An "entity" refers here to an identifiable organization that has a legally recognized form, e.g., a corporation or a partnership. An "institution" refers to a widespread type of interpersonal activity in a society that is essential to the functioning of the society. The sociological concept of "institution" is defined supra in note 3.
172. For example, higher rates of homicide in U.S. counties have been found to lower the probability of conviction for defendants charged with homicide and to shorten the length of the prison terms that such convicted defendants receive. Mark Cooney and Callie Harbin Burt, "Less Crime, More Punishment," *American Journal of Sociology* 114 (2008): 491. Homicide thus does not seem to be deterred by punishment occurring through the institution of law, i.e., by conviction and imprisonment. Ibid., 494–95, 514. The finding, if applicable to all types of crime, adds to the evidence in note 6 supra that patterns of social behavior in a society have a material effect on, but are not materially affected by, the institution of law in the society.

5

The Public–Private Dichotomy in Morality and Law*

This chapter advances the thesis that the doctrines and concepts of law are attributable to the properties of society and to the forces molding these properties. The thesis, after being illustrated with the federal Investment Advisers Act, is assessed quantitatively using data from a survey of a national sample of adults in U.S. households. The survey, which was conducted in 1991, ascertained whether interviewees classified morality as a private matter or as a public issue. The public or private nature of morality in social values was the dependent variable in a study that assumed (a) law does not attempt to regulate an activity, or explicitly protects the activity from regulation, when society designates the activity as private, and (b) the doctrines of law designed to regulate activities that are designated public embody the doctrines of prevailing morality.

Because social values on whether morality is private or public comprised the dependent variable, the factors that mold these values have the potential to prevent or permit law designed to regulate socially significant activities. Logistic regression was used to estimate the relationship to the dependent variable of two sets of factors that may influence whether morality is designated private or public. One set was factors that structure (e.g., stratify) a society and that have important societal correlates and consequences. The other set was comprised of modes of thought and conduct that are cultural dimensions of a society. Notable relationships to the dependent variable were found for the structural factors of gender and, among women, educational attainment. In terms of gender, the odds that morality would be considered a private matter were approximately three-and-a-half times higher among women than among men. In terms of education, the odds that morality would be considered private were approximately three-fourths lower among women with thirteen or more years of schooling than among women with twelve or fewer years of schooling. The chapter suggests that, because the odds of placing morality in the private sphere are appreciably greater among women, gains in the status of women may help to explain U.S. Supreme Court decisions that construed the Constitution to restrict government regulation of sexual activity and its incidents.

I. The Rule and Role of Law in Society

"When they discover the center of the universe, a lot of people will be disappointed to discover they are not it."

—Bernard Bailey[1]

A. The Rule of Law

The concept underlying the phrase "the rule of law" conveys a specific image both of the nature of law and of the role of law in society. The concept is pertinent to the instant chapter because it is embedded in Anglo-Saxon jurisprudence[2] and is generally believed to be a key to the success of modern societies.[3] In the United States, the concept enjoys widespread support,[4] and if this support accurately gauges the prevalence of the concept and of the image of law linked to the concept, a large fraction of Americans believe law to be a significant aspect of their country. Not surprisingly, persons in law-related occupations share that belief, and they may assign even greater importance than the public to "the rule of law." In their view, both the structure and operation of U.S. society depend on law.[5] Thus, the concept of "the rule of law" has been employed to suggest that the existence[6] and equilibrium[7] of a society are impossible without law. According to this view, "we have survived and prospered as a free nation because we have adhered to the rule of law."[8]

What, however, is "the rule of law"? When does "the rule of law" exist? A concept, to be useful, must have an identifiable referent, but the concept of "the rule of law" has no generally accepted referent or set of referents.[9] Nonetheless, "the rule of law" would seem to be associated with the presence of at least four conditions[10]: (1) the law of the society has unambiguous standards; (2) the standards are the same for, and are applied in the same way to, all members of a category of human beings or entities; (3) the categories that are used by law to differentiate human beings and entities, and the standards of each category, are accepted by the society; and (4) the standards for a given category are manifested in the behavior and activities of the members of the category. The preceding list of attributes of "the rule of law" is consistent with conclusions regarding law that courts and scholars have reached—that law must be fair[11] in content,[12] appearance,[13] and application.[14] However, despite its importance to maintaining cohesion in a society,[15] fairness does not seem to be the primary focus of the concept of "the rule of law." Instead, the concept by its very name highlights the idea of *rule*. With this emphasis, the concept of "the rule of law" suggests that the law of a society controls,[16] and thus is followed by, the individuals and entities in the society.[17] Indeed, the concept means literally that, in a society characterized by the rule of law, there is obedience to law.[18] Law, in a word, regulates.

B. Law as a Regulator

In the United States, then, law is believed to be at the heart of society, and the belief seems to rest heavily on the assumption that, in a society whose structure is complex and whose population is large and diverse, law is a highly effective means of guiding the behavior of individuals and the activities of groups. But is law successful when it seeks to regulate, i.e., control, important aspects of social life? An explicit or implicit intent to regulate, directly or indirectly, is embedded in law as an institution[19]—to the degree that a society deems behavior X to be desirable and public in nature, the law of the society will seek to increase the frequency of X, and to the extent that a society deems behavior Y to be undesirable and public, the law of the society will be designed to eliminate (or at least reduce) the occurrence of Y. However, if law does not fulfill its regulatory goal, i.e., if law does not appreciably affect the behaviors and activities it targets, the contention that law is critical to a society must either be abandoned or, if retained, justified on other grounds.

Unfortunately for the advocates of the contention that law is an effective regulatory mechanism, a substantial body of well-designed quantitative research has found that law does not appreciably and permanently alter social patterns. Briefly stated, the research indicates that the impact on targeted social behavior of law-based regulation is generally just minimal in the long term, and if and when the impact is substantial, it is short-lived.[20] Moreover, regulation can have effects that are unwanted by or harmful to society.[21] Accordingly, the center of the universe is unlikely to be either law as a set of ideas or the individuals who write and apply the doctrines of law. If the universe has a sociological center, it is evidently not a particular institution but society itself.[22]

C. Law in a Macrosociological Framework

The thesis of the present chapter is that the concepts and doctrines of law are macrosociological phenomena. Law is thus treated in the chapter as a component of a larger social system, i.e., of a society. In this framework, law as a societal component is deemed to be an institution—i.e., a pattern of human interaction that is common in, and a contributor to the functioning of, the society in which it exists.[23] The concepts and doctrines of the institution of law are assumed by the framework to result from the properties of society and the forces that mold these properties. In the United States, however, such a framework contradicts conventional thinking because the framework considers individual human beings, including those who are prominent in politics and those who are charismatic, to have no long-term impact on the core content of law in a democracy.[24] Although my framework recognizes that an individual can trigger a lasting change in the doctrines of law in a democracy, it contends that an individual can do so only when society-level properties and forces create the trigger. A particular individual who triggers such a change is not essential to the change, however, because other individuals could and would also have done so. In my macrosociological framework, then, explanations of non-ephemeral change in the central ideas of law in a democracy are wrong when they attribute the change to specific individuals, because the process that shapes these ideas involves fungible individuals.

While quantitative research bearing on this framework is in its infancy, the findings of currently available studies are consistent with it. What does existing research suggest are the most important societal properties that produce concepts and doctrines of law?[25] In answering the question, I will also touch on the key societal forces that seem to be responsible for changing the societal properties pertinent to law. The discussion of the properties and forces will inform the analyses undertaken in subsequent parts of the instant chapter.

One property that evidently affects the law of a society is the educational attainment of the members of the society. The importance of education may arise from the relationship that exists between educational level and rationality. Specifically, education is at least a concomitant, and is probably a cause, of the extent of rationality in a society. As a societal property, educational attainment is likely to result from one large-scale force in particular—the quantity and quality of knowledge that is being used by a society.[26]

A second property that apparently has a bearing on the content of law in a society is the degree of urbanization in the society or, more precisely, the proportion of the inhabitants of the society who are exposed to high population density. Rationality is heightened among individuals who live and/or work in large cities, theory suggests, because these individuals are exposed to a wide range of changing stimuli.[27] The density of population in a society, of course, results from the rates of fertility and mortality in the society, from the pace and patterns of migration within the society, and from the rates of immigration into and emigration out of the society.

A third property that may shape the content of law in a society is the extent and severity of social, cultural, and economic divisions within the population of the society. The law of a society results from conditions that have an impact on the society, and a plausible argument can be made that law can be affected by social, cultural, and economic fractures in the population of the society, e.g., by cleavages on the basis of race,[28] national origin, and/or income. For example, as the population of a society becomes more heterogeneous in terms of national origin, the law of the society is more likely to incorporate doctrines that are symbols[29] in order to counteract the reduction in social cohesion caused by the heterogeneity.[30]

A further aspect of divisions within a society merits a brief discussion here. Given a split in a society, law can be formulated to pursue one of two objectives. First, law may accept the continuation of the division but concern itself with curbing unwanted activities (e.g., crime) to which the division is believed to be a contributor.[31] Second, law may be concerned with erasing the division, as in the case of statutes banning discrimination in employment. Unfortunately, the societal conditions producing law that has the former concern rather than the latter concern have yet to be identified,[32] but the existence of one concern rather than the other may depend, inter alia, on the degree to which the division creates friction between the different sides of the division. Whatever the reason, the doctrines of law do not occur by accident; rather, they are adopted in response to, and are designed to improve, the conditions of social life.

However, if law exists to benefit society, the question is *why* law acts in the interests of society. What explains the subservience of law to the society in which the law exists? In my framework, a society is a system, and a system, by definition, is organized.[33] Being organized, a system is more than the simple combination of its components, and a society, therefore, is a discrete entity with distinct properties of its own. Alternatively expressed, a society is comprised of structured networks of interaction between members of a population, and both the network structure and the population possess properties that their members do not have.[34]

If a system comprised of institutions—i.e., a society—has an existence that is independent of its components (institutions), as a macrosociological framework contends, the system will tend to persist. A society, being a system, will normally be supported by its institutions, according to the framework, and it will therefore generally be characterized by inertia and by a propensity for self-preservation. This reasoning, if correct, permits the question posed in the prior paragraph to be answered tentatively—a society develops and utilizes particular concepts and doctrines of law because it is, and the concepts and doctrines of law help to make it, a self-sustaining entity.

A related, and important, macrosociological proposition is that, being a system composed of institutions, a society is independent of the individual human beings in it even though, at a given time, the society operates through these human beings. From a macrosociological perspective, individuals are irrelevant. As a result, the particular individuals who populate a society are believed to have no direct, enduring influence on the institution of law. In the macrosociological framework of this chapter, the content of law in a society, and the impact of law on patterns of social activity, are thus expected to be affected no more than temporarily by the individuals who write and enforce statutes, administrative agency rules, and court decisions.

Why are individuals unable to have a substantial, permanent impact on law—at least in a society such as the United States that has a large, heterogeneous population and a complex set of institutions? The chief reason is probably that individuals live their lives in a *system* and the system changes in response to system-level forces. Furthermore, individuals have, in historical terms, just a relatively brief presence in the system, i.e., in a society.[35] A society, on the other hand, lasts to the extent that it is supported by its institutions, and a society will normally have this support because it possesses a built-in tendency to persist. Over the long run, accordingly, the institution of law responds to, and helps to fulfill, the needs of the system, not the wishes of the individuals in the system.[36]

D. The Role of Law

On the surface, the framework I am proposing may seem to imply that law is merely a puppet of the society in which it exists and that law performs no significant role in social life. The framework, however, warrants no such conclusion. If law were unimportant to society, law would not have lasted. Since the United States was founded, major changes have occurred in the concepts and doctrines of law, of course, but notably the institution of law was not abandoned. Instead, the institution of law continued to be used, although with revisions to its content, and it persisted because law was an instrument that had utility to society.

The durability of law in the United States,[37] in short, is evidence that law *does* something for society and that the societal benefits of law are not trivial. Because concepts of law (including the concept of "the rule of law") and doctrines applying these concepts operate within a larger social system, their sociological functions must be understood in terms of that system.[38] However, if my framework is helpful in understanding law, the societal contributions made by the concepts and doctrines of law in the United States differ appreciably from the contributions that these concepts and doctrines are widely believed to make. In my framework, the concept of "the rule of law" is useful to a society as an ideal,[39] but the present meaning of the concept[40] gives the concept undeserved importance because current assumptions regarding the societal functions of law are incorrect. A reassessment of the concept is thus required, even though the reassessment may prove uncomfortable and will lead to much less emphasis on the "rule of law."

What are the societal contributions of law? The contributions are probably the same in the United States and in other countries with similar sociological, economic, and demographic characteristics. At present, unfortunately, the sociology of law has an insufficient body of empirically grounded knowledge to provide a definitive list of the contributions that law makes to society. Nonetheless, a society possessing characteristics similar to those of the United States seems likely to benefit from law in at least three important ways: (1) law provides symbols that endorse prevailing social values, (2) law contributes to preserving or improving the reputation of socially and economically important segments of society, and (3) law assists in maintaining trust and perceptions of fairness or, when trust and perceptions of fairness have been damaged, in rebuilding them.[41] Through these contributions, law strengthens the ties that individuals have to their society.

Under the above line of reasoning, the function of law in a complex, heterogeneous society is primarily sociological rather than economic. This conclusion, if correct, has important ramifications for understanding the societal bases of law. More precisely, assuming that law exists mainly for sociological reasons, the origin and evolution of law can be expected to develop and change in response to sociological factors, i.e., system-level properties and forces that are social in character. To illustrate, I next consider investment advisers and their regulation by the federal government.

II. Investment Advisers

What is an investment adviser? Broadly defined, investment advisers supply investment advice, i.e., guidance on a potential or an existing commitment of economic resources to any type of property from which monetary profit is sought. In this chapter, however, investment advice is construed more narrowly, and investment advice, while obviously involving investment,[42] is deemed to be rendered only when the subject of the advice is a security.[43] Investment advisers, then, are concerned with, and only with, securities.

As will be explained in Part II-B infra, Congress has adopted a statute that defines the occupation of "investment adviser" and authorizes the Securities and Exchange Commission to regulate the members of the occupation. The statute is the Investment Advisers Act ("Act"),[44] but before turning to its provisions, I describe the importance of investment advisers in the United States.

A. Investment Advisers in the Economy

In general terms, an investment adviser is a party (i.e., individual or entity) that makes or recommends decisions to acquire and dispose of securities for particular clients.[45] To be within the statutory definition, the decisions and recommendations, which may involve specific securities (e.g., the common stock of corporation X) or a specific type of security (e.g., common stock in general), must have been reached through the exercise of judgment.[46] Thus, decisions and recommendations are not investment advice if they arise mechanically (e.g., from a computer program) and if the human inputs into the mechanical process are disregarded. However, the decisions and recommendations that constitute investment advice are not entirely unfettered because the securities involved in the advice are, or are to be, owned by another party. An adviser is an agent for a client who is investing in securities and, as agent, must act in line with restrictions that the client has imposed on the type(s) of securities that can be bought and sold.[47]

In this regard, it is important to keep in mind that the instruments being purchased and sold are *securities*. Federal securities statutes do not identify the elements of a security but only list types of securities.[48] Unfortunately, the referent of the word "security" is neither certain nor constant. Whether or not an instrument is a security is context-dependent, can differ between societies at a given point in time, and can change within a society over time.[49] Nonetheless, widespread agreement seems to exist regarding one element of a security. In particular, the concept of a security connotes profit,[50] and as a result, the decisions and recommendations of an investment adviser are primarily, if not solely, aimed at producing economic gain for the clients of the adviser rather than change in social policies.

How important are investment advisers in the economy of the United States? Surprisingly, data are scarce, but the Securities and Exchange Commission ("Commission") has estimated that, in the twelve months ending on May 3, 2010, investment advisers that were registered with the Commission managed client assets worth[51] in excess of $38 trillion.[52] This amount is large in absolute terms, of course, and it is large in relative terms, too.

The relative size of the assets entrusted to Commission-registered investment advisers is illustrated by two economic yardsticks. The first is the gross domestic product (GDP) of the United States.[53] In the fourth quarter of 2009, approximately the midpoint of the period for which the Commission estimated the assets managed by registered investment advisers, the United States domestically produced goods and services worth almost $14.3 trillion.[54] Consequently, the wealth controlled by these investment advisers was, in amount, roughly 2.7 times the size of the GDP of the United States economy. Otherwise stated, the economy of the United States would have needed about 2.7 years to generate the wealth over which registered investment advisers had management authority between May 2009 and May 2010.

GDP, however, may not be the most appropriate gauge of the relative importance of investment advisers in the economy of the United States. While the assets controlled by investment advisers and GDP are both monetary in nature, the former is a measure of financial resources that the United States has accumulated—in a sense, a nest egg of the country. GDP, on the other hand, is a measure of the output of the economy of a country in a single year from labor and property situated in the country. Comparing the two measures may be juxtaposing apples and oranges.

A measure that may be more suitable for judging the societal significance of investment advisers is the monetary value of fixed assets in the United States. Fixed assets are buildings (residential and non-residential), equipment, and software of private parties and governments.[55] Like assets managed by investment advisers, fixed assets constitute accumulated wealth, and a comparison of the two is thus likely to be more appropriate than a comparison of the assets managed by investment advisers and GDP. Moreover, adviser-managed assets and fixed assets do not overlap because they are different forms of wealth. Assets managed by investment advisers represent financial wealth; fixed assets represent nonfinancial wealth.

Unfortunately, data on both measures could not be obtained for the same point in time, and as a result, some error exists in comparing the data. Nonetheless, a comparison is useful, because fixed assets are central components of the level of American affluence. At the end of 2009, the market value of fixed assets in the United States was approximately $44 trillion.[56] The wealth managed by Commission-registered investment advisers (during the twelve months from early May 2009 to early May 2010) was thus equal to roughly 86 percent of the wealth in fixed assets (at year-end 2009). Otherwise expressed, for every $100 of fixed assets, there were about $86 under the management of registered investment advisers.

Whichever yardstick is preferred—GDP or fixed assets—it is clear that the occupation of investment adviser has become an important component of the financial sector of the United States. As the Commission has noted, "investment advisers play a key role in the economic life of America today."[57] However, securities and the society in which they trade are inextricably linked, and although the point is not often made explicitly, the occupation of investment adviser cannot be divorced from the society in which the occupation functions. As a result, the occupation has been a topic of legislation by Congress and, pursuant to the legislation, subject to oversight by the Commission.

B. Investment Advisers Act

Important federal legislation dealing with securities was not enacted in the United States until the economic depression of the 1930s.[58] In 1933, Congress passed the first piece of legislation, the Securities Act,[59] and a year later adopted the Securities Exchange Act.[60] In 1940, Congress approved the Investment Advisers Act[61] and the Investment Company Act.[62] These four statutes supply most of the foundation for the regulation of securities and the securities industry in the United States today. Of the four statutes, however, we will be concerned with just one—the Investment Advisers Act ("Advisers Act").

As shown above,[63] the occupation of investment adviser is currently of major significance to the financial sector in the United States, but the salience of the occupation is not recent. Investment advisers became a noticeable feature of the sector initially during the 1930s.[64] The expansion of the occupation at this time has been attributed to the volatility of stock prices that started in the latter half of 1929[65] and that caused investors to be wary of long-term commitments to constant sets of securities.[66] Although the exact monetary value of assets managed by investment advisers in the 1930s is unknown, the amount under management was believed by Congress to be sufficiently large to warrant enactment of a statute—the Advisers Act—authorizing regulation of the occupation by the federal government.[67] In writing the Act, therefore, Congress not surprisingly incorporated an explicit statement that the impact of the occupation on the economy in general and the financial sector in particular had been nationwide in scope and material in degree.[68]

1. Statutory Definition

Section 202(a)(11) of the Advisers Act, stripped of its statutory exclusions,[69] defines an investment adviser as:

> any person who, for compensation, engages in the business of advising others, either directly or through publications or writings, as to the value of securities or as to the advisability of investing in, purchasing, or selling securities, or who, for compensation and as part of a regular business, issues or promulgates analyses or reports concerning securities.[70]

The above definition ("statutory definition"), like any law that is designed to achieve breadth, employs concepts of general application. Given this generality and the resulting ambiguities in the statutory definition, the staff of the Commission has found it necessary to publish two interpretations of the definition.[71] The initial interpretation appeared in 1981,[72] but a second interpretation—Release IA-1092—superseded it in 1987, i.e., just six years later.[73] Because Release IA-1092 is important to understanding the statutory definition of investment adviser, a review of pertinent portions of the Release is warranted.

2. Release IA-1092

According to Release IA-1092, a person is an investment advisor for purposes of the Advisers Act if all of the following conditions exist:

(i) The person furnishes advice, reports, or analyses that deal with securities;
(ii) The services in (i) constitute a business[74]; and
(iii) The services in (i) are supplied for compensation.[75]

An additional condition, however, is embedded in (i). While the additional condition is not expressly addressed by the Release, it is basic to the statutory definition of investment adviser. The condition, which arises from the construction of the Advisers Act by the United States Supreme Court,[76] recognizes that advice, reports, and analyses regarding securities—the services in (i)—can be of different types. For a person to qualify as an investment adviser under the Advisers Act, however, the person needs to provide a particular type of service. Specifically,

(iv) The services in (i) must involve individualized treatment of the recipient of the services.

Thus, if the services do not take into account the financial and psychological profile of the person receiving the services—i.e., if the services are not tailored to the recipient—the person delivering the advice, reports, or analyses will not be an investment adviser.[77]

It is unfortunate that condition (iv) is not discussed in Release IA-1092.[78] An in-depth discussion of this condition would have probably suggested indicators of the presence or absence of individualized treatment under the Advisers Act. In doing so, the discussion would have underscored the prominence of individualism in the culture of the United States.[79] Individualism, often a concomitant or component of privacy, is manifested in doctrines of U.S. law on a variety of topics, including employment discrimination,[80] immigration,[81] pornography,[82] sexuality and reproduction,[83] and violent crime.[84] Individualism also forms a cornerstone of U.S. law on securities,[85] and its appearance in the Advisers Act, therefore, should not be unexpected.

Condition (iv), however, is not alone in having relevance to the macrosociological framework of this chapter. Conditions (ii) and (iii) are pertinent, too. With regard to (ii)—which focuses on the business element of the statutory definition—the Release concludes that a person is engaged in the business of being an investment adviser if the person makes public representations that the person is an investment adviser, if the person receives identifiable compensation that is linked to furnishing advice on securities, or if the person other than sporadically provides clients with recommendations, analyses, or reports focusing on particular securities or particular types of securities.[86] Because the Release separates these conditions with the word "or," it contemplates that any one of the conditions will suffice to create a business under the Advisers Act.[87]

The Release, of course, is an interpretation of a statute by an administrative agency, and as such, it is not binding on the judiciary.[88] If Congress has not defined a word in a statute, federal courts rather than federal executive-branch agencies are the ultimate arbiters of the meaning of the word.[89] Notably, neither the Advisers Act itself[90] nor the legislative history of the Act[91] supplies a definition of the word "business." To date, moreover, no federal court seems to have departed from the Release when interpreting the word "business" in the Advisers Act definition of investment adviser, but inasmuch as the judiciary is not compelled to follow the Release, the judiciary may eventually assign to the word "business" the meaning that was generally accepted in the United States when the Advisers Act was adopted.[92] Indeed, the meaning of the word "business" to the public at the time the statutory definition was incorporated into the Advisers Act may be preferred by the judiciary[93] inasmuch as Congress has not altered the definition since formulating it in 1940.[94]

A reason for believing that the general understanding of the word "business" in 1940 comports more fully with congressional intent than the criteria for the existence of a business[95] that were developed by the staff of the Commission is that the two Releases were issued by the staff in the 1980s. The Advisers Act, however, was adopted by Congress in 1940, four decades earlier. Because the Releases reflect social and economic conditions at the time they were written, their criteria for a business cannot be blindly accepted. On the contrary, their criteria should be approached with some skepticism.

If the judiciary were to construe the word "business" in accordance with the way the word was employed in public discourse when Congress approved the Advisers Act, what would be the meaning of the word? According to two dictionaries published in the first half of the 1930s, a period close to the year (1940) in which the Act was adopted, "business" includes:

> Any particular occupation or employment habitually engaged in, esp. for livelihood or gain.[96]
>
> 12. A person's official or professional duties as a whole; stated occupation, profession, or trade. 13. In general sense: Action which occupies time, demands attention and labour; *esp.* serious occupation, work, as opposed to pleasure or recreation... 14.b. A particular occupation; a trade or profession.[97]

To combine the above, a business is a recurring,[98] profit-seeking activity of a person (human being or entity). In addition, the society in which the activity occurs must identify the activity as a business rather than as a form of relaxation or a means of amusement. A business, consequently, has the purpose of obtaining an economic return and is an activity that society classifies as a business.

The preceding composite of the dictionary meanings ("composite"), however, is at variance with the position taken by the Release. In this regard, two of the factors listed in the Release are pertinent. First, public representations by a person that the person is an investment adviser suffice to put the person into business as an investment adviser.[99] Second, the receipt of compensation for furnishing advice on securities is enough to cause a person to be in business as an investment adviser.[100] According to the Release, either factor by itself creates a business.[101]

Unlike the Release, the composite of the dictionary definitions does not allow any one factor to cause an activity to be a business. Under the composite, a person would be in the business of being an investment adviser only if the person actually furnished clients with advice, reports, or analyses dealing with securities; if the person did so repeatedly (i.e., on a regular basis); *and* if the person expected or accepted a monetary payment for these activities. To illustrate the composite, a company that publicly portrays itself as an investment adviser would not be in the investment adviser business unless it actually has clients and serves them as an investment adviser. Similarly, an individual would not be in the investment adviser business under the composite simply because he or she is paid, or expects to be paid, a sum of money for acting as an investment adviser to a single client on a single occasion. If the position adopted in the Release is used, on the other hand, both the company and the individual would be in the investment adviser business.

Before leaving the composite, a final point merits emphasis. Under the composite, a necessary condition for an activity to be designated a business is that the society in which the activity takes place must label the activity as a business rather than as entertainment. However, a society has latitude in how it classifies and deals with phenomena. Thus, a society may consider a particular activity to be unacceptable, as in the case of prostitution, and when it does so, it will attempt to eliminate the activity through informal means and/or through law.[102] On the other hand, a society may not be cognizant of or concerned with the impact of a phenomenon that is materially affecting it. An illustration is the size and continuing growth of population, a topic that is relevant to the content of law because population density shapes law.[103] In recent decades, the population of the world has been increasing by more than three-quarters of a billion people every ten years,[104] but the ramifications of population growth in the United States[105] and elsewhere for economic prosperity and social stability[106] are not currently attracting much attention among Americans.[107]

The way in which a phenomenon is perceived by a society, in short, does not depend solely on the nature of the phenomenon. It is also a function of societal conditions, including the cultural dimensions of social life, and in this sense, the problems that confront a society are socially constructed.[108] For the Advisers Act, the social character of societal designations means that whether a particular undertaking is deemed to be a "business"—and, as discussed infra, whether the undertaking is "*for* compensation" and whether an item *is* compensation—depends on circumstances in the society that hosts the undertaking. Unfortunately, the sociological variables bearing on whether an activity is considered to be the business of investment advising are unknown and will remain so until they have been the subject of rigorous research.

Finally, we consider condition (iii)—the compensation element—in the statutory definition of investment adviser. While the condition does not require a lengthy exploration, two points should be made. First, insofar as compensation is economic in nature—a position that seems to be taken by the Release[109]—it is a component of a business, which is condition (ii).[110] Thus, when compensation is economic, its treatment as a separate element is unnecessary.[111]

The second point involves the matter of whether all compensation is economic. In this regard, it is pertinent that section 17(e)(1) of the Investment Company Act forbids a person who is affiliated with a Commission-registered investment company from accepting non-salary or non-wage compensation for selling property to, or buying property from, the investment company if, in the transaction, the affiliated person is an agent.[112] Notably, section 17(e)(1) is part of a statute that was a companion to the Advisers Act,[113] and both in section 17(e)(1) and in section 202(a)(11) of the Advisers Act, Congress incorporated compensation as an element. Neither piece of legislation defines the word "compensation," but inasmuch as the two statutes were adopted together, Congress is unlikely to have wanted the word to be defined in one way in the Investment Company Act and in a different way in the Advisers Act.

Because an affiliate of an investment company includes the investment adviser to the company,[114] section 17(e)(1) covers investment advisers to registered investment companies.[115] Under existing case law, an item is compensation under section 17(e)(1) as long as the item is *thought* to be a benefit by the person accepting it,[116] i.e., the attractiveness of an item to a person determines whether, for that person, the item constitutes compensation. Of course, while an item may be attractive for an economic reason, it may also be attractive for a reason that is not economic. Therefore, an item would apparently qualify as compensation under section 17(e)(1) even if it has no significant economic (e.g., monetary) value as long as it has significant psychological (e.g., emotional) value or significant social (e.g., reputational) value to the person who wants or receives it.[117]

Assuming that Congress wanted the word "compensation" to have the same meaning in section 202(a)(11) of the Advisers Act as it has in section 17(e)(1) of the Investment Company Act, a person could become an investment adviser either from compensation that is economic or from compensation that is not economic. If this conclusion is correct—i.e., if compensation under section 202(a)(11) can be economic or non-economic—the statutory definition of investment adviser fits comfortably within a macrosociological framework. For example, the relative appeal of money versus an item other than money evidently varies across subcultures within a society,[118] and the relative appeal of one type of non-money item versus another is almost certainly a function of culture, too.[119] If these propositions are correct, the issue of whether a person satisfies the compensation element (as well as other elements) of the statutory definition of investment adviser is not determined by factors internal to the institution of law but by factors external to the institution. The latter factors can be expected to include mainly macrosociological variables.

III. An Empirical Study of Determinants of Law

A premise of this chapter is that law does not arise randomly but is anchored in society. Under this view, the concepts and doctrines of law that are central to a society are not attributable to individuals and personalities, but are explained instead by sociological, demographic, and/or economic conditions in the society. However, the premise requires appreciably more empirical support than it currently possesses.[120] Relevant evidence seems likely to be produced by research on the societal factors that may lie behind the conditions that are the immediate determinants of regulatory law (i.e., law designed to suppress or encourage a particular type of activity). If a factor that potentially affects an immediate determinant of regulatory law can be measured quantitatively, a multivariate statistical test can ascertain whether the factor is related to the determinant and can estimate the strength of any relationship found.

In Part II supra, I examined federal law on the occupation of investment adviser as an example of regulation by government. This law and the occupation it regulates were intended to be a case study, and the regulation of investment advisers was reviewed on the assumption that law concerned with one type of activity can lead to an understanding of the determinants of regulatory law on multiple types of activity that are important to society. Notably, the Advisers Act embodies a concern with morality,[121] a concern whose presence in the Act should not be surprising since law generally is grounded in morality.[122] Any factor that molds morality, therefore, is likely to help in explaining the development and disappearance of law-based regulation directed at the many activities in a society that are tied to morality.

In this Part of the chapter, I present an analysis of quantitative data that was undertaken to identify factors that may affect whether morality is classified by adults in the United States as a public issue or a private matter. Because law in a democracy eventually incorporates prevailing morality, law and morality cannot be divorced. However, the assignment of a morality-linked form of behavior to the public sphere or to the private sphere is critical to the presence or absence of regulatory law addressing such behavior. The factors that are responsible for defining morally relevant behavior as public or private thus potentially account for whether law exists to regulate the behavior.

The data that I analyzed are from the General Social Survey ("GSS"). The GSS, which began in 1972, annually or biennially samples adults residing in the United States and, through face-to-face interviews, gathers information on a wide range of topics. The topics covered by the GSS, however, are not identical in every survey. The data for the instant study are from the GSS that was conducted in 1991 because of the set of variables measured in that year. The 1991 GSS used multistage cluster sampling to choose blocks of dwelling units and then, within chosen blocks, quota sampling to select individuals. In 1991, the GSS was confined to English-speaking residents.[123]

A. Variables

The dependent variable—the phenomenon that I sought to explain—was derived from responses to two questions in the 1991 GSS that focus on a fundamental dimension of social life, and I therefore regard the responses as measures of values rather than of opinions.[124] The GSS assigns mnemonic labels to its variables, and the labels for the two questions that formed the basis of the dependent variable in my study were PERRIGHT and SOCRIGHT. The wording of each question is reproduced in Table 5.1, and as is evident from their wording, both questions dealt with morality. In the sociology of law, morality and the factors that affect it are important subjects for research because different views of morality are central to divisive issues facing government[125] and because law will not usually regulate an activity in a democratic society unless the society considers the activity to be immoral[126] and public.[127] Although PERRIGHT and SOCRIGHT concentrated on morality in general rather than on the morality of a specific type of behavior, the general is likely to inform the specific, and the factors that shape morality in its generic form can be expected to offer insight into the content of law at a particular time and change in law over time.

Table 5.1 Variables in Regression Model[129]

Mnemonic label of variable	Measurement of variable
Dependent variable	
MORALITY	MORALITY was measured as a dummy variable (i.e., respondents were coded 0 or 1) and was based on the answers to two GSS questions, namely, PERRIGHT and SOCRIGHT. Respondents who disagreed with PERRIGHT and agreed with SOCRIGHT were coded 0 on MORALITY. Respondents who agreed with PERRIGHT and disagreed with SOCRIGHT were coded 1 on MORALITY.
Components of MORALITY	
PERRIGHT	"Do you agree or disagree with the following statements... Right and wrong should be a matter of personal conscience."
SOCRIGHT	"Do you agree or disagree with the following statements... Right and wrong should be decided by society."
Independent variables	
AGE	Age of the respondent in years. In the data analysis, AGE was a variable with three categories. Respondents who were 18–44 years of age were coded 1; respondents who were 45–64 years of age were coded 2; and respondents who were 65 years of age or older were coded 3.
BORN	"Were you born in this country?" In the data analysis, BORN was a dummy variable. Respondents who answered "yes" were coded 0, and respondents who answered "no" were coded 1.
EDUC	The number of years of formal schooling that a respondent reported she or he had completed. In the data analysis, EDUC was a dummy variable. Respondents who had finished no more than twelve years of schooling were coded 0, and respondents who had finished at least thirteen years of schooling were coded 1.

(Continued on the next page)

Table 5.1 (*Continued*)

Mnemonic label of variable	Measurement of variable
FATALISM	"Do you agree or disagree with the following... There is little that people can do to change the course of their lives." In the data analysis, FATALISM was a dummy variable. Respondents were coded 0 if they answered "strongly agree" or "agree," and they were coded 1 if they answered "disagree" or "strongly disagree."
PRAYFREQ	"Now thinking about the present, about how often do you pray?" In the data analysis, PRAYFREQ was a variable with three categories. Respondents were coded 1 if they reported praying "never," "less than once a year," "about once or twice a year," or "several times a year." Respondents were coded 2 if they reported praying "about once a month," "2–3 times a month," "nearly every week," "every week," or "several times a week." Respondents were coded 3 if they reported praying "once a day" or "several times a day."
RACE	Race of the respondent as reported by the respondent. In the data analysis, RACE was a dummy variable. Respondents who reported that they were "White" were coded 0, and respondents who reported that they were "Black" were coded 1.
REALINC	Family income of the respondent in constant (1986) dollars. In the data analysis, REALINC was a dummy variable. Respondents were coded 0 if their family income was less than $20,000 and were coded 1 if their family income was $20,000 or more.
SEX	Sex of the respondent. In the data analysis, SEX was a dummy variable. Males were coded 0, and females were coded 1.

Mnemonic label of variable	Measurement of variable
TRUST	"Generally speaking, would you say that most people can be trusted or that you can't be too careful in life." In the data analysis, TRUST was a dummy variable. Respondents who believed that "most people can be trusted" were coded 0, and respondents who believed that "you can't be too careful" were coded 1.
XNORCSIZ	Level of urbanization of the place of residence of the respondent. In the data analysis, XNORCSIZ was a variable with three categories. Respondent's place of residence was coded 1 if it was "not within an SMSA (within a county)" *and* was one of the following: "open country within larger civil divisions," "an incorporated area less than 2,500 or an unincorporated area of 1,000 to 2,499," "a town or village (2,500 to 9,999)," or "a small city (10,000 to 49,999)." Respondent's place of residence was coded 2 if it was "within an SMSA" *and* was one of the following: "an unincorporated area of a medium central city," "an unincorporated area of a large central city (division, township, etc.)," "a suburb of a medium size central city," or "a suburb of a large central city." Respondent's place of residence was coded 3 if it was "within an SMSA" *and* was one of the following: "a medium size central city (50,000 to 250,000)" or "a large central city (over 250,000)." SMSA is the acronym for a Standard Metropolitan Statistical Area.

Respondents who agreed with PERRIGHT and disagreed with SOCRIGHT were assumed to consider morality a private matter; conversely, respondents who disagreed with PERRIGHT and agreed with SOCRIGHT were assumed to view morality as a public issue.[128] To capture the dimension that links PERRIGHT and SOCRIGHT, a new variable was created, and on the new variable, the former respondents were coded 1 and the latter respondents were coded 0. The new variable was labeled MORALITY and was used in the regression model as the dependent variable. Respondents who could not be coded 1 or 0 on MORALITY—e.g., respondents who agreed both with PERRIGHT and with SOCRIGHT—were omitted from the analysis. As a result, the use of MORALITY as the dependent variable imposed on the data analysis a ceiling of 305 respondents, of whom 145 were coded 1 and 160 were coded 0.

What variables ("independent variables") are promising as explanations of the dependent variable in the instant study? The combination of already published research on the determinants of the content of law on specific topics,[130] other pertinent social science research,[131] and existing law on investment advisers[132] suggest two sets of independent variables. One set structures (e.g., stratifies) a societal system, and the other set is comprised of dimensions of its culture.[133] Table 5.1 presents the variables in the two sets, the questions in the 1991 GSS that were used for the variables, and the manner in which each variable was measured in the instant study. A maximum of three categories were employed for an independent variable because, as discussed infra in Part III-B, the number of respondents in the data analysis was relatively small. Three-category independent variables were assumed to be interval scales.[134]

For the first set of independent variables—i.e., the structural variables—the regression equation included factors that have been significant in organizing the societal system in the United States. Each of the variables, accordingly, has important social correlates and consequences. The variables were the respondent's age (AGE),[135] educational attainment (EDUC), national origin (BORN), race (RACE), family income (REALINC), and sex (SEX) as well as the degree of urbanization of the area where the respondent resided (XNORCSIZ). Because of their importance in society, structural features such as the foregoing have traditionally been the core of the discipline of sociology[136] and cannot be ignored in any effort to explain social values that differentiate private from public in morality as a determinant of regulatory law.

The second set of independent variables in the regression model included modes of thought and conduct that are cultural dimensions of a society. Whether law seeks to regulate a particular activity is evidently a function in part of culture, i.e., of how the participants in a society perceive, and hence react to, their social world. For example, public support for a state law banning same-sex marriage is higher when same-sex marriage is seen as jeopardizing traditional social values regarding family and sex roles.[137] Because law is shaped by morality and because morality is a function of culture, the content of law can be expected to respond to and incorporate the content of culture.

The variables employed in the regression model as aspects or indicators of culture were the respondent's beliefs as to whether individuals are in control of their lives (FATALISM) and whether trust in people is warranted (TRUST). An additional cultural variable was the frequency of prayer by respondents (PRAYFREQ), which was assumed to be a measure of the more-general factor of religiousness. While no quantitative study seems to have been done on the relationship between any of these three independent variables and the dependent variable in the instant study, such relationships are suggested by logic and/or by some empirical research. The view that morality is a private issue, and thus a subject that is inappropriate for regulation by government, seemed likely to vary with inter alia (a) the belief that the participants in the society are able to manage their future,[138] (b) a belief by participants in the trustworthiness of other participants,[139] and (c) commitment to religion.[140]

B. Data Analysis

In the instant study, maximum-likelihood logit coefficients were estimated for the independent variables in the regression model. Linear (least squares) regression could not be used because the dependent variable was dichotomized; a dataset with such a dependent variable requires logistic regression.[141] Given the use of logistic regression and the coding employed for the dependent variable, the regression coefficient and odds ratio computed for an independent variable express, for each change in category on the independent variable, the change in the odds that morality was regarded as private.[142] In this regard, the reader should keep two points in mind. First, the regression coefficient and odds ratio for an independent variable estimate the impact of that independent variable on MORALITY while holding constant the effects of the other independent variables in the regression model. Second, an independent variable that increases the likelihood that morality will be deemed private evidently reduces the likelihood that regulatory law will be adopted. In the United States, an activity is not explicitly addressed by law, or is explicitly protected by law from regulation, when the activity is designated as private by a substantial share of the population.[143]

Because the GSS selected interviewees with cluster sampling—i.e., because the GSS sampled *sets* of individuals[144]—an adjustment was made to the standard errors that were calculated by the statistics program (Stata) in estimating the regression coefficients.[145] Specifically, each standard error from the estimation by Stata was multiplied by the square root of 1.42, i.e., by 1.19, in an attempt to remedy the effect of the sampling design.[146] Tables 5.2 and 5.3 infra report the regression coefficients, the adjusted standard errors for the coefficients, and the two-tailed levels of statistical significance for the coefficients based on the adjusted standard errors. The tables also show the constant in the regression equation and label it α.

Regression coefficients were initially estimated using data on 164 respondents.[147] With a significance level of .10 as the criterion for rejecting the null hypothesis,[148] three independent variables—educational attainment, sex, and frequency of prayer—were related to the dependent variable. The relationships can be more easily understood by converting each regression coefficient into the percentage change in the odds that a respondent will be coded 1 on MORALITY when the independent variable in question rises by a measurement category. Considered in these terms, the odds that morality would be deemed a private matter were 70 percent lower for respondents with thirteen or more years of schooling than for respondents with twelve or fewer years schooling, were 246 percent higher for females than for males, and rose by 87 percent for each increase in category of prayer frequency.[149]

To determine whether the results obtained might be misleading, a check was made for outliers, i.e., interviewees whose coding on the dependent variable differed from the coding that was predicted by the regression model. Outliers can materially distort the coefficients estimated in a regression analysis, and in order to identify influential outliers in the study, Cook's Statistic was calculated.[150] Unfortunately, the process of locating influential outliers is subjective,[151] and thus I visually examined the distribution of Cook's Statistic.[152] Doing so revealed that Cook's Statistic was far higher for two of the interviewees than for any of the others.[153] Accordingly, I omitted these interviewees and re-estimated the regression model. In re-estimating the coefficients, however, Stata dropped the variable BORN, because the code of 1 on BORN perfectly predicted the code of 0 on MORALITY and thereby prevented an estimation of maximum likelihood.[154]

Given the problem with BORN, the regression analysis was confined to the remaining independent variables. Tables 5.2 and 5.3 report the regression coefficients estimated for the independent variables without BORN and without the two interviewees who had the largest Cook's Statistic. The coefficients in Tables 5.2 and 5.3 are thus based on data for 162 interviewees. In addition to presenting the regression coefficients, the tables show the adjusted standard error for each coefficient, the *z* score obtained with the adjusted standard error of the coefficient, and the two-tailed statistical significance level for the *z* score.[155]

The regression model without BORN yielded results that were similar to the regression model with BORN. The signs and magnitudes of the coefficients that were statistically significant at or below .10 did not differ materially between the two models. Based on Table 5.2, the odds that morality would be regarded as a private matter were 68 percent lower for respondents with thirteen or more years of schooling than for respondents with twelve or fewer years of schooling, were 263 percent higher for females than for males, and rose by 97 percent with each increase in category of prayer frequency.[156] Because the

Table 5.2 Logit Coefficients and Significance Levels from Regression of MORALITY on Independent Variables

Independent variable (mnemonic label)	Regression coefficient	Adjusted standard error	z	p>|z|
Structural variables				
AGE	.297	.307	.97	.34
EDUC	−1.151	.456	−2.52	.02
RACE	−.104	.662	−.16	.88
REALINC	.295	.481	.61	.55
SEX	1.289	.468	2.75	.01
XNORCSIZ	.232	.324	.72	.48
Cultural variables				
FATALISM	−.744	.777	−.96	.34
PRAYFREQ	.677	.286	2.37	.02
TRUST	.385	.456	.84	.41
α	−2.441	1.322	−1.85	.07

impact of an independent variable is estimated holding constant the impact of every other independent variable in the regression model, the percentage change in odds produced by a rise in category on an independent variable is net of the percentage change in odds produced by a rise in category on every other independent variable.

In considering the results reported in Table 5.2, a possibility that must be explored is whether interaction existed between independent variables. If the relationship of one independent variable to the dependent variable differed across categories or levels of another independent variable—i.e., if interaction was present—the results in Table 5.2 do not accurately explain MORALITY. The failure to uncover interaction thus would yield incorrect conclusions regarding the manner in which independent variables act on the dependent variable.

Theory rather than statistics should guide the selection of independent variables to evaluate for potential interaction.[157] In light of this principle, it is notable that women in general have been found by research to be more religious than men in general, and theory has been advanced that ascribes this divergence in religiosity to sex-based differences in biology.[158] Consequently, I investigated the possibility that there was interaction between SEX and PRAYFREQ by estimating the regression coefficients for the independent variables (other than SEX) separately for women (n = 95) and for men (n = 67). The results are presented in Table 5.3, with the results for women in the top panel of the table and the results for men in the bottom panel.

Perhaps the most notable finding that emerges from Table 5.3 is the failure of even one explanatory variable to have regression coefficients that were statistically significant both among women and among men. Among women, only education had a significant coefficient. When this coefficient is converted into an odds ratio, the odds that morality would be considered private are found to be 73 percent lower for women who had thirteen or more years of schooling than for women who had twelve or fewer years of schooling. Among men, frequency of prayer had the sole significant coefficient; the conversion of this coefficient into an odds ratio shows that the odds that morality would be deemed private rise 148 percent for each category increase in PRAYFREQ.[159] However, the relationships uncovered by these coefficients have no discernible logical connection to each other, and without an identifiable pattern to the relationships, the coefficients in Table 5.3 for EDUC among women and PRAYFREQ among men stand on their own.

Table 5.3 Logit Coefficients and Significance Levels by Sex from Regression of MORALITY on Independent Variables

Independent variable (mnemonic label) by sex	Regression coefficient	Adjusted standard error	z	p>|z|
Women				
Structural variables				
AGE	.232	.424	.55	.59
EDUC	−1.318	.592	−2.23	.03
RACE	.000	.856	.00	1.00
REALINC	.247	.576	.43	.67
XNORCSIZ	.341	.418	.82	.42
Cultural variables				
FATALISM	−1.724	1.382	−1.25	.22
PRAYFREQ	.475	.398	1.19	.24
TRUST	.377	.571	.66	.51
α	.184	1.935	.10	.92
Men				
Structural variables				
AGE	.306	.480	.64	.53
EDUC	−.936	.798	−1.17	.25
RACE	.247	1.135	.22	.83
REALINC	.503	.979	.51	.61
XNORCSIZ	−.001	.571	.00	1.00
Cultural variables				
FATALISM	−.261	1.277	−.20	.85
PRAYFREQ	.908	.454	2.00	.05
TRUST	.418	.805	.52	.61
α	−3.276	2.318	−1.41	.16

C. Discussion

When the regression model employed in this study is evaluated with the results in Tables 5.2 and 5.3, just one independent variable is able to claim a general relationship to whether adults in the United States regard morality as private or as public.[160] Net of the other independent variables in the model, gender alone had an unconditional effect on social values defining morality as private or public. The influence that gender exercised, moreover, was far from trivial: the odds that morality would be deemed private were fully three-and-a-half times greater among women than among men.[161]

Tables 5.2 and 5.3, however, do not exhaust the insights that can be gleaned from the data. A fuller understanding of the effect of gender can be obtained from the accuracy with which independent variables in the instant study predicted whether interviewees would view morality as private or as public. Accuracy was determined first by regressing MORALITY on just SEX (Model 1) and then by regressing MORALITY on the three independent variables—EDUC, SEX, and PRAYFREQ—whose coefficients in Table 5.2 were found to be statistically significant (Model 2). The regression analyses used the same 162 interviewees as Tables 5.2 and 5.3. The measure of accuracy is the percentage of all predictions by a model that were correct. The percentages are in Table 5.4.[162]

I begin with Model 1. For predictions with SEX alone, accuracy was 63.6 percent when considering both predictions of interviewees who would classify morality as private *and* predictions of interviewees who would classify morality as public. However, the overall percentage masks a difference: Model 1 was noticeably less successful in predicting interviewees who would view morality as a private matter (59 percent) than in predicting interviewees who would view morality as a public matter (70.2 percent).

I turn now turn to Model 2, which retains gender as an independent variable but adds educational attainment and prayer frequency. As Table 5.4 shows, the use of the three independent variables together greatly improved success in predicting the interviewees who would regard morality as private and the interviewees who would regard

Table 5.4 Predictions by Independent Variables: Correct Predictions as a Percentage of All Predictions

Prediction	Correct predictions from	
	Model 1: SEX	Model 2: EDUC, SEX, and PRAYFREQ
Morality private or morality public	63.6%	72.2%
Morality private	59.0%	67.8%
Morality public	70.2%	77.3%

morality as public. Specifically, the three independent variables jointly increased the accuracy of predictions by not less than seven percentage points. Although educational attainment influences the designation of morality as private or public only among women and prayer frequency influences the designation only among men (see Table 5.3), the two variables enhance the ability of gender to identify persons in terms of their social values on the private or public nature of morality.

IV. Change in the Status of Women and the Content of Law

Perhaps it should not be surprising that women and men differ materially in their social values on whether morality is a private matter or a public issue. After all, much if not most of social life is affected to some extent by the attribute of biological sex and by the different roles in society that are attached to this attribute.[163] In the discussion that follows, however, I focus not on the sociology of gender but on the importance for law of the findings in Tables 5.2–5.4 that pertain to gender. The findings, I suggest, may help to explain the change in the interpretation of the United States Constitution by the U.S. Supreme Court with respect to set of related issues that were presented in cases spanning almost forty years.[164] Unfortunately, the paradigm that currently dominates the legal profession is unlikely to recognize the contribution to the change that may have been made by the gender difference in social values on morality. That paradigm, by embodying the concept of "the rule of law," assumes the primacy of law. In doing so, the paradigm ignores the subservience of law to conditions in the social system.

The law to which the findings are relevant involves sexuality. Currently, the U.S. Constitution is construed to bar government penalties for nonpublic, noncommercial sexual activity—homosexual as well as heterosexual—between adults who consent to the activity and who are capable of giving consent.[165] The prohibition on penalties for such activity is based largely on a right of privacy that the U.S. Supreme Court believes emanates from the liberty guarantee that is explicit in the two due process clauses of the Constitution.[166] Indeed, the line of cases through which the Court announced that the Constitution protects sexual activity between adults that is consensual, nonpublic, and noncommercial began with a case decided in 1965 in which the Court explicitly employed the concept of a right of privacy.[167] Notably, the Court has expressed a concern with privacy even when, in invalidating government penalties for sexual activity and closely related matters, it seems to have relied on other grounds—for instance, the liberty guarantee alone[168] or the equal protection guarantee.[169] By accepting privacy as an important concern, the Court implied that the right at issue was a right to privacy even though its holding was not explicitly based on privacy.

The preceding change in law, I believe, is explained partially by the findings reported in Part III of this chapter. In order to develop the explanation, I turn to a quantitative indicator of the social status of men relative to the social status of women in the United States. The indicator, which is portrayed graphically in Figure 5.1, is the difference between the percentage of men and the percentage of women who, at age 25–29, possessed at least a bachelor's degree in each decennial census year from 1940 to 2000.[170] Because the data are for seven equally spaced time points covering a total of sixty years, Figure 5.1 supplies a census-based measure of social status differences grounded on gender during most of the twentieth century.

To appreciate fully the importance of the data in Figure 5.1, it is necessary to realize that the male–female difference in educational attainment in the United States for most of the century-and-a-half after the Civil War was mainly at the college level.[171] The difference between men and women in college completion, therefore, is a

Figure 5.1 Sex Gap at Age 25-29 in Percentage with Bachelor's or Higher Degree

United States, 1940 to 2000

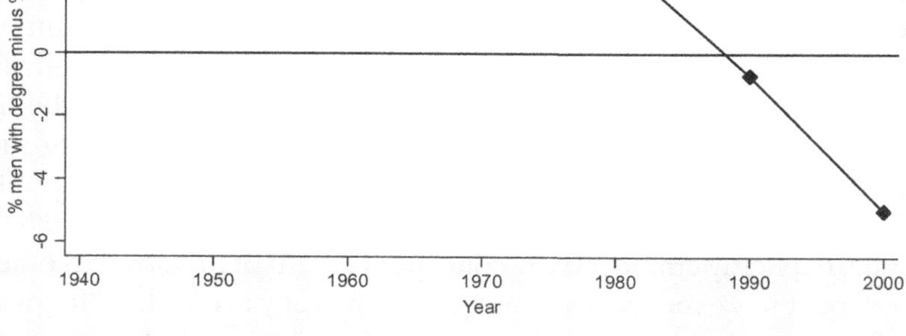

useful barometer of the relative status of each sex at a single point in time and of change in the relative status of each sex over time.[172] The indicator does not capture every dimension of sex roles and status, of course. However, the indicator is useful because it measures an attribute of individuals early in their lives, and the attribute has the potential to affect markedly later stages of the life cycle, especially in terms of occupation and income from employment. Unfortunately, the figure cannot be extended further back in time—i.e., cannot cover years prior to 1940—because the census did not gather information on educational attainment until 1940.[173]

The shift in law on sexuality and related matters that the United States experienced from the mid-1960s onward is likely to be attributable partially to the shift in the status of women that Figure 5.1 reveals.[174] Understanding this link will be aided by a brief explanation of the figure. In particular, Figure 5.1 was constructed from the *difference* between the percentage of men 25–29 years old and the percentage of women 25–29 years old who, in the census year specified, possessed a bachelor's degree or a higher degree. Because the percentage for women was subtracted from the percentage for men, a number above zero means that proportionally more men than women held a degree; conversely, a number below zero means that proportionally more women than men held a degree. The horizontal line across Figure 5.1 serves as a reference and marks the point at which the percentage for men is equal to the percentage for women. When the trend line—the line connecting the male–female difference in degrees in each census year—is moving *away* from the horizontal line, the gender gap in college completion is expanding, and when the trend line is moving *toward* the horizontal line, the gender gap is contracting.

Figure 5.1 shows that the male advantage in bachelor's and graduate degrees at age 25–29 rose substantially from 1940 to 1960, fell slightly from 1960 to 1970, and then began a steep descent. Indeed, the decline after 1970 was so large in magnitude and rapid in speed that by 1990 a slightly larger percentage of women than of men in the 25–29 age group held a bachelor's or higher degree.[175] In the history of a nation, alterations in social structure of this size and swiftness are probably infrequent.

The change in the gender gap that is portrayed in Figure 5.1 is likely to have contributed to the change that took place after the middle of the twentieth century in law on sexuality and its incidents. In evaluating the plausibility of such a link, an important point to keep in mind is that the gender gap in Figure 5.1 is measured by college completion among individuals who were 25–29 years old. The age range that was used for the measure (i.e., age 25 through age 29) is important for two reasons. First, since most first-year college students in the last half of the twentieth century evidently matriculated in college shortly before or after their eighteenth birthday,[176] the pursuit of a bachelor's degree by persons who hold such a degree at age 25–29 started normally when these persons were much younger—specifically, an average of about nine or ten years younger. Thus, the societal changes that affected educational attainment at age 25–29, but did so differently among women than among men, happened (or at least began) approximately a decade before women and men were in this age range. Second, the societal conditions that determine the college matriculation rates of women and of men probably do not have an instantaneous effect. Rather, the conditions are likely to operate with a time lag, and although the number of years that must pass for the effect to materialize is unknown, a half-decade could be required. When the two preceding points are combined, the small contraction of the sex gap between 1960 and 1970, and the large contraction that started in 1970, must be understood as responses to societal changes that took place or that had their inception more than a decade earlier. Consequently, the societal foundation for the higher status of men relative to women was evidently beginning to erode by 1950, and in the 1960s and later, the pace of the erosion markedly increased.

What societal consequences flowed from the changes that occurred in the gender-based status differential during the last half of the twentieth century? The answer may be the following. Because the odds that morality will be treated as a private matter are much higher among women than among men, the changes in the societal foundation for the status of women vis-a-vis men during the 1950s and 1960s—the changes that altered the course of the trend line in Figure 5.1—probably enhanced the prominence and influence of the view that issues of morality are not appropriately handled in a public setting or by a public body. As the status of women rose, in other words, the values of women were increasingly a factor in social life and were incorporated into law. Sexuality and related matters, therefore, gradually came to be regarded as beyond the scope of government regulation. In 1965, the U.S. Supreme Court held that government prohibitions on the use by married couples of items to prevent pregnancy were inconsistent with a constitutionally based right of privacy.[177] This ruling may not have represented a major jurisprudential step because the law had traditionally considered the relationship between spouses to be private.[178] Subsequently, however, the view that sexual activity and its incidents are private rather than public matters was extended to other government restrictions on adults. Thus, complete or almost-complete bans on aborting pregnancies were held unconstitutional not only when directed at an adult female who is unmarried,[179] but also when directed at an adult female who is married and cannot secure the consent of her husband.[180] Most recently, the view that sexuality is a private concern was responsible for the invalidation on constitutional grounds of government prohibitions on same-sex sexual activity between adults that is consensual, nonpublic, and noncommercial.[181]

If the higher social status of women had an impact on law governing sexuality, how large was the impact? Unfortunately, an answer to the question is not possible at the present time, because the answer needs to deal with the *net* impact of the change in women's social status. The findings in Tables 5.2–5.4—together with the data in Figure 5.1—suggest that there were two effects on social values bearing on whether morality is public or private and that to some degree these effects offset one another. According to the findings in Tables 5.2 and 5.3, social values that classify morality as private are affected by gender, and they are affected even more when educational attainment and prayer frequency are added to gender as causal agents. However, while the odds that morality will be considered a private issue are appreciably higher among women than men, the regression coefficient for educational attainment among women is negative in Table 5.3. Accordingly, social values that assign morality to the private sphere become *less* widespread as women acquire more schooling.

In short, the enhanced status of women in society, as represented by sex differences in rates of college completion, poses a problem for understanding whether and how the law was influenced by social values on whether morality is a private matter or a public issue. If the reasoning I have proposed is correct, the changing societal conditions that improved the status of women relative to the status of men magnified the effect of sex per se, thus expanding the prevalence and influence of social values that deem morality to be a private matter and an unacceptable subject for regulation through law. On the other hand, the societal forces that were responsible for the higher status of women resulted in more years of college-level schooling for a larger proportion of women.[182] The increases in educational attainment among women, in turn, reduced the extent to which the social values of women designated morality as private and, presumably, the influence of these values in society.

Was the change in social values that was brought about by gender on its own neutralized by the change in social values that was brought about by gains in college attendance and completion among women? The question is important because the answer has the potential to advance our understanding of the processes involved in the shift in law on sexuality that the United States underwent starting in the mid-1960s. Regrettably, an answer is not possible with the evidence that is currently available, and additional research is required. However, it is unlikely to be a coincidence that the odds of classifying morality as private are much higher among women than among men *and* that the status of women was rising relative to the status of men during the same period in history in which law was liberalizing on sexual activity and its incidents. Like every society, the United States is a social system, and in a system, concurrent phenomena are presumptively interconnected, not independent. Therefore, the proposition is at least plausible, and indeed seems probable, that the influence in society of social values treating morality as private was affected appreciably more by the sex attribute and associated social roles than by the extent to which women achieved a college-level education.

V. Conclusion

The biological attribute of sex has been and remains a cornerstone of social structure in the United States,[183] and to the extent the societal significance of the attribute results from male–female differences in hormones that cause male–female differences in behavior,[184] sex-based distinctions will not be eliminated from social life even if they are prohibited by law. Notably, during the last half of the twentieth century, U.S. law incorporated a doctrine of female–male equality and disapproved various socially significant sex-based distinctions. When interpreting the Constitution, for example, the U.S. Supreme Court discarded traditional beliefs regarding the place of women in society and endorsed the view that women are entitled to go beyond the roles of wife and mother.[185] The same view appeared in federal statutes.[186]

A description of a shift in law, of course, is only a first step; an explanation of the shift and its timing is also needed. In my macrosociological framework, the shift in law on the sex attribute is presumed to have resulted from substantial change in the degree to which and/or the manner in which the attribute was organizing society. While all of the aspects of the changed sex basis of social structure are probably still unknown, Figure 5.1 reveals that the status of women increased relative to the status of men after 1960. However, the shift in U.S. law was not confined to female–male distinctions per se; as discussed in Part IV, the shift extended to sexuality.[187] Unless the breadth of the shift is assumed to be happenstance—which would not accord with the tenet of science that the world is orderly—it can be explained. The results of the data analysis in Part III suggest that at least a partial explanation is a sex difference in social values regarding morality as a private or public matter. If so, these values are a link in a chain of causation between women's relative status in society and law bearing on the sex attribute and sexuality.

The macrosociological framework I have proposed, however, is not limited to a single topic or to a single set of related topics. On the contrary, the framework contends that, in a democratic nation, all of the fundamental concepts and doctrines of law are attributable to their societal context. The framework thus denies that law is self-contained and self-determined, that law has primacy over other elements of the social system, and that law is permanently shaped by individual personalities. Instead, the framework maintains that the important concepts and doctrines of law found in a democracy (a) are generated by the properties of society (e.g., average educational attainment) and (b) undergo change as the properties of society are altered by large-scale forces (e.g., the growth of knowledge). The framework also maintains that the impact of the macro-level forces on societal properties typically occurs slowly (and perhaps at an uneven pace) and that the societal properties affected by these forces normally produce new law when (and because) thresholds are reached.

Although a macrosociological framework does not accord with any paradigm that is widely accepted at the present time in scholarship on law, such a framework merits investigation. The framework not only is consistent with a considerable body of empirical evidence, but it can benefit social life by promoting research on the societal causes of law. In particular, research on the jurisdiction-level causes of law can be expected to lead to predictions of new law. If the proposed framework has utility, such predictions can be made well in advance of the emergence of the law being predicted, because alterations in jurisdiction-level properties usually occur over many years before generating law. Although the predictions will not always be accurate, they are likely to be correct much more often than they are incorrect. If so, quantitative studies of the jurisdiction-level conditions that shape law will allow a democratic nation to (a) prepare for new law and (b) appreciate that important doctrines in its law do not depend in the long run on individuals, no matter how influential the individuals seem to be. Insofar as (b) is prevalent, there will be less socially harmful conflict in a democracy over law that deviates from traditional cultural values. Especially if it involves violence and threats of violence, conflict can undermine the social order, as illustrated in the United States with regard to law on abortion and the provision of, and access to, abortion services.[188] Because law on important aspects of social life at a given point in history expresses the character of society rather than the idiosyncrasies of individuals, however, conflict directed at such law will not—indeed, cannot—have an enduring effect, and efforts to eliminate the law will have no more than temporary success. To the extent the foregoing is acknowledged, conflict over law that breaches social convention will be understood as futile. The probable result will be that such conflict will not occur as frequently, and when it occurs, it will not be as protracted.

Notes

*Chapter 5 is from Larry D. Barnett, "The Public-Private Dichotomy in Morality and Law," *Journal of Law and Policy* 18 (2010): 541. Part II-A of the chapter has been updated.

1. The Quotations Page, http://www.quotationspage.com/quotes/Bernard_Bailey (accessed April 9, 2011).
2. Michael H. Davis and Dana Neacsu, "Legitimacy, Globally: The Incoherence of Free Trade Practice, Global Economics and Their Governing Principles of Political Economy," *UMKC Law Review* 69 (2001): 733, 753 (referring to "the rule of law" as "the bedrock of western law").
3. See, e.g.,, Martin Krygier and Whit Mason, *Violence, Development and the Rule of Law* (Univ. of N.S.W., Research Paper No. 2008-8, 2008), 2 (noting that "The rule of law is so popular these days that there is little it is not called upon to do or to fix.").
4. James L. Gibson, "Changes in American Veneration for the Rule of Law," *DePaul Law Review* 56 (2007): 593, 603–5.
5. Craftsman Builder's Supply, Inc. v. Butler Mfg. Co., 974 P.2d 1194, 1223 (Utah 1999) (Stewart & Durham, JJ, concurring) (contending that the rule of law and the protections it affords are necessary for a capitalist economy and personal safety).
6. See Port Auth. of New York and New Jersey v. SST Concorde Alert Program, 394 N.Y.S.2d 364, 367 (Sup. Ct. 1977) (contending that "History proves that our society can survive only by law or else be consumed and destroyed by man....").

7. See Morrissey v. Brewer, *United States Reports* 408 (1972), 471, 499 (Douglas, J., dissenting in part) (stating that "The rule of law is important in the stability of society.").
8. Gore v. Harris, 772 So.2d 1243, 1272 (Fla. 2000) (Harding & Shaw, JJ., dissenting).
9. See Marc O. DeGirolami, "Faith in the Rule of Law," *St. John's Law Review* 82 (2008): 573, 576 (explaining the difficulty in defining the rule of law).
10. The elements of the rule of law that have been enumerated in "leading modern accounts" of the concept are summarized in Richard H. Fallon, Jr., "'The Rule of Law' as a Concept in Constitutional Discourse," *Columbia Law Review* 97 (1997): 1, 8–9. Professor Fallon indicates that the concept of "the rule of law" is an ideal but points out that agreement has not been reached on the elements of the ideal. Ibid., 10, 55.
11. See County of Sacramento v. Lewis, *United States Reports* 523 (1998), 833, 846–47 (noting that the enforcement of law is unconstitutional when it fails to "comport with traditional ideas of fair play and decency"); see also People ex. rel. Clancy v. Superior Court, 705 P.2d 347, 351 (Cal. 1985) (noting that law cannot be useful "[W]ithout a belief by the people that the system [of law] is just and impartial").
12. See David Gray, "An Excuse-Centered Approach to Transitional Justice," *Fordham Law Review* 74 (2006): 2621, 2640 ("[L]aws on the books play an essential role in the fair and just exercise of legal force").
13. Wheat v. United States, *United States Reports* 486 (1988), 153, 160 (pointing out the importance that "legal proceedings appear fair to all who observe them"); Marshall v. Jerrico, Inc., *United States Reports* 446 (1980), 238, 242 (remarking that the judiciary must provide "the appearance and reality of fairness" in order to "generat[e] the feeling, so important to a popular government, that justice has been done").
14. Truax v. Corrigan, *United States Reports* 257 (1921), 312, 332 (observing that law in the United States demands equality in its development and execution).
15. See Joel Brockner et al., "The Influence on Prior Commitment to an Institution on Reactions to Perceived Unfairness: The Higher They Are, the Harder They Fall," *Administrative Science Quarterly* 37 (1992): 241.
16. City of Akron v. Akron Ctr. for Reprod. Health, *United States Reports* 462 (1983), 416, 420 (referring to the United States as "a society *governed* by the rule of law" (emphasis added)). The word "rule" is defined to include "[a] principle, regulation, or maxim *governing* individual conduct." *Oxford English Dictionary*, vol. 14, 2nd ed. (1989), 228 (emphasis added). The word "govern" has among its definitions "to direct and control the actions and affairs of (a people, a state or its members)…." *Oxford English Dictionary*, vol. 6, 2nd ed. (1989), 709.
17. Roger Cotterrell, *Law's Community* (Oxford: Clarendon Press; New York: Oxford University Press, 1995), 259–60. See Gibson, supra note 4, at 597 (arguing that "[T]he essential ingredient of the rule of law is universalism—the law should be universally heeded") (emphasis omitted).
18. Joseph Raz, *The Authority of Law* (Oxford: Clarendon Press; New York: Oxford University Press, 1979), 213.

19. Wesley Newcomb Hohfeld, *Fundamental Legal Conceptions as Applied in Judicial Reasoning* (New Haven, CT: Yale University Press, 1919), 75; Elie Mischel, Note, "'Thou Shalt Not Go About as a Talebearer Among Thy People': Jewish Law and the Private Facts Tort," *Cardozo Arts & Entertainment Law Journal* 24 (2006): 811, 821.
20. Notable studies are cited and summarized in Larry D. Barnett, "Law as Symbol: Appearances in the Regulation of Investment Advisers and Attorneys," *Cleveland State Law Review* 55 (2007): 289, 300–1 nn.65–67 [hereinafter *Law as Symbol*] and in Larry D. Barnett, "The Regulation of Mutual Fund Boards of Directors: Financial Protection or Social Productivity?" *Journal of Law & Policy* 16 (2008): 489, 528–29 nn.163–66, 530 n.168, 545 n.217 [hereinafter *Regulation of Mutual Fund Boards of Directors*]. Notes 65 and 67 in *Law as Symbol* are reproduced as revised in Part II of Chapter 8 infra, where they are numbered notes 66 and 67, respectively; notes 163–66, 168 and 217 in *Regulation of Mutual Fund Boards of Directors* are reproduced as revised in Chapter 3 supra, where they are numbered notes 160–63, 165, and 209, respectively.
21. See, e.g., Thomas B. Marvell and Carlisle E. Moody, "The Lethal Effects of Three-Strikes Laws," *Journal of Legal Studies* 30 (2001): 89 (finding a substantial rise in homicides from the enactment of state statutes that require individuals, upon a third conviction for a violent crime, to be sentenced to a lengthy prison term without possibility of parole); David Neumark and Wendy A. Stock, "The Labor Market Effects of Sex and Race Discrimination Laws," *Economic Inquiry* 44 (2006): 385, 411 (finding that the earnings of employed white women and of employed black women are reduced in the short term, though raised in the long term, by state statutes banning sex-based differentials in pay and that employment in these groups is reduced by such statutes in the short term).
22. See Larry D. Barnett, *Mutual Funds, Hedge Funds, and the Public-Private Dichotomy in a Macrosociological Framework for Law* (Interuniversity Ctr. for Research on the Sociology of Law, Info. and Legal Insts., Working Paper No. 34, 2008), 38–39, http://www.cirsdig.it/Pubblicazioni/barnett.pdf (accessed April 9, 2011) [hereinafter *Public-Private Dichotomy in a Macrosociological Framework*].
23. Sociologically, an institution is a set of statuses and roles (a) that a society defines and endorses and (b) that involve interpersonal relationships through which a socially approved type of activity takes place in the society. Howard B. Kaplan, "The Concept of Institution: A Review, Evaluation, and Suggested Research Procedure," *Social Forces* 39 (1960): 176, 179.
24. Individualism is a dominant theme in the culture and law of the United States. See infra notes 79–85 and accompanying text.
25. The most persuasive of these studies are reviewed in *Public-Private Dichotomy in a Macrosociological Framework*, supra note 22, at 11–13. That review is the basis for the discussion which follows in the text.
26. Ibid., 25–26; Larry D. Barnett, "The Roots of Law," *American University Journal of Gender, Social Policy & Law* 15 (2007): 613, 630–32, 677–79 [hereinafter *The Roots of Law*]. Pages 630–32 and 677–79 in *The Roots of Law* are reproduced in Part II and Part IV-B, respectively, of Chapter 6 infra.

27. Georg Simmel, "The Metropolis and Mental Life," in *The Sociology of Georg Simmel*, ed., trans. Kurt H. Wolff (Glencoe, IL: Free Press , 1950), 409–10.
28. See Joe Soss et al., "Why Do White Americans Support the Death Penalty?" *Journal of Politics* 65 (2003): 397, 415–16 (finding with cross-sectional data that, among Caucasians, approval of the death penalty for individuals convicted of murder varies with, inter alia, prejudice toward blacks).
29. *Law as Symbol*, supra note 20, at 315, 324, 328–29 (reproduced in Parts IV-B, IV-C, and IV-D, respectively, of Chapter 8 infra).
30. Hilde Coffé and Benny Geys, "Community Heterogeneity: A Burden for the Creation of Social Capital?" *Social Science Quarterly* 87 (2006): 1053, 1065, 1068.
31. David Jacobs and Jason T. Carmichael, "The Political Sociology of the Death Penalty: A Pooled Time-Series Analysis," *American Sociological Review* 67 (2002): 109, 111.
32. One study has found that certain indicators of state-level social and economic divisions predict whether states have statutes that authorize the death penalty. Ibid., 121–22. However, the study did not include a control for, and thus did not remove, state differences in knowledge use and, hence, in rationality. Ibid. For example, differences between states in the educational attainment and occupational composition of their inhabitants were not controlled by the study with data on, respectively, the percentage of state inhabitants that had completed four (or more) years of college and the percentage of state inhabitants employed in white-collar occupations. Ibid. Differences between education levels as well as differences between occupations result from differences in quantity and quality of knowledge. *The Roots of Law*, supra note 26, at 630–31, 678 (reproduced in Parts II and IV-B, respectively, of Chapter 6 infra). Support for the death penalty is affected by educational level. Soss et al., supra note 28, at 408, 415; Steven F. Messner et al., "Distrust of Government, the Vigilante Tradition, and Support for Capital Punishment," *Law & Society Review* 40 (2006): 559, 576. Support for the death penalty probably varies by occupation, too, because occupations differ in the amount and type of knowledge required for their duties. Thus, state differences in knowledge use could account for the relationship between social and economic divisions in states, on the one hand, and the existence of state death-penalty statutes, on the other.
33. A system is "[a] set or assemblage of things connected, associated, or interdependent, so as to form a complex unity; a whole composed of parts in orderly arrangement according to some scheme or plan...." *Oxford English Dictionary*, vol. 17, 2nd ed. (1989), 496.
34. Bruce H. Mayhew, "Structuralism Versus Individualism: Part 1, Shadowboxing in the Dark," *Social Forces* 59 (1980): 335, 338–39.
35. In 2006, life expectancy at birth in the United States was 77.7 years. Melonie Heron et al., "Deaths: Final Data for 2006," *National Vital Statistics Report* 57, no. 14 (April 17, 2009): 26, table 7 (combining both sexes and all races), http://www.cdc.gov/nchs/data/nvsr/nvsr57/nvsr57_14.pdf (accessed April 9, 2011).
36. The needs of the system, however, are likely to be manifested typically in the expressed wishes of individuals. The concept of societal need is explained

in *The Roots of Law*, supra note 26, at 672–77 (reproduced in Part IV of Chapter 6 infra).

37. An indicator of the durability of law in England and the United States is the commonly used phrase "the Western legal *tradition*." As used in the phrase, the word "tradition" is an activity that has persisted over a considerable period of time. See *Webster's Third New International Dictionary*, 3rd ed. (1993), 2422.
38. Krygier and Mason, supra note 3, at 9–10.
39. Cotterrell, supra note 17, at 271.
40. Supra notes 16–18 and accompanying text.
41. Larry D. Barnett, "Social Productivity, Law, and the Regulation of Conflicts of Interest in the Investment Industry," *Cardozo Public Law, Policy, & Ethics Journal* 3 (2006): 793, 812, 814–27 [hereinafter *Social Productivity*]; *Regulation of Mutual Fund Boards of Directors*, supra note 20, at 535–36 (reproduced in Part IV of Chapter 3 supra). Pages 812 and 814–827 in *Social Productivity* are reproduced in Part IV of Chapter 2 infra; pages 535–36 in *Regulation of Mutual Fund Boards of Directors* are reproduced in Part IV of Chapter 3 supra.
42. In the present context, the word "investment" refers to "[t]he conversion of money or circulating capital into some species of property from which an income or profit is expected to be derived in the ordinary course of trade or business." *Oxford English Dictionary*, vol. 8, 2nd ed. (1989), 48.
43. The elements of a security are discussed in *Social Productivity*, supra note 41, at 829–32 (reproduced in Part VI-A of Chapter 2 supra).
44. 15 U.S.C.S. §§ 80b-1 to -21 (2010).
45. Jeffrey J. Haas and Steven R. Howard, *Investment Adviser Regulation In A Nutshell* (St. Paul, MN: Thomson West, 2008), 11–12.
46. Ibid.
47. See Deborah A. DeMott, "The Mechanisms of Control," *Connecticut Journal of International Law* 13 (1999): 233–34.
48. In the Advisers Act, the list of securities is in section 202(a)(18). 15 U.S.C.S. § 80b-2(a)(18) (2010).
49. *Social Productivity*, supra note 41, at 829–31 (reproduced in Part VI-A of Chapter 2 supra).
50. See United Hous. Found., Inc. v. Forman, *United States Reports* 421 (1975), 837, 852–53 (reasoning that profit has been an element in "all of the Court's decisions defining a security"); Reves v. Ernst & Young, *United States Reports* 494 (1990), 56, 66 (concluding that one criterion for whether an instrument is a security is whether the motivation for acquiring the instrument is profit).
51. Form ADV, which a registered investment adviser must file annually with the Commission, requires the adviser to report the value of the assets it manages. 17 C.F.R. § 275.204-1 (2009); Sec. & Exch. Comm'n, Uniform Application for Investment Advisor Registration, Form ADV: Instructions for Part 1A, 5–8, http://www.sec.gov/about/forms/formadv-instructions.pdf (accessed April 9, 2011).
52. Amendments to Form ADV, Release No. IA-3060, 75 Fed. Reg. 49,234, 49,234 & n.2 (July 28, 2010). The estimate by the Commission is "more than $38 trillion" and is just for Commission-registered investment

advisers. Ibid. If the estimate included advisers registered with states, the total assets being managed by all investment advisers nationwide would, of course, be larger. An investment adviser is required to register with the Commission if its "principal office and place of business" is in a state that does not regulate advisers *or* if it has as a client an investment company that is registered with the Commission. Any other investment adviser cannot register with the Commission unless it manages assets worth at least $25 million. 15 U.S.C.S. § 80b-3a(a) (2010). An investment adviser in a state that regulates advisers has the option of registering with the Commission if it manages assets of at least $25 million but less than $30 million, and such an investment adviser must register with the Commission if it manages assets worth $30 million or more. 17 C.F.R. § 275.203A-1(a) (2009).

53. Gross domestic product (GDP) is "the total output of goods and services produced by labor and property located in the United States, valued at market prices." U.S. Census Bureau, *Statistical Abstract of the United States: 2008*, 127th ed. (Washington, DC: U.S. Government Printing Office, 2007), 425. Gross national product (GNP), on the other hand, is "the output attributable to all labor and property supplied by United States residents." Ibid., 426. GDP is the output of labor and property that are within the United States; the labor and property may be that of residents of the United States or residents of other countries. Carol S. Carson, "Replacing GNP: The Updated System of National Economic Accounts," *Business Economics*, July 1992, 44, 46. GNP is the output of the labor and property of residents of the United States, but the labor and property may be situated in any country. Ibid., 46. GDP has replaced GNP as the chief measure of economic production in the United States. Ibid., 44.
54. Bureau of Economic Analysis, National Economic Accounts table 1.1.5, http://www.bea.gov/national/nipaweb/Index.asp (follow "Frequently Requested NIPA Tables" hyperlink) (accessed August 2, 2010).
55. *Bureau of Economic Analysis, U.S. Dep't of Commerce, Fixed Assets and Consumer Durable Goods in the United States*, 1925-97 M-5 (2003), http://www.bea.gov/national/pdf/Fixed_Assets_1925_97.pdf (accessed April 9, 2011).
56. Bureau of Economic Analysis, Table 1.1: Current-Cost Net Stock of Fixed Assets and Consumer Durable Goods (2010), http://www.bea.gov/national/FA2004/SelectTable.asp (follow "Table 1.1. Current-Cost Net Stock of Fixed Assets and Consumer Durable Goods" hyperlink) (accessed September 17, 2010).
57. Investment Adviser Year 2000 Reports, 1998 SEC LEXIS 1339, at *4.
58. Mindy Olson, Note, "The Securities Fraud Deterrence and Investor Restitution Act: More Effective Than Current Regulation?" *Iowa Journal of Corporate Law* 30 (2005): 425, 427–28.
59. Securities Act of 1933, Pub. L. No. 73-22, 48 Stat. 74 (1933) (codified as amended at 15 U.S.C. §§ 77a to 77z-3 (2006)).
60. Securities Exchange Act of 1934, Pub. L. No. 73-291, 48 Stat. 881 (1934) (codified as amended at 15 U.S.C. §§ 78a to 78oo (2006)).
61. Investment Advisers Act, ch. 686, title II, 54 Stat. 847 (1940) (codified as amended at 15 U.S.C.S. §§ 80b-1 to 80b-21 (2010)). The Investment

Advisers Act took effect on November 1, 1940. Ibid., title II, § 221, 54 Stat. 857 (codified at 15 U.S.C.S. § 80b-21 (2010)).

62. Investment Company Act, ch. 686, title I, 54 Stat. 789 (1940) (codified as amended at 15 U.S.C. §§ 80a-1 to 80a-64 (2006)).
63. Supra Part II-A.
64. S. Rep. No. 76-1775, at 21 (1940); H.R. Rep. No. 76-2639, at 27 (1940).
65. A chart of the Dow Jones Industrial Average on each trading day from January 1920 through December 1939 is available at http://stockcharts.com/charts/historical/djia19201940.html (accessed April 9, 2011).
66. H.R. Doc. No. 76-477, at 5 (1939); *Investment Trusts and Investment Companies, Hearings on S. 3580 Before a Subcomm. of the Sen. Comm. on Banking & Currency*, 76th Cong. 1004 (1940) (statement of Research Dep't, Ill. Legis. Council), available at HeinOnline, U.S. Federal Legislative History Library. A study of financial markets has ascribed the shift from passive to active management of securities portfolios, and the adoption of the techniques currently used to reduce risk in securities portfolios, to the volatility of stock prices during the 1970s and to the investment in securities of large sums by entities at that time. Peter L. Bernstein, *Capital Ideas: The Improbable Origins of Modern Wall Street* (New York: Free Press, 1992), 7–9. A chart of the Dow Jones Industrial Average on each trading day from January 1960 through December 1980 is available at http://stockcharts.com/charts/historical/djia19601980.html (accessed April 9, 2011).
67. S. Rep. No. 76-1775, at 21 (1940); H.R. Rep. No. 76-2639, at 27 (1940).
68. Investment Advisers Act, 15 U.S.C.S. § 80b-1 (2010).
69. Ibid. 15 U.S.C.S. § 80b-2(a)(11)(A)-(G) (2010).
70. Ibid. 15 U.S.C.S. § 80b-2(a)(11) (2010). A "person" can be a human being or an entity. Ibid. 15 U.S.C.S. § 80b-2(a)(5), -2(a)(16) (2010).
71. The interpretations are those of the staff of the Division of Investment Management. Ibid. The current structure of the Commission includes five Divisions and eighteen Offices. Sec. & Exch. Comm'n, Division and Offices Homepages, http://www.sec.gov/divisions.shtml (accessed January 27, 2010). The Division of Investment Management is responsible for construing the Investment Advisers Act and the Investment Company Act. See Sec. & Exch. Comm'n, Division of Investment Management, http://www.sec.gov/divisions/investment.shtml (accessed January 27, 2010).
72. Applicability of the Investment Advisers Act to Financial Planners, Pension Consultants, and Other Persons Who Provide Investment Advisory Services as an Integral Component of Other Financial Related Services, Investment Advisers Act Release No. IA-770, 46 Fed. Reg. 41,771 (August 18, 1981) [hereinafter Release IA-770].
73. Applicability of the Investment Advisers Act to Financial Planners, Pension Consultants, and Other Persons Who Provide Investment Advisory Services as a Component of Other Financial Services, Investment Advisers Act Release No. IA-1092, 52 Fed. Reg. 38,400 (October 16, 1987) [hereinafter Release IA-1092].
74. The statutory definition, which is reproduced in the text accompanying note 70 supra, seems to cover two distinct types of business activity that differ in, inter alia, frequency. Haas and Howard, supra note 45, at 13. One type entails a "business" of providing advice on securities; the other type

entails a "regular business" of providing analyses or reports on securities. 15 U.S.C.S. § 80b-2(a)(11) (2010). However, the staff has taken the position that the two references to business in section 202(a)(11) apply to just a single type of activity. Release IA-1092, supra note 73, at 38,402.

75. Release IA-1092, supra note 73, at 38,402.
76. Lowe v. Sec. & Exch. Comm'n, *United States Reports* 472 (1985), 181.
77. Ibid., 207–8 (concluding that "[t]he Act was designed to apply to those persons ... who provide personalized advice attuned to a client's concerns, whether by written or verbal communication").
78. The Release, in answering question (i), refers to a recipient of the services as a *client*. Release IA-1092, supra note 73, at 38,402. The Release, accordingly, may have implicitly recognized question (iv) and incorporated the position of the U.S. Supreme Court in *Lowe*.
79. Frank B. Cross, "Law and Trust," *Georgetown Law Journal* 93 (2005): 1457, 1526 (finding with data from the World Values Survey that, among twenty-five countries, the United States had the highest level of individualism).
80. See *The Roots of Law*, supra note 26, at 631–35 (reproduced in Part II of Chapter 6 infra).
81. E.g., McLeod v. Peterson, 283 F.2d 180, 183 (3d Cir. 1960).
82. Stanley v. Georgia, *United States Reports* 394 (1969), 557.
83. Eisenstadt v. Baird, *United States Reports* 405 (1972), 438, 452–53.
84. E.g., Winston v. Lee, *United States Reports* 470 (1985), 753.
85. Barbara Black and Jill I. Gross, "Economic Suicide: The Collision of Ethics and Risk in Securities Law," *University of Pittsburgh Law Review* 64 (2003): 483, 486.
86. Release IA-1092, supra note 73, at 38,402.
87. Ibid.
88. Bureau of Alcohol, Tobacco & Firearms v. Fed. Labor Relations Auth., *United States Reports* 464 (1983), 89, 97.
89. See Bedroc Ltd. v. United States, *United States Reports* 541 (2004), 176, 182–84.
90. 15 U.S.C.S. § 80b-2(a) (2010).
91. S. Rep. No. 76-1775, at 20–22 (1940); H.R. Rep. No. 76-2639, at 27–28 (1940).
92. See Smith v. United States, *United States Reports* 508 (1993), 223, 228; Norman J. Singer, *Statutes and Statutory Construction*, vol. 2A, 6th ed. (St. Paul, MN: West Group, 2000), 123–24.
93. Bedroc Ltd., *United States Reports* 541, at 184. In ascertaining the referents of three words in a section of the Securities Exchange Act, the U.S. Supreme Court has relied on a dictionary published in the year the Act was adopted by Congress. Ernst & Ernst v. Hochfelder, *United States Reports* 425 (1976), 185, 199 nn.20, 21.
94. *Compare* Investment Advisers Act of 1940, ch. 686, title II, § 202(a)(11), 54 Stat. 847, 848 (1940) *with* 15 U.S.C.S. § 80b-2(a)(11) (2010).
95. The criteria can be found in Release IA-770, supra note 72, at 41,772–73, and in Release IA-1092, supra note 73, at 38,402–3.
96. *Webster's New International Dictionary of the English Language* (1932), 296–97 (def. 2.b).
97. *Oxford English Dictionary*, vol. 1 (1933), 1205.

98. Sec. & Exch. Comm'n v. Fifth Ave. Coach Lines, Inc., 289 F. Supp. 3, 31 (S.D.N.Y. 1968) (defining words in a section of the Investment Company Act and observing that the word "'Business' implies continued activity"), *aff'd*, 435 F.2d 510 (2d Cir. 1970).
99. Supra note 86 and accompanying text.
100. Ibid.
101. Ibid.
102. As of 2006, prostitution was unlawful in every state of the United States except in certain counties of Nevada and except in certain circumstances in Rhode Island. Lauren M. Davis, "Prostitution," *Georgetown Journal of Gender and the Law* 7 (2006): 835, 836–37.
103. E.g., Kenneth D. Wald et al., "The Politics of Gay Rights in American Communities: Explaining Antidiscrimination Ordinances and Policies," *American Journal of Political Science* 40 (1996): 1152.
104. See U.S. Census Bureau, *Total Midyear Population for the World: 1950–2050* (2011), http://www.census.gov/ipc/www/idb/worldpopinfo.php. The U.S. Census Bureau estimates that the population of the world was 4.45 billion in 1980 and 6.85 billion in 2010. Ibid.
105. The resident population of the United States, according to the decennial census, was 151.3 million in April 1950 and 281.4 million in April 2000. U.S. Census Bureau, supra note 53, at 7 table 1. The U.S. resident population is estimated to have been 307.0 million on July 1, 2009. U.S. Census Bureau, *Annual Estimates of the Resident Population For the United States, Regions, States, and Puerto Rico: April 1, 2000 to July 1, 2009* (2009), http://www.census.gov/popest/states/NST-ann-est.html (accessed April 9, 2011).
106. Jared Diamond, *Collapse: How Societies Choose to Fail or Succeed* (New York: Viking, 2005), 6–7 (finding that human population growth was a factor causing the disappearance of societies in the past).
107. Derek Seabury Hoff, "Are We Too Many? The Population Debate and Policymaking in the Twentieth-Century United States" (unpublished PhD diss., University of Virginia, January 2006), 10–12 (on file with Widener University Library). The present failure to address the problem of U.S. population growth also characterizes scholarship on law. A notable exception is Carter J. Dillard, "Rethinking the Procreative Right," *Yale Human Rights & Development Law Journal* 10 (2007): 1.
108. Joseph W. Schneider, "Social Problems Theory: The Constructionist View," *Annual Review of Sociology* 11 (1985): 209, 210–12 (examining social problems as societal constructs).
109. Release IA-1092, supra note 73, at 38,403; Haas and Howard, supra note 45, at 16.
110. Supra note 86 and accompanying text.
111. The Release raises a further point when, in discussing the compensation element, it refers to "the receipt of any economic benefit," to whether a "fee is charged," and to whether compensation is "paid." Release IA-1092, supra note 73, at 38,403. The statutory definition of investment adviser requires only that covered activities be "*for* compensation." 15 U.S.C.S. § 80b-2(a)(11) (2010) (italics added). Consequently, the compensation element of the statutory definition is probably satisfied not only by a receipt/payment of compensation but also by an expectation of compensation. Whether such

an expectation is present in a situation undoubtedly depends in part on social convention and culture.

112. 15 U.S.C. § 80a-17(e)(1) (2006). The wording of section 17(e)(1) has not been amended since the Investment Company Act was adopted in 1940. *Compare* Investment Company Act, ch. 686, title I, § 17(e)(1), 54 Stat. 789, 816 (1940) *with* 15 U.S.C. § 17(e)(1) (2006). Section 17(e)(1) covers both a "first-tier" affiliated person (i.e., a person affiliated with a registered investment company) and a "second-tier" affiliated person (i.e., a person affiliated with a first-tier affiliated person). 15 U.S.C. § 80a-17(e)(1) (2006). "Affiliated person" is defined in section 2(a)(3) of the Investment Company Act. 15 U.S.C. § 80a-2(a)(3) (2006).

113. The Investment Company Act and the Advisers Act were included in Public Law No. 76-768. Investment Company Act of 1940, ch. 686, tit. I, 54 Stat. 789 (1940); Investment Advisers Act of 1940, ch. 686, tit. II, 54 Stat. 847 (1940). The stated purpose of Public Law No. 76-768 was inter alia "[t]o provide for the registration and regulation of investment companies and investment advisers…." Ibid., 54 Stat. at 789.

114. 15 U.S.C. § 80a-2(a)(3)(E) (2006). The adviser is a first-tier affiliated person of the investment company. Ibid.

115. Officers, employees, and directors of an investment adviser are affiliated with the investment adviser. 15 U.S.C. § 80a-2(a)(3)(D) (2006). As first-tier affiliated persons of the investment adviser, they are second-tier affiliated persons of an investment company that is served by the adviser. Section 17(e)(1) covers both first-tier and second-tier affiliated persons of a registered investment company. Supra note 112. Consequently, if an investment company is registered with the Commission, section 17(e)(1) applies not only to its investment adviser but also to the officers, employees, and directors of the adviser. 15 U.S.C. § 80a-17(e)(1) (2006).

116. United States v. Ostrander, 999 F.2d 27, 31 (2d Cir. 1993).

117. *Ostrander*, 999 F.2d at 31. This conclusion, which is derived from case law, is consistent with definitions of "compensation" in dictionaries published shortly before the Investment Company Act was adopted. The Investment Company Act was enacted in 1940, as was the Advisers Act. Ch. 686, title I, 54 Stat. 789 & title II, 54 Stat. 847 (1940). Definitions in a contemporary dictionary are evidence of the meaning of words in a statute. Ernst & Ernst v. Hochfelder, 425 U.S. 185, 199 & nn.20, 21 (1976).

Webster's New International Dictionary of the English Language (1932), 455, 1784, defines "compensation" to include "[t]hat which constitutes, or is regarded as, an equivalent or recompense," and defines "recompense" as a noun to encompass "[a]n equivalent returned for anything done, suffered, or given." A synonym listed for "compensation" and for "recompense" is "reward." Ibid. *Accord, Oxford English Dictionary*, vol. 2 (1933), 717 (definitions 1 and 2 of "compensation); *Oxford English Dictionary*, vol. 8 (1933), 259 (definition 3 of "recompense" in its substantive sense). Under the foregoing definitions, compensation can be non-economic.

118. See R. L. Stirrat, "Money, Men and Women," in *Money and the Morality of Exchange*, ed. J. Parry and M. Bloch (Cambridge and New York: Cambridge University Press, 1989), 94, 98–99 (describing differences between women and men in money-related views and behavior in a village in Sri Lanka). Cf.

Celia J. Falicov, "The Cultural Meanings of Money: The Case of Latinos and Anglo-Americans," *American Behavioral Scientist* 45 (2001): 313, 314, 321, 326 (contending that social considerations, especially ties within nuclear and extended families, are more important as incentives to working-class Latinos in the United States than to middle-class Anglo-Americans and that the uses of money accordingly differ between the two subcultures). See generally Maurice Bloch and Jonathan Parry, "Introduction: Money and the Morality of Exchange," in *Money and the Morality of Exchange*, supra, at 1, 1 (concluding from anthropological studies that the way money is viewed and used is not the same in all cultures); Viviana A. Zelizer, "The Social Meaning of Money: 'Special Monies,'" *American Journal of Sociology* 95 (1989): 342, 351 (contending that the uses, users, allocation, and sources of money in a society are affected by culture and social structure).

119. Cf. Stacey Menzel Baker et al., "From Despicable to Collectible: The Evolution of Collective Memories for and the Value of Black Advertising Memorabilia," *Journal of Advertising* 33 (2004): 37 (describing a type of item whose appeal changed over time in the United States). See generally Geert Hofstede and Robert R. McCrae, "Personality and Culture Revisited: Linking Traits and Dimensions of Culture," *Cross-Cultural Research* 38 (2004): 52, 62–64, 79 (finding that differences in culture are associated with differences in personality and hypothesizing that the former produce the latter).
120. The most persuasive of the empirical studies that support the premise are summarized in *Public-Private Dichotomy in a Macrosociological Framework*, supra note 22, at 11–13. A recently published study has found that higher rates of homicide in U.S. counties lower the probability that defendants charged with homicide will be convicted; for defendants who are convicted, higher rates of homicide shorten the prison terms imposed. Mark Cooney and Callie Harbin Burt, "Less Crime, More Punishment," *American Journal of Sociology* 114 (2008): 491. Homicide, accordingly, seems to be undeterred by punishment through the institution of law, i.e., by conviction and imprisonment. Ibid., 494–95, 514. This finding is consistent with the evidence from social science research that, in a society, patterns of social activity materially affect, but are not materially affected by, the institution of law. Supra note 20.
121. Sec. & Exch. Comm'n v. Capital Gains Research Bureau, Inc., *United States Reports* 375 (1963), 180, 186–87.
122. Don Welch, "The State As a Purveyor of Morality," *George Washington Law Review* 56 (1988): 540, 542–43, 549.
123. *Nat'l Opinion Research Ctr., General Social Surveys, 1972–2010: Cumulative Codebook* (2011), 3089, http://www.norc.org/GSS+Website/Documentation (accessed April 9, 2011) (follow "Entire GSS Codebook" hyperlink).
124. Social values and opinions are defined and distinguished as concepts in *Public-Private Dichotomy in a Macrosociological Framework*, supra note 22, at 14.
125. David L. Schecter, "Legislating Morality Outside of the Legislature: Direct Democracy, Voter Participation and Morality Politics," *Social Science Journal* 46 (2009): 89, 101–4.

126. The United States Supreme Court has observed that "[t]he law... is constantly based on notions of morality." Bowers v. Hardwick, *United States Reports* 478 (1986), 186, 196. The holding in *Bowers*—that a statute prohibiting private same-sex sexual relations is not unconstitutional—was overruled seventeen years later in Lawrence v. Texas, *United States Reports* 539 (2003), 558, 578. However, the Court in *Bowers* was not incorrect in writing that the substance of morality shapes the doctrines of law. Following the decision in *Bowers* in 1986, the belief that "homosexuality should be considered an acceptable alternative lifestyle" became increasingly frequent among adults in the United States, and by 1999, a slight majority held this belief. Public Agenda, Acceptance of Homosexuality Has Grown Significantly, http://www.publicagenda.org/charts/acceptance-homosexuality-has-grown-significantly-0 (accessed February 14, 2010). Morality has been defined as the "conduct conforming to the customs or accepted standards of a particular culture or group." *Webster's Third New International Dictionary*, 3rd ed. (1993), 1469. As so defined, the state of morality at the time of *Lawrence* forms a foundation of the holding of the Supreme Court in the case.
127. See *Public-Private Dichotomy in a Macrosociological Framework*, supra note 22, at 15–18.
128. Interviewees whose response was "strongly agree" or "agree" were classified as having agreed; interviewees whose response was "disagree" or "strongly disagree" were classified as having disagreed.
PERRIGHT was answered by 1,287 interviewees, 315 of whom stated that they "neither agree nor disagree" or that they "don't know." SOCRIGHT was answered by 1,282 interviewees, 368 of whom stated that they "neither agree nor disagree" or that they "don't know." Calculated from *Nat'l Opinion Research Ctr.*, supra note 123, at 2454. A total of 638 interviewees gave one of the foregoing answers to PERRIGHT and/or to SOCRIGHT. These 638 interviewees were not included in the data analysis.
129. The wording of the GSS questions for PERRIGHT and SOCRIGHT, and the wording of the GSS questions for the independent variables, are in *Nat'l Opinion Research Ctr.*, supra note 123.
130. A summary of the most credible of these studies is in *Public-Private Dichotomy in a Macrosociological Framework*, supra note 22, at 11–13.
131. James A. Davis, *Background Variables and Opinions in the 1972–1977 NORC General Social Surveys: Ten Generalizations about Age, Education, Occupational Prestige, Race, Religion, and Sex, and Forty-Nine Opinion Items* (1979), http://publicdata.norc.org:41000/gss/DOCUMENTS/REPORTS/Topical_Reports/TR02.pdf (accessed April 9, 2011).
132. Supra notes 116–119 and accompanying text.
133. In the instant chapter, the word "culture" refers to the fundamental assumptions that shape the perceptions and behavior of the members of a society. Edgar H. Schein, "Culture: The Missing Concept in Organization Studies," *Administrative Science Quarterly* 41 (1996): 229, 236.
134. An explanation of scale types—nominal, ordinal, interval, and ratio—is in Anwer Khurshid and Hardeo Sahai, "Scales of Measurements: An Introduction and a Selected Bibliography," *Quality & Quantity* 27 (1993): 303, 304–5, 308–10. Although the scale types have been clearly defined,

universal agreement is lacking on the criteria for determining the scale type of a particular measurement procedure. Ibid., 311–12. Moreover, evidence exists that, when three or more ordered categories are used to measure an independent variable, the advantages of treating the categories as an interval scale (rather than an ordinal scale) outweigh the disadvantages. Sanford Labovitz, "The Assignment of Numbers to Rank Order Categories", *American Sociological Review* 35 (1970): 515; Mark Traylor, "Ordinal and Interval Scaling," *Journal of Market Research Society* 25 (1983): 297. In general, then, three or more ordered categories should be considered an interval scale unless there is a specific reason for using them as an ordinal scale.

In analyzing data, a reference category is needed for an independent variable that is measured with an ordinal scale. J. Scott Long and Jeremy Freese, *Regression Models for Categorical Dependent Variables Using Stata*, 2nd ed. (2006), 415–18. A reference category is not required with an interval scale (or a ratio scale). In data analyses in a pair of earlier studies, I employed ordered three-category independent variables as interval scales by not having a reference category for each variable, but I incorrectly referred to the categories as ordinal scales. *Law as Symbol*, supra note 20, at 320 n.166; *The Roots of Law*, supra note 26, at 655 n.140. Especially because the categories for each of these independent variables were derived from a ratio scale, the categories were justifiably used as interval scales.

135. In general, age differences in social values probably result from differences between generations in educational attainment, i.e., age itself probably has little effect on most social values. See Davis, supra note 131, at 62. *Aging*, on the other hand, can affect values. Nicholas L. Danigelis et al., "Population Aging, Intracohort Aging, and Sociopolitical Attitudes," *American Sociological Review* 72 (2007): 812; David J. Harding and Christopher Jencks, "Changing Attitudes Toward Premarital Sex: Cohort, Period, and Aging Effects," *Public Opinion Quarterly* 67 (2003): 211, 225. The effect of the aging process on values can be measured with cross-sectional data from sample surveys, but only if the surveys have been conducted in different years and cover a substantial time span. The effect of aging cannot be measured using information on age from a single survey. GSS surveys have not gathered the data required to assess the possible influence of the aging process on MORALITY. See *Nat'l Opinion Research Ctr.*, supra note 123, at app. U.

136. Xavier Hansen, "Back to the Future: The Origins and Return of Sociology as the Scientific Study of Societal Development" (paper presented at the 2004 annual meeting of the American Sociological Association, San Francisco, August 2004) (on file with author).

137. Rory McVeigh and Maria-Elena D. Diaz, "Voting to Ban Same-Sex Marriage: Interests, Values, and Communities," *American Sociological Review* 74 (2009): 891, 907.

138. Among individuals, degree of fatalism and at least one aspect of morality depend in part on degree of self-direction. Carmi Schooler et al., "Occupational Self-Direction, Intellectual Functioning, and Self-Directed Orientation in Older Workers: Findings and Implications for Individuals and Societies," *American Journal of Sociology* 110 (2004): 161, 185 figure 4.

Fatalism and morality, therefore, are correlated in some ways and to some extent.

139. Trust among the members of a group having a subsistence economy seems to be necessary for the group to survive. See W. G. Runciman, "Stone Age Sociology," *Journal of Royal Anthropological Institute* 11 (2005): 129, 134–35 (contending that during the Stone Age the survival of a group depended on cooperation among its members and the expectation of such cooperation). Not surprisingly, therefore, research has found that trust broadly affects other types of groups, including social systems that are affluent and complex. *Social Productivity,* supra note 41, at 825–27 (reproduced in Part V-C of Chapter 2 supra). In light of this research, a relationship between trust and morality is plausible a priori.
140. See Ramona Houmanfar et al., "Religion and Cultural Survival," *Psychological Record* 51 (2001): 19, 27–28 (discussing the link between religion and morality).
141. Fred C. Pampel, *Logistic Regression* (Thousand Oaks, CA: Sage Publications, 2000), 1–10, Monograph No. 132; Alfred DeMaris, "A Tutorial in Logistic Regression," *Journal of Marriage & Family* 57 (1995): 956–58.
142. An understanding of logistic regression requires that two concepts—probability and odds—be distinguished. A probability is a proportion, while odds are a ratio of two probabilities. Pampel, supra note 141, at 11–13. As explained infra in Part III-B of the text, the regression results reported in Tables 5.2 and 5.3 are based on data for 162 interviewees. Of the 162, 76 were coded 1 on MORALITY and 86 were coded 0. Therefore, the probability that morality would be regarded as private by an interviewee in this group was 76 ÷ 162 = .469, the probability that morality would be regarded as public was 86 ÷ 162 = .531, and the odds that morality would be regarded as private was .469 ÷ .531 = .883.
143. *Public-Private Dichotomy in a Macrosociological Framework,* supra note 22, at 15–18.
144. See Wikipedia, Cluster Sampling, http://en.wikipedia.org/wiki/Cluster_sampling (accessed February 15, 2010).
145. The coefficients and their unadjusted standard errors were estimated with Stata Release 10.0 using the LOGIT command. StataCorp., *Stata Base Reference Manual: Release 10,* vol. 2 (2007), 178–93 [hereinafter Stata Reference Manual]. The estimation procedure did not employ either sampling weights or household-size weights. Sampling weights for the GSS require data on the cluster variable. StataCorp., *Stata User's Guide: Release 10* (2007), § 20.17.3, at 280. Data on the cluster variable, however, were not available. The adjustment that was made to the estimated standard errors, as described in the text, is an imprecise way of compensating for the omission of sampling weights and the cluster variable.
Household-size weights were considered unnecessary because they are unlikely to alter materially the results obtained when analyzing GSS data. C. Bruce Stephenson, *Weighting the General Social Surveys for Bias Related to Household Size* (1978), 1, http://publicdata.norc.org:41000/gss/DOCUMENTS/REPORTS/Methodological_Reports/MR003.pdf (accessed April 9, 2011). In addition, household-size weights have the disadvantage that they reduce the statistical efficiency of population parameter estimators

such as regression coefficients. Ibid., 3. Efficient estimators are preferred because they are likely to be closer to their population parameters than inefficient estimators. Ronald J. Wonnacott and Thomas H. Wonnacott, *Econometrics*, 2nd ed. (New York: Wiley, 1979), 58–60.

146. The need for the adjustment, and the use of $\sqrt{1.42}$ for the adjustment, are explained in *Public-Private Dichotomy in a Macrosociological Framework*, supra note 22, at 33–34.

147. A score (0 or 1) on MORALITY was available for 305 respondents. See the text following supra note 128. However, the regression results were based on no more than 164 of these respondents because data on one or more of the independent variables did not exist for 141 respondents. Two factors were primarily responsible for the inability to use the 141 respondents in the regression analysis. First, the 1991 GSS gathered data on certain variables only from subsamples of the full sample; of the independent variables in the instant study, TRUST was not measured in one of the three subsamples in the 1991 GSS. *Nat'l Opinion Research Ctr.*, supra note 123, at 3508, 3524. Because the full sample was not asked the question for TRUST, there were interviewees with data on MORALITY but not on TRUST. Second, some interviewees who had a score of 0 or 1 on the dependent variable and who were asked all of the questions measuring the independent variables either did not answer a question for one (or more) of the independent variables or responded to a question on an independent variable with an answer that was outside the coding employed by the instant study (which coding is described in Table 5.1).

148. As discussed in *Public-Private Dichotomy in a Macrosociological Framework*, supra note 22, at 35 n.84, caution is required when relying upon tests of statistical significance.

149. The odds ratios for these three variables were –.298, 3.4647, and 1.873, respectively. Percentage changes were obtained from the regression coefficients with the LISTCOEF command. Long and Freese, supra note 134, at 94–98, 464–67.

150. Ibid., 128.

151. David W. Hosmer and Stanley Lemeshow, *Applied Logistic Regression*, 2nd ed. (New York: John Wiley, 2000), 175–76.

152. A visual examination of the distribution is suggested in Long and Freese, supra note 134, at 151.

153. For these two interviewees, Cook's Statistic was .99 and 2.16. For the other interviewees, Cook's Statistic was less than .60.

154. A maximum-likelihood regression coefficient cannot be estimated for an independent variable that predicts the dependent variable without any error. Hosmer and Lemeshow, supra note 151, at 138.

155. The null hypothesis was used to compute the z scores in Tables 5.2 and 5.3, i.e., every independent variable was assumed to be unrelated to the dependent variable in the population from which the sample was drawn. Each z score in the tables, accordingly, is the number of standard errors by which the regression coefficient obtained from the sample deviated from a regression coefficient of zero in the population that was sampled. Emilio J. Castilla, *Dynamic Analysis in the Social Sciences* (Amsterdam: Elsevier, 2007), 154–55.

156. The odds ratios were .316 for EDUC, 3.631 for SEX, and 1.969 for PRAYFREQ.
157. James Jaccard and Robert Turrisi, *Interaction Effects in Multiple Regression*, 2nd ed. (Thousand Oaks, CA: Sage Publications, 2003), 3–4, Monograph No. 72.; William D. Berry, *Understanding Regression Assumptions* (Thousand Oaks, CA: Sage Publications, 1993), 30–31, Monograph No. 92.
158. Rodney Stark, "Physiology and Faith: Addressing the "Universal" Gender Difference in Religious Commitment," *Journal for the Scientific Study of Religion* 41 (2002): 495–500, 504.
159. The odds ratio for EDUC among women was .268; the odds ratio for PRAYFREQ among men was 2.480.
160. The reader should keep in mind that the instant study utilizes cross-sectional data and that, because change over time cannot be observed, such data produce erroneous conclusions regarding causal relationships more often than longitudinal data. *Public-Private Dichotomy in a Macro-sociological Framework*, supra note 22, at 33.
161. Supra note 156 and accompanying text.
162. The percentages were computed in Stata with the *estat classification* command and its default probability cutoff, i.e., >= .5. *Stata Reference Manual*, supra note 145, at 166–67.
163. Kathleen E. Hull and Robert L. Nelson, "Gender Inequality in Law: Problems of Structure and Agency in Recent Studies of Gender in Anglo-American Legal Professions," *Law & Social Inquiry* 23 (1998): 681, 697.
164. My reasoning assumes that the relationships reported in Tables 5.2 and 5.3 are not confined to 1991, the year in which the data for these tables were obtained. The assumption is plausible at least with regard to gender. As reported supra in note 156 and accompanying text, gender had a very large impact on whether morality is deemed to be a public issue or a private matter. An impact of this magnitude is unlikely to occur in just a single year.
165. Val D. Ricks, "Marriage and the Constitutional Right to Free Sex: The State Marriage Amendments as Response," *Florida Coastal Law Review* 7 (2005): 271.
166. Francisco Valdes, "Anomalies, Warts and All: Four Score of Liberty, Privacy and Equality," *Ohio State Law Journal* 65 (2004): 1341. The Fifth Amendment and the Fourteenth Amendment contain similarly worded liberty guarantees. U.S. Const. amend. V ("No person shall... be deprived of life, liberty, or property, without due process of law"); U.S. Const. amend. XIV, § 1 ("nor shall any State deprive any person of life, liberty, or property, without due process of law"). While the liberty guarantee in the Fifth Amendment is applicable to the federal government, the liberty guarantee in the Fourteenth Amendment covers state government. Heiner v. Donnan, *United States Reports* 285 (1932), 312, 326.
167. Griswold v. Connecticut, *United States Reports* 381 (1965), 479, 485–86. In *Griswold*, the Supreme Court inferred a right of privacy from a number of constitutional provisions. Ibid., 485. In 1973, the Court attached the right of privacy to the liberty guarantee of due process, at least insofar as the right pertains to marriage, family, and sexuality. Roe v. Wade, *United States Reports* 410 (1973), 113, 152–53.

168. Government penalties for nonpublic, noncommercial, consensual same-sex sexual activity were held unconstitutional in Lawrence v. Texas, *United States Reports* 539 (2003), 558. Although the Court repeatedly refers to the liberty guarantee in the Constitution, it concludes that the state statute at issue "furthers no legitimate state interest which can justify its intrusion into *the personal and private life* of the individual." Ibid., 578 (italics added). The Court thus explicitly focused on privacy, suggesting that the constitutional right at issue is a right directed at protecting privacy. Ibid. Furthermore, the Court in *Lawrence* approved a passage in an opinion it had previously authored that described sexually relevant activities as entailing "the most *intimate and personal* choices a person may make in a lifetime." Ibid., 574 (quoting Planned Parenthood of Se. Pa. v. Casey, *United States Reports* 505 (1992), 833, 851) (italics added). In crafting its opinion in *Lawrence*, the Court also adopted a passage from a dissenting opinion written for an earlier case; the passage stated that the "*intimate* choices by unmarried as well as married persons" were beyond the constitutional powers of government to regulate. Ibid., 578 (quoting Bowers v. Hardwick, *United States Reports* 478 (1986), 186, 216 (Stephens, J., dissenting)) (italics added). The word "intimate" connotes privacy. *American Heritage Dictionary of the English Language*, 3rd ed. (1992), 945 (defining "intimate" as an adjective to include "[m]arked by informality and privacy" and "[v]ery personal; private").
169. U.S. Const. amend. XIV, § 1 ("No State shall make or enforce any law which shall... deny to any person within its jurisdiction the equal protection of the laws... ."). In ruling that a state statute violated the equal protection guarantee by restricting to married persons the distribution of items to be used for preventing pregnancy, the Court emphasized the relevance of a constitutional right of privacy. Eisenstadt v. Baird, *United States Reports* 405 (1972), 438, 453.
170. The data for Figure 5.1 are from U.S. Census Bureau, *A Half-Century of Learning: Historical Census Statistics On Educational Attainment in the United States, 1940 to 2000: Detailed Tables* table 2: Percent of the Population 25 Years and Over with a Bachelor's Degree or Higher by Sex and Age, for the United States: 1940 to 2000 (2006), http://www.census.gov/hhes/socdemo/education/data/census/half-century/tables.html (accessed April 9, 2011).
171. James P. Smith and Michael P. Ward, *Women's Wages and Work in the Twentieth Century* (1984), 39, table 20, http://www.rand.org/pubs/reports/2007/R3119.pdf (accessed April 9, 2011); Andrea Adams, *U.S. Census Bureau, Population Profile of the United States: Educational Attainment* (2008), http://www.census.gov/population/www/pop-profile/educattn.html (accessed April 9, 2011). In addition, see infra note 173 and accompanying text.
172. Figure 5.1 provides just a measure of the magnitude of a status differential between men and women in a given year. The figure thus assumes that, at each point in time, a male–female difference in social status is correlated with the male–female difference in rates of college completion. Figure 5.1 makes no assumption as to whether or how the two variables (social status and college completion) are causally connected.

173. Adams, supra note 171. Data from the census of 1940 have been employed in conjunction with other data to estimate years of schooling completed and degrees received by five-year cohorts born in 1866–1870 and later. Smith and Ward, supra note 171, at 35 nn.6 and 7. However, the estimates are for educational attainment of each birth cohort during the lifetime of the cohort, not at a specific age.
174. The data described in supra note 173 have been used to show that the sex gap in college-level education generally predicts U.S. Supreme Court decisions during most of the twentieth century on whether the national Constitution is violated by government policies that distinguish males and females. Larry D. Barnett, *Legal Construct, Social Concept* (New York: Aldine De Gruyter, 1993), 50–55.
175. It is probably not coincidence that, after removing the effects of the different choices that men and women in the United States make due to sex roles, there was only a small gender gap in compensation from employment in 2000. June O'Neill, "The Gender Gap in Wages, Circa 2000," *American Economic Review* 93 (May 2003): 309, 313 table 3, at table 3 (models 2 and 3). Because current compensation evidently involves a lengthier process than educational attainment, a gender-linked compensation differential can be expected to respond more slowly than a gender-linked education differential to the societal forces that alter the status of women vis-à-vis men.
176. For example, at the time of the 1970 census (which occurred on or around April 1, 1970), 83.6 percent of all first-year college students (male and female) who were younger than twenty-five had been seventeen, eighteen, or nineteen years old when the 1969–70 academic year started (or, more precisely, on October 1, 1969). Calculated from U.S. Census Bureau, *1970 Census of Population*, vol. II. Series PC(2). 5A *Subject Reports: School Enrollment* (1970), 119 table 5, http://www2.census.gov/prod2/decennial/documents/42045400v2p5a5cch01.pdf (accessed April 9, 2011). In late 1969, consequently, five out of six first-year college students who had not reached age twenty-five were a maximum of one year away from age eighteen. The proportion of these students who earned a bachelor's degree is unknown. However, among women who are enrolled in college when they are younger than twenty, relatively few seem not to complete a bachelor's degree before their thirtieth birthday. See Jerry A. Jacobs and Rosalind Berkowitz King, "Age and College Completion: A Life-History Analysis of Women Aged 15–44," *Sociology of Education* 75 (2002): 211, 219 figure 1 (cumulative completion rates estimated from Figure 1).
177. Griswold v. Connecticut, *United States Reports* 381 (1965), 479.
178. Trammel v. United States, *United States Reports* 445 (1979), 40, 43–44 (describing the purpose and historical roots of the privilege against adverse testimony by a person against her/his spouse). During the last half of the twentieth century, the privilege that allows a married person to bar testimony against the person by his or her spouse when the testimony involves confidential marital matters became less prevalent, and the conditions under which the privilege could be exercised were narrowed. Ibid., 48–50. These changes are consistent with the evident intensification of individualism that has occurred in the United States since the middle of

the century and with the equalization of the status of men and of women that accompanied or resulted from greater individualism. Individualism and gender equality are probably the result of the long-term growth of knowledge. *Law as Symbol*, supra note 20, at 336–37 (reproduced in Part V of Chapter 8 infra); *The Roots of Law*, supra note 26, at 628–32, 678–79 (reproduced in Part II and in Part IV-B, respectively, of Chapter 6 infra).

179. Roe v. Wade, *United States Reports* 410(1973), 113, 153–54, 165 n.67.
180. Planned Parenthood of Cent. Mo. v. Danforth, *United States Reports* 428 (1976), 52, 70–71.
181. Lawrence v. Texas, *United States Reports* 539 (2003), 558. In addition, see supra note 168.
182. Smith and Ward, supra note 171, at 36 table 18 (rates of college attendance and completion among women by birth cohort); U.S. Census Bureau, supra note 170 (percentage of women twenty-five to twenty-nine years old who had received at least a bachelor's degree by census year from 1940 to 2000). See also U.S. Census Bureau, Table A-2: Percentage of the Population 3 Years Old and Over Enrolled in School, by Age, Sex, Race, and Hispanic Origin: October 1947 to 2008, http://www.census.gov/population/socdemo/school/TableA-2.xls (accessed February 15, 2010) (percentages of women at age 18–19, 20–21, 22–24, and 25–59 who were enrolled in school between 1947 and 2008).
183. Kathy A. Thomack, "Centering Men's Experience: Norah Vincent's Self-Made Man Complicates Feminist Legal Theorists' Views of Gender," *Buffalo Women's Law Journal* 15 (2006): 1, 30 (contending that the sex attribute is the most influential of societally defined characteristics in shaping social behavior and self-conception).
184. J. Richard Udry, "Biological Limits of Gender Construction," *American Sociological Review* 65 (2000): 443.
185. Norman T. Deutsch, "*Nguyen v. INS* and the Application of Intermediate Scrutiny to Gender Classifications: Theory, Practice, and Reality," *Pepperdine Law Review* 30 (2003): 185, 220–60.
186. *The Roots of Law*, supra note 26, at 632–34 (federal statutes prohibiting sex-based discrimination in employment). Pages 632–34 in *The Roots of Law* are reproduced in Part II of Chapter 6 infra.
187. Supra notes 165–169, 177–181.
188. S.Rep. No. 103–117 (1993), available at 1993 WL 286699. From the late 1970s to the early 1990s, "[a] nationwide campaign of anti-abortion blockades, invasions, vandalism and outright violence" in the United States was found to be "endangering the lives and well-being of the health care providers who work there and the patients who seek their services." Ibid., 3.

Jurisdiction Properties and Law

6

Jurisdiction Properties and Law on Social Issues in the United States*

Chapter 6 examines shifts in law in the United States on a number of subjects, including law setting the age of majority and law regulating access to abortion, and it links these shifts to changes in specific aspects of U.S. society. Data from the 1950 and 1960 censuses of the population of the forty-eight coterminous states are analyzed with logistic regression to identify system-level properties distinguishing states that liberalized their law on abortion between 1967 and 1972 (i.e., before the U.S. Supreme Court ruling in Roe v. Wade) from states that did not. The regression analysis, in conjunction with time-series data for the nation as a whole, suggests that the liberalization by states and by *Roe* of law-imposed restrictions on abortion was associated with increases in school enrollment and educational level among young women. The chapter advances the premise that long-term growth in the quantity of knowledge broadly affected the American social system and its law, and ascribes the rising prevalence and longer duration of education among women—as antecedents of the liberalization of law on abortion—primarily to the expansion of knowledge. The chapter thus provides empirical support for the macrosociological thesis that the concepts and doctrines of law are determined by the properties of society and the large-scale forces that are responsible for these properties.

I. Introduction

Distinct concepts and principles characterize every profession,[1] and the reality perceived by members of one profession therefore differs to some extent from the reality perceived by members of another profession.[2] Because an understanding of the world is never complete—perhaps because "[r]eality is nothing but a collective hunch"[3]—no single profession has a monopoly on truth, and research that brings together different professions has the potential to yield new insights. Accordingly, Chapter 6 draws on two professions—law and sociology—in an attempt to answer a pair of related questions. First, why does the law of a society contain certain concepts and doctrines at one point in history but not at another? Second, why at a given point in time does the law of one society contain certain concepts and doctrines while the law of another society does not? I believe that both questions have a common answer and that the answer is supplied by the discipline of macrosociology. Specifically, my thesis is that the properties of society form the roots of law and that these properties, and the forces behind them, shape the content of law in the social system in which the law develops and operates.

As a social science, macrosociology assumes that the doctrines of law are not random occurrences. Instead, macrosociology contends that identifiable system-level factors account for differences in law both across time in any particular jurisdiction and across jurisdictions at any particular point in time. The macrosociological approach employed in the instant chapter (a) views law as an institution of a society and, hence, as a component of a system[4]; (b) assumes that, as an institution, law aids society by promoting the equilibrium and cohesiveness of the system in the long run[5]; (c) contends that, for law to benefit society, the content of law—i.e., the concepts and doctrines of law—must manifest the properties of society, not the personalities of individuals; and (d) expects, therefore, that law will change as large-scale forces alter the properties of society. The preceding principles, although generally ignored in research on law,[6] form the foundation of the present chapter, and the fourth principle, which follows from the three that precede it, is the focus of the chapter.

Several illustrations can be given in support of the fourth principle, i.e., the principle that law evolves in response to large-scale forces that alter the properties of society. These illustrations rely on studies (including, when available, quantitative data) that concern a long time interval prior to the change in law under consideration. Shifts that take place in the concepts and doctrines of law can be traced in most instances to change in societal properties that began much earlier and that occurred gradually.

A. Sex Roles

The first illustration is the manner in which American law during the nineteenth and twentieth centuries treated the biological trait of sex. In 1872, the United States Supreme Court, with just one dissenting justice, ruled that a state could deny a woman a license to practice law even if she were eligible for a license in a state where she had formerly resided.[7] The Court deferred to the state's police power, under which states regulate occupations, and concluded that an inconsistency between states in the requirements for admission to the bar does not nullify the requirements of the more-restrictive state, even though the restriction involves the sex of the applicant and the applicant had resided in a less-restrictive state. Notably, three justices, concurring in the decision, explained the ruling with their view that:

> The natural and proper timidity and delicacy which belongs to the female sex evidently unfits it for many of the occupations of civil life. The constitution of the family organization, which is founded in the divine ordinance, as well as in the nature of things, indicates the domestic sphere as that which properly belongs to the domain and functions of womanhood.[8]

A full century would pass before Supreme Court jurisprudence on sex-based differences in government policy underwent substantial change. Since the 1970s, the Court has required government to justify policies that treat women differently than men[9] and to do so with a rationale that is "exceedingly persuasive."[10] However, a quantitative measure of differences over time in the roles of women and men indicates that the shift in Supreme Court doctrine on gender just mirrored societal change in sex roles[11] and that the Court accepted gender egalitarianism only after sex-role equality had markedly increased.[12]

The preceding conclusion, of course, conflicts with the belief that law on gender shapes sex roles as well as with the assumption on which the belief is based. The assumption—viz., that the causal link between law and society is *from* law *to* society—is unfortunate for at least two reasons. First, the assumption undoubtedly is responsible for the dearth of quantitative research on whether and how societal conditions affect law, including law relevant to women. Second, the assumption is just that—an assumption—and as an assumption, it may not be true. At the very least, the assumption should not be taken for granted. Indeed, it is rejected by the macrosociological framework that I propose. In my framework, law is a mechanism that facilitates the operation of the societal system, and the concepts and doctrines used by the law of a society necessarily respond to the properties of the society. While considerable time frequently (if not typically) elapses before law harmonizes with societal conditions, eventually law must be congruent with societal circumstances for law to remain a viable institution of society. Thus, American law on gender evolved because it was adapting to change that had occurred in social life.

I turn now to two additional topics that illustrate the proposition that law is rooted in societal conditions.

B. The Investment Company Act and the Concept of "Person"

The Investment Company Act ("Act"),[13] which Congress adopted in 1940,[14] governs vehicles in the United States that (a) issue and sell securities to investors and (b) with the assets obtained from the sale of their securities, invest in securities issued by others, which are usually business entities, governments, and/or government agencies. Because the Act is the basis for the regulation of mutual funds by the Securities and Exchange Commission,[15] it is a prominent aspect of law pertinent to finance in the United States and significant to the American public. An indicator of the societal importance of mutual funds is that at the end of 2009 U.S. mutual funds managed net assets totaling $11.1 trillion, and during the first decade of the twenty-first century their investors included more than two out of five households in the country.[16]

As specified in Section 3 of the Act, an investment company must inter alia be an "issuer,"[17] and given the definition of issuer in Section 2 of the Act, an issuer must be a "person."[18] Therefore, the conceptualization of person is fundamental to an investment company: an investment vehicle cannot be an investment company unless it is a person. Of relevance here, the Act defines a person to include a "company,"[19] and by doing so, Congress placed entities—i.e., artificial persons—within the scope of the Act.[20]

By encompassing an artificial being, is the Act's definition of person consistent with the way society at large employs the word? This question is important because my thesis contends that the meaning of concepts in law is compatible with their meaning in the general population. Research in etymology suggests that, in referring to artificial beings, the definition of person in law was preceded by a similar definition in society. The word *person* came into English from the Old French word *persone*, which in turn was derived from the Latin word *persona*.[21] Before the end of fourteenth century, the

English concept of person referred not only to a human being but also to "[a] character sustained or assumed in a drama or the like, or in actual life; part played; hence function, office, capacity."[22] The latter meaning can include fictionalized characters, and by extending the word *person* to such characters, the English language abstracted artificial beings from interpersonal activities and recognized artificial beings as separate from the human beings who were involved in these activities.

Prior to the fifteenth century, therefore, English as a language possessed the ability to conceptualize an intangible dimension of human interaction such as business arrangements and to treat this dimension as distinct from the human participants in the arrangement. Because the idea of an artificial person had become possible in the English language, a necessary condition existed for English law to recognize this type of person—including what we call a corporation and a partnership.[23] Notably, it was in the fifteenth century that corporations and partnerships were brought within the definition of person in the law of England.[24] Artificial beings thus appeared in the lexicon of English law only after they appeared in the English language, and the sequence is not simply coincidence. Business arrangements that today would be labeled partnerships, companies, and guilds had become an important element in the economy of England well before the fifteenth century began.[25] The experience of society is the impetus for the emergence and meaning of concepts,[26] and the nature of economic activity required artificial persons to be part of the language of England and of its law.[27]

When American law included artificial beings within the definition of person, therefore, it followed a long-established practice[28] and accepted a meaning for the word that had already been adopted outside the institution of law. However, if the macrosociological framework employed in the instant chapter is applicable to the concepts used by law, the word "person" is only illustrative of a general principle, namely, that all concepts and rules of law develop within and are molded by the social system and culture in which the law is embedded. This principle accounts for abstractions from interpersonal relationships involving economic activity and the acceptance by law in the United States of artificial beings as persons: corporations and partnerships are, and long have been, central to the U.S. economy,[29] indicating that these forms of business organization have been an important, if not essential, aspect of U.S. society.

C. Age of Majority

For a macrosociological theory of law, a compelling topic is the age of majority, i.e., the age at which society ceases to define an individual as a child and confers all of the rights, and imposes all of the duties, of adulthood. The topic is important sociologically for two related reasons. First, age, like gender, is a factor that organizes social life in every technologically advanced society, including the United States.[30] Second, the age of majority provides a salient line in the social order of the United States—for persons who do not suffer from a physical or psychological disability, the line separates individuals deemed dependent by American society from individuals deemed independent.[31] Given its societal importance, the age of majority is designated by law, and "[y]oung people eagerly anticipate their legal 'adulthood.' At the age of majority, our society puts them on notice that they are assuming an array of rights and responsibilities which they never had before."[32]

In examining the age of majority designated by law, I will limit myself to the forty-eight states in the continental United States. I exclude Alaska and Hawaii because I consider a period that extends to the start of the twentieth century, and Alaska and Hawaii were not states until the end of the sixth decade of that century.[33] In addition, I omit all non-state jurisdictions. Thus, the District of Columbia is excluded along with non-state jurisdictions located outside the continental United States, such as Puerto Rico, Guam, and the Virgin Islands.[34]

The table in the Appendix to the instant chapter summarizes state law on the age of majority. Column 2 of the table shows, by state, the age of majority that was in force during most of the twentieth century. Column 3 gives, for each state, the age of majority that replaced the age in column 2, and column 4 specifies the year in which each state legislature approved the age in column 3. In reviewing the table, the reader should keep two points in mind. First, column 4 specifies the year in which the legislature revised the age of majority, but the year of legislative approval may not have been the first year that the age of majority was in force. Some states did not implement the new age of majority until the year following its approval by the legislature. Because my interest is whether law setting the age of majority responds to its social environment, the point at which a law-making body approves a statute seems more significant than the point at which government officially implements it. Second, the legislation altering the age of majority may have amended an existing statute or it may have altered the common law, i.e., doctrine in court decisions. Under the common law, the age of majority was twenty-one.[35]

A review of the table in the Appendix yields a number of conclusions. Of greatest importance, states generally reduced the age of majority to eighteen, or in a few instances to nineteen, during a relatively short time span, viz., in the first half of the 1970s. Additionally, this period witnessed the elimination of different ages of majority for males and females by states that had such differences. However, states whose age of majority contained a gender distinction were few in number, and all but one of these states (Illinois) had small populations.[36] Gender differences in the age of majority had thus largely disappeared prior to the 1970s. Moreover, change in statutory law preceded rather than followed the emergence of constitutional law on the subject. In 1975, the U.S. Supreme Court concluded that, for purposes of child support, a gender-based distinction in the age of majority violates the equal protection guarantee of the Constitution,[37] but when the Court announced its decision in April 1975, the states (shown in the table) that had been using different ages of majority for women and men were no longer doing so.[38] The age of majority, therefore, was a product of the legislative process, not the judicial process.

Whether new law is developed by legislatures or by courts (or by executive-branch agencies), however, is not of central concern to my thesis. As an institution, law must aid the operation of its society in the long run, and through legislation, judicial action, or agencies of the executive branch, the doctrines of law will come to embody the character of the social system and the forces shaping it. Let me accordingly attempt to identify the forces that contributed to reducing the age of majority in the early 1970s. Since the reduction occurred in most states during a short span of time, the forces that were involved evidently operated on a national scale and affected much of the population to roughly the same degree. But what social forces were at work?

One force behind the reduction in the age of adulthood was probably the changing age structure of the United States that resulted from the baby boom after World War II and the historical context of the baby boom. Specifically, because of low levels of fertility before World War II, especially during the Depression of the 1930s, the post-war baby boom created a large bulge in the demographic structure of the population, and as the passage of time moved the bulge into successive age categories, these age categories seriatim noticeably and rapidly increased in relative size. During the three decades after the war, therefore, the salience and significance of younger age groups rose dramatically. This demographic situation is likely to have contributed to the collective decision during the early 1970s to reduce the age of majority. Research on other topics suggests that the age makeup of the U.S. population has had distinct effects,[39] and the changing age distribution of the country after World War II is logically a key factor altering the age of majority in the 1970s.

The historical context and demographic dimensions of the baby boom may be understood with data on annual births. Estimates of fertility in the United States as a whole are available by individual year starting in 1909. From 1909 until the mid-1920s, the crude birth rate (the number of births per one-thousand members of the population) was consistently above twenty-five. Subsequently, the rate declined, reaching a low of 18.4 in the mid-1930s, and then moved slightly upward until World War II ended in 1945. Once World War II was over, births rose substantially: from 1946 to 1959, the crude birth rate was between 24.1 and 26.6.[40] The comparatively low birth rate before and during the war, together with the materially higher birth rate after the war, had a dramatic effect on the age structure of the population.

If a society is to avoid upheaval, it must absorb its youth socially as well as economically. Since my goal is to ascertain whether the post-World War II baby boom helps to explain the reduction in the age for adult status during the first half of the 1970s, the ages directly affected by the change—viz., eighteen, nineteen, and twenty—necessarily are included in my analysis. In addition, persons close to their eighteenth birthday presumably contributed to lowering the age of majority, because in the 1960s they were relatively numerous and their share of the population was growing rapidly. The appreciable expansion of the segment of the population that was approaching age twenty-one—an expansion attributable to the baby boom following World War II and occurring in the decade-and-a-half prior to 1970—confronted society with the necessity of assimilating a large group that would soon be adults and was probably a major source of pressure on the American social system.

Given these theoretical considerations, my focus is on the fraction of the population fifteen to twenty years of age and the manner in which this fraction changed over time. Striking shifts in this fraction may be infrequent in the history of a society, but when they occur, they have the ability to create conspicuous social and economic problems. Figure 6.1 shows the percentage of the U.S. population that was fifteen through twenty years old in each year from 1900 to 1980.[41] Particularly important is the period from 1940 to 1970: the percentage declined by more than one-fourth between 1940 and 1954 (from 11.2 percent to 7.9 percent) and then rose by one-half between 1955 and 1976 (from 7.9 percent to 11.8 percent), with most of the rise occurring before 1970. Thus, during the three decades that preceded the reduction of the age of majority to eighteen, there was a sharp decline and rebound in the demographic presence of the age group most directly affected by whether majority was attained at age twenty-one or at age eighteen. The rapidity and magnitude of the rebound undoubtedly increased the salience of youth, and the prominence of young persons in the population is likely to have promoted law that reduced the age for adulthood.

Figure 6.1 also shows that the percentage of the population fifteen to twenty years of age was relatively high in the early decades of the twentieth century. Why was the age of majority not reduced to eighteen at this time? One possibility is that the substantial swing after 1940 in the proportion of persons fifteen to twenty years old by itself

Figure 6.1 Percentage of Population 15-20 Years Old

United States, 1900 to 1980

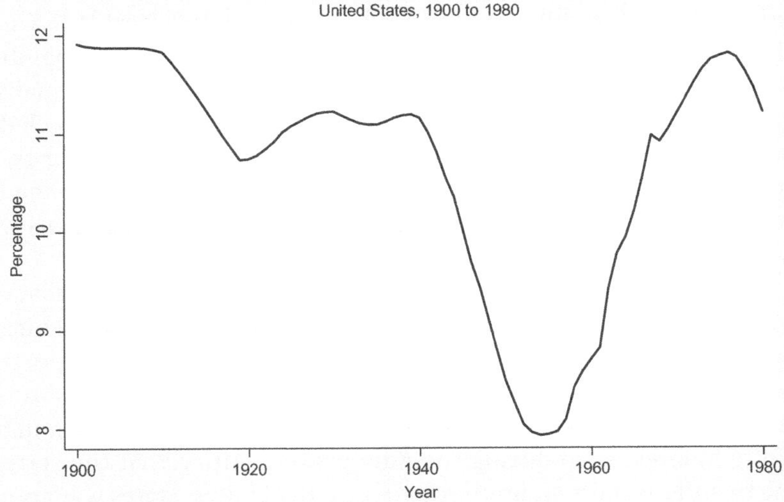

reduced the age of majority to eighteen. Under this hypothesis, the magnitude and speed of the change in the proportion was decisive. A second possibility is that the relatively large percentage of fifteen to twenty year olds in the population during the second half of the twentieth century (rather than the volatility of the percentage) acted in conjunction with at least one other factor that was present at the time—a factor that did not exist or was not adequate in strength at the start of the twentieth century. According to the second hypothesis, the level of the percentage, and not its change, was critical, but the level of the percentage was unable by itself to alter the age of majority; a further factor was required as well. A third possibility, of course, is that the reduction of the age of majority to eighteen in the 1970s was the product of the large pre-reduction swing in the relative size of the age group fifteen to twenty years old in conjunction with one or more other factors. Under the last hypothesis, the change in, and not the level of, the relative size of the age group combined with additional factors to lower the age of majority. Because social phenomena are typically complex, the second alternative and third alternative are more plausible than the first, and the age structure of the population probably did not act alone to reduce the age of majority in the 1970s.

What else may have been at work? One potential factor was the transformation that occurred during the twentieth century in the traits that American parents wanted to inculcate in their children. Specifically, independence increased and obedience decreased as characteristics desired for children, and both changes were sizeable.[42] These changes may have stemmed from the large, complex, and expanding body of knowledge found in the United States, because individualism and personal autonomy become more prevalent when knowledge grows or reaches a certain threshold.[43] A lower age of majority, of course, is consistent with a societal emphasis on independence for youth, while a higher age of majority can be expected a priori in a social system that stresses obedience to authority.[44]

By way of conclusion, the reduction of the age of majority that occurred during the first half of the 1970s should be regarded as a means by which American society, through its law, adjusted to an important group. The assimilation of large, distinct groups—a process that probably happens in most social systems—has long been significant in the United States, even during the nineteenth century.[45] At the start of the twentieth century, immigration into the United States was appreciable, and a large part of the immigrant stream originated in central, eastern, and southern Europe.[46] Adaptation to and the assimilation of groups that did not share the culture of northwestern Europe—the dominant culture of the United States—were essential to the effective operation of the American social system. By the 1970s, on the other hand, cultural diversity was no longer a major problem for American society,[47] but the baby boom after World War II had created another substantial group, defined by age rather than culture, to which the social order needed to adjust if it was to avoid disruption. One means employed in the adjustment process was to lower the age of majority to eighteen. Law setting the age of majority was thus a societal device to facilitate a macrosociological process.

II. Knowledge as a Societal Property

If a macrosociological framework for law is to develop, a critical area for research is multi-jurisdiction change in law. Such a framework posits that jurisdiction characteristics account for the content of law and that alterations in the former will thus lead to alterations in the latter. In this regard, two types of situations merit study—(1) situations in which multiple jurisdictions acquire a particular doctrine during a relatively brief period and (2) situations in which multiple jurisdictions, one at a time, acquire the doctrine over a lengthy period.

Concurrent transformations in the law of numerous jurisdictions—the first type of situation—may on the surface seem more important as a research topic because they are more salient, and they may be more attractive as a research topic because their causes may be easier to identify. However, inasmuch as prediction is a central goal of the scientific enterprise, coincident shifts in law across multiple jurisdictions can complicate the task of social science. For example, concurrent multi-jurisdiction shifts in law can stem from massive but aperiodic events such as natural disasters and wars. These events are difficult, perhaps impossible, to anticipate far in advance, and as a result, uncertainty as to the timing (if not the content) of the law they can be expected to engender may be unavoidable.

In addition, doctrines of law that, over an extended period, undergo modification in multiple jurisdictions one at a time may not be simple to study either. Such modifications may have been produced by forces that developed gradually and that had their effects when thresholds were reached. This route to multi-jurisdiction change in law is probably much more common than the first, and the changes in law that it generates will be hard to anticipate when there is more than a single threshold at which slowly building pressure precipitates a new doctrine of law. Two or more thresholds for a given doctrine will be present whenever law is transformed by different combinations of societal properties and their interactions, a situation that is likely to exist in most, and perhaps all, structurally complex societies. The threshold(s) for a particular doctrine of law may thus differ between jurisdictions.

Regardless of whether jurisdictions adopt novel doctrines of law in a brief period or over an extended period, the properties of a social system and the forces that affect these properties must be the focus of attention if the doctrines are to be understood and their emergence is to be predicted. In my macrosociological framework, the individuals in the system—including those who participate in law-making bodies such as legislatures, agencies of the executive branch, and courts—do not account for the content of law. Rather, pervasive forces that mold the characteristics of the social system determine the decisions of these individuals with regard to the content of law,[48] and explanations of law that are based on personalities, even personalities of prominence and charisma, treat the institution of law superficially. The character of society and the substance of its law are not formed by individuals, but by large-scale forces that operate through the actions of individuals.

In this part of Chapter 6, I will focus on one such force that I believe shaped the social order and doctrines of law in the United States during the twentieth century and that can be expected to remain a potent influence on U.S. law for the foreseeable future. The role of this force, however, seems not to have been fully appreciated by either social scientists or law-trained scholars. The force is the expansion of knowledge. Undoubtedly, other forces (e.g., increases in population density[49]) influenced the character of American society and the content of its law, but I concentrate on knowledge because I believe that it had, and will continue to have, a major impact on the United States. Possibly because accumulating knowledge has shaped social life for so long, its role in the social system has not received the attention it deserves. We simply have become accustomed to improvements in knowledge.

In order to show the increase of knowledge over time, I begin with a quantitative measure of knowledge. Perhaps not surprisingly, knowledge is difficult to study because it is an abstract concept and must be operationalized. The concept of knowledge is necessarily an abstraction because knowledge assumes different forms (e.g., a chemical compound or mechanical process in manufacturing, a statistical technique for data analysis in science), and in some forms (e.g., mathematics) it is composed entirely of written signs. Being an abstract concept, knowledge is not directly observable and must be measured by its manifestations.

What indicators can be used to determine the magnitude and growth of knowledge? The question does not have an easy answer, because no single indicator or set of indicators seems to be accepted by social scientists[50] even though the amount of knowledge available to Americans is believed to be expanding dramatically.[51] The absence of a generally accepted measure or set of measures is unfortunate. The availability of a relatively simple indicator that correctly gauges the quantity of knowledge, together with long-term data on the indicator, would benefit macrosociological analyses in general and a macrosociological framework for doctrines of law in particular.

Although at present no single indicator adequately depicts the volume and expansion of knowledge in the aggregate, Figure 6.2 shows the annual number of patents for inventions that U.S. residents have received from the U.S. Patent and Trademark Office.[52] In the United States, patents are issued for inventions, for natural plants, and for

Figure 6.2 Number of Patents Granted Yearly for Inventions

United States, 1790 to 2009

designs, but of the three, patents for inventions are the most accurate indicator of knowledge since they are awarded for "any new and useful process, machine, manufacture, or composition of matter, or any new and useful improvement thereof," that was not obvious to a person of average skill in the field in which the invention originated.[53] An invention thus constitutes a technological innovation, and since technology employs knowledge, the number of patents granted for inventions over time can serve as an indicator of change in the quantity of accumulated knowledge.

In considering Figure 6.2, the reader should keep in mind that patented inventions represent only one form of knowledge and are just a rough indicator of such knowledge. Patented inventions cannot serve as an accurate indicator of knowledge as a whole for at least two reasons: (1) an addition to knowledge may not be incorporated into a patentable invention; and (2) all patented inventions do not utilize the same amount of knowledge. The two problems are distinct. The first exists because many types of knowledge are not within the term "invention" as defined by law, and hence they cannot be patented. For example, a new measure of sex segregation in occupations[54] is a contribution to knowledge, but it is not patentable. Moreover, even when knowledge generates patented inventions, the quantum of knowledge used is not the same in every invention. To illustrate, less knowledge is probably required to create appliances for the home than to create drugs that treat serious diseases. Unfortunately, neither of the two problems can be corrected at the present time. The first problem could be mitigated by data on copyrights issued for scientific articles and books. However, while copyrights for scientific publications could be employed as an indicator (albeit imperfect) of advances in scientific knowledge,[55] long-term data on these copyrights do not exist. The second problem necessitates a technique to measure the amount of knowledge in an invention, but such a technique has yet to be devised. As a result, time-series data are unavailable on the total amount of knowledge in patented inventions.

Figure 6.2 shows a secular rise in the number of patents granted for inventions. Even during the periods when the number declined, knowledge continued to accumulate; the gains in knowledge simply were less in these periods than in the years that preceded them. Moreover, the intervals of decline in patent issuance are relatively brief when viewed historically, and the discovery process is cumulative, i.e., the inventions in one year build on inventions (knowledge) from earlier years. For the last two centuries, then, knowledge expanded in the United States. Notably, the pace of the expansion accelerated starting in the mid-1980s, which may reflect developments in computer hardware and software.

A sustained increase in knowledge is likely to generate broad changes in the character of society,[56] and the changes resulting from this increase probably include two that are critical to understanding the content and evolution of law. The first of the two changes is an expansion of economic wealth. All else remaining constant, advances in knowledge add to the wealth of a society by augmenting economic productivity and permitting more efficient and/or more complete exploitation of natural resources. Wealth, in turn, allows individuals to pursue and fulfill their personal goals, i.e., wealth promotes secular individualism.[57] The second likely change is an increase in rationality. The progress of knowledge encourages rationality in part by producing a greater understanding of events and experiences; comprehension, in turn, fosters reason. Additionally, the progress of knowledge increases rationality by enlarging the portion of the labor force that works with information[58] and that thus relies on intellectual rather than physical skills. Concomitantly, the progress of knowledge enlarges the number of jobs that are self-directed, i.e., that involve complex, non-methodical tasks and that are not subject to close supervision.[59] In short, occupations concerned with information and characterized by self-direction encompass more people as knowledge advances, and they enhance analytical abilities, i.e., reasoning, in every facet of life.[60] The U.S. commitment to scientific research has thus had widespread effects on American society.[61]

Assuming that the growth of knowledge reshapes society, in what ways did expanding knowledge alter doctrines of law in the United States during the twentieth century? The growth of knowledge undoubtedly had many effects, but this chapter will suggest just two. Specifically, greater individualism and rationality, as consequences of knowledge growth, probably created and intensified expectations that expertise, rather than characteristics irrelevant to occupational skill and performance, would be the basis for employment-related decisions. Evidence that such change in expectations occurred with regard to gender is the declining sex differential in compensation since the early part of the twentieth century: the disparity between American women and men in skill levels due to work experience decreased with the passage of time, and the average pay of women rose more rapidly than the average pay of men.[62] Indeed, the gains of women in the United States seem to be a manifestation of an apparently universal phenomenon, because economic development—a process in which new knowledge is introduced and utilized in an economy[63]—has been found to augment the presence of women in information-based, self-directed occupations in numerous countries.[64] One of the attributes of these occupations is higher income.[65]

Advancing knowledge, in short, enlarges the number of jobs that require intellectual skill rather than physical strength, and it produces, or at least facilitates, pressure on employers to focus their personnel practices on job skills rather than on demographic attributes. In the United States, individualism and rationality seem to have become sufficiently pervasive and intense to generate statutes that authorized the imposition of penalties on employers that use demographic characteristics such as age, race, and sex in decisions regarding current employees and applicants for employment. Antidiscrimination statutes represent one of the striking innovations in law during the last half of the twentieth century, and because they illustrate—though by no means exhaust—the doctrines of law produced by advancing knowledge, I review below the major antidiscrimination statutes at the federal level that deal with employment.[66]

I begin with a statute enacted by Congress in 1870 that prohibits race discrimination in contracts and that has been applied to employment contracts.[67] The statute originally was aimed at slavery and associated conditions,[68] and it was extended to employment only in the 1970s.[69] Insofar as it is concerned with job discrimination, therefore, the statute is a creation of the last part of the twentieth century.

The Equal Pay Act of 1963 was the first federal statute explicitly fashioned to combat employment discrimination.[70] The Act requires that, except when differential compensation is attributable to certain specified factors (e.g., a seniority program), women and men in the same establishment must receive identical compensation for work that is "equal," that demands "equal skill, effort, and responsibility," and that occurs under "similar working conditions."[71] Congress directed the Equal Pay Act at the "ancient but outmoded belief that a man, because of his role in society, should be paid more than a woman even though his duties are the same."[72] It is notable, however, that this belief had already been abandoned by Americans. In a 1954 national survey, fully 87 percent of respondents approved, and just 13 percent disapproved, of equal compensation for male and female employees with the same occupational duties.[73]

While the Equal Pay Act of 1963 is confined to gender and covers only compensation, the Civil Rights Act of 1964 includes a provision (Title VII) that bans discrimination involving "race, color, religion, sex, or national origin" in all facets of employment.[74] The aim of Title VII is to require employers, labor organizations, and employment agencies to base employment decisions on job-related qualifications and to eliminate from these decisions groundless stereotypes that have been maintained by social inertia. In addition, Title VII renders reliance on statistical differences between groups impermissible in employment decisions without a compelling justification. For example, employment decisions cannot be based on the statistically demonstrable fact that women with minor children more often have primary responsibility for child care than men with minor children.[75] "Title VII prohibits the use of popular stereotypes or even statistical data to attribute general group characteristics to each individual member of the group."[76] Under Title VII, potential and current employees must be evaluated individually using criteria that are pertinent to job performance.

Because it encompassed the entire employment relationship and multiple demographic attributes and also established a governmental agency (the Equal Employment Opportunity Commission) to deal with discrimination covered by Title VII,[77] the Civil Rights Act of 1964 has been the most prominent federal legislation to date on employment discrimination. The Civil Rights Act of 1964 did not, however, include all demographic characteristics important to the structure of American society. In particular, the Act did not cover age, an omission that Congress corrected three years later when it adopted legislation to prohibit discrimination in employment against persons forty to sixty-five years old. Like Title VII, the Age Discrimination in Employment Act of 1967 ("ADEA") extends to all aspects of employment, with exceptions for some types of employers,[78] and was designed to suppress "inaccurate and stigmatizing stereotypes" about age.[79] Under both statutes, decisions that affect employment must rely on factors relevant to job performance and on evaluations of individuals in terms of these factors.

The next, and last, major federal statute on employment discrimination was adopted more than two decades later. In 1990, Congress approved the Americans with Disabilities Act ("ADA") in order to prevent employers, labor organizations, and employment agencies from engaging in unwarranted discrimination against persons who have, or who are thought to have, physical or psychological disabilities.[80] Like other legislation dealing with employment discrimination, the ADA was designed to require that job-related decisions be based on the qualifications of current and potential employees, and it reflected the dissatisfaction of society with preconceptions that preclude evaluations of individuals in terms of these qualifications.[81] In enacting the ADA, "Congress acknowledged that society's accumulated myths and fears about disability and disease are as handicapping as are the physical limitations that flow from actual impairment."[82]

The four statutes described above—the Equal Pay Act of 1963, Title VII of the Civil Rights Act of 1964, the Age Discrimination in Employment Act of 1967, and the Americans with Disabilities Act of 1990—comprise the main innovations in federal law concerned with employment discrimination in the United States and serve as the central tools of the institution of law at the national level for efforts to promote social and economic justice in employment. Indicative of the importance of these statutes to American society is that the number of employers subject to the statutes has generally been expanded over time.[83] Of particular relevance to a macrosociological framework is that the four statutes, as well as related federal legislation,[84] confer an identifiable character on the period from 1963 to 1990. By differentiating the period, the statutes form a unitary sociological phenomenon, and their enactment is presumptively not fortuitous.

In conclusion, novel doctrines are a core concern in a macrosociological approach to law, and an especially important macrosociological topic is any novel doctrine that several major pieces of legislation incorporate. Part II of the instant chapter has focused on the impact of a growing stock of knowledge and has linked this factor to a salient development in recent law in the United States—federal antidiscrimination legislation. However, if the properties of a society have effects that are broad and fundamental, the substantial increase in knowledge is likely to have been responsible for new doctrines of law on a variety of subjects. In Part III below, I present evidence that additions to knowledge reshaped law on abortion by increasing the prevalence and lengthening the duration of schooling among young women.[85]

III. Law and Abortion

Because law on abortion underwent a transformation during a relatively short period in the United States, the subject of abortion affords an opportunity not only to identify societal properties and forces shaping law but also to call attention to an important point in the macrosociological thesis that I am advancing. If the concepts and principles that dominate law are attributable to the society in which they are embedded, the distinction between branches of government—the legislature, the executive branch, and the judiciary—is not of major importance, and prevailing doctrines of law do not depend on whether they are in statutes enacted by legislatures, in regulations issued by administrative agencies, or in decisions rendered by judicial bodies. In a macrosociological perspective, broad forces that determine the properties of society shape the governing doctrines of law, and the doctrines respond in the long run to these forces/properties in a manner that protects the equilibrium of the society and maintains, or increases, commitment to the society on the part of its participants. One of the branches of government will supply a doctrine of law that a society needs, because a society is a system and because law is a component that contributes to the system. Thus, merely identifying the branch of government that produces a given doctrine is insufficient for understanding why the doctrine exists. An inquiry of greater depth is necessary. The branches of government form a dependent, not an independent, variable in my framework, and the branch that happens to originate a particular doctrine is a fact requiring an explanation, not a fact providing one.[86]

In asserting that the branch of government from which any particular doctrine emanates cannot explain the content and evolution of law, I am implicitly challenging at least one widely accepted belief, namely, that the political process is an important factor determining doctrines of law. As explained supra in Part II-A of Chapter 1, I reject this assumption at the same time I concede that politics is a precursor of law. The role of politics differs across the branches of government—a difference that is particularly apparent between the judicial branch, where politics operates through the appointment and election of judges, and the legislative and executive branches, where politics operates not just through the election of officeholders but also through lobbying efforts directed at them. In my framework, however, political activity is merely the vehicle by which societal needs and values shape doctrines of law, and political analyses—despite their popularity—are not useful for understanding either why certain concepts and principles of law are dominant in a society at a given point in time or why such concepts and principles change over time. The political process in a viable social system, I contend, primarily functions to communicate the requirements of society to the institution of law. Thus, social science research has found that the expenditure patterns and legislative subjects of government are not affected materially by whether the persons comprising the governing elite are replaced or retained.[87] Societal imperatives, not political considerations, drive the domestic policies of government.

The preceding points are pertinent to law governing the use of abortion, and I therefore turn to a review of the change that occurred in this law during the late 1960s and early 1970s.

A. Change in Law on Abortion, 1967–1973

Roe v. Wade,[88] the January 1973 decision of the U.S. Supreme Court that held unconstitutional government action intended to impose severe restrictions on access to abortion, has been regarded not just as a milestone in the rights that law accords women,[89] but more broadly as a landmark in the history of constitutional interpretation.[90] The salience of *Roe,* however, diverts attention from an important forerunner that occurred at the state level. Specifically, in the years immediately preceding *Roe,* many states, either through legislation or court decision, substantially liberalized their law on access to therapeutic abortion. The liberalization of state law began in 1967, and by 1972, sixteen states in the coterminous United States had appreciably relaxed the conditions under which women were allowed to terminate pregnancies lawfully.[91] While not all of the states that revised their law permitted women to terminate pregnancies as easily as they could under *Roe,* the important point is that a substantial number of states expanded access to abortion before the Supreme Court announced *Roe* in 1973. *Roe,* therefore, must be understood to be a part of a movement that had already begun within law to reduce government barriers to therapeutic abortion.

B. Factors Affecting Decisions by Women to Abort Pregnancies

To identify the societal properties and forces that are pertinent to law on abortion, I will begin with a review of research conducted by social scientists on variables hypothesized to be possible influences on the decisions of pregnant women whether to abort their pregnancies. The review is based on the assumption that the variables having such an effect on individuals suggest the factors determining the strength of the societal need for access to medically approved methods of terminating pregnancy. Unfortunately, social science research dealing with the antecedents of induced abortion among women is scarce, and none of the existing research employs longitudinal, i.e., time-series or panel, data. The absence of longitudinal data seriously limits the conclusions that can be drawn regarding causal relationships, because longitudinal data allow temporal sequences to be studied and are thus more likely than cross-sectional data to identify causes accurately.[92]

The studies I review involved multivariate analyses of data on samples of women in the United States and focused on whether induced abortions among these women were associated with at least two of the following variables: (1) female employment; (2) female education (years of school completed or present school attendance); and/or (3) female marital status. The decisions made by women whether to end pregnancies by abortion are believed to be based on the costs of childbearing[93] and/or on the manner in which women define their role in society.[94] Because each of the three enumerated variables can affect these costs and reflect sex-role definitions, each variable has the potential to influence the proportion of pregnancies that women seek to avoid through contraception and to terminate through abortion. More precisely, insofar as any of the variables burdens childbearing and/or offers socially acceptable alternatives to childbearing, the variable(s) will enhance the need of the social system for ready access to abortion and for law that endorses such access. As a result, this chapter examines social science research on the variables to ascertain if one or more of them influences the likelihood that women will end pregnancies through abortion.

Before turning to these studies, it is worth mentioning that the variables being considered—the employment, education, and marital status of women—possess three important attributes. First, the relationship to abortion of each variable has been the subject of at least one reasonably well-designed study, and the effect on abortion of each variable can be ascertained tentatively. Quantitative research of acceptable quality will thus be the basis for decisions regarding which of the variables might create a societal need for a change in law on abortion. Second, for each variable, reliable annual data that start soon after World War II are obtainable. Since the reform of abortion law in the United States commenced in the last half of the 1960s when some states began to ease their restrictions on abortion, a variable can produce a need for this reform if, during earlier years, there was an increase in its rate or in the prevalence of certain of its components. Accordingly, the period covered by the data should commence well before the 1960s and, because World War II is a landmark in U.S. history, should ideally begin in the last half of the 1940s or in the early 1950s. Third, data on states from the decennial censuses of 1950 and 1960 are available for each of the three variables, and these data can be used to examine system-level properties that may differentiate the states that liberalized their law on abortion in the late 1960s and early 1970s from the states that did not.

In light of the attention that the abortion issue has attracted in the political arena, it is surprising that few well-designed social science studies with large data sets have been conducted on the factors affecting the likelihood that women who conceive will choose to abort their pregnancies. Indeed, I was able to locate just two such studies. Like all research, the studies have methodological limitations that need to be understood in evaluating their findings. Therefore, I will discuss each study in some detail.

The first study was based on the 1976 cycle of the National Survey of Family Growth ("NSFG").[95] The NSFG sampled females fifteen to forty-four years old who resided in the coterminous United States. A female in this population was eligible for the sample if (a) she was currently or previously married, or (b) even though she had never married, she had borne a child who was living with her.[96] In imposing these eligibility criteria, however, the sample excluded childless females who had never married. Since females in the latter category (i.e., childless never-married females) comprised most of the women who were undergoing abortions in the mid-1970s,[97] a serious question exists whether the findings of the study can be generalized to all women who experienced a pregnancy at this time.

Because the dependent variable in the study was whether a woman had ever opted to abort a pregnancy, the study was confined to women who reported they had been pregnant.[98] In examining the dependent variable, the study dichotomized the respondents—respondents who reported having had an abortion were placed in one category and respondents who did not report an abortion were placed in another category.[99] However, subsequent research indicates that many women in the survey did not admit that they had aborted pregnancies. Indeed, married interviewees in the 1976 NSFG are estimated to have revealed just 45 percent of the abortions they actually obtained.[100] If the misreporting of abortions was not random but systematically associated with certain attributes of women, the findings of the study may misstate whether, how, and/or the degree to which the attributes are linked to the abortion decisions of women.

In terms of the independent variables that are of interest here, education was determined by the NSFG at the time of pregnancy and scaled with a dichotomy that separated (a) women who were still in school from (b) women who had finished their education or whose educational status was uncertain.[101] Consequently, the study measured school attendance, not educational attainment. Employment status of respondents was generally unknown for the point in time when respondents became pregnant, but information existed on whether respondents were economically active outside the home when they were interviewed for the NSFG. The study used the latter information on employment, and hence the variable as measured refers to a point subsequent to the occurrence of pregnancy.[102] While the study assumed that the employment status of women was the same at the time of the pregnancy as at the time of the interview, the assumption may have often been inaccurate given the tendency of women in the 1970s to withdraw from the labor force when they carried pregnancies to term.[103] The findings of the study, accordingly, may be incorrect with regard to the relationship between employment and abortion.

The final independent variable of interest was marital status. For this variable, the study grouped women into two categories: (a) those who were married when they became pregnant or ended their pregnancy; and (b) those who, when they became pregnant or aborted their pregnancy, had never been married, were married but separated or divorced from their husbands, or were widowed. The study deemed women in the first category to be married and women in the second category to be unmarried.[104] However, the NSFG did not interview, and the second category therefore omits, never-married females who were childless. The exclusion of the latter females prevents the study from comparing women who were married at the time of their pregnancies to all other women and undermines the ability of the study to assess marital status as an explanatory variable.

What did the statistical analysis reveal? As the investigator recognized,[105] the problems characterizing the research design require that considerable caution be exercised in drawing conclusions from the findings. Nevertheless, the findings are plausible and hence noteworthy. With a range of other variables held constant,[106] a relationship emerged between school attendance and abortion use: the probability that a woman would end a pregnancy was higher among females who were attending school than among females who were not.[107] The relationship to abortion use of both employment status and marital status, however, differed between women who were not mothers when they became pregnant and women who were.[108] In terms of employment status, non-mothers were more likely to abort a pregnancy when they were employed, full-time or part-time, than when they were not employed, but among mothers, employment status was unrelated to the probability of abortion. In terms of marital status, non-mothers were not characterized by a relationship between marital status and abortion probability, but mothers were less likely to terminate pregnancies when they were married than when they were not.

Two points emerge from the above findings and merit some emphasis. First, school attendance was the sole independent variable that did not interact with another factor; the effects of the other two independent variables were contingent on whether the woman was already a mother when she became pregnant. Consequently, school attendance—and, by implication, educational attainment—offers particular promise as a factor generating a societal need for abortion. Second, standardized regression coefficients from ordinary least-squares regression indicated that school attendance had by far the strongest effect, as well as the most uniform effect, on the likelihood of aborting a pregnancy.[109]

A second study of the antecedents of abortion use was conducted on the pregnancy outcomes of females who resided in eight states or in New York City and whose pregnancies ended during 1980.[110] The data included information on more than a half-million pregnancies involving women twenty years of age and older, but while an impressively large number of cases could be used to assess the factors influencing pregnancy outcome, the data possessed three limitations that should be kept in mind.

The first limitation of the study is that the data set covered pregnancy outcomes of the residents of just a few geographic areas and therefore included only a portion of all pregnancies—specifically, only one out of nine pregnancies—that occurred in the United States among women age twenty and older and that had an outcome in 1980.[111] While this sampling fraction is much higher than the sampling fraction used in most surveys of large populations, the women included in the data were not chosen randomly from a broad universe. Because the women studied may not be representative of all U.S. women in the same age range, considerable caution should be exercised in deciding whether relationships found between the independent variables and the dependent variable apply to women in general.

The second limitation of the study is that information was unavailable on the employment status of women whose pregnancies were included in the study. Thus, one of the three variables of concern in this chapter was omitted from the data analysis undertaken by the study.[112] To the extent that differences in employment are related not only to differences in the probability of aborting a pregnancy but also to differences in education and/or marital status, the study may yield inaccurate conclusions. Notably, available research has identified relationships between employment, education, and marital status.[113]

The third limitation is that the data did not include information on spontaneous fetal deaths when gestation length was twenty weeks or less. The omission of data on early spontaneous fetal deaths, the investigators point out, causes the abortion rate to be overstated, but they contend that the omission does not bias their conclusions regarding the impact on abortion use of the explanatory variables that are of interest here. When the variables produce differences between groups in rates of abortion, the investigators argue, the magnitude of the differences will be correctly gauged because rates of early spontaneous fetal mortality are unlikely to differ between these groups.[114] However, if the investigators are mistaken in this regard, their estimates of the impact of the variables on the probability of abortion may be biased, because while fetal deaths were relatively uncommon in 1980,[115] the fetal deaths that were omitted from the data accounted for roughly three out of four such deaths that took place.[116]

In examining the findings of the study, I concentrate on women who were at least twenty years old, because the study combined younger females into a single category that included ages eighteen and nineteen and ages below eighteen.[117] Women who were at least twenty years old were thus the only group studied that had attained adulthood and had acquired new rights from the reform of abortion law.[118] In this group, unmarried women had a much higher probability of aborting a pregnancy than currently married women, an effect that was net of differences on the remaining independent variables. The relationship between marital status and abortion was found even among women who were childless; indeed, childless unmarried women were ten times more likely than childless married women to abort a pregnancy. This is contrary to the Badagliacco study, which concluded that marital status did not affect the probability of abortion among childless women.

While marital status exhibited a simple relationship to abortion use, educational attainment did not. As the number of years of schooling increased, so did the likelihood that a pregnancy would end in an abortion, but when the study examined potential interactions, it found that the impact of education varied with the number of previous live births and with marital status. As to number of prior births, a clear difference existed between women who had not borne a child and women who had: the probability of an abortion generally rose with years of schooling for women who were childless, but for women having one or more births, the probability increased only to twelve years of completed schooling and then remained essentially constant. More important, however, is the finding that the effect of education depended on marital status. Among unmarried women, the proportion of pregnancies terminated by abortion rose consistently with education, but among married women, the relationship was ∩ in shape: the probability of abortion increased as the level of completed schooling went from eight or fewer years to twelve years and then fell back to its initial level as the level of completed schooling rose to sixteen or more years.

Let me now attempt to integrate the findings of the two studies. While their results are not conclusive, the studies indicate that abortion use rises with educational attainment and school enrollment and is more common among unmarried women than among married women,[119] but whether abortion is generally and substantially affected by employment is uncertain.[120] Educational achievement may not possess a linear relationship to the probability of abortion among married women, but it must be kept in mind that unmarried women were by far the chief source of abortions in the United States in the decade-and-a-half that followed Roe v. Wade, whether measured by the proportion of pregnancies ended by abortion or by the proportion of females of childbearing age who had an abortion.[121] Among women as a whole, then, a higher level of schooling is associated with a higher likelihood that a woman will terminate a pregnancy.

Before concluding this section, I would like to raise an important, but largely unrecognized and unexplored, methodological issue. The two studies reviewed above focused exclusively on the characteristics of individual women and used these characteristics to estimate the probability that a woman would abort a pregnancy. Neither study, however, examined whether the characteristics of geographic areas that form law-defined jurisdictions such as states are related to jurisdiction-level rates of abortion. For instance, the two studies defined marital status by the marital status of each woman in the sample, and the studies examined whether the marital status of a woman was related to whether she aborted a pregnancy. The studies did not consider whether a relationship existed between the percentage of women who were currently married or unmarried in each state and the percentage of all pregnancies in the state that were aborted. Individual-level attributes and jurisdiction-level attributes are distinctly different types of information, and when studied for their relationship to a state-level measure of abortion use, they may not yield the same conclusions. Unfortunately, while some investigators have attempted to estimate the incidence of abortion from the characteristics of jurisdictions, their research designs have serious limitations.

Future work, then, must address the question whether the antecedents of change in law on induced abortion are more readily and accurately identified using data on the characteristics of jurisdictions (e.g., states), data on the characteristics of individuals in these jurisdictions, or data on both. From a macrosociological perspective, law as an institution is a component of a social system, and the antecedents of the doctrines of law are expected to stem from the system. A number of social science studies using a multivariate statistical technique support the assumption that characteristics of states shape doctrines of state law.[122] The research reported infra in Part III-D extends this type of study to the subject of abortion law.

C. Time-Series Indicators of a Societal Need for Abortion

While employment among women may or may not be generally related to the demand for abortion, according to the studies reviewed above, the marital status and education of women are evidently important factors affecting the likelihood that women in the United States will abort their pregnancies. These two variables, therefore, may shape the need for and lawfulness of abortion. Which variable—education or marital status—more accurately predicts abortion use cannot be ascertained from research conducted to date, but each variable seems to have a definite bearing on the probability an individual woman will choose to end a pregnancy, and each variable may thus be an indicator of a system-level determinant of law on induced abortion.

In light of the above findings with regard to marital status and school enrollment, I consider whether, among women in the United States, the incidence of particular marital statuses and the level of school enrollment changed over time in a manner suggesting that these variables produced a need for lawfully induced abortion prior to the shift in abortion law that occurred from 1967 to 1973.[123] Figure 6.3 deals with marital status.[124] Specifically, the figure shows, for each year in the time period covered, the percentage of women at age twenty to twenty-four and at age twenty-five to twenty-nine who had not been married; these women are designated "never married." The figure also shows the percentage of women in each of the two age ranges who had been married previously but who were no longer married due to divorce. I confine my attention to currently unmarried women because they accounted for the vast majority of abortions in the years following Roe v. Wade[125] and, presumably, in the years before as well.

For marital status to be a plausible factor creating and heightening a societal need for abortion, the percentage of reproductive-age women who are unmarried, whether from having never married or from divorce, would have had to rise *before* abortion law was reformed. As explained above, the principal doctrinal changes in

Figure 6.3 Marital Status of Women in the United States

By age and year

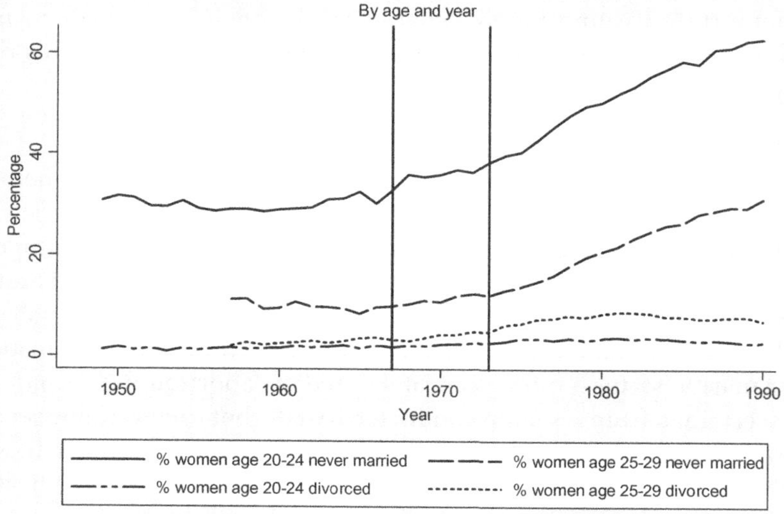

that reform occurred between 1967, when some states began to ease substantially the grounds for a lawfully induced abortion, and 1973, when the Supreme Court decided Roe v. Wade.[126] (The two years are marked by vertical lines in Figure 6.3 as well as in Figures 6.4 and 6.5.)

Figure 6.4 School Enrollment among Women in the United States

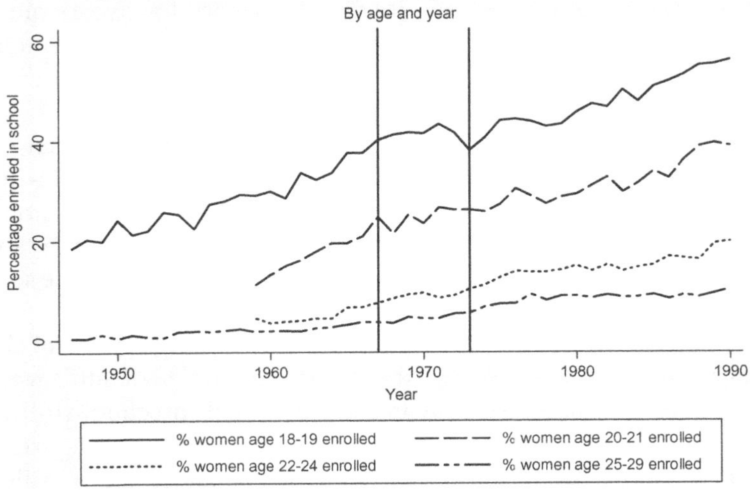

Figure 6.5 Labor Force Participation among Women in the United States

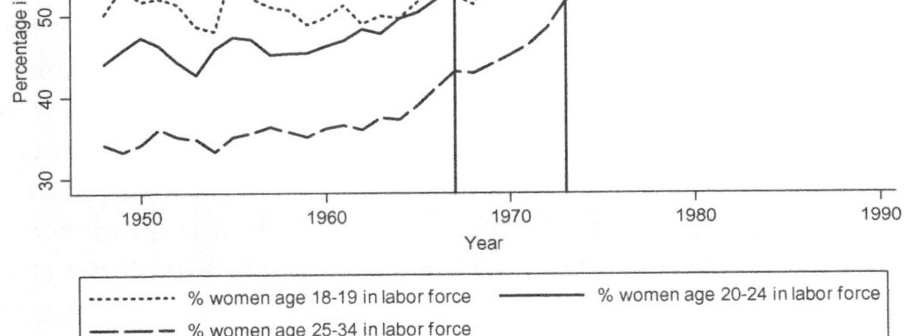

The years from 1967 to 1973 thus constitute the period of abortion law reform, and the years prior to this period are critical to deciding whether change in the incidence of certain marital statuses produced a societal need to liberalize abortion law.

During the pre-reform period, as is evident from Figure 6.3, the proportion never married and the proportion divorced are essentially stable among women twenty to twenty-four years old and women twenty-five to twenty-nine years old. Distinct movement in these proportions is found only during and/or after the period when reform occurred, and during the reform period (1967–1973), the movements are generally modest. As a consequence, there is no persuasive evidence that change in the prevalence of unmarried women in the population engendered a societal need for the liberalization of abortion law in the 1960s. If there was a need on the part of the social system to relax the grounds for abortion permitted by law, the source of the need evidently lies elsewhere.

I turn now to the rate of school enrollment among women of childbearing age. Figure 6.4 shows the yearly percentage of adult women in each of four age groups who were enrolled in school (full-time or part-time).[127] Schools of all levels are included in the figure. The data, therefore, cover enrollments in high schools, junior colleges, colleges granting baccalaureate and graduate degrees, and professional schools.

Substantial growth in school enrollment rates among women eighteen to nineteen years old and among women twenty to twenty-one years old characterizes most of the time interval covered by Figure 6.4. Notably, the trend commences prior to the period (1967–1973) when abortion doctrine underwent its main change. The trend was present well in advance of this period among women eighteen to nineteen years old, for whom enrollment rates begin in 1947. A rise in enrollment rates prior to the abortion-law liberalization period also is found among women twenty to twenty-one years old, for whom rates begin in 1959. Finally, an increase in enrollment rates among women twenty-two to twenty-four years old and among women twenty-five to twenty-nine years old is evident before this period, although each increase is small in absolute magnitude and does not commence until shortly before the liberalization of abortion law began. (Rates start in 1959 for women twenty-two to twenty-four years old[128]; rates start in 1947 for women twenty-five to twenty-nine years old.) Thus, school enrollment in all of the age groups of women shown in the figure—but especially in the two youngest age groups—was changing in a manner that permitted schooling to create a societal need for lawfully induced abortion and promote legalization of the procedure. Indeed, school enrollment rates, by rising before as well as during the time that states significantly eased restrictions on access to abortion, behaved exactly as they would be expected to behave if they were creating and intensifying a need in American society for liberalized abortion doctrine.[129] Macrosociological research on law regulating access to abortion, accordingly, must consider the variable.

Finally, I consider female employment. Although a relationship between the employment status of a woman and the probability she will abort a pregnancy has not been established, a relationship between these variables has not been disproved. Social science research to date does not allow a conclusion to be drawn regarding such a relationship, because studies of the relationship are too few in number and suffer from too many limitations. However, a link between female employment and abortion has been posited by theory, and thus such a link is a possibility that should not be dismissed out of hand. For this reason, I examine the labor force participation rate, i.e., the percentage of individuals in a demographically defined group who currently are employed or are engaged in finding employment.

Figure 6.5 presents the seasonally adjusted rate of labor force participation among civilian women in each of three age groups, viz., eighteen to nineteen, twenty to twenty-four, and twenty-five to thirty-four.[130] The data in the figure are for the fourth quarter of each year from 1948 through 1990. Labor force participants are persons (a) who are presently working or (b) who are not working but who are available for work and have sought work during the prior four weeks.[131] Labor force participants who are unemployed—the members of group (b)—are thus persons who are motivated to work and have an attachment to work; women in this group presumably would view a pregnancy similarly to women who are employed.

Notably, Figure 6.5 reveals that the labor force participation rate of both women who were twenty to twenty-four years old and women who were twenty-five to thirty-four years old started to increase at least five years in advance of the period of abortion law reform. Among women eighteen to nineteen years old, the labor force participation rate remained relatively flat before 1967, but the absence of change is probably due to the growing school enrollment of women in this age group that is observable in Figure 6.4.

D. System-Level Properties and the Liberalization of State Abortion Law

Did change involving the role of women reshape law on abortion in the United States between 1967 and 1973 in order to expand access to the procedure? If law is a macrosociological phenomenon, the properties of society rather than the idiosyncrasies of individuals or the operation of chance determine the concepts and principles that dominate law at any particular point in history. In terms of sex roles, such properties may include the level of educational attainment, extent of labor force participation, and distribution of marital status among women in the population. Because the three variables have been the focus of social science theory on sex roles, their potential to account for the modification of law on abortion in the United States during the period from 1967 to 1973 was considered in Figures 6.3—6.5. To supplement these figures, the question whether the three variables contributed to liberalizing abortion law will be addressed with a different type of quantitative data and a different data-analysis tool.

The study that I report below involved the application of maximum-likelihood logistic regression—a statistical technique that is being used increasingly in social science research[132]—to state-level data on a number of "independent" variables, i.e., variables that are to be tested for their ability to account for a phenomenon. In the instant study, the phenomenon to be explained (i.e., the dependent variable) was whether states liberalized their law on abortion in the 1967–1972 period, and in an attempt to explain differences between states in this regard, twelve independent variables (discussed below) were included in the regression equation. Table 6.1 gives the mnemonic label for, and a definition of, each variable. The data for all of the independent variables were confined to women and were obtained from the censuses of the U.S. population conducted in 1950 and 1960.[133] The age ranges used for the independent variables were largely dictated by the age ranges for which the census reported data. All of the forty-eight states in the coterminous United States were included in the study.[134]

The twelve independent variables can be divided into two categories, with each category containing half of the variables. The six variables (by mnemonic label) in the first category involved the educational attainment (PCTCOLL2529), income (INCFEM2534), labor force participation (LABOR2024 and LABOR2529), and marital status

Table 6.1 Variables in Regression Model

Variable by mnemonic label	Description of variable
Dependent variable	
ABORTIONLAW	Whether the state liberalized its law on therapeutic abortion during the years 1967 through 1972, i.e., prior to the decision of the U.S. Supreme Court in Roe v. Wade. Each state was coded either 0 or 1. A state was coded 0 if it did *not* liberalize its law on abortion and was coded 1 if it did liberalize its law on abortion.
Independent variables	
PCTCOLL2529	The percentage of all women twenty-five to twenty-nine years old in each state in 1960 who had completed at least four years of college as of 1960.
CHNGCOLL2529	The percentage change between 1950 and 1960 in PCTCOLL2529.
INCFEM2534	The median income, in dollars, in 1959 of all women in each state who were twenty-five to thirty-four years old in 1960 and who received any income in 1959.
CHNGINC2534	The percentage change between 1949 and 1959 in INCFEM2534.
LABOR2024	The percentage of all women twenty to twenty-four years old in each state in 1960 who were in the labor force in 1960.
CHNGLABOR2024	The percentage change between 1950 and 1960 in LABOR2024.
LABOR2529	The percentage of all women twenty-five to twenty-nine years old in each state in 1960 who were in the labor force in 1960.
CHNGLABOR2529	The percentage change between 1950 and 1960 in LABOR2529.
MARR2024	The percentage of all women twenty to twenty-four years old in each state in 1960 who were currently married, i.e., who in 1960 were married.
CHNGMARR2024	The percentage change between 1950 and 1960 in MARR2024.

(Continued on the next page)

Table 6.1 (*Continued*)

Variable by mnemonic label	Description of variable
MARR2529	The percentage of all women twenty-five to twenty-nine years old in each state in 1960 who were currently married, i.e., who in 1960 were married.
CHNGMARR2529	The percentage change between 1950 and 1960 in MARR2529.

(MARR2024 and MARR2529) of women who resided in each state. Except for income, the independent variables in the first category were measured as of 1960; income was measured as of 1959. The six variables in the second category involved the rate of change over the prior ten years in each of the variables in the first category. These variables were CHNGCOLL2529, CHNGINC2534, CHNGLABOR2024, CHNGLABOR2529, CHNGMARR2024, and CHNGMARR2529. The rate of change in a state was measured by percentages, not by percentage points. Thus, the ten-year state change in an independent variable was computed using the formula below:

$$\left[\frac{\text{(data from 1960 census)} - \text{(data from 1950 census)}}{\text{(data from 1950 census)}} \times 100\right]$$

In sum, the independent variables in the first category measure amounts of possible explanatory factors at a single point in time while the independent variables in the second category measure the ten-year difference in these amounts (expressed as a percentage). The independent variables in the first category thus assume that, to explain state differences in law on induced abortion, the quantity of a factor is critical; the independent variables in the second category focus on the rate at which a factor changed. Amount and speed are separate dimensions of a factor, and because they are not necessarily correlated, one dimension of the factor may affect a phenomenon while the other does not. Every independent variable in the first category thus has an analog in the second category, and to allow each pair to be easily identified, the variables comprising the pair are listed together in Table 6.1.

In order to provide further insight into the independent variables, I discuss each variable in some depth. The discussion focuses on the amounts of the variables, and thus on the data obtained from the 1960 census, because the immediate antecedent of state differences in law on induced abortion is expected to be state differences in societal properties, which are measured in amounts, shortly before the period (1967–1972) when state law on abortion changed. Data from the 1950 census were employed solely for ascertaining the rate of change in these properties during the ten years between the 1950 census and the 1960 census. The ten-year changes were incorporated into the study as independent variables on the belief that they are indicators of the forces responsible for the societal properties altering law on therapeutic abortion and that the forces developed well before the properties were able to alter this law. The impact of these forces may not be accurately gauged by the study, however, if the forces operate over periods substantially exceeding ten years.

In the instant study, education was measured by the percentage of women twenty-five to twenty-nine years old who had finished four or more years of college. The variable involved the number of years of college completed, not the receipt of a degree (for which data are unavailable in the state reports from the 1960 census). The age range twenty-five to twenty-nine was preferable to the age range twenty to twenty-four, because college enrollment in 1960 was relatively infrequent among women twenty-five to twenty-nine years old compared to women twenty to twenty-four years old.[135] By age twenty-five to twenty-nine, that is, women who will ultimately finish at least four years of college will have generally done so.

The independent variable measuring the income of women was used in the regression equation on the assumption that, as their personal income rises, women possess not only the economic resources required to abort pregnancies but, in addition, an economic incentive to do so because childrearing will compete with other activities for at least some of their income.[136] A macrosociological perspective suggests that a social system will eventually permit and endorse the solutions wanted by its members for serious problems they are experiencing. With gains in the income of women, accordingly, a social system becomes more likely to accept a solution (abortion) sought by its female members to a problem (unwanted pregnancy) that solely or disproportionately affects them.

In terms of problems faced by women, pregnancy was evidently creating social and economic difficulties for many women when states began to liberalize their statutes on abortion, because during

1960–1965, women in the United States did not want a substantial proportion of their pregnancies.[137] Notably, in the third quarter of the twentieth century, the birth and rearing of children reduced employment among women in the United States[138] and thus interfered with women's career goals. Moreover, much of the status difference between female and male sex roles, as indicated by the extent of sex segregation in occupations during the twentieth century, had been erased before the liberalization of state abortion law started.[139] In the context of reduced sex-role inequality, the likelihood that women would seek to eliminate unwanted pregnancies can be expected to increase with their personal income, because income supplies the financial resources and incentives to terminate pregnancies. The income of women, consequently, is a potentially important variable in the reform of abortion law.

As its measure of the amount of income, the instant study used the median number of dollars of income in 1959 received by women twenty-five to thirty-four years old who had income in that year.[140] While income at age twenty-five to twenty-nine might have been preferable to income at age twenty-five to thirty-four, income at age twenty-five to thirty-four was utilized because the U.S. Census Bureau did not report income by state for age twenty-five to twenty-nine separately. Instead, in publishing state data on income from the 1960 census, the Bureau combined age twenty-five to twenty-nine with age thirty to thirty-four and placed the two five-year age ranges into a single ten-year age range, i.e., twenty-five to thirty-four. State-level data on income were reported for the five-year age range twenty to twenty-four. However, age twenty-five to thirty-four was deemed more appropriate for the measure of income, because compared to women in the twenty-five to thirty-four age range, a materially higher percentage of women in the twenty to twenty-four age range were in school in 1960.[141] School enrollment, of course, interferes with earning income, and as a result, income at age twenty to twenty-four is not a suitable gauge of the income of a cohort.

Even though the twenty-five to thirty-four age bracket includes numerous women who were older than women on whom the other independent variables were based (who were either age twenty to twenty-four or age twenty-five to twenty-nine), income at age twenty-five to thirty-four is important because women at this age generally have a high level of fecundity.[142] For them, unwanted pregnancy is a salient possibility, and law on abortion is a potentially important issue.

Moreover, because in most situations a social system changes at a slow pace, the system is able to anticipate the approximate average income that a cohort of women, as well as a cohort of men, will earn after its members have gone through the education institution and acquired the knowledge that is available to the cohort. The experience of the cohort that is currently twenty-five to thirty-four years old is the basis for making a generally accurate prediction regarding what younger persons will collectively experience when they reach age twenty-five to thirty-four, because the cohort that is in the latter age range (i.e., twenty-five to thirty-four) has been affected by the forces that have recently shaped the economy. The income of women who are twenty-five to thirty-four years of age thus is likely to have meaning to women who are younger, and therefore is a useful measure of the financial fortunes of adult women during their main childbearing years.

With regard to labor force participation and marital status, the study estimated odd ratios for each of these variables in two age ranges—age twenty to twenty-four and age twenty-five to twenty-nine. That is, the dependent variable (whether states revised their law to increase access to abortion during 1967–1972) was regressed on inter alia labor force participation among women twenty to twenty-four years old *and* among women twenty-five to twenty-nine years old. In addition, the study regressed the dependent variable on marital status among women twenty to twenty-four years old as well as among women twenty-five to twenty-nine years old. Both age groups are indisputably important in studying abortion: from 1973 to 1988, women in the two age groups produced approximately one-half of all lawful abortions induced annually, and because these yearly percentages were remarkably consistent over time,[143] the percentage probably characterizes 1967 to 1972, the period of interest here. The two age groups were thus included in the instant study.

Table 6.2 presents the regression results for the forty-eight coterminous states from an analysis of the data with logistic regression.[144] Although the table presents levels of statistical significance, the discussion of the results will rely on the magnitude of the relationships alone and, in particular, on the odds ratios. As explained elsewhere,[145] tests of statistical significance are inappropriate when, as here, maximum-likelihood logistic regression is applied to a small number of cases,[146] and they are unnecessary when, as here, the cases comprise the entire universe under study rather than a sample drawn from the universe.[147] Nonetheless, Table 6.2 reports the two-tailed significance

Table 6.2 Odds Ratios, Regression Coefficients, and Two-tailed Significance Levels for Regression of ABORTIONLAW on Independent Variables: Forty-eight States

Independent variable (mnemonic label)	Odds ratio	Regression coefficient	Standard error of regression coefficient	*z*	*p*>|*z*|
PCTCOLL2529	4.699	1.547	.647	2.39	.017
CHNGCOLL2529	.998	−.002	.048	−.04	.967
INCFEM2534	.999	−.001	.004	−.32	.752
CHNGINC2534	1.076	.074	.063	1.17	.241
LABOR2024	1.288	.253	.409	.62	.536
CHNGLABOR2024	.872	−.137	.137	−1.00	.317
LABOR2529	1.053	.051	.298	.17	.864
CHNGLABOR2529	1.156	.145	.139	1.05	.295
MARR2024	1.553	−.440	.458	.96	.336
CHNGMARR2024	.783	−.244	.256	−.96	.339
MARR2529	.803	−.219	.764	−.29	.774
CHNGMARR2529	1.770	.571	.645	.88	.376
CONSTANT		−39.867	43.55	−.92	.360

Regression model
Number of observations = 48
Log likelihood = −18.436124
Likelihood ratio chi-squared (12) = 24.23
Probability > chi-square = .0189
Pseudo R^2 = .3966

levels of the regression coefficients and odds ratios for readers who want this information.

The regression results discussed below furnish estimates of the relationship of each independent variable to whether states changed their abortion law during 1967–1972. Like other forms of regression, logistic regression estimates the relationship to the dependent variable by each independent variable on its own, i.e., separately from the relationship of every other independent variable in the same regression equation. Whether a particular independent variable is related to the dependent variable depends on the degree to which the odds ratio for the independent variable deviates from 1.000. The closer an odds ratio for an independent variable is to 1.000, the less the dependent variable is altered by increases in the independent variable, and an odds ratio that is exactly (or approximately) 1.000 indicates that the independent variable has no effect on the dependent variable. In the instant analysis, logistic regression estimated the increase or decrease in the odds that a state eased its law on abortion for every increase of one measurement unit in a given independent variable.[148]

Table 6.2 presents the results obtained when all twelve independent variables in the study are simultaneously included in the data analysis. Before considering these results, however, let us examine the relationships to the dependent variable estimated in two separate regression analyses—one containing only the six independent variables in the first category and the other containing only the six independent variables in the second category.

When the relationships to the dependent variable (ABORTIONLAW) were calculated for just the independent variables in the first category, a substantial odds ratio was found for PCTCOLL2529—viz., 3.161—and a not-insubstantial odds ratio was found for LABOR2529—viz., 1.442. When the regression was confined to the independent variables in the second category, no independent variable had a material influence on ABORTIONLAW. Nonetheless, a relationship emerged that is pertinent to the results in Table 6.2. Specifically, CHNGMARR2529 (odds ratio = .786) was inversely related to ABORTIONLAW.

The odds ratios in Table 6.2 indicate that three of the twelve independent variables had an appreciable relationship to the dependent variable (ABORTIONLAW). Two of the variables are the percentage of women twenty to twenty-four years old who were currently married (MARR2024), for whom the odds ratio was 1.553, and the rate of change between 1950 and 1960 in the percent of all women twenty-five to twenty-nine years old who were currently married (CHNGMARR2529), for whom the odds ratio was 1.770. Since an odds ratio is converted into a percentage by subtracting 1.000 and multiplying the remainder by 100,[149] the odds that a state liberalized its abortion law rose by approximately 55.3 percent for each increase of one percentage point in MARR2024 and by 77.0 percent for each increase of one percentage point in CHNGMARR2529. On the other hand, when MARR2529 was absent from the regression analysis (see above), the odds ratio for CHNGMARR2529 was .786, i.e., gains in CHNGMARR2529 reduced the odds that a state would ease its statutory grounds for inducing an abortion. Although CHNGMARR2529 without MARR2529 did not have a large impact on ABORTIONLAW, both of these independent variables are evidently required in a regression equation to assess the effect on abortion law of marital status at age twenty-five to twenty-nine.

The independent variable in Table 6.2 that had the largest odds ratio was PCTCOLL2529, the percentage of women twenty-five to twenty-nine years old who had finished four or more years of college. For this variable, the odds ratio was 4.699. Otherwise expressed, the odds that a state would relax its law-imposed restrictions on induced abortion rose by approximately 370 percent for each percentage-point increase in PCTCOLL2529. The rate of change between 1950 and 1960 in PCTCOLL2529, on the other hand, was unrelated to ABORTIONLAW.

The odds ratios in Table 6.2 cannot be accepted, however, until several matters are considered. The first is the possibility that the results of the regression analysis were seriously affected by one or more outliers, i.e., states whose classification (0 or 1) on the dependent variable (ABORTIONLAW) was substantially different from the classification that the regression model predicted. An indication that an influential outlier may exist is the odds ratio in Table 6.2 for MARR2024: each increase of one percentage-point in the percent of women twenty to twenty-four years old who were currently married raised the odds that a state would liberalize its abortion law by about 55 percent. However, the odds ratio for MARR2024, in substantially exceeding 1.000, is inconsistent with the data in Figure 6.3, according to which the marital-status variables should be unrelated to change in state abortion law. The odds ratio for MARR2024 is also inconsistent with theory, which suggests that increases in the prevalence of marriage among women will reduce, not raise, the odds of abortion law liberalization. It is also curious that, according to the odds ratio for MARR2529 (i.e., .803), gains in MARR2529 may somewhat lower the odds of ABORTIONLAW. If this were the case, MARR2024 and MARR2529 would have had opposing effects on ABORTIONLAW. Such effects cannot be explained by current theory.

No procedure for identifying potentially influential outliers seems to be generally accepted by statisticians. The procedure I chose for the instant study involved calculating Cook's Statistic and visually inspecting a graph that plotted the values obtained from the calculation.[150] The procedure thus had both a quantitative component and a qualitative component. Relatively large values on Cook's Statistic were evident for five states—viz., Arkansas, Nevada, New York, Vermont, and Wyoming. Therefore, I re-estimated the relationship of each of the twelve independent variables to ABORTIONLAW by eliminating one of these states at a time, i.e., the odds ratios for the twelve independent variables were re-estimated based on forty-seven states.

Of the five states named above, the elimination of two notably altered the odds ratios for several of the independent variables. The two states were New York and Wyoming. As to the latter, a suspiciously large odds ratio (viz., 26.499) was estimated for PCTCOLL2529 when Wyoming was removed from the data. Because an odds ratio of this magnitude is implausible, the exclusion of Wyoming seemed inadvisable. Wyoming, therefore, was not considered an influential outlier.[151]

Table 6.3 reports the results of the regression analysis when New York is omitted. A comparison of Table 6.2 with Table 6.3 reveals that, without New York in the data, the most notable difference in results was in the odds ratio for MARR2529. Specifically, the odds ratio for MARR2529 moved from slightly below unity in Table 6.2 (New York included) to markedly above unity in Table 6.3 (New York excluded)—to be exact, from .803 to 2.079. The odds ratios for MARR2024 remained essentially the same and above unity in both analyses—1.553 in Table 6.2 and 1.593 in Table 6.3. In the coterminous United States outside of New York, accordingly, each percentage-point increase in marriage prevalence among women twenty to twenty-nine years old materially raised the odds of abortion law liberalization. Given the consistency between the odds ratios for MARR2024 and MARR2529 when New York was excluded, New York seems to have acted as an outlier that distorted the relationship that is reported in Table 6.2 between MARR2529 and ABORTIONLAW.[152]

Odds ratios substantially above 1.000 for MARR2024 and MARR2529, however, are inconsistent with theory and Figure 6.3. These inconsistencies raise the question whether New York was an outlier that caused the differences between Tables 6.2 and 6.3 in the odds ratios for MARR2529. An additional difference between Tables 6.2 and 6.3 may suggest that one or more other factors were at work. Specifically, the odds ratio for CHNGMARR2529 is 1.770 when New York is in the data (Table 6.2) but 4.071 when it is not

Table 6.3 Odds Ratios, Regression Coefficients, and Two-tailed Significance Levels for Regression of ABORTIONLAW on Independent Variables: Forty-seven Coterminous States Excluding New York

Independent variable (mnemonic label)	Odds ratio	Regression coefficient	Standard error of regression coefficient	*z*	*p*>|*z*|
PCTCOLL2529	4.820	1.572	.785	2.00	.045
CHNGCOLL2529	1.084	.081	.067	1.21	.226
INCFEM2534	1.002	.002	.005	.37	.715
CHNGINC2534	1.067	.064	.073	.89	.375
LABOR2024	.783	−.245	.486	−.50	.614
CHNGLABOR2024	1.036	.036	.155	.23	.818
LABOR2529	1.739	.554	.422	1.31	.189
CHNGLABOR2529	.969	−.031	.158	−.20	.844
MARR2024	1.593	.465	.583	.80	.425
CHNGMARR2024	.706	−.348	.278	−1.25	.210
MARR2529	2.079	.732	1.070	.68	.494
CHNGMARR2529	4.071	1.404	.994	1.41	.158
CONSTANT		−130.562	72.86	−1.79	0.73

Regression model
- Number of observations = 47
- Log likelihood = −15.192
- Likelihood ratio chi-squared (12) = 28.48
- Probability > chi-square = .005
- Pseudo R^2 =.484

(Table 6.3). With both odds ratios, of course, an increase in the rate of change in MARR2529 raised the odds that a state would amend its law to expand access to abortion, but without New York, the impact of CHNGMARR2529 more than doubles. Because the amount variable (MARR2529) *and* the change variable (CHNGMARR2529) are affected by New York among women twenty-five to twenty-nine years old, a marriage-linked factor may have been responsible for the relationships to ABORTIONLAW that were estimated for the marital-status variables among women. New York itself may not be a problem.

If New York was not an influential outlier, what marriage-relevant factor(s) might have affected the estimations of the impact of the marital-status variables among women? One possibility is that the data on marital status suffer from measurement error that is sufficiently widespread to affect the odds ratios for marriage among women. Under this view, marital status was inaccurately reported often enough to affect appreciably the proportion of women who were counted as married. Such an effect could have distorted the results of the regression analysis undertaken in the instant study for the marital-status variables among women. Different sources of data on the number of marriages in any particular year exhibit inconsistencies as well as suffer from errors,[153] and data on marital status in the census contain errors, too.[154]

Let me mention three reasons that marital status may have been misreported in the 1960 census with sufficient frequency to have a material effect on the odds ratios for the marital-status variables. First, the 1960 census gathered data using a questionnaire that respondents received by mail, and was the first census to rely on a mailed, respondent-completed questionnaire for the country as a whole.[155] Thus, respondents in the 1960 census classified themselves as married or unmarried.[156] Second, an unknown but appreciable number of cohabiting persons in 1960 are likely to have incorrectly identified themselves as married.[157] Misidentification probably was facilitated because respondents, on their own, completed the census questionnaire. Third, the census considered individuals who were in common-law marriages to be married,[158] and respondents who did not know whether common-law marriage existed in their jurisdiction or whether their relationship satisfied the requirements of a common-law marriage could often have recorded marital status incorrectly. The potential extent of the misunderstanding is suggested by the relatively low educational attainment of persons who were twenty-five to twenty-nine years old in 1960: in the United States as a whole, 72.6 percent of men and 81.0 percent of women in this age range had no more than a high-school education.[159]

Figure 6.3 and theory are consistent with the contention that errors in marital status in the 1960 census distorted the odds ratios for the marital-status variables in Tables 6.2 and 6.3. Figure 6.3 shows that, prior to 1967, change over time was minimal in the prevalence of never-married and divorced young women, and thus marital status was not a variable that could have altered state law on abortion during

1967–1972. Theory[160] suggests that an increase in the percentage of women who are married will reduce the odds of abortion law liberalization, but the odds ratios for MARR2024 and MARR2529 in Table 6.3 indicate that, in terms of marriage prevalence among women twenty to twenty-nine years old, just the opposite happens. Moreover, according to Table 6.2, MARR2024 and MARR2529 moved ABORTIONLAW in different directions. In short, the odds ratios reported in Tables 6.2 and 6.3 for marriage prevalence among women twenty to twenty-nine years old are suspect. New York, therefore, will not be treated as an influential outlier.

A second matter regarding the regression results—namely, collinearity[161]—will be considered just briefly. Was the correlation of any pair of independent variables sufficiently strong to keep regression from estimating reliable odds ratios for the variables? The correlation coefficients for pairs of independent variables in Tables 6.2 and 6.3 were often substantial.[162] However, the logistic regression program did not halt the computation of the odds ratio for any independent variable due to excessive collinearity with another independent variable. Because the program did not find the covariation of pairs of independent variables to be problematic, I concluded that collinearity did not exist.

Finally, I turn to the possibility that the relationship of an independent variable to the dependent variable may not be the same within all categories or at all levels of another independent variable. This is the question of interaction,[163] and the independent variables I consider here are those that theory suggests are related. Of the independent variables in the regression equations, two meet this criterion—namely, labor force participation and marital status. Notably, a relationship between these two variables is posited by both theory in economics and theory in sociology. Economic theory has postulated that, ceteris paribus, the inclination of women to marry varies inversely with the attractiveness of their opportunities in the economy. Under this view, marriage in a society will be less beneficial to, and less popular among, women to the extent that women have enticements (e.g., high monetary compensation) to engage in paid employment outside the home. According to economic theory, then, marriage will become less common among women as the labor force provides incentives that draw women into non-household work.[164]

Sociological theory, which incorporates social values as a central concept,[165] expects marital status and employment status (of men as well as of women) to conform to the prevailing values of a society. In 1960, conventional values regarding marriage seem to have still been dominant in the United States,[166] and thus paid employment outside the home was envisioned for the husband but not the wife. Only later in the decade of the 1960s did traditional values concerning marriage start to come under attack and begin to erode.[167] Notably, patterns of employment in the United States in 1960 were consistent with the traditional view regarding marriage and employment among women: labor force participation at age twenty to twenty-four existed among fully 73 percent of never-married women in 1960 but among only 31 percent of currently married women whose husband was present; at age twenty-five to twenty-nine, labor force participation existed among 79 percent of never-married women but among just 27 percent of currently married women whose husband was present.[168]

To ascertain the possible existence of an interaction, I created two new variables—one by multiplying the values of LABOR2024 and MARR2024 and the other by multiplying the values of LABOR2529 and MARR2529. Each of the new variables was added, one at a time, to the regression equation. The odds ratios for the two variables deviated from 1.000 by less than ±.050 when all forty-eight states were included in the regression analysis.[169] Because the two variables created to test for interaction had no clear relationship to ABORTIONLAW, interaction was assumed to be absent from the data.

What conclusions can be drawn from the data? In answering the question, I will focus on the data that include all forty-eight coterminous states and will refer to the results in Table 6.2, not Table 6.3.[170] Disregarding the marital-status variables because of the likelihood that they were subject to appreciable measurement error, two general conclusions emerge. The reader should keep in mind that the estimated relationship to ABORTIONLAW of each of the independent variables below was net of the influence of the other independent variables in the regression model, i.e., the remaining independent variables were held constant.

First, educational attainment among young women had a strong, positive relationship to the liberalization of state abortion law. A positive (as opposed to an inverse) relationship between PCTCOLL2529 and ABORTIONLAW is consistent with the findings of research on the attributes of women that predict the probability of aborting a pregnancy[171] and with the trends disclosed by the time-series data in Figure 6.4. The odds that a state would relax its law on induced abortion, according to Table 6.2, rose by roughly 370 percent for each one-point increase in the percentage of women twenty-five to twenty-nine years old who had finished at least four years of college.[172]

Second, labor force participation among women twenty to twenty-nine years old had little if any relationship to liberalization of state abortion law. The lack of a clear, substantial relationship between labor force participation and the dependent variable is perhaps not surprising given the uncertain relationship between employment and the likelihood a woman will surgically terminate a pregnancy.[173]

In light of the evidence that increases in the prevalence of schooling and the duration of education among young women were important in easing restrictions found in state law on access to abortion, let us turn to Table 6.4. The table is confined to women in the United States who were twenty-five to twenty-nine years old in each census year from 1940 to 2000. For the year specified in the first (i.e., left-hand) column of the table, the second column reports the percentage of women twenty-five to twenty-nine years old who held at least a bachelor's degree, and for each pair of sequential percentages in the second column, the third column reports the percentage change that occurred from the earlier to the later year. The third column thus shows, for women who were twenty-five to twenty-nine years old, the percentage change from one census year to the next in the prevalence of college graduation.

The trend that is apparent in the second column of Table 6.4 is consistent with the trend that is seen in Figure 6.4 for women younger than age twenty-five and with the data that note 128 presents on the mounting school enrollment rate between the last part of the 1940s

Table 6.4 Women 25–29 Years Old with a Bachelor's Degree or Higher, 1940–2000[174]

Year	Percentage of women age 25–29 holding at least a bachelor's degree (%)	Percentage change from prior year (%)
1940	4.9	—
1950	5.9	20.4
1960	7.8	32.2
1970	13.3	70.5
1980	20.5	54.1
1990	22.4	9.3
2000	29.7	32.6

and last part of the 1950s among women in the age range twenty to twenty-four. Table 6.4 shows that the percentage of women with a bachelor's degree or higher at age twenty-five to twenty-nine rose steadily from 1940 onward (second column) and that the decadal pace of the rise accelerated from 1940 to 1970 (third column). Figure 6.4 and note 128, which complement Table 6.4, suggest that the proportion of women who received at least a bachelor's degree while twenty to twenty-four years old climbed rapidly during the 1950s and the first half of the 1960s. As these women grew older, the percentage of women with a college degree at age twenty-five to twenty-nine increased.[175] The increase from 1960 to 1970 is particularly notable; indeed, the largest percentage change found in the third column of Table 6.4 is that occurring between 1960 and 1970. Therefore, prior to 1967 as well as during the period of abortion law liberalization that commenced in 1967, young women were increasingly entering college and earning bachelor's and graduate degrees. These trends are indicators of a fundamental shift in the role of women, and the occurrence of the shift before the modification of abortion law during 1967–1973 is unlikely to be mere coincidence.

E. The Conway–Butler Study

A fuller understanding of the research reported in Part III-D supra can be obtained by comparing it to another study of the relationship between the characteristics of jurisdictions and the law on abortion existing in the jurisdictions prior to Roe v. Wade.[176] As I explain below, while the latter study (the Conway–Butler study) has the same subject matter as mine, there are critical differences in objectives, data, and procedures.

To begin, the Conway–Butler study, after an initial analysis, omitted women's educational attainment as a variable from its refined regression models, partly because the investigators assumed that the chief impact of educational attainment would be manifested through two other variables that they included in these models, namely, women's labor force participation rate and income.[177] Given the omission of education from the refined models, the Conway–Butler study could not thoroughly evaluate the effect of that variable on abortion law or estimate the magnitude of any effect of the variable—an aspect of the study whose importance cannot be underrated in light of the trends in Figure 6.4 supra and the odds ratio for PCTCOLL2529 in Table 6.2 supra.

With regard to the variables that were included in the regression models of both the Conway–Butler study and my study, a difference in procedure between the studies markedly affected the interpretation of the regression results. Professors Conway and Butler relied on tests of significance; for reasons given earlier,[178] I did not. Using tests of statistical significance, the Conway–Butler study found that the restrictiveness of abortion law in a jurisdiction in 1970 was not associated with either the rate of labor force participation or the prevalence of marriage among women in the jurisdiction.[179] This conclusion, however, takes into account only whether the probability of the regression coefficient for each variable was at or below .10 if no relationship with the dependent variable existed in the universe from which the investigators drew their sample.[180] If the regression coefficients themselves are considered[181] and their significance levels are disregarded, then the Conway–Butler study indicates that abortion law became more liberal with increases in the percentage of women in a jurisdiction who are married. This finding is consistent with the results of my study for women who were in the age range twenty to twenty-four but is not consistent with the results of my study for women who were in the age range twenty-five to twenty-nine (Table 6.2). Moreover, the finding of the Conway–Butler study regarding the positive relationship between marital status and law on abortion, like the finding of my study for women twenty to twenty-four years old, cannot be reconciled with Figure 6.3 supra[182] or with theory.[183] With regard to labor force participation, the regression results in the Conway–Butler study indicate that the odds of liberal abortion law *decline* with increases in the percentage of women in a jurisdiction who participate in the labor force. This finding is not consistent with the odds ratios I obtained for women's labor force participation (Table 6.2), with the trends shown in Figure 6.5 supra, and with theory.[184] The discrepant findings of the two studies as to labor force participation may be due to the omission of education as an independent variable in the Conway–Butler study and/or to one, or a combination, of the following differences between the studies.

The reader should note that the manner in which the dependent variable was measured was not the same in both studies. Professors Conway and Butler placed each state into one of three levels of restrictiveness in terms of its abortion law prior to *Roe*—viz., abortion unrestricted, significantly restricted, or prohibited[185]—while I measured the dependent variable with just two categories—viz., whether or not the state had eased its restrictions on abortion in the years preceding *Roe*. Undoubtedly of much greater potential importance to the regression results, however, is that the studies classified three states differently in terms of their abortion law before *Roe*. Professors Conway and Butler designated Florida as a state that banned abortion, and designated Alabama and Massachusetts as states that significantly restricted access to abortion.[186] My study, on the other hand, classified Florida as a state that liberalized its abortion law, because the state had done so in 1972.[187] Furthermore, my study classified Alabama and Massachusetts as states that did not liberalize their abortion law, partly because the last pre-*Roe* change in abortion law that was made by these two states occurred, respectively, in 1951[188] and in 1944,[189] not in the 1960s.

An additional difference between the studies is that the Conway–Butler study included Alaska, Hawaii, and the District of Columbia,[190] but my study omitted them. I omitted Alaska and Hawaii for reasons explained earlier,[191] and I omitted the District of Columbia in order to confine the analysis to states. The difference in the jurisdictions covered by the two studies could have markedly affected the regression results of the studies, and the difference is not simply coincidence. Professors Conway and Butler included the three jurisdictions (Alaska, Hawaii, and the District of Columbia), and I excluded them, because our studies had different purposes. Professors Conway and Butler wanted to predict the content of law on abortion in each major jurisdiction of the United States if the U.S. Supreme Court overrules *Roe*, and their refined regression models thus evidently included the District of Columbia even though the investigators had identified this jurisdiction as "a very influential outlier."[192] My goal, on the other hand, was to help build a sociological theory of law, and to this end, my study examined a universe that was more circumscribed in order to reduce the likelihood of contamination by unmeasured factors.[193]

In sum, the regression results of the Conway–Butler study appear not to be helpful in isolating the causes of existing law on induced abortion. Professors Conway and Butler focused on predicting the law on access to abortion that jurisdictions can be expected to adopt if Roe v. Wade is overturned—an entirely legitimate focus when the goal is to understand the political process. Their study, however, was not primarily concerned with a theory of law. My study, on the other hand, places a heavy emphasis on theory.

IV. The Concept of Societal Need

All theories contain key concepts, and the macrosociological theory that lies behind the instant chapter is no exception. Specifically, this chapter employs the concept of need and contends that need is a principal determinant of law. My focus, however, has been on the needs of society, not on the needs of individuals, and although the two may influence one another and change concurrently in content and intensity, they possess distinctly different referents. To use abortion as an illustration, a woman who seeks to end a pregnancy does so for one or more reasons *she* considers important—because, for example, the fetus she is carrying is jeopardizing her physical health or financial goals—but *her* need to terminate a pregnancy is an individual-level attribute. I have focused instead on the degree to which *society*, in responding to the forces affecting it, requires the availability of abortion and the existence of supporting doctrine in law. Need in my lexicon accordingly emerges from the properties of society and from the forces that mold these properties, and it involves the propensity of every social system in the long run to (a) retain and/or strengthen the commitment of its participants to the system and (b) operate smoothly. In accounting for the rules of social life—both those that are formal (e.g., law) and those that are informal—I believe that the concept of societal need can make a distinct and important contribution.

By considering need as an attribute of society, I do not mean to disparage the concept of need as an attribute of individuals or suggest that scientific inquiry should avoid the subject of the needs of individuals. Rather, I contend that individual need is unlikely to be a particularly helpful concept in accounting for the content and evolution of doctrines in law. Law is concerned with the ways in which individuals interact, but "relations among people have a material character which is largely independent of individual control or conscious action."[194] Doctrines in law must accordingly be understood by reference to conditions beyond the individual, i.e., by reference to the society in which the doctrines exist. In particular, I maintain that law, as a macrosociological phenomenon, is a response to societal needs and cultural values and that the need for law with a particular content on a given topic is the need of the social system.

Need, whether used in reference to social systems or to individuals, is an abstract concept, i.e., a concept that is not directly observable but that has observable manifestations. Accordingly, need is a concept with potential uses in theory. Science employs such concepts because they have the ability to provide a coherent view of the world. With theoretical concepts, numerous and varied observations can be transformed into a manageable set of ideas and organized in ways that permit events not yet observed to be anticipated. The concept of gravity, for example, is found in physics for this reason.

A theoretical concept, however, does not exist for its own sake. Science is an inherently practical undertaking, and unless a concept is useful to the scientific enterprise—i.e., unless a concept furthers understanding and aids prediction—it must and will be abandoned. The history of science contains instances of theoretical concepts that did not advance the goals of science and were dropped. In the 1700s, for example, the concept of phlogiston was believed to be an invisible substance produced by combustion that accounted for certain observable changes associated with heat, but the concept was finally discarded because it could not be reconciled with the results of experiments in the emerging discipline of chemistry.[195]

If the concept of need in social science is not to suffer the same fate as the concept of phlogiston in physical science, it must be shown to aid the scientific enterprise, i.e., contribute to the explanation and prediction of phenomena. The present chapter has considered several topics, and for each, the concept of need is useful. Specifically, a defensible argument can be made that, because of change in system-level conditions, society developed a need for new law on sex roles, on the age of majority, and on abortion. Societal need, in short, offers promise as an efficacious concept in a macrosociological theory of law.

A. Functionalism

In order to understand the concept of societal need, the sociological theory from which it derives must be described, and the criticisms directed at the theory must be considered. The theory is functionalism. As an approach to the nature of social life, functionalism was the first theory propounded by sociologists, and revised versions of the theory remain influential.[196] The central premise of functionalism is that a society is composed of interrelated components that promote the operation and, in turn, the continuation of the society.[197] Specifically, functionalism considers society to be a system—i.e., an interrelated whole—and contends that the components of society facilitate the performance of the system. A component that becomes unable to assist the system, according to the functionalist perspective, either will change so that it once again serves the system, or it will cease to exist. A component thus does not emerge and/or persist unless it is supportive of society. However, the emergence of, change in, or the disappearance of a component may not be immediate; on the contrary, these processes probably occur in the main over and/or after a substantial interval. Normally, then, the propositions of the functionalist school apply just in the long run.

What are the components of a society? In my macrosociological framework, the components are denominated "institutions,"[198] and one of them is law. Law, like every institution, possesses a distinct set of concepts and a distinct set of principles (doctrines), and the central doctrines of law reflect conditions in society, although usually with a time lag. Among the conditions shaping law are the values that govern the society.[199] The conformity of the content of law to social values should not be surprising, for without this conformity, the institution of law would not be accepted and could not contribute to the operation of society.

With this general outline, let me take up the principal criticisms that have been directed at the functionalist school insofar as the criticisms are relevant to doctrine in law and the theoretical framework employed in the instant book.[200] The first criticism is that, because functionalism emphasizes stability and persistence in social systems, it cannot deal effectively with change, at least change that involves an important aspect of system structure and a major departure from established patterns. In terms of the framework I am employing for doctrines of law, the criticism is unfounded, because my framework, though based on functionalism, demands that shifts in doctrine be studied. Indeed, the larger the magnitude of a doctrinal shift, the greater the importance of investigating the shift because major change is more likely than minor change to reveal (a) the societal properties and forces molding law and (b) the effects of law—two issues with which any theory-based framework for law must be concerned. It is thus not happenstance that the instant chapter examines abortion law. The subject was selected because of the striking change that abortion law underwent in the United States during the 1960s and 1970s, and because of the availability of considerable data to study the change.

A second criticism of functionalism has been that it is teleological, a criticism that implicates the concept of need. Functionalism relies heavily on the concept of need; indeed, the concept is "what is distinctive about functional analysis."[201] Traditionally, functionalism incorporated the concept of need by contending that every society requires a certain degree of internal integration and equilibrium in order to survive. In advancing this argument, functionalism becomes teleological if it assumes that the goal of satisfying the need produces the features of social life that accomplish the goal, and it becomes incapable of being empirically tested if at the same time it cannot generate hypotheses identifying these features in advance.[202] Specifically, to the extent functionalism argues that the needs of society call forth processes and structures that meet the needs, functionalism assumes the existence of an inherent design in society and relies on ends to explain means. Such reliance, though teleological, does not preclude empirical testing as long as functionalism also is able to predict the means that can reach the ends, and that therefore may emerge and be observed, in a given situation. Unfortunately, however, functionalist theory seems to be insufficiently developed at this point in time to permit such predictions to be consistently generated.

The preceding problem is associated with a third criticism of the functionalist school, namely, that the societal needs named by the school are so general that empirical research cannot disprove their existence. According to this criticism, functionalists have assumed that amorphous needs such as integration and equilibrium govern the social system, but the assumption cannot be rigorously tested because of the elusive nature of these needs. One prominent theorist in sociology has concluded that, because need is unverifiable as well as teleological, functionalism as an approach is of questionable scientific utility.[203]

The obscure quality and problematic testability of needs in the functionalist perspective is closely linked to and largely responsible for a fourth problem that has plagued the perspective, namely, tautological reasoning. The problem arose because functionalists, having specified needs in highly abstract terms, rely upon the conditions believed to satisfy the needs as evidence that the needs are a reality. According to the functionalist argument, the existence of need X is shown by the presence of condition Y, and the fact that condition Y exists and can satisfy need X is proof that need X is real. This is reasoning that is circular and tautological; when need is employed in this fashion, it is intellectually empty.

To recapitulate, the concept of societal need has introduced problems of teleology, indefiniteness, and tautology into the macrosociological theory of functionalism. These problems, however, are not inherent in the concept of need, and they can be avoided. To do so in the present chapter, I defined need in specific rather than general terms—e.g., as the need of the system for a particular type of law on therapeutic abortion rather than as the need for integration and equilibrium—and I identified observable variables from which conclusions can be drawn regarding the degree to which a societal need exists for a specific doctrine in law, e.g., acceptance of access to abortion. The latter step—identifying a measure of need—is particularly important and warrants further comment.

Operationalizing a theoretical concept is essential if science is to use the concept and ascertain the contribution the concept can make to explanation and prediction.[204] In the instant chapter, the criterion for determining the extent of a societal need for a particular doctrine of law, both at a given point in time and over time, was (a) the distribution in the population of the characteristic (e.g., age) that is the subject of the doctrine and/or (b) the magnitude of a system-level factor that prior research on individuals suggests has an influence on the behavior that is the subject of the doctrine (e.g., decisions by women to end pregnancies). Thus, a societal need to expand the grounds for an induced abortion was deemed to have existed when, before restrictions imposed by law on access to abortion were removed, an increase occurred in a system-level variable that has been found to affect the probability that individual women will choose to terminate pregnancies.

Need, however, remains a concept that organizes and summarizes observations and that is itself unobserved. Need thus continues to be a theoretical construct, but as used here, it does not introduce the problems of teleology, indefiniteness, and tautology for which functionalism has been attacked. First, need was not regarded in this chapter as controlling the variable being employed to measure need. Rather, my focus was on a variable that was believed responsible for producing a need, and quantitative data on the variable were employed to judge the intensity of the need. The variable, as reflected in data on its rate or distribution in the population, was accordingly viewed as creating a need rather than as satisfying a need that already exists. Used in this manner, the concept of need does not generate a teleological explanation. Second, need was empirically assessed in this chapter with quantitative data on phenomena that were defined in a relatively unambiguous and precise manner. The referents of need, therefore, were definite, not obscure. Third, and finally, inferences regarding the intensity of need were based on the level of and trends in the quantitative variables employed—variables (e.g., age) that were themselves the subject of the doctrines of law under study or variables that research had found influence the frequency of behaviors (e.g., women's decisions to end pregnancies) that were the focus of the doctrines of law under study. In this way, conclusions regarding the existence and intensity of a need do not arise from a presumption regarding the need but, instead, from change in one or more variables that are logically causes of the need and that are independently measured. Such an approach involves inferences in only one direction and precludes tautological reasoning.

B. Societal Need and Abortion

Let me return to the subject of abortion. In Part III of this chapter, evidence was adduced that increases in the prevalence and duration of schooling among women in their main reproductive years were key to the creation of a societal need for the nonrestrictive abortion law that materialized during the last half of the 1960s and the first half of the 1970s. The apparent impact on abortion law of schooling among females does not end the inquiry, however, because a macrosociological framework for law cannot be confined to the immediate antecedents of law doctrines if the framework is to maximize its ability to explain and predict doctrinal content and change. Rather, the framework must include the forces molding these antecedents, and an explanation, therefore, is required for the fact that, as seen in Figure 6.4 and Table 6.4, school enrollment and college graduation underwent an appreciable rise among young women during the 1950s and 1960s. Identification of the causes of the rise is also a prerequisite to understanding the full range of effects of the large-scale forces that altered the properties of society pertinent to the liberalization of law on therapeutic abortion. For example, the greater extent and length of schooling among young women seems to have been accompanied by a shift, albeit delayed, in the meaning that children have for women,[205] and all of these changes, as contributors to or concomitants of the liberalization of abortion law, may have stemmed from a common source. To obtain a complete picture of the societal setting in which abortion law evolved, an exploration of the reasons for higher rates of school enrollment and college graduation among young women is essential.

What forces expanded the pursuit of education by young women in the United States during the last half of the twentieth century? The research necessary for a definitive answer to this question remains to be done, but I suspect two forces were important—viz., increases in the stock of knowledge and increases in the density of population. Elsewhere I have discussed why I believe these forces enlarged the number of court decisions during the 1960s and 1970s that dealt with the constitutional guarantee of equal protection.[206] Here, I would like to briefly explain why I think the two forces made school enrollment and college graduation more common among young women and, in turn, helped to produce law that accepted induced abortion.

I begin with growth in the stock of knowledge because I believe that, with respect to abortion, it is the more influential of the two forces. Increases in the quantity and quality of knowledge, and associated advances in technology, are presumably responsible for changes observed in the occupational structure of the United States—specifically, the noticeable enlargement during the 1950s and 1960s of the part of the occupational structure devoted to information.[207] These changes can also be seen during the twentieth century in the expanding size of the professional and technical workforce, an expansion that was especially rapid after World War II: during the fifty years from 1900 to 1950, the proportion of professional and technical workers in the economically active population rose by approximately four percentage points, but in the twenty years from 1950 to 1970, the magnitude of the rise was some five percentage points.[208] Decadal growth in professional and technical workers was thus considerably larger in the two decades that followed 1950 than in the five decades that preceded it.

The effect of knowledge and its increase are not confined to the occupational structure, however, but extend to the pursuit of education, for the greater size of the professional and technical workforce has, since the middle of the twentieth century, fostered school attendance after high school.[209] Change in the volume of knowledge, that is, altered the occupational system in a way that affected the incidence of tertiary education. Consequently, the post-World War II increase among young women in school enrollment and college completion (seen in Figure 6.4 and Table 6.4, respectively) was not happenstance, and it was undoubtedly a key factor in the movement of employed females into the professions after 1950.[210] Collectively, these changes—which stemmed from the enlarged store of knowledge—promoted the rationality of society and, hence, individual choice on a variety of matters.[211] In short, the volume and growth of knowledge had a major impact on the American social system at this time, an impact manifested in changes involving the role of women and, in turn, in law pertinent to women. Law banning gender-based discrimination in employment[212] and law specifying the grounds for therapeutic abortion are illustrative.

With regard to population density, it is notable that the fraction of the U.S. population residing in a relatively populous area grew steadily during the twentieth century and that the fraction was appreciable in the period preceding and accompanying the reform of abortion law. To be exact, the percentage of the U.S. population residing in a metropolitan setting doubled between 1910 and 1950 (28 percent to 56 percent). It continued to mount between 1950 and 1960 (56 percent to 63 percent) and between 1960 and 1970 (63 percent to 69 percent).[213] How did exposure to an urban environment of a large and expanding share of the population contribute to the evolution of abortion law? Research indicates that, because its residents are more frequently college graduates,[214] such an environment is characterized by views, and presumably actions, that deviate from tradition.[215] Indeed, the impact of urbanism on civil liberties may be greatest in terms of the role of women.[216] Therefore, increases in metropolitan residence, by fostering or at least allowing the acceptance of nontraditional behavior, probably promoted the schooling and educational attainment of women.

In sum, I believe that, for the reasons above, growth in knowledge and increases in population density were instrumental in modifying abortion law in the United States. As forces reshaping the American social order, they changed the core of society in a number of ways that encouraged young women to enroll in school and complete college. Specifically, increases in the volume of knowledge and the density of population are likely to have altered the social system in a manner that increased the ratio of burdens to benefits from childbearing and broadened the range of nonreproductive activities that attract women. From a functionalist perspective, society-provided constraints and inducements mold the acts of individual human beings, and growth in the stock of knowledge and the density of population were capable of changing the constraints and inducements that affect women with respect to bearing and rearing children. In the social environment that resulted, the education of women began to expand, and the expansion affected fertility-related decisions. As the process unfolded, society needed to remove conspicuous restrictions imposed by law that were thought to prevent adult women from terminating unwanted pregnancies. Since participation in and progress through the education institution, and the nonreproductive activities that stem from this participation/progress, would not be fully available to young women unless induced abortion was accessible, the existence of appealing alternatives to childbearing would have required that the institution of law acknowledge the importance of abortion access and eliminate doctrines regarded as major obstacles to abortion use.[217]

Appendix

Age of Majority Specified by Law in Each State[218]

State	Column 2: Age of majority before adoption of age of majority in column 3	Column 3: Age of majority that replaced the age in column 2	Column 4: Year of approval by legislature of age of majority in column 3
Alabama	21	19	1975
Arizona	21	18	1972
Arkansas	21 (males); 18 (females)	18	1975
California	21; 18 if married	18	1971
Colorado	21	18	1973
Connecticut	21	18	1972
Delaware	21	18	1972
Florida	21	18	1973
Georgia	21	18	1972
Idaho	21 (males); 18 (females)	18	1972
Illinois	21 (males); 18 (females)	18	1971
Indiana	21	18	1973
Iowa	21 or upon marriage	19 or upon marriage	1972
	19 or upon marriage	18 or upon marriage	1973
Kansas	21; 18 if married	18	1972
Kentucky	21	18	1964
Louisiana	21	18	1972
Maine	21	20	1969
	20	18	1972

State	Column 2: Age of majority before adoption of age of majority in column 3	Column 3: Age of majority that replaced the age in column 2	Column 4: Year of approval by legislature of age of majority in column 3
Maryland	21	18	1973
Massachusetts	21	18	1973
Michigan	21	18	1971
Minnesota	21	18	1973
Mississippi	21	21	----
Missouri	21	18	[See Missouri in Sources list for table.]
Montana	21 (males); 18 (females)	19	1971
	19	18	1973
Nebraska	21 or upon marriage	20 or upon marriage	1969
	20 or upon marriage	19 or upon marriage	1972
Nevada	21 (males); 18 (females)	18	1973
New Hampshire	21	18	1973
New Jersey	21	18	1972
New Mexico	21	18	1971
New York	21	18	1974
North Carolina	21	18	1971
North Dakota	21 (males); 18 (females)	18	1971
Ohio	21	18	1973
Oklahoma	21 (males); 18 (females)	18	1972
Oregon	21 or upon marriage	18 or upon marriage	1973
Pennsylvania			[See Pennsylvania in Sources list for table.]

(Continued on the next page)

Appendix (*Continued*)

State	Column 2: Age of majority before adoption of age of majority in column 3	Column 3: Age of majority that replaced the age in column 2	Column 4: Year of approval by legislature of age of majority in column 3
Rhode Island	21	18	1972
South Carolina	21	18	1975
South Dakota	21 (males); 18 (females)	18	1972
Tennessee	21	18	1972
Texas	21	18	1973
Utah	21 (males); 18 (females); or upon marriage	18 or upon marriage	1975
Vermont	21	18	1971
Virginia	21	18	1972
Washington	21	18	1970, 1971
West Virginia	21	18	1972
Wisconsin	21	18	1972
Wyoming	21	19	1973
	19	18	1993

Sources:

Alabama: Act of July 22, 1975, No. 77, 1975 Ala. Acts 554; *Ex parte* Bayliss, 550 So. 2d 986, 989 (Ala. 1989) ("From 1852 to 1975, the age of majority in Alabama was 21 years.").

Arizona: Ariz. Rev. Stat. § 1-215 (1956); Act of May 22, 1972, ch. 146, 1972 Ariz. Sess. Laws 1002.

Arkansas: Ark. Code. § 57-103 (1947); Act of April 4, 1975, No. 892, 1975 Ark. Acts 2321.

California: Act of December 14, 1971, ch. 1748, 1971 Cal. Stat. 3736; Act of September 7, 1955, ch. 183, 1955 Cal. Stat. 648.

Colorado: Colo. Rev. Stat. § 2-4-211 (1989); Act of June 25, 1973, ch. 158, 1973 Colo. Sess. Laws 543.

Connecticut: Act of May 9, 1972, No. 127, 1972 Conn. Acts 129 (Reg. Sess.); Altieri v. Altieri, 155 A.2d 758, 760 (Conn. Super. Ct. 1959) ("Under the common law, which has been adopted in our jurisdiction, the age of majority is twenty-one years.").

Delaware: Act of June 16, 1972, ch. 439, 1972 Del. Laws 1351-52; Wife v. Husband, 412 A.2d 724, 725 (Del. Fam. Ct. 1980) (referring to the June 16, 1972 statutory reduction in the age of majority from twenty-one to eighteen years).

Florida: Act of May 9, 1973, ch. 73-21, 1973 Fla. Laws; Act of November 6, 1829, § 1, 1829 Fla. Laws 8-9; Riley v. Holmer, 131 So. 330, 331 (Fla. 1930) ("Under our law, both males and females are minors till they reach the age of twenty-one years. This was the common law rule.").

Georgia: Ga. Code Ann. § 74-104 (1964); Act of March 10, 1972, No. 862, 1972 Ga. Laws 193–99.

Idaho: Idaho Code ann. § 32-101 (1932); Act of March 10, 1972, ch. 117, 1972 Idaho Sess. Laws.

Illinois: Act of July 24, 1939, § 131, 1939 Ill. Laws 37; Act of August 24, 1971, No. 77-1229, 1971 Ill. Laws 2201.

Indiana: Ind. Code Ann. § 34-1-67-1 (1973, repealed 1990); Act of April 16, 1973, no. 313, 1973 Ind. Acts 1715-17; McClain v. Chavez, 383 N.E.2d 414, 415 (Ind. Ct. App. 1978) ("The Legislature changed the age of majority from 21 to 18 years effective as of July 26, 1973").

Iowa: Iowa Code § 599.1 (1950); Act of April 19, 1972, ch. 1027, 1972 Iowa Acts 83; Act of March 7, 1973, ch. 140, 1973 Iowa Acts 311.

Kansas: Act of April 7, 1978, ch. 155, 1978 Kan. Sess. Laws 683 (reducing the age of majority to sixteen if married); Act of March 26, 1972, ch.161, 1972 Kan. Sess. Laws 606; Act of April 19, 1965, ch. 274, 1965 Kan. Sess. Laws 546.

Kentucky: Act of March 10, 1964, ch. 21, 1964 Ky. Acts 96 (establishing eighteen as the age of majority; approved in 1964 and implemented on January 1, 1965); Showalter v. Showalter, 497 S.W.2d 420, 421 (Ky. 1973) ("In 1965 the age of majority was lowered from twenty-one to eighteen years by the General Assembly").

Louisiana: La. Civ. Code Ann. art. 37 (vacated by amendment 1987); Act of June 25, 1972, No. 98, 1972 La. Acts 336.

Maine: The age of majority was reduced from twenty-one to twenty in 1969 and from twenty to eighteen in 1971. Act of October 1, 1969, ch. 433, 1969 Me. Laws 1150–68; Act of June 9, 1972, ch. 598, 1971 Me. Laws 164-180 (Spec. Sess.).

Maryland: Act of May 24, 1973, ch. 651, 1973 Md. Laws 1300; Monticello v. Monticello, 315 A.2d 520, 523 (Md. 1974) (quoting legislative history stating that, except for liquor, the 1973 Act "lower[s] the age of majority from twenty-one to eighteen years of age in all areas of the common law, in all sections and articles of the Annotated Code of Maryland, and in all counties of the State of Maryland").

Massachusetts: Act of October 17, 1973, ch. 925, 1973 Mass. Acts 938-53; Orlandella v. Orlandella, 347 N.E.2d 665, 665 (Mass. 1976) ("Effective January 1, 1974, the age of majority was changed from twenty-one to eighteen years of age.").

Michigan: Mich. Const. of 1963, art. III, § 7; Act of August 4, 1971, no. 79, 1971 Mich. Pub. Acts 142.

Minnesota: Minn. Stat. § 645.45 (1947); Act of May 24, 1973, ch. 725, 1973 Minn. Laws 2082.

Mississippi: Miss. Code Ann. § 1-3-27 (1999); Miss. Code Ann. § 1-3-27 (1972).

Missouri: Owens v. Owens, 854 S.W.2d 52, 54 (Mo. Ct. App. 1993) ("In 1974 the Legislature attempted to change the age of majority from twenty-one to eighteen years of age for all purposes except for the purchase of alcoholic beverages. However, the Supreme Court held unconstitutional this blanket attempt to change the age of majority through an improper amendment. State *ex rel.* McNary v. Stussie, 518 S.W.2d 630, 634, 637 (Mo. 1974). Since then, the Legislature has piecemeal changed the age of majority to eighteen in certain instances.") See also *In re* Marriage of Orth, 637 S.W.2d 201, 205 (Mo. Ct. App. 1982) ("The age of majority is, for most purposes, eighteen in Missouri.").

Montana: The age of majority was reduced to nineteen for all persons in 1971 and to eighteen for all persons in 1973. Mont. Code Ann. § 64-101 (1949); Act of March 6, 1973, ch. 94, 1973 Mont. Laws 109; Act of March 9, 1971, ch. 240, 1971 Mont. Laws 993.

Nebraska: Until 1965, majority was reached at twenty-one or, for females only, upon marriage. Neb. Rev. Stat. § 38-101 (1944). From 1965 to 1969, majority was reached at twenty-one or upon marriage for both males and females. Act of May 12, 1965, ch. 207, 1965 Neb. Laws 613. The age of majority was reduced from twenty-one to twenty in 1969 and from twenty to nineteen in 1972, with marriage conferring majority at younger ages. Act of March 13, 1969, ch. 298, 1969 Neb. Laws 1072; Legis. 1086, 1972 Leg. (Neb. 1972).

Nevada: Act of May 3, 1973, ch. 753, 1973 Nev. Stat. 1577-83.

New Hampshire: N.H. Const., pt. 2, art. 90; Act of April 4, 1973, ch. 72, 1973 N.H. Laws 51.

New Jersey: Act of July 5, 1972, ch. 81, 1972 N.J. Laws 457; Act of December 28, 1972, ch. 206, 1972 N.J. Laws 790; Green v. Auerbach Chevrolet Corp., 606 A.2d 1093, 1095 (N.J. 1992) ("Effective January 1, 1973, the Legislature lowered the age of majority in New Jersey from twenty-one to eighteen.").

New Mexico: Act of April 2, 1971, ch. 213, 1971 N.M. Laws 727; Montoya de Antonio v. Miller, 34 P. 40, 41 (N.M. 1893) ("the common law fixes the beginning of [full legal age] on the day preceding the twenty-first anniversary of birth, and the same has not been changed by any statute of this territory.").

New York: N.Y. Dom. Rel. Law § 2 (Thompson 1964); Act of June 15, 1974, ch. 920, 1974 N.Y. Laws 2213.

North Carolina: N.C. Gen. Stat. § 4-1 (1986); Act of June 17, 1971, ch. 585, 1971 N.C. Sess. Laws 510.

North Dakota: N.D. Cent. Code §§ 14-10-01, 14-10-02 (1960); Act of February 26, 1971, ch. 145, 1971 N.D. Laws 230.

Ohio: Ohio Rev. Code Ann. § 3109.01 (1972); Act of November 21, 1973, No. 1, 1973 Ohio Laws 7.

Oklahoma: Okla. Stat. tit. 15, §§ 13, 14 (1966); Act of April 7, 1972, ch. 221, 1972 Okla. Sess. Laws 332.

Oregon: Or. Rev. Stat. §§ 109.510, 109.520 (1971); Act of July 20, 1973, ch. 827, 1973 Or. Laws 2417.

Pennsylvania: 23 Pa. Cons. Stat. § 5101 (1991); Act of December 6, 1972, No. 300, 1972 Pa. Laws 1404; 1 Pa. Cons. Stat. § 1991 (1995); Act of May 28, 1937, No. 282, 1937 Pa. Laws 1019; Sutliff v. Sutliff, 528 A.2d 1318, 1322 n.4 (Pa. 1987) ("The age of majority for substantive purposes in civil matters remains twenty-one.").

Rhode Island: Act of March 29, 1972, ch. 20, 1972 R.I. Pub. Laws 62, which "changed the age of majority in Rhode Island from twenty-one to eighteen." Vaillancourt v. Vaillancourt, 449 A.2d 885, 886 n.2 (R.I. 1982).

South Carolina: Act of July 2, 1976, no. 695, 1976 S.C. Acts 1886; Act of February 6, 1975, No. 15, 1975 S.C. Acts 13.

South Dakota: S.D. Codified Laws § 26-1-1 (1967); Act of February 17, 1972, ch. 154, 1972 S.D. Sess. Laws 185.

Tennessee: Act of March 30, 1972, ch. 612, 1972 Tenn. Pub. Acts 494; Cardwell v. Bechtol, 724 S.W.2d 739, 745 (Tenn. 1987) ("That the Legislature has adopted [18 years] for attainment of majority indicates persuasively that conditions in society have changed to the extent that maturity is now reached at earlier stages of growth than at the time that the common law recognized the age of majority at 21 years.").

Texas: Act of June 16, 1973, ch. 626, 1973 Tex. Gen. Laws 1722; Dallas Joint Stock Land Bank of Dallas v. Dolan, 92 S.W.2d 1111, 1112 (Tex. Civ. App. 1936) ("By the common law and the law of this state, the status of minority of appellee continues up to the age of 21.").

Utah: Utah Code Ann. § 15-2-1 (1953); Act of March 24, 1975, ch. 39, 1975 Utah Laws 121.

Vermont: Vt. Stat. Ann. tit. 1, § 173 (1958); Act of April 16, 1971, No. 90, 1971 Vt. Acts & Resolves 208.

Virginia: Act of April 10, 1972, ch. 824-25, 1972 Va. Acts 1472-97; Hurdle v. Prinz, 235 S.E.2d 354, 355 (Va. 1977) ("On July 1, 1972, ... [chapters 824 and 825] became effective lowering the age of majority from 21 years to 18.").

Washington: The age of majority was reduced from twenty-one to eighteen in 1970 for specified purposes (e.g., contractual obligations, civil litigation) and in 1971 for all purposes. Age Qualifications Act, ch. 292, 1971 Wash. Sess. Laws 1601; Act of February 20, 1970, ch. 17, 1970 Wash. Sess. Laws 145; Act of March 10, 1923, ch. 72, 1923 Wash. Sess. Laws 222.

West Virginia: W. Va. Code § 2-1-1 (1999); Act of March 11, 1972, ch. 61, 1972 W. Va. Acts 310; Dimitroff v. Dimitroff, 218 S.E.2d 743 (W. Va. 1975).

Wisconsin: Wis. Stat. § 990.01 (1958); Act of March 22, 1972, ch. 213, 1971 Wis. Sess. Laws 509.

Wyoming: The age of majority was reduced from twenty-one to nineteen in 1973 and from nineteen to eighteen in 1993. Wyo. Stat. Ann. § 8-1-101 (1999); Act of February 16, 1993, ch. 1, 1993 Wyo. Laws 1; Act of March 5, 1973, ch. 213, 1973 Wyo. Sess. Laws 312.

Notes

*Chapter 6 is an extensive revision of Larry D. Barnett, "The Roots of Law," *American University Journal of Gender, Social Policy & the Law* 15 (2007): 613. The revision includes substantial change in the design of the study that is reported in Part III-D infra.

1. Larry D. Barnett, "When is a Mutual Fund Director Independent? The Unexplored Role of Professional Relationships under Section 2(a)(19) of the Investment Company Act," *DePaul Business & Commercial Law Journal* 4 (2006): 155, 173–78 (summarizing the central elements of a profession) [hereinafter *When is a Mutual Fund Director Independent?*].
2. According to research in linguistics, "the world is presented in a kaleidoscopic flux of impressions which has to be organized by our minds—and this means largely by the linguistic systems in our minds. We cut nature up, organize it into concepts, and ascribe significances as we do, largely because we are parties to an agreement to organize it in this way—an agreement that holds throughout our speech community and is codified in the patterns of our language." Benjamin Lee Whorf, "Science and Linquistics," in *Language, Thought, and Reality: Selected Writings of Benjamin Lee Whorf*, ed. John B. Carroll (Cambridge: Technology Press of Massachusetts Institute of Technology, 1956), 207, 213; see also Benjamin Lee Whorf, "Language, Mind, and Reality," in *Language, Thought, and Reality*, supra at 246–47 (stating that "[e]very language...incorporates certain points of view and certain patterned resistances to widely divergent points of view"). Professions as well as societies differ in the concepts they use, and the concepts unique to a particular profession accordingly provide its members with perceptions that do not exist among the members of a different profession.
3. Jane Wagner, quoted in Michael Moncur's (Cynical) Quotations, The Quotations Page, http://www.quotationspage.com/quotes/Jane_Wagner (accessed May 30, 2010).
4. Macrosociology assumes that, as a system, a society is characterized by cohesiveness and is comprised of interacting, interdependent components. See John Scott, *Sociological Theory: Contemporary Debates* (Aldershot: Edward Elgar, 1995), 138–39, 150, 153. The findings of quantitative research are consistent with this assumption. See Sung-Soon Clara Kim, Dimensions of Social Integration: Solidarity and Deviance in American Cities (1985) (unpublished Ph.D. diss., University of Virginia), 9–28, 142–48 (on file with Widener University School of Law Delaware Campus Library).
5. In my macrosociological framework, law furthers both social integration and system integration. Social integration involves the relationships between the individuals, and between the groups of individuals, in a society; system integration involves the relationships between the structural components of a society. David Lockwood, "Social Integration and System Integration," in *Explorations in Social Change*, ed. George K. Zollschan and Walter Hirsch (Boston, MA: Houghton Mifflin, 1964), 244, 245.
6. Daniel J. Elazar, *American Federalism: A View from the States* (New York: Thomas Y. Crowell Company, 1966), 97, 135–36 (exemplifying an early use of principle (iv)). The statistical techniques available in the 1960s would not have allowed Professor Elazar to undertake the type of regression analysis reported in Part III-D of the instant chapter.

7. Bradwell v. State, 83 U.S. 130, 139 (1872). See generally Caroline Goddard and Gwen Hoerr McNamee, "Myra Colby Bradwell," in *Bar None: 125 Years of Women Lawyers in Illinois: Eight Women Lawyers in Illinois*, ed. Gwen Hoerr McNamee (Chicago, IL: Chicago Bar Association, 1998), 3–7.
8. *Bradwell*, 83 U.S. at 141 (Bradley, Swayne, and Field, JJ., concurring). A similar view appears in a majority opinion of the Court rendered in 1908 on a state statute that limited the number of hours a woman, but not a man, could work during a twenty-four hour period. See Muller v. Oregon, 208 U.S. 412, 421–22 (1908).
9. United States v. Virginia, 518 U.S. 515, 532–34 (1996).
10. Ibid., 533; *accord* Nev. Dep't of Human Res. v. Hibbs, 538 U.S. 721, 728–30, 740 (2003) (holding constitutional a federal statute that, in banning sex-based employment discrimination, removed the sovereign immunity of states that engaged in such discrimination).
11. Larry D. Barnett, *Legal Construct, Social Concept* (New York: Aldine de Gruyter, 1993), 50–55 [hereinafter *Legal Construct, Social Concept*].
12. Ibid., 52–55. Between 1910 and 1990, the largest decadal decline in sex segregation in occupations occurred from 1930 to 1940. See Kim A. Weeden, "Revisiting Occupational Sex Segregation in the United States, 1910-1990: Results from a Log-Linear Approach," *Demography*, 35 (1998): 475, 480 index A. Notable decreases in such segregation took place in two subsequent decades (1940–1950 and 1960–1970), but these decreases were much smaller in magnitude than the decline between 1930 and 1940. See ibid.
13. 15 U.S.C. § 80a (2006).
14. Act of August 22, 1940, ch. 686, title 1, 54 Stat. 789 (1940).
15. 15 U.S.C. § 80a-37 (2006). The Securities and Exchange Commission defines a mutual fund as an open-end management investment company, i.e., as an investment company that issues securities redeemable by the company. Disclosure of Proxy Voting Policies and Proxy Voting Records by Registered Management Investment Companies, Investment Company Act Release No. IC-25922, 68 Fed. Reg. 6564, 6565 n. 6 (February 7, 2003); 15 U.S.C. §§ 80a-2(a)(32), 80a-4, 80a-5(a) (2006).
16. Investment Company Institute, *2010 Investment Company Fact Book*, 50th ed. (2010), 80, 126 (including net assets of money market funds in total net assets of mutual funds), http://www.ici.org/about_ici/annuals/fact_books (accessed April 10, 2011).
17. 15 U.S.C. § 80a-3 (2006).
18. Ibid., § 80a-2(a)(22) (defining "issuer" as "every person who issues or proposes to issue any security, or has outstanding any security which it has issued").
19. 15 U.S.C. § 80a-2(a)(28) (2006) (defining "person" as "a natural person or a company"); 15 U.S.C. § 80a-2(a)(8) (2006) (defining "company" to include corporations and partnerships).
20. Other federal securities statutes—viz., the Securities Act of 1933, the Securities Exchange Act of 1934, and the Investment Advisers Act of 1940—also extend the word "person" to an entity. 15 U.S.C §§ 77b(a)(2), 77b(a)(4) (2006) (Securities Act); 15 U.S.C. § 78c(a)(9) (2006) (Securities Exchange Act); 15 U.S.C. §§ 80b-2(a)(5), -2(a)(16) (2006) (Investment Advisers Act).

21. *Webster's Dictionary of Word Origins* (New York: Smithmark Publishers, 1995), 353–55 .
22. *Oxford English Dictionary*, ed. J.A. Simpson and E.S.C. Weiner, vol. 11, 2nd ed. (Oxford: Clarendon Press; New York: Oxford University Press, 1989), 596–97 (using definition I.1); see also Oxford English Dictionary, http://www.oed.com (search "find word" for "person;" then select "person, n.;" then follow "Date Chart" hyperlink) (showing dates of meaning usage in English literature).
23. Because they are accepted by law, corporations and partnerships are logically characterized as artificial persons that *result from* fictionalizing rather than as artificial persons that *are* a fiction. However, the judiciary does not necessarily take this approach. "If [a corporation] is a fiction it is a fiction created by law with intent that it should be acted on as if true. The corporation is a person." Klein v. Bd. of Tax Supervisors, 282 U.S. 19, 24 (1930).
24. *Webster's Dictionary of Word Origins*, supra note 21, at 354; Beth Stephens, "The Amorality of Profit: Transnational Corporations and Human Rights," *Berkeley Journal of International Law* 20 (2002): 45, 54.
25. Shepard Bancroft Clough and Charles Woolsey Cole, *Economic History of Europe* (Boston, MA: D.C. Heath and Company 1941), 56, 75, 148; A. B. Hibbert, "The Economic Policies of Towns," in *Cambridge Economic History of Europe*, vol. 3, ed. M. M. Postan et al. (Cambridge: Cambridge University Press, 1963/1965), 157, 170, 190–95; see Shael Herman, "Trusts Sacred and Profane: Clerical, Secular, and Commercial Uses of the Medieval Commendatio," *Tulane Law Review* 71 (1997): 869, 891–94; R. de Roover, "The Organization of Trade," in *Cambridge Economic History of Europe*, 42, 113.
26. S. I. Hayakawa, *Language in Thought and Action*, 2nd ed. (New York: Harcourt Brace & World, 1964), 11–14.
27. Cf. Sylvia L. Thrupp, "The Gilds," in *Cambridge Economic History of Europe*, 230, 231–32, 244 (describing the development of occupational guilds in England during the late thirteenth century: "[t]heir organization was important...in bringing more formal deliberation to bear on the shaping of the law and custom and on the administrative procedures through which orderly relations were maintained among buyers and sellers").
28. Bank of the United States v. Deveaux, 9 U.S. (5 Cranch) 61, 88 (1809).

> As our ideas of a corporation, its privileges and its disabilities, are derived entirely from the English books, we resort to them for aid in ascertaining its character. It is defined as a mere creature of the law, invisible, intangible, and incorporeal. Yet, when we examine the subject further, we find that corporations have been included within terms of description appropriated to real persons.

Ibid. See generally Franklin A. Gevurtz, "The Historical and Political Origins of the Corporate Board of Directors," *Hofstra Law Review* 33 (2004): 89 (outlining the historical antecedents of boards of directors of corporations).

29. Business receipts—data on which are available for corporations, partnerships, and nonfarm proprietorships—evidence the economic importance of corporations and partnerships in the United States. Of all receipts (in

billions of dollars) for the three types of business organization combined, corporations and partnerships have accounted for no less than 95 percent in recent years. Calculated from U.S. Census Bureau, *Statistical Abstract of the United States: 2010*, 129th ed. (2009), 483 table 728, http://www.census.gov/prod/www/abs/statab2006_2010.html (accessed April 10, 2011).

Unfortunately, data that use a consistent definition of proprietorship over a long period of time are unavailable. Corporations were not a customary form of conducting business in the United States before 1850. See William W. Bratton, Jr., "The New Economic Theory of the Firm Critical Perspectives from History," *Stanford Law Review* 41 (1989): 1471, 1485. Sole proprietorships, too, seem not to have been the norm prior to 1850. Rather, businesses at this time were predominantly partnerships. Lawrence M. Friedman, *A History of American Law*, 3rd ed. (New York: Simon & Schuster, 2005), 130. Nonetheless, corporations were being formed in the decades preceding 1850, usually by special acts of state legislatures. William C. Kessler, "Incorporation in New England: A Statistical Study, 1800–1875," *Journal of Economic History* 8 (1948): 43, 45–47, 50. Notably, the business corporations in existence during this period "tended to function in vital, sensitive parts of the economy, such as banking and transportation. They tended to be the largest economic organizations and concentrations of economic power." Stephen A. Siegel, "Understanding the Nineteenth Century Contract Clause: The Role of the Property-Privilege Distinction and "Takings" Clause Jurisprudence," *Southern California Law Review* 60 (1986): 1, 68. The economy of the United States, therefore, is likely to have been dominated by corporations and/or partnerships almost since the nation began. See James Willard Hurst, *The Legitimacy of the Business Corporation in the Law of the United States, 1780–1970* (Charlottesville: University Press of Virginia, 1970), 14–18.

Law manifests the pivotal economic function of artificial beings both in legislation (e.g., state statutes on corporations and partnerships) and in judicial opinions. See Marshall v. Balt. & Ohio R.R. Co., 57 U.S. (16 How.) 314, 327 (1850) (explaining that corporations exist because "[t]he necessities and conveniences of trade and business require that [natural persons] ... should act by representation, and have the faculty of contracting, suing, and being sued in a factitious or collective name").

30. Gunhild O. Hagestad and Peter Uhlenberg, "The Social Separation of Old and Young: A Root of Ageism," *Journal of Social Issues* 61 (2005): 343, 344–47.
31. Sy Moskowitz, "American Youth in the Workplace: Legal Aberration, Failed Social Policy," *Albany Law Review* 67 (2004): 1071, 1081–82.
32. Schwan v. Riverside Methodist Hosp., 452 N.E.2d 1337, 1339 (Ohio 1983).
33. Proclamation No. 3269, 24 Fed. Reg. 81 (1959) (declaring Alaska a state); Proclamation No. 3309, 24 Fed. Reg. 6868 (1959) (declaring Hawaii a state).
34. From 1960 to 1980, these jurisdictions accounted for just 1.8 percent of all residents of areas that were under United States sovereignty. Calculated from U.S. Bureau of the Census, *U.S. Dep't of Commerce, Statistical Abstract of the United States: 1985*, 105th ed. (1984), 12 Table 12, 826 Table

1451, http://www.census.gov/prod/www/abs/statab.html (accessed April 10, 2011).

35. Homer H. Clarke, Jr., *The Law of Domestic Relations in the United States*, 2nd ed. (St. Paul, MN: West Publishing Company, 1988), 309.

36. U.S. Bureau of the Census, *U.S. Dep't of Commerce, Statistical Abstract of the United States: 1998*, 118th ed. (1998), 28 Table 26, http://www.census.gov/prod/ www/abs/statab.html (accessed April 10, 2011).

37. Stanton v. Stanton, 421 U.S. 7, 17 (1975) (suggesting twice that its holding applied only in "the context of child support").

38. Stanton v. Stanton, 517 P.2d 1010 (Utah 1974) (upholding the different age of majority for men and women), *rev'd*, 421 U.S. 7 (1975) (decided April 15, 1975). The U.S. Supreme Court announced its ruling in *Stanton* on April 15, 1975. Ibid. Two of the nine states, Arkansas and Utah, eliminated the sex difference in their age of majority in 1975, but both states acted before April 15: a gender-neutral age of majority was approved by the Utah legislature on March 24, 1975 and by the Arkansas legislature on April 7, 1975. Act of April 7, 1975, No. 892, 1975 Ark. Acts 2321; Act of March 24, 1975, ch. 39 § 15-2-1, 1975 Utah Laws 121. In adopting a uniform age of majority, the Utah legislature thus was not responding to an adverse court decision.

39. See Guy N. Burkhardt, Population Determinants of Social Change: An Analysis of the Age Composition of the United States from 1920 to 1983 (unpublished Ph.D. diss., Portland State University, 1988) (on file with Widener University School of Law Delaware Campus library); see also Henry M. McMillan and Jerome B. Baesel, "The Macroeconomic Impact of the Baby Boom Generation," *Journal of Macroeconomics* 12 (1990): 167 (finding that the age composition of the U.S. population affected real interest rates, income, inflation, and unemployment); Michael D. Mumford et al., "Age-Related Changes in the Likelihood of Major Contributions," *International Journal of Aging & Human Development* 29 (1989): 171, 175; Raymond K. Oldakowski, The Influence of Population Change on Municipal Fiscal Policy (unpublished Ph.D. diss., University of Illinois at Urbana-Champaign, August 1987) (on file with author) (finding that age structure and other population characteristics generate changes in municipal fiscal policy).

40. National Center for Health Statistics, *Vital Statistics of the United States: 1993, Vol. I, Natality* (1999), at Table 1-1, http://www.cdc.gov/nchs/products/vsus.htm (accessed April 10, 2011).

41. The percentages were calculated for each year from 1900 through 1980. Percentages are based on the resident population of the forty-eight states for 1900–1939 and on the total population for 1940 and later years. Alaska and Hawaii are included by the Census Bureau in total population starting in 1950. U.S. Bureau of the Census, *Estimates of the Population of the United States, by Single Years of Age, Color, and Sex: 1900 to 1959*, Current Population Rep., Series P-25, No. 311 (1965); U.S. Bureau of the Census, *Estimates of the Population of the United States, by Age, Sex, and Race: April 1, 1960 to July 1, 1973*, Current Population Rep., Series P-25, No. 519 Table 1 (1974); U.S. Bureau of the Census, *Preliminary Estimates of the Population of the United States, by Age, Sex,*

and Race: 1970 to 1981, Current Population Rep., Series P-25, No. 917 Table 1 (1982).

42. Duane F. Alwin, "From Obedience to Autonomy: Changes in Traits Desired in Children, 1924–1978," *Public Opinion Quarterly* 52 (1988): 33, 43.
43. *Legal Construct, Social Concept*, supra note 11, at 22–23.
44. It is probably not coincidence that, prior to the reduction during the 1970s in the age of majority established by law, loyalty to religion also became less important in the values that American parents had for their children. See Alwin, supra note 42, at 43.
45. See Oscar Handlin, *Immigration as a Factor in American History* (Englewood Cliffs, NJ: Prentice-Hall, 1959), 1–3.
46. U.S. Bureau of the Census, *U.S. Dep't of Commerce, Statistical Abstract of the United States*, 118th ed. (1998), 10 Table 5, http://www.census.gov/prod/www/ abs/statab.html (accessed April 10, 2011); U.S. Bureau of the Census, *Historical Statistics of the United States: Colonial Times to 1970, Part I*, (Series C 89-119) (1975), 105–9, http://www.census.gov/prod/www/abs/statab.html [hereinafter *Historical Statistics*].
47. See Campbell J. Gibson and Emily Lennon, *Historical Census Statistics on the Foreign-Born Population of the United States: 1850 to 1990*, (U.S. Census Bureau, Population Division Working Paper No. 29, 1999), Table 1, http://www.census.gov/population/www/documentation/twps0029/twps0029.html (accessed April 10, 2011). (showing that foreign-born persons comprised no less than 13.2 percent of the U.S. population between 1860 and 1920 but were just 4.7 percent of the population in 1970).
48. I am not implying that history is governed by a master plan and moves in a preordained direction; my contention is only that certain factors precede societal change and the new concepts and doctrines of law that are generated by such change.
49. *Legal Construct, Social Concept*, supra note 11, at 23–24; Larry D. Barnett, "Population Growth, Population Organization Participants, and the Right of Privacy," *Family Law Quarterly* (1978): 37.
50. See G. Nigel Gilbert, "Measuring the Growth of Science," *Scientometrics* 1 (1978): 9; Mumford et al., supra note 39, at 175.
51. Graham T.T. Molitor, "Trends and Forecasts for the New Millenium," *Futurist* (August–September 1998), 53, 59.
52. The data in Figure 6.2 are from U.S. Patent & Trademark Office, *U.S. Patent Activity, Calendar Years 1790 to the Present* (2011), http://www.uspto.gov/web/offices/ac/ido/oeip/taf/h_counts.pdf (accessed April 10, 2011).
53. 35 U.S.C. §§ 101, 103(a) (2006).
54. See generally Weeden, supra note 12 (using a margin-free method to measure sex segregation in occupations in the United States from 1910 to 1990).
55. Publications such as books and articles can be copyrighted only if they are original. Marshall Leaffer, *Understanding Copyright Law*, 4th ed. (Newark, NJ: Lexisnexis, 2005), § 2.07. Copyrighted publications in science, therefore, represent contributions to scientific principles and/or concepts.
56. See Patrick Nolan and Gerhard Lenski, "Technology, Ideology, and Societal Development," *Sociological Perspectives* 39 (1996): 23, 33 (finding

with cross-sectional data that, compared to ideology, improvements in subsistence technology had a larger effect on societies).

57. Ron Lesthaeghe, "A Century of Demographic and Cultural Change in Western Europe: An Exploration of Underlying Dimensions," *Population and Development Review* 9 (1983): 411, 429–30.

58. See Clifford I. Nass, Society as Computer: The Structure and Skill of Information Work in the United States, 1900–1980, (unpublished Ph.D. diss., Princeton University, October 1986), 92, 94 (on file with Widener University School of Law Delaware Campus Library) (finding that between 1900 and 1980 the proportion of the U.S. labor force in occupations dealing with information rose by 5.5 percent per decade, and that in 1980 two out of five workers were engaged in these occupations).

59. Melvin L. Kohn and Kazimierz M. Slomczynski, *Social Structure and Self-Direction* (Cambridge, MA: B. Blackwell, 1990), 108.

60. See Nass, supra note 58, at 204 (identifying information as the primary substance of nonmanual occupations, not of manual occupations); see also Melvin L. Kohn and Carrie Schoenbach, "Class, Stratification, and Psychological Functioning," in *Work and Personality*, ed. Melvin L. Kohn and Carmi Schooler (Norwood, NJ: Ablex Publishing, 1983), 154, 185 (finding that nonmanual occupations, including white-collar workers, have a higher level of self-direction than manual, i.e., blue-collar, occupations). Additions to knowledge thus seriatim enlarge the number of nonmanual positions in an economy, increase intellectual autonomy and flexibility, and heighten reasoning. Cf. Melvin L. Kohn and Carmi Schooler, "Job Conditions and Personality: A Longitudinal Assessment of Their Reciprocal Effects," in *Work and Personality*, 125, 147 (finding that self-direction in an occupation is associated with reduced authoritarianism and ideational conformity); Kohn and Slomczynski, supra note 59, at 235 (finding that self-direction in work produces more intellectual flexibility and a less-conformist orientation to society). See generally Kohn and Schoenbach, supra, at 154 (exploring the impact of occupational self-direction and social stratification on values, orientations, and cognitive functioning).

61. See Kenneth C. Land and Fred C. Pampel, "Indicators and Models of Changes in the American Occupational System, 1947–73," *Social Indicators Research* 4 (1977): 1, 18–19 (finding that expenditures on science raised the mean prestige of the occupational structure in the United States between 1950 and 1973). Because professional and other white-collar occupations are highest in prestige, advances in science and hence in knowledge, which presumably resulted in part from expenditures on science, increased the prevalence of these occupations. By definition, a profession possesses a substantial quantity of complex knowledge. See *When is a Mutual Fund Director Independent?*, supra note 1, at 177 (identifying a large body of abstract concepts and complex principles as one of five attributes presently fundamental to the existence of a profession in the United States).

62. See James P. Smith and Michael Ward, "Women in the Labor Market and in the Family," *Journal of Economic Perspectives* 3 (1989): 9, 10–11.

63. Cf. Eric A. Hanushek and Dongwook Kim, Schooling, Labor Force Quality, and Economic Growth 34 (Working Paper 5399, Nat'l Bureau of Economic

Research, 1995) (finding that national rates of economic growth rise with the level of student mastery of mathematics and science).

64. Roger Clark, "Contrasting Perspectives on Women's Access to Prestigious Occupations: A Cross-National Investigation," *Social Science Quarterly* 72 (1991): 20, 28–29.
65. Kohn and Slomczynski, supra note 59, at 133.
66. I confine myself to federal law, and exclude state law, because my focus is on the stock of knowledge of the nation as a whole. However, a macro-sociological framework is also applicable at the state level, as exemplified infra in Parts III-C and III-D. Thus, variations between states in knowledge growth and use can be expected to create differences in the content of state law.
67. Act of May 31, 1870, ch. 114, § 16, 16 Stat. 144 (codified at 42 U.S.C. § 1981 (2006)).
68. See Long v. Ford Motor Co., 496 F.2d 500, 504 (6th Cir. 1974).
69. See Johnson v. Railway Express Agency, Inc., 421 U.S. 454, 459–60 & n.6 (1975).
70. Equal Pay Act of 1963, Pub. L. No. 88-38, 77 Stat. 56 (1963). The Act is concerned with employees who are, or whose employers are, "engaged in commerce or in the production of goods for commerce". § 2(a), 77 Stat. 56. The Act was in force as of 1964. § 4, 77 Stat. 57.
71. 29 U.S.C. § 206(d) (2006).
72. S. Rep. No. 88-176, at 1 (1963).
73. George H. Gallup, *The Gallup Poll: Public Opinion 1935–1971*, ed. William P. Hansen and Fred L. Israel, vol. 2 (New York: Random House, 1972), 1240.
74. Pub. L. No. 88-352, § 703, 78 Stat. 241, 255-56 (1964) (codified at 42 U.S.C. § 2000e-2 (2006)). The Civil Rights Act was in force as of 1965. § 716, 78 Stat. 266. The Act applied to employers having an impact on interstate commerce and a minimum of twenty-five employees each working day during at least twenty calendar weeks in either the current or the preceding calendar year. § 701, 78 Stat. 253. The Act also prohibited labor organizations and employment agencies from discriminating. § 703, 78 Stat. 255.
75. See Phillips v. Martin Marietta Corp., 400 U.S. 542, 543 (1971) (per curiam).
76. Mitchell v. Mid-Continent Spring Co., 583 F.2d 275, 281 (6th Cir. 1978) (internal quotation marks omitted), *cert. denied*, 441 U.S. 922 (1979).
77. See Pub. L. No. 88-352, §§ 705-709, 78 Stat. 241, 258 (1964).
78. See Pub. L. No. 90-202, 81 Stat. 602 (1967) (codified at 29 U.S.C. § 623 (2006)). The ADEA was in force as of 1968 and banned age discrimination by employers, employment agencies, and labor organizations. Ibid. The term "employer" has identical definitions in the ADEA and in Title VII but somewhat different exceptions. Although the ADEA originally did not cover persons who were older than sixty-four, a maximum age was subsequently removed for all but a few occupations. Pub. L. No. 95-256, § 3, 92 Stat. 189 (1978); Pub. L. No. 99-592, §§ 2-3, 100 Stat. 3342 (1986).
79. Hazen Paper Co. v. Biggins, 507 U.S. 604, 610–11 (1993).
80. Pub. L. No. 101-336, 104 Stat. 327 (1990) (codified at 42 U.S.C. §§ 12101–17 (2006)). The ADA, which was in force as of 1992, covered the disabled

individual, i.e., one who possesses "a physical or mental impairment that substantially limits one or more of the major life activities ... or [who is] regarded as having such an impairment." Ibid. With some exceptions, the ADA covered an employer that had an impact on interstate commerce and a minimum of fifteen employees each working day during at least twenty calendar weeks in either the present or the prior calendar year. Ibid. §§ 3(2), 101(5), 108.

81. In 1977, i.e., thirteen years before the ADA, a national sample of adults in the United States was asked whether the government should enact legislation designed to ensure equal job rights for individuals who are physically handicapped. Four out of five respondents endorsed the enactment of such legislation. *CBS News & New York Times*, July 19–25, 1977.
82. Sutton v. United Air Lines, Inc., 527 U.S. 471, 489 (1999).
83. See, e.g., Equal Employment Opportunity Act of 1972, Pub. L. No. 92-261, § 2, 86 Stat. 103 (1972); Fair Labor Standards Amendments of 1974, Pub. L. No. 93-259, § 28, 88 Stat. 55, 74 (1974); Congressional Accountability Act of 1995, Pub. L. No. 104-1, 109 Stat. 3 (1995).
84. See, e.g., Rehabilitation Act of 1973, Pub. L. No. 93-112, § 504, 87 Stat. 355, 394 (1973).
85. See Richard Rubinson and John Ralph, "Technical Change and the Expansion of Schooling in the United States, 1890–1970," *Sociology of Education* 57 (1984): 134 (finding that advances in technology boosted enrollments in primary and secondary schools in the United States). However, Professors Rubinson and Ralph did not investigate whether advances in technology affected the likelihood of attending college. A study of four countries in Western Europe concluded that economic development between 1900 and 1985 increased the rate at which women enrolled in institutions of higher education. Joan Mary Hermsen, Gendering Higher Education Expansion: Explaining the Growth in Women's University Enrollment Rates in Britain, France, Germany, and Italy During the Twentieth Century (unpublished Ph.D. diss., University of Maryland at College Park, 1997), 41, 49, 111–12 (on file with author). Economic development requires the application of knowledge. Because economic development promoted college attendance in four European nations, it also is likely to have done so in the United States.
86. *Legal Construct, Social Concept*, supra note 11, at 168 (suggesting that: (1) that the branches of government are mechanisms acting in response to their social environment; and (2) that a comprehensive theory focusing on doctrines of law must explain why one branch reacts rather than another).
87. Gregory G. Brunk and Thomas G. Minehart, "How Important Is Elite Turnover to Policy Change?" *American Journal of Political Science* 28 (1984): 559, 568; David J. Falcone, "Legislative Change and Policy Change: A Deviant Case Analysis of the Canadian House of Commons," *Journal of Politics* 41 (1979): 611, 632; Harold Wolman et al., "Does Changing Mayors Matter?" *Journal of Politics* 58 (1996): 201, 219–21.
88. Roe v. Wade, 410 U.S. 113 (1973).
89. Amy S. Cleghorn, Comment, "Justice Harry A. Blackmun: A Retrospective Consideration of the Justice's Role in the Emancipation of Women," *Seton Hall Law Review* 25 (1995): 1176, 1189 (describing *Roe as* "the first victory

cry for women in the fight to claim emotional and legal independence in a male-dominated world")

90. The U.S. Supreme Court regards Roe v. Wade as one of its most socially significant decisions during the last half of the twentieth century. In 1992, the Court described *Roe* as "a watershed decision" and added that *Roe*

> calls the contending sides of a national controversy to end their national division by accepting a common mandate rooted in the Constitution.
>
> The Court is not asked to do this very often, having thus addressed the Nation only twice in our lifetime, in the decisions of *Brown* [*v. Board of Education* holding unconstitutional purposeful racial segregation in public schools] and *Roe*.

Planned Parenthood of Southeastern Pennsylvania v. Casey, 505 U.S. 833, 867 (1992).

91. Fifteen of the sixteen states eased their restrictions on the use of therapeutic abortion through legislation. The fifteen states were Arkansas, California, Colorado, Delaware, Florida, Georgia, Kansas, Maryland, New Mexico, New York, North Carolina, Oregon, South Carolina, Virginia, and Washington. In Washington, the legislation was drafted by the legislature, but by its terms, the legislation could become law only after it was approved by the voters in a general election. Jon F. Merz et al., "A Review of Abortion Policy: Legality, Medicaid Funding, and Parental Involvement, 1967-1994," *Women's Rights Law Reporter* 17 (1995): 1. The pertinent session laws were: Act of February 17, 1969, § 2, 1969 Ark. Acts 177–78; Act of June 15, 1967, ch. 327, 1967 Cal. Stat. 1521; Act of April 25, 1967, ch. 190, 1967 Colo. Sess. Laws 284; Act of June 17, 1969, ch. 145, 57 Del. Laws 409; Act of April 12, 1972, ch. 72-196, 1972 Fla. Laws 608; Act of April 10, 1968, ch. 26-12, 1968 Ga. Laws 1277; Act of April 23, 1969, ch. 180, § 21-3407, 1969 Kan. Sess. Laws 452; Act of May 7, 1968, ch. 470, 1968 Md. Laws 870; Act of March 21, 1969, ch. 67, 1969 N.M. Laws 225; Act of April 11, 1970, ch. 127, 1970 N.Y. Laws 852; Act of May 9, 1967, ch. 367, 1967 N.C. Sess. Laws 394; Act of June 16, 1969, ch. 684, 1969 Or. Laws 1782; Act of January 29, 1970, No. 821, 1970 S.C. Acts 1892; Act of April 4, 1970, ch. 508, 1970 Va. Acts 1101; Act of February 4, 1970, ch. 3, 1970 Wash. Sess. Laws 23. The Washington legislation was approved in an election held on November 3, 1970. Wash. Rev. Code §§ 9.02.060, 9.02.070 (1977).

The sixteenth state that expanded access to therapeutic abortion prior to *Roe* was Vermont, which did so through judicial decision. Specifically, in January 1972, the Supreme Court of Vermont held unconstitutional a state statute that subjected a person who performed an abortion to imprisonment unless the pregnancy threatened the life of the woman; the statute expressly exempted from punishment the woman whose pregnancy was aborted. Beecham v. Leahy, 287 A.2d 836, 840 (Vt. 1972). Following *Beecham*, a pregnancy could be terminated lawfully in Vermont for any reason before the fetus was capable of moving in the uterus, i.e., prior to quickening. Ibid., 839.

Under Mississippi law prior to 1966, a woman could abort a pregnancy only when the pregnancy jeopardized her life. *Miss. Code Ann.* § 2223(1) (1942, recompiled 1956). In 1966, Mississippi revised its abortion statute and added rape as a permissible ground for terminating a pregnancy. Act of May 8, 1966, ch. 358, § 1, 1966 Miss. Laws 661; Merz et al., supra, at 33. Because the statutory change did not substantially expand access to abortion, the instant study treats Mississippi as a state that did not alter its abortion law before *Roe*.

As the result of state court decisions rendered prior to *Roe*, Massachusetts allowed a pregnancy to be terminated "to preserve the woman's life or physical or mental health." Merz et al., supra, at 30. The court decisions conflicted with the state statute on abortion, which did not permit abortion for any reason. *Mass. Gen. Laws Ann.* ch. 272, § 19 (1970). The highest court in Massachusetts established the exception for the life or health of the woman at least as early as 1944. Commonwealth v. Wheeler, 53 N.E.2d 4, 5 (Mass. 1944). Because my focus is on the states that eased restrictions on abortion starting in the 1960s, I classify Massachusetts as a jurisdiction that did not liberalize its law. An additional basis for doing so is that the case law of the highest court in Massachusetts during the 1960s is unclear as to whether a serious threat to the mental or physical health of the pregnant woman was necessary to abort a pregnancy lawfully or whether a health threat of any degree justified an abortion. *Compare* Commonwealth v. Brunelle, 171 N.E.2d 850, 852 (Mass. 1961) (requiring that an abortion be based on a reasonable belief that the health of the pregnant woman was placed in "great peril" by her pregnancy and that her health was in danger of "serious impairment" unless the pregnancy was terminated) *with* Kudish v. Bd. of Registration in Med., 248 N.E.2d 264, 266 (Mass. 1969) (citing *Brunelle* and earlier decisions without specifying the degree to which a pregnancy must endanger the health of the pregnant woman to justify an abortion). Massachusetts would have been categorized in the instant study as a state that liberalized its law on abortion prior to *Roe* if it had clearly changed its law to allow an abortion to be performed legally for health reasons without regard to the level of risk that the pregnancy posed. (For the same reasons, the instant study treats Alabama as a state that did not liberalize its law on abortion before *Roe*: its pre-*Roe* statute allowing an abortion for health reasons was enacted in 1951, as indicated in the text accompanying note 188 infra, and I could find no evidence that the statute permitted an abortion regardless of the severity of the health risk created by the pregnancy.)

In 1970, a three-judge federal district court issued a judgment declaring a Wisconsin statute to be unconstitutional in banning abortions during the first trimester of pregnancy and later issued an injunction against enforcement of the statute. The U.S. Supreme Court declined to rule on the declaratory judgment, but it vacated the injunction of the district court and directed the district court to reconsider the injunction. Babbitz v. McCann, 310 F. Supp. 293 (E.D. Wis. 1970), *appeal dismissed*, 400 U.S. 1 (1970); Babbitz v. McCann, 320 F. Supp. 219 (E.D. Wis. 1970), *vacated*, 402 U.S. 903 (1971). The remand of the case on the issue of the injunction has no subsequent judicial history, but since Wisconsin prosecutors and the Wisconsin judiciary were evidently continuing to enforce the state abortion statute during the appeal of the district court declaratory judgment, enforcement presumably continued until the Supreme Court decided *Roe* in January 1973. See *Babbitz,* 320 F. Supp. at 223 (justifying the injunction because "the state judiciary has failed to discourage the prosecutors from trespassing on the federal rights in question. The reaction of the state authorities to our judgment relegates our ruling to nothing more than a gratuitous, advisory opinion"). Accordingly, I do not consider Wisconsin to be a state that liberalized its abortion law prior to *Roe.*

In 1972, a three-judge federal district court, in a declaratory judgment, ruled unconstitutional the New Jersey statute that imposed criminal penalties on physicians who performed abortions, but the court did not enjoin enforcement of the statute. Young Women's Christian Ass'n v. Kugler, 342 F. Supp. 1048 (D. N.J. 1972), *aff'd,* 463 F.2d 203 (3d Cir. 1972), *cert. denied,* 415 U.S. 989 (1974). Because enforcement of the statute could continue while appellate courts considered the district court ruling, I do not deem New Jersey to be a state that liberalized its abortion law before *Roe.*

92. *Legal Construct, Social Concept,* supra note 11, at 5–7; Joanna M. Shepherd, "Deterrence versus Brutalization: Capital Punishment's Differing Impacts Among States," *Michigan Law Review* 104 (2005): 203, 213.
93. Lawrence B. Finer et al., "Reasons U.S. Women Have Abortions: Quantitative and Qualitative Perspectives," *Perspectives on Sexual and Reproductive Health* 37 (2005): 110, 117.
94. Steven L. Nock, "The Symbolic Meaning of Childbearing," *Journal of Family Issues* 8 (1987): 373.
95. Joanne M. Badagliacco, Who Has Abortions: Determinants of Abortion Choice among American Women (unpublished Ph.D. diss., Columbia University, 1987) (on file with Widener University School of Law Delaware Campus Library).
96. Ibid., 33.
97. Ibid., 38.
98. Ibid., 54.
99. Ibid., 56.
100. Elise F. Jones and Jacqueline Darroch Forrest, "Underreporting of Abortion in Surveys of U.S. Women: 1976 to 1988," *Demography* 29 (1992): 113, 115.
101. Badagliacco, supra note 95, at 64.
102. Ibid.
103. Gus Haggstrom et al., *Changes in the Lifestyles of New Parents* (Santa Monica, CA: Rand, 1984), 146.
104. Badagliacco, supra note 95, at 61.
105. Ibid., 76–77.
106. Among the variables controlled was whether the pregnancy occurred before or after the U.S. Supreme Court decided Roe v. Wade. Ibid., 62, 160.
107. Unless otherwise noted, I base my summary of the findings on the logistic regression equations, not the ordinary least-squares equations, estimated by the investigator. Badagliacco, supra note 95, at 158–61.
108. Ibid., 67.
109. Ibid., 143, 165.
110. Katherine Trent and Eve Powell-Griner, "Differences in Race, Marital Status, and Education Among Women Obtaining Abortions," *Social Forces* 69 (1991): 1121.

111. Computed from ibid., 1126 and from Stephanie J. Ventura et al., "Trends in Pregnancies and Pregnancy Rates, United States, 1980–88," *Monthly Vital Statistics Report* 41 (November 16, 1992): table 1, http://www.cdc.gov/nchs/data/mvsr/supp/mv41_06s.pdf (accessed April 10, 2011).
112. In addition to educational attainment and marital status, the following independent variables were included: age, metropolitan versus nonmetropolitan residence, prior number of live births, race, and state of residence. Trent and Powell-Griner, supra note 110, at 1126.
113. Among women, educational level and marital status are related to employment status under at least some conditions. Diane H. Felmlee, "A Dynamic Analysis of Women's Employment Exits," *Demography* 21 (1984): 171, 178, 180. In addition, the educational level and the employment status of wives affect the likelihood of marital disruption, suggesting that educational level and employment status of wives are linked to current marital status. Steven Ruggles, "The Rise of Divorce and Separation in the United States, 1880–1990," *Demography* 34 (1997): 455, 456, 463; Scott South and Glenna Spitze, "Determinants of Divorce Over the Marital Life Course," *American Sociological Review* (1986): 583, 587–88.
114. Trent and Powell-Griner, supra note 110, at 1125.
115. Fetal deaths occurred in just one out of eight pregnancies that ended in 1980. Computed from Ventura et al., supra note 111, at table 2.
116. Computed from U.S. Dep't of Health & Human Servs., *Vital Statistics of the United States: 1980, Vol. IIA, Mortality* (1985), table 3-3, http://www.cdc.gov/nchs/data/vsus/mort80_2a.pdf (accessed April 10, 2011).
117. Trent and Powell-Griner, supra note 110, at table 2 (reporting the findings).
118. Because the study focused on pregnancies having an outcome in 1980, all of the pregnancies in the study occurred after Roe v. Wade. *Roe* was applicable to adult women but not to females who were minors. 410 U.S. 113, 165 n.67. The constitutional right of minors to procure an abortion developed after *Roe* and is more circumscribed than the right of adults. Planned Parenthood Ass'n of Kansas City v. Ashcroft, 462 U.S. 476 (1983).
119. Another study that finds unmarried women are more likely to end pregnancies is Kanhaiya Lal Vaidya, Unintended Pregnancy and Abortion in the United States: Evidence from the National Survey of Family Growth, Cycle IV, 1988, (unpublished Ph.D. diss., Bowling Green State University, 1995), 79, 85 (on file with author). However, the study did not include a control for the current educational level, schooling status, or employment status of women. Ibid., 69–70, 94.
120. Among females who terminated pregnancies in 1987, the age-standardized use of abortion varied less with employment status than with school enrollment or marital status. Stanley K. Henshaw and Jane Silverman, "The Characteristics and Prior Contraceptive Use of U.S. Abortion Patients," *Family Planning Perspectives* 20 (1988): 158, 162.
121. Stanley K. Henshaw and Jennifer Van Vort, *Abortion Factbook: Readings, Trends, and State and Local Data to 1988* (New York: Alan Guttmacher Institute, 1992), 176–77.
122. E.g., Larry D. Barnett, "Law as Symbol: Appearances in the Regulation of Investment Advisers and Attorneys," *Cleveland State Law Review* 55

(2007): 289, 314–29 [hereinafter *Law as Symbol*]; Rich Geddes and Dean Lueck, "The Gains from Self-Ownership and the Expansion of Women's Rights," *American Economic Review* (2002): 1079, 1084–90. Pages 314–29 of *Law as Symbol* are reproduced infra in Part IV of Chapter 8. A state can be regarded as a system per se or as a subsystem in a larger system, namely, the United States as a society.

123. The U.S. Census Bureau gathered the data on marital status and school enrollment in the Current Population Survey. Although the years before rather than after 1967–1973 determine the possible role of marital status and school enrollment in the need for lawful abortion, the time-series I present extends to 1990.

124. The data on marital status start in 1949 for women twenty to twenty-four years old and in 1957 for women twenty-five to twenty-nine years old; the data are limited to the civilian population in some years but not others. Data on marital status for all years except 1990 are from U.S. Bureau of the Census, *Statistical Abstract of the United States* (71st ed. through the 111th ed.). Data for 1990 are from U.S. Bureau of the Census, *Marital Status and Living Arrangements: March 1990, Current Population Reports*, Series P-20, No. 450 (May 1991), at Table 1.

125. Henshaw and Van Vort, supra note 121.

126. I regard the change in abortion law during this period as a national movement, and hence use data on marital status and school enrollment for the United States as a whole, because a decision of the highest federal court ended the period and because in 1972, 39 percent of the population of the United States resided in the sixteen states whose law was changed from 1967 through 1972 to expand access to abortion. The percentage of the population was calculated from U.S. Bureau of the Census, *Statistical Abstract of the United States: 1974*, 95th ed. (1974), Table 11, http://www.census.gov/prod/www/abs/statab.html (accessed April 10, 2011).

127. The figure uses yearly rates of school enrollment for women in the civilian noninstitutionalized population. The rates are in U.S. Census Bureau, Table A-2: Percentage of the Population 3 Years Old and Over Enrolled in School, by Age, Sex, Race, and Hispanic Origin: October 1947 to 2008, http://www.census.gov/population/www/socdemo/school.html (accessed April 10, 2011) [hereinafter Table A-2].

128. Ibid. (providing school enrollment rates from 1947 to 1958 for the age category twenty to twenty-four). From 1959 onward, Table A-2 separates this age range into two categories, namely, age twenty to twenty-one and age twenty-two to twenty-four. Ibid. The three-year mean percentage of women enrolled in school at age twenty to twenty-four doubled from 3.7 percent in 1947–1949 to 7.4 percent in 1956–1958. Calculated from ibid.

129. After the U.S. Supreme Court decided Roe v. Wade, women eighteen to twenty-nine years old were the source of approximately seven out of ten lawful abortions performed in the United States, and the proportion varied little over time. Henshaw and Van Vort, supra note 121, at Table 1. Given the consistency of this proportion in the years that followed *Roe*, the same proportion is likely to have prevailed in the years that preceded the ruling. If women eighteen to twenty-nine years old provided most

of the pregnancies that were surgically terminated in the period prior to 1967–1973, their rising rate of school enrollment before abortion law underwent liberalization had the ability to spawn and magnify a need for the liberalization.

130. The data in the figure are from the Current Population Survey and are published by the U.S. Bureau of Labor Statistics. U.S. Bureau of Labor Statistics, Current Population Survey, http://data.bls.gov:8080/PDQ/outside.jsp?survey=ln (accessed June 4, 2010).

131. *Handbook of U.S. Labor Statistics*, ed. Eva E. Jacobs, 8th ed. (Lanham, MD: Bernan Press, 2005), 4, 5.

132. David W. Hosmer and Stanley Lemeshow, *Applied Logistic Regression*, 2nd ed. (New York: John Wiley, 2000), ix.

133. The data used for abortion law, the dependent variable, are from supra note 91.

Six independent variables—PCTCOLL2529, INCFEM2534, LABOR2024, LABOR2529, MARR2024, and MARR2529—use data from the 1960 census of population. The data for these variables were derived from the state reports for the 1960 census. U.S. Bureau of the Census, *U.S. Dep't of Commerce, Census of Population: 1960. Vol. 1, Characteristics of the Population: Part 1, United States Summary* (1963), http://www.census.gov/prod/www/abs/decennial/1960cenpopv1.htm (accessed April 10, 2011). The following lists, by independent variable, the table(s) used in each state report for the 1960 census:

PCTCOLL2529 - tables 37 and 103
INCFEM2534 - table 134
LABOR2024 - table 115
LABOR2529 - table 115
MARR2024 - table 105
MARR2529 - table 105

The ten-year percentage change in each of the above is measured by six other independent variables—CHNGCOLL2529, CHNGINC2534, CHNGLABOR2024, CHNGLABOR2529, CHNGMARR2024, and CHNGMARR2529. The percentage-change calculations employ data from the state reports for the 1950 census. U.S. Bureau of the Census, *U.S. Dep't of Commerce, Census of Population: 1950. Vol. II, Characteristics of the Population: Part I, United States Summary* (1952), http://www.census.gov/prod/www/abs/decennial/1950cenpopv2 .html (accessed April 10, 2011). The following lists, by independent variable, the table used in each state report for the 1950 census:

CHNGCOLL2529 - table 65
CHNGINC2534 - table 89
CHNGLABOR2024 - table 69
CHNGLABOR2529 - table 69
CHNGMARR2024 - table 56
CHNGMARR2529 - table 56

134. Alaska and Hawaii were omitted from the data in order to exclude the possibility that their law on abortion was influenced by factors different from and/or additional to the factors operating in the coterminous states. If such factors were present in Alaska and/or Hawaii, the inclusion of the

two states could have affected the findings from the data analysis. The possibility exists that Alaska and Hawaii were subject to different and/or additional factors because both jurisdictions (a) are geographically distant from the coterminous states and (b) were not states at the time of the 1950 census and had become states in just the year prior to the 1960 census. See supra note 33.

135. In the coterminous United States in 1960, just 1.5 percent of women twenty-five to twenty-nine years old were enrolled in college. The percentages were much higher at younger ages; for example, 15.4 percent of women twenty years old, 11.0 percent of women twenty-one years old, and 5.2 percent of women twenty-two years old were enrolled in college. U.S. Bureau of the Census, *U.S. Dep't of Commerce, U.S. Census of Population: 1960. Vol. I, Characteristics of the Population. Part 1, United States Summary* (1964), table 167, http://www.census.gov/prod/www/abs/decennial/1960cenpopv1.html (accessed April 10, 2011) [hereinafter United States Summary: 1960].

136. See generally Marshall H. Medoff, "Constituencies, Ideology, and the Demand for Abortion Legislation," *Public Choice* 60 (1989): 185, 186. The proportion of pregnancies aborted has been found to rise with the family income of women. Badagliacco, supra note 95, at 64, 165.

137. Women who bore children during 1960–1965 indicated that approximately one out of five of their births was unwanted and would not have been wanted under any circumstances. The pregnancies resulting in an additional two out of five births were regarded by the women involved as occurring earlier than they desired. Larry Bumpass and Charles F. Westoff, "The Perfect Contraceptive Population," *Science* 169 (1970): 1177, 1178–80. Because the preceding proportions refer to *births* and because an unknown number of pregnancies in this time period did not end in births due to miscarriage or induced abortion, the proportion of births that were unwanted was lower than the proportion of pregnancies that were unwanted.

138. Haggstrom, supra note 103, at 146; Felmlee, supra note 113, at 180–81.

139. Weeden, supra note 12, at 480 index A.

140. Because every source of income was included, not all of the income received by a woman was necessarily from paid employment. However, in the United States as a whole, nine out of ten females age fourteen and over reported earned income in 1959. *United States Summary: 1960*, supra note 135, at table 98. Therefore, the assumption seems warranted that compensation from employment supplied most of the income received in 1959 by a majority of women twenty-five to thirty-four years old.

141. In the United States as a whole, the percentage of women enrolled in school in 1960 was, for example, 19.3 percent among women who were twenty years old, 13.9 percent among women who were twenty-one years old, and 7.2 percent among women who were twenty-two years old. On the other hand, just 3.1 percent of all women twenty-five to twenty-nine years old, and 2.4 percent of all women thirty to thirty-four years old, were enrolled in school. Ibid., table 165.

142. In 1960, the number of live births per one hundred women in the United States was 19.7 among women who were twenty-five to twenty-nine years old and 11.3 among women who were thirty to thirty-four years old. Nat'l

Center for Health Statistics, *U.S. Dep't of Health, Education & Welfare, Vital Statistics of the United States: 1960. Vol. I, Natality, at Table 1-E* (1964), http://www.cdc.gov/nchs/products/pubs/pubd/vsus/1963/1963.htm (accessed April 10, 2011). Women who were twenty-five to thirty-four years old accounted for a large proportion (42 percent) of all live births in the United States in 1960. Calculated from ibid., table 2-16.

143. Henshaw and Van Vort, supra note 121, at Table 1.
144. All statistical analyses were performed with Stata Release 10.1. Regression results were generated by the LOGISTIC and LOGIT commands. Stata Corp., *Stata Base Reference Manual: Release*, vol. 2 (College Station, TX: Statacorp, 2007), 10, 144, 178.
145. *Law as Symbol*, supra note 122, at 321–22. Pages 321–22 of *Law as Symbol* are reproduced infra in Part IV-C of Chapter 8.
146. States are the cases in the instant regression analysis. As explained earlier, sixteen of the forty-eight states in the continental United States substantially revised their law during 1967–1972 to expand access to abortion. See supra note 91 and accompanying text. Since the remaining thirty-two states did not liberalize their law on abortion, the number of states characterized by the least-frequent outcome on the dependent variable was sixteen. Given the latter number, the regression equation in Table 6.2 has eleven too many independent variables for tests of statistical significance to be used. See Hosmer and Lemeshow, supra note 132, at 346–47.
147. The universe for the present study is all states in the coterminous United States. See supra note 134 and accompanying text.
148. See *Law as Symbol*, supra note 122, at 327–28 for an explanation of probability, odds, and odds ratio.
149. See J. Scott Long and Jeremy Freese, *Regression Models for Categorical Dependent Variables Using Stata*, 2nd ed. (2006), 178, 180.
150. Ibid., 151.
151. In a study, a component of a system should be set aside with caution. Because a state is an individual jurisdiction within a larger, more-encompassing jurisdiction (viz., the United States), it is part of a system. The elimination from a system of a member of the system may in effect dismantle the system.
152. Cook's Statistic is compatible with the conclusion that New York was an influential outlier. New York had a very large Cook's Statistic (namely, 11.88) that is well above the usual threshold for being an influential outlier (namely, 1.00). Hosmer and Lemeshow, supra note 132, at 180. However, that this threshold was exceeded by New York is not definitive proof New York was an influential outlier because other states also had a Cook's Statistic at or above 1.00.
153. Ellen Linna Jamison and Donald S. Akers, "An Analysis of the Differences Between Marriage Statistics from Registration and Those from Censuses and Surveys," *Demography* 5 (1968): 460, 461.
154. *United States Summary: 1960*, supra note 135, at liv.
155. Ibid., xiv. After the questionnaire was mailed, a Census Bureau enumerator conducted an interview, but the purpose of the interview was only to "correct omissions and obviously wrong entries" in the questionnaire as filled out. Ibid.

The yearly data on marital status that are the basis of Figure 6.3 are from the Current Population Survey. See supra notes 123 and 124. Since the Census Bureau assumed responsibility for the methodological aspects of the Survey in the early 1940s, each respondent in the Survey has remained in the sample for a period totaling several months, and at least the initial interview of respondents has been conducted in the home of the respondent by Census Bureau personnel unless the respondent has requested a telephone interview. U.S. Census Bureau, *U.S. Dep't of Commerce, Technical Paper 63RV, Current Population Survey: Design and Methodology 2-1, 2-2, 7-1, 7-3, 7-4* (2002), http://www.census.gov/apsd/techdoc/cps/cps-main.html (accessed April 10, 2011). As a source of data on marital status, consequently, the Current Population Survey is probably more accurate than the 1960 census.

156. Jamison and Akers, supra note 153, at 462.
157. Catherine Fitch et al., *The Rise of Cohabitation in the United States: New Historical Estimates* (paper prepared for presentation at annual meeting of the Population Association of America, Philadelphia, 2005), 19, http://www.hist.umn.edu/~ruggles/cohab-revised2.pdf (accessed April 10, 2011).
158. *United States Summary: 1960*, supra note 135, at liv; Jamison and Akers, supra note 153, at 462.
159. Calculated from *United States Summary: 1960*, supra note 135, at table 173.
160. See supra notes 93 and 94 and accompanying text.
161. William D. Berry, "Understanding Regression Assumptions," *Quantitative Applications in the Social Sciences* 92 (1993): 1, 24–27.
162. The correlation coefficients were computed with the CORRELATE command in Stata. Stata Corp., *Stata Base Reference Manual: Release 10*, vol. 1, (2007), 321.
163. James Jaccard and Robert Turrisi, "Interaction Effects in Multiple Regression," *Quantitative Applications in the Social Sciences* 72, 2nd ed. (2003): 1, 3–4.
164. Sara McLanahan and Lynne Casper, "Growing Diversity and Inequality in the American Family," in *State of the Union: America in the 1990s* , vol. 2, ed. Reynolds Farley (New York: The Russell Sage Foundation, 1995), 1, 32–35; Francine D. Blau et al., "Understanding Young Women's Marriage Decisions: The Role of Labor and Marriage Market Conditions," *Industrial and Labor Relations Review* 53 (2000): 624, 626, 645.
165. E.g., Francisco Parra-Luna, "An Axiological Systems Theory: Some Basic Hypotheses," *Systems Research & Behavioral Science* (2001): 479, 481.
166. While this assertion cannot be documented with quantitative data from a sample survey of the U.S. population, the observation that the traditional conception of marriage prevailed at least as late as 1960 has been made by others. McLanahan and Casper, supra note 164, at 35. No national survey of attitudes conducted in the 1950s, or even in the early 1960s, assessed the extent to which Americans endorsed the conventional ideal of marriage. From 1969 to 1988, national sample surveys often asked interviewees to indicate whether they approved or disapproved of paid employment on the part of a married woman whose husband was "capable of supporting

her" or "able to support her." During the years from 1946 through 1968, however, national surveys included no such measure. See Richard G. Niemi et al., *Trends in Public Opinion: A Compendium of Survey Data* (New York: Greenwood Press, 1989), 225.

167. See McLanahan and Casper, supra note 164, at 35; accord, Elizabeth S. Scott, "The Legal Construction of Norms: Social Norms and the Legal Regulation of Marriage," *Virginia Law Review* 86 (2000): 1901, 1935–36.
168. *United States Summary: 1960*, supra note 135, at table 196.
169. In a regression analysis that excluded New York, the odds ratio was 1.1237 for the variable testing for interaction between labor force participation and marriage prevalence among women who were twenty to twenty-five years of age. However, the presence of the variable testing for interaction generated very large odds ratios for certain of the independent variables, and the accuracy of the odds ratio estimated for the interaction-testing variable is thus suspect.
170. I thus do not consider New York to be an influential outlier.
171. See the text accompanying supra note 119.
172. The range of PCTCOLL2529 was 6.3 percent to 11.2 percent. The total impact of PCTCOLL2529 may not be correctly estimated by multiplying the odds ratio for PCTCOLL2529 and the number of percentage points in this range (11.2 – 6.3 = 4.9). Long and Freese, supra note 149, at 216.
173. See supra note 120 and accompanying text.
174. The data in column 2 are from U.S. Census Bureau, U.S. Dep't of Commerce, *A Half-Century of Learning: Historical Statistics on Educational Attainment in the United States, 1940 to 2000* (2006), Table 2, http://www.census.gov/population/www/socdemo/education/phct41.html (accessed June 5, 2010).
175. Most women who hold a bachelor's degree at age twenty-five to twenty-nine evidently entered college when they were eighteen or nineteen years old. See, e.g., *United States Summary: 1960*, supra note 135, at table 168; U.S. Bureau of the Census, U.S. Dep't of Commerce, *Census of Population: 1970. Vol. I, Characteristics of the Population. Part 1, United States Summary – Section 2* (1973), table 197, http://www.census.gov/prod/www/abs/decennial/1970cenpopv1.htm (accessed April 10, 2011). Therefore, an increase in the percentage of women with a bachelor's degree at age twenty-five to twenty-nine is an indicator of change in the female sex role that took place as much as a decade prior to the increase.
176. Karen Smith Conway and Michael R. Butler, "State Abortion Legislation as a Public Good — Before and After Roe v. Wade," *Economic Inquiry* 30 (1992): 609.

    In several social science studies that considered state differences on matters pertinent to law on abortion, the dependent variable was not differences in current law on abortion. Elizabeth Adell Cook et al., "State Political Cultures and Public Opinion about Abortion," *Political Research Quarterly* 46 (1993): 771, 772; Leo H. Kahane, "Political, Ideological and Economic Determinants of Abortion Position: An Empirical Analysis of State Legislatures and Governors," *American Journal of Economics & Sociology* 53 (1994): 347, 348–50; Medoff, supra note 136.

177. Conway and Butler, supra note 176, at 615, 618. The refined models are the models that Conway and Butler label the "'Best' Model" and the "Private Demand" model. Education, although included in the model that Conway and Butler label the "Broadest model," was not in the refined models, while the labor force participation rate and income of women eighteen to forty-four years old were in all of these models. Ibid., 618.
178. See supra notes 146 and 147 and accompanying text.
179. Conway and Butler, supra note 176, at 618.
180. Ibid., 619 (notes to table III).
181. Ibid., 618 (reporting the regression coefficients).
182. See the text accompanying Figure 6.3.
183. See supra notes 93 and 94 and accompanying text.
184. Ibid.
185. Conway and Butler, supra note 176, at 616, 621–22. Another study classified states into three levels of restrictiveness in terms of their law on access to abortion before Roe v. Wade. Sharon Kay Parsons, Abortion Policy in the Fifty States: A Comparative Analysis (unpublished Ph.D. diss., Florida Atlantic University, 1991), 96, 166–67 (on file with Widener University School of Law Delaware Campus Library). However, the study by Parsons is not useful for two reasons. First, the Parsons study employed factor analysis to create clusters of independent variables, and it assessed the relationship of just the clusters to the restrictiveness of state abortion law prior to *Roe*. Ibid., 114–19. Because a cluster is global in nature, reliance on clusters rather than on the independent variables that form the clusters precludes a direct comparison of the findings of the Parsons study with the findings of my study. The relationship of a cluster of independent variables to a dependent variable, moreover, supplies information that is much less precise than the relationship to the dependent variable of each of the independent variables comprising the cluster. The second reason the Parsons study is not helpful is that the study employed least-squares regression, but for analyzing relationships to a dependent variable that is measured in categories, least-squares regression is dubious and, accordingly, has been replaced by logistic regression. The results reported in the Conway–Butler study, which was carried out at almost the same time as the Parsons study, are based on logistic regression, and least-squares regression was not employed. Conway and Butler, supra note 176, at 615.
186. Conway and Butler, supra note 176, at 621–22.

    To classify states in terms of the restrictiveness of their law on abortion prior to *Roe*, Professors Conway and Butler relied on information in a book authored by a social scientist. Ibid., 613 n.6. The book explicitly discloses that its information on abortion law was current as of January 1971. Nanette J. Davis, *From Crime to Choice: The Transformation of Abortion in America* (Westport, CT: Greenwood Press, 1985), 254–57. Because the book was published fourteen years after January 1971, Professors Conway and Butler may have assumed that, from January 1971 until the Court announced *Roe* in January 1973, no other jurisdiction liberalized its law on abortion. However, such an assumption is mistaken as to Florida. See infra note 187 and accompanying text.

187. Act of April 12, 1972, ch. 72-196, 1972 Fla. Laws 608; Merz et al., supra note 91, at 19–20.
188. Act of September 12, 1951, no. 956, 1951 Ala. Laws 1630 (amending *Ala. Code tit.* 14, § 9 (1940)).
189. See supra note 91.
190. Conway and Butler, supra note 176, at 621–22.
191. See supra note 134.
192. Conway and Butler, supra note 176, at 623 n.17.
193. Two further differences between the studies should be mentioned. First, Professors Conway and Butler measured their independent variables as of 1970. Ibid., 616. However, 1970 was either concurrent with or after the point at which action had been taken by most of the jurisdictions that eased restrictions on abortion. See supra note 91. In my study, on the other hand, the data on the independent variables were for 1959 (in the case of income) or 1960 or for change in these variables over the prior ten years. Accordingly, the independent variables in my study involve time points that *precede* the alterations in state law on abortion. Because causation involves temporal sequences, potential causes of a phenomenon should be measured at a time that is before the occurrence of the phenomenon.

    Second, Professors Conway and Butler measured their independent variables with data for women eighteen to forty-four years old. Conway and Butler, supra note 176, at 616–17. On the other hand, I used data for women in the age range twenty to twenty-nine to measure all of the independent variables except income, for which the data were for women twenty-five to thirty-four years old. See supra Table 6.1. In the decade-and-a-half from 1973 to 1988 (and presumably in the years before 1973), women twenty to twenty-nine years old were the source of approximately half of all abortions, while women thirty years of age and older accounted for fewer than one out of five abortions. Henshaw and Van Vort, supra note 121, at 172–73. Accordingly, the characteristics of females under thirty years old are probably the chief determinants of the existence and degree of pressure on a social system to allow ready access to abortion.
194. Bruce H. Mayhew, "Structuralism versus Individualism: Part 1, Shadowboxing in the Dark," *Social Forces* 59 (1980): 335, 345.
195. Gerald Holton and Duane H. D. Roller, *Foundations of Modern Physical Science* (Reading, MA: Addison-Wesley, 1958), 269–73.
196. Jonathan H. Turner, *The Structure of Sociological Theory*. 7th ed. (Belmont, CA: Wadsworth Thomson, 2003), 34, 37 n.31 ; Scott, supra note 4, at 139.
197. Mark Abrahamson, *Functionalism* (Englewood Cliffs, NJ: Prentice-Hall, 1978), 5.
198. In the instant book, an institution refers to a set of statuses and roles (a) that a society defines and endorses and (b) that involve interpersonal relationships through which a socially approved type of activity occurs in the society. Howard B. Kaplan, "The Concept of Institution: A Review, Evaluation, and Suggested Research Procedure, *Social Forces* 39 (1960): 176, 179.

199. Thomas R. Marshall, *Public Opinion and the Supreme Court* (Boston, MA: Unwin Hyman, 1989), 192–93; Christopher Z. Mooney and Mei-Hsien Lee, "The Influence of Values on Consensus and Contentious Morality Policy: U.S. Death Penalty Reform, 1956–82," *Journal of Politics* (2000), 223, 234; Matthew E. Wetstein and Robert B. Albritton, "Effects of Public Opinion on Abortion Policies and Use in the American States," *Publius* 25 (1995): 91, 102. Government policy generally manifests the attitudes of the public when crystallized attitudes exist. Paul Burstein, "Bringing the Public Back In: Should Sociologists Consider the Impact of Public Opinion on Public Policy?," *Social Forces* 77 (1998): 27, 41.
200. My review of these criticisms is based on Abrahamson, supra note 197, at 37–49; John Rex, *Key Problems of Sociological Theory* (London: Routledge & Kegan Paul, 1961), 60–77; Turner, supra note 196, at 23–37; Peter A. Munch, "The Concept of "Function" and Functional Analysis in Sociology," *Philosophy of Social Science* 6 (1976): 193; Jonathan H. Turner and Alexandra R. Maryanski, "Is 'Neofunctionalism' Really Functional?," *Sociological Theory* 6 (1988): 110, 115–17.
201. Turner and Maryanski, supra note 200, at 117.
202. Cf. ibid., 116.
203. Rex, supra note 200, at 76.
204. Holton and Roller, supra note 195, at 218–22.
205. Nock, supra note 94, at 388–92.
206. *Legal Construct, Social Concept*, supra note 11, at 22–24.
207. Nass, supra note 58, at 206.
208. Professional, technical, and kindred workers comprised 4.3 percent of the economically active population in 1900, 8.6 percent in 1950, and 13.7 percent in 1970. Computed from *Historical Statistics*, supra note 46, at 140 (Series D 233-682).
209. Pamela Barnhouse Walters, "Occupational and Labor Market Effects on Secondary and Postsecondary Educational Expansion in the United States: 1922 to 1979," *American Sociological Review* 49 (1984): 659, 668.
210. James P. Smith and Michael P. Ward, Rand Corp., *Women's Wages and Work in the Twentieth Century* (Santa Monica, CA: The RAND Corporation, 1984), 40, http://www.rand.org/content/dam/rand/pubs/reports/2007/R3119.pdf (accessed April 22, 2011).
211. See supra notes 56–64 and accompanying text; *Law as Symbol*, supra note 122, at 336–37. Pages 336–37 of *Law as Symbol* are reproduced infra in Part V of Chapter 8.
212. See supra notes 70–76 and accompanying text.
213. Frank Hobbs and Nicole Stoops, *U.S. Census Bureau, U.S. Dep't of Commerce, Demographic Trends in the 20th Century: Census 2000 Special Reports, at A-5* (2002). A geographic area that is labeled "metropolitan" contains "a large population nucleus, together with adjacent communities having a high degree of social and economic integration with that nucleus." Ibid., B-4.
214. Laura M. Moore and Seth Ovadia, "Accounting for Spatial Variation in Tolerance: The Effects of Education and Religion," *Social Forces* 84 (2006): 2205, 2214.

215. Thomas C. Wilson, "Urbanism, Migration, and Tolerance: A Reassessment," *American Sociological Review* 56 (1991): 117, 119–21.
216. Thomas C. Wilson, "Urbanism and Nontraditional Opinion: Another Look at the Data," *Social Science Quarterly* 73 (1992): 610, 612, at table 1.
217. While the growing demand for education among young women was critical to easing restrictions placed on abortion by law, the change in abortion policy did not appreciably further the schooling of these women: the liberalization of abortion law between 1967 and 1973 did not raise the educational level of white women, and it added just a quarter-year to the average educational achievement of black women. Maya H. Klein, *The Effects of Abortion Legislation on Women's Educational Attainment in the United States* (unpublished Ph.D. diss., University of California, Berkeley, 1997), 83–84, 106, 109, 113–14 (on file with Widener University School of Law Delaware Campus library). This is further evidence that, prior to 1967, women who wished to terminate pregnancies were in general doing so, even if the terminations violated existing law, and that the chief benefit to society from the liberalization of law on abortion was symbolic. *Law as Symbol*, supra note 122, at 299–301. Pages 299–301 of *Law as Symbol* are reproduced infra in Part II of Chapter 8.
218. The age of majority that is given applies both to males and to females unless otherwise indicated.

7

Jurisdiction Properties and Law on Same-Sex Relationships in Europe*

In a macrosociological framework, law is assumed to be inextricably tied to the society in which it is found. A proposition central to such a framework is that (1) differences in social, economic, and demographic conditions explain differences in law between countries and (2) changes in social, economic, and demographic conditions explain changes in law within countries. To test the foregoing proposition, societal antecedents of law authorizing same-sex non-marital partnerships and same-sex marriage were ascertained using pooled time-series data on country-level characteristics of fourteen European Union (EU) nations. The odds that such law had been adopted by a country were found to increase with the level of wealth and education of the population of the country and with the fraction of the population of the country residing in urbanized areas having a large number of inhabitants. Implications of the findings for understanding law as a societal institution are discussed, and suggestions for future research are made.

I. The Societal Context

One of the subjects that sociological theory must address is the variability of institutions between nation-states.[1] Unfortunately, however, the factors responsible for this variability are difficult to investigate. The difficulty exists for two reasons. First, nation-states are not numerous and therefore constitute a relatively small universe for study. Second, the data needed to measure the hypothesized causes of the variability of the institutions of nation-states are generally limited in amount and often problematic in quality.[2] Nonetheless, because the countries of the world are heterogeneous and few of them are static, students of social systems would do well to devote more of their efforts to identifying the reasons that an institution differs between nations at any specific time and changes within a nation over time. If such differences and changes can be explained, they can be anticipated, and policy will be improved by an ability to make predictions regarding institutions with an accuracy rate that exceeds chance. The findings of the study reported infra in Part III may thus have important practical ramifications.

In the text to follow, we focus on two important institutions of societies—marriage and law—and attempt to explain cross-spatial and cross-temporal variation that exists in these institutions. In particular, we consider the factors that may account for the doctrine of law that a country adopts on same-sex non-marital partnerships and same-sex marriage, and we do so by considering differences between, and change within, countries in this doctrine.

Quantitatively, change must be measured by reference to a baseline, and for the present discussion, the most useful baseline is no change.[3] What conditions are likely to be responsible for a lack of change in a society and its institutions? Three plausible theoretical propositions can be suggested[4]:

1. A society remains unchanged if it does not interact with another society whose social values and institutions differ.
2. A society remains unchanged if its supply of knowledge—i.e., the information at its disposal to solve problems—is constant.
3. A society remains unchanged if it is not densely populated.[5]

If the above propositions are correct, few nation-states in the world today can be expected to experience no significant social change over time. Moreover, although each proposition assumes that all else is equal, the three sources of change that the propositions identify are likely to act in conjunction with one another more often than they act independently. In combination, the effects of the sources are probably multiplicative rather than additive.

The discussion that follows will focus on propositions 2 and 3, not proposition 1. However, it should be kept in mind that in part because of expanding inter-nation ties (proposition 1), a country is unlikely to avoid increases in its store of knowledge (proposition 2), or to maintain a low population density (proposition 3).[6] Currently, ties between countries are being promoted most notably by the Internet, but the rate of growth of these ties was probably rising throughout the twentieth century.[7]

A. Supply of Knowledge

Proposition 2 contends that a society is shaped by inter alia the nature and quantity of the knowledge that it employs.[8] If the proposition is correct, the rapidity and content of change in a society are direct consequences of the degree to which the society acquires and applies new knowledge. The acquisition of new knowledge by a society, of course, can derive from knowledge generated within the society and/or from knowledge that is imported from outside the society. Among the countries of the world, both avenues have been used,[9] and given the advances in technology that have raised the speed and reduced the cost of communication in recent decades, both are likely to contribute substantially to the knowledge used by a society in the future. Indeed, the tempo of knowledge accumulation may increase geometrically rather than arithmetically through a self-reinforcing cycle in which improvements in communication allow knowledge to be disseminated more quickly and less expensively, facilitating additions to knowledge that make communication even speedier and cheaper.

The growth of knowledge has been posited as a source of broad consequences for the institutions of a society, including the institution of law.[10] Although all of these consequences may not be easily traceable to the expansion of knowledge, each can be plausibly attributed at least partly to it. The source of the consequences is most readily identified when their concrete manifestations are considered, and these consequences are likely to include many of the prominent issues that have been confronted during the last half of the twentieth century by the institutions of Western countries. One such issue is same-sex relationships that involve sexual activity. Although this type of relationship is inconsistent with the traditional definition of the institution of marriage in societies generally,[11] societies have discarded and replaced customary social patterns in the past. Slavery and its abolition are illustrative.[12] Accordingly, the substitution of new patterns for established patterns can be expected to happen in the future, and probably not infrequently. As such substitutions occur, permanent same-sex relationships involving sexual activity may come to be recognized and accommodated in the law of a society even though at an earlier point in time such relationships conflicted with deeply entrenched, prevalent social values.[13]

B. Social Classifications and the Concept of Discrimination

Because an expanded supply of knowledge is likely to have been (and is likely to continue to be) a major factor in the emergence of new social arrangements, the enlargement of the store of knowledge in Western countries may be responsible for changing law and policy on same-sex relationships. Why would the growth of knowledge have this effect? Increases in knowledge are probably a key factor intensifying individualism and rationality.[14] Individualism—the social philosophy that accords priority to the interests, preferences, and wishes of individuals over those of groups—has contributed to the acceptance by public policy and law of same-sex sexual activity,[15] and rationality has probably been influential, too. Individualism is antithetical to classifications in a society, and rationality is hostile to stereotypes associated with classifications.[16] Therefore, as individualism and rationality become more prevalent and more intense, an inhospitable environment is created for social classifications and stereotypes. This environment leads to law requiring that evaluations of human beings be based on the type and degree of skill possessed by the human beings who are evaluated, not on predilections of these human beings that pose no threat to others.[17] Recognition by law of same-sex relationships, therefore, becomes more likely with increases in the quantity and quality of knowledge.

Since the middle of the twentieth century, a salient development in the law of Europe,[18] Canada, and the United States[19] has been the application of the word "discrimination" to social behaviors and arrangements that have come to be regarded as unacceptable. Conceptually, discrimination is a problem for a society and banned by its law when a classification that the society deems unnecessary, and an associated stereotype that the society deems unwarranted, are employed in social life. Of course, a classification and the stereotype linked to it are not inherently problematic for a society. Rather, a classification and stereotype are a problem only when certain conditions prompt a society to treat them as a problem,[20] and as history demonstrates, these conditions—social, demographic, and economic—are not constant over time. The role of societal conditions in determining whether a particular classification and stereotype are a problem, moreover, is complicated by the context-specific impact of the conditions. A classification and stereotype will not be a problem in all contexts; instead, the classification and stereotype may be deemed problematic in some contexts and continue to be accepted in others.

The context-specific nature of social problems is illustrated by the evolution and treatment of sex roles in the United States.[21] Societal distinctions made between males and females, although favored during much of U.S. history, have come to be regarded by social values and law as unacceptable in certain contexts such as education and employment. In these contexts, distinctions between males and females are labeled discrimination, but in other contexts, gender-based distinctions continue to receive widespread approval. Thus, the first-names that parents choose for their newborn female children differ from the first-names they choose for their newborn male children,[22] and government will record and require the use of these names even though the names classify on the basis of sex.[23]

Discrimination, then, is a label that possesses a societal context and can be understood only in that context. At the present point in history, classifications and stereotypes are labeled discrimination and banned by law when they conflict with the premise that people are individuals and when they are regarded as not rational.[24] The importance of individualism and rationality at the present time is evident in the following passage from an opinion written in 1991 by an appellate court in the United States:

> Discrimination stems from a reliance on immaterial outward appearances that stereotype an individual with imagined, usually undesirable, characteristics thought to be common to members of the group that shares these superficial traits. It results in a stubborn refusal to judge a person on his merits as a human being. Our various statutes against discrimination express the policy that this refusal to judge people who belong to various, particularly disadvantaged, groups is too costly to be tolerated in a society committed to equal individual liberty and opportunity.[25]

Individuality and reason, in short, are incompatible with discrimination, and because individuality and reason are central features of a society that has an appreciable store of knowledge, they shape the law of the society. For the institution of law to facilitate the operation of society, as it will in the long run, the concepts and doctrines of law must address impediments to the effective functioning of the social system. It is not coincidence, therefore, that the scope of law has included the topic of marriage and that the doctrines of law on marriage have evolved as the nature of marital relationships has changed.[26]

C. Population Density

Population density has been theorized as a variable that affects the degree of change occurring in a society. Specifically, a geographic area in which population density is high is expected to have a greater probability of changing, and of changing more, than an area in which population density is low. This expectation is grounded on three general propositions that have been propounded in sociology. First, the number of individuals in a geographic area who are inclined to engage in a particular activity rises with population concentration. Second, increases in population density facilitate encounters between individuals who have the same goal and simplify the formation of a group around the goal, thereby bolstering support for the goal and expanding acceptance of it.[27] Third, geographic areas characterized by high population density contain more numerous and diverse stimuli than areas characterized by low population density, and as a result, the inhabitants of the former develop a higher level of rationality than the inhabitants of the latter.[28] It is not coincidence, then, that an individual who resides in a metropolitan setting "reacts with his head instead of his heart"[29] and that, given the collective impact of the sociological processes suggested by the foregoing propositions, unconventional activity occurs more often, and is more likely to become acceptable, in an area of high population density. Simply put, tradition and urban life tend to be incompatible because of the group-level effects that a large number of people ineluctably have.

The utility of the just-described theory of urban life has yet to be determined, because the quantitative research necessary to assess it fully has not been conducted.[30] In this regard, a recent study merits discussion. The study found that, in the United States, unorthodox beliefs and behavior are more commonly tolerated in metropolitan areas than in nonmetropolitan areas because, and only because, college graduates are a higher percentage of the population of metropolitan areas.[31] Population density itself did not matter. The study, however, does not disprove the theory of urbanism because the data analyzed in the study suffered from several key limitations.

The first limitation of the data was in the definition of a "metropolitan area." An area is classified as "metropolitan" on the basis of the number of its inhabitants, i.e., the number of its residents,[32] and the criteria for a metropolitan area are established by the U.S. Census Bureau. As the concept was defined during the years covered by the study, a metropolitan area could have had as few as seventy-five thousand residents in New England and as few as one hundred thousand residents in other regions.[33] The effect of urbanism, however, may not be detectible with the relatively small population size that may be present in metropolitan areas, i.e., the effect may not occur until the number of residents is appreciably larger than one hundred thousand. Second, the impact of population density may be affected as much or more by population density in the geographic location where persons are employed than by population density in the location where they reside, but the study considered only the latter. Third, tolerance of unorthodox beliefs and behavior may not increase linearly with population density.[34] Instead, tolerance may change little or not at all until thresholds of population density are reached, and then it may change markedly.[35] The thresholds may be numerous, moreover, and none of them may be at the demographic point that differentiates metropolitan areas from nonmetropolitan areas.[36]

For these reasons, the study does not refute the theory of urbanism—either its general proposition that urban living raises tolerance or the paths it hypothesizes for the transmission of the impact of urban living on tolerance. The theory, therefore, cannot be disregarded in research to which the theory may be pertinent.

D. The Institution of Marriage

A consideration of sociological factors that determine the acceptability by a society and its law of a specific form of marriage should not distract attention from another question regarding marriage. The question, simply expressed, is why marriage is and has been common in social life, i.e., why marriage is an institution of society. Even though a large percentage of marriages terminate in divorce,[37] most persons beyond the initial years of adulthood are married. European countries are illustrative. In 2005, the percentage of all adults 30–59 years old who were currently married was 62 percent in France, 64 percent in Germany, and 75 percent in Italy.[38] Similar percentages are found in the United States, where adults who were currently married and living with their spouse in 2008 comprised between 57 percent and 68 percent of all adults at ages 30–34 to 65–74.[39]

The societal properties that are responsible for the form(s) of marriage accepted by a society and its law at a particular time, and that are responsible for changing the accepted form(s) of marriage,[40] probably cannot be completely separated from the reasons that marriage is an institution. The attenuation or disappearance of any of the reasons that marriage is ingrained in a society can be expected to promote the emergence of new types of relationships (marital and/or non-marital) that the society will be pressured to recognize in its law. The continuation or dissipation of these reasons is likely to depend, in turn, on the properties of the society.

An explanation of the institutional nature of marriage begins with the assumption that a society is a system, i.e., an organized set of components. If the assumption is correct, marriage did not become and has not remained a societal institution as the result of chance. Rather, marriage is an institution because it has played an important role in the larger social system. Not coincidentally, the Congress of the United States has described marriage as "an essential institution of a successful society."[41] Although the congressional statement does not explain *why* marriage is essential to a society, the explanation may be found by treating marriage as social capital.[42] From the perspective of social capital, the institution of marriage is important to a society because marriage acts as a *resource*. Marriage, that is, supplies benefits to a society.

What exactly are the benefits that society derives from marriage? Three major benefits of marriage will be enumerated below.[43] The listed benefits, it will be noted, partly overlap and can reinforce each other.

One contribution of marriage to a society is in perpetuating the society. More exactly, marriage is the social arrangement that a society employs, or emphasizes as an ideal, for rearing children. A child who is being raised by a married couple may be the genetic product of one or both of the current members of the marriage; alternatively, the child may be the genetic product of other individuals and have been reared (as the result of, for example, adoption) by one or both of the current members of the marriage. Children who grow up with their genetic parents, however, are more likely to enjoy a variety of advantages (e.g., in physical and mental health) than children who spend their years as minors in other settings.[44] Thus, to the extent that intact marriages are increased by the ideal that Western countries have established for marriage, the social systems in these countries possess an especially effective mechanism promoting their continuation. During recent decades, however, the importance of this benefit in European nations and in the United States has evidently been eroded by increases in the proportion of married women who bear no children.[45]

Childrearing, however, is not the sole societal benefit of marriage. Marriage acts as a resource of society in a second way—it contributes to the welfare of the population of the society. For example, marriage improves the psychological health of the married couple (and of their children) if the marriage remains unbroken.[46] Additionally, marriage is associated with financial well-being; i.e., income and wealth are higher among individuals who are married than among individuals who are not.[47] In turn, the enhanced financial assets of married couples aid the children who they rear. Indeed, the greater financial assets of a married couple seem to explain many of the advantages possessed by the children raised by the couple.[48]

Lastly, marriage serves as a resource for society in at least one additional way—by helping to strengthen communities. Because of the social roles attached to marriage,[49] life styles are substantially altered by marriage, and in spite of sex differences in marital roles, marriage embeds individuals in more social networks. To be precise, marriage leads men (but not women) to join voluntary associations, and it reduces withdrawals by both men and women from voluntary associations.[50] The positive effect of marriage on membership in voluntary associations has consequences that bolster communities. Greater participation in voluntary associations in the United States improves the performance of state governments,[51] and in both the United States and Europe, greater participation in voluntary associations increases the trust that individuals have in other people.[52] Trust is an especially important benefit of involvement in voluntary associations, because trust has a pervasive impact on societal quality. Thus, a rise in the level of trust in a society promotes the quality of government[53] and fosters not only adequate physical infrastructure in a country but adequate educational facilities as well.[54] An increase in trust in a country also lowers the overall homicide rate.[55]

A society is thus broadly, albeit indirectly, benefited by the institution of marriage, and even if the benefits are not fully recognized by the members of the society, the benefits will cause a society to resist change in the form(s) of marriage that it accepts and that its law thus authorizes. More generally, a society will not alter its law for any new social arrangement that it considers a threat to key societal values. To the extent a change in law is incompatible with social values, the change will destabilize the society, and if the disruption is severe, the change eventually will be reversed. In the United States, for example, the acceptance of liquor manufacture, transportation, and sale was replaced in the early part of the twentieth century by a nationwide ban on these activities. However, the ban seems to have materially increased crime and just temporarily reduced liquor consumption, and it was rescinded thirteen years later.[56]

Given the uncertainties that accompany any major change in an important aspect of social life, there should be no surprise that a society resists altering its law in order to accommodate a new and unconventional social arrangement. Same-sex non-marital partnerships and same-sex marriage are such arrangements, of course. However, some countries in Europe have concluded that same-sex non-marital partnerships and same-sex marriage are socially beneficial and have adopted law allowing these relationships.[57] We now review this law.

II. Law in Europe on Same-Sex Non-Marital Partnerships and Same-Sex Marriage

The present study is confined to fourteen countries that were members of the European Union ("EU")[58] from 1995 through 2003. Twelve countries were members of the EU when it was formally established in 1993,[59] and three more countries became members in 1995.[60] All of the fifteen countries that comprised the EU from 1995 through 2003 were located in the geographic regions generally labeled Northern Europe, Southern Europe, and Western Europe.[61] Of the fifteen countries, however, one—Germany—was omitted from the study because until 1990 it was divided between separate sovereign nation-states (West Germany and East Germany)[62] each of which had its own social and economic institutions.[63] For historical reasons, then, Germany and data on it are not comparable before and after 1990.

The next expansion of the European Union occurred in May 2004, when ten countries were added as EU members.[64] The ten countries appreciably increased the social, cultural, and economic heterogeneity of the EU,[65] however, and as a result, the universe of the study reported in Part III infra was limited to the countries (other than Germany) that comprised the EU from 1995 through 2005. In alphabetical order, the countries in the study were Austria, Belgium, Denmark, Finland, France, Greece, Ireland, Italy, Luxembourg, The Netherlands, Portugal, Spain, Sweden, and the United Kingdom. The preceding set of fourteen countries avoids the greater heterogeneity of the EU stemming from the countries added in 2004, and because the fourteen countries belong to a recognized geographic region, they are a meaningful universe.

Of the fourteen countries included in the study, ten adopted statutes that explicitly recognized same-sex non-marital partnerships or same-sex marriage; all did so during the time period covered. The year 1989 starts the time period because that is the first year in which any of the fourteen countries adopted such law;[66] the year 2005 ends the time period because none of the fourteen countries adopted such law during 2006, 2007, or 2008.[67]

The ten countries that have law conferring a formal status on same-sex non-marital partnerships or same-sex marriage are listed below. Two text boxes are used: Box 1 identifies the countries with legislation approving same-sex non-marital partnerships; Box 2 identifies the countries with legislation approving same-sex marriage.[68] The year of adoption of the legislation in each country is shown in parentheses immediately after the name of the country. Two countries—The Netherlands and Sweden—are in both boxes because after adopting law that authorized same-sex non-marital partnerships, they approved legislation that authorized same-sex marriage.

Box 1: Countries Legalizing Same-Sex Non-marital Partnerships

Denmark (1989)
Finland (2001)
France (1999)
Luxembourg (2004)
The Netherlands (1998)
Portugal (2001)
Sweden (1994)
United Kingdom (2004)

Box 2: Countries Legalizing Same-Sex Marriage

Belgium (2003)
The Netherlands (2001)
Spain (2005)
Sweden (2009)

III. Antecedents of Law on Same-Sex Non-Marital Partnerships and Same-Sex Marriage

The research to be reported in Part III tests the assumption that law on same-sex non-marital partnerships and same-sex marriage does not develop by chance. Instead, differences between countries and change within countries in social, demographic, and/or economic conditions are believed to account for variation in such law. As a result, the dependent and independent variables in the present research are measured at the country level and thus are aspects of societies, not of individuals.

A. Independent Variables

To identify variables that potentially explain between-country differences and within-country change in the law of EU countries on same-sex non-marital partnerships and same-sex marriage, we start by examining quantitative studies that focused on the relationship between the characteristics of jurisdictions and the likelihood of adoption by the jurisdictions of law pertinent to interpersonal sexual activity. The law that was the subject of these studies either expressed a preference for opposite-sex sexual activity over same-sex sexual activity or explicitly repudiated policies grounded on such a preference. In the text that follows, we review six such studies. Our review begins with the only one of the six (viz., "the Soule study") that involved the topic of marriage.[69]

As of 2006, ninety percent of the states in the United States explicitly prohibited same-sex marriage through their state constitution and/or through a state statute,[70] a situation that is in line with the antipathy that is prevalent among Americans toward the legalization of same-sex marriage.[71] Using the thirty-five states that had adopted such a prohibition by 2000, the Soule study regressed whether a state did so at a particular time between 1973 and 2000 on a series of state-level independent variables.[72] Most of the independent variables were political in nature, however, because the study was concerned with the role of political elites, processes, and protesters in altering law.[73] Nonetheless, three sociological–demographic characteristics of states were included as independent variables—viz., the geographic region in which each state was located (South versus non-South); the percentage of the inhabitants of each state that resided in an urban area; and the percentage of the inhabitants of each state that had earned a college degree.[74]

None of the three sociological–demographic variables in the Soule study was found to have a statistically significant relationship to the dependent variable, i.e., to whether a state adopted an explicit ban on same-sex marriage.[75] Statistically significant relationships to the dependent variable existed for independent variables measuring the presence in states of political-interest organizations, but if law is a macrosociological phenomenon, these relationships are not surprising. In a macrosociological framework, political-interest organizations are expected to be precursors of law because the properties of society are believed to create societal needs that give rise to such organizations that, in turn, shape law. Political-interest organizations thus transmit the needs of society to lawmaking bodies. If this line of reasoning is correct, political-interest organizations offer just a superficial explanation of the content of law at a particular point in history and of the shifts that occur over time in the concepts and doctrines of law. Instead, the roots of law lie elsewhere.

The seeming lack of influence of the sociological–demographic variables in the Soule study merits discussion. In this regard, two features of the study are notable. The first concerns the reliance by the study on tests of statistical significance to decide whether a relationship existed between an independent variable and the dependent variable. The study did not obtain its data using a sample drawn from a universe but, rather, included all members of the universe, viz., all states in the United States during the time period covered by the study. Because sampling was not employed, tests of statistical significance were unnecessary.[76] Moreover, even when tests of statistical significance are applied to data from a sample, it should be kept in mind that significance levels are arbitrary criteria for reaching decisions on null hypotheses and that unthinking reliance on a significance level can cause relationships that exist and that are important to be overlooked.[77]

If the statistical significance of the regression coefficients in the Soule study is disregarded, two of the sociological–demographic variables in the study—education and geographic region—have utility as predictors of the odds that a state will formally ban same-sex marriage. Specifically, the percentage of state inhabitants who held a college degree was inversely related to the odds of a ban, i.e., lower educational attainment was associated with a greater likelihood that same-sex marriage would be formally proscribed. In addition, states located in the South were more likely to prohibit same-sex marriage than states located in other regions.[78]

The second feature of the Soule study that warrants mention is its measurement of the other sociological–demographic variable it included—the degree to which state populations were urbanized. For this variable, the Soule study evidently used U.S. Census Bureau data on "urban" areas,[79] but at least since 1970—the earliest year for which the study included data on the variable[80]—an area could be classified as urban with as few as 2,500 inhabitants.[81] However, the theory of urbanism discussed supra in Part I-C contemplates that population density will generate the effects only when the number of people in an area far exceeds 2,500. The theory, therefore, was not tested by the Soule study.

The second study to be reviewed was concerned with country-level characteristics that explain differences between countries in law on consensual same-sex sexual activity ("the Frank–McEneaney study").[82] The study is pertinent here because whether law accepts such activity is likely to be correlated (albeit imperfectly) with whether law recognizes same-sex non-marital partnerships and same-sex marriage; i.e., all else being equal, countries that change their law to allow consensual same-sex sexual activity will be more inclined to alter their law to authorize same-sex non-marital partnerships and same-sex marriage.[83] In accounting for the degree to which the law of countries allows consensual same-sex sexual activity, the Frank–McEneaney study emphasized inter-country variation in individualism and employed country-level indicators of individualism, especially (1) an index of the degree of commitment by each country to human rights, (2) whether the dominant religious tradition of each country was Anglo-American Protestant, and (3) the extent of authorships in each country of articles in professional journals in psychology.[84] Additional country-level variables were included as explanatory or control variables, e.g., gender equality, involvement in world affairs, population size, and gross domestic product per capita.

Based on levels of statistical significance, the main finding of the Frank–McEneaney study was that an increase in individualism raised the likelihood that the law of a country would allow same-sex sexual activity among men. On the other hand, variation between countries in individualism was not related to the degree to which the law of countries permitted same-sex sexual activity among women. As to egalitarianism in sex roles—which the investigators viewed as a correlate of individualism[85]—the study found that greater gender equality contributed to the adoption by countries of law accepting same-sex sexual activity both among men and among women. Neither gross domestic product per capita nor population size, however, affected the content of law on same-sex sexual activity.[86]

Unfortunately, the Frank–McEneaney study furnishes just minimal assistance in pinpointing independent variables for the data analysis to be undertaken infra. One reason the Frank–McEneaney study is not of major help is that its chief independent variable was individualism and its concern was with whether individualism was a cause of law on same-sex sexual activity. However, the macrosociological framework for the data analysis below regards individualism as a general factor that *includes* same-sex sexual activity and the social arrangements for it, not a factor that *affects* the acceptability of such activity and arrangements. Furthermore, even if the Frank–McEneaney study had been concerned with the determinants of individualism, it may not have contributed to understanding multiple types of social activities and arrangements, because individualism is unlikely to be a single social form with homogeneous content. Instead, individualism probably encompasses a variety of social forms, and the social activities and arrangements comprising individualism may not have a common set of societal causes. Thus, even though same-sex sexual activity, same-sex non-marital partnerships, and same-sex marriage share some similarities on the surface, they may differ sufficiently as social forms that their antecedents are not identical.

In a similar vein, the degree to which nations are involved in world affairs, though found by the Frank–McEneaney study to be a predictor of the lawfulness of same-sex sexual activity,[87] would be treated as a dependent variable in the macrosociological framework employed here. In this framework, the manner and extent of participation of nations in world affairs is considered to be a response to nation-level economic, technological, and demographic conditions.

The explanatory variables for the data analysis that follows, in short, omit a measure of individualism in a country as well as a measure of the involvement of a country in world affairs. While both were key independent variables in the Frank–McEneaney study, they are not regarded as independent variables by the framework that prompted the research reported infra.

However, one explanatory variable for the instant data analysis can be derived from the Frank–McEneaney study, although the variable is of uncertain promise. The variable is societal wealth. If statistical significance is set aside as a criterion for decisions on the null hypothesis,[88] the Frank–McEneaney study indicates that higher gross domestic product per capita expands the adoption of law that accepts same-sex sexual activity among men but that gross domestic product per capita has essentially no impact on the adoption of law that accepts same-sex sexual activity among women. The difference in impact by the sex of participants in sexual activity is potentially important. If law that permits same-sex sexual activity is germane to law that permits same-sex non-marital partnerships and same-sex marriage, as suggested earlier,[89] the effect of wealth on the latter law may vary with the sex of the participants in the relationship. Specifically, the impact of wealth on law directed at such relationships may be limited to relationships between men.

The remaining four studies to be reviewed will be considered together because of the similarity of their dependent variables. All of the studies were concerned with whether law prohibiting discrimination on the basis of sexual preference had been adopted by the governments of states, counties, or cities in the United States. The law that was examined in these studies barred discrimination in employment, in housing and/or public accommodations, and/or in lending[90]—topics on which state and local governments in the United States traditionally legislate. The preceding topics, although involving facially different activities, are closely related in terms of whether law covers them, i.e., the law of a jurisdiction is unlikely to ban discrimination on one of the topics without banning discrimination on others.[91]

A further reason to consider the four studies jointly is that, while two of the studies have notable limitations that should be kept in mind,[92] the findings of the four studies in combination are not inconsistent. Consequently, the four studies together help in identifying the antecedents of law on discrimination that is directed at persons who prefer to engage in sexual activity with members of their own sex.

What independent variables for the current project are suggested by these four studies? On the one hand, law banning sexual-preference discrimination in a jurisdiction may become more common with increases in the educational attainment of jurisdiction inhabitants[93] and with increases in the numerical size of jurisdiction populations.[94] On the other hand, law banning sexual-preference discrimination is not predicted by the income of jurisdiction inhabitants under the most commonly used criteria for statistical significance,[95] but if statistical significance is ignored, jurisdictions are more likely to have such law as the income of their inhabitants rises.[96]

The research that we report infra employs four explanatory variables measured at the country level. All were suggested by the macrosociological framework that was considered infra in Part I of the present chapter and/or by the studies that were just reviewed. Three of the variables—education, population density, and wealth—have sociological substance or accompaniments. Each of the three variables is a plausible antecedent of whether law recognizes same-sex non-marital partnerships and same-sex marriage, because rising levels of education, population density, and wealth are believed to increase rationality and individualism.[97] As rationality and individualism intensify and diffuse in a society, at least some of the established lifestyles of the society will become less acceptable to participants in the society. Among the lifestyles that may come under pressure to change is the conventional form of marriage.

The fourth explanatory variable included in the instant research is cultural in nature. Three out of the six prior studies of the impact of jurisdiction conditions on jurisdiction law have included an indicator of culture, e.g., the composition of state populations in terms of religion or the geographic region in which states were located.[98] Another study—of factors that affect voting by the public on state prohibitions of same-sex marriage—lends additional credence to the proposition that law is shaped by culture.[99] In the research undertaken here, the indicator of culture is the total fertility rate (TFR). The TFR is the projected number of children that one thousand females who are fifteen years old in a given year will have during their childbearing period, i.e., from age fifteen through age forty-nine.[100] The TFR is not a measure of actual lifetime childbearing, because it is calculated by summing the number of births per one thousand women at all ages from fifteen through forty-nine in a particular year. The calculation thus assumes that the age-specific birth rates in the year for which the calculation is done will remain constant for the next thirty-five years. However, even though the TFR depicts no more than "the completed fertility of a synthetic cohort of women,"[101] it is a potentially useful indicator of culture relevant to marriage. A relationship exists between childbearing and social values relevant to the role of women,[102] and due to the way the TFR is computed, the TFR quickly incorporates changes in birth rates. In doing so, the TFR rapidly reflects shifts in social values pertinent to gender roles[103] and, given the link between gender-role beliefs and whether couples marry or cohabit,[104] to marriage. As a result, the TFR offers a potentially useful measure of culture in a society, i.e., of the key assumptions that characterize a society and that mold the views and behavior of its population.[105]

B. Measurement of Variables and Sources of Data

The instant study employed a combination of time-series data and cross-sectional data. Such a dataset, which is commonly labeled "pooled time-series,"[106] permits variation to be examined both across space and across time.[107] Pooled time-series, therefore, are particularly appropriate for attempts to explain differences between and changes in the law of nation-states. As explained in Part II,[108] the instant study focused on fourteen countries that were members of the EU during the period from 1995 through 2003, and it includes data on these countries through 2005.[109] In order to capture fully the variation in all of the variables of interest to the study, the dependent variable (law on same-sex unions) was coded, and data on the independent variables were included, for each country for every fifth year from 1970 through 2005. We chose 1970 as the initial year because (1) 1970 is approximately two decades prior to the year (1989) in which the first country in the study approved legislation to recognize same-sex non-marital partnerships or same-sex marriage and because (2) we assume that changes in law, although often sudden, are typically responses to shifts in the properties of societies that have occurred slowly.[110] Because at least two decades of data were used for the independent variables prior to the adoption of law authorizing same-sex unions in the ten countries whose law was changed between 1989 and 2005 to authorize such unions,[111] we believe that the data allow results from which causality can be plausibly inferred.

In coding the dependent variable (which was assigned the mnemonic label LAW), a statute authorizing same-sex non-marital partnerships was not distinguished from a statute authorizing same-sex marriage. No distinction was made between the two types of statutes because of the small number of countries with law recognizing same-sex marriage.[112] The dependent variable was thus coded as a dummy, i.e., 0 or 1. A country with a statute permitting same-sex unions (either non-marital partnerships or same-sex marriage) was coded 1 starting in the year in which its statute was adopted and was coded 0 in each prior year. A country that did not have such a statute between 1970 and 2005 was coded 0 in all years.[113] The code of 1, once applied to a country, continued until the end of the time-series for the country since no country adopted and subsequently rescinded legislation that authorized same-sex unions. Furthermore, of the four countries with a statute authorizing same-sex marriage, two (The Netherlands and Sweden) had initially adopted law permitting same-sex non-marital partnerships and later adopted law permitting same-sex marriage. Each of these countries was coded 1 from the year in which it had a statute permitting same-sex non-marital partnerships.

Let us now turn to the independent variables, i.e., the variables that have been hypothesized as explanations of the dependent variable. Given the time period for which data were required, it is not surprising that the available measures of the independent variables were not numerous, and as a result, the measures that were chosen for the study were not necessarily ideal. Nonetheless, the measures that were used permit a credible test of the ability of each independent variable to predict the presence or absence of law on same-sex unions. An assessment of the relationship, if any, between the former and the latter is thus possible.

We list below each independent variable and specify the measure that we used for it. The name of the independent variable is followed in parentheses by the mnemonic label that the regression equation used for the variable. Data on the independent variables were included in the regression analysis for eight years, viz., 1970, 1975, 1980, 1985, 1990, 1995, 2000, and 2005. Country-level data were used for all of the independent variables. Missing data were infrequent.[114]

- *Wealth* (mnemonic label GDP). The indicator of wealth was the gross domestic product per person in each country. Gross domestic product per person was measured in current U.S. dollars and took into account differences in prices between countries.[115]
- *Culture* (mnemonic label TFR). As explained in Part III-A supra,[116] culture was measured by the total fertility rate.[117]
- *Education* (mnemonic label EDUCALL). The measure of education is school-life expectancy in each country of both males and females, i.e., of males and females combined.[118] School-life expectancy is calculated for a country by summing the enrollment ratios[119] that exist during a designated school year at all of the ages within an age range. Because it assumes that these age-specific enrollment ratios do not change with the passage of time, school-life expectancy estimates the total number of years of schooling for a child who reaches school age in the designated year.[120] In the instant study, the calculation of school-life expectancy included all levels of education (primary, secondary, and tertiary).
- *Population density* (mnemonic label URBANPOP). The measure of population density in each country was the percentage of the population

residing in an area that was classified as an "urban agglomeration" and that, in 2007, had at least 750,000 people.[121] Although the definition of "urban" may not have been uniform across countries[122] and the population of an "urban agglomeration" in a country may have been less than 750,000 in some of the eight years, the measure we use here gauges the percentage of the population of a country that was living in large urbanized centers during the period from 1970 to 2000. The measure thus allows a test of the impact of population density that has been propounded by the theory of urbanism.[123]

Based on the empirical and theoretical work that has been reviewed in this chapter,[124] the odds that a country will by law authorize same-sex non-marital partnerships or same-sex marriage can be expected to rise with increases in the wealth (GDP), school-life expectancy (EDUCALL), and density of the population (URBANPOP) of the country. As each of the foregoing explanatory variables increases, rationality and individualism are likely to become more intense and/or more prevalent. On their face, greater rationality and individualism are incompatible with law that is designed to restrict personal choice and, hence, with law that does not authorize same-sex unions. If the prior reasoning is correct, the odds ratios for GDP, EDUCALL, and URBANPOP will exceed 1.00.[125]

The sole independent variable expected to have an odds ratio below 1.00 is the TFR. Cultural values that do not favor childbearing probably promote unconventional arrangements between women and men, including unconventional forms of pairings for sexual activity and marriage. If so, the odds that a country will adopt law recognizing same-sex unions will be related inversely to the TFR of the country, i.e., a secular decline in TFR can be expected to raise the odds that such law will be enacted. Given the coding of the dependent variable, the odds ratio for TFR is hypothesized to be less than 1.00.[126]

C. Statistical Technique[127]

The data in the present study were analyzed with maximum-likelihood logistic regression. Least-squares (i.e., linear) regression was unsuitable[128] because the dependent variable was coded 0 or 1 and hence was binary.[129] However, while the measurement of the dependent variable dictated the form of regression, it did not require a particular type of regression model. When data comprise pooled time-series, different types of models are available. In the instant research, the question was whether a fixed-effects regression model or a random-effects regression model was appropriate. Unfortunately, a clear answer to the question does not exist because of the nature of the data and of the phenomenon under investigation. A brief review of the reasons for the lack of certainty may be helpful.

Studies of the societal factors that shape law do not select cases with a probability sampling procedure but include all or almost all of the jurisdictions in a bounded geographic area. In this respect, the instant study is typical. Fixed-effects models do not assume that the jurisdictions in a study of the societal antecedents of law have been chosen with a random sampling procedure or that the dependent variable is distributed normally.[130] Using this criterion, accordingly, a fixed-effects model would be preferable to a random-effects model for the data analysis infra.

However, fixed-effects models also pose a disadvantage in studies of the societal antecedents of law, because such models do not create confidence that the findings they produce can be applied to jurisdictions (e.g., nations) other than those included in the data.[131] Fixed-effects models assume that jurisdictions influence law in unique ways; random-effects models do not make this assumption.[132] In believing that jurisdictions themselves influence only by chance the relationship to law of each independent variable, random-effects models are more compatible with the goal of building theory,[133] a goal of the sociological framework that underlies the present study.

The type of model that was most appropriate for the present study, therefore, was unclear—each type of model has a feature that recommends it for research on the societal antecedents of law, and each has a feature that makes it of uncertain suitability for such research. Nonetheless, a choice had to be made, and while neither type of model is entirely satisfactory, a random-effects model was selected. One of the bases for the choice was that the number of countries in the study (viz., fourteen) was evidently insufficient for a fixed-effects model but adequate for a random-effects model.[134] In addition, a random-effects model was preferable because of the advantages it offers even if the number of countries had been adequate for a fixed-effects model.[135]

The findings reported in Part III-D later are from data analyses performed with Stata release 10.1. The XTLOGIT command for a random-effects model was used to estimate the regression coefficients and odds ratios for the independent variables.[136]

D. Data Analysis

The XTLOGIT command, in estimating the regression coefficient and odds ratio for an independent variable in a model, computes the standard error of the regression coefficient and reports the probability under the null hypothesis that the independent variable is unrelated to the dependent variable. Tables 7.1 and 7.2 (presented infra) include all of the preceding information for readers who are interested in it, but the conclusions reached in the instant study were *not* grounded on the probability that a coefficient or odds ratio reported by Stata would have occurred by chance if the null hypothesis was accurate; i.e., our conclusions were not based on the level of statistical significance of a coefficient or odds ratio. Levels of statistical significance were ignored for two reasons. First, the data were analyzed with maximum-likelihood regression. While the minimum number of observations needed to obtain credible results from tests of statistical significance

Table 7.1 Regression of LAW on GDP, EDUCALL, and URBANPOP (default quadrature method)

Variable	Odds ratio	Regression coefficient	Standard error of regression coefficient	*Z*	*p*>|z|
GDP	1.000799	.000799	.000679	1.18	.239
EDUCALL	1.377840	.320517	.923837	.35	.729
URBANPOP	1.405618	.340477	.463411	.73	.463
constant		−38.280300	36.259020	−1.06	.291

Notes: Regression model
Number of observations = 110
Number of groups (countries) = 14
Observations per group (country)
Minimum = 6
Maximum = 8
Average = 7.9
Log likelihood = −24.323267
Wald $chi^2(3)$ = 1.96
Probability > chi^2 = .5801
$\ln(\sigma_v^2)$ = 4.273009
Standard error of $\ln(\sigma_v^2)$ = 1.868620
σ_v = 8.469780
Standard error = 7.913399
ρ = 0.9561509
Standard error = .0783444
Likelihood-ratio test of ρ = 0:
$Chibar^2(01)$ = 7.75, probability>= $chibar^2$ = .003.

Table 7.2 Regression of LAW on GDP, EDUCALL, and URBANPOP (fifteen quadrature points)

Variable	Odds ratio	Regression coefficient	Standard error of regression coefficient	*Z*	*p*>|z|
GDP	1.001221	.001221	.0008148	1.50	.134
EDUCALL	1.504103	.408196	1.2334540	.33	.741
URBANPOP	1.828459	.603473	.4715783	1.28	.201
Constant		−57.938500	39.3373700	1.47	.141

Notes: Regression model
Number of observations = 110
Number of groups (countries) = 14
Observations per group (country)
Minimum = 6
Maximum = 8
Average = 7.9
Log likelihood = −24.272617
Wald $chi^2(3)$ = 2.45
Probability > chi^2 = .4841
$\ln(\sigma_v^2)$ = 5.099070
Standard error of $\ln(\sigma_v^2)$ = 1.422154
σ_v = 12.801150
Standard error = 9.102608
ρ = .9803190
Standard error = .0274386
Likelihood-ratio test of ρ = 0:
$Chibar^2(01)$ = 7.85, probability>= $chibar^2$ = .003.

for maximum-likelihood regression has not been extensively investigated,[137] the use of such tests with fewer than one hundred observations has been labeled "risky," and even fewer than five hundred observations may be insufficient.[138] Under these guidelines, the use of tests of statistical significance in the instant study was dubious because the number of observations was just 110.

The second reason that statistical significance was not a criterion in drawing conclusions from the data in this study involves a fundamental assumption of the tests that compute statistical significance. Specifically, such tests presuppose that the data to which they are applied come from a relatively small number of cases selected from a substantially large universe and that the cases selected for study were obtained with a random sampling procedure.[139] The instant investigation, however, covered every country in the defined universe whose government exercised sovereignty over an unchanged geographic area during the time span of interest. Because the countries in the study were not chosen randomly out of a larger universe, tests of statistical significance are unnecessary if not inappropriate.

The initial regression analysis employed data on all fourteen countries and all four independent variables,[140] but the odds ratio for TFR was suspect. Specifically, the odds ratio for TFR diverged from 1.00 in the opposite direction from what had been predicted,[141] and the magnitude of the odds ratio for TFR appeared implausible.[142] Accordingly, there seemed to be a distinct possibility that TFR was affected by one or more influential outliers and/or that TFR was subject to excessive collinearity. An influential outlier is a case (here, a country) that, on the dependent variable, diverges from the prediction made by the regression model for that case (country), and the divergence distorts the odds ratio obtained for an independent variable.[143] Excessive collinearity exists when change in the amount or condition of one independent variable in a regression model corresponds so closely to change in the amount or condition of another independent variable that, when both independent variables are included in the regression model, their odds ratios are unstable and cannot be estimated with an acceptable degree of confidence.[144]

We begin with the potential problem of influential outliers. Unfortunately, a recommended statistical procedure for locating such an outlier from a regression analysis of data with a binary dependent variable[145] is unavailable for the XTLOGIT command, but even if the procedure could have been used, the detection of an influential outlier remains a largely subjective process.[146] Given the uncertainty involved in investigating and identifying influential outliers, we attempted to ascertain whether an influential outlier might be present in our data by using the XTLOGIT command with a series of datasets from each of which one of the fourteen countries had been removed. Because a different country was omitted *seriatim*, each resulting thirteen-country dataset differed in terms of one country.

A finding from the above procedure was that the odds ratios for TFR (as well as for EDUCALL) was appreciably altered by the omission of two countries—namely, Luxembourg and Sweden—but in a study that has just fourteen cases (countries), a major impact of one or two cases is not necessarily surprising and may not jeopardize the credibility of the conclusions reached from all of the cases included in the study. A plausible proposition is that the present study is dealing with countries that form a *system*. By definition,[147] a system—or at least a system that is viable—has components that do not severely or consistently disadvantage one other,[148] and even when a component deviates on a specific dimension from what was anticipated, the component can still be integral to the system. Furthermore, an unexpected deviation on a dimension by a component of a system will not be an abnormality if (1) the system allows or encourages its components to be within a certain range on the dimension and (2) the deviating component is within that range. In such a situation, the component should be retained in the data even though it is an outlier and influences the results obtained from the set of all components.

What determines whether a component is an outlier that should be removed from a dataset? The question must be answered by the model for the study,[149] and the model will be based on theory.[150] Macrosociological theory, however, has not developed sufficiently to permit a researcher to distinguish (1) an outlier component whose inclusion in a dataset produces biased results from (2) an outlier component whose inclusion is essential for unbiased results.[151] On the other hand, the question may be answered in the instant study by theory regarding the nature of the European Union. A necessary condition for the formation of the EU was undoubtedly that the founding nations were similar on certain dimensions, and a necessary condition for the continuation and growth of the EU is undoubtedly the persistence of this similarity. Indeed, the EU has been funding projects designed to reduce differences among its member nations in economy-related conditions.[152] Assuming as the instant study does that the EU is a system of countries and that the system is viable, a particular country should not be eliminated from the data of the instant study unless a compelling reason exists for doing so. This conclusion is reinforced by the small number of countries that are components of the system (EU); the relevance of each component to a system is presumably greater in a system that has few components than in a system that has many. For the instant study, in short, the retention of a country in the data is likely to be important, and may be essential, if error is to be avoided in identifying the societal antecedents of law in EU nations.[153]

We turn now to the possibility that TFR suffered from an unacceptable degree of collinearity with another independent variable in the regression model. Collinearity is a frequent problem in data on a set of nations,[154] but in the instant study, Stata kept all of the independent variables in the regression model when it computed the odds ratios even though it drops an independent variable that exceeds its criterion for collinearity.[155] Nonetheless, the failure to abandon a variable is not conclusive evidence that the degree of collinearity is acceptable. Indeed, the retention by any statistics software of an independent variable in a regression model does not ensure that excessive collinearity is absent.[156]

Because the odds ratio obtained for TFR may have been biased by collinearity between TFR and another independent variable, TFR was taken out of the regression model, and the odds ratios for the remaining three independent variables (GDP, EDUCALL, and URBANPOP) were estimated. Notably, the odds ratios for the three independent variables in the three-variable model were not dissimilar in magnitude to the odds ratios for these variables in the four-variable model, and the direction of the relationship between each independent variable and the dependent variable (LAW) was the same in both models.[157] In terms of the direction of the relationships, the odds ratios for each independent variable exceeded 1.00 in both models.[158]

Why not retain TFR in the regression model and eliminate another independent variable? Besides the unexpected direction and suspect magnitude of the relationship of TFR to LAW, TFR was excluded because, during the time period covered by the study (1970–2005), a secular decline occurred in the total fertility rate of each of the four EU countries that did *not* enact law authorizing same-sex unions, namely, Austria, Greece, Ireland, and Italy. The decline is presented graphically in Figure 7.1. Under the rationale we followed for placing TFR in the regression model, the direction in which the total fertility rate moved in these four countries would have raised the odds that the countries would approve legislation recognizing same-sex unions. None of the four countries adopted such legislation, however, and their inaction in this regard undoubtedly had an appreciable impact on the odds ratio that was estimated for TFR using data on all of the fourteen countries.

Tables 7.1 and 7.2 report the results of the regression analysis for the three-variable model.[159] The results in Table 7.1 were generated by the default quadrature approximation in XTLOGIT; the results in Table 7.2 were generated by XTLOGIT with fifteen quadrature points.[160] Significance levels, which are derived from the standard

Figure 7.1 Countries Not Authorizing Same-Sex Unions: Total Fertility Rate from 1970 to 2005

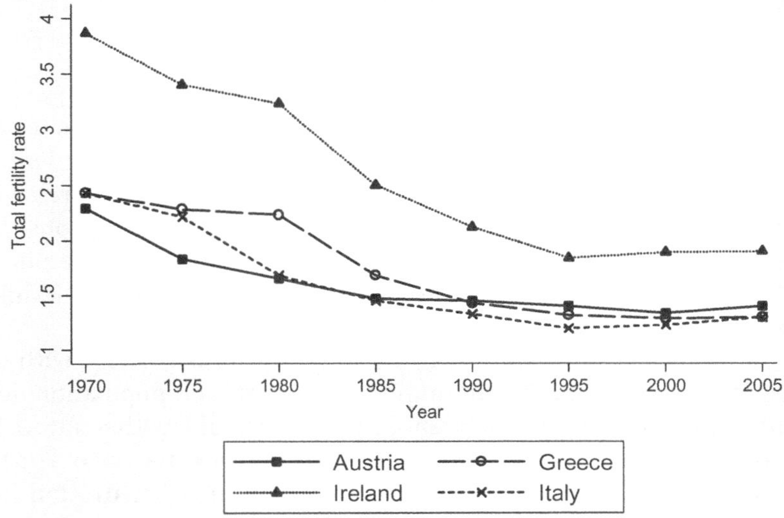

errors of the regression coefficients, are given for two-tailed tests,[161] but as explained earlier, the criterion for drawing conclusions about an independent variable in the regression model was the odds ratio for the variable—whether, the degree to which, and the direction in which the odds ratio deviated from 1.00.

According to the odds ratios in Table 7.2—on which we will focus in summarizing the results of the data analysis—the odds that legislation would be enacted by a country to authorize same-sex unions increased by .1221 percent for every additional U.S. dollar of gross domestic product per person[162]; increased by 50.4 percent for every additional year of school-life expectancy; and increased by 82.8 percent for every additional percentage point in the share of the population that resided in an urban agglomeration.[163] In multiple regression, of course, an odds ratio (and coefficient) for an independent variable estimates the impact of that independent variable on the dependent variable *after* the effects of the other independent variables in the regression model have been statistically removed. For the countries and the time period covered by the instant study, therefore, growth in each independent variable—wealth, education, and urbanism—raised the odds that a country would enact law authorizing same-sex unions, and the contribution of each independent variable to the enactment of such law was evidently of practical importance.[164]

IV. Discussion

The findings presented in Part III-D are consistent with the results of earlier research with regard to education and population density, and they are not inconsistent with the results of earlier research with regard to wealth. The relationships to law on same-sex unions that the instant study uncovered, therefore, seem unlikely to be due to chance or to any of the numerous problems that potentially undermine research in the social sciences.

Notably, the findings of the instant study are consistent with the theory of urbanism. The findings indicate that high population density contributes to the emergence of doctrines of law that authorize same-sex non-marital partnerships and same-sex marriage. For the institution of law, then, the level of population concentration in a society matters. Furthermore, the findings as to wealth and education lend credibility to the proposition that the knowledge used by a society exercises a powerful influence on the character of the society and, in turn, on the content of its law. Specifically, improvements in the quality and quantity of knowledge during the last hundred years (if not longer) are likely to have augmented the wealth and educational level of the population of Western nations; increases in wealth and educational attainment probably raised the degree and expanded the prevalence of individualism and rationality; and greater individualism and rationality are likely to have shaped the concepts and doctrines of law in these nations. The extent and magnitude of the impact of the stock of knowledge has not been understood, however, because the impact has been mainly if not entirely indirect.

Perhaps some appreciation of the ability of growing wealth, education, and urbanism to shape law on same-sex non-marital partnerships and same-sex marriage can be gained from a visual presentation of the changes that have occurred in these factors in EU nations. Figure 7.2 includes three graphs, each of which shows the *mean* of the fourteen countries on one factor at the eight time points from 1970 to 2005. The trends in the graphs are probably known in general terms by most readers, but the graphs delineate precisely the level of each factor and its course over time. Perusal of the graphs indicates that, during the

Figure 7.2 Explanatory Variables
Yearly Means: 1970 to 2005

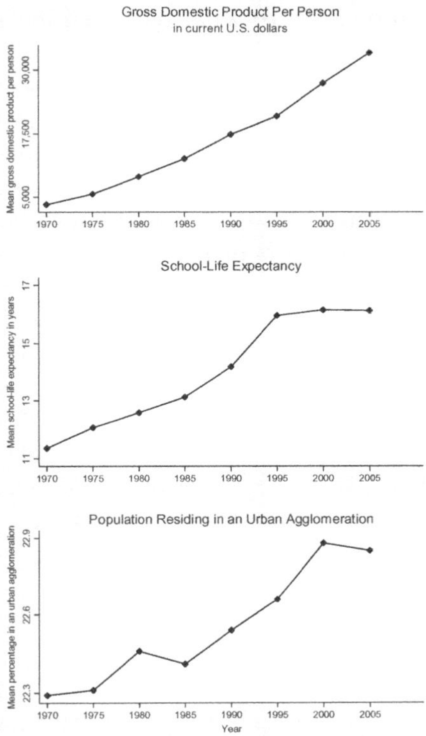

period covered, there were secular increases in all three factors. The upward movement of the factors, together with the magnitude of the movement in wealth and in education, adds credibility to the odds ratios that were reported in Tables 7.1 and 7.2. In short, countries are evidently pushed to adopt law authorizing same-sex non-marital partnerships and same-sex marriage by growth in the stock of knowledge and in urbanism.

Although we hope that our study has contributed to understanding the emergence of law recognizing same-sex non-marital partnerships and same-sex marriage, we want to stress that our study should not be taken as an ending point—indeed, it is only a beginning. We are under no illusion that our study provides the definitive word on the societal properties that prompt jurisdictions to adopt law authorizing same-sex unions. On the contrary, our study is no more than a small step in the search for these properties. Nevertheless, we hope that the study adds to what has been learned from prior research on the antecedents of law and that it will prompt others to undertake their own research. The properties of societies that shape law on all types of activities and entities would benefit from the efforts of additional investigators, and in order to assist them, we want to suggest two independent variables that were absent from our explanatory model but that we believe hold promise for understanding the antecedents of law on same-sex unions and on at least some other topics as well.

One of the variables that we recommend for inclusion in future research is the status of women relative to the status of men. Unfortunately, we were unable to find data for a suitable measure of gender status in the years and countries included in our study. The relative status of women may help to account for whether law authorizes same-sex unions because, in research that was recently completed on a nationwide sample of adults in the United States, the odds that morality would be deemed a private matter (as opposed to a public issue) were found to be much higher among women than among men.[165] Given the evidence that social values shape law,[166] a plausible argument can be made that, in the United States, (1) gains in the status of women increased the influence of social values classifying morality as private and (2) this shift in social values moved the U.S. Supreme Court to rule in a series of cases that the national Constitution is offended by government action designed to penalize adults for consensual, noncommercial, nonpublic sexual activity and its incidents.[167] The cases were decided during the period from 1965 to 2003, and included law-imposed penalties for consensual, noncommercial, nonpublic sexual activity when it involves adults who are of the same sex.[168] Same-sex sexual activity, therefore, has come to be viewed as a private choice under the Constitution of the United States, and it cannot be suppressed by government.[169] Assuming that the appreciably greater inclination of women than of men to assign morality to the private sphere is not limited to the United States, the status of women can be expected to shape law targeting same-sex relationships in numerous nations. If so, improvements in the status of women in a country, ceteris paribus, raise the likelihood that same-sex non-marital partnerships and same-sex marriage will be treated as a private matter and that the law of the country will permit such unions.[170] In sum, future studies of this law, as well as of law targeting social behaviors and arrangements bearing on sexual activity, may benefit from incorporating the status of women into their models.

The second independent variable that we recommend for inclusion in future research is relevant to law on all topics rather than to just law on same-sex unions. The variable is the ease with which a country can modify the concepts and doctrines in its law. Unfortunately, a satisfactory measure of this variable does not seem to exist for the countries and years covered by our study. The variable, in being concerned with the process by which concepts and doctrines enter law, involves all lawmaking entities—legislatures, judicial bodies, and administrative agencies. The variable is potentially important insofar as it affects the speed with which law is harmonized with societal properties. Extremes in the structure of the lawmaking process probably arise from major historical events such as wars and economic depressions; i.e., a country may be so disrupted by an event that its lawmaking procedures are reorganized for the purpose of allowing, or of preventing, a material delay in or complete thwarting of new law. In the instant study, the structure of the lawmaking process would have been treated as a factor intervening between (1) the other explanatory variables and (2) the content of law regarding same-sex unions. The impact of (1) on (2) would be expected to occur with a delay in countries whose lawmaking process allows alterations in law to be readily blocked. In these countries, the threshold at which law is altered by change in societal properties is likely to be materially higher than in countries whose lawmaking process is conducive to revisions in law.

Appendix

A social scientist who we asked to critique the instant study questioned whether our regression model was correct in assuming that the independent variables (EDUCALL, GDP, and URBANPOP) concurrently affected the dependent variable (LAW). The independent variables, he believed, have a temporal sequence, and he recommended that our model, and hence our data analysis, incorporate this sequence. Specifically, the reviewer advanced the following propositions: (1) GDP is an immediate antecedent both of EDUCALL and of URBANPOP; (2) EDUCALL and URBANPOP are immediate antecedents of LAW; and, consequently, (3) the influence of GDP on LAW occurs indirectly through EDUCALL and URBANPOP.[171] The propositions are portrayed in the following diagram:

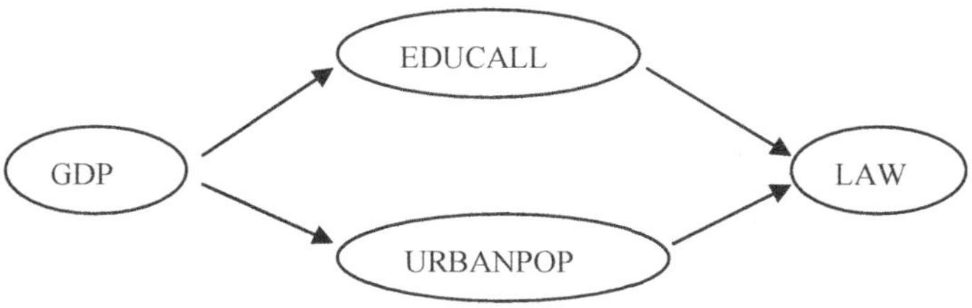

Although no rationale was provided for the foregoing propositions, the reviewer may have reasoned that basic goods such as food and minerals are not produced by full-time students or by inhabitants of densely populated areas, but that these goods are nonetheless required for full-time schooling and residence in a large city. Under this reasoning, basic goods are the foundation for wealth (as measured by GDP), and the wealth of a society determines the proportion of the population of the society that is able to engage in activities that do not themselves generate basic goods. Societal wealth would thus be the cornerstone for, and possibly would be the driving force behind, average educational attainment and degree of urbanization.

The above reasoning is logical and therefore appealing, but the model it yields is dubious. Indeed, the model advanced by the reviewer masks the considerable disagreement that exists regarding the direction of causality between societal wealth, schooling, and the share of the population residing in metropolitan areas.[172] Two particular factors, however, undermine the credibility of the model proposed by the reviewer. First, proposition 1 of the reviewer is not supported by quantitative research. Average educational attainment has been found to contribute to growth in societal wealth, but an impact of the latter on the former—i.e., an impact of societal wealth on educational attainment—is apparently weak.[173] The direction of causality, therefore, seems to be chiefly from educational attainment to wealth. Moreover, in most of the nations that were included in the instant study, societal wealth does not affect the density of population. Indeed, the reverse evidently occurs in these nations, i.e., degree of urbanization affects the level of wealth.[174]

The model proposed by the reviewer is implausible for a second reason as well, namely, the findings presented in Part III-D supra. Specifically, the model of the reviewer treats EDUCALL and

URBANPOP as variables intervening between GDP and LAW, but if this model is correct and no other variables are positioned between GDP and LAW, a relationship between GDP and LAW should be absent in Table 7.2 because EDUCALL and URBANPOP are held constant in computing whether GDP is related to LAW. Controls for EDUCALL and URBANPOP, that is, should have removed the ability of GDP to affect LAW if the impact of GDP on LAW occurred through (and only through) EDUCALL and URBANPOP. As Table 7.2 shows, however, GDP had an appreciable influence on LAW despite the controls for EDUCALL and URBANPOP.[175] Of course, even with controls for EDUCALL and URBANPOP, GDP would continue to have an impact on LAW if GDP affects LAW through other intervening variables, but these other intervening variables have yet to be identified and the manner in which they operate is unknown. Indeed, a problem underlying all models that seek to explain the content and evolution of law is that they are in territory that social scientists have only begun to chart.

In the end, then, the reader should keep in mind that social science remains uncertain about whether and how EDUCALL, GDP, and URBANPOP are related to each other. The uncertainty may exist in part because the three variables may not possess simple causal interconnections,[176] but regardless of its source, the uncertainty is a compelling reason to entertain models other than that advanced by the reviewer. A consideration of other models is especially important for the instant study given that the concern of the study is the relationships of these variables to *law* rather than to each other. One plausible model suggests that, in general, average educational attainment and population density are antecedents, not results, of wealth,[177] and that each of the three variables (EDUCALL, URBANPOP, and GDP) have their own impact on LAW. In this model, greater educational attainment and urbanization (1) improve economically relevant skills in a society and (2) increase rationality, both of which contribute to enlarging gross domestic product per person, i.e., wealth. With gains in wealth and in rationality, increases in individualism can be expected.[178] Contrary to the model proposed by the reviewer, educational attainment and population density may thus start the sequence, with growth in these societal forces adding to wealth and sharpening analytical skills.

In the model just described, the components and concomitants of individualism (e.g., rationality and analytical skills) are fostered by an increase in education, an increase in population density, and an increase in wealth. Individualism is important to the instant chapter for two reasons. First, an intensification and expansion of individualism may have been a central and defining feature of global change in recent history.[179] Second, individualism involves or creates challenges to the conventions of societies. Since opposition to societal conventions from rising and spreading individualism is likely to be broad rather than narrow, individualism undermines traditional lifestyles as a whole, including traditional forms of marriage. As conventional lifestyles become less accepted and less enforceable in a society, law authorizing alternative lifestyles can be expected to follow.

Under the above rationale, then, the relationships between EDUCALL, URBANPOP, and GDP, on the one hand, and LAW, on the other, differ materially from those suggested by the reviewer. The relationships posited by the above rationale can be diagrammed as follows:

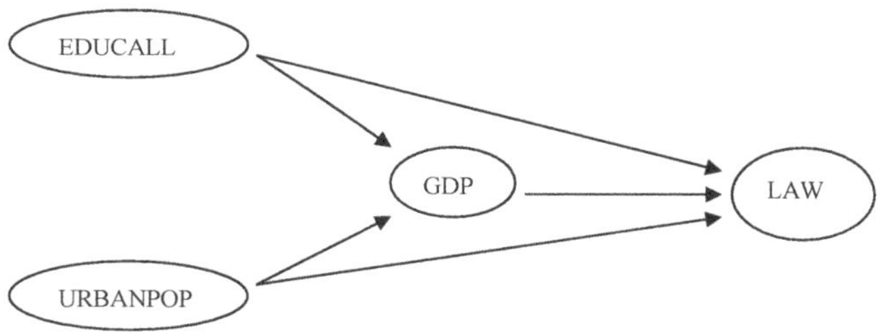

What is the most appropriate model for the instant study? The systematic exploration of the societal antecedents of law is in its infancy, and not surprisingly, the picture of these antecedents that social scientists have painted to date is hazy. Because the three independent variables (EDUCALL, GDP, and URBANPOP) in the present study do not clearly have a temporal order in explaining the content of law at any single point in time or over time, they were assumed by the model that was employed in Part III-D supra to have concurrent effects on LAW.[180] Models are not developed in a vacuum, of course, and they should not be based solely on existing theory or solely on an analysis of data; rather, models should be grounded on a combination of theory and information from prior empirical studies.[181] The model that was chosen for the instant study satisfies this criterion, and the credibility of the model is bolstered by the findings reported in Table 7.2. Accordingly, unless future social science research and theory applicable to the societal antecedents of law recommend a model in which EDUCALL, GDP, and URBANPOP are temporally ordered, the most prudent course is to assume that the effects of the variables on law are concurrent.

Notes

*Chapter 7 is a reprint with some revision of Larry D. Barnett and Pietro Saitta, "Societal Properties and Law on Same-Sex Non-Marital Partnerships and Same-Sex Marriage in European Union Nations," *Journal of Civil Rights and Economic Development* 25: (2011). Professor Saitta is Assistant Professor of Sociology in the Department of Economics, Statistics, Mathematics, and Sociology at the University of Messina (Italy).

1. In the instant chapter, an institution is considered to be a set of statuses and roles (1) that a society defines and endorses and (2) that involve interpersonal relationships through which a socially approved type of activity takes place in the society. Howard B. Kaplan, "The Concept of Institution: A Review, Evaluation, and Suggested Research Procedure," *Social Forces* 39 (1960): 176, 179. An institution, as the word is used in the chapter, is not a specific organization (e.g., a particular corporation in the private sector or a particular agency in the public sector), but a general pattern of interpersonal behavior. Together, the institutions of a society determine the character and effectiveness of the society.
2. Bruce Western and Simon Jackman, "Bayesian Inference for Comparative Research," *American Political Science Review* 88 (1994): 412, 412, 414.
3. Alternative baselines would be change of various types (e.g., linear versus curvilinear) and change at various rates. However, the alternative baselines are numerous and diverse, and the criteria for choosing among them are uncertain.
4. The three propositions are not intended to list all of the factors that are responsible for the absence of change in societies and their institutions. None of the propositions, for example, deals with the impact of unique but massive events such as wars, natural disasters, and economic depressions. Unfortunately, the degree to which such events affect social patterns in the long run has infrequently been the subject of research applying a multivariate statistical test to a large dataset. A notable exception is the study by Claudia D. Goldin, "The Role of World War II in the Rise of Women's Employment," *American Economic Review* 81 (1991): 741. Professor Goldin found that, contrary to popular belief, World War II did not produce a substantial rise in employment among women in the United States. Ibid., 755. The economic depression of the 1930s, however, was associated with a marked reduction in differences in the sex composition of occupations in the United States. Kim A. Weeden, "Revisiting Occupational Sex Segregation in the United States, 1910–1990: Results from a Log-Linear Approach," *Demography* 35 (1998): 475, 480 table 2 (index A).
5. As to propositions 2 and 3, see Larry D. Barnett, *Legal Construct, Social Concept: A Macrosociological Perspective on Law* (New York: Aldine De Gruyter, 1993): 22–24 [hereinafter Legal Construct, Social Concept].
6. During the period from 1967 to 2010, the population of the world is estimated to have increased by no less than 70 million people per year. U.S. Census Bureau, Total Midyear Population for the World 1950–2050,

http://www.census.gov/ipc/www/idb/worldpoptotal.php (accessed April 13, 2011). Migration between countries is thought to have also increased. The number of people whose country of residence was not the country of their birth is estimated to have more than doubled from 76 million in 1965 to 188 million in 2005. J. Edward Taylor, "International Migration and Economic Development," in *United Nations International Symposium on International Migration and Development* (2006), 1, 22, http://www.un.org/esa/population/migration/turin/Symposium_Turin_files/P09_SYMP_Taylor.pdf (accessed April 13, 2011). Inter-nation migration can cause population growth in a country in which the birth rate is equal to the death rate, and it can prevent population size from declining in a country in which the birth rate is less than the death rate.

7. Christian Fuchs, "Transnational Space and the 'Network Society,'" *21st Century Society* 2 (2007): 49, 56, 61. Inter-country ties in a world economy based on capitalism may have started to increase as early as 1500 AD. Immanuel Wallerstein, *The Essential Wallerstein* (New York: New Press, 2000), 140.
8. Proposition 3 is discussed infra Part I-C.
9. See Evan Schofer, "Cross-national Differences in the Expansion of Science, 1970–1990," *Social Forces* 83 (2004): 215 (studying change from 1970 to 1990 in an index of science infrastructure in countries differing in type of government, dominant religion, and level of economic development).
10. Larry D. Barnett, "The Roots of Law," *American University Journal of Gender Social Policy & the Law* 15 (2007): 613, 630–35, 677–79 [hereinafter *The Roots of Law*]. For a measure of the accumulation of knowledge in the United States, see ibid., 628–30. Pages 628–35 and 677–79 in *The Roots of Law* are reproduced in Parts II and IV-B, respectively, of Chapter 6 supra.
11. Peter Lubin and Dwight Duncan, "Follow the Footnote or the Advocate as Historian of Same-Sex Marriage," *Catholic University Law Review* 47 (1998): 1271, 1324.
12. Slavery, although rare at the present time, was not uncommon in the world prior to the twentieth century. Karen E. Bravo, "Exploring the Analogy between Modern Trafficking in Humans and the Trans-Atlantic Slave Trade," *Boston University International Law Journal* 25 (2007): 207, 266–67.
13. Among adults who reside in households in the United States, the percentage disagreeing with the statement (MARHOMO) that "homosexual couples should have the right to marry one another" was 55 percent in 2004 and 48 percent in 2008, but in 1988, the percentage was 73 percent. The preceding percentages were weighted with COMPWT and are the totals of "disagree" and "strongly disagree." SDA Archive, GSS 1972–2008 Cumulative Data File, http://sda.berkeley.edu/cgi-bin/hsda?harcsda+gss08 (accessed April 13, 2011). Although opposition to same-sex marriage was evidently less in the first decade of the twenty-first century than in the 1980s, same-sex marriage is still at variance with social values in the United States. Lynn Marie Kohm, "The Homosexual "Union": Should Gay and Lesbian Partnerships be Granted the Same Status as Marriage?" *Journal of Contemporary Law* 22 (1996): 51, 62. Currently, law in just two states (Massachusetts and Connecticut) allows same-sex marriage, and law in eleven other states

and the District of Columbia offers some type of recognition to same-sex non-marital unions. Louis Thorson, Comment, "Same-Sex Divorce and Wisconsin Courts: Imperfect Harmony?" *Marquette Law Review* 92 (2009): 617, 623–34.

14. Larry D. Barnett, "Law as Symbol: Appearances in the Regulation of Investment Advisers and Attorneys," *Cleveland State Law Review* 55 (2007): 289, 336–37 [hereinafter *Law as Symbol*]; *The Roots of Law*, supra note 10, at 630–31. Pages 336–37 of *Law as Symbol* are reproduced in Part V of Chapter 8 infra.
15. David John Frank and Elizabeth H. McEneaney, "The Individualization of Society and the Liberalization of State Policies on Same-Sex Sexual Relations, 1984-1995," *Social Forces* 77 (1999): 911.
16. Cf. *Legal Construct, Social Concept*, supra note 5, at 20–24 (discussing the frequency of use by United States courts of the constitutional guarantee that limits classifications by U.S. governmental entities and linking change in this frequency to the growth of knowledge and population density).
17. *The Roots of Law*, supra note 10, at 632–35 (reviewing federal statutes that require employment-related decisions to be based on the skills of the individuals affected by the decisions rather than on the demographic attributes of the individuals).
18. Sandra Fredman, *Discrimination Law* (Oxford: Oxford University Press, 2002), 6–7, 69, 75, 85–86, 89–90. The European Economic Community (now named the European Community) was established by a treaty signed in 1957; the European Union was created by a treaty signed in 1992. Tore Totdal, "An Introduction to the European Community and to European Community Law," *North Dakota Law Review* 75 (1999): 59, 59–65.
19. Colleen Sheppard, "Equality Rights and Institutional Change: Insights from Canada and the United States," *Arizona Journal of International and Comparative Law* 15 (1998): 143, 144–46.
20. Joseph W. Schneider, "Social Problems Theory: The Constructionist View," *Annual Review of Sociology* 11 (1985): 209, 210–12.
21. For evidence that the evolution over time of sex role differences in the United States has affected Supreme Court decisions, see *Legal Construct, Social Concept*, supra note 5, at 47–55; Larry D. Barnett, "The Public-Private Dichotomy in Morality and Law," *Journal of Law & Policy* 18 (2010): 541, 593–603 [hereinafter Morality and Law].
22. Stanley Lieberson et al., "The Instability of Androgynous Names: The Symbolic Maintenance of Gender Boundaries," *American Journal of Society* 105 (2000): 1249, 1260–61, 1274.
23. Under Anglo-American common law, an individual is allowed to change her/his given name as long as the new name does not involve fraud and is not obscene. Omi Morgenstern Leissner, "The Problem That Has No Name," *Cardozo Women's Law Journal* 4 (1998): 321, 335–36. Accurate data do not seem to exist on the frequency with which individuals in the United States replace first-names that are linked to their sex with names that are sex-neutral or with names that are associated with the opposite sex. Such changes, however, are probably rare. Ibid.
24. Samuel R. Bagenstos, "'Rational Discrimination,' Accommodation, and the Politics of (Disability) Civil Rights," *Virginia Law Review* 89 (2003): 825, 877

(observing that discrimination is banned by law because discrimination is not rational).

25. Bennun v. Rutgers State Univ., 941 F.2d 154, 173 (3d Cir. 1991), *cert. denied*, *United States Reports* 502 (1992), 1066.

26. Law governing the dissolution of marriage has not had an appreciable, enduring impact on the rate at which marriages dissolve. Frans van Poppel and Joop de Beer, "Measuring the Effect of Changing Legislation on the Frequency of Divorce: The Netherlands, 1830-1990," *Demography* 30 (1993): 425, 439; Thorsten Kneip and Gerrit Bauer, "Did Unilateral Divorce Laws Raise Divorce Rates in Western Europe?," *Journal of Marriage and Family* 71 (2009): 592; Justin Wolfers, "Did Unilateral Divorce Laws Raise Divorce Rates? A Reconciliation and New Results," *American Economic Review* 96 (2006): 1802. If the divorce rate is not materially affected in the long run by changes in law on divorce, the latter presumably reflects the former, i.e., change in law on divorce is likely to be attributable to secular change in the divorce rate.

27. Thomas C. Wilson, "Community Population Size and Social Heterogeneity: An Empirical Test," *American Journal of Sociology* 91 (1986): 1154, 1155–57; Claude S. Fischer, "The Subcultural Theory of Urbanism: A Twentieth-Year Assessment," *American Journal of Sociology* 101 (1995): 543, 544–46.

28. Georg Simmel, "The Metropolis and Mental Life," in *The Sociology of Georg Simmel*, ed. and trans. Kurt H. Wolff (Glencoe, IL: Free Press, 1950), 409, 410 (theorizing that a metropolitan area provides a sensory rich environment that promotes intellectual development).

29. Ibid., 410.

30. Fischer, supra note 27, at 568.

31. Laura M. Moore and Seth Ovadia, "Accounting for Spatial Variation in Tolerance: The Effects of Education and Religion," *Social Forces* 84 (2006): 2205, 2217.

32. U.S. Census Bureau, *Statistical Abstract of the United States: 2000*, 120th ed. (2000), 908, http://www.census.gov/prod/www/abs/statab.html (accessed April 13, 2011).

33. Ibid.

34. See Simmel, supra note 28, at 419 (hypothesizing that, after a threshold has been reached, the advantage in intellectual sophistication possessed by city dwellers over persons outside cities advances geometrically).

35. The hypothesis that social change typically occurs abruptly rather than gradually—i.e., that social change typically involves thresholds—is consistent with the thesis that metropolitan areas increase the intensity of and conflict between subcultures. Fischer, supra note 27, at 545, 548. Intensity and conflict, by their very nature, are conducive to sudden change.

36. The thresholds at which population density effects a change may not be the same in all geographic areas. Instead, the thresholds may differ between geographic areas, and the difference(s) may depend on such variables as economic structure and social values. Claude S. Fischer, "Toward a Subcultural Theory of Urbanism," *American Journal of Sociology* 80 (1975): 1319, 1330.

37. The rate at which marriages fail is most accurately measured with cohort data. In the United States, almost half of all first marriages that occurred

during the 1980s among ever-married women who were 15–44 years old in 2002 had ended in divorce by 2002. Anjani Chandra et al., *Nat'l Ctr. for Health Statistics, Fertility, Family Planning, and Reproductive Health of U.S. Women: Data from the 2002 National Survey of Family Growth 90 table 51, Vital and Health Statistics*, Series 23, No. 25 (2005), http://www.cdc.gov/nchs/data/series/sr_23/sr23_025.pdf (accessed April 13, 2011).

38. Computed using data obtained from the United Nations Economic Commission for Europe, UNECE Statistical Database (Population), Population 18 and plus, Selected Age Groups, by Marital Status and Sex, http://w3.unece.org/pxweb/database/STAT/30-GE/01-Pop/?lang=1 (accessed April 13, 2011).
39. U.S. Census Bureau, *Table A1. Marital Status of People 15 Years and Over, by Age, Sex, Personal Earnings, Race, and Hispanic Origin*, 2008 (2009), http://www.census.gov/population/www/socdemo/hh-fam/cps2008.html (accessed April 13, 2011).
40. The forms of marriage that a society may approve are not confined to opposite-sex marriage and same-sex marriage, both of which may be permitted. Other forms of marriage are defined by the number of spouses that an individual is allowed. The latter forms are monogamy (in which an individual can have just one spouse at a time), polyandry (in which a female can have two or more husbands concurrently), and polygyny (in which a male can have two or more wives concurrently). By definition, a society that requires monogamy does not permit polyandry or polygyny, but a society that does not limit itself to monogamy can permit both polyandry and polygyny.
41. Personal Responsibility and Work Opportunity Reconciliation Act of 1996, Pub. L. No. 104–193, § 101(2), 110 Stat. 2105, 2110 (1996).
42. See James S. Coleman, "Social Capital in the Creation of Human Capital," *American Journal of Sociology* 94 (1988): S95 (proposing the concept of, and discussing forms of, social capital).
43. The enumerated benefits are derived from research that was conducted during the last half-century in the United States. These benefits, however, may be partially or completely absent in other historical eras and in societies that are not similarly structured. For instance, the enumerated benefits were identified from research on a nation whose ideal form of marriage has been monogamy involving persons of opposite sex; different benefits may be found in social systems with opposite-sex polygyny and/or polyandry. Claude Lévi-Strauss, *The Elementary Structures of Kinship*, trans. James Harle Bell et al., rev. ed. (Boston, MA: Beacon Press, 1969), 38, 43–44, 267, 371. See Thomas V. Pollet and Daniel Nettle, "Market Forces Affect Patterns of Polygyny in Uganda," *Proceedings of the National Academy of Sciences of the United States of America* 106 (2009): 2114 (finding that the likelihood of polgyny was related to land ownership among men and to the sex ratio). Cf. R. Jean Cadigan, "Woman-to-Woman Marriage: Practices and Benefits in Sub-Saharan Africa," *Journal of Comparative Family Studies* 29 (1998): 89 (finding social benefits from same-sex marriage between women). Moreover, the research that underlies the benefits enumerated in the text has reached conclusions that have been questioned. Pietro Saitta, *La Genitorialità Sociale e la Sua Regolazione. Una Rassegna Europea* 17

Working Paper No. 18, Interuniversity Centre for Research on Sociology of Law, Information and Legal Institutions, University of Messina (2006), http://www.cirsdig.it/indexeng.html (accessed April 13, 2011). Accordingly, the benefits we name in the text are intended to be a provisional list. The reader should keep in mind, however, that the popularity of marriage in a society is evidence that marriage furnishes important benefits in the society even though these benefits (1) may be other than, or in addition to, the listed benefits, (2) may not be the same in all types of societies, and (3) may be altered by change in social, economic, and demographic conditions.

44. Linda J. Waite and Evelyn L. Lehrer, "The Benefits from Marriage and Religion in the United States: A Comparative Analysis," *Population and Development Review* 29 (2003): 255, 259.
45. Gunnar Andersson et al., "Cohort Fertility Patterns in the Nordic Countries," *Demographic Research* 20 (article 14) (2009): 313, 323, 332 (on file with author), http://www.demographic-research.org/Volumes/Vol20/14/default .htm (accessed April 13, 2011); Laurie Chancey, Voluntary Childlessness in the United States: Recent Trends by Cohort and Period 18–21 (May 2006) (unpublished M.A. thesis, Louisiana State University) (on file with author); Tomas Frejka, "Parity Distribution and Completed Family Size in Europe: Incipient Decline of the Two-Family Model," *Demographic Research* 19 (article 4) (2008): 47, 49–50, 52, 54, 56, 58, 61 (on file with author), http://www.demographic-research.org/Volumes/Vol19/4/default.htm (accessed April 13, 2011).
46. Waite and Lehrer, supra note 44, at 257–59; Richard A. Easterlin, "Explaining Happiness," *Proceedings of the National Academy of Sciences* 100 (2003): 11176, 11178–11179; Steven Stack and J. Ross Eshleman, "Marital Status and Happiness: A 17-Nation Study," *Journal of Marriage and Family* 60 (1998): 527.
47. Waite and Lehrer, supra note 44, at 258, 264.
48. Ibid., 264.
49. Thomas Rotolo, "A Time to Join, A Time to Quit: The Influence of Life Cycle Transitions on Voluntary Association Membership," *Social Forces* 78 (2000): 1133, 1136–37 (noting that studies have found that, following marriage, women are more likely to focus on activities inside the home and men are more likely to focus on activities outside the home).
50. Ibid., 1146–47, 1150–51, 1155–56. The impact of marriage was independent of the impact of childbearing and the age of children. The impact of marriage, therefore, may be partly a function of the difference in marital roles that is a component of current differences in gender roles.
51. Stephen Knack, "Social Capital and the Quality of Government: Evidence from the States," *American Journal of Political Science* 46 (2002): 772, 779.
52. Paul Dekker and Andries van den Broek, "Civil Society in Comparative Perspective: Involvement in Voluntary Associations in North America and Western Europe," *Voluntas: International Journal of Voluntary and Nonprofit Organizations* 9 (1998): 11, 23 n.9, 33. See Paul Dekker and Andries van den Broek, "Involvement in Voluntary Associations in North America and Western Europe: Trends and Correlates 1981–2000," *Journal*

of Civil Society 1 (2005): 45, 53–56 (finding that higher levels of voluntary association participation were related to higher levels of trust but concluding that the direction of causality could not be established). The ranking of the United States and European nations on rates of participation in voluntary associations varies with the type of association that is the basis for the ranking. James E. Curtis et al., "Voluntary Association Membership in Fifteen Countries: A Comparative Analysis," *American Sociological Review* 57 (1992): 139.

53. Knack, supra note 51, at 779; Rafael La Porta et al., "Trust in Large Organizations," *American Economic Review* 87 (May 1997): 333, 335–36.
54. La Porta, supra note 53, at 335–36. The study omitted "socialist" countries. Ibid., 334. In measuring the adequacy of infrastructure, the study considered air transportation, ports, power supply, roads, and telecommunications. Ibid., 335 table 1.
55. Daniel Lederman et al., "Violent Crime: Does Social Capital Matter?" *Economic Development and Cultural Change* 50 (2002): 509, 529; Richard Rosenfeld et al., "Social Trust, Firearm Prevalence, and Homicide," *Annals of Epidemiology* 17 (2007): 119, 124.
56. The history and impact of the amendment to the U.S. Constitution that was the basis for the ban, and of the federal legislation that implemented the amendment, are described in Joshua Kaplan, "Unmasking the Federal Marriage Amendment: The Status of Sexuality," *Georgetown Journal of Gender and the Law* 6 (2005): 105, 115–18, 121–22.
57. An historical marker for the inception of these changes is the Resolution on Equal Rights for Homosexuals and Lesbians in the EC, Eur. Parl. Doc. A3-0028, 1994 O.J. (C 61) 40.
58. The structure of the European Union is described in Duncan E. Alford, *European Union Legal Materials: A Guide for Infrequent Users* (2005), http://www.aallnet.org/products/pub_llj_v97n01/2005-03.pdf (accessed April 13, 2011).
59. Treaty on European Union, July 29, 1992, 1992 O.J. (C 191) art. R, http://eur-lex.europa.eu/en/treaties/dat/11992M/htm/11992M .html (accessed April 13, 2011). The twelve original members were Belgium, Denmark, France, Germany, Greece, Ireland, Italy, Luxembourg, The Netherlands, Portugal, Spain, and the United Kingdom. Ibid. The Treaty, which required ratification by signatory countries, was in effect as of November 1, 1993. Volker Roben, "Constitutionalism of the European Union After the Draft Constitutional Treaty: How Much Hierarchy?" *Columbia Journal of European Law* 10 (2004): 339, 340 n.3.
60. Europa, The History of the European Union: 1995, http://europa.eu/abc/history/1990-1999/1995/index_en .htm (accessed April 13, 2011). The three countries that joined the EU in 1995 were Austria, Finland, and Sweden. Ibid.
61. Wikipedia, Northern Europe, http://en.wikipedia.org/wiki/Northern_Europe (accessed April 13, 2011); Wikipedia, Southern Europe, http://en.wikipedia.org/wiki/Southern_Europe (accessed April 13, 2011); Wikipedia, Western Europe, http://en.wikipedia.org/wiki/Western _Europe (accessed April 13, 2011). Several nation-states in these regions—most notably, Iceland, Norway, and Switzerland—have not become EU members.

Europa, The EU at a Glance, http://europa.eu/abc/european_countries/eu_members/index_en.htm (accessed April 13, 2011).

62. Arthur B. Gunlicks, "The Impact of Unification on German Federalism," in *The Berlin Republic: German Unification and A Decade of Changes*, ed. Winand Gellner and John D. Robertson (London: Frank Cass, 2003): 131, 131–36 [hereinafter *The Berlin Republic*].
63. Mi-Kyung Kim and John D. Robertson, "Analysing German Unification: State, Nation and the Quest for Political Community," in *The Berlin Republic*, supra note 62, at 3, 7; Winand Gellner and Gerd Strohmeier, "The 'Double' Public: Germany After Reunification," in *The Berlin Republic*, supra note 62, at 59, 60–61.
64. Europa, The History of the European Union: 2000–Today, http://europa.eu/abc/history/2000_today/index_en.htm (accessed April 13, 2011). The ten countries were Cyprus, Czech Republic, Estonia, Hungary, Latvia, Lithuania, Malta, Poland, Slovak Republic, and Slovenia. Ibid.
65. Natalie Shimmel, "Welcome to Europe, but Please Stay Out: Freedom of Movement and the May 2004 Expansion of the European Union," *Berkeley Journal of International Law* 24 (2006): 760, 774–76.
66. Of the fourteen countries, only one (Denmark) changed its law before 1995 to recognize same-sex unions. Denmark was a member of the European Economic Community, the forerunner of the European Union. Treaty on European Union, art. G, supra note 59, at art. G; Roger J. Goebel, "The Treaty of Amsterdam in Historical Perspective: Introduction to the Symposium," *Fordham International Law Journal* 22 (1999): S7, S18–19; Roger J. Goebel, "The European Union in Transition: The Treaty of Nice in Effect; Enlargement in Sight; A Constitution in Doubt," *Fordham International Law Journal* 27 (2004): 455, 473 n.73. Accordingly, the pre-1995 change in law by Denmark is included in the study.
67. The data for the study were compiled in 2009.
68. Ian Curry-Sumner, *All's Well that Ends registered? The substantive and private international law aspects of non-marital registered relationships in Europe* (Antwerp: Intersentia, 2005); Patrick Festy, "Legalizing Same-Sex Unions in Europe: Innovations and Paradoxes," *Population & Societies* (June 2006): 1; ILGA—Europe, Marriage and Partnership Rights for Same-Sex Partners: Country-by-Country, http://doc.ilga.org/europe/issues/marriage_and_partnership/marriage_and_partnership_rights_for_same_sex_partners_country_by_country (accessed April 13, 2011); Marriage Law Foundation, International Survey of Legal Recognition of Same-Sex Couples (no date), http://marriagelawfoundation.org/publications/International.pdf (accessed February 18, 2011); Kees Waaldijk et al., *More or Less Together: Levels of Legal Consequences of Marriage, Cohabitation and Registered Partnership for Different-Sex and Same-Sex Partners: A Comparative Study of Nine European Countries* (2004), http://www.ined.fr/fichier/t_publication/1034/publi_pdf1_document_de_travail_125.pdf; Wikipedia, Timeline of Same-Sex Marriage, http://en.wikipedia.org/wiki/Timeline_of_same-sex_marriage (accessed April 13, 2011).
69. Sarah A. Soule, "Going to the Chapel? Same-Sex Marriage Bans in the United States, 1973-2000," *Social Problems* 51 (2004): 453.

70. Justin Reinheimer, "Same-Sex Marriage through the Equal Protection Clause: A Gender-Conscious Analysis," *Berkeley Journal of Gender, Law & Justice* 21 (2006): 213, 214–15.
71. David Masci, Pew Forum on Religion & Public Life, Public Opinion on Gay Marriage: Opponents Consistently Outnumber Supporters (July 9, 2009), http://pewforum.org/docs/?DocID=424 (accessed April 13, 2011).
72. Soule, supra note 69, at 456 n.3, 457, 463.
73. Ibid., 454–55, 459–62.
74. Ibid., 465–66. The three sociological–demographic variables were considered by the investigator to be control variables. Accordingly, they were included in the regression equation only for the purpose of removing their influence on the dependent variable so that the impact of each political variable on the dependent variable could be estimated. Nonetheless, the investigator reports the regression coefficients for each of the three sociological–demographic variables. Ibid., 467 table 2, 470 table 3.
75. Ibid., 467 table 2, 469, 470 table 3.
76. Denton E. Morrison and Ramon E. Henkel, "Significance Tests Reconsidered," *American Sociologist* 4 (1969): 131, 134 (noting that significance tests are inappropriate when analyzing data on all of the members of a population).
77. James K. Skipper, Jr. et al., "The Sacredness of .05: A Note Concerning the Uses of Statistical Levels of Significance in Social Science," *American Sociologist* 2 (1967): 16, 16–17.
78. Soule, supra note 69, at 467 table 2, 470 table 3.
79. Ibid., 465–66.
80. Ibid.
81. U.S. Bureau of the Census, *Statistical Abstract of the United States: 1970*, 91st ed. (Washington, DC: U.S. Government Printing Office, 1970), 2, http://www.census.gov/prod/www/abs/statab.html (accessed April 13, 2011); U.S. Bureau of the Census, *Statistical Abstract of the United States: 1980*, 101st ed. (Washington, DC: U.S. Government Printing Office, 1980), 2, http://www.census.gov/prod/www/abs/statab.html (accessed April 13, 2011); U.S. Bureau of the Census, *Statistical Abstract of the United States: 1990*, 110th ed. (Washington, DC: U.S. Government Printing Office, 1990), 4, http://www.census.gov/prod/www/abs/statab.html (accessed April 13, 2011); U.S. Bureau of the Census, *Statistical Abstract of the United States: 2000*, 120th ed. (Washington, DC: U.S. Government Printing Office, 2000), 4, http://www.census.gov/prod/www/abs/statab.html (accessed April 13, 2011).
82. Frank and McEneaney, supra note 15.
83. For law in the United States, see Lawrence v. Texas, *United States Reports* 539 (2003), 558, 604–5 (Scalia, J., Rehnquist, C.J., and Thomas, J., dissenting). The dissent in *Lawrence* argued that the rationale used by the Court to protect private same-sex consensual sexual activity under the liberty guarantee of the federal constitution gives same-sex couples a constitutional right to marry. Ibid.

    The adoption of law that permits consensual same-sex sexual activity may not be followed immediately by the adoption of law that authorizes same-sex non-marital partnerships and same-sex marriage. However, the time elapsing between the former and the latter is unlikely to be long when judged in historical terms.

84. Frank and McEneaney, supra note 15, at 924.
85. Ibid., 917–18.
86. Ibid., 932–33 table 3.
87. In all models, the regression coefficients were positive and statistically significant for the relationship between the extent to which countries were involved in world affairs and the extent to which the law of the countries permitted same-sex sexual activity among men and among women. Ibid., 932–33 table 3. The lawfulness of same-sex sexual activity was measured by an ordinal-level variable. Ibid., 922 table 1.
88. The Frank–McEneaney study was confined to countries that were independent in 1984 as well as in 1995, and it had data for eighty-four such countries. Ibid., 921, 937 n.11. The number of countries that were independent in both years but were omitted from the study is not reported. Consequently, whether the study encompassed all of the countries in its defined universe cannot be ascertained. Assuming that the study had data for less than its entire universe, the procedure for deciding whether to include a country should have been, but was not, described by the investigators. See ibid., 921. If a random sampling procedure was not used, a prerequisite to the use of tests of statistical significance was absent. Earl R. Babbie, *Survey Research Methods* (1973), 307–9.
89. See supra note 83 and accompanying text.
90. John B. Dorris, "Antidiscrimination Laws in Local Government: A Public Policy Analysis of Municipal Lesbian and Gay Public Employment Protection," in *Gays and Lesbians in the Democratic Process*, ed. Ellen D.B. Riggle and Barry L. Tadlock (New York: Columbia University Press, 1999), 39; Donald P. Haider-Markel and Kenneth J. Meier, "The Politics of Gay and Lesbian Rights: Expanding the Scope of the Conflict," *Journal of Politics* 58 (1996): 332; Marieka Klawitter and Brian Hammer, "Spatial and Temporal Diffusion of Local Antidiscrimination Policies for Sexual Orientation," in *Gays and Lesbians in the Democratic Process*, supra, at 22; Kenneth D. Wald et al., "The Politics of Gay Rights in American Communities: Explaining Antidiscrimination Ordinances and Policies," *American Journal of Political Science* 40 (1996): 1152.
91. Haider-Markel and Meier, supra note 90, at 335–36.
92. The study by Klawitter and Hammer was limited to counties having a population of at least one hundred thousand. Klawitter and Hammer, supra note 90, at 26. In the study by Haider-Markel and Meier, the dependent variable was whether discrimination based on sexual preference was prohibited by states. However, a state whose government had not adopted law against sexual-preference discrimination was evidently counted as having such law as long as a minimum percentage of the population of the state resided in cities that had such law. See Haider-Markel and Meier, supra note 90, at 335. The investigators do not identify the threshold percentage that determined the classification of states on the dependent variable.
93. Dorris, supra note 90, at 48–49; Haider-Markel and Meier, supra note 90, at 341 table 1. In the study by Haider-Markel and Meier, however, education had a regression coefficient that was statistically significant at or below .10 for just law barring sexual-preference discrimination in public-sector

employment and law barring sexual-preference discrimination in private-sector employment. With the .10 significance level as the maximum for rejecting the null hypothesis, the educational attainment of jurisdiction inhabitants was not related to the presence in the jurisdictions of law forbidding sexual-preference discrimination in credit, education, housing, public accommodations, or union practices. The sign and magnitude of coefficients that had a significance level above .10 are not reported. Haider-Markel and Meier, supra note 90, at 342 table 2.

The study by Klawitter and Hammer, in which the dependent variable was whether county and city law barred sexual-orientation discrimination in private-sector employment, found that none of the levels of the ordinal scale for educational attainment had a regression coefficient that was statistically significant at or below .10; i.e., the regression coefficients for the dummy variables for educational attainment did not differ from the reference category (education beyond a bachelor's degree) at .10 or below. Klawitter and Hammer, supra note 90, at 29 table 2.1, 33.

The study by Wald et al. did not estimate the relationship between the educational attainment of jurisdiction inhabitants and whether the jurisdictions had law forbidding sexual-orientation discrimination. Instead, the study included two independent variables for the relative presence of higher education in a jurisdiction—(1) the number of colleges and universities in each jurisdiction and (2) the aggregate number of students enrolled in the colleges and universities of a jurisdiction as a percentage of the population of the jurisdiction. Wald et al., supra note 90, at 1160. These independent variables had regression coefficients that were not statistically significant at or below .05. Ibid., 1165 table 2.

94. Dorris, supra note 90, at 48–49; Klawitter and Hammer, supra note 90, at 29 table 2.1, 33; Wald et al., supra note 90, at 1165–66. The study by Haider-Markel and Meier included an independent variable for the percentage of the inhabitants of a state who resided in an urban area as of 1990. Haider-Markel and Meier, supra note 90, at 339, 347. The study did not report the regression coefficient for this variable because the coefficient failed to reach statistical significance at .10 or below. Ibid., 341 table 1, 342 table 2. However, an area was "urban" only if it was classified as such by the U.S. Census Bureau. Ibid., 347, 349. The minimum population for an urban area in 1990 was 2,500. U.S. Bureau of the Census, *Statistical Abstract of the United States: 1992*, 112th ed. (Washington, DC: U.S. Government Printing Office, 1992), 4, http://www.census.gov/prod/www/abs/statab.html (accessed April 13, 2011). Urban areas, because of the small populations they can contain, are inappropriate for assessing the theory of urbanism. See supra text accompanying and following note 81.

95. Dorris, supra note 90, at 48–49; Klawitter and Hammer, supra note 90, at 29 table 2.1, 33. See Wald et al., supra note 90, at 1163–65, 1172. In the study by Wald et al., the .05 significance level was employed in deciding whether to reject the null hypothesis; the sign and magnitude of the regression coefficient for income are not reported. Ibid., 1165 table 2.

The study by Haider-Markel and Meier contained no measure of income or of any other aspect of wealth. Haider-Markel and Meier, supra note 90, at 339, 347.

96. Dorris, supra note 90, at 48–49; Klawitter and Hammer, supra note 90, at 29 table 2.1, 33. The study by Dorris used data on almost all cities with a law prohibiting sexual-preference discrimination; these cities were compared to a randomly chosen sample of cities that had a population of at least 2,500 but did not have a law prohibiting sexual-preference discrimination. Dorris, supra note 90, at 46, 54–57. For the study by Klawitter and Hammer, the universe was counties with at least one hundred thousand inhabitants in 1980, and data were obtained for almost all of these counties. Klawitter and Hammer, supra note 90, at 26, 36 n.3. While tests of statistical significance may be appropriate in the study by Dorris, they are inappropriate in the study by Klawitter and Hammer.
97. *The Roots of Law*, supra note 10, at 630–31, 678–79; Simmel, supra note 28, at 409–10.
98. Dorris, supra note 90, at 47–48; Soule, supra note 69, at 465; Wald, supra note 90, at 1161–62.
99. Rory McVeigh and Maria-Elena D. Diaz, "Voting to Ban Same-Sex Marriage: Interests, Values, and Communities," *American Sociological Review* 74 (2009): 891, 907 (finding that, in counties in which sex roles and families were conventionally structured, voters tended to be strongly opposed to same-sex marriage).
100. Sharon Estee, "Natality: Measures Based on Vital Statistics," in *The Methods and Materials of Demography*, ed. Jacob S. Siegel and David A. Swanson, 2nd ed. (Amsterdam: Elsevier, 2004), 371, 391–93.
101. Ibid., 392 (describing the TFR as a depiction of "the completed fertility of a synthetic cohort of women").
102. Gayle Kaufman, "Do Gender Roles Matter?" *Journal Family Issues* 21 (2000): 128.
103. Childbearing has been found to be a function of traditionalism in sex roles. S. Philip Morgan and Linda J. Waite, "Parenthood and the Attitudes of Young Adults," *American Sociological Review* 52 (1987): 541, 544; Steven L. Nock, "The Symbolic Meaning of Childbearing," *Journal of Family Issues* 8 (1987): 373, 385, 388.
104. Marin Clarkberg et al., "Attitudes, Values, and Entrance into Cohabitational versus Marital Unions," *Social Forces* 74 (1995): 609, 622 (finding that, for women and for men, nontraditional views of sex roles raise the likelihood of cohabitation and reduce the likelihood of marriage).
105. Edgar H. Schein, "Culture: The Missing Concept in Organization Studies," *Administrative Science Quarterly* 41 (1996): 229, 236.
106. Another name often applied to this type of data is "cross-sectional time-series."
107. Lois W. Sayrs, "Pooled Time Series Analysis," in *Quantitative Applications in the Social Sciences*, (Sage University Paper No. 70, 1989), 1, 7.
108. See the text accompanying supra notes 58 through 65.
109. See the text accompanying supra note 67.
110. *The Roots of Law*, supra note 10, at 616; *Law as Symbol*, supra note 14, at 334. Page 616 of *The Roots of Law* is reproduced in Part I of Chapter 6 supra; page 334 of *Law as Symbol* is reproduced in Part V of Chapter 8 infra.
111. See supra notes 66–68 and accompanying text.

112. See text accompanying supra note 68.
113. Sweden was coded 0 in all of the years included in the study, because its law recognizing same-sex marriage was not enacted until 2009.
114. Because the study included fourteen countries and sought data on four independent variables for each country in eight years, the number of cells requiring data was 448 (14 × 4 × 8 = 448). Three of the 448 cells had no data for the regression analysis. (See, in addition, infra note 121.) Of the three cells with no data, two were for school-life expectancy (discussed in the text infra) in Luxembourg in 1990 and 1995; the third cell was for the TFR in Luxembourg in 1975. We assume that the missing data were not a function of what would have been observed and were thus "missing at random." The present study employed maximum-likelihood estimates of regression coefficients and odds ratios, which estimates are not rendered inaccurate by data that are missing at random. Sophia Rabe-Hesketh and Anders Skrondal, *Multilevel and Longitudinal Modeling Using Stata*, 2nd ed. (College Station, TX: Stata Press, 2008), 207.
115. The data on gross domestic product per person are from Organization for Economic Cooperation and Development OECD.StatExtracts, *Gross Domestic Product: GDP per Head, US $, Current Prices, Current PPPs*, http://stats.oecd.org/index.aspx?queryid=558 (accessed January 19, 2011). The data are based on purchasing power parities, which are discussed in *Organization for Economic Cooperation and Development, Eurostat-OECD Methodological Manual on Purchasing Power Parities* (2006), 261, http://www.oecd.org/std/ppp/manual (accessed January 19, 2011).
116. See the text accompanying supra notes 98–105.
117. The data on TFRs are from the following sources: U.N. Dep't of Econ. & Soc. Affairs, Population Div., *Partnership and Reproductive Behaviour in Low-Fertility Countries*, U.N. Doc. ESA/WP.177 (May 2003), 72 table 22 http://www.un.org/esa/population/publications/reprobehavior/partrepro.pdf (accessed April 13, 2011) (data for 1970 through 2000); U.N. Econ. Comm'n for Europe, *Total Fertility Rate*, http://w3.unece.org/pxweb/Dialog/varval.asp?ma=02_GEFHFertilityRate_r&ti=Total%20Fertility%20Rate%20by%20Country%20and%20Year&path=../DATABASE/Stat/30-GE/02-Families_households/&lang=1 (data for 2005) (accessed April 19, 2011).
118. The data on school-life expectancy that were used in the instant study are from UNESCO Institute for Statistics, Historical Data, Table 3—Total Enrolment, School Life Expectancy and Expenditure on Education, http://www.uis.unesco.org/ev.php?ID=7660_201&ID2=DO_TOPIC (accessed June 1, 2009) (on file with author).
119. UNESCO Institute for Statistics, Education Indicators: Technical Guidelines (2009), 7, http://www.uis.unesco.org/ev.php?ID=5202_201&ID2=DO_TOPIC (follow "English" hyperlink) (accessed January 19, 2011).
120. Ibid., 7.
121. U.N. Dep't of Econ. & Soc. Affairs, Population Div., *World Urbanization Prospects: The 2007 Revision Population Database, Panel 2: Urban Agglomerations – Population Residing in Agglomeration as Percentage of Total Population* (2008), http://esa.un.org/unup/index.asp?panel=2 (accessed April 13, 2011). The term "urban agglomeration" is defined as

"the de facto population contained within the contours of a contiguous territory inhabited at urban density levels without regard to administrative boundaries. It usually incorporates the population in a city or town plus that in the sub-urban areas lying outside of but being adjacent to the city boundaries." U.N. Dep't of Econ. & Soc. Affairs, Population Div., *World Urbanization Prospects: The 2007 Revision Population Database, Glossary* (2008), http://esa.un.org/unup/index.asp?panel=6 (accessed April 13, 2011).

The United Nations Population Division reports "no data available" for Luxembourg on this measure. U.N. Dep't of Econ. & Soc. Affairs, Population Div., *World Urbanization Prospects: The 2007 Revision Population Database, Panel 2: Urban Agglomerations – Population Residing in Agglomeration as Percentage of Total Population* (2008), http://esa.un.org/unup/index.asp?panel=2 (accessed April 13, 2011). In the instant study, URBANPOP for Luxembourg was coded zero in each of the eight years from 1970 to 2005, because in none of these years did urban areas of Luxembourg have a combined population of 750,000 or more. Indeed, the largest total population of urban areas of Luxembourg during this period was 378,000 in 2005. U.N. Dep't of Econ. & Soc. Affairs, Population Div., *World Urbanization Prospects: The 2007 Revision Population Database, Panel 1: Urban* and Rural Areas – *Urban Population* (2008), http://esa.un.org/unup/index.asp?panel =1 (accessed April 13, 2011).

122. U.N. Dep't of Econ. & Soc. Affairs, Population Div., *World Urbanization Prospects: The 2007 Revision Population Database, Glossary* (2008), http://esa.un.org/unup/index.asp?panel=6 (accessed April 13, 2011) (noting in the definition of "urban population" that "areas [are] classified as urban according to the criteria used by each area or country").
123. See supra Part I-C.
124. See supra Parts I and III-A.
125. When interpreting the data, odds ratios rather than regression coefficients were considered because, unlike regression coefficients, odds ratios have intuitive meaning. See *Law as Symbol*, supra note 14, at 327–28 (explaining the concepts of probability, odds, and odds ratios). Pages 327–28 of *Law as Symbol* are reproduced in Part IV-D of Chapter 8 infra. Moreover, as explained in note 164 infra, regression coefficients in the instant study could not be compared in terms of the magnitude of their impact on the dependent variable.
126. Each hypothesis in this and the preceding paragraph assumes, of course, that all other causal variables remain constant.
127. The authors want to thank Antonio Di Pino for commenting on the statistical aspects of their research. These aspects are described in Parts III-C and III-D.
128. An explanation of the difference between least-squares regression and logistic regression, and the reason for using the latter when the dependent variable is binary, is found in J. Scott Long and Jeremy Freese, *Regression Models for Categorical Dependent Variables Using Stata*, 2nd ed. (College Station, TX: Stata Press, 2006), 113–16 and in Fred C. Pampel, "Logistic Regression: A Primer," in *Quantitative Applications in the Social Sciences*, (Sage University Paper No. 132, 2000), 1, 1–18.

129. See the text accompanying supra notes 112–113.
130. See Rabe-Hesketh and Skrondal, supra note 114, at 61; Michael M. Ward and J. Paul Leigh, "Pooled Time Series Regression Analysis in Longitudinal Studies," *Journal of Clinical Epidemiology* 46 (1993): 645, 650.
131. Ward and Leigh, supra note 130, at 649 ("[T]he results of fixed effects models are restricted to, or conditional upon, the individuals included in the study, and generalization to other groups can be problematic.").
132. See Emilio J. Castilla, *Dynamic Analysis in the Social Sciences* (Amsterdam: Elsevier, 2007), 97, 108–09.
133. Random-effects models are more suitable than fixed-effects models when the findings of a study can be generalized beyond the cases included in the study. Joseph M. Hilbe, *Logistic Regression Models* (Boca Raton, FL: CRC Press 2009), 503.
134. See Rabe-Hesketh and Skrondal, supra note 114, at 51, 62 (noting that a random-effects model is appropriate when the number of clusters—here, the number of countries—exceeds ten and when, for "a good number of clusters," cluster size—here, the number of years for each country—is at least two; but that a fixed-effects model requires "large" cluster sizes to estimate parameters specific to clusters).
135. Castilla, supra note 132, at 108–09.
136. StataCorp., *Stata Longitudinal/Panel-Data Reference Manual Release 10*, (College Station, TX: Stata Press, 2007), 205–21.
137. David W. Hosmer and Stanley Lemeshow, *Applied Logistic Regression*, 2nd ed. (New York: John Wiley, 2000), 339.
138. J. Scott Long, *Regression Models for Categorical and Limited Dependent Variables* (Thousand Oaks, CA: Sage Publications, 1997), 54.
139. Babbie, supra note 88, at 308.
140. For this analysis, the number of observations was 109.
141. See the text accompanying supra note 126.
142. The odds ratio for TFR was 170.949.
143. John Fox, "Regression Diagnostics," in *Quantitative Applications in the Social Sciences* (Sage University Paper No. 79, 1991), 1, 21–24.
144. Ibid., 10–11.
145. The procedure has been proposed by Long and Freese, supra note 128, at 151.
146. Vic Barnett and Toby Lewis, *Outliers in Statistical Data*, 3rd ed. (Chichester: John Wiley, 1994), 7.
147. A system is "[a] group of interacting, interrelated, or interdependent elements forming a complex whole." *American Heritage Dictionary of the English Language*, 3rd ed. (Boston, MA: Houghton Mifflin, 1992), 1823.
148. Because conflict between the components of a system can undermine the stability of the system, a system presumably requires some degree of system integration. Cf. David Lockwood, *Solidarity and Schism* (Oxford: Clarendon Press, 1992), 400 (differentiating "system integration" from "social integration").
149. Barnett and Lewis, supra note 146, at 7, 17.
150. Babbie, supra note 88, at 5–6, 227–28.
151. See Bruce Western, "Vague Theory and Model Uncertainty in Macrosociology," *Sociological Methodology* 26 (1996): 165, 166 (observing that

current theories in macrosociology are not helpful in analyzing quantitative data).

152. Council Regulation No. 1164/94, Establishing a Cohesion Fund, 1994 O.J. (L 130) 1, 3–4; European Union, *Cohesion Policy 2007-13: National Strategic Reference Frameworks* (2008), 3, 5–7, http://ec.europa.eu/regional_policy/atlas2007/fiche/nsrf.pdf (accessed April 13, 2011); European Commission, *Guide to the Cohesion Fund 2000–2006* (2000), 4, http://ec.europa.eu/regional_policy/sources/docoffic/working/doc/vademecum_cf_en.pdf (accessed April 13, 2011); European Commission, European Social Fund, *What is the ESF?* http://ec.europa.eu/employment_social/esf/discover/esf_en.htm (accessed January 19, 2011). In projects and programs that it funds, the European Union prohibits discrimination based on social and demographic attributes. Council Decision, Community Strategic Guidelines on Cohesion, 2006 O.J. (L 291) 11, 14.
153. See generally Part III-D of Chapter 9 infra.
154. Western and Jackman, supra note 2, at 414.
155. See *StataCorp.*, supra note 136, at 9, 205, 207.
156. Hosmer and Lemeshow, supra note 137, at 140.
157. In the four-variable regression model—i.e., in the model that included TFR as an independent variable—the odds ratios for GDP, EDUCALL, and URBANPOP were 1.000609, 1.76051, and 1.349848, respectively. The odds ratios for these variables in the three-variable model are reported infra Tables 7.1 and 7.2.
158. After eliminating from a regression model an independent variable affected by collinearity, the odds ratios for the remaining independent variables may be biased. Fox, supra note 143, at 15–19. Given the consistency between the odds ratios for GDP, EDUCALL, and URBANPOP in the three-variable model and in the four-variable model, the elimination of TFR does not seem to have created such bias.
159. The entries in the bottom panel of the tables are explained in *StataCorp.*, supra note 136, at 210–11, and in Rabe-Hesketh and Skrondal, supra note 114, at 58, 102–4.
160. Quadrature approximation is discussed in: Rabe-Hesketh and Skrondal, supra note 114, at 258–62; Marc Callens and Christophe Croux, "Performance of Likelihood-based Estimation Methods for Multilevel Binary Regression Models," *Journal of Statistical Computation & Simulation* 75 (2005): 1003, 1007. As recommended by Rabe-Hesketh and Skrondal, supra note 114, at 261, the number of quadrature points for the results presented in Table 2 was selected by repeating the regression estimation with an increasing number of points.
161. Stata supplies the significance levels for two-tailed tests. Significance levels under a one-tailed test are one-half those shown in the tables.
162. The percentage change in the odds of such legislation that is due to a change of one unit in a given independent variable is calculated by (1) subtracting 1.000 from the odds ratio for that independent variable and (2) multiplying the result by 100. For example, the percentage change in the odds of such legislation from a one-dollar gain in gross domestic product per capita is computed by subtracting 1.000 from the odds ratio for GDP and multiplying by 100, i.e., $1.001221 - 1.000000 = .001221 \times 100 = .1221\%$. However,

the percentage change resulting from an increase of more than one unit in an independent variable may not be accurately estimated when multiplying (1) the percentage change attributable to one unit of the independent variable by (2) the number of units in a larger amount. Long and Freese, supra note 128, at 216. Accordingly, if gross domestic product per capita rises by $2,500, the percentage change in the odds of enacting legislation that recognizes same-sex unions may be more or less than .1221 × 2,500.

163. The measures of these variables are described in the text accompanying supra notes 115 and 118–122.

164. When pooled time-series data are employed—i.e., when the XTLOGIT command is used—there are no generally accepted Stata statistical techniques that compare regression coefficients for the independent variables in a model and estimate the relative impact of each independent variable on the dependent variable. For example, the LISTCOEF command is unavailable with XTLOGIT, and as a result, the instant study was unable to obtain standardized regression coefficients. The LISTCOEF command is described in Long and Freese, supra note 128, at 94–98, 464–67. In addition, the PRCHANGE command does not work with XTLOGIT, precluding an alternative approach to assessing the magnitude of the impact of each independent variable in the study. The PRCHANGE command is described in ibid., 118–22, 216–17.

As explained in note 162 supra, the percentage change in the odds of LAW may be inaccurately estimated if the percentage change in these odds due to a one-unit change in a specific independent variable is multiplied by a larger number of units of the same independent variable. Nonetheless, the importance of an independent variable to explaining the dependent variable *may* be roughly indicated by the size of the range (i.e., the difference between the maximum and minimum number of units) of the independent variable in conjunction with the magnitude of the odds ratio for that independent variable. See Long and Freese, supra note 128, at 216. In the data for the independent variables in the present study, the largest difference within a country over time, or between countries at a single point in time, was $62,678 for GDP, 7.3 years for EDUCALL, and 38.6 percentage points for URBANPOP.

165. *Morality and Law*, supra note 21, at 588 & n.156, 591 (finding, in an analysis of data from the 1991 General Social Survey, that the odds were 263 percent higher for women than for men that morality would be considered a private matter). *Morality and Law* is reproduced in Chapter 5 supra.

166. *The Roots of Law*, supra note 10, at 674 n.189 (citing empirical studies that found that social values affected doctrines of law). Note 189 in *The Roots of Law* is reproduced in Part IV-A of Chapter 6 supra, where it is numbered note 199.

167. *Morality and Law*, supra note 21, at 593–603 (presenting the argument). Pages 593–603 of *Morality and Law* are reproduced in Part IV of Chapter 5 supra.

168. Lawrence v. Texas, *United States Reports* 539 (2003), 558.

169. *Morality and Law*, supra note 21, at 594 & n.168. Page 594 of *Morality and Law* is reproduced in Part IV of Chapter 5 supra; note 168 in *Morality and Law* has the same number in Chapter 5

170. See supra note 83 and accompanying text.
171. E-mail from Antonio Di Pino (August 17, 2009, 8:55:03 EST; August 17, 2009, 11:39:54 EST) (translated by Pietro Saitta) (on file with authors).
172. Krishna Mazumdar, "An Analysis of Causal Flow Between Social Development and Economic Growth: The Social Development Index," *American Journal of Economics & Sociology* 55 (1996): 361, 361–63.
173. Angela Martin Crowly et al., "Quantitative Cross-National Studies of Economic Development: A Comparison of the Economics and Sociology Literatures," *Studies in Comparative International Development* 33 (1998): 30, 39. See Evan Schofer and John W. Meyer, "The Worldwide Expansion of Higher Education in the Twentieth Century," *American Sociological Review* 70 (2005): 898, 900, 916 (concluding from empirical studies that economic development in countries does not materially enlarge enrollment rates in "education at any level").
174. Mazumdar, supra note 172, at 364, 365, 367, 373. Dr. Mazumdar found that, in high-income countries and in low-income countries, the percentage of the population that resides in urban locations affected, but was unaffected by, per capita real gross domestic product; in middle-income countries, the two variables affected each other. Ibid., 373. The study by Dr. Mazumdar included ninety-two countries, while our study included fourteen. (The fourteen nations in our study are listed in the text in Part II supra.) Ten of the fourteen nations in our study were classified as high-income countries by Dr. Mazumdar; three of the nations in our study (viz., Greece, Ireland, and Portugal) were classified as middle-income countries by Dr. Mazumdar. One nation in our study (viz., Luxembourg) was not in the study by Dr. Mazumdar. Mazumdar, supra note 172, at 367.
175. Supra notes 162–164 and accompanying text.
176. See Mazumdar, supra note 172, at 373, 378, 380 (summarizing from an analysis of country-level data the relationships found between education indicators, gross domestic product per capita, and urban population within each of three levels of gross domestic product per capita).
177. Supra notes 173 (education) and 174 (urbanization) and accompanying text.
178. See *The Roots of Law*, supra note 10, at 630–31, 677–79 (contending that increases in knowledge lead to increases in economic wealth and rationality, each of which fosters individualism). A similar sequence of effects from the growth of knowledge is traced in *Law as Symbol*, supra note 14, at 336 & n.224.
179. Frank and McEneaney, supra note 15, at 912.
180. Because average educational attainment, societal wealth, and degree of urbanization are correlated, just one of the three was used to capture the influence of all of them in a study of jurisdiction-level antecedents of law. Frank and McEneaney, supra note 15, at 926. However, the three variables are different phenomena and should not be deemed interchangeable; each is important in its own right. Thus, the theory of urbanism (explained in the text accompanying supra notes 27–29) cannot be tested without a measure of population density, but a test of the theory must also include a measure of average educational attainment and a measure of wealth. The inclusion of data on educational attainment and on wealth allows these variables to

be controlled and their effects to be removed so that the impact (if any) of urban life on law can be isolated.

181. David A. Belsley, "Model Selection in Regression Analysis, Regression Diagnostics and Prior Knowledge," *International Journal of Forecasting* 2 (1986): 41, 43–45.

8

Jurisdiction Properties and State Regulation of Lawyers

From a macrosociological perspective, law is an institution of society, is shaped by conditions in society, and facilitates social life by, inter alia, producing symbols. Law accordingly adopts concepts and principles that focus on the appearance to society of certain phenomena and that are symbols when the phenomena are socially significant. As an illustration of symbols in law, Chapter 8 examines the standard for ethical conduct that requires attorneys to avoid appearances of impropriety. If symbolic concepts and principles in law are tied to the properties of society, the acceptance of the appearance-of-impropriety standard by a state will be related to one or more system-level properties. In an analysis of data with logistic regression, differences between states in whether the standard was in use in 2010 were found to be associated mainly with differences between states in the levels in 1980 of two such properties: cultural heterogeneity, which was measured in each state by the percentage of inhabitants who had been born outside the United States; and population concentration, which was measured in each state by the percentage of inhabitants who resided in a metropolitan area. Specifically, increases in cultural heterogeneity raised, and increases in population concentration lowered, the odds that a state was using the standard. Because the appearance-of-impropriety standard for attorneys is symbolic, the two properties affected whether symbolism developed in law. The findings also suggest that information on societal properties and the forces behind them can be used to predict, albeit imperfectly, the symbolic concepts and principles of law that will exist at future points in time.

I. Symbols in Law and Society

Every intellectual discipline has a set of unique concepts. Indeed, disciplines are set apart from one another by, inter alia, their concepts. Macrosociology, the discipline that is concerned with the system-level features of societies, places heavy reliance on the concept of "institution." The referent of "institution," however, is not the same in macrosociology as it is in much of everyday discourse—a difference that can perhaps be understood by starting with what an institution is *not*. Specifically, an institution is not a physical facility—i.e., a building or a group of buildings—devoted to a particular public purpose.[1] In macrosociology, rather, an institution is an abstraction from observable social life—a set of statuses and roles (a) that a society defines and endorses and (b) that involve interpersonal relationships through which a socially approved type of activity occurs in the society.[2] Examples of institutions are law, the family, and religion.

Why is the concept of "institution" central to a macrosociological analysis? From the perspective of macrosociology, institutions are intermediaries between a society and individuals, and they serve as the vehicles through which social life is conducted. Institutions are thus the basic components of a society and key to its continuation.[3] Moreover, because a society is a system, the institutions in a society can affect one another, and thereby intensify or reduce the impact of any one institution.

To function smoothly, a society must, of course, be comprised of institutions that contribute to it in positive ways. These contributions occur to the extent that institutions fulfill the recognized needs and embody the paramount values of their society. Indeed, if an institution does not aid the operation of the system in which it exists, the institution will change so that it does so. Sociological imperatives, not individual personalities, ultimately mold the character of institutions.[4]

Unfortunately, the preceding principles of macrosociology seem rarely to be the concern of research on the institution of law. With few exceptions, scholarship in law simply takes for granted the institutional character of law, and the societal foundation of the institution is, therefore, generally ignored. However, law must be understood in its societal context, for law would not be an institution unless it was a sociological necessity. Law, that is, *does* something vital for society. But what? The answer, in part, seems to be that law allows each participant in a potential interpersonal relationship to expect certain behavior from the other participant(s).[5] This function is important sociologically because reliance on expectations of others' behavior is at the foundation of interpersonal relationships, and the fulfillment of such expectations is necessary for a viable social order. But while law helps to make possible interpersonal relationships and hence a social system,[6] *how* it performs this function has yet to be established. The particular mechanisms involved, and the exact role and relative importance of each mechanism, have not been widely agreed upon by social scientists and scholars who study law.

The present chapter focuses on one mechanism that has been of interest to researchers—viz., symbols. Students of the institution of law have long contended that law has a symbolic character[7] and that the symbols of the institution can strengthen the fabric of social life and promote the cohesion of society.[8] Although a social system will, over time, change its specific symbols of law and the prominence given to such symbols generally, law-related symbols may be attracting more attention from the average American now than in the past. Indeed, one scholar has suggested that a central characteristic of the United States is "the development of public reverence for the symbols of law."[9]

While the particular symbols of law in a society may shift over time and may be less important at some points in history than at others, symbols of law are probably never completely absent from a society and never completely unimportant. Societies uniformly seem to develop and use symbols[10] because "[s]ymbols help citizens organize their beliefs, reinforce core values, and provide a rallying point for those who believe in them, thus reducing the costs of organization."[11] Symbols from the institution of law seem to be beneficial, and are probably indispensable, for sustaining a social system. The societal importance of symbols of law is indicated by the diversity of these symbols,[12] which include far more than the well-known blindfolded female figure holding balanced scales and a sword.[13] Indeed, a symbol of the institution of law may be drawn from another institution in the society,[14] and under certain conditions, a symbol of the institution may be an individual who has intentionally violated a statute and committed a felony.[15]

The present chapter focuses on symbolic concepts and doctrines in statutes and in court rules and opinions.[16] Symbolism has been noted in statutes that label behavior as criminal[17]; in legislation that recognizes marriage and specifies the sex composition of the married couple[18]; and in the Securities Act of 1933,[19] the original (and still a fundamental) federal statute dealing with securities.[20] Accordingly, it is logical to assume that there is symbolism in the concepts and doctrines of other statutes and in the concepts and doctrines of rules adopted by regulatory bodies. Part III of this chapter illustrates the assumption with the federal Investment Advisers Act.[21] Part IV pursues the assumption further with a very different subject, namely, the appearance-of-impropriety standard for assessing attorney behavior. Specifically, Part IV employs the standard in an attempt to isolate some of the societal conditions that contribute to symbolism in the doctrines of law. The attempt will advance the understanding of law provided by the discipline of macrosociology, which rests on the assumption that the properties of a society have broad effects on the institutions of the society.

Unfortunately, while scholars trained in the discipline of law have understood that law has a symbolic nature, they have not undertaken, or joined with sociologists in undertaking, rigorous quantitative research on the circumstances in which, the variations in the degree to which, and the paths by which law as symbol affects and is affected by the social order. These questions must be answered, however, if a useful body of knowledge is to be developed on law as an institution. Key questions regarding law that involves symbolism, therefore, have not been studied with the research tools offering the greatest power and precision. The situation exists partly because few scholars trained in law appreciate that numeric information can be used to investigate the questions and that, in seeking answers to the questions, quantitative data can be analyzed with statistical techniques.[22] The situation is probably compounded by a resistance on the part of law school faculty-scholars to acknowledging that the content of law is closely tied to—indeed, that the content of law directly results from—the character of the society in which law is embedded.[23] Nonetheless, well-designed research on law-as-symbol is missing not just from the professional output of law-trained scholars. Even sociologists, many of whom are highly skilled in measurement and data analysis, have undertaken few quantitative studies of symbols relevant to law and of the role of these symbols in social life.[24] The situation in sociology is notable given the existence in the discipline of a school whose very name—symbolic interaction—directs attention to symbols.[25] The rudimentary state of present knowledge regarding symbols in law and society thus cannot be explained solely by the work of scholars educated in law, but is attributable also to researchers educated in sociology.

Because symbols are central to this chapter, their defining characteristics need to be identified. In doing so, the concept of "symbol" must be juxtaposed with the concept of "sign," and the similarities as well as the differences between symbols and signs must be identified. In terms of similarities, neither symbols nor signs on their own have intrinsic meanings. Instead, symbols and signs represent other things, which may be tangible or intangible, and they produce responses because their referents have been learned. Symbols and signs, consequently, are alike in the societal function they perform—each transmits meaning and, in doing so, is integral to the development and operation of societies.[26] Without symbols and signs, a society is probably incapable of having an economy of even modest complexity, a population of even modest size, or technology of even modest sophistication.

What distinguishes symbols from signs? Collectively, signs form a language employed in a society,[27] i.e., the signs in a human group are the vehicles that make possible mutual understanding and interpersonal coordination.[28] To be effective in a language, of course, a sign (which can be verbal or nonverbal) must have a specific referent; a sign whose meaning is ambiguous impedes rather than facilitates social interaction. A symbol, on the other hand, possesses meanings that are of greater complexity. Thus, a symbol communicates a message that is broader and more complicated than the message communicated by a sign. Moreover, a symbol is more likely than a sign to have an impact on individuals that is emotional in nature[29] and that, for neurological reasons, occurs partly at a subconscious level.[30] For instance, the word "flag" is a sign whose referent is immediately intelligible and readily explained, but a flag in cloth or other tangible form is a symbol with a complex meaning that is, by comparison to its sign, less easily comprehended through oral or written descriptions.[31] The importance to a human group of the referent of a symbol, furthermore, confers importance on the symbol; thus, the cloth flag of a nation is socially significant in its own right as a symbol of the nation.[32]

The preceding explanation of the nature of symbols may be aided by a dictionary definition of the word "symbol." Although dictionaries vary in the way they define the word, an illuminating definition depicts a symbol as:

> 5. an object or act that represents a repressed complex through unconscious association rather than through objective resemblance or conscious substitution[;] 6. an act, sound, or material object having cultural significance and the capacity to excite or objectify a response.[33]

A symbol, then, carries a broad, intricate meaning in standing for something else, and is visible, audible, and/or touchable. A visible, touchable symbol includes the fabric flag of a country and a metal or wood religious artifact such as the Latin cross. An audible symbol is exemplified by a musical composition that has been formally adopted by a government as the official anthem of the country—the "Star Spangled Banner" in the case of the United States[34]—or that is closely but informally identified with the country, e.g., the song "God Bless America" by the composer Irving Berlin. However, an item cannot be a symbol for a group unless the participants in the group recognize the referent(s) of the item. That is, a particular item is symbolic only if the meaning of the item is apprehended. The intention of the producer of the item is insufficient by itself to make the item a symbol.

What is the function of symbols for society?[35] Macrosociology defines a society as a human group that operates through and is maintained by institutions. Consequently, if an institution begins to damage its society, the institution will change—although possibly with a substantial time lag—so that it ceases to do so and, instead, supports the social order.[36] Thus, as an institution, law in all of its forms—including statutes, administrative agency and court rules, and court decisions—manifests the acknowledged needs[37] and represents the prevailing values of society, and in the long run, the concepts and doctrines of law act as the sociological equivalent of a magnet, attracting participants to their society rather than driving them away. Law promotes the overall functioning of society by, in part, supplying symbols that solidify social life,[38] and because law as an institution must not weaken the bond between a social system and its participants,[39] the symbols of law will change as large-scale forces alter the properties of society.

But how do we know when law is operating as a symbol? Otherwise expressed, by what observable measure(s) can we determine whether a particular concept or doctrine is a symbol? Unless the question is answered, quantitative research cannot be undertaken on the societal role of symbols of law, for such research requires that the presence—and, when appropriate, the magnitude—of every relevant variable be accurately identified. Whether a particular concept or doctrine of law is a symbol or is not a symbol involves a variable, because there are two mutually exclusive states one of which logically must exist. Moreover, for law that has become a symbol, the strength or importance of the symbol is a variable because strength/importance, by definition, is characterized by gradations; strength/importance can differ between symbols at any given point in time and can differ over time for any particular symbol. Consequently, the symbolic aspect of law unavoidably involves at least one variable—viz., whether or not law is a symbol—and law that is a symbol will involve a second variable—viz., the intensity or salience of the symbol.

The concern of the instant chapter is with the first variable: How can an investigator decide when a given concept or doctrine of law is a symbol? The decision can probably be made using a number of alternative criteria, and given the limited state of social science knowledge regarding symbols, it would be presumptuous to believe that the criteria can be definitively and exhaustively listed at this time. Nonetheless, one criterion can be suggested.

II. Appearances and Symbolism in Law

Social science research will someday determine whether the comment that "[t]he world is governed more by appearances than realities"[40] is correct and whether the characterization of the 1980s and 1990s in the United States as "an Age of Appearances"[41] is apt. Should these claims be proven wrong, however, they are likely to have erred merely in degree. If most of social life is not influenced by appearances, much undoubtedly is.

How do appearances achieve such influence? Let me suggest the following explanation. Social order, by definition, requires predictability in the behavior of individuals and groups. Such predictability, in turn, seems to depend partially on the existence of statuses (social positions) and roles. In a group—even one with relatively few members—differentiated statuses and roles emerge for individuals,[42] and in a society, distinct statuses and roles develop for groups. Given the presence of statutes and roles among both individuals and groups, the social attributes of individuals and groups affect interpersonal and intergroup relationships. However, attributes can be socially relevant only when they are perceived, and perception unavoidably entails interpretation. Indeed, the inherent character of attributes may be less significant to a society than the perception and interpretation of the attributes. Research has found that the way in which the attributes of individuals and groups are perceived, as well as the context in which they are perceived, affects the treatment of and responses to the individuals and groups involved.[43] In short, appearances—"the action or state of appearing or seeming to be (to eyes or mind); semblance;

looking like"[44]—are an inherent and unavoidable aspect of living in a society.[45]

Two illustrations may help. First, almost all parents give each of their children a name that their culture associates with the biological sex of the child.[46] Sociologically, the name of an individual is not merely a label. Where gender distinctions are prevalent in the social fabric, as they are in the United States,[47] sex-appropriate names for individuals facilitate social interaction by contributing to the appearance of the named individuals. To be exact, sex-linked names assist a society in placing individuals in gender roles, and like all social roles, gender roles involve conventions regarding appropriate behavior towards, as well as by, the occupants of the roles.[48] In the context of gender, then, the names of individuals shape appearances and, in doing so, aid the functioning of society. Second, evaluations of the physical features of an individual affect judgments that others make of the individual.[49] Thus, student beliefs about the physical attractiveness of their college professors markedly influence the students' ratings of the teaching quality of the professors[50]; judgments of the relative competence of opposing candidates for Congress that are based on the candidates' faces evidently have a major bearing on the outcome of elections[51]; and the degree to which the facial traits of cadets at a military academy indicate dominance (rather than submissiveness) affects the rank achieved by the cadets at the academy.[52] In short, the appearance of an individual has an impact on responses to the individual by others.

My concern, however, is not with appearances qua appearances but with appearances as symbols. What is responsible for infusing appearances with symbolism? The question encompasses appearances in many contexts, but I will consider just one, namely, law. In particular, my hypothesis is that law acts as a symbol when, inter alia, it addresses (e.g., regulates) appearances of a phenomenon that is significant to society,[53] and law that is explicitly directed at protecting (or eliminating) a recognized symbol of a socially significant phenomenon is symbolic, too. The symbolism of such law results from stimulus generalization, a phenomenon identified in the 1920s by the noted scientist Ivan Pavlov that has come to be regarded by psychologists as an "undeniable characteristic" of human learning.[54] Stimulus generalization, simply described, involves a stimulus to which individuals learn a particular response and which is subsequently joined by at least one additional stimulus that spontaneously produces the response. Thus, stimulus generalization begins with the establishment of a link between an initial stimulus and a certain reaction through positive and/or negative reinforcement, i.e., reward and/or punishment; after the connection between the initial stimulus and the reaction has been created, another stimulus generates the reaction without any reinforcement.[55] In the present chapter, the initial stimulus would be appearances, the second stimulus would be law that deals with appearances, and the response to each stimulus would be the social meaning that constitutes a symbol. The meaning that makes law symbolic is thus determined socially[56] and important sociologically.

By way of illustration, the national flag of the United States, as a tangible representation (i.e., appearance) of the country, is an acknowledged symbol.[57] The symbolism of the flag exists because the referent of the flag—the Nation—is socially significant, and to promote and preserve this symbolism, federal statutes specify the settings, circumstances, and manner in which the flag is to be displayed.[58] Thus, a federal statute seeks to preserve the symbolism of the flag by explicitly providing, inter alia, that "[n]o disrespect should be shown to the flag of the United States of America; the flag should not be dipped to any person or thing."[59] Through stimulus generalization, statutes such as these acquire symbolism from the symbolism of the flag.

Stimulus generalization has been employed in theoretical analyses to explain social phenomena[60] and in empirical research to account for symbolism in a law-based government program.[61] If it is widespread in social life, stimulus generalization can be expected to occur with law that deals with appearances of socially important phenomena, and the learned reaction that confers symbolism on such appearances will be transferred to law focusing on these appearances. The present chapter specifically assumes that stimulus generalization does so, although the assumption has not been tested empirically by social scientists. Under the thesis of the chapter, then, dress codes for students imposed by public schools are symbolic. The symbolism of dress codes arises because the codes target physical appearances that have social meaning; through stimulus generalization, the meaning of the physical appearances attaches to the dress codes applicable to the appearances and makes the codes symbolic.[62]

While tangential to the chapter, law that does not focus on appearances may also be symbolic. Specifically, law can serve as a symbol when it directly applies to or images the particular phenomenon for which it was formulated. At least two types of law in a society are in this category. They are symbolic because their function "is not so much to guide society, as to comfort it."[63]

The first type of law that is symbolic, even though it does not focus on appearances, is law designed to regulate a socially significant activity.[64] Law of this type is expected by participants in the society that adopts it to be effective in substantially altering the frequency of the activity, but, in fact, the law has little or no influence on the incidence of the activity. Illustrations of such law include: (a) state statutes that authorize the death penalty for individuals who commit the crime of murder, and (b) statutes that on their face are intended to prohibit abortion. In spite of the widespread, relatively intense feelings that have accompanied each of these topics[65]—feelings that have undoubtedly helped to instill symbolism into law on the topics—such law has evidently not had an appreciable impact on the murder rate[66] or on the percentage of pregnancies that women choose to terminate.[67]

The second type of law that does not emphasize appearances but is symbolic is law that merely expresses dominant values of the society. Law of this type does not directly regulate activity but, rather, affirms salient social ideals, and it is illustrated by the federal Defense of Marriage Act. The pertinent provision of the Act permits states and other U.S. jurisdictions (territories, possessions, and Indian tribes) to deny recognition to same-sex marriages from another jurisdiction even though the marriages are lawful in the latter.[68] The Act endorses both the traditional conception of marriage (and its associated gender roles[69]) and the longstanding authority of states to define marriage.[70] Indeed, an express purpose of the Act was to affirm state sovereignty over marriage so that a state can, if it chooses, exclude from the status of marriage couples comprised of individuals of the same sex.[71] Because the Act merely recognizes the existing authority of states to regulate marriage rather than altering that authority, the Act is purely symbolic.[72]

In the present chapter, however, I concentrate on appearances that a phenomenon is present, and I contend that law dealing with appearances of a socially salient phenomenon is symbolic. Although not all law applies to such appearances, some law probably must do so. Why do these appearances become the subject of law? The answer is that attitudes and behaviors toward a group (including an institution)[73] are shaped by beliefs regarding whether the group acts in a just manner,[74] and these beliefs are molded by appearances. Thus, although jurisprudence and scholarship on it have long distinguished "substance" from "form"[75] and often expressed a preference for substance over form,[76] the appearances generated by the form of judicial proceedings have been recognized as a factor that affects the trust of the public in the institution of law.[77]

In sum, appearances of phenomena that are important to a social system give symbolism to law addressing the appearances, and symbolic law aids a society in securing the commitment of its participants.[78] For every group, of course, the commitment of its participants is vital, because to the extent that participant commitment is lacking, the ability of a group to operate smoothly and effectively will be hampered.[79] If a society is to benefit from an institution, moreover, the institution must be perceived as fair, i.e., viewed as just. Not surprisingly, the institution of law has acknowledged the necessity of perceptions of fairness; in the words of the United States Supreme Court, "justice must satisfy the appearance of justice."[80]

As defined in this chapter, then, a symbol is a stimulus that is visible, audible, or touchable and that represents a thing having significance to society; such stimuli include appearances that society deems important. Two additional illustrations of the symbolism of appearances and of pertinent law may be helpful. First, American ideals require a substantial distance between the institution of government and the institution of religion,[81] a requirement that is embodied in the Religion Clauses of the First Amendment to the United States Constitution.[82] Consequently, appearances that powers of government are being shared with religious entities have been found by the United States Supreme Court to constitute symbols that implicate (and violate) the First Amendment.[83] As a second illustration, certain physical attributes of individuals generate reactions by others,[84] and one of the attributes that does so is body hair. Numerous cultures specify the manner of dealing with body hair,[85] and in the United States, the social definition of females and males involves unequivocal sex-based differences as to the management of hair. For instance, "[t]he gender norm that says that women's skin should be smooth and bare (and the social opprobrium that accordingly rains down on any woman who goes unshaven)" contribute to sex-based differences in grooming.[86] Body hair, being a factor in the appearances of gender, is symbolic because it is linked to social roles and thus is significant to society. In terms of law, constitutional and statutory doctrines have arisen from sex distinctions in the policies of government entities and private employers regarding the length of head hair,[87] and through stimulus generalization, these doctrines have become symbols.

In concluding Part II, let me identify the key points that underlie the macrosociological perspective I am proposing. A society, to operate effectively, must have the commitment of its participants generally, but such commitment requires that the participants trust the institutions of their society and regard the institutions as fair.[88] Otherwise expressed, a society will be viable to the extent its participants believe that the institutions of the society provide social justice.[89] Given that the content of law is a response to the recognized needs and dominant values of society,[90] the concepts and doctrines of law, and the definitions of social justice that they advance,[91] undergo change when societal conditions are altered.[92]

The present chapter, in focusing on concepts and doctrines of law that operate as symbols, contends that such law in the long run strengthens the bond that participants in a society have to the society. The symbols of law do so because they incorporate established notions of social justice and "[a]ppearance—symbolism—is critical in any system of justice."[93] Symbolic concepts and doctrines of law thus aid society even though law does not materially alter the incidence of socially important activities, and concepts and doctrines of law are symbolic when, inter alia, they are applied to appearances of socially significant phenomena because the symbolism of the latter is, through stimulus generalization, acquired by law.

Because system-level factors are the focus of macrosociology, the fact that law is an institution of society is not attributed to the efforts of particular individuals or thought to be the result of chance. Instead, law is an institution because, in a macrosociological framework, law is regarded as a servant rather than a master of society,[94] and as such, law is assumed to furnish invaluable benefits to the social system. These benefits are supplied partially through symbols, a mechanism that permits the existence of widespread interpersonal relationships and, hence, social life.

III. The Statutory Definition of the Occupation of Investment Adviser

A statutory provision may not on its face encompass appearances, but it may be extended to appearances through interpretation by courts and administrative agencies. The application of law to appearances, therefore, may not be obvious and easily ascertained; instead, whether appearances have been brought within the scope of a statute may be determinable only from documents construing the statute.

To illustrate this point, I will use the occupation of investment adviser and, in particular, the definition of the occupation under federal law. The topic demonstrates the often-subtle role of appearances in law.[95]

Congress has defined the occupation of "investment adviser" in both the Investment Company Act and the Investment Advisers Act ("Advisers Act"), but the definition in the former Act is concerned exclusively with the parties furnishing recommendations to investment companies regarding the acquisition and/or disposition of securities by the companies.[96] The definition in the Advisers Act contains no such limitation. Specifically, section 202(a)(11) of the Advisers Act declares an investment adviser to be

> [A]ny person who, for compensation, engages in the business of advising others, either directly or through publications or writings, as to the value of securities or as to the advisability of investing in, purchasing, or selling securities, or who, for compensation and as part of a regular business, issues or promulgates analyses or reports concerning securities.[97]

Subject to certain exceptions, a person satisfying this definition ("Advisers Act definition") must register with, and abide by applicable rules of, the Securities and Exchange Commission if the person uses the mail system or any channel of interstate commerce in the United States to engage in business as an investment adviser.[98]

The discussion below will focus solely on the Advisers Act definition, because this definition is applicable to a much larger number of persons—and is therefore of much greater practical importance—than the definition of investment adviser in the Investment Company Act. Any investment adviser under the latter Act will be an investment adviser under the Advisers Act,[99] but an investment adviser under the Advisers Act may not be an investment adviser under the Investment Company Act because a person meeting the Advisers Act definition of investment adviser can serve clients that are not investment companies. As a result, investment advisers under the Advisers Act are responsible for the securities portfolios of not just investment companies (e.g., mutual funds) but of other clients as well, and all of the securities portfolios they manage have a combined market value that far exceeds the market value of the securities portfolios of investment companies.[100]

Why is the occupation of investment adviser of *social* significance in the United States? The answer may not be immediately obvious inasmuch as the products with which investment advisers work (viz., securities) are, on the surface, economic in character. Nonetheless, the occupation of investment adviser has important implications for American society. Economic matters can have major social consequences,[101] and in the case of investment advisers, such consequences are unavoidable because the occupation directly affects a large portion of the public. One reason the occupation does so is the popularity of mutual funds (the most common form of investment company). Specifically, since 1998, no less than two out of five households in the United States have owned shares of at least one mutual fund.[102] In the latest year for which data are available (viz., 2009), two-thirds of the households that owned mutual fund shares had more than half of their financial assets in the funds.[103]

An examination of the definition of investment adviser in the Advisers Act reveals that the definition encompasses more than a single type of activity. Specifically, the definition designates as an investment adviser "any person *who*" (italics added), employs the word "who" not once but twice, and precedes the second "who" with the word "or." Each "who" is accompanied by a description of a set of activities, moreover, and the descriptions differ markedly in their wording. Given the significance of individual words in a statute,[104] two separate classes of activity are within the scope of the definition of investment adviser in section 202(a)(11). The subject of both classes, however, is conduct that is business in nature.

Although one class of activity under the Advisers Act definition involves a "business" and the other class involves a "regular business," the Division of Investment Management ("Division") of the Securities and Exchange Commission has taken the position that the business element of the definition has the same character in each of the two classes of activity comprising the occupation of investment adviser as defined in section 202(a)(11).[105] Regardless of whether the Division is correct in this regard, the concept of "business" is basic to the definition. Accordingly, there must be a "business" that supplies investment advice, or furnishes reports or analyses, regarding securities, and the fundamental attributes of a business inhere in every type of advisory service provided. But what are these attributes?

One of the attributes that can place a person in the investment advisory business, according to the Division, is "hold[ing] himself out as an investment adviser or as one who provides investment advice."[106] Notably, the "[h]olding oneself out" attribute also has a bearing at other points in the definition of investment adviser in section 202(a)(11). For example, the section excludes lawyers, accountants, engineers, and teachers from the definition of investment adviser when their investment advice "is solely incidental to the practice of [their] profession,"[107] and the staff has concluded that the exclusion is unavailable to any of the designated professionals who holds herself/himself out publicly as an investment adviser.[108] Similarly, section 202(a)(11) excludes brokers and dealers from the definition of investment adviser if, inter alia, they supply investment advice in a manner that is "solely incidental" to their broker–dealer business.[109] This exclusion, under a Commission rule, is unavailable when a broker or dealer, in furnishing advice that is a component of a financial plan or that is related to financial planning, "holds itself out generally to the public as a financial planner or as providing financial planning services."[110] Brokers and dealers that, in the context of a comprehensive analysis of the long-term financial requirements of a client, supply advice about securities to the client will not be doing so in connection with their brokerage business when they have portrayed themselves as engaged in investment advising.[111] Any appearance of being an investment adviser, accordingly, renders these brokers and dealers ineligible for the statutory exclusion from the definition of investment adviser and triggers the status of investment adviser.

In short, the "hold oneself out" standard is a recurring aspect of section 202(a)(11). That the standard is not uncommon in the definition of investment adviser may be traceable to section 203 of the Advisers Act. Paragraph (a) of section 203 mandates registration with the Securities and Exchange Commission of an investment adviser that employs mail or interstate commerce "in connection with his or its business."[112] However, paragraph (b)(3) of the section exempts from registration inter alia an investment adviser who has had no more than fourteen clients in the prior twelve months, who is not an investment adviser to an investment company that is registered with the Commission under the Investment Company Act, and who does not "hold[] himself out generally to the public as an investment adviser."[113] Thus, the "hold oneself out" standard is explicitly embedded in the Advisers Act.

To hold out a thing as existing, of course, generates appearances of the thing.[114] For investment advisory services, a wide range of actions can portray an entity or individual as an investment adviser and produce appearances that the services are offered by a business.

For example, an entity will evidently be deemed to have held itself out publicly as being in the investment advisory business if the entity has an office in a building whose directory lists the name of the entity and identifies the entity as an "investment adviser."[115] Furthermore, an entity that furnishes recommendations to a bank regarding securities for the portfolio of a common fund operated by the bank as a trustee, executor, administrator or guardian will be holding itself out publicly as an investment adviser if (a) current or prospective participants in the fund are supplied with information they request about the entity and its significant personnel and investment strategies, (b) meetings to discuss these matters are conducted with the officers of the entity at the request of current and prospective participants, and (c) even one or two conferences, attended by representatives of the entity, are arranged each year by the bank for current and prospective participants.[116] In short, persons recommending securities for purchase and/or sale will hold themselves out as investment advisers unless investment-pertinent information about and from them is restricted.[117] If these persons are not circumspect in making available such information, they may appear to be offering investment advice to potential clients and, therefore, may be required to register with the Commission as investment advisers.

IV. The Appearance-of-Impropriety Standard for Attorney Conduct

This chapter rests on the macrosociological proposition that the concepts and doctrines of law, partly if not chiefly by being symbols, in the long run promote the commitment of participants to their society and hence strengthen the social order. Like all scientific propositions, the proposition that law furnishes symbols supporting the social system is empirically testable, albeit indirectly. The proposition is based on the related assumptions that concepts and doctrines of law are responses to identifiable properties of society; that, being responses to societal properties, concepts and doctrines of law are suitable for the properties responsible for them; and that the responses are manifested in measurable relationships between the societal properties, on the one hand, and the concepts and doctrines, on the other.[118] The proposition and the assumptions behind it necessarily follow from the conceptualization of a society as a *system*.[119] By definition, a system is organized, and organization is the antithesis of randomness.[120] Therefore, the concepts and doctrines of law as an institution of society can be expected not to occur randomly but to be tied to conditions in the system. I report below the results of a study that examines whether societal properties predict the use by states of a specific symbolic concept and doctrine in defining ethical standards for attorneys.

A. Model Ethical Standards Promulgated by the American Bar Association

Explicit standards for the behavior of attorneys were initially adopted by the American Bar Association ("ABA") during the first decade of the twentieth century.[121] However, not until the third decade of the twentieth century do any ABA documents exhibit a concern with the appearances that the actions of attorneys generate, and the focus at this time was on attorneys in limited types of situations.[122] In 1969, the ABA promulgated the Model Code of Professional Responsibility ("Model Code"),[123] and under the Code, all attorneys were instructed to "avoid even the appearance of impropriety."[124] The admonition was evidently intended to build trust in the institution of law[125] and to promote a belief in the fairness of the institution.[126] Being an institution, law is by definition of major social significance, and given the prominence of law among the professions,[127] those who perform the central tasks of the institution—viz., attorneys and judges—are unavoidably salient to the public. Accordingly, the ethical standards applied by the institution to appearances generated by its professionals operate as symbols in society.[128]

In specifying ethical requirements for attorneys, the Model Rules of Professional Conduct ("Model Rules"), which were released by the ABA in 1982,[129] omitted the appearance-of-impropriety standard[130] on the ground that the standard was ambiguous.[131] Nonetheless, the ABA applies the standard to judges—and has done so since 1924 when it approved the Canons of Judicial Ethics. Canon 4 in the 1924 formulation required, inter alia, that "[a] judge's official conduct should be free from impropriety and the appearance of impropriety."[132] In 1972, this canon became the basis of Canon 2 of the Model Code of Judicial Conduct.[133] Canon 2 stated that "A Judge Shall Avoid Impropriety and the Appearance of Impropriety in All of the Judge's Activities," and the same wording was employed in the 1990 version[134] as well as in the 2007 version[135] of the Model Code of Judicial Conduct. The persistence over eight decades of the appearance-of-impropriety standard for judges is notable, for it is an implicit concession that appearances mold the public's view of the institution of law. Indeed, the importance to the institution of appearances does not seem to have been disputed in formulating the Model Rules. The appearance-of-impropriety standard was abandoned in the Model Rules because it was thought to be incapable of consistent, non-invidious application rather than because appearances are irrelevant to the social standing of the institution of law.[136]

Even though the most recent paradigm of ethical standards for attorneys promulgated by the ABA does not include an explicit appearance-of-impropriety test, an indicator of the importance to society of appearances of ethical behavior is that, during the last two decades of the twentieth century, a widespread concern with appearances of unethical conduct existed in the United States.[137] The concern cannot be dismissed as a sociological fortuity. On the contrary, the concern may be unavoidable in a society that possesses a large population and a complex society, because complete information about others is difficult to procure in such a setting.[138] Accordingly, appearances of ethical conduct and appearances of unethical conduct by participants in a group are commonly understood to affect the degree of trust that prevails in the group.[139] Moreover, appearances have been acknowledged as a factor that shapes the reputation of the judiciary and the police,[140] and appearances thus affect the reputation of the institution of law itself. Because trust and reputation—two social outputs that are critical to every group[141]—are influenced by appearances of ethical behavior and appearances of unethical behavior, American society places considerable emphasis on these appearances.

To ascertain whether symbolic concepts and doctrines of law are reactions to societal conditions, I report below the results of a study that examined the use by states of the appearance-of-impropriety standard for the conduct of attorneys. The Model Code, which incorporated the standard, and the Model Rules, which omitted the standard, are simply proposals of the ABA. The standards of ethics that govern an attorney are set and enforced by the particular state in which the attorney practices. Moreover, a state that declines to formulate its own standards but bases its ethical standards on the Model Code or Model Rules is not obligated to adopt verbatim the content of either; indeed, states have modified the Model Code and especially the Model Rules.[142] In addition, the courts in a state through case law can alter the ethical standards of the state without revising the wording of the standards that were derived from the Model Code or Model Rules. Consequently, although by 2008 the Model Rules were in effect (albeit with modifications) in forty-seven states and the District of Columbia,[143] neither the Model Rules nor the Model Code by themselves can be assumed to disclose accurately the current ethical standards that are applied to attorneys in a jurisdiction. Rather, both the codified standards of a state and the opinions of the highest court of the state determine whether the appearance-of-impropriety standard is being used.

B. Research Design

In September 2010, I undertook a state-by-state review to ascertain whether, as of that time, the appearance-of-impropriety standard for attorneys either was an explicit provision of the written ethical requirements of the state or had been employed by the highest court of the state after the Model Rules (or modified version thereof) were adopted by the state.[144] Given that the purpose of my research was to identify societal properties that foster or hinder acceptance of the standard by states, I wanted to minimize the possibility that properties unique to a state could influence the findings, and I therefore did not include the two states (Alaska and Hawaii) that are geographically distant from the coterminous United States. Of the remaining forty-eight states, two are excluded from the study, because for each of these states, I was unable to determine with a high degree of confidence that the appearance-of-impropriety standard either was currently utilized or was not currently utilized.[145] The data analysis reported below is thus limited to forty-six states.[146] Twenty-seven of the states were found to be applying the standard to attorneys as of September 2010,[147] and nineteen of the states were found not to be applying the standard to attorneys.[148]

Four system-level properties were identified a priori as potential influences on whether the appearance-of-impropriety standard would be employed by a state. The properties were cultural heterogeneity, population concentration, social system rationality, and societal stability. The level of each property in a state seemed, on logical grounds, to be capable of affecting the likelihood that the state would accept the standard, as I explain below. The explanation is based on the assumption that, as to each property, all else is equal.

- *Cultural heterogeneity.* Logically, a culture characterized by diversity could be inhospitable to explicit prohibitions on appearances of impropriety because the culture may lack a substantial body of common values, which may be a prerequisite for general agreement on the types of conduct that are to be regarded as improper. Without such agreement, bans on appearances of impropriety may not be adopted.

However, an alternative and opposing prediction is possible. Specifically, a high level of cultural heterogeneity could facilitate the adoption of explicit bans on appearances of impropriety and make such bans more frequent, because the bans can provide culturally diverse groups with a set of common focal points and thereby promote the commitment of the groups to the more-encompassing social system.

- *Population concentration.* Logically, a high level of population concentration in a state could increase the likelihood that the state will expressly prohibit appearances of impropriety. When population density is high, unseemly conduct could be noticed by a larger number of people and produce more condemnation. On this reasoning, a densely populated society will benefit more than a sparsely populated society from explicit bans on appearances of impropriety and hence will more often accept such bans for lawyers. Alternatively, however, a high level of population concentration may reduce the viability, and thus the incidence, of explicit prohibitions on appearances of impropriety. A dense population may have a social structure that is complex, which could expand the range of conduct that must be accepted and render official proscriptions of appearances of improper conduct difficult or impossible to apply.
- *Social system rationality.* Logically, express bans on appearances of impropriety are not required to the extent a population recognizes the importance of avoiding such appearances. If such recognition results from rationality, a high level of rationality in a society[149] could reduce the necessity of the appearance-of-impropriety standard for lawyers and make the standard less likely. On the other hand, the opposite could happen. Specifically, insofar as rationality in a society fosters awareness of the social problems created by appearances of impropriety, explicit bans on these appearances could become more acceptable and, in turn, more frequent.
- *Societal stability.* On logical grounds, a stable society could require fewer symbols than an unstable society because a stable society probably has a higher level of internal cohesion. A cohesive society may gain little from explicit bans on appearances of impropriety insofar as the bans are symbols that bolster participants' attachment to their society. When this attachment is already high, as it would be in a cohesive society, such bans will presumably not strengthen social life appreciably, and to the extent the bans are unnecessary for societal cohesion, they will presumably be adopted less often. The result would be fewer explicit prohibitions on appearances of impropriety in a stable society than in an unstable society. However, the opposite is logically possible, too. A stable society could have a larger number and variety of symbols than an unstable society, because the former may experience less-frequent change in key social values, including those that underlie symbols. To the degree that central social values are constant, the fit between express prohibitions on appearances of impropriety and the existing social fabric can be expected to improve,

making such prohibitions more socially acceptable and, in turn, more common. Under this reasoning, bans on appearances of impropriety would have a greater prevalence in societies that are stable than in societies that are not.

In short, logic furnishes a basis for linking all four system-level properties to the appearance-of-impropriety standard for lawyers; i.e., in principle, each property is capable of affecting the likelihood the standard will be present in a state. However, as the preceding discussion reveals, a prediction cannot be made as to whether this likelihood is raised or lowered by growth or intensification of a given property.

The necessity of relying entirely on logic, and the inability to predict the direction of change in the likelihood of the appearance-of-impropriety standard as a societal property increases, stem from the inadequate level of social science knowledge of law as an institution. The study reported here attempts to contribute to a research-based sociological theory that deals with the existence and nature of the links between the system-level properties identified above, on the one hand, and doctrines of law, on the other. If a society is a system—i.e., if the components of society do not operate haphazardly—the symbols of law do not develop fortuitously, and a relationship can be expected to exist between one or more of the properties discussed above and the appearance-of-impropriety standard for attorneys.

In order to ascertain the relationship, if any, between the properties and the adoption by states of the appearance-of-impropriety standard for lawyers, the properties must be empirically measured. Because the properties are potential building blocks for a theory, their conceptualization is necessarily abstract, and each property must be represented in the statistical analysis by a measurable variable that quantitatively and accurately captures the property. Table 8.1 provides descriptions of, as well as the mnemonic labels for, the variables that were utilized in the regression model. The independent variable that served as the empirical indicator of each societal property was as follows:

System-level property	**Independent variable (mnemonic label)**
Cultural heterogeneity	FOREIGNPOP
Population concentration	METROPOP
Social system rationality	PCT4YRSCOLL
Societal stability	CRIMERATE

For cultural heterogeneity in a state, an obvious indicator is the percentage of the population of the state that was born outside the United States,[150] and for population concentration in a state, an obvious indicator is the percentage of inhabitants of the state who reside in a metropolitan area. Accordingly, these variables require no justification. For social system rationality in a state, the indicator is the percentage of state inhabitants twenty-five years of age and older who had completed a minimum of four years of college. The percentage is logically tied to the level of rationality in a social system.[151] For societal stability in a state, the indicator employed is the crime rate in the state, because crime reduces interpersonal contacts[152] and hence impairs the ability of a social system to function smoothly.

Table 8.1 Variables in Regression Model[153]

Variable (mnemonic label)	Description of variable
APPEARIMPROP	Each state was coded 0 or 1. A state was coded 0 when, as of 2010, the appearance-of-impropriety standard was not explicit in the enumerated ethical standards for lawyer conduct that were in force in the state and had not been applied to a lawyer by the highest court of the state while the current enumerated standards have been in force. A state was coded 1 when, as of 2010, the appearance-of-impropriety standard was explicit in the enumerated ethical standards for lawyer conduct that were in force in the state or, if not explicit in the current enumerated standards, had been applied to a lawyer by the highest court of the state while the current enumerated standards have been in force.
PCT4YRSCOLL	The percentage of state inhabitants twenty-five years of age and older in 1980 who had finished at least four years of college.
CRIMERATE	The number of Crime Index crimes in each state in 1980 per one thousand state residents who were at least fifteen years of age. Crime Index crimes are murder and non-negligent manslaughter, forcible rape, robbery, aggravated assault, burglary, larceny-theft, and motor-vehicle theft.
FOREIGNPOP	The percentage of all inhabitants of each state in 1980 who were born outside the United States.

(Continued on the next page)

Table 8.1 *(Continued)*

METROPOP	The percentage of all inhabitants of each state in 1980 who resided in a "metropolitan area," as defined by the U.S. Census Bureau. A "metropolitan area" encompassed (a) a core area that had a substantial population and (b) communities adjoining the core that were integrated, economically as well as socially, with the core. Every metropolitan area included either: • At least one city with a population of not less than fifty thousand; or • Both (a) an urbanized area, as determined by Census Bureau criteria, with a population of not less than fifty thousand and (b) a total metropolitan area population of not less than one hundred thousand (seventy-five thousand in New England).[154]

For every variable, data were obtained on each of the forty-six states that were included in the study. The independent variables are measured as of 1980. The year 1980 was chosen for two reasons. First, data on all of the independent variables were available for that year.[155] Second, 1980 preceded the introduction of the Model Rules,[156] and by 1980 all of the forty-six states in the study had endorsed the appearance-of-impropriety standard for attorneys.[157] Since the Model Rules rejected the standard, 1980 is a useful temporal point (a) for marking the start of the period in history during which many states dropped the standard and (b) for ascertaining whether and how the variables measuring the four system-level properties predict state retention or rejection of the standard.

A final but important matter involving the research design requires discussion. Specifically, the reader should keep in mind that the findings of the study do not furnish a basis for definitive conclusions regarding the impact of the properties. Caution in interpreting the findings is necessary for at least two reasons. First, the system-level properties under consideration are poorly understood because they have not been extensively studied by social scientists. Future research may reveal, for example, that each property possesses multiple aspects and that each aspect requires a different empirical indicator. Accordingly, the selection of indicators (independent variables) for the instant study was grounded on logic and supposition, not substantial empirical research, and the indicator chosen for a property may not fully capture the property. Second, the relationship of the four properties to the presence or absence of the appearance-of-impropriety standard was not assessed with repeated, regular (e.g., yearly) measures of the variables that were used to represent the properties and with data on the year in which the states that abandoned the standard did so. Such data, especially when they cover numerous points in time both prior and subsequent to the occurrence of a phenomenon, are the most appropriate for identifying causes of the phenomenon.[158]

C. Data Analysis

The preceding limitations of the research design did not directly affect the data analysis, but another aspect of the study did. That aspect is the number of states (observations) in the study. Researchers have devoted scant attention to the question of the minimum number of observations needed for the accurate estimation of statistical significance by maximum-likelihood logistic regression,[159] and hence the number is uncertain. Nevertheless, currently available guidelines suggest that the number of observations in the instant study (viz., forty-six) is substantially fewer than the number that is required to generate reliable, unbiased estimates of the characteristics of a larger universe.[160] With these guidelines, accordingly, there is no support for using tests of statistical significance in the study.

If statistical significance cannot be computed accurately, do the odds ratios estimated by logistic regression for the current data have any utility? The answer, I believe, is that they do, because the odds ratios for the four independent variables in the model can stand on their own. Indeed, little if anything has been lost in the instant study because of the absence of meaningful estimates of the statistical significance of the odds ratios. To understand why, the role in research of tests of statistical significance needs to be explained. As I hope to convey in the explanation that follows, measures of statistical significance are unnecessary in the instant study even though they are justifiable in much, if not most, quantitative social science research. The odds ratios themselves can be the basis for identifying relationships to the appearance-of-impropriety standard of the system-level properties posited as antecedents of the standard.

The goal of the social and behavioral sciences is to ascertain conditions in and characteristics of *universes* of human individuals or human organizations. However, data cannot be acquired from all of the members of most universes due to the economic cost and/or time that would be expended. As a result, a sample must typically be drawn from the universe that is under investigation, and conclusions about the universe must be reached from data supplied by the sample. The function of tests of statistical significance is to allow such data to be employed to reach one type of conclusion regarding the universe with knowledge of the likelihood that the conclusion is wrong. Specifically, a test of significance whose assumptions (e.g., as to sampling procedure) are satisfied identifies the probability of error when deciding to reject the "null hypothesis"—the hypothesis that, in the universe, no relationship exists between two variables or no difference exists between two groups on a particular attribute. In what percentage of samples from the universe would a particular relationship between variables or a particular difference between groups be found if there is actually no relationship or no difference in the universe, i.e., if the null hypothesis correctly portrays the universe? The answer is the level of statistical significance. The level of statistical significance thus discloses the probability of erring when the null hypothesis is rejected on the basis of data garnered from a relatively small number of members of a universe who have been selected with a probability (e.g., random) sampling procedure.

In short, information on the statistical significance of an odds ratio presupposes that a *sample* has furnished the data from which the odds ratio and its statistical significance have been estimated. If the data used in a study to compute the odds ratio come from the entire universe of interest, however, statistical significance is irrelevant. That is the situation in the instant study. The universe for the study is the states in the continental United States whose acceptance or nonacceptance of the appearance-of-impropriety standard for attorneys could be determined as of 2010. Because the data for the study include *all* states in the continental United States that had an ascertainable position on the standard in 2010, the data do not result from sampling, and a test of statistical significance is inappropriate.

However, skepticism of conclusions—especially conclusions regarding causal relationships—is not eliminated simply because the data underlying the conclusions cover the entire universe under investigation. While estimates of statistical significance (even if based on an adequate number of observations) contribute little or nothing to the present study,[161] the study has potentially major limitations that arise from the two problems discussed in the last paragraph of Part IV-B supra of the instant chapter, namely, possible defects in the measurement of the system-level properties posited as determinants of whether states preserve the appearance-of-impropriety standard and the absence of time-series data on the variables chosen as indicators of these properties.

With this background, I turn to the results of the data analysis.[162] Table 8.2 presents the regression coefficients and odds ratios from the regression of the appearance-of-impropriety standard (APPEARIMPROP) on the four independent variables. In addition, the table supplies the two-tailed level of statistical significance of each of the regression coefficients and odds ratios for readers who prefer to ground decisions regarding a regression model on this information.

Inherent in the regression coefficients and odds ratios reported in Table 8.2 are a number of assumptions regarding the statistical attributes of the data, and the accuracy of these assumptions must be probed before the regression coefficients and odds ratios are used to draw conclusions regarding relationships between the independent variables and APPEARIMPROP. The first assumption is that outliers did not affect the odds ratios. Outliers are cases (here, states) characterized by a substantial disparity between the actual (i.e., observed) outcome on the dependent variable (APPEARIMPROP) and the outcome predicted by the regression equation. Cook's Statistic, a measure used to identify influential outliers,[163] was distinctly higher for California than for any other state.[164] To be exact, Cook's Statis-

Table 8.2 Odds Ratios and Two-tailed Significance Levels for Regression of APPEARIMPROP on Independent Variables: Forty-six States

Variable	Regression coefficient	Standard error of regression coefficient	Odds ratio	z	$p>\|z\|$
PCT4YRSCOLL	−.101	.149	.904	−.68	.498
CRIMERATE	.050	.032	1.051	1.57	.115
FOREIGNPOP	.133	.142	1.142	.94	.349
METROPOP	−.074	.029	.928	−2.54	.011
constant	2.893	2.217		1.30	.192

Notes: Regression model

Number of observations = 46

Log likelihood = −26.377

Likelihood ratio chi-squared (4) = 9.62

Probability > chi-square = .047

Pseudo R^2 = .154

tic for California was 1.24; the next highest Cook's Statistic was .70 (for South Dakota), which was followed closely by four states with numerical values of more than .30 on Cook's Statistic.[165] Consequently, the regression model in Table 8.2 was re-estimated with California omitted. For one independent variable—viz., FOREIGNPOP—the exclusion of California proved noteworthy. The results from regressing APPEARIMPROP on the independent variables using forty-five states (i.e., without California) are reported in Table 8.3.

The second assumption requiring examination prior to accepting the results in Table 8.2 and/or Table 8.3 is that variation in one independent variable in the regression model does not correspond closely to variation in any other independent variable. The assumption is important because a correlation (i.e., collinearity) between two independent variables, if sufficiently strong, can prevent the calculation of a reliable estimate of the odds ratio and coefficient for one or both of these independent variables. Regression supplies an estimate of the amount of change in the dependent variable that is associated with a unit of change in a particular independent variable (X_1), but in order to estimate accurately the amount of change in the dependent variable that is due to this independent variable (X_1) rather than to another independent variable (X_2), the influence of the latter independent variable (X_2)

Table 8.3 Odds Ratios and Two-tailed Significance Levels for Regression of APPEARIMPROP on Independent Variables: forty-five States (California omitted)

Variable	Regression coefficient	Standard error of regression coefficient	Odds ratio	z	$p>\|z\|$
PCT4YRSCOLL	−.119	.157	.888	−.76	.449
CRIMERATE	.053	.034	1.055	1.58	.115
FOREIGNPOP	.279	.181	1.322	1.54	.123
METROPOP	−.086	.032	.918	−2.66	.008
constant	3.197	2.267		1.41	.159

Notes: Regression model
Number of observations = 45
Log likelihood = −24.832
Likelihood ratio chi-squared (4) = 10.91
Probability > chi-square = .028
Pseudo R^2 = .180

must be statistically removed. If a strong relationship exists between independent variables X_1 and X_2, however, the amount of change in the dependent variable that is attributable to independent variable X_1 may not be separable from the amount of change in the dependent variable that is attributable to independent variable X_2. When two independent variables are highly correlated with each other, in short, regression may not generate reliable estimates of the amount of change that takes place in the dependent variable when a unit of change occurs in each of these correlated independent variables.[166]

A reason to believe that collinearity might preclude the reliable estimation of odds ratios in the instant study is found in the nontrivial zero-order correlation coefficients for pairs of the independent variables. The independent variables in Tables 8.2 and 8.3 are the indicators for the system-level properties that have been proposed as possible antecedents of the appearance-of-impropriety standard (the dependent variable). In the forty-six-state data set, three of the six correlation coefficients were .63 or higher; in the forty-five-state data set, three of the six coefficients were .61 or higher.[167] However, the regression program employed in the data analysis automatically notifies the investigator when an unacceptable level of collinearity is present,[168] and it did not do so for the results reported either in Table 8.2 or in Table 8.3.[169] Accordingly, collinearity was evidently not a problem, and the second assumption was accepted.

I turn now to the third assumption of the regression model that needs to be tested. The assumption is that the nature and strength of the relationship between each system-level property (as measured by its independent variable) and APPEARIMPROP is not conditional on any other system-level property. If the assumption is wrong, the relationship of independent variable X_1 to the dependent variable differs across the levels or categories of independent variable X_2.[170] Such a conditional relationship, in statistical terminology, involves "interaction" between X_1 and X_2. Interaction can occur when the two independent variables are related both to each another *and* to the dependent variable.[171] As pointed out above in the discussion of collinearity, the four independent variables in the instant study were characterized by nontrivial correlation coefficients in their relationships to one another, and Tables 8.2 and 8.3 suggest that some of the independent variables may have a nontrivial relationship to APPEARIMPROP. Accordingly, the assumption that no interaction is present in the data may be incorrect, and if it is incorrect, one or more of the system-level properties measured by the independent variables is moderating the relationship between a system-level property and APPEARIMPROP.

To ascertain interaction between independent variables in a data set, any pair of the independent variables can be used to create a new variable ("interaction variable") that will serve as an additional independent variable. In the instant study, the numerical values of an interaction variable can be obtained by multiplying, for each state, the numerical values on the two independent variables comprising the interaction variable. However, if the objective of research is to build theory, the choice of independent variables to examine for potential interaction should be based on existing or proposed theory. That is, theory on a subject should guide the selection of the properties of the system that can be expected to interact and whose possible interaction should be investigated.[172] Current macrosociological theory addresses two sets of the system-level properties in the instant study.[173] Specifically, theory suggests that (a) cultural heterogeneity and population density reinforce one another[174] and (b) cultural heterogeneity and societal stability are related.[175] Moreover, as explained supra,[176] theoretical grounds exist for believing that each of the foregoing properties can affect whether states formally prohibit appearances of impropriety.

In short, there is reason to include in the regression model two interaction variables—one created from FOREIGNPOP and METROPOP, and one created from FOREIGNPOP and CRIMERATE—and to ascertain whether they are related to APPEARIMPROP. If an interaction variable is related to APPEARIMPROP, the impact on APPEARIMPROP of one of the components of the interaction variable is not the same at every level or in every category of the other.

The numerical values of FOREIGNPOP and of METROPOP, and the numerical values of FOREIGNPOP and CRIMERATE, were multiplied to generate the interaction variables, which were included separately and jointly with the original four independent variables in data analyses. The expanded models were used both for the data set that contained forty-six states and for the data set that contained forty-five states (i.e., the data set omitting California). The odds ratios for the two interaction variables, whether present simultaneously or separately, departed less than ±.03 from 1.000 in the two data sets. There was, consequently, no evidence of a relationship between either interaction variable and APPEARIMPROP—or at least a relationship of any practical utility.[177] As measured by their independent variables, accordingly, the system-level properties in the instant study did not seem to interact in their effect on the dependent variable.

D. Discussion of Findings

Before the findings of the data analysis can be discussed, a choice must be made between Table 8.2 and Table 8.3. That choice, of course, depends on whether California is an influential outlier. A decision to classify California as an influential outlier requires a cogent justification, because California is part of a system of jurisdictions—viz., the United States—and as explained infra in Part III-D of Chapter 9, there are potentially important implications when a particular jurisdiction in a system of jurisdictions is designated an influential outlier.

Notably, California has consistently been a leading jurisdiction in the United States not only for change in law and policy[178] but also for change in technology. To illustrate, California was the first U.S. state to authorize no-fault divorce and thereby substantially ease the statutory criteria for dissolving a marriage[179]; California was the first U.S. jurisdiction to criminalize harassment and violence prompted by hate of specific categories of individuals[180]; and California has been among the earliest states to accept new doctrines of tort law.[181] Moreover, the growth of innovation in technology (as measured by the number of patented inventions) has for several decades been more rapid in California than in all but a handful of other U.S. states.[182]

Sociologically, therefore, California is differentiable from other jurisdictions within the United States, a conclusion that is pertinent to the question at hand. To be exact, the sociological distinctiveness of California, I believe, justifies classifying the state as an influential outlier in the instant study. The discussion that follows, accordingly, will focus on Table 8.3, not on Table 8.2.

How well did the regression model in Table 8.3 predict whether the appearance-of-impropriety standard for attorneys is or is not applied to lawyers in a state? As Table 8.4 shows, the model in Table 8.3—i.e., the model with four independent variables—accurately predicted the presence and absence of the standard in 73 percent of the forty-five states.[183] If the predictions had been made randomly, 50 percent of the states would have been correctly identified. The model as a whole, therefore, contributes substantially to explaining whether the standard is present. Moreover, the benefit of the full model was uniform. To be precise, the model with all of the independent variables

Table 8.4 Accuracy of Predictions of APPEARIMPROP from Regression with Forty-five States (California omitted)

	Correct predictions as a percentage of all predictions of states using and states not using the appearance-of-impropriety standard for lawyers		
Variables in model	**Predictions of states using and states not using (%)**	**Predictions of states using (%)**	**Predictions of states not using (%)**
Four variables: PCT4YRSCOLL, CRIMERATE, FOREIGNPOP, METROPOP	73	74	72
Three variables: PCT4YRSCOLL, CRIMERATE, METROPOP	67	85	39
Three variables: PCT4YRSCOLL, CRIMERATE, FOREIGNPOP	60	100	0
Three variables: PCT4YRSCOLL, FOREIGNPOP, METROPOP	67	74	56
Three variables: CRIMERATE, FOREIGNPOP, METROPOP	71	74	67
Two variables: FOREIGNPOP, METROPOP	64	74	50

correctly predicted 74 percent of the states that used the standard and 72 percent of the states that did not.

If the goal of research is to build theory, the regression model per se is not as important as the particular independent variables in the model and the theory behind each of them.[184] Theory is constructed from independent variables that are related to the dependent variable, and advances in theory depend on uncovering these variables. Thus, I consider next the question of whether each of the four independent variables in the regression model had an influence of meaningful magnitude on state differences in the presence/absence of the appearance-of-impropriety standard.

Table 8.4 suggests an answer to the question by allowing models with three independent variables to be compared to the four-variable model. Considering predictions of states expected by the model to be applying the appearance-of-impropriety standard as well as predictions of states expected by the model not to be applying the standard, the percentages of states that were accurately predicted by a three-variable model were noticeably different from the four-variable model when FOREIGNPOP and METROPOP were removed seriatim from the data analysis. The differences that resulted from omitting these two variables suggest that both of the variables are nontrivial determinants of whether a state focuses on appearances of unseemly conduct by lawyers. According to the bottom row in Table 8.4, FOREIGNPOP and METROPOP are important in predicting the states that apply the appearance-of-impropriety standard rather than in predicting the states that do not apply the standard.

By how much and in what way did FOREIGNPOP and METROPOP affect APPEARIMPROP? The answer to this question requires an explanation of three statistical concepts—probability, odds, and odds ratio.

The *probability* of occurrence of a phenomenon is the proportion of the combined number of occurrences and nonoccurrences that are occurrences, while the probability of nonoccurrence of a phenomenon is the proportion of the combined number of occurrences and nonoccurrences that are nonoccurrences.[185] To illustrate, I will use the instant data on the forty-five states that are the basis of Table 8.3. The probability that the appearance-of-impropriety standard for attorneys was being used in a state is calculated through the division of 27, the number of states employing the standard, by 45, the total number of states. Thus, the probability of occurrence of the standard was 27/45 = .60. Conversely, the probability that the standard was not being used in a state is calculated through the division of 18, the number of states not employing the standard, by 45. The probability of nonoccurrence, therefore, is 18/45 = .40.

The probability of a phenomenon, however, differs from the *odds* of the phenomenon. When the probability of occurrence of a phenomenon is divided by the probability of its nonoccurrence, the result is the odds of occurrence, and when the probability of nonoccurrence of a phenomenon is divided by the probability of occurrence, the result is the odds of nonoccurrence.[186] In the data on the forty-five states, the odds that the appearance-of-impropriety standard for attorneys was being employed in a state is the ratio of .60 (the probability of occurrence) to .40 (the probability of nonoccurrence), while the odds that a state was not employing the standard is the ratio of .40 to .60. Thus, the odds that a state was utilizing the standard is .60/.40 = 1.50 (alternatively expressed as 1.5 to 1), while the odds that a state was not utilizing the standard is .40/.60 = .67 (or .67 to 1).

The third statistical concept is the *odds ratio*, i.e., a ratio of two odds. The numerator in the odds ratio in logistic regression is the odds of the *dependent* variable for a given number of units (i.e., amount) of an *independent* variable that is measured as an interval or ratio scale; the denominator is the odds of the dependent variable when the number of units of the same independent variable is less by one.[187] Accordingly, the odds ratio for an independent variable in the instant study specifies the factor by which the odds of APPEARIMPROP are multiplied when the independent variable increases by one unit[188]—by one percentage point in the case of PCT4YRSCOLL, FOREIGNPOP, and METROPOP, and by one Crime Index crime per 1,000 state residents 15+ years old in the case of CRIMERATE. An independent variable affects APPEARIMPROP to the degree that its odds ratio deviates from 1.000.[189]

Let us now consider the odds ratios in Table 8.3. With the other independent variables held constant, the odds that the appearance-of-impropriety standard was being used in a state as of 2010 (a) rose by a factor of 1.322 for each increase of one percentage point in the share of the state population that, as of 1980, had been born outside the United States, and (b) declined by a factor of .918 for each increase of one percentage point in the share of the state population that, as of 1980, resided in a metropolitan area. That is, removing the effects of the other independent variables, the odds of employing the standard are multiplied by 1.322 when a state moves up one percentage point in the size of its foreign-born population and by .918 when a state moves up one percentage point in the size of its metropolitan-area population. The two variables thus work in opposite directions with regard to whether a state applies the appearance-of-impropriety standard. Expressed in percentages, each percentage-point rise in foreign-born population was associated with roughly a 32 percent *increase*, and each percentage-point rise in metropolitan-area population was associated with roughly an 8 percent *decrease*, in the odds that the standard was being used in a state.[190]

The discussion above raises a further question. Specifically, did FOREIGNPOP and METROPOP affect APPEARIMPROP to roughly the same degree, or was the impact of one of these independent variables materially larger than the impact of the other? The question cannot be answered by comparing the odds ratios for percentage-point changes in two independent variables because, inter alia, each independent variable will have a different range and/or a different variance. However, an answer to the question can be derived from a standardization procedure that supplies the odds ratio for FOREIGN-POP and the odds ratio for METROPOP based on their respective standard deviations.[191] When each odds ratio in Table 8.3 is measured in terms of the standard deviation of its independent variable, the odds ratio is 2.277 for FOREIGNPOP and .154 for METROPOP.[192] In other words, the odds that a state would have a formal ban on appearances of impropriety by lawyers were enlarged by a factor of 2.277 (i.e., by approximately 128 percent) when there was an increase of one standard deviation in the percentage of the state population that had been born outside the United States, and the odds were reduced by a factor of .154 (i.e., by approximately 85 percent) when there was an increase of one standard deviation in the percentage of the state population that resided in a metropolitan area. Using the standard deviation of each independent variable thus indicates that FOREIGNPOP had a somewhat greater effect than METROPOP.

In sum, the data analysis suggests that the appearance-of-impropriety standard for attorneys is not a randomly occurring doctrine of law and that the presence or absence of the standard is tied to specific system-level properties. Although indicators rather than direct measures of hypothesized societal properties were employed in the data analysis, cultural heterogeneity and population concentration evidently contribute materially to whether a state adopts or rejects the standard. This conclusion is buttressed by trends over time (discussed in Part V below) in each property. The conclusion is also buttressed by the potential utility of each property in a sociological theory of law.[193]

V. Conclusion

This chapter, adopting the perspective of macrosociology, has deemed law to be an institution of society and has accordingly considered law to be a component of a system. If law is embedded in a system, the concepts and doctrines of law are shaped by conditions in that system and facilitate the operation of the system. In this regard, the chapter contended that symbols are among the products of law, that symbols are responses to societal circumstances, and that symbols promote societal cohesion in the long run. Specifically, the chapter examined concepts and doctrines of law that are concerned with the appearance to society that certain things are present. The chapter hypothesized that, through stimulus generalization, these concepts and doctrines become symbols when the things to which the concepts and doctrines refer are socially significant. Because lawyering as an occupation is important in the United States and generates appearances to which the public is attentive,[194] the appearance-of-impropriety standard for judging attorney behavior is among the concepts and doctrines of law that are symbolic.

If macrosociology is correct in treating a society as a *system*—i.e., as a set of interacting, interdependent parts—symbolic concepts and doctrines are not random but, instead, are responses to identifiable aspects of the society in which they exist. Accordingly, an analysis was undertaken, with logistic regression, of state-level quantitative measures of four system-level properties—cultural heterogeneity, population concentration, social system rationality, and societal stability—to determine whether any of the four properties predicted the odds that the appearance-of-impropriety standard for attorneys would be present in, rather than absent from, a state. Two of the properties were found to have substantial predictive power. Specifically, higher cultural heterogeneity raised the odds, while higher population concentration lowered the odds, that the standard was being used in a state. For each state, the two properties were measured, respectively, by the percentage of inhabitants in 1980 who had been born outside the United States and by the percentage of inhabitants in 1980 who resided in a metropolitan area.

If social, demographic, and/or economic conditions outside the institution of law are responsible for concepts and doctrines inside the institution, law is not a self-contained component of society that operates independently of other components. Instead, law as an institution is inextricably tied to the social system in which it exists, and the border between law and other institutions is porous. Unfortunately, a decision on the utility of the macrosociological approach to law that has been developed here will not be possible until an appreciable body of well-designed quantitative research that is pertinent to the approach has accumulated.[195] However, the approach receives support from not just the instant study but from other studies as well.[196] In finding that cultural heterogeneity and population density were related to whether the appearance-of-impropriety standard for attorneys was maintained or discontinued by states, the instant study strengthens the thesis that law is a sociological phenomenon and that the concepts and doctrines of law can be understood only by placing them in their societal context.

In order to explore more fully the implications of the instant study, I will assume that cultural heterogeneity and population concentration operated as causes of state acceptance or rejection of the appearance-of-impropriety standard. If each property was adequately captured by its independent variable, the juxtaposition of Table 8.3 supra and Table 8.5 infra suggests that the two properties, and the forces behind them, worked concurrently over time. With regard to Table 8.5, the top panel (panel A) shows, for each specified year, the percentage of the total population of the United States that had been born outside the United States.[197] As measured by this percentage, cultural heterogeneity declined moderately from the middle of the twentieth century until about 1970 and then increased substantially over the next three decades. The bottom panel (panel B) shows, for each specified point in time, the percentage of the population in the United States as a whole that resided in a metropolitan area.[198] As measured by this percentage, population concentration rose steadily from 1950 to 2000.

All of the states in the study had adopted an appearance-of-impropriety standard for attorneys by 1980,[199] and the states without the standard in 2010 had dropped it after 1980. Can the findings in Tables 8.3 and 8.4, their accompanying analyses, and the data in Table 8.5

Table 8.5 Metropolitan-Area Population and Foreign-Born Population: United States, 1950–2000

	1950	1960	1970	1980	1990	2000
Panel A: Percent of U.S. population born outside U.S. (%)	6.9	5.4	4.7	6.2	7.9	11.1
Panel B: Percent of U.S. population residing in a metropolitan area (%)	56.1	63.3	69.0	74.8	77.5	80.3

help to explain the shift from universal to partial acceptance of the standard? I believe that the answer is affirmative and, in particular, that four conclusions are warranted. First, declining cultural heterogeneity, perhaps acting synergistically with rising population concentration, reduced the societal need for the appearance-of-impropriety standard from 1950 to 1970 and thus could have been a factor in the subsequent abandonment of the standard by some states. Second, in reversing direction from 1970 to 2000, cultural heterogeneity increased the societal benefit of the standard and therefore contributed to preserving the standard in the states that kept it after 1980. Third, population density, by increasing from 1950 to 2000, eroded the social utility of the standard before as well as during the period when numerous states stopped using it, and accordingly was a force leading these states to terminate the standard.

Fourth, the effects of both properties—cultural heterogeneity and population density—were substantial, but the importance of cultural heterogeneity in retaining the appearance-of-impropriety standard after 1980 seems to have modestly exceeded the importance of population density in eliminating the standard.[200] That is, much if not most of the pressure after 1980 to use the standard evidently stemmed from increasing cultural heterogeneity, and much if not most of the pressure to discontinue the standard evidently resulted from growing population density. Assuming that the estimated weights of these properties were accurately gauged, it is notable that the relative magnitude of the impact of each property is roughly consistent with the number of states having and the number of states not having the appearance-of-impropriety standard in 2010: greater cultural heterogeneity was associated somewhat more strongly with retention of the standard than greater population concentration was associated with non-retention of the standard, and among the forty-six states studied, the number of states preserving the standard (twenty-seven) was somewhat larger than the number of states discarding it (nineteen).

In short, the retention of the appearance-of-impropriety standard for attorneys was not due to inertia, and the abandonment of the standard was not due to chance. Instead, two system-level properties were evidently major contributors to whether a state kept the standard during the time period covered by the study, and these properties helped to shape the decision on the standard by the courts and committees in the state that made the decision. Because the appearance-of-impropriety standard for attorneys is symbolic, the two properties affected whether symbolism occurred in law.

Before leaving the appearance-of-impropriety standard, a comment on investment advisers is in order. Investment advisers, like attorneys, work in a government-regulated occupation: an attorney must abide by requirements imposed by the judiciary of the state(s) in which the attorney is licensed to practice law; an investment adviser must be registered either with the Securities and Exchange Commission ("Commission") or with a regulatory body of the state in which the adviser has its main office and business site, and must conform to applicable statutes and agency rules.[201] In two cases, the Commission has expressed concern with appearances of impropriety in the conduct of investment advisers.[202] Notably, however, such cases are not found after the early 1980s, precisely the point in time when the prevalence of the appearance-of-impropriety standard for attorneys began to decline in the United States, and it is unlikely to be coincidence that, since the early 1980s, the Commission has not mentioned appearances of impropriety in the context of the duty owed by investment advisers to their clients. Because the movement away from the appearance-of-impropriety standard was not confined to one occupation, logic suggests that the movement was not fortuitous. Its explanation, instead, is presumably found in broadly operating forces.

A final, but controversial, point should be made regarding the macrosociological approach to law on which this chapter rests. Specifically, the approach offers the possibility of predicting, far in advance, the existence and emergence of law on socially significant topics. To the extent that system-level properties determine the concepts and doctrines of law, information on the level of and change in pertinent properties can be used to forecast the law that a society will possess a decade or more in the future. Predictions will not be uniformly correct, of course, but if the predictions are grounded on well-designed quantitative research, they will be accurate more often than they are flawed. At the present time, however, rigorous quantitative research on the macrosociological aspects of law is scarce, and the existence and emergence of law on a wide variety of topics cannot be predicted with confidence.

Why is prediction possible? From a macrosociological perspective, particular personalities—no matter how charismatic or colorful they might be—are merely the vehicles through which the properties of society, and the large-scale forces that determine the properties, mold the fundamental content of law and generate socially meaningful shifts in this content. The negligible importance of individuals in shaping law is evidenced, inter alia, by the similarity of concepts and doctrines of state law across the country,[203] because the legislators, judges, and government-agency officials promulgating law in one state are not the individuals who are the legislators, judges, and government-agency officials promulgating law in another state.[204] Society-level properties, on the other hand, have broad effects and are likely to be at work throughout the United States (although their level/intensity may differ between states). In addition, society-level properties generally seem to develop at a gradual pace, not abruptly. As a result, the ideas of law whose emergence, modification, and abandonment are due to such properties can in principle be anticipated well in advance. In the study reported in the instant chapter, differences between states in the level/intensity of two particular system-level properties were found to predict use of the appearance-of-impropriety standard for attorneys three decades later.

Given the potential predictability of law, let me revisit and assess a prediction I made in a publication in 1993.[205] Specifically, I contended that, as the result of societal changes, law in the United States was likely "in the next two decades" explicitly to authorize physicians to assist in terminating the lives of mentally competent individuals who requested assistance to end their suffering from physically stressful, incurable medical conditions that were expected to be fatal.[206] In the years since this prediction was made, two states—Oregon in 1997 and Washington in 2009[207]—have implemented statutes allowing physician-assisted suicide under such conditions, and the United States Supreme Court has rejected an attempt by the executive branch of the federal government to prohibit physicians from using federally regulated medications to aid individuals in ending their lives in accordance with the requirements and procedures of a state statute.[208] On the other hand, the number of U.S. states that have thus far legalized physician-assisted suicide is just two, and the Supreme Court has ruled that statutes barring physician-assisted suicide do not violate either the due process guarantee[209] or the equal protection guarantee[210] of the national Constitution.

Statutes on physician-assisted suicide are a type of symbolic law[211] because physician-assisted suicide is a socially important topic and is unlikely, if legalized, to alter existing practices. As to the social importance of the topic, more than three out of five adults in the United

States rejected the conclusion of the Supreme Court that statutory prohibitions on physician-assisted suicide are constitutional[212] and thus believed that they possess an inherent right under certain conditions to end their lives with the aid of a physician. At the same time, a majority of adults in the country as a whole consider the enactment of a statute legalizing physician-assisted suicide to be important.[213] As to the impact of legalizing physician-assisted suicide, just one-eighth of one percent of all deaths in Oregon has resulted from a lethal dose of medication obtained under the terms of the state statute allowing physician-assisted suicide.[214] Therefore, like law generally that deals with social issues,[215] law on physician-assisted suicide does not substantially alter a society but, instead, manifests the existing attributes of the society and serves as a symbol.

My 1993 prediction that physician-assisted suicide would be explicitly and widely legalized in the United States over the course of the following two decades will almost certainly prove wrong in terms of timing. Formal approval of the practice continues to be likely—e.g., through legislation and/or through written interpretations of existing statutes by state attorneys general—but it will involve a much longer period of time than I anticipated. Probably the main cause of the delay is that physician-aided suicide has been largely legalized de facto. That is, a substantial number of physicians in the United States evidently help terminally ill patients to end their lives,[216] and even though the practice is not authorized by statute, physicians are rarely prosecuted for it.[217] Because the practice has been legalized de facto, there is less pressure on society to revise existing statutes that ban the practice.

Nonetheless, physician-assisted suicide is likely to be expressly and widely authorized by state law in the future. Legalization de jure of physician-assisted suicide can be expected because of social values—Americans generally accept the practice and want law that allows it. For example, according to national sample surveys of adults in the United States conducted from 1995 to 2005, no less than three out of five respondents prefer that their state adopt a statute allowing physician-aided suicide with conditions and requirements comparable to those in the Oregon act.[218] Moreover, legalization of physician-aided suicide is a subject that seems to be of more than minimal concern to most Americans. In a sample survey of adults in the United States conducted during 2001, almost three out of five respondents believed that passage "within the next year" of a federal statute allowing physician-assisted suicide[219] in cases of terminal illness was "important," "very important," or "extremely important," while somewhat less than two out of five respondents thought such a statute either was "not important" or should not be adopted.[220] Notably, broad support for the legalization of physician assistance to end the lives of terminally ill patients is not recent—legalization has been favored by a majority of Americans since the mid-1980s.[221] Over time, furthermore, support for legalization will likely become stronger in the United States as the older generation, which is less inclined than the younger generation to endorse legalization, is removed from the population by death.[222] Law formally permitting physician-assisted suicide can thus be expected to emerge in most if not all states in the future.

Why are social values supportive of a change in law on this topic? One plausible factor—indeed, the factor that has probably been primary—is a higher level and greater prevalence of rationality, which seems to have reached the point in the United States where most adults want the option of selecting the manner and timing of their deaths if they develop a progressive, terminal illness. As the United States has added to its stock of knowledge, reason and individualism have increased,[223] resulting in an erosion of public acceptance of rules that deny personal choice. Rationality, however, is unlikely to have acted alone in fostering social values favorable to the adoption of law accepting physician-assisted suicide. A second plausible factor is the increased share of the American population living in areas having a highly concentrated population. Such areas, because of the variety of people they attract and the variety of stimuli they produce, presumably possess a relatively complex social structure and experience a relatively fast rate of social change. Complexity and change, however, are incompatible with rules that prevent flexibility and constrain individual choice. The exposure of more Americans to densely inhabited areas, therefore, logically promoted, and will continue to promote, the development of social values that are averse to such rules,[224] including law that bars physician-assisted suicide.

Notes

*Chapter 8 is an extensively revised version of Larry D. Barnett, "Law as Symbol: Appearances in the Regulation of Investment Advisers and Attorneys," *Cleveland State Law Review* 55 (2007): 289 [hereinafter *Law as Symbol*].

1. *American Heritage Dictionary*, 3rd ed. (1992), 936 (defining an institution to include "3.a. [a]n established organization or foundation, especially one dedicated to education, public service, or culture. b. The building or

buildings housing such an organization. c. A place for the care of persons who are destitute, disabled, or mentally ill").

2. Howard B. Kaplan, "The Concept of Institution: A Review, Evaluation, and Suggested Research Procedure," *Social Forces* 39 (1960): 176, 179.
3. Donald N. Levine, "Introduction," in *Georg Simmel: On Individuality and Social Forms: Selected Writings*, ed. Donald N. Levine (Boston, MA: Houghton Mifflin, 1971), xv–xvii, xxvi.
4. Larry D. Barnett, *Legal Construct, Social Concept* (1993): 14–19.
5. Larry D. Barnett, "Social Productivity, Law, and the Regulation of Conflicts of Interest in the Investment Industry," *Cardozo Public Law, Policy and Ethics Journal* 3 (2006): 793, 794–95 [hereinafter *Social Productivity*]. *Social Productivity* is reproduced (with revision) infra in Chapter 2.
6. Street v. Nat'l Broad. Co., 645 F.2d 1227, 1237 (6th Cir. 1981) (stating that "[s]ocial order is based on law,....").
7. E.g., Thurman W. Arnold, *The Symbols of Government* (New Haven, CT: Yale University Press, 1935).
8. E.g., John W. Ragsdale, Jr., "Anasazi Jurisprudence," *American Indian Law Review* 22 (1998): 393, 423.
9. Christopher E. Smith, "Imagery, Politics, and Jury Reform," *Akron Law Review* 28 (1994): 77, 78–79.
10. Karen A. Cerulo, *Identity Designs: The Sights and Sounds of a Nation* (New Brunswick, NJ: Rutgers University Press, 1995), 12.
11. Steven G. Calabresi, "Federalism and the Rehnquist Court: A Normative Defense," *Annals of the American Academy of Political and Social Science* 574 (2001): 24, 34.
12. *Social Productivity*, supra note 5, at 821–24. Pages 821–24 in *Social Productivity* are reproduced in Part V-B of Chapter 2 supra.
13. E.g., Glover v. State, 386 S.E.2d 699, 702 (Ga. Ct. App. 1989) (Benham, J., concurring).
14. Sally Engle Merry, "Legal Pluralism," *Law & Society Review* 22 (1988): 869, 882.
15. Paul Kooistra, "Criminals as Heroes: Linking Symbol to Structure," *Symbolic Interaction* 13 (1990): 217.
16. Concepts and doctrines in the Constitution of the United States, and in court decisions interpreting the Constitution, can also be symbols. Calabresi, supra note 11, at 34; see Gene R. Nichol, "Toward a People's Constitution," *California Law Review* 91 (2003): 621, 621 (book review) ("The Constitution is not quite as potent a symbol to us as the flag, but it occupies a close second."). Indeed, since the Constitution is the charter of the nation as a sovereign entity, the clauses in it that express cultural ideals are inescapably symbolic, and the document as a whole is, too. Max Lerner, "Constitution and Court as Symbols," *Yale Law Journal* 46 (1937): 1290, 1299–1300; see Dennis v. United States, *United States Reports* 341 (1950), 494, 523.
17. E.g., V. F. Nourse, "Twenty-five Years of George P. Fletcher's Rethinking Criminal Law: Rethinking Crime Legislation: History and Harshness," *Tulsa Law Review* 39 (2004): 925, 934 ("[C]rime legislation is a powerful symbol of public and political order and stability.").

18. Kathleen E. Hull, "The Cultural Power of Law and the Cultural Enactment of Legality: The Case of Same-Sex Marriage," *Law & Social Inquiry* 28 (2003): 629, 638.
19. Securities Act of 1933, 15 U.S.C. §§ 77a–77z-3 (2006).
20. Roberta S. Karmel, "Realizing the Dream of William O. Douglas—The Securities and Exchange Commission Takes Charge of Corporate Governance," *Delaware Journal of Corporate Law* 30 (2005): 79, 142.
21. Investment Advisers Act, 15 U.S.C.S. §§ 80b-1 to 80b-21 (2010).
22. Douglas W. Vick, "Interdisciplinarity and the Discipline of Law," *Journal Law and Society* 31 (2004): 163, 185, 192. Moreover, scholars in the field of law who conduct empirical studies typically do so without employing the rules of scientific inference. Lee Epstein and Gary King, "Empirical Research and the Goals of Legal Scholarship: The Rules of Inference," *University of Chicago Law Review* 69 (2002): 1, 6. Therefore, these studies supply "considerably less accurate information about the empirical world than the studies' stridently stated, but overly confident, conclusions suggest." Ibid., 6–7.
23. Edward L. Rubin, "Social Movements and Law Reform: Passing Through the Door: Social Movement Literature and Legal Scholarship," *University of Pennsylvania Law Review* 150 (2001): 1, 78–80.
24. The studies that have been conducted are: Cerulo, supra note 10; Karen A. Cerulo, "Sociopolitical Control and the Structure of National Symbols: An Empirical Analysis of National Anthems," *Social Forces* 68 (1989): 76; Lauren B. Edelman, "Legal Ambiguity and Symbolic Structures: Organizational Mediation of Civil Rights Law," *American Journal of Sociology* 97 (1992): 1531.
25. Cf. Fred Davis, "On the 'Symbolic' in Symbolic Interaction," *Symbolic Interaction* 5 (1982): 111 (contending that symbolic interaction as an approach has focused on interaction and ignored symbols).
26. See Benjamin Lee Whorf, "The Relation of Habitual Thought and Behavior to Language," in *Language, Culture, and Personality: Essays in Memory of Edward Sapir*, ed. Leslie Spier et al. (Menasha, WI: Sapir Memorial Publication Fund, 1941), 75, reprinted in *Language, Thought, and Reality: Selected Writings of Benjamin Lee Whorf*, ed. John B. Carroll (Cambridge: Technology Press of Massachusetts Institute of Technology, 1956), 134, 154, 156, 159; Ino Rossi, *From the Sociology of Symbols to the Sociology of Signs* (New York: Columbia University Press, 1983), 23, 52–53.
27. Roberta Kevelson, *The Law As a System of Signs* (New York: Plenum Press, 1988), 4.
28. Garth Gillan, *From Sign to Symbol* (Brighton, Sussex: Harvester Press, 1982), 7.
29. Ute Krudewagen, "Political Symbols in Two Constitutional Orders: The Flag Desecration Decisions of the United States Supreme Court and the German Federal Constitutional Court," *Arizona Journal of International & Comparative Law* 19 (2002): 679, 679, 681–83.
30. David D. Franks, "Mutual Interests, Different Lenses: Current Neuroscience and Symbolic Interaction," *Symbolic Interaction* 26 (2003): 613.
31. See J. Steven Ott, *The Organizational Culture Perspective* (1989), 21–22.

32. For this reason, statutes have prohibited intentional damage to tangible forms of the national flag of the United States. As applied to individuals who have deliberately damaged U.S. flags that they personally owned and who did so for the purpose of communicating a political message, the statutes have been judicially invalidated under the First Amendment to the Constitution. United States v. Eichman, *United States Reports* 496 (1990), 310, 313, 315–16. However, First Amendment case law does not deny the meaning attached to physical forms of the flag; rather, this case law is an indicator of the greater weight placed by society on the cultural value(s) protected by the First Amendment.
33. *Webster's Third New International Dictionary*, unabridged ed. (1993), 2316.
34. 36 U.S.C. § 301 (2006).
35. To the extent that symbols perform the function subtly—which may happen often—measurement of the function is difficult.
36. See Larry D. Barnett, "When Is a Mutual Fund Director Independent? The Unexplored Role of Professional Relationships Under Section 2(a)(19) of the Investment Company Act," *DePaul Business and Commercial Law Journal* 4 (2006): 155–60.
37. A societal need is any condition that is required for a society to be workable and that is accommodated by an institution. The concept of "societal need" is discussed in Larry D. Barnett, "The Roots of Law," *American University Journal of Gender, Social Policy and the Law* 15 (2007): 613, 672–77 [hereinafter *The Roots of Law*]. Pages 672–77 in *The Roots of Law* are reproduced in Part IV of Chapter 6 supra.
38. Three justices of the United States Supreme Court recognized the symbolic aspect of law, but seem to have underestimated its societal importance, when they wrote: "We cannot ignore that rules of law also have a symbolic power that may vastly exceed their utility." New Jersey v. T.L.O., *United States Reports* 469 (1985), 325, 373 (Stevens, Marshall, and Brennan, JJ., dissenting). For the social system, however, the utility of law stems partially from the symbols generated by law. Furthermore, in some situations, the utility of the symbolic aspect of law probably equals or surpasses other benefits to society furnished by the institution of law. Law, for example, furnishes a social system with symbols that express cultural ideals, and these symbols, "by creating a realm...where all our dreams of justice in an unjust world come true," in the long run promote the equilibrium of the system. Arnold, supra note 7, at 34–35.
39. See Cerulo, supra note 10, at 120–21, 164, 168.
40. Daniel Webster, quoted in Michael Moncur's (Cynical) Quotations, The Quotations Page, http://www.quotationspage.com (accessed July 31, 2010).
41. Peter W. Morgan and Glenn H. Reynolds, *The Appearance of Impropriety* (New York: Free Press, 1997), 2.
42. See John M. Levine and Richard L. Moreland, "Small Groups," in *The Handbook of Social Psychology*, ed. Daniel T. Gilbert et al., vol. 2, 4th ed. (Boston, MA: McGraw-Hill 1998), 415, 425–27 [hereinafter *Handbook of Social Psychology*].
43. Theodore N. Greenstein and J. David Knottnerus, "The Effects of Differential Evaluations on Status Generalization," *Social Psychology Quarterly* 43 (1980): 147; Jolanda Jetten et al., "Group Distinctiveness and Intergroup

Discrimination," in *Social Identity: Context, Commitment, Content,* ed. Naomi Ellemers et al. (Malden, MA: Blackwell Publishers, 1999), 107.

44. *Oxford English Dictionary,* vol. 1, 2nd ed. (1989), 566.
45. To employ a colloquialism, "'[r]eality' is the only word in the English language that should always be used in quotes." Author unknown, quoted in *Cole's Quotables,* The Quotations Page, http://www.quotationspage.com (accessed November 7, 2006).
46. Stanley Lieberson et al., "The Instability of Androgynous Names: The Symbolic Maintenance of Gender Boundaries," *American Journal of Sociology* 105 (2000): 1249, 1260–61, 1274.
47. Traditional sex roles have been rejected in principle by no less than two out of three adults in the United States since at least the late 1980s. Kim Parker, "The Harried Life of the Working Mother," *Social and Demographic Trends* (2009), http://pewsocialtrends.org/pubs/745/the-harried-life-of-the-working-mother (accessed September 30, 2010). Nonetheless, Americans retain a commitment to traditional sex roles. Among parents in the United States who had children age sixteen or younger in 2009, fewer than half as many working mothers (37 percent) as working fathers (79 percent) wanted to be employed full-time. Ibid. (sample survey conducted July 20, 2009 to August 2, 2009). Public support for traditional sex roles, moreover, has evidently increased. Among working mothers with children younger than eighteen, the percentage who preferred full-time employment declined by about one-third between 1997 and 2007. Pew Res. Ctr., "From 1997 to 2007: Fewer Mothers Prefer Full-time Work," *Social and Demographic Trends Report* (July 2007): 1, 13, http://pewsocialtrends.org/assets/pdf/WomenWorking.pdf (accessed April 11, 2011).
48. See Mary R. Jackman and Mary Scheuer Senter, "Images of Social Groups: Categorical or Qualified?" *Public Opinion Quarterly* 44 (1980): 341, 355, 358; Tom Langford and Neil J. Mackinnon, "The Affective Bases for the Gendering of Traits: Comparing the United States and Canada," *Social Psychology Quarterly* 63 (2000): 34.
49. Robert B. Cialdini and Melanie R. Trost, "Social Influence: Social Norms, Conformity, and Compliance," in *Handbook of Social Psychology,* supra note 42, at 151, 174.
50. James Felton et al., "Web-based Student Evaluations of Professors: The Relations Between Perceived Quality, Easiness, and Sexiness," *Assessment & Evaluation in Higher Education* 29 (2004): 91, 100–1, 106.

    The heavy reliance that colleges and universities place on student-completed teaching evaluation questionnaires is illustrative of the importance of appearances, even in organizations that are ostensibly committed to rationality and empirically grounded knowledge. Research indicates that the questionnaires are not highly accurate measures of the degree to which students master assigned material. Larry D. Barnett, "Are Teaching Evaluation Questionnaires Valid? Assessing the Evidence," *Journal of Collective Negotiations* 25 (1996): 335. Moreover, relatively little is known about the negative effects of the questionnaires on faculty members and students. Ibid., 343. Appearances, therefore, are the primary basis for the use of the questionnaires in personnel decisions by organizations of higher education.

51. Alexander Todorov et al., "Inferences of Competence from Faces Predict Election Outcomes," *Science* 308 (2005): 1623, 1623.
52. Allan Mazur et al., "Military Rank Attainment of a West Point Class: Effects of Cadets' Physical Features," *American Journal of Sociology* 90 (1984): 125, 140.
53. If law is symbolic when it deals with appearances of activities that are significant to society, empirical research must be able to distinguish activities that are "significant" from activities that are not. Unfortunately, theory in the sociology of law currently seems to be of little or no help to researchers who are seeking to measure societal significance, which is potentially ascertained from objective measures, from subjective measures, or from both. Objectively, societal significance might be determined from quantitative data on conditions in the society; such data on the United States are found inter alia in studies of the population of the country undertaken by federal government agencies. Subjectively, societal significance might be determined from the attitudes and values of the participants in society; data on attitudes and values are available from surveys conducted by organizations in the private sector using samples drawn from the population. The study of symbols in law will be scarce until sociological theory aids researchers in selecting both the most suitable approach to societal significance—objective, subjective, or an objective–subjective combination—and the most appropriate data within the approach.
54. David I. Mostofsky, "Introduction," in *Stimulus Generalization*, ed. David I. Mostofsky (Stanford, CA: Stanford University Press, 1965), 1–2.
55. Ibid., 1.
56. Corrado Roversi, "Constitutive Rules in Context," *Archiv für Rechts- und Sozialphilosphie* 96 (2010): 223, 235, 238.
57. E.g., Texas v. Johnson, *United States Reports* 491 (1989), 397, 405.
58. 4 U.S.C. §§ 6, 7 (2006).
59. Ibid., § 8.
60. Robert A. LeVine, "*The Role of Family in Authority Systems: A Cross-Cultural Application of Stimulus-Generalization Theory,*" *Behavioral Science* 5 (1960): 291; Richard M. Merelman, "Learning and Legitimacy," *American Political Science Review* 60 (1966): 548, 558; Robert Frank Weiss, "Defection from Social Movements and Subsequent Recruitment to New Movements," *Sociometry* 26 (1963): 1.
61. David O. Sears et al., "Whites' Opposition to "Busing": Self-Interest or Symbolic Politics?" *American Political Science Review* 73 (1979): 369, 381.
62. In a survey conducted during 2002, a nationwide sample of adults in the United States was asked whether "[s]etting dress codes in public schools that stop students from wearing clothes that are too revealing or sloppy" would be "an effective solution for improving people's behavior." In answering the question, respondents selected one of the following: "very effective," "somewhat effective," "not too effective," "not effective at all." More than half (55 percent) of the respondents thought dress codes would be "very effective." Public Agenda Foundation (January 2–23, 2002). *Accord*, Public Agenda Foundation (March 11–18, 2004)(national sample of adult parents of public school students who were in grades 5–12). Because the personal attire under consideration breached accepted social standards

(i.e., because the attire was "too revealing or sloppy"), the behavior that would be "improved" by dress codes presumably violated social standards, too. The belief that dress codes are a means of reducing socially unacceptable behavior links attire to the character of social life. This link—which confers meaning on personal attire and, in turn, dress codes—is evidently well-entrenched and widespread in the United States inasmuch as most respondents believed that dress codes would be highly effective in enhancing social behavior. School codes that bar grooming that deviates from social norms seem to have been generally favored by Americans since at least the mid-1960s. See Gallup Organization (September 16–21, 1965).

Under my thesis, most if not all of the physical appearances targeted by dress codes are symbolic even if the individuals affected by the codes have no intent to communicate a political or social message through their physical appearance. My thesis, therefore, is broader than existing case law on the constitutionality of government-decreed dress codes. See Wendy Mahling, Note, "Secondhand Codes: An Analysis of the Constitutionality of Dress Codes in the Public Schools," *Minnesota Law Review* 80 (1996): 715. Furthermore, my thesis contends that the dress codes themselves are symbolic when they address physical appearances characterized by symbolism.

63. Arnold, supra note 7, at 34.
64. The regulatory law discussed in this paragraph is not concerned with appearances, but regulation is the goal of much, if not most, of the law that focuses on appearances. Regulatory law dealing with appearances is the subject of Parts III and IV of the instant chapter.
65. In 1984, seven out of ten adults in the United States thought that the death penalty was "one of the most important" issues facing the country (13 percent) or that the death penalty was an "important" issue (58 percent). General Social Survey, http://www.norc.org/GSS+Website (follow "Data Analysis using SDA" hyperlink). The data are from the GSS question CAPIMP and are weighted with COMPWT.

    In 1982 and 1984, more than half of all adults in the United States believed that abortion was "one of the most important" issues in the country (12 percent in 1982 and 18 percent in 1984) or that abortion was an "important" issue (44 percent in 1982 and 45 percent in 1984). Ibid. The data are from the GSS question ABIMP are weighted with COMPWT. Among registered voters in the United States, the percentage regarding abortion as "very important" fluctuated between 39 percent and 47 percent during the years from 2004 to 2008. Pew Forum on Religion & Public Life, *More Americans Question Religion's Role in Politics* (2008), 47–48, http://people-press.org/reports/pdf/445.pdf (accessed April 11, 2011).

    Given the significance of capital punishment and abortion to society, both can be expected to spawn important social products—in particular, symbols. See *Social Productivity*, supra note 5, at 821–24. Pages 821–24 in *Social Productivity* are reproduced in Part V-B of Chapter 2 supra.
66. Tomislav V. Kovandzic et al., "Does the Death Penalty Save Lives? New Evidence from State Panel Data, 1977 to 2006," *Criminology & Public Policy* 8 (2009): 803; Kevin B. Smith, "Explaining Variation in State-Level Homicide Rates: Does Crime Policy Pay?" *Journal of Politics* 59 (1997): 350,

355, 360–61. A rigorous study of the impact of the death penalty, which used annual data on counties for the period 1977 through 1996, found that the impact of capital punishment differed between states and that executions, while reducing the number of murders in some states, increased the number of murders or had no effect in other states. When the effects in all of the states were aggregated, the net number of murders that executions were estimated to have prevented in 1977–1996 was roughly 1,672. Joanna M. Shepherd, "Deterrence Versus Brutalization: Capital Punishment's Differing Impacts Among States," *Michigan Law Review* 104 (2005): 203, 232. During the twenty years covered by the study, however, the number of recorded murders in the United States totaled 427,600. Calculated from U.S. Bureau of the Census, *Statistical Abstract of the United States: 1988*, 108th ed. (1987), table 263, available at http://www.census.gov/prod/www/abs/statab .html (accessed April 11, 2011); U.S. Bureau of the Census, *Statistical Abstract of the United States: 1998*, 108th ed. (1998), table 335, available at http://www.census.gov/prod/www/abs/statab.html (accessed April 11, 2011). Consequently, executions between 1977 and 1996 reduced the number of murders that would have occurred in these years by 1,672/(427,600 + 1,672) = 1,672/429,272 = .00389 x 100 = .389%, i.e., by approximately four-tenths of 1 percent.

In addition, statutes on prison sentences for criminal conduct have a negligible influence on the overall rate of major crimes. Elsa Y. Chen, "Impacts of "Three Strikes and You're Out" on Crime Trends in California and Throughout the United States," *Journal of Contemporary Criminal Justice* 24 (2008): 345; Tomislav V. Kovandzic, "The Impact of Florida's Habitual Offender Law on Crime," *Criminology* 39 (2001): 179; Tomislav V. Kovandzic et al., "'Striking Out' as Crime Reduction Policy: The Impact of 'Three Strikes' Laws on Crime Rates in U.S. Cities," *Justice Quarterly* 21 (2004): 207; Thomas B. Marvell and Carlisle E. Moody, "The Impact of Enhanced Prison Terms for Felonies Committed with Guns," *Criminology* 33 (1995): 247; Lisa Stolzenberg and Stewart J. D'Alessio, "'Three Strikes and You're Out': The Impact of California's New Mandatory Sentencing Law on Serious Crime Rates," *Crime & Delinquency* 43 (1997): 457; Tamasak Witayapanyanon, Criminal Justice Policy in the United States: A Pooled Time-Series Analysis of Sentencing Reform Acts (unpublished PhD diss., Southern Illinois University, 1989), 211–12, 223–24 (on file with Widener University Library).

67. The liberalization of law on induced abortion in the United States had no more than a small impact on the aggregate number of births in the nation as a whole and in individual states. Timothy D. Hogan, "An Intervention Analysis of the Effects of Legalized Abortion Upon U.S. Fertility," *Population Research & Policy Review* 3 (1984): 201, 214–15. See also Kenneth J. Meier et al., "The Impact of State-Level Restrictions on Abortion," *Demography* 33 (1996): 307 (finding that twenty-three state laws and policies, individually and collectively, had no statistically significant impact on the number of abortions occurring in the states per one thousand females age 15–44); Matthew E. Wetstein, "The Abortion Rate Paradox: The Impact of National Policy Change on Abortion Rates," *Social Science Quarterly* 76 (1995): 607 (finding that the U.S. Supreme Court decision in Roe v. Wade

had no effect on the ratio of abortions to live births in the United States as a whole). If law that banned induced abortion had been a major obstacle for women who wanted to end pregnancies, the elimination of such law would have been followed by a substantial decline in births, ceteris paribus. Because no such decline occurred, law that was intended to restrict induced abortion was evidently having little effect on the frequency with which women terminated pregnancies.

The failure of law to have a material impact on the incidence of induced abortion is not confined to the United States. The rate at which women residing in Spain opted to abort pregnancies was unaffected when that country in 1985 expanded the grounds for lawfully terminating a pregnancy. Rosana Peiró et al., "Does the Liberalisation of Abortion Laws Increase the Number of Abortions? The Case Study of Spain," *European Journal of Public Health* 11 (2001): 190.

The preceding studies, in supporting the conclusion that law on abortion has minimally influenced the proportion of pregnancies that are intentionally interrupted, suggest that such law serves chiefly as a symbol.

68. 28 U.S.C. § 1738C (2006).
69. See Sylvia A. Law, "Homosexuality and the Social Meaning of Gender," *Wisconsin Law Review* 1988 (1988): 187, 196.
70. H.R. Rep. No. 104–664, at 2 (1996), reprinted in 1996 U.S.C.C.A.N. 2905, 2906.
71. Ibid., 2–3, 25, 27, reprinted in 1996 U.S.C.C.A.N. 2905, 2906, 2907, 2929, 2931.
72. Denise C. Morgan and Rebecca E. Zietlow, "The New Parity Debate: Congress and Rights of Belonging," *University of Cincinnati Law Review* 73 (2005): 1347, 1385.
73. Since the word "group" is employed here to refer to an organized set of individuals, an institution is a type of group.
74. Tom R. Tyler and Heather J. Smith, "Social Justice and Social Movements," in *Handbook of Social Psychology*, supra note 42, at 595, 595, 606, 611–12.
75. E.g., Holmes v. Jennison, *United States Reports* 39 (1840), 540, 573.
76. E.g., John T. Parry, "The Virtue of Necessity: Reshaping Culpability and the Rule of Law," *Houston Law Review* 36 (1999): 397, 462; Ronald H. Jensen, "Of Form and Substance: Tax-Free Incorporations and Other Transactions Under Section 351," *Virginia Tax Review* 11 (1991): 349, 372.
77. United States v. Lastra, 973 F.2d 952, 956 (D.C. Cir. 1992).
78. See Cerulo, supra note 10, at 15–27. The promotion of societal cohesion is among the goals sought to be achieved by government in regulating the physical appearance of individuals. See Miller v. School Dist. No. 167, 495 F.2d 658, 664 (7th Cir. 1974). Government regulation of individuals' physical appearance is discussed earlier in this chapter. See supra note 62 and accompanying text.
79. Levine and Moreland, supra note 42, at 428; Charles A. O'Reilly III et al., "Work Group Demography, Social Integration, and Turnover," *Administrative Science Quarterly* 34 (1989): 21, 33–34. See Wayne Busby, Social Integration and Community Health (unpublished PhD diss., Univ. of Oklahoma, 1985), 79–81, 86; Sung-Soon Clara Kim, Dimensions of Social

Integration: Solidarity and Deviance in American Cities (unpublished PhD diss., University of Virginia, 1985), 142–48 (on file with Widener University Library); Thorolfur Thorlindsson and Jón Gunnar Bernburg, "Durkheim's Theory of Social Order and Deviance: A Multi-level Test," *European Sociological Review* 20 (2004): 271. See also Uberto Gatti et al., "Civic Community and Juvenile Delinquency," *British Journal of Criminology* 43 (2003): 22 (data analysis consistent with an inverse relationship between degree of social integration and incidence of the most serious violent crimes). Cf. Thomas A. Petee et al., "Levels of Social Integration in Group Contexts and the Effects of Informal Sanction Threat on Deviance," *Criminology* 32 (1994): 85 (concluding that the ability of informal sanctions to prevent illegal behavior rises with the degree of social integration in a group).

80. Offutt v. United States, *United States Reports* 348 (1954), 11, 14; *In re* Murchison, *United States Reports* 349 (1955), 133, 136.
81. A survey of a national sample of adults in the United States found in 2002 that eight out of ten respondents "completely" or "mostly" agreed with the statement that "Religion is a matter of personal faith and should be kept separate from government policy." Princeton Survey Res. Assoc. (August 19–September 8, 2002). The United States Supreme Court has incorporated this ideal into jurisprudence on the national constitution. Lee v. Weisman, *United States Reports* 505 U.S. (1992), 577, 589 (observing that "[t]he design of the Constitution is that preservation and transmission of religious beliefs and worship is a responsibility and a choice committed to the private sphere...").
82. "Congress shall make no law respecting an establishment of religion, or prohibiting the free exercise thereof." *U.S. Const.* amend. I. These provisions also apply to the states and their subdivisions. Elk Grove Unified Sch. Dist. v. Gordon, *United States Reports* 542 (2004), 1, 8 & n.4.
83. Bd. of Educ. v. Grumet, *United States Reports* 512 (1994), 687, 696–97. See also Doe v. Shenandoah County Sch. Bd., 737 F. Supp. 913, 918 (W.D. Va. 1990).
84. See supra notes 49–52 and accompanying text.
85. Deborah Pergament, "It's Not Just Hair: Historical and Cultural Considerations for an Emerging Technology," *Chicago-Kent Law Review* 75 (1999): 41.
86. Louise M. Antony, "Back to Androgeny: What Bathrooms Can Teach Us About Equality," *Journal of Contemporary Legal Issues* 9 (1998): 1, 7.
87. Pergament, supra note 85, at 52–54, 56. See also Stacey S. Baron, "Note, (Un)Lawfully Beautiful: The Legal (De)Construction of Female Beauty," *Boston College Law Review* 46 (2005): 359 (discussing sex-based head hair grooming policies as part of "appearance discrimination" generally and labeling court decisions and statutes on appearance discrimination as "appearance law").
88. Joel Brockner et al., "The Influence of Prior Commitment to an Institution on Reactions to Perceived Unfairness: The Higher They Are, The Harder They Fall," *Administrative Science Quarterly* 37 (1992): 241 [hereinafter Brockner I]; Joel Brockner et al., "When Trust Matters: The Moderating Effect of Outcome Favorability," *Administrative Science Quarterly* 42 (1997): 558.

89. Instances of perceived social *in*justice reduce commitment to a group among participants who are strongly committed, but instances of perceived social justice do not seem to increase commitment among participants who are weakly committed. Consequently, "it may be much easier to break, rather than build[,]...organizational commitment." Brockner I, supra note 88, at 260.
90. Barnett, supra note 4, at 16–19.
91. In this regard, the English jurist William Blackstone was correct in his observation that "[l]aw is the embodiment of the moral sentiment of the people." *Classic Quotes,* The Quotations Page, http://www.quotationspage.com (accessed November 7, 2006).
92. Collins v. United Mine Workers of Am. Welfare & Ret. Fund, 298 F. Supp. 964, 968 (D. D.C. 1969), *aff'd,* 439 F.2d 494 (D.C. Cir. 1970); Hay v. Med. Ctr. Hosp., 496 A.2d 939, 944 (Vt. 1985); Semler v. Oregon State Bd. of Dental Exam'rs, 34 P.2d 311, 313 (Or. 1934).
93. Eugene R. Fidell, "The Culture of Change in Military Law," *Military Law Review* 126 (1989): 125, 132.
94. See George v. Jordan Marsh Co., 268 N.E.2d 915, 918 (Mass. 1971) (referring to the "ever changing conditions of the society which the law is intended to serve.").
95. See Greenberg v. Kimmelman, 494 A.2d 294, 299 (N.J. 1985) (state statute regulating employment in casinos must be "concerned not only with impropriety, but also with its appearance, which is always more subtle than impropriety itself.").
96. 15 U.S.C. § 80a-2(a)(20) (2006). A party supplying securities advice will not be an investment adviser under the Investment Company Act unless the entity receiving the advice qualifies as an investment company. The statutory criteria for an investment company are in section 3 of the Act. 15 U.S.C.S. § 80a-3 (2010).
97. 15 U.S.C.S. § 80b-2(a)(11) (2010). A "person" is either "a natural person or a company"; a company includes "a corporation, a partnership, an association, a joint-stock company, a trust, or any organized group of persons, whether incorporated or not...." Ibid., §§ 80b-2(a)(5), 80b-2(a)(16) (2010).
98. 15 U.S.C.S. § 80b-3(a) (2010).
99. 15 U.S.C.S. § 80b-3(b)(3) (2010); Cornelius C. Rose Associates, Inc., SEC No-Action Letter, 1978 SEC No-Act. LEXIS 360, at *2 (January 6, 1978).
100. During the twelve months that ended on May 3, 2010, the assets managed by investment advisers registered with the Securities and Exchange Commission were estimated to be worth more than $38 trillion. Amendments to Form ADV, Release No. IA-3060, 75 Fed. Reg. 49,234, 49,234 & n.2 (July 28, 2010). The estimate is based on Form ADV, which a registered investment adviser must file annually with the Commission. Form ADV requires the adviser to report the value of the assets it manages. 17 C.F.R. § 275.204-1 (2009); Sec. & Exch. Comm'n, Uniform Application for Investment Advisor Registration, Form ADV: Instructions for Part 1A, 5–8, http://www.sec.gov/about/forms/formadv-instructions.pdf (accessed April 11, 2011).

Advisers registered with states were omitted from the estimate, but if they had been included, the total assets being managed by investment advisers nationwide would have been larger. An investment adviser is required to register with the Commission if its "principal office and place of business" is in a state that does not regulate advisers *or* if it has as a client an investment company that is registered with the Commission. Any other investment adviser cannot register with the Commission unless it manages assets worth at least $25 million. 15 U.S.C.S. § 80b-3a(a) (2010). An investment adviser in a state that regulates advisers has the option of registering with the Commission if it manages assets of at least $25 million but less than $30 million, and such an investment adviser must register with the Commission if it manages assets worth $30 million or more. 17 C.F.R. § 275.203A-1(a) (2009).

At the end of 2009, the net assets of mutual funds amounted to $11.1 trillion, while the other common forms of investment companies—closed-end funds, exchange-traded funds, and unit investment trusts—had assets worth, respectively, $228 billion, $777 billion, and $38 billion. Investment Company Institute, *2010 Investment Company Fact Book*, 50th ed. (2010), 9, http://www.ici.org/about_ici/annuals/fact_books (accessed April 11, 2011).

101. Caroline Hodges Persell, "The Interdependence of Social Justice and Civil Society," *Social Forces* 12 (1997): 149.
102. Investment Company Inst., "Ownership of Mutual Funds, Shareholder Sentiment, and Use of the Internet, 2009," *Research Fundamentals* (December 2009), 16, http://www.ici.org/pdf/fm-v18n7.pdf (accessed April 11, 2011).
103. Investment Company Inst., "Characteristics of Mutual Fund Investors, 2009," *Research Fundamentals* (December 2009), 6, http://www.ici.org/pdf/fm-v18n8.pdf (accessed April 11, 2011).
104. Norman J. Singer, *Statutes and Statutory Construction*, vol. 2A, 6th ed. (2000), § 46.06.
105. Applicability of the Investment Advisers Act to Financial Planners, Pension Consultants, and Other Persons Who Provide Investment Advisory Services as a Component of Other Financial Services, Investment Advisers Act Release No. IA-1092, 52 Fed. Reg. 38,400, 38,402 (October 16, 1987) [hereinafter Release No. IA-1092].
106. Ibid. Investment advising is not the only occupation of which an individual can be deemed a member when the individual holds himself or herself out as being in the occupation. Thus, the ethical rules governing attorneys have been applied to an individual who, although not admitted to the bar, presented himself as an attorney. Triffin v. DiSalvo, 643 A.2d 118 (Pa. Super. Ct. 1994), *appeal denied*, 661 A.2d 874 (Pa. 1995).
107. 15 U.S.C.S. § 80b-2(a)(11)(B) (2010).
108. Release No. IA-1092, supra note 105, at 38,403. *Accord*, Hungerford, Aldrin, Nichols and Carter, SEC No-Action Letter, 1991 SEC No-Act. LEXIS 1420, at *2–3 (December 10, 1991).
109. 15 U.S.C.S. § 80b-2(a)(11)(C) (2010).
110. 17 C.F.R. § 275.202(a)(11)-1(b)(2)(i) (2009); Certain Broker-Dealers Deemed Not To Be Investment Advisers, Extension of Compliance Date, Investment Advisers Act Release No. IA-2426, 2005 SEC LEXIS 2343 (September 12, 2005).

111. Sec. Indus. Ass'n, SEC No-Action Letter, 2005 SEC No-Act. LEXIS 853, at *2–3 (December 16, 2005).
112. 15 U.S.C.S. § 80b-3(a) (2010).
113. 15 U.S.C.S. § 80b-3(b)(3) (2010). Section 203(b)(3) does not exclude a person from the definition of investment adviser but permits a person qualifying as an investment adviser to conduct an investment advisory business through mail and interstate commerce without registering with the Commission.
114. See, e.g., *Restatement (Second) of Agency* (1958), § 27 (creation of apparent authority); Andrews v. John E. Smith's Sons Co., 369 So.2d 781, 785 (Ala. 1979) (imposition of liability on successor corporations for acts of their predecessor corporations).
115. Mr. Bate, SEC No-Action Letter, 1988 SEC No-Act. LEXIS 847, at *2 (June 28, 1988). The reply of the staff in this case dealt with section 203(b)(3) of the Advisers Act, the pertinent portion of which is discussed in the prior paragraph in the text. The staff seems to consider the activities that comprise "holding out" under section 203(b)(3) to be the same activities that comprise "holding out" under the exclusions from the definition of investment adviser in section 202(a)(11). See George J. Dippold, SEC No-Action Letter, 1990 SEC No-Act. LEXIS 748, at *4 (May 7, 1990). It is logical to presume, therefore, that these activities are also applicable to and determinative of the business element in the definition of investment adviser in section 202(a)(11).
116. Resource Bank & Trust, SEC No-Action Letter, 1991 SEC No-Act. LEXIS 624 (March 29, 1991).
117. See Thomson Financial, Inc., SEC No-Action Letter, [2002 Transfer Binder] Fed. Sec. L. Rep. (CCH) ¶ 78,318, at 78,517 (July 9, 2002), available at 2002 SEC No-Act. LEXIS 635.
118. See John W. Mohr, "Measuring Meaning Structures," *Annual Review of Sociology* 24 (1998): 345.
119. See John Scott, *Sociological Theory* (Brookfield, VT: Edward Elgar 1995), 138–39; Kim, supra note 79, at 9–28, 142–51.
120. Dictionary definitions of the word "system" include "[a] set or assemblage of things connected, associated, or interdependent, so as to form a complex unity; a whole composed of parts in orderly arrangement according to some scheme or plan." *Oxford English Dictionary*, vol. 17, 2nd ed. (1989), 496.
121. James M. Altman, "Considering the A.B.A.'s 1908 Canons of Ethics," *Fordham Law Review* 71 (2003): 2395.
122. Edward C. Brewer, III, "Some Thoughts on the Process of Making Ethics Rules, Including How to Make the 'Appearance of Impropriety' Disappear," *Idaho Law Review* 39 (2003): 321, 323–24.
123. Ibid., 324.
124. *Model Code of Prof'l Responsibility Canon* (1981), 9.
125. Peter W. Morgan, "The Appearance of Propriety: Ethics Reform and the Blifil Paradoxes," *Stanford Law Review* 44 (1992): 593, 595.
126. Brown v. Eighth Jud. Dist. Ct., 14 P.3d 1266, 1269 n.4 (Nev. 2000).
127. A measure of the relative importance to society of law as a profession is the number of Juris Doctor (J.D.) and Bachelor of Laws (LL.B.) degrees in relation to the total number of first-professional degrees. J.D. and LL.B. degrees from law schools accredited by the American Bar Association

comprised between 46 percent and 51 percent of all first-professional degrees awarded during the period from the 1970–71 academic year to the 2005–06 academic year. Calculated at five-year intervals from 1970–71 to 2005–06 using data in the following sources: Am. Bar Ass'n, Enrollment and Degrees Awarded, 1963–2008, http://www.abanet.org/legaled/statistics/stats.html (follow "Enrollment and Degrees Awarded" hyperlink) (accessed August 3, 2010); Nat'l Ctr. For Educ. Statistics, Digest of Education Statistics: 2009, (2010), table 268, http://nces.ed.gov/pubsearch/pubsinfo.asp?pubid=2010013 (accessed April 11, 2011).

128. See William T. Gallagher, "Ideologies of Professionalism and the Politics of Self-Regulation in the California State Bar," *Pepperdine Law Review* 22 (1995): 485, 619–21.
129. Brewer, supra note 122, at 324.
130. However, the Model Rules explicitly bar attorneys from publicly holding themselves out as admitted to practice in jurisdictions where they are not members of the Bar. *Model Rules of Prof'l Conduct R. 5.5(b)* (2003). The Rules, therefore, continue to prohibit appearances of one type.
131. Brewer, supra note 122, at 324–25.
132. American Bar Association, *Opinions of the Committee on Professional Ethics and Grievances with the Canons of Professional Ethics Annotated and the Canons of Judicial Ethics Annotated* (1936), 29, 30.
133. Lisa L. Milord, *The Development of the ABA Judicial Code* (Chicago, IL: American Bar Association, Center for Professional Responsibility, 1992), 13.
134. American Bar Association, *Annotated Model Code of Judicial Conduct* (Chicago, IL: American Bar Association, Center for Professional Responsibility, 2004), 29.
135. American Bar Association, *ABA Model Code of Judicial Conduct* (2007), Canon 1 ("A judge . . . shall avoid impropriety and the appearance of impropriety."), http://www.abanet.org/judicialethics/approved_MCJC.html (accessed April 11, 2011).
136. See Morgan, supra note 125, at 602–03, 616–17.
137. Morgan and Reynolds, supra note 41, at 2–5.
138. See Dennis F. Thompson, *Ethics in Congress* (Washington, DC: Brookings Institutions, 1995), 126 ("[A]ppearances are usually the only window that citizens have on official conduct.").
139. E.g., Deborah Hellman, "The Importance of Appearing Principled," *Arizona Law Review* 37 (1995): 1108, 1126; Susan P. Shapiro, "Bushwhacking the Ethical High Road: Conflict of Interest in the Practice of Law and Real Life," *Law & Social Inquiry* 28 (2003): 87, 177.
140. E.g., *In re* Complaint of Fadeley, 802 P.2d 31, 40 (Ore. 1990) (judiciary); Auburn Police Union v. Carpenter, 8 F.3d 886, 902 (1st Cir. 1993) (law enforcement officers and associations).
141. *Social Productivity*, supra note 5, at 814–21, 825–27. Pages 814–21 and 825–27 in *Social Productivity* are reproduced in Parts V-A and V-C, respectively, of Chapter 2 supra.
142. Stephen Gillers, *Regulation of Lawyers: Problems of Law and Ethics*, 8th ed. (New York, NY: Aspen Publishers, 2009), 9–10.
143. Ibid., 10.
144. The review was completed on September 9, 2010.

145. The two states excluded for this reason were Connecticut and Maine.
146. In order to confine the study to states, the District of Columbia was omitted from the statistical analysis.
147. The twenty-seven states applying the standard were Arizona, Arkansas, Florida, Georgia, Idaho, Illinois, Kansas, Kentucky, Louisiana, Maryland, Michigan, Minnesota, Mississippi, Missouri, Montana, Nebraska, Nevada, New Hampshire, New Mexico, New York, North Carolina, North Dakota, Texas, Utah, Vermont, West Virginia, and Wyoming.
148. The nineteen states not applying the standard were Alabama, California, Colorado, Delaware, Indiana, Iowa, Massachusetts, New Jersey, Ohio, Oklahoma, Oregon, Pennsylvania, Rhode Island, South Carolina, South Dakota, Tennessee, Virginia, Washington, and Wisconsin.
149. The level of rationality in a society is probably an effect of the degree to which the society produces and uses sophisticated knowledge and disseminates that knowledge to its participants through the education institution.
150. See Olof Dahlbäck, "Modelling the Influence of Societal Factors on Municipal Theft Rates in Sweden: Methodological Concerns and Substantive Findings," *Acta Sociologica* 41 (1998): 37, 47–48 (using as its measure of the cultural source of variation in societal commitment among the municipalities of a country the percentage of inhabitants of the municipalities who were not citizens of the country).
151. See Michael B. Tannen, "The Investment Motive for Attending College," *Industrial and Labor Relations Review* 31 (1978): 489, 496 (finding that differences between states in the rationality of economic decisions were responsible for state differences in college enrollment rates among males fourteen to twenty-four years old).
152. Allen E. Liska and Barbara D. Warner, "Functions of Crime: A Paradoxical Process," *American Journal of Sociology* (1991): 1441, 1460–61.
153. The data for the variables were obtained or computed from the following sources:

APPEARIMPROP: Search of Lexis databases conducted by the author in September 2010.

PCT4YRSCOLL: U.S. Bureau of the Census, *Statistical Abstract of the United States: 1986*, 106th ed. (1985), 134 table 217, http://www.census.gov/prod/www/abs/statab1951-1994.htm (accessed April 11, 2011).

CRIMERATE: U.S. Dep't of Justice, *Uniform Crime Reports: Crime in the United States*, (Washington, DC: U.S. Government Printing Office, 1981), 42–47 table 3; U.S. Bureau of the Census, *Statistical Abstract of the United States: 1982–83*,103rd ed. (Washington, DC: U.S. Government Printing Office, 1982), 28 table 32, http://www.census.gov/prod/www/abs/statab1951-1994.htm (accessed April 11, 2011).

FOREIGNPOP: Campbell J. Gibson and Emily Lennon, U.S. Census Bureau, Historical Census Statistics on the Foreign-born Population of the United States: 1850–1990 (February 1999), table 13: Nativity of the Population, for Regions, Divisions, and States: 1850 to 1990, http://www.census.gov/population/www/documentation/twps0029/twps0029.html (accessed September 9, 2010).

METROPOP: U.S. Bureau of the Census, *Statistical Abstract of the United States: 1993*, 113th ed. (1993), 36 table 41, http://www.census.gov/

prod/www/abs/statab1951-1994.htm (accessed April 11, 2011) [hereinafter *Statistical Abstract: 1993*].

154. *Statistical Abstract: 1993*, supra note 153, at 916–17.

155. An effort was made to include, as an indicator of social system stability, the state divorce and annulment rate in 1980, i.e., the number of divorces and annulments granted in 1980 in each state per one thousand inhabitants who were at least fifteen years of age. However, data on divorces and annulments in 1980 were incomplete for one of the forty-six states (viz., Louisiana). Sally C. Clarke, Nat'l Ctr. for Health Statistics, "Advance Report of Final Divorce Statistics, 1989 and 1990," *Monthly Vital Statistics Report* (March 22, 1995): 10–11 table 2, http://www.cdc.gov/nchs/data/mvsr/supp/mv43_09s.pdf (accessed April 11, 2011). As a result, the divorce-annulment rate was omitted from the statistical analysis. For the forty-five states in the study for which the divorce-annulment rate in 1980 was determinable, the zero-order correlation coefficient between the divorce-annulment rate and the crime rate was .422. (The crime rate is denominated CRIMERATE in Table 8.1 in the text.) Therefore, only about one-sixth of the variation in each rate is linked to variation in the other ($r^2 = (.422)^2 = .178 \times 100 = 17.8\%$), and although the two rates are to some extent overlapping indicators of societal stability, they are for the most part independent.

The correlation coefficient was computed with the CORRELATE command in Stata 10.1. StataCorp., *Stata Base Reference Manual: Release 10*, vol. 1 (2007), 321–28 [hereinafter *1 Stata Manual*].

156. The Model Rules were promulgated in 1982. Brewer, supra note 122, at 324–25.

157. Canon 9 of the Model Code of Professional Responsibility, which was issued by the ABA in 1969, provided that "a lawyer should avoid even the appearance of impropriety." *Model Code of Prof'l Responsibility* Canon 9 (1980); Brewer, supra note 122, at 324. By 1980, according to a survey by the ABA, Canon 9 had been adopted in all states with the possible exception of California, Delaware, Georgia, Maine, Montana, and New Mexico. *ABA Nat'l Ctr. for Prof'l Responsibility, Code of Professional Responsibility by State x* (1980). Of these six states, Maine was not included in the data. Supra note 145. The remaining five states had adopted, no later than 1980, either Canon 9 or a common-law appearance-of-impropriety standard for attorneys. Comden v. Superior Court, 576 P.2d 971, 973 (Cal. 1978) (California); *Del. Code Ann.*, vol. 16, at 562, 589 (1974) (Canon 9 adopted in 1971) (Delaware); *Ga. Code Ann.* tit. 9 App. Rule 3-109 (Harrison 1973) (Canon 9 in effect in 1973) (Georgia); *In re* Estate of Sauter, 615 P.2d 875, 878 (Mont. 1980) (Montana); John H. Clough, "Federalism: The Imprecise Calculus of Dual Sovereignty," *John Marshall Law Review* 35 (2001): 1, 36 n.209 (finding that Canon 9 was adopted by the Supreme Court of New Mexico in 1974) (New Mexico).

158. Shepherd, supra note 66, at 213–14.

159. David W. Hosmer and Stanley Lemeshow, *Applied Logistic Regression* 2nd ed. (2000), 339.

160. A minimum of one hundred observations has been recommended for tests of significance calculated by maximum-likelihood logistic regression.

J. Scott Long, *Regression Models for Categorical and Limited Dependent Variables* (Thousand Oaks, CA: SAGE Publications, 1997), 53–54.

161. Tests of statistical significance, even though common in social science research, have fundamental limitations that are often unrecognized or ignored, and use of the tests may be unjustified even for samples containing an adequate number of observations. Lancelot Hogben, *Statistical Theory: The Relationship of Probability, Credibility and Error* (London: Allen & Unwin, 1957), 332–44.
162. All analyses of the data in this study were conducted with Stata Release 10.1. The Stata commands LOGIT and LOGISTIC generated the results in Table 8.2 as well as the results in Table 8.3. StataCorp., *Stata Base Reference Manual: Release 10*, vol. 2 (2007), 144–52, 178–89 [hereinafter *2 Stata Manual*].
163. J. Scott Long and Jeremy Freese, *Regression Models for Categorical Dependent Variables Using Stata*, 2nd ed. (2006), 151.
164. One recommendation that has been made by statisticians is to treat Cook's Statistic as generally large in magnitude when it exceeds 1.0. Hosmer and Lemeshow, supra note 159, at 180. Another recommendation is to regard Cook's statistic as large when it is more than the result obtained from dividing the number 2 by the square root of the number of observations; in the present analysis, the threshold from this recommendation would be $2/\sqrt{46} = .3$. David A. Belsley et al., *Regression Diagnostics* (Hoboken, NJ: Wiley-Interscience, 2004), 28. As is evident from the different recommendations, there is no generally accepted quantitative criterion for identifying outliers whose influence may be undermining regression results; the process of determining such influence is acknowledged to be subjective. Hosmer and Lemeshow, supra note 159, at 176; Long and Freese, supra note 163, at 148.
165. Given the recommendation by Belsley supra in note 164, a numerical value of .30 on Cook's Statistic is used as the cut-off in the text. However, because Cook's Statistic was so much larger for California than for any other state, only California was selected for investigation as a possible influential outlier.
166. William D. Berry, *Understanding Regression Assumptions* (Newbury Park, CA: Sage Publications, 1993), 24–27, Monograph #92.
167. The largest correlation coefficient was .67 in the 46- state data set and .66 in the 45-state data set. The coefficients were computed with the CORRELATE command in Stata. *1 Stata Manual*, supra note 155, at 321–28.
168. James Hardin, StataCorp., Why Do Estimation Commands Sometimes Omit Variables? (July 2009), http://www.stata.com/support/faqs/stat/drop.html (accessed September 19, 2010); *2 Stata Manual*, supra note 162, at 292, 299.
169. Excessive collinearity is evidenced by very large standard errors. Berry, supra note 166, at 27; Hosmer and Lemeshow, supra note 159, at 141. Visual inspection of Tables 8.2 and 8.3 indicates that the standard errors are not abnormal in size.
170. James Jaccard and Robert Turrisi, *Interaction Effects in Multiple Regression*, 2nd ed. (Thousand Oaks, CA: SAGE Publications, 2003), 3, Monograph #92.

171. Ibid.
172. Ibid., 3–4; Berry, supra note 166, at 30–31.
173. Other potential interactions in the instant study lack a theoretical foundation and, therefore, are not considered. The possibility of an interaction between CRIMERATE and METROPOP nevertheless deserves mention, because urban areas are evidently characterized by higher rates of crime overall than are rural locations. Edward L. Glaeser and Bruce Sacerdote, "Why Is There More Crime in Cities?" *Journal of Political Economy* 107 (1999): S225. Certain types of major crime, however, are not more frequent in urban settings. Claude S. Fischer, "The Subcultural Theory of Urbanism: A Twentieth-Year Assessment," *American Journal of Sociology* 101 (1995): 543, 560–65. Since urban size is not related to all types of serious crime, the role of the former in the latter is unclear, and an interaction variable based on CRIMERATE and METROPOP was omitted from the regression model.
174. Fischer, supra note 173, at 545–46, 552.
175. Dahlbäck, supra note 150, at 37–39.
176. See the discussion supra in Part IV-B of the text.
177. The strength of the effect of an interaction variable is measured by the magnitude of its regression coefficient and/or odds ratio. Jaccard and Turrisi, supra note 170, at 28.
178. Jack. L. Walker, "The Diffusion of Innovations among the American States," *American Political Science Review* 63 (1969): 880, 883 table 1.
179. Lynn D. Wardle, "No-Fault Divorce and the Divorce Conundrum," *BYU Law Review* (1991): 79, 83–84.
180. Ryken Grattet et al., "The Homogenization and Differentiation of Hate Crime Law in the United States, 1978 to 1995: Innovation and Diffusion in the Criminalization of Bigotry," *American Sociological Review* 63 (1998): 286, 289, 295.
181. James M. Lutz, "Regional Leaders in the Diffusion of Tort Innovations among the American States," *Publius* 27 (1997): 39, 55–56 table 4.
182. Brian Ceh, "Regional Innovation Potential in the United States: Evidence of Spatial Transformation," *Papers in Regional Science* 80 (2001): 297, 313–14.
183. The calculation was performed by the Stata command *estat classification. 2 Stata Manual,* supra note 162, at 166–67. The calculation used the default predicted probability of the dependent variable, namely, ≥ .5. Ibid., 167. The output from *estat classification* includes the percentages for the "sensitivity" and the "specificity" of the model, which terms are defined in ibid., 176.
184. Long and Freese, supra note 163, at 108.
185. Fred C. Pampel, *Logistic Regression: A Primer* (Thousand Oaks, CA: SAGE Publications,v 2000), 11, Monograph #92.
186. Ibid., 11–12.
187. Ibid., 12–13, 35–36.
188. Ibid., 36–37.
189. Ibid., 12.
190. Factor changes (here, 1.322 and .918) are translated into percentages by subtracting 1.000 from each factor change and multiplying the remainders by 100.

191. Standardization was done with the LISTCOEF command for Stata. Long and Freese, supra note 163, at 177–78. However, while standardized dependent and independent variables measured with interval or ratio scales furnish a meaningful basis in ordinary least-squares regression for ascertaining the relative magnitude of the influence on the dependent variable of each independent variable, standardized independent variables in logistic regression do not allow a definitive comparison of independent variables measured with interval or ratio scales when, as in the instant study, the dependent variable is a dummy (i.e., coded 0 or 1). See Pampel, supra note 185, at 32. Nonetheless, logistic regression can provide a useful ranking of the degree to which a dummy dependent variable is affected by each of two independent variables when the independent variables are measured with an interval or ratio scale and the standard deviations on those scales are used. Robert L. Kaufman, "Comparing Effects in Dichotomous Logistic Regression: A Variety of Standardized Coefficients," *Social Science Quarterly* 77 (1996): 90, 108; Scott Menard, "Six Approaches to Calculating Standardized Logistic Regression Coefficients," *American Statistician* 58 (2004): 218, 222.
192. When standardized in this way, the odds ratio for CRIMERATE was 2.555 and the odds ratio for PCT4YRSCOLL was .717.
193. See Hosmer and Lemeshow, supra note 159, at 184 (stressing the importance of developing useful theory).
194. Evidence on the public perception of lawyers is in Marc Galanter, "The Faces of Mistrust: The Image of Lawyers in Public Opinion, Jokes, and Political Discourse," *University of Cincinnati Law Review* 66 (1998): 805, 808–16.
195. See Michael Heise, "The Past, Present, and Future of Empirical Legal Scholarship: Judicial Decision Making and the New Empiricism," *University of Illinois Law Review* 2002 (2002): 819, 824; Daniel Klerman, "Statistical and Economic Approaches to Legal History," *University of Illinois Law Review* 2002 (2002): 1167, 1173–76.
196. E.g., Part III-D in Chapter 6 supra; Part III in Chapter 7 supra; Kenneth D. Wald et al., "The Politics of Gay Rights in American Communities: Explaining Antidiscrimination Ordinances and Policies," *American Journal of Political Science* 40 (1996): 1152.
197. The percentages in Panel A are from the following sources: Gibson and Lennon, supra note 153; U.S. Census Bureau, *Statistical Abstract of the United States: 2004–2005*, 124th ed. (2004), table 42, http://www.census.gov/prod/www/abs/statab.html (accessed April 11, 2011).
198. The percentages in Panel B are from Frank Hobbs and Nicole Stoops, U.S. Census Bureau, *Demographic Trends in the 20th Century* (Census 2000 Special Reports, Series CENSR-4, 2002), 33 figures 1–15, 35 figures 1–16.
199. See supra note 157 and accompanying text.
200. Supra note 191 and accompanying text.
201. 15 U.S.C.S. §§ 80b-3, 80b-3a (2010). An investment adviser, even though registered with a state and not with the Commission, remains subject to the prohibition against fraud imposed by section 206 of the federal Investment Advisers Act and implementing rules adopted by the Com-

mission. 15 U.S.C.S. § 80b-6 (2010); Rules Implementing Amendments to the Investment Advisers Act of 1940, Release No. IA-1601, 61 Fed. Reg. 68,480, 68,490 (December 27, 1996); Investment Advisers Act Release No. IA-1633, 62 Fed. Reg. 28,112, 28,127, 28,128 (May 22, 1997).

202. *In re* Steadman Security Corp., Sec. & Exch. Comm'n Admin. Proc. File No. 3-3101, 1974 SEC LEXIS 3639, at *103, *104 (December 20, 1974); Report of Investigation in the Matter of Bull & Bear Management Corp., Investment Advisors Act Release No. 769, 1981 SEC LEXIS 931, at *8 (August 7, 1981).

203. The commonality of law in the United States is illustrated by "model" statutes and rules. The large number of, and wide range of subjects covered by, such statutes and rules is indicated by the contents of the "Model Acts & Uniform Laws" database in LEXIS (follow "Legal" hyperlink to "Secondary Legal"). While the statutes and rules as adopted undoubtedly differ in some ways between states, they necessarily possess an underlying similarity.

204. In the macrosociological approach I am advocating, the rate of replacement of—i.e., the rate of personnel turnover among—the individuals who are legislators, judges and government-agency officials may affect the *timing* of a basic change in law but does not determine *whether* the change occurs.

205. Barnett, supra note 4, at Chapter 6.

206. Ibid., 140.

207. Shelly A. Cassity, Note, "To Die or Not to Die: The History and Future of Assisted Suicide Laws in the U.S.," *Journal of Law and Family Studies* 11 (2009): 467, 473–74.

208. Gonzales v. Oregon, *United States Reports* 546 (2006), 243.

209. Washington v. Glucksberg, *United States Reports* 521 (1997), 702.

210. Vacco v. Quill, *United States Reports* 521 (1997), 793.

211. See supra notes 61, 63–67 and accompanying text.

212. Humphrey Taylor, "Physician-Assisted Suicide," *The Harris Poll*, August 1997, 1, 3.

213. International Communications Research (April 25–May 20, 2001. The findings of this survey are presented infra note 220 and its accompanying text.

214. From the first full calendar year in which the Oregon physician-assisted suicide legislation was in force through the most recent completed calendar year—i.e., from 1998 through 2009—a total of 460 Oregon residents ended their lives in accordance with the legislation. Oregon Dep't of Human Services, Table 1: Characteristics and End-of-Life Care of 460 DWDA Patients who Died After Ingesting a Lethal Dose of Medication, by year, Oregon, 1998–2009, http://oregon.gov/DHS/ph/pas/ar-index.shtml (follow "Table 1(pdf)" hyperlink) (accessed September 25, 2010). During the same twelve-year period, deaths in Oregon are estimated to have been 366,834. Computed from Oregon Dep't of Human Services, Center for Health Statistics—Health Statistics/Data, Death Data, http://www.dhs.state.or.us/dhs/ph/chs/data/death/death.shtml (accessed September 25, 2010). Physician-assisted suicide in Oregon was thus responsible for 460/366834 = .00125 x 100 = .125% of all deaths.

215. Barnett, supra note 4, at 162.

216. Timothy E. Quill, "Risk Taking by Physicians in Legally Gray Areas," *Albany Law Review* 57 (1994): 693, 699; Brief for American College of Legal Medicine as Amicus Curiae, Vacco v. Quill, *United States Reports* 521 (1997), 793 (No. 95-1858) and Washington v. Glucksberg, *United States Reports* 521 (1997), 702 (No. 96-110), 1996 U.S. S. Ct. Briefs LEXIS 674, at *44 (November 12, 1996).
217. Stephen J. Ziegler, "Physician-Assisted Suicide and Criminal Prosecution: Are Physicians at Risk?" *Journal of Law Medicine & Ethics* 33 (2005): 349, 355 (noting that "the number of physicians prosecuted for participating in [physician-assisted suicide] is virtually non-existent.").
218. Taylor, supra note 212, at 4; Harris Interactive (December 14–19, 2001; April 5–10, 2005).
219. Under current U.S. Supreme Court jurisprudence, a federal statute that authorizes physician-assisted suicide in contravention of state law probably exceeds the power of Congress under the Commerce Clause. See Brian Boyle, "Comment, The Oregon Death with Dignity Act: A Successful Model or a Legal Anomaly Vulnerable to Attack?" *Houston Law Review* 40 (2004): 1387, 1400–6.
220. International Communications Research (April 25–May 20, 2001). The alternatives "important," "very important" and "extremely important" were chosen by 21 percent, 23 percent, and 13 percent of the respondents, respectively.
221. O. D. Duncan and L. F. Parmelee, "Trends in Public Approval of Euthanasia and Suicide in the US, 1947-2003," *Journal of Medical Ethics* 32 (2006): 266, 267.
222. Ibid., 269; Barnett, supra note 4, at 145–46, 148–52.
223. The level of knowledge in a society is manifested in the efficiency and effectiveness of its technology. Change in the level of knowledge in the United States, therefore, can be measured by the annual number of patents issued for inventions. *The Roots of Law*, supra note 37, at 628–31. Pages 628–31 of *The Roots of Law* are reproduced in Part II of Chapter 6 supra.

    The impact of the growth of knowledge on reason and individualism may have involved a two-step process. In the first step, advances in technology (knowledge) raised enrollments in primary and secondary schools. Richard Rubinson and John Ralph, "Technical Change and the Expansion of Schooling in the United States, 1890-1970," *Sociology of Education* 57 (1984): 134. The number of students was boosted partly by the higher personal income that schooling generates. Kathryn Wilson, "The Determinants of Educational Attainment: Modeling and Estimating the Human Capital Model and Education Production Functions," *Southern Economic Journal* 67 (2001): 518, 545. In the second step, higher personal income increased individualism. Ron Lesthaeghe, "A Century of Demographic and Cultural Change in Western Europe: An Exploration of Underlying Dimensions," *Population & Developmental Review* 9 (1983): 411, 429–30. By definition, individualism is characterized by rationality: individualism entails "a mode of life in which the individual...follows out his own ideas; free and independent individual...thought." *Oxford English Dictionary*, vol. 7, 2nd ed. (1989), 880.
224. Supra Part I-C in Chapter 7.

9

Research on the Societal Determinants of Law

I. Introduction

A puzzle is assembled piece by piece, and scientific progress in understanding a phenomenon normally occurs in small increments, too. A single work of scholarship thus typically constitutes no more than a limited step in the long-term expansion of knowledge, and the most for which a scholar can reasonably hope is that he or she will make a modest addition to this expansion. The instant book is offered with that hope. The book deals with topics that have long been part of the sociology of law but challenges popular assumptions about these topics by bringing to bear a considerable number of social science studies that indicate the assumptions are mistaken. Indeed, the crux of the book is the challenge it mounts to the assumptions, and I submit that the challenge merits consideration *because* the assumptions continue to be widely accepted despite the body of credible evidence that contradicts them. The success or failure of this challenge will undoubtedly be critical to whether the book is ultimately judged a useful contribution to knowledge or a misguided undertaking.

In broad terms, the book attempts to further the development of theory on the role of law in social life. The basis of the attempt is the belief that pertinent quantitative research must be intimately and continually involved in building theory. The results of quantitative studies can be wrong, of course, but such studies are advantageous both because they offer greater precision than research based solely on impression and because they can more easily be repeated in order to check the accuracy of their findings. Consequently, when a pattern is discernible in the results of quantitative studies, as it is for the place of law in society, the results must not be ignored.

I am cognizant that the findings of the research compiled in the instant book, and the inferences I have drawn from these findings, conflict sharply with widely held beliefs about law and that the book, therefore, will be uncomfortable for many readers. However, progress in understanding a complex phenomenon is unavoidably hard and rarely, if ever, fast. The book is concerned with a prominent institution of society, raises important questions about that institution, and proposes answers to the questions by relying on an array of evidence—evidence that must not be summarily dismissed simply because it and its implications clash with established views. Given the quantity and quality of this evidence, further study of the questions is plainly warranted, and for me, the book will have been a worthwhile effort if it leads just a few scholars to reconsider their position on the role of law in society. In this regard, the following point by Albert Einstein bears repeating because it is as relevant today as when it was made almost a century ago:

> Concepts that have proven useful in ordering things easily achieve such authority over us that we forget their earthly origins and accept them as unalterable givens. Thus they might come to be stamped as 'necessities of thought,' 'a priori givens,' etc. The path of scientific progress is often made impassable for a long time by such errors.[1]

II. Macrosociology and Law

Law, I have argued in the preceding chapters, is a macrosociological phenomenon—or, more precisely, an institution with concepts and doctrines that is a component of a society.[2] By setting law *within* a social system, the framework I have proposed directs attention to the source and function of law in a society. What originates and changes the concepts and doctrines of law in a society? What accounts for the persistence of the institution of law in a society, i.e., what benefit(s) does a society obtain from law? The answers to the preceding questions are indispensable to understanding law, and the formulation and application of law will therefore be inefficient, or even counterproductive, if the societal source and function of law are seriously misapprehended. Unfortunately, this is evidently the situation today. Scholars and the public continue to believe that concepts and doctrines of law on activities at the heart of society are the product of individuals and that law can furnish effective solutions to social problems. Neither belief, however, is likely to be correct. The former belief is rendered implausible by the similarity of concepts and doctrines that is often the outcome of concurrent multi-jurisdiction change in law on important societal activities,[3] and it is being undercut by a small but growing body of research on the links between the characteristics and law of jurisdictions.[4] The latter belief—the belief that law cures social ills—cannot be squared with an impressive array of social science studies of the effects of law.[5] Simply put, the commonly accepted understanding of the societal place of law is wrong.

For practical reasons alone, then, the development of a useful macrosociological theory of law is important. Such a theory cannot be fashioned, however, until a substantially larger body of rigorous quantitative research has accumulated. This research must include studies on the two general topics mentioned in the prior paragraph, viz., the determinants of the content of law and the effects of law.

Let me begin with the effects of law (statutes, administrative-agency rules, and court decisions) on the behavior of individuals and entities. The topic encompasses both effects that are sought by law and effects that are not. The effects that are sought—i.e., the intended effects—involve the influence of law on the frequency and/or prevalence of the activities specifically addressed by the law. The instant book has referenced some, but not all, of the studies done on this topic. I have been selective because quantitative studies of the intended effects of law not-infrequently have seriously flawed designs.[6] In writing the book, I have tried to avoid citing them.

In addition to examining the degree to which law has intended effects, research must ascertain the effects of law that were neither expected nor desired. These are side effects—i.e., the costs of law—and whether or not law alters targeted activities, law may have costs that are socially and economically significant. Unfortunately, research in sociology seems rarely to investigate these costs, probably in part because many if not most of the unanticipated, unwanted consequences of law are insidious and difficult to locate. However, *all* effects must be accounted for in a macrosociological treatment of law, and investigators should be wary of the assumption that law inflicts no social and economic harm. The assumption may be incorrect, and the costs of law, even if infrequent, may be severe.

The second general topic that a macrosociological theory of law must cover is the societal causes of law, i.e., the sociological, demographic, and economic characteristics of jurisdictions that are responsible for the concepts and doctrines of law that exist in the jurisdictions. Because there have been relatively few studies on the topic, the remainder of the instant chapter will discuss matters that need to be resolved, or at least considered, in undertaking such studies in the future. The present chapter draws on my experience in conducting this type of research—in particular, the studies that were reported in Chapters 6–8 supra—and I hope that the experience will help other investigators to improve on the research that I have done. Science, being a cumulative process, should benefit from the mistakes made and the insights gained in earlier endeavors.[7]

III. Jurisdiction Characteristics as Causes of Law: Research Issues

Among the research-related matters that I take up in Chapter 9, some were mentioned in prior chapters but are discussed again because they deserve emphasis. The other research-related matters to be considered in Chapter 9 were inherent in prior chapters but need to be made explicit. All of the matters I discuss, however, are relevant to conducting rigorous empirical research on the society-level determinants of the content of law. The matters deserve thought so that research can maximize its contribution to the formulation of theory that is able to explain current, and predict new, concepts and doctrines of law.

I divide the matters into four general categories. Although a specific matter may involve more than one category, the classification is helpful in organizing the discussion. The categories are concerned with:

A. Independent variables
B. Types of data and measurement of variables
C. Data analysis
D. Generalizability of a relationship found between jurisdiction attributes and law

A discussion of the above matters is warranted because research on the societal conditions that shape the concepts and doctrines of law is relatively recent and the number of studies in this line of research is still quite small, at least if the count is confined to studies that analyzed quantitative data with a multivariate statistical technique. Indeed, I am aware of fewer than twenty such studies that were published before 2010, the first of which was a Ph.D. dissertation that was finished in 1991.[8] Although studies of the influence of jurisdiction characteristics on the content of law are undoubtedly more numerous than the ones I have encountered, such studies are almost certainly much less common than studies of the effects of law. Sophisticated research on the societal determinants of law thus is in its intellectual infancy.

Let me now discuss the matters that I believe warrant consideration in this line of research.

A. Independent Variables

The content of law can be fully explained and accurately predicted only if, inter alia, the factors that mold this content are known. Without intending to belabor the obvious, all of the factors—probably even most of the factors—have yet to be identified. Because the societal factors that shape law have not been fully enumerated, investigators who study these factors must consider additional independent variables for their models.[9] The importance of doing so cannot be overstated, because if a particular variable is omitted from a research model, its possible impact on law will not be ascertained. Indeed, an investigator whose model lacks an independent variable that affects the content of law will have no reason to gather data on the variable and thus will be unable to uncover, even serendipitously, the impact of the variable.

In this part of Chapter 9, I want to discuss two independent variables that may benefit future studies. The first variable is the presence or absence of an organized religion that opposes certain doctrines of law, and favors other doctrines of law, on core social activities. The potential significance of the variable is illustrated by the apparent ability of the Catholic Church to prevent, at least for a while, the legalization of abortion in Italy[10] and Spain.[11] The variable merits study even though opposition by a religiously motivated entity to a doctrine of law on a key social activity seems not to affect *whether* a jurisdiction adopts the doctrine; rather, such opposition appears to affect only *when* the jurisdiction does so. An ability to block a particular doctrine will not be permanent, because in historical terms, the life span of human beings is brief. The leaders of an organized religion who tenaciously resist a particular doctrine of law will eventually leave their positions through death or retirement, and when they do, their successors—whether immediate or remote—are unlikely to stand in the way of that doctrine of law even though the doctrine conflicts with the original position of the religion. In the long term, the leaders of a religion will quietly if not openly accept a doctrine of law that is needed by societal conditions because individuals cannot overcome these conditions.[12]

Let me turn to the second independent variable that may operate as a societal determinant of law. That variable is language. Although an impact it has on law may not be easy to detect, language possesses the potential to influence the content of law because differences between languages can produce dissimilar perceptions of social and physical environments.[13] More precisely, language can shape the manner in which situations and events are experienced, and by doing so, it may affect the existence and/or intensity of a societal need for a particular doctrine of law.

An investigator who wants to include language as an independent variable in quantitative research will undoubtedly face numerous challenges. Let me mention several. First, a language is characterized by complexities and nuances, but a study that seeks to incorporate language into its explanatory model will be required to quantify language, e.g., code words for the presence or absence of specific meanings. The quantification process will not be free of uncertainty. Another likely problem involves the aspects of language that may influence the content of law. Multiple aspects may be promising influences, and thus several independent variables for language may be necessary in a model. Finally, the sheer number of languages may pose a challenge. While the exact count of languages depends on the criteria used to classify a means of communication as a "language," the total number of languages currently in use is indisputably large. In the world as a whole, between five thousand and ten thousand active languages are presently recognized.[14] Even a study that includes a small fraction of all languages may face a formidable task in measuring the meanings and dimensions of words.

B. Types of Data and Measurement of Variables

In social science research on the existence and magnitude of a causal connection between an independent variable and a dependent variable, data of two general types have been employed—cross-sectional data and longitudinal data. The former in its pure form involves measuring all variables at the same point in time,[15] while the latter involves measuring at least the dependent variable at multiple points in time. However, the dichotomy between cross-sectional data and longitudinal data is only the starting point for a discussion of data forms, because there are variations on and combinations of cross-sectional data and longitudinal data.

The selection of data for a study is based on a number of factors. Data can be used, of course, only if they are available, but assuming that researchers have access to data of different types, the form of data chosen should be that which is most conducive to uncovering causal relationships.[16] Given the temporal sequence that is presumed by the concept of causality, a phenomenon that is a cause must precede the phenomenon that is its effect. In the case of some phenomena, little time may separate cause and effect, but in the case of most aspects of societies, the interval between onset of the cause and occurrence of the effect is probably substantial. The data selected for studying the societal determinants of law must comport with the way in which societies operate.

In light of the above, a study that seeks the societal causes of law should avoid measuring its independent variables at the same point in time that the content of law (the dependent variable) is measured. A study that does so would be using pure cross-sectional data, but such data usually provide no basis for deciding whether an independent variable occurred before the dependent variable. Pure cross-sectional data, accordingly, furnish weak evidence regarding the existence and strength of a causal relationship. Indeed, such data have a greater propensity than longitudinal data to produce mistakes when used to estimate a relationship between an independent variable and a dependent variable.[17] Although cross-sectional data will gradually be displaced by longitudinal data as the latter become increasingly available, most social science studies today cannot, unfortunately, avoid using cross-sectional data in some form.

The studies that are reported in Chapters 6 and 8 supra involved a variation on cross-sectional data. In a sense, each study employed data from two cross-sections of states—one cross-section for the dependent variable, which as coded was measured at a single point in time, and one cross-section for the independent variables, which were measured at an earlier point in time.[18] Although the coding of the dependent variable indicated only *whether* law having a particular content was present and did not indicate the exact year in which each jurisdiction adopted that content, the data for every independent variable were for a time point that was earlier than the time point for the dependent variable. Consequently, the data offered assurance that the dependent variable temporally followed the independent variables, and the certainty of the time sequence enhanced the credibility of conclusions regarding causality.

The data used for the studies in Chapters 6 and 8 nonetheless suffered from a major limitation. In the studies, the dependent variable and the independent variables were each measured at a single point in time rather than at multiple time points. The data sets for the studies thus involved only *differences* between states on the dependent variable and on the independent variables. In this regard, the reader should keep in mind that quantitative differences between jurisdictions on an independent variable at one time point may hide multiple within-jurisdiction changes over time in the independent variable, and that all of the changes may not be in same direction and of the same magnitude. An independent variable, for example, may both rise and fall appreciably in quantity, or it may increase a lot for a brief period and then increase a little for an extended period. In addition, the dependent variable (law) may have changed more than once in jurisdictions, and differences between jurisdictions in their law at a single time point may mask within-jurisdiction changes in that law over time. Thus, some jurisdictions may have altered their law on an activity but subsequently reversed these alterations. In short, the studies reported in Chapters 6 and 8 did not employ longitudinal data for the independent and dependent variables, and they therefore could not ascertain whether and when a particular change in an independent variable was followed temporally by a particular change in the dependent variable.

On the other hand, the study reported in Chapter 7 employed a form of longitudinal data. In particular, the study in Chapter 7 used pooled time-series data, which quantitative social science studies have been employing with apparently greater frequency because of the advantages such data offer for identifying causal relationships. Pooled time-series data are a combination of time-series data and cross-sectional data, and they allow an assessment of the overall impact that an independent variable has on the dependent variable due to both (a) within-jurisdiction change over time in the independent variable and (b) between-jurisdiction differences on the independent variable at each point in time.[19] In the diagram below, I have attempted to portray the structure of this data type for the study in Chapter 7. A row in the diagram is for one jurisdiction (nation), and a column is for one year. The data for the study arose from measuring the dependent variable *and* the independent variables in each of fourteen jurisdictions (j_1 through j_{14}) in each of eight years (t_1 through t_8).

An example may help to understand the diagram. Let us assume that Austria was jurisdiction j_1. The law of Austria on same-sex non-marital partnerships and same-sex marriage was ascertained in and coded for 1970 (t_1), the first of eight time points, and for every fifth year thereafter through 2005 (t_2 to t_8). In addition, the amounts of each independent variable in Austria were determined for the same years. The numerical values obtained for j_1 were the time-series data for Austria and are represented in the diagram by the Greek letter ν. Similarly, the law of each of the remaining countries (j_2 through j_{14}) in the study was coded, and the numerical values of the independent variables in each of these countries were ascertained, for 1970 (t_1) and for every fifth year after 1970 (t_2 through t_8). The resulting data for all of the time points within all of the countries were included in a single regression analysis. The time series data for the countries were, in a word, pooled.

The advantages of pooled time-series data are obvious. Indeed, pooled time-series data may allow the most rigorous test today of whether, and the degree to which, jurisdiction characteristics are responsible for the content of law. However, data from multiple jurisdictions and multiple time points can pose problems when studying the societal determinants of law. Especially if the jurisdictions being studied are nations and the nations materially differ in their sociological attributes, problems may exist with the comparability of the

Diagram of Pooled Time-Series Data

Jurisdiction	**Time**							
	t_1	t_2	t_3	t_4	t_5	t_6	t_7	t_8
j_1	ν	ν	ν	ν	ν	ν	ν	ν
j_2	ν	ν	ν	ν	ν	ν	ν	ν
j_3	ν	ν	ν	ν	ν	ν	ν	ν
j_4	ν	ν	ν	ν	ν	ν	ν	ν
j_5	ν	ν	ν	ν	ν	ν	ν	ν
j_6	ν	ν	ν	ν	ν	ν	ν	ν
j_7	ν	ν	ν	ν	ν	ν	ν	ν
j_8	ν	ν	ν	ν	ν	ν	ν	ν
j_9	ν	ν	ν	ν	ν	ν	ν	ν
j_{10}	ν	ν	ν	ν	ν	ν	ν	ν
j_{11}	ν	ν	ν	ν	ν	ν	ν	ν
j_{12}	ν	ν	ν	ν	ν	ν	ν	ν
j_{13}	ν	ν	ν	ν	ν	ν	ν	ν
j_{14}	ν	ν	ν	ν	ν	ν	ν	ν

data on an independent variable. For example, all of the nations in a study may not use the same definition of the independent variable; even if a single, uniform definition is used, some of the nations in the study may have incomplete data on the independent variable or may inaccurately measure it. In a particular nation, furthermore, the definition of an independent variable and the accuracy of the data on that variable may not be constant over time. For data that are partially cross-sectional and partially longitudinal, therefore, data assembled by a supranational government or quasi-government agency will typically be preferable to data available from the government agencies of individual countries.

Let us turn to another data-related matter, namely, the starting and ending times for data on multiple time points. When time-series data are to be used, what should be the first time point in the series and what should be the last? The answer to the question is important because the time period chosen for a study can affect the results obtained from an analysis of the data for the study.[20] The choice of the beginning and ending time points should not be arbitrary, as it would be if an investigator includes all time points for which data can be obtained. Instead, the choice should stem from the historical context of the phenomenon being studied. In other words, research on a phenomenon that uses data covering a period of time must respect history, and the period must be historically meaningful.[21]

The above principle is pertinent to the study that is reported in Part III-D of Chapter 6. The study, which obtained the data for its independent variables from the decennial censuses of 1950 and 1960, intentionally refrained from using data from any census conducted before 1950. The decision to avoid pre-1950 censuses stemmed from a concern with the impact of World War II and the economic depression of the 1930s. Both events were milestones in the history of the United States and are likely to have affected social life in ways difficult or impossible to detect. In order to avoid the direct consequences of these events, the data for the independent variables in the study were confined to years that followed them.

Unfortunately, in some (and perhaps most) studies of jurisdiction characteristics that mold jurisdiction law, the temporal boundaries of the pertinent historical period will be uncertain. Given the scarcity of research on the societal causes of law, this uncertainty should not be surprising. Period boundaries are important, however, and their selection should be based on established guidelines. Eventually, these guidelines will be formulated, but the process of doing so is unlikely to be either simple or quick.

C. Data Analysis

Change occurs in a doctrine of law of a jurisdiction when an existing doctrine is partially modified or entirely replaced by the action of a government body that is authorized to promulgate law in the jurisdiction. Even when the law-promulgating body delays implementing the change after announcing it, the amount of time involved in the shift from the old to the new doctrine is not long. At least for law on behavior that is central to social life, however, a change in law is often, even perhaps typically, preceded by a lengthy period in which organized groups favoring and opposing the change emerge and become engaged in the political process. The pre-change period and the advocacy groups in it can last decades.[22]

The social movements that are dedicated to altering doctrines of law, and the political process through which their participants realize or do not realize their goals, present my macrosociological framework with an important question. The framework assumes that, in the long run, little is added to a new doctrine of law either by the social movement that advocated the doctrine in the political process or by the political process itself.[23] In my framework, the social movement is assumed to emerge from change in the properties of society, and a doctrine of law that develops and endures is assumed to be the doctrine of law that is required by societal properties. These assumptions, however, do not explain markedly dissimilar durations between two social movements each of which pursues a different issue and both of which realize the changes in the law they advocate. Why does a long time elapse before the social movement on issue X is able to claim victory, while in just a short period the social movement on issue Y witnesses approval of the law it has championed?

The answer to the preceding question will require that research pinpoint thresholds at which doctrines of law develop. One doctrine of law displaces another doctrine presumably when a threshold is attained, i.e., when the amounts of change-inducing properties of society become sufficient to substitute the former doctrine for the latter. Thresholds are likely to be common given that, when a given doctrine of law undergoes a shift, the shift happens in a relatively short time span.

How can thresholds explain differences between social movements in the time that passes before the law they back is adopted? For the movement whose success occurred less quickly, the societal properties (independent variables) that generated the law presumably rose or fell at an appreciably slower speed, and/or by an appreciably greater amount, before a threshold was reached for the development of the law that the movement espoused. Empirical tests of the preceding hypothesis, however, can be expected to unearth considerable complexity, because more than one threshold for a given doctrine of law will probably be common. Multiple thresholds may exist when, for instance, there is interaction between properties that are responsible for a particular doctrine of law. Thus, a given doctrine of law could be generated at threshold A on independent variable X_1 when the amount of independent variable X_2 is small, but when the amount of X_2 is large, the doctrine could be generated at threshold B on X_1. However, the doctrine could emerge at threshold C when both independent variable X_2 and independent variable X_3 are small in amount and at threshold D when both X_2 and X_3 are large in amount. Multiple thresholds may also accompany variation in the pace at which a societal property changes. Thus, the development of a particular doctrine of law may require the attainment of threshold E on independent variable X_4 when X_4 is changing at a slow rate but it may require the attainment of threshold F on X_4 when X_4 is changing at a moderate rate and of threshold G when X_4 is changing at a fast rate.

Let me turn to another matter. When analyzing data in a study of jurisdiction characteristics as predictors of the content of law, the existence of thresholds argues for using *ranges* of numerical values for independent variables, not the exact numerical values for these variables. However, ranges will be useful in such research only if one range ends just under a threshold and the next range begins at the threshold. Indeed, the selection of ranges that miss the threshold(s) for a particular independent variable may result in severely distorted estimates of the impact of that independent variable. Because the current state of theory on the societal antecedents of law does not furnish a basis for selecting specific ranges, an investigator has only the data at hand to justify the use of a set of ranges. A data-driven decision in one study, of course, will not necessarily be in harmony with a data-driven decision in another study, a situation that may not be uncommon among studies using different sets of jurisdictions. To the extent this happens with studies of the same doctrine of law, obvious problems arise for constructing theory.[24]

Let me mention a final matter involving the analysis of data, a matter that I believe must be confronted. A serious question exists regarding the legitimacy of using statistical significance as a criterion for identifying relationships between variables. Although statistical significance is no more than a tool and a particular significance level is arbitrary, statistical significance frequently serves as a substitute for judgment in science.[25] The situation is regrettable because advances in knowledge are not necessarily facilitated, and may be hampered, by statistical significance. Indeed, disagreement exists with regard to both the function of statistical significance in quantitative research[26] and the circumstances in which statistical significance should be employed in such research. As pointed out in earlier chapters, statistical significance may not be an appropriate criterion for assessing the impact of jurisdiction conditions on law. In such assessments, therefore, investigators expose themselves to the risk of drawing erroneous conclusions if they reflexively rely on statistical significance.

D. Generalizability of Study Findings

In research on the determinants of law, can the findings of a study done on one historical era in a society be generalized to other historical eras in that society? Or are the societal properties that are responsible for the content of law unique to each era? Research to date cannot provide an answer.[27] To the extent the activities targeted by law differ between eras, the societal properties that shape law may not be the same across time. On the other hand, the activities addressed by law in one era may have aspects in common with the activities addressed by law in other eras. Should that be the case, the law on these activities in all eras may have resulted from some or even most of the same societal properties.

Does an historical era recur in a society? If it does, the societal causes of law can be expected to operate at more than one point in time. The question is accordingly important, but it raises several issues. One is that, if the answer to the question is affirmative, the time interval between two occurrences of an era is probably very long. An era involves a specific mix of sociological, economic, and demographic conditions, and the same mix must be present in the initial era as well as in the subsequent era. A given mix is unlikely to be repeated soon, however, and complete, comparable data on the two eras may be difficult or impossible to obtain. Fortunately, a long temporal distance between eras may not indefinitely pose an insurmountable obstacle to quantitative research on the eras, because numeric data are being extracted from historical records[28] and are being developed from historical documents composed of words.[29]

Another issue is inherent in the question of whether historical eras happen more than once in a society. In particular, a workable definition of the term "historical era" is required, but a definition is not possible until all of the dimensions (i.e., elements) of an historical era are known. Identifying these dimensions will be difficult to the extent that the dimensions vary over time as the referents of the idea of history evolve.[30] Other issues will arise from defining the concept of historical era. For instance, societal properties probably change gradually in most cases before they reach the thresholds that generate new law. Given a slow pace of change in a property over a lengthy period, should the entire period during which the property changed be within the historical era in which the law was modified? The decision may be complicated by an important event, e.g., a natural disaster with long-lasting consequences. Assuming that such an event occurred but affected just a few of the jurisdictions in a multi-jurisdiction system, should the event alter the start and end points of the historical era for the system as a whole? A macrosociological theory of law must satisfactorily deal with such issues.

The preceding discussion brings us to the final, but nonetheless exceedingly important, matter of outliers. When analyzing data with regression, a researcher who must decide whether to designate a particular jurisdiction as an influential outlier faces a dilemma if the jurisdiction is part of an identifiable system, e.g., states within the United States or nations within the European Union. On the one hand, the researcher must consider the possibility that, even though a jurisdiction deviates markedly from the other jurisdictions in the system, the deviation is natural. In other words, the deviation may have attracted attention only because of a flawed understanding of the character of the system.[31] If the deviation is a normal aspect of the system—i.e., if the deviating jurisdiction is not an aberration—the theoretical model being used by the researcher may need to be revised.

The alternative, unfortunately, is not any less problematic for a researcher. When a researcher concludes that a deviating jurisdiction is an influential outlier, the jurisdiction will be removed from the data,[32] but the removal of the jurisdiction unavoidably leads to a series of difficult questions. The questions begin with whether the remaining jurisdictions form a system. They may not. If they do, however, the system they comprise may not be the equivalent of the original system, and if the system without the jurisdiction materially differs from the system with the jurisdiction, the system without the jurisdiction may not be socially meaningful. Should this be the case, the researcher faces the possibility that the new system is not a worthwhile subject for study. Moreover, even if the researcher-created set of jurisdictions is a socially significant system, the absence of a component (state or nation) from the data for investigating the genesis of law in one historical era may preclude application of the findings of the study to another historical era in which all of the components are present. Statistical procedure thus has a bearing on whether the results of research can be generalized beyond the historical era on which the research was done.

Notes

1. Albert Einstein, http://en.wikiquote.org/wiki/Albert_Einstein (accessed April 7, 2011).
2. An institution, as the word has been used in this book, is a set of statuses and roles (a) that a society defines and endorses and (b) that involve interpersonal relationships through which a socially approved type of activity occurs in the society. Howard B. Kaplan, "The Concept of Institution: A Review, Evaluation, and Suggested Research Procedure," *Social Forces* 39 (1960): 176, 179. Because language is needed for sustained interaction between human beings, concepts and doctrines in linguistic form are inherent in an institution.
3. See Part II-A of Chapter 1 supra.
4. See Chapters 6–8 supra.
5. This research is found supra in Part III-E of Chapter 3 (notes 160-63, 165, and 209), in Part I-B of Chapter 5 (notes 20 and 21), and in Part II of Chapter 8 (notes 66 and 67).
6. For a thorough discussion of the manner in which research must be designed in order to ascertain the impact of law on the activity it targets, see Chester Britt et al., "A Reassessment of the D.C. Gun Law: Some Cautionary Notes on the Use of Interrupted Time Series Designs for Policy Impact Assessment," *Law & Society Review* 30 (1996): 361.
7. Chapter 9 is grounded on the assumption that, in the long run, the findings of quantitative research on the societal determinants of law cannot be ignored by theory on the subject. Of course, advances in knowledge involve the interplay of research and theory, and the treatment of matters that seem on the surface to involve just research may be helped by theory. In the end, however, the results of well-designed empirical studies must be incorporated into theory, especially if the results of the studies form a pattern and/or have been replicated.
8. Sharon Kay Parsons, Abortion Policy in the Fifty States: A Comparative Analysis (unpublished Ph.D. diss., Florida Atlantic University, 1991) (on file with Widener University School of Law Delaware Campus Library). Because the dissertation was not in a scholarly journal or in a book, it is designated as "unpublished" by established rules of citation. *The Bluebook: A Uniform System of Citation* § 17.1.2, at 148 (18th ed., 2005). Nonetheless, I regard the dissertation as having been published because, after being

accepted for the Ph.D. degree, it became available through University Microfilms International (UMI). Of the faculty members and university administrators who were required to accept the dissertation, the Dean of Graduate Studies evidently was responsible for giving final approval and did so on November 18, 1991. Parsons, supra, ii. The title page of the dissertation is dated December 1991. The initial month in which the dissertation could be obtained from UMI is unknown, but that month, even if in 1992, was presumably before publication of the next study on the societal determinants of law. The latter study was in the October 1992 issue of the journal that published it. Karen Smith Conway and Michael R. Butler, "State Abortion Legislation as a Public Good—Before and After Roe v. Wade," *Economic Inquiry* 30 (1992): 609.

9. Unfortunately, political ideology can motivate and control research (including quantitative research) on the societal determinants of law. By influencing the choice of independent variables for a model, political ideology can shape the findings that are obtained from data. The findings of a politically inspired study should, of course, be treated with considerable caution.
10. Erica DiMarco, "The Tides of Vatican Influence In Italian Reproductive Matters: From Abortion to Assisted Reproduction," *Rutgers Journal of Law & Religion* 10 (2009): i, 6–9, 12.
11. Rishona Fleishman, Comment, "The Battle Against Reproductive Rights: The Impact of the Catholic Church on Abortion Law in Both International and Domestic Arenas," *Emory International Law Review* 14 (2000): 277, 292–300; Adrienne Fulco, "Secularization and Its Discontents: Courts and Abortion Policy in the United States and Spain," in *Secularism, Women and the State*, ed. Barry A. Kosmin and Ariela Keysar (2009), 195, 203–5, http://www.trincoll.edu/secularisminstitute (accessed April 7, 2011).
12. The changes experienced by a society will usually occur at a slow pace and may extend over decades. The doctrines of law in a society, therefore, will typically lag behind—indeed, they may often lag appreciably behind—social, economic, and demographic conditions in the society. One factor that may affect the length of the lag is the presence or absence of a particular religious group even though the group cannot indefinitely avoid a doctrine of law that is needed by social life.
13. Benjamin Lee Whorf, "Science and Linguistics," in *Language, Thought, and Reality: Selected Writings of Benjamin Lee Whorf*, ed. John B. Carroll (Cambridge: Technology Press of Massachusetts Institute of Technology, 1956), 207, 213.
14. *Language Family*, Wikipedia, http://en.wikipedia.org/wiki/Language_group (accessed July 25, 2010).
15. Pure cross-sectional data were used in the study that is reported in Part III of Chapter 5 supra.
16. I am not implying that a study should proceed as long as *some* pertinent data are at hand. The data for a study can suffer from one or more deficiencies whose severity makes the study inadvisable. To illustrate, data on particular characteristics of jurisdictions can yield incorrect estimates of the effect of these characteristics on the content of law if (a) the explanatory model omits an independent variable because the investigator has not obtained data on that variable, (b) the omitted independent variable is an

important determinant of the content of law, and (c) the omitted variable is related to another determinant of the content of law that is included in the regression model. One independent variable that is evidently important in explaining the content of law is the educational attainment of jurisdiction populations. Larry D. Barnett, *Mutual Funds, Hedge Funds, and the Public-Private Dichotomy in a Macrosociological Framework for Law*, Working Paper No. 34, Interuniversity Centre for Research on Sociology of Law, Information and Legal Institutions, University of Messina (2008), 11–13, http://www.cirsdig.it/indexeng .html (accessed April 7, 2011). Data on the educational level in jurisdictions, accordingly, should be routinely gathered and analyzed in research on the societal causes of the concepts and doctrines of law.

Similarly, in order to assess accurately the existence, magnitude, and duration of an impact of law on a targeted activity, data must exist on, inter alia, the incidence of the activity over a long period of time both before *and* after change occurred in the law. If data are lacking for a lengthy period prior to and following a change in law, a study cannot establish whether the law had an effect and, if it did, the size and permanence of the effect. See Christoper Winship and Stephen L. Morgan, "The Estimation of Causal Effects from Observational Data," *Annual Review of Sociology* 25 (1999): 659, 687–88 (observing that, without repeated measures of a phenomenon prior to and following an event, the entire range of possible impacts of the event cannot be investigated and the exact type of impact, if any, of the event cannot be determined).

In the above situations, the risk of erroneous conclusions is simply too great to warrant undertaking a study. Such conclusions should be avoided not only because the resources used to produce them were wasted but also because they can lead to the unnecessary expenditure of additional resources in future research.

17. E.g., Norval D. Glenn, "Quantitative Research on Marital Quality in the 1980s: A Critical Review," *Journal of Marriage & Family* 52 (1990): 818, 820–21.
18. In the study that is reported in Chapter 6, a single year supplied the data for half of the independent variables, each of which had a corresponding independent variable that measured change over a ten-year period. The single year for each independent variable in the former group was the last year of the period for its corresponding variable in the latter group. The data analysis examined *differences* between states on the independent variables in each group; such an analysis involves the use of cross-sectional data.
19. Emilio J. Castilla, *Dynamic Analysis in the Social Sciences* (Amsterdam, Netherlands: Academic Press, An Imprint of Elsevier, 2007), 43–44.
20. Larry W. Isaac and Larry J. Griffin, "Ahistoricism in Time-Series Analyses of Historical Process: Critique, Redirection, and Illustrations from U.S. Labor History," *American Sociological Review* 54 (1989): 873, 879–81.
21. Ibid., 873 (observing that "[n]o sociological account, however theoretically or technically sophisticated, is valid if it denies or masks important features of historical reality").
22. Verta Taylor, "Social Movement Continuity: The Women's Movement in Abeyance," *American Sociological Review* 54 (1989): 761.

23. The emergence of the United States as a sovereign nation may be thought to contradict my framework. The social movement that led to the creation of the United States arose from the populace of the colonies when the belief became widespread that the government of Britain was, at best, indifferent to the colonies and was, at worst, vindictive in dealing with them. T. H. Breen, *American Insurgents, American Patriots: The Revolution of the People* (New York: Hill and Wang, 2010), 25, 45–46, 52–53, 65–66, 76–77. However, the social movement that produced independence from Britain was aimed at preserving the ideals of the law of England; its objective was not to replace the law of England on core social activities with law having markedly different substance. Ibid., 42; John Phillip Reid, *Constitutional History of the American Revolution: The Authority of Rights* (Madison, WI: University of Wisconsin Press, 1986), 15, 23–26, 209–11. Therefore, the states that originally constituted the United States accepted in general the law of England that existed at the time of the American Revolution. Louis Henkin, "International Law as Law in the United States," *Michigan Law Review* 82 (1984): 1555, 1555–56; Arturo Gandara, "Contracts in Wonderland: A Fable Regarding the Administrative Adjudication of Qualifying Facility Contracts in California," *San Diego Law Review* 31 (1994): 307, 369; R. Ben Brown, "Judging in the Days of the Early Republic: A Critique of Judge Richard Arnold's Use of History in Anastasoff v. United States," *J. Appellate Practice and Process* 3 (2001): 355, 365–66.

In my framework, social values are assumed to be among the society-level factors that mold the content of law in a jurisdiction, and social movements are regarded as intermediaries in the link between these factors and law. Deeply entrenched, widely endorsed social values, inter alia, can thus explain social movements that develop to retain the ideals found in the law of a jurisdiction. The American Revolution is compatible with my framework because it was a popular uprising. Breen, supra, 25 (opposition to Britain involved "a huge percentage of the colonial population on the eve of independence"). That is, the colonists generally viewed the British government as disregarding the social values underlying the ideals of law. Ibid., 42; Reid, supra. The broad social movement in the colonies for the Revolution is an indication that strongly held, prevalent social values were believed to be in jeopardy.

24. These problems prompted me to alter the way I measured the independent variables in the studies that are reported in the journal articles on which Chapters 6 and 8 supra are based. In the articles, I used ranges of numerical values when assessing the impact of the independent variables. In reanalyzing the data for these studies, I used the actual numerical values of the independent variables. The results reported in Chapters 6 and 8 are from the reanalysis.

25. M. J. R. Healy, "Comments on the Paper by Lindley," *Statistician* 49 (2000): 321.

26. Henry F. Inman, "Karl Pearson and R. A. Fisher on Statistical Tests: A 1935 Exchange from *Nature*," *American Statistician* 48 (1994): 2, 7–10.

27. In addition, research is needed on the impact of law in different eras. Whether law has an effect on a targeted activity may vary between eras; when an effect occurs, the magnitude and permanence of the effect may not

be the same in every era. If such differences exist, the societal function(s) of law may change over time, and the benefit(s) that a society receives from law may be era-specific.

28. Roderick Floud, "Quantitative History: Evolution of Methods and Techniques," *Journal of the Society of Archivists* 5 (1977): 407, 414–15.
29. Roberto Franzosi, "Narrative as Data: Linguistic and Statistical Tools for the Quantitative Study of Historical Events," *International Review of Social History* 43 (1998): 81.
30. Gerald A. Press, "History and the Development of the Idea of History in Antiquity," *History and Theory* 16 (1977): 280, 282–83, 293–95.
31. See Vic Barnett and Toby Lewis, *Outliers in Statistical Data*, 3rd ed. (Chicester, NY: Wiley, 1994), 36 (noting that a phenomenon may be characterized by inherent variation and that a model of the phenomenon will be inadequate if it does not recognize and incorporate this variation).
32. An outlier may offer insight into the relationship between the attributes and law of jurisdictions. An investigator, by carefully studying an outlier, may identify attributes that are possible causes of the content of law but that have not previously been considered. Rebecca Jean Emigh, "The Power of Negative Thinking: The Use of Negative Case Methodology in the Development of Sociological Theory," *Theory and Society* 26 (1997): 649; Ke-Hai Yuan and Peter M. Bentler, "Effect of Outliers on Estimators and Tests in Covariance Structure Analysis," *British Journal of Mathematical and Statistical Psychology* 54 (2001): 161, 171. When examining an outlier, qualitative research methods are likely to prove helpful and may be essential.

Author Index

Subject Index

For Product Safety Concerns and Information please contact our EU representative GPSR@taylorandfrancis.com Taylor & Francis Verlag GmbH, Kaufingerstraße 24, 80331 München, Germany